HOLLYWOOD ON HOLLYWOOD

by
James Robert Parish
and
Michael R. Pitts
with
Gregory W. Mank

The Scarecrow Press, Inc.
Metuchen, N.J. & London
1978 63817

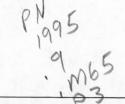

Library of Congress Cataloging in Publication Data

Parish, James Robert.
    Hollywood on Hollywood.

    1. Moving-picture industry in motion pictures—
Catalogs. 2. Moving-pictures—United States—Catalogs.
I. Pitts, Michael R., joint author. II. Mank,
Gregory W., joint author. III. Title.
PN1995.9.M65P3   016.79143   78-15513
ISBN 0-8108-1164-2

For

MISS MAE WEST

The Legendary Lady Who Announced
Upon Arriving in Hollywood in June 1932:

"I'm not a little girl from a little town
makin' good in a big town.
I'm a big girl from a big town
makin' good in a little town."

"All you need in movies is looking sincere and believe me brother, in this town, that's hard work."
Carol Kane to Rudolf Nureyev in <u>Valentino</u> (1977).

ACKNOWLEDGMENTS

Research Associates:

JOHN ROBERT COCCHI and FLORENCE SOLOMON

Introduction:

DeWITT BODEEN

Grateful thanks for their helpfulness to:

Academy of Motion Picture
    Arts & Sciences (Anthony
    Slide)
Richard Braff
Jim Butler
Jon Davison
Morris Everett, Jr.
Film Favorites (Bob Smith
    and Charles Smith)
Pierre Guinle
Ken D. Jones
John Kane
Gary Kramer
William T. Leonard
Library of Congress, Motion
    Picture Section (Patrick
    J. Sheehan)

John Malone
Barbra Mank
Albert M. Manski
Alvin H. Marill
Doug McClelland
Jim Meyer
Peter Miglierini
Don Miller
Screen Facts (Alan G. Barbour)
Mrs. Peter Smith
Charles K. Stumpf
T. Allan Taylor
Lou Valentino
Bill Werneth

And special thanks to Paul Myers, curator of the Theatre Collection at the Lincoln Center Library for the Performing Arts, and his staff: Monty Arnold, David Bartholomew, Rod Bladel, Donald Fowle, Maxwell Silverman, Dorothy Swerdlove, Betty Wharton, and Don Madison of Photo Reproductions.

by DeWitt Bodeen

Hollywood has always done better by Hollywood than it has
any other American industry. From the very beginning this has
been true. Once it was discovered that movie audiences were fascinated by seeing how a movie was made, with what went on behind
camera, and what the moviemakers themselves did when they weren't
making movies, then Hollywood as a background, as a story setting,
was willingly shown to those who regularly put down their nickels,
then their dimes, and now their four dollars at the box-office for
an admission ticket. It was not difficult in the old days, making
these pictures; the studios were right there and could be utilized as
places of action; the streets of Hollywood itself, the streets of downtown Los Angeles, the desert at Mojave, and the beach at Santa
Monica were backgrounds for free.

It's changed now. The studios are gone; the celebrities
aren't around; most of them don't even live in the Hollywood area
any more; the whole face of Southern California has changed, and
hardly for the better. Nor is it so simple any longer, making a
film about the Hollywood that was. It's gone, and has to be recon-
structed if it's to be used as a setting. Nevertheless, during the
1975-1976 seasons, there was a flurry of interest about using Hollywood stories on the screen again, but the films that emerged were
either seriously flawed, like The Day of the Locust, The Last Tycoon, and Nickelodeon, or they were simply dull, ineptly-made features like Gable and Lombard and W. C. Fields and Me.

Up till the present, however, Hollywood could be very proud
of most of the movies its producers have made about itself and its
most famous industry. Characters and stories, either based upon

1

fact or completely fictional, have had the semblance of truth up
there on the screen.   This was not a shadow world, nor were the
people in it merely shadows.   Reality has always been the forte of
the film, its very keynote, and Hollywood became a very real place
to filmgoers during the first fifty years of cinema history.   Indeed,
they knew Hollywood far better and more accurately than they did
Los Angeles.   Back in the good old days, one never got a <u>China-
town</u>, with its wealth of Los Angeles history--but tales about Hollywood were legion.   Their stories were told with both humor and
wit; they didn't avoid real tragedy or comedy or outrageous scandal;
they were not afraid of passion and pathos.   Characters, it is true,
were frequently glamourized; but, with tongue in cheek, they were
more often deglamourized.   Most importantly, the people in those
stories were always human, seldom stock characters, people who
worked hard and lived hard, people who rose to the heights and fell
to the most deplorable depths of obscurity.

        And the ironic note is that there never really was a town or
village in Southern California called Hollywood; it was only an un-
defined community within the city of Los Angeles.   It still is.   And
most of the studios, even more ironically, were never located within that community.   MGM was in Culver City; Universal, in Universal City; Warner Bros. , in Burbank; Republic, in San Fernando
Valley; 20th Century-Fox, in West Los Angeles.   Only Paramount,
RKO/Radio, Columbia, United Artists, and the old Fox Studios on
Western Avenue existed within the boundaries of Hollywood.

        But in that very word, "Hollywood," there has always been
magic for the layman, and while Hollywood showed its audiences the
allure and magic of movie-making, it was nonetheless not afraid to
show the other side of the picture--the failure, the despair, the
fears, the brevity of fame, the phony tawdriness behind the mask.

        In the beginning, there was an occasional feature, a ro-
mance like World's <u>A Girl's Folly</u> (1916), written by Frances Marion with Maurice Tourneur, the latter also directing; it showed film-
making as it was in the Eastern studios before production was con-
centrated in the West, and it was recognized as an honest, charm-

ing, work-a-day romance. And later for Paramount, Miss Marion also wrote an amusing character comedy about the Hollywood film studios, The Goat (1918), starring Fred Stone.

It was the short comedies, however, rather than an occasional feature that first captured the interest and then familiarized moviegoers with life as it was behind the cameras, with what happened on the sets when the camera wasn't being cranked.

The Mack Sennett comedies were always showing life behind the scenes. Mabel Normand, Roscoe Arbuckle, Ford Sterling, and Charlie Chaplin made a series of one- and two-reel comedies with Hollywood backgrounds that delighted movie audiences. The best, in my opinion, remains Chaplin's 1914 comedy for Sennett, The Masquerader, wherein, dressed in alluring drag and behaving as archly and coyly as any Tarkington heroine, the one and only Charlie fascinates all the men on the set, and is a veritable siren of the studio until he is unmasked as a masculine interloper. When Chaplin left Sennett and went over to Essanay and then to Mutual, he continued to make more than an occasional comedy with a studio setting.

Universal, Vitagraph, Christie, and, finally, Hal Roach jumped on the bandwagon, and also turned out a quantity of these short-reelers that could find a place on any exhibitor's program. Mack Sennett filmed a feature-length comedy about Hollywood, A Small Town Idol (1921), that was immensely popular; and sometime later in the twenties, Mabel Normand was the star of Sennett's The Extra Girl (1924), a feature-length comedy romance with a studio setting.

During the twenties, Hollywood often showed itself on film for what it was, and was not. Even Cecil B. DeMille displayed the making of a movie in his 1918 sex exposé, We Can't Have Everything, in which Wanda Hawley, a rising baby vamp who makes her living before the camera, is wooed between takes by Elliott Dexter, as a California millionaire. A night fire which actually broke out on the Lasky lot was immediately utilized for a sequence in the film, and DeMille gained added value for his feature with this photographic reality.

Among the first, and also the best, are two that are now accounted "lost films," both made at Paramount and both directed by
James Cruze--Merton of the Movies (1924), starring Glenn Hunter
with Viola Dana, and the all-star Hollywood (1923). The first,
based on the novel by Harry Leon Wilson and the successful stage
dramatization by George S. Kaufman and Marc Connelly, had some
marvelous moments behind the scenes. All the world sympathized
with poor Merton Gill, movie-struck country boy, who comes to
the film capitol, determined to become a great dramatic star.
Every night he prays, "Dear God, please make me a good movie
actor." When he finally gets inside the studio, his money is gone,
and he daren't leave the sacred precincts, stealing sleep on a bedroom set. Ever scornful of slapstick, he nevertheless becomes a
sensation when he finally gets a chance to play a screen role. He
plays the character with earnest fervor, absolutely straight, but
when it is projected, he comes across as a superlative comedian.
And so Merton Gill does become a movie star, not a new Valentino,
but a slapstick hero, who in private life takes to wife the only girl
who has stuck by him, a studio stunt girl, Flips Montague, whom
he has come to characterize, even after marrying her, as "my best
pal and severest critic."

There was genuine pathos and a lot of not-so-gentle satire in
Merton of the Movies, but the previous year, 1923, James Cruze
had made an equally biting comedy from a Frank Condon story,
Hollywood, which not only had a movie-struck heroine named Angela Whitaker as its protagonist, but boasted a series of cameos
that presented nearly every contract player then on the Paramount
lot, as well as other stars from other lots. Angela Whitaker
(played by an unknown, Hope Drown, who ironically never made another movie) comes to Hollywood with her family from the Middle
West. She has stars in her eyes, but in the end gets exactly nowhere in the world of the silver screen. Every member of her
family, however, from Grandpa to her hick-town sweetheart, gets
a job in the movies. Finally, Angela, resigning herself to marriage with her smalltown lover, now a maker of popular Western

thrillers, settles down to keep house for the whole family, including the pets and Angela's newly-born twins, "Mary and Doug," all
of whom are in top demand for studio work.

Early in the twenties, too, came a unique little comedy from
Metro, starring Buster Keaton as a movie projectionist studying to
become a detective. It was called Sherlock, Jr., and there is an
admirable sequence in it, where Keaton falls asleep in the projection booth, and his other self rises to go down the aisle and into
the action upon the screen, trying to redirect the destinies of the
players. Sherlock, Jr. was shown recently at the D. W. Griffith
Theatre in Manhattan, along with a revival of the early Fox talkie,
Hound of the Baskervilles, and it so enchanted critics that they gave
more space to the Keaton film than to the main attraction.

Romantic melodrama had its day, too, when Samuel Goldwyn
presented a Rupert Hughes feature, Souls for Sale (1923), with a
cast of rising young players, supplemented by cameo appearances
of established stars playing themselves. I myself had been to Hollywood during several summers prior to seeing Souls for Sale in the
Kinema Theatre in my hometown, Fresno, California. I had never
thought of Hollywood as glamourville. From the time I was a boy,
I had seen movie stars on the boulevards, in the shops, and dining
in restaurants; I had been on studio sets and seen companies at
work. As far as I was concerned, anything that happened was part
of a day's work, and it never seemed as if much happened except
a lot of waiting and horsing around. Seeing a movie shot had none
of the magic of going backstage in a theatre, of being allowed to sit
in an auditorium and watch a professional rehearsal in progress.
Going to the Kinema and seeing the latest film attractions starring
Norma Talmadge, or Charles Ray, Wallace Reid, or Mary Pickford,
could not be compared to going to a matinee of the local legitimate
playhouse, the White Theatre, and seeing Ruth Chatterton, Nazimova, Pauline Frederick, or Elsie Ferguson alive onstage. I was
stagestruck then, and it was the theatre that spelt glamour and
symbolized another world. Movie-making and movies were all too
realistic. And also, when you watched a scene being shot, those

waits between takes were interminable, with no sense of continuity, and there was none of that lovely world of illusion that was always there on stage. Inside the theatre, as a matter of fact, it was there the minute you walked across the doorway. The theatre was multi-dimensional because of its spell of illusion, and I missed it on the screen.

So I thought until I saw Souls for Sale.

With this incredible, trashy, romantic thriller, I found my-self transported for the first time to a wonderland beyond reality. What Souls for Sale provided was what every romantic melodrama should provide--escape. And that it should also show film-making as_exciting and colorful gave that escape drama a real extra fillip.

Souls for Sale is the story of a smalltown girl, Remember Sedden (played by Eleanor Boardman), who marries a no-good op-portunist (Lew Cody). He has made a career of marriage, insuring his brides and then making sure that they all meet with mortal ac-cidents so that he can collect the insurance. Remember, on the train bound west for her honeymoon, learns the truth about the man she has married in time to escape when the train pauses for a mo-ment during the night in the desert. Alone in the wilderness, she stumbles over the hot, sun-withered sands, finally collapsing at the foot of a dune. And then, on the dune's summit, she sees an Arab in sheik-like garb, mounted on his horse. He rides down and res-cues her, and Remember finds that she is lost neither in a distant world nor on another planet, but has stumbled upon a movie com-pany shooting on location. The company takes her in, and she falls in love with the young director (Richard Dix), who makes of her a star and saves her, finally, from death when her husband returns to expose and claim her.

It was not only all the background of a film company on lo-cation that entranced me, but the dangers they faced from a giant wind machine, as well as all the petty jealousies occasioned in such a group by actresses like Barbara La Marr, Mae Busch, and Aileen Pringle. As a story, Souls for Sale was admittedly melodramatic clap-trap, but it caught and held my interest. You never lost sight

of the fact that you were watching an escape melodrama being created by real people who were living their own real-life melodramas.
From that time on, movies were magic time, and every instance
when I went on a movie set, I felt as if I had gone through the
looking-glass and were in a really make-believe land, where the
false fronts were real, and only off the lot was there any show of
untruths.

Only a few years ago at London's National Film Theatre, I
saw a special showing of Goldwyn's Doubling for Romeo (1921),
starring Will Rogers with Sylvia Breamer. It was not only a fun
comedy, with lots of satire and tongue-in-cheek romance, but one
of Will Rogers' best adventures for the silent screen; and it also
had the extra attraction of showing a real film company shooting a
movie on the studio sets as they were then.

Inez from Hollywood (1924), directed by Alfred E. Green for
First National, presented that always admirable actress from Sweden, Anna Q. Nilsson, as a girl who becomes a Hollywood star
known as "the wickedest woman on the screen." She tries to keep
her stardom secret from a younger sister, and when she finds that
the young girl has met a movie magnate and is in love with him,
she reveals herself for what she is, only to find out that the magnate is a very nice guy and sincerely in love with her sister.

Marshall Neilan created a dazzling movie about a girl who
becomes an overnight star, but does not last (how true and familiar
a story that was in real life!) from Adela Rogers St. Johns' novel,
The Skyrocket (1926), starring America's foremost gold digger,
Peggy Hopkins Joyce, whom Neilan turned for this one film into a
real star who could act her way in diamonds.

And at the very end of the silent era, King Vidor made a
very funny and very poignant romantic comedy about two people in
Hollywood who fall in love and learn that they cannot be happy without one another, no matter what their status professionally; it was
called Show People (1928), and starred Marion Davies with William
Haines. It had a lovely moment when Miss Davies, as the heroine,
sees a star get out of her car, and asks who she is. "Marion

Davies," she is told.   The heroine only wrinkles her nose disdain-
fully, and says, "I don't think so much of her."

One of Hollywood's most dramatic treatments of itself also
came at the end of the silent era, a Josef von Sternberg drama,
The Last Command (1928), starring Emil Jannings, with Evelyn
Brent and William Powell.   In it Jannings played a onetime great
Russian general who had fallen upon bad times and has made his
way to Hollywood, where, as an extra, he gets a bit as a general
leading an attack much as he did in real life--but this time it is in
a film directed by the very revolutionary who had ruined him, now
a top film director.

Early in 1929, MGM released a charming, down-to-earth
love story (with sound and music, but no dialogue), A Man's Man,
in which William Haines, as a soda jerker, saves up enough money
to bring his movie-mad wife (Josephine Dunn) to Hollywood.   She
fancies herself as a Garbo, and one of the best moments comes
when she sees the real Garbo with John Gilbert attending a premiere and senses that she can never touch the greatness of Garbo.
And she also learns that the agent who has promised her stardom
wants only to get her into his bed.   Her husband punches the agent
in the kisser, and takes his wife away from Hollywood, back home
to the soda fountain job, and she is happy to know that she is loved,
and that's better than being a movie star.

One of the best of all pictures about Hollywood came early in
the talking era when George Cukor directed at RKO/Pathé Adela
Rogers St. Johns' story about a Brown Derby waitress who is
made into a big star by an alcoholic director.   It was What Price
Hollywood (1932), acted brilliantly and with becoming warmth by
Constance Bennett and Lowell Sherman, neither of whom glossed the
cynicism that rules the town.   In its story line, too, was the gene-
sis for Selznick's A Star Is Born (1937), with Janet Gaynor and
Fredric March, and its sturdiest remake as a romance with mu-
sic, also called A Star Is Born (1954), and also directed by George
Cukor, certainly on very familiar ground, and this time starring
Judy Garland, with James Mason.   Time has played tricks with this

triumvirate of three films on a similar theme, with the same basic
story as a springboard, and Jack Warner's last-minute cutting of
the third version nearly ruined it.   It's not too astonishing that today it is What Price Hollywood that suffers least, holding up as the
truest, the most biting and dramatic of the three, all verity with
only enough schmaltz to spice the action.

By this time I had become a genuine Hollywood convert.   I
had divided my love for the theatre with an equal affection for the
motion picture.   And it's only recently, on looking back, that I've
realized it was that silly melodrama about movies and their makers,
Souls for Sale, that was responsible for the division.   I've treated
at length this initial period of the films about Hollywood, because
when the talking film came of age there was hardly a season that
did not boast of at least one movie with a Hollywood background.
And some of them have been of sterling worth.

Merton of the Movies was remade twice, first as Make Me
a Star, with Stuart Erwin and Joan Blondell (1932), and again, this
time at MGM, as a vehicle for Red Skelton, under its original title
(1947).   Neither could reach the touching comedy of the original silent.   I understand that the Museum of Modern Art in Manhattan has
nearly succeeded in putting together a presentable version of that
first production of Merton, and I know that if they succeed and it
is publicly shown, the modern moviegoer is in for a treat.

The book which follows treats at some length all the newer
entries, and some of them are really top of the list, like Sullivan's
Travels, a Preston Sturges film for Paramount (1942), with Joel
McCrea and Veronica Lake; it was a satiric comedy with a strong
social impact about a director who becomes personally involved with
a frighteningly realistic, sordid and cruel episode in a prison down
South.   When he gets back to Hollywood, he plans to devote himself
to filming only comedies, because in them he has seen that the
world can escape from its pain and misery to find surcease in the
humor of a celluloid world.

Nobody can forget Sunset Boulevard (1950), that superlative
Brackett and Wilder melodrama, with its bizarre story boasting two

magnificent performances by the ageless Gloria Swanson and Erich
von Stroheim, who, ironically, caught in the change-over period
from silents to sound with a half-finished silent film, Queen Kelly,
were forced to abandon it, and then, thanks to Miss Swanson, some
of her most captivating close-ups from Queen Kelly were used in
Sunset Boulevard to show Norma Desmond, the character she played,
at her height. Norma Desmond became so real a character for
audiences, especially those younger ones not familiar with Swanson
films, that Gloria Swanson almost lost her own identity in playing
the role. Audiences thought of her as being Norma Desmond,
when, as a matter of fact, there was very little of Swanson herself
in the character of the half-mad has-been movie queen.

From MGM came The Bad and the Beautiful (1952), probably
the most adult and polished of stories about Hollywood and its people that has ever been filmed; it also permitted Lana Turner to
show the depths and variety of characterization that can be hers
when she has a more than one-dimensional role.

And also in that same year from MGM came Singin' in the
Rain, unquestionably the best musical comedy about Hollywood ever
made, and the only one that achieved any distinction as a satire,
dramatizing all the vagaries inherent in the changeover from silents
to talkies. Musical performances in it by Debbie Reynolds and
Donald O'Connor were so brilliant that they have rarely excelled
them, and Jean Hagen gave one of the funniest performances ever
put on screen as the silent movie queen who could neither talk nor
sing.

Two very funny Broadway comedies, Once in a Lifetime by
George S. Kaufman and Moss Hart, and Boy Meets Girl by Sam
and Bella Spewack, were successfully filmed, but they were actually
photographed stage plays. Much better was MGM's Bombshell (aka
Blonde Bombshell) (1933), which gave Jean Harlow a chance to show
that she had a real flare for comedy, and was one of Victor Fleming's most successful adventures into satire and good humor.

In 1958 came John Cromwell's The Goddess, from an original screenplay by Paddy Chayevsky, undoubtedly the most sympa-

thetic story ever made about a young actress who symbolizes sex to millions and becomes known as a goddess, but who is always lonely, friendless, and afraid, and ends a sick psychopath in the charge of a possessive nurse. As played by Kim Stanley, the girl was heartbreakingly real. Miss Stanley turned a bravura role, for which she was actually miscast, into a wonderfully bravura performance.

The feature film about films had come a long way from a simple studio romance like A Girl's Folly (1916).

Perhaps Hollywood did so well with films about Hollywood that other countries were tempted to show off the world behind film-making as it exists in their own studios. From Italy, memorably, there emerged all the Fellini studies of himself in his world of Rome's Cinecittà--La Dolce Vita, $8\frac{1}{2}$, and Juliet of the Spirits. And from France came those two unforgettable comedies--René Clair's charming romance of silent film-making in Paris, Le Silence est d'or, in which the perfect combination of Clair and Chevalier wrought sheer filmic magic; and the more recent François Truffaut film, Day for Night (1973), with the exquisite Valentina Cortese giving a divinely inspired performance of a star who not only can't remember her lines but can't coordinate her action.

The genre itself, Hollywood on Hollywood, has become so international that today it should probably be broadened to read, "Films on Film-Making." What happens in Hollywood also happens in Paris, in Rome, in London, in Stockholm, in Prague, in Moscow and Tokyo, and whatever films any nation has to show that deal with studios and film people will find audiences anywhere in the world. Even, and especially, in Hollywood itself, where interest in what they did and the rest of the world is doing on film has never died. Hollywood has never been able to resist just one more look at itself.

ABBOTT AND COSTELLO IN HOLLYWOOD (MGM, 1945) 83 min.

Producer, Martin Gosch; director, S. Sylvan Simon; story, Nat Perrin and Martin Gosch; screenplay, Perrin and Lou Breslow; songs, Ralph Blaine and Hugh Martin; choreography, Charles Walters; music director, George Bassman; orchestrator, Ted Duncan; art directors, Cedric Gibbons and Wade B. Rubottom; set decorator, Edwin B. Willis; assistant director, Earl McAvoy; sound, Douglas Shearer; camera, Charles Schoenbaum; editor, Ben Lewis.

Bud Abbott (Buz Kurtis); Lou Costello (Abercrombie); Frances Rafferty (Claire Warren); Robert Stanton (Jeff Parker); Jean Porter (Ruthie); Warner Anderson (Norman Royce); Rags Ragland (Himself); Mike Mazurki (Klondike Pete); Carleton G. Young (Gregory Le Maise); Donald MacBride (Dennis Kavanaugh); Katharine [Karin] Booth (Louise); The Lyttle Sisters (Quartette); Marion Martin (Miss Milbane); Dean Stockwell and Sharon McManus (Child Stars); Lucille Ball, Preston Foster, Robert Z. Leonard, and Jackie "Butch" Jenkins (Themselves).

ABBOTT AND COSTELLO MEET THE KEYSTONE KOPS (Universal, 1955) 79 min.

Producer, Howard Christie; director, Charles Lamont; story, Lee Loeb; screenplay, John Grant; assistant directors, William Holland and Ira S. Webb; costumes, Jay Morley, Jr.; music director, Joseph Gershenson; camera, Reggie Lanning; editor, Ed Curtiss.

Bud Abbott (Harry Pierce); Lou Costello (Willie Piper); Fred Clark (Joseph Gorman); Lynn Bari (Leota Van Cleef); Frank Wilcox (Rudolph Snavely); Maxie Rosenbloom (Hinds); Henry Kulky (Brakeman); Sam Flint (Conductor); Mack Sennett, Heinie Conklin, and Hank Mann (Themselves); Harold Goodwin (Cameraman); Roscoe Ates (Wagon Driver); Paul Dubov (Jason); Marjorie Bennett (Stout Woman); Joe Besser (The Hunter); Carole Costello (Theatre Cashier).

During the years that Abbott and Costello starred in films they spent most of their screen time at odds with a variety of monsters. But they did find time to make two features which kidded Hollywood, neither of which were up to the team's best standards.
Abbott and Costello in Hollywood was the first film to use the team's name in a title; it benefitted from good MGM production values and a deft director (S. Sylvan Simon). Also the picture's sight gags were above average and it boasted a good supporting cast, including Rags Ragland as a barbershop victim of Costello's,

13

Lynn Bari, Lou Costello, and Fred Clark, with Bud Abbott recum-
bent, in Abbott and Costello Meet the Keystone Kops (1955).

and Lucille Ball, Preston Foster, and director Robert Z. Leonard
as themselves performing a soundstage love scene ruined by plump
Costello.

Briefly the film had Abbott as a barber and Costello as his
shoeshine pupil. The boys want to be talent agents and get the opportunity after a former manicurist in Abbott's salon makes it in
the movies. The boys take over the management of singer Robert
Stanton after fading movie idol Carleton G. Young cheats him out
of a screen role. After disturbing much of the Mammoth Studio
backlot (actually MGM), Bud decides to have Lou get Young into a
fight to cause his suspension. In that manner Parker can have the
coveted role. The action takes place in a harbor and Young knocks
Lou into the water and he and Bud think he has drowned the Fat
Fellow. Young makes a getaway, Lou turns up safe, and Stanton
wins the part. The film concludes with Abbott and Costello as successful agents with money pouring out of their telephone.

The rather unsatiric film, however, did not have the same

fate; it proved a box-office mediocrity and as a result MGM dropped
the team's option for an annual film thereafter.

Bud and Lou then took full residence at Universal (-International) where several of their films (i. e. Abbott and Costello Meet
Frankenstein, 1948) were good box-office. However, by the mid-fifties their screen material had become stale and their films pedestrian.   One of the more disappointing of their latter efforts was
Abbott and Costello Meet the Keystone Kops.   Taking place in 1912,
the feature presented the boys as being conned by Fred Clark into
buying the Edison Studios.   Eventually they realize they have been
bilked and head West to recover their investment.   In Hollywood they
win jobs as stuntmen at Amalgamated Pictures and eventually catch
Clark.   (At one point in his career, Lou Costello had been a stunt-man in 1920s' Hollywood.)   Clark is now a director trying to steal
money from the company.   The pursuit leads to the airport where
aided by the Keystone Kops, they finally catch the hoodlum.

Outside of good stunt chases by Universal's squad of dare-devils and the brief appearance of Mack Sennett as himself and
Harold Goodwin, Hank Mann, and Heinie Conklin repeating their
original roles as Keystone Kops, the film had little to offer.   Not
even the presence of Lynn Bari, with a pungent portrayal of a mov-ie queen, nor the well-staged chase at the finale, did much to ele-vate the overall calibre of the production.   It provided little of the
promise in its title.

ACTORS AND SIN (United Artists, 1952) 85 min.

Producer/director, Ben Hecht; co-director, Lee Garmes;
screenplay, Hecht; set decorator, Howard Bristol; music, George
Antheil; camera, Garmes; editor, Otto Ludwig.

Actor's Blood: Edward G. Robinson (Maurice Tillayou);
Marsha Hunt (Marcia Tillayou); Dan O'Herlihy (Alfred O'Shea); Ru-dolph Anders (Otto Lachsley); Alice Key (Tommy); Rick Roman
(Clyde Veering).

Woman of Sin: Eddie Albert (Orlando Higgens); Alan Reed
(J. B. Cobb); Tracey Roberts (Miss Flannigan); Paul Guilfoyle (Mr.
Blue); Doug Evans (Mr. Devlin); Jenny Hecht (Daisy Marcher); Jody
Gilbert (Mrs. Egelhofer); John Crawford (Movie Hero).

This two-part feature dealt with different facets of show busi-ness; the first focused on the stage, while the second segment,
Woman of Sin, was situated in Hollywood.

The story is set in 1930s' Hollywood and concerns a fast-talking and none-too-honest talent agent (Eddie Albert) who sells a
romantic story to a movie studio.   To his surprise, Albert dis-covers that the story was written by an evil nine-year old (Jenny
Hecht), who subsequently gives him a great deal of trouble.   The
fast-thinking ten-percenter, however, turns the situation in his favor
when he blackmails the studio into giving the girl a five-year con-tract rather than give the human interest account to the media.   The
grasping agent, of course, gets a nice piece of the child's upcoming

earnings. The New York Times found the Woman of Sin episode a "screamingly funny wind-up" to the film, "a howl. "

THE AFFAIRS OF ANNABEL (RKO, 1938) 69 min.

Producers, Lee Marcus and Lou Lusty; director, Lew Landers; based on the story "Menial Star" by Charles Hoffman; screenplay, Bert Granet and Paul Yawitz; music director, Roy Webb; camera, Russell Metty; editor, Jack Hively.

Jack Oakie (Lanny Morgan); Lucille Ball (Annabel Allison); Ruth Donnelly (Josephine); Bradley Page (Howard Webb); Fritz Feld (Vladimir Dukoff); Thurston Hall (The Major); Elisabeth Risdon (Margaret Fletcher); Granville Bates (Jim Fletcher); James Burke (Officer Pat Muldoon); Lee Van Atta (Robert Fletcher); Edward Marr (Martin); Anthony Warde (Bailey); Leona Roberts (Mrs. Hurley); Maurice Cass (Dr. Rubnick the Jiu-Jitsu Teacher); John Sutton (Man at News Stand); Kane Richmond (Detective); Charles Coleman (Perkins the Butler); Wade Crosby (Scriptwriter); George Irving (Warden); Stanley Blystone (Cop).

Lucille Ball portrayed a harried and overworked film star who was the victim of countless publicity stunts and tricks employed by her energetic press agent to promote the features she turned out for Wonder Pictures. The end result was two films which were moderately budgeted (about $150,000 per film) and successful at the box-office. RKO, in fact, planned a whole series with Ball and Jack Oakie (who played the high-pressure press agent), but the latter's salary demands were too great and the series idea was dropped after only two entries. The Affairs of Annabel told of diminished film star Annabel Allison whose bad temper has made her unpopular with the studio. Pompous and fast-talking publicity man Oakie, however, devises a barrage of gimmicks to retain her name before the public. He is sure his efforts will make her films once again profitable in distribution. When she makes a prison picture he devises a scheme which lands her in jail, although it thereafter takes a month for her to be released. Next she is cast on the soundstage as a maid, so he hires her out as a domestic despite the fact she has no household abilities whatsoever. Still later when she is to undertake a movie about smugglers, he gets her involved in a publicity caper that tangles the actress with gangsters. Once again she finds herself in jail. The Affairs of Annabel was successful enough for RKO to rush the two contract performers into Annabel Takes a Tour (q. v. for credits and photo), also directed by Lew Landers. This outing, however, was much weaker than the first, despite the presence of Ruth Donnelly who added comedy relief as Annabel's pal Josephine. The tepid plotline had the actress on a promotional tour and still trying to cope with Oakie's silly, and often entangling, publicity stunts. One such effort has her engaged to a British "nobleman". This situation goes awry when the studio demands she break the engagement after it is learned the man is not all he seems.

Jack Oakie and Lucille Ball in The Affairs of Annabel (1938).

_____

       With this follow-up the series met an early demise.   Perhaps
it was just as well as the downward trend begun in the second film
might have continued with subsequent installments.   As it remains,
Ball and Oakie are remembered for having performed in two moderately funny minor efforts which poked polite fun at bad-tempered
stars and the harebrains who write their puff pieces.

AFTER THE FOX (aka CACCIA ALLA VOLPE) (United Artists,
     1966) Color, 102 min.

       Producer, John Bryan; director, Vittorio De Sica; screenplay,
Neil Simon and Cesare Zavattini; second unit directors, Giorgio
Stegani and Richard Talmadge; music director, Burt Bacharach; song,
Bacharach and Hal David; costumes, Piero Tosi; titles, Maurice
Binder; art director, Mario Garbuglia; camera, Leonida Barboni;
editor, Russell Lloyd.

       Peter Sellers (Aldo Vanucci); Britt Ekland (Gina Romantica);
Lidia Brazzi (Teresa Vanucci); Victor Mature (Tony Powell); Paolo
Stoppa (Pollo); Tino Buazzelli (Siepi); Mac Ronay (Carlo); Akim

Tino Buazelli; Mac Ronay, Britt Ekland, Paolo Stoppa, Peter Sellers, and Victor Mature in After the Fox (1966).

Tamiroff (Okra); Martin Balsam (Harry); Maria Grazia Buccelli (Okra's Sister); Lando Buzzanca (Captain of the Guardia); Tiberio Murgia (Policeman); Enzo Fiermonte (Raymond); Carlo Croccolo (Cafe Proprietor); Maurice Denham (Chief of Interpol); Pier Luigi Pizzi (Doctor).

     After the Fox is one of those features which seemed to have all the proper ingredients in its favor: a big name comedy star (Peter Sellers), a top-flight director (Vittorio De Sica), and a rising author (Neil Simon) providing his debut screenplay. Unfortunately none of these ingredients jelled into a coherent or consistently funny film. The movie did have its moments, mainly from Victor Mature's surprisingly good performance as an egomaniacal has-been star and Britt Ekland's comely good looks. But the European-lensed film's comedy premise went afoul, resulting in a colorful but limp movie exercise.

     Simon had a novel idea in that a slick Italian hoodlum (Sellers) devises a major gold robbery to be executed in the course of filming a neo-realistic movie on the Italian seacoast. Drawn into the plan is one-time cinema idol Tony Powell (Mature) who is to star in the film and be the decoy to forestall suspicion among the law enforcers. The robbery is carried off as the film is being made.

All the participants are captured and in court they each plead
innocent.

The most amusing scene in the film takes place in the courtroom where the film depicting the robbery is screened--showing
nothing more than a poorly-shot sequence of a long line of people
loading gold bars onto a waiting ship.   After the footage is unreeled,
a psuedo-intellectual movie critic rises up in the courtroom and de-
clares the film a "masterpiece" only to be overruled by the court.

Perhaps the true weakness of the picture is that Sellers appears in nearly every frame of the proceedings.   As a cameo or
character player the British comedian can be marvelous, but in a
full-length performance he frequently overstays his welcome.   Sadly
the emphasis of the movie was on crook Sellers and not on Mature's
in-depth portrayal of a faded muscle-man movie star, as his performance was excellent.   More than once he stole a scene from Sellers.
Also offering a diverting performance was Martin Balsam as Mature's
harried agent.

The reviews were not kind.   "After the Fox presents Peter
Sellers in a garlicky farce that could barely make the late late show
on Sicilian TV ..." (Time).   "Probably everyone concerned with
After the Fox, a completely exemplary lot, was so busy congratulat-
ing himself for being in such august company (Peter Sellers, Vittorio
De Sica, Neil Simon, and composer Burt Bacharach) that he completely overlooked the fact that there was also a little matter of
getting a show on the road" (Saturday Review).   Variety did laud
Mature's "... generous and delightful piece of self-parody...."

ALEX IN WONDERLAND (MGM, 1970) Color, 111 min.

Producer, Larry Tucker; associate producer, Anthony Ray;
director, Paul Mazursky; screenplay, Tucker and Mazursky; assistant
director, Anthony Ray; costumes, Moss Mabry; music, Tom O'Hor-
gan; production designer, Pato Guzman; choreography, Paula Kelly;
makeup, John G. Holden; sound, Jerry Jost; camera, Laszlo Kovacs;
editor, Stuart H. Pappe.

Donald Sutherland (Alex Morrison); Ellen Burstyn (Beth Mor-
rison); Meg Mazursky (Amy Morrison); Glenna Sergent (Nancy Mor-
rison); Viola Spolin (Mother); Andre Philippe (Andre); Michael Lerner
(Leo); Joan Delaney (Jane); Neil Burstyn (Norman); Leon Frederick
(Lewis); Carol O'Leary (Marlene); Moss Mabry (Mr. Wayne); Feder-
ico Fellini and Jeanne Moreau (Themselves); Sophia Krischer (Sophia);
Gene Krischer (Gene); Paul Mazursky (Hal Stern); Ed Long (Border
Guard); George Reynolds (Chauffeur).

A young cinema director (Donald Sutherland) has completed
his first film, which is labeled a masterpiece, and he must devise
a suitable follow-up to the initial production.   He is in a dilemma
as to what to photograph and he discusses the problem with his
wife (Ellen Burstyn) and the changes that will undoubtedly occur in
their lives with his new-found success.

Jeanne Moreau and Donald Sutherland on Hollywood Boulevard in <u>Alex in Wonderland</u> (1970).

Problems soon develop over the matter in the young man's life and he consults a psychiatrist, visits numerous friends, has a falling out with his spouse, and finally experiments with LSD. During these various interludes he imagines himself in various situations which he might employ for a new movie, including being a victim of an African tribal ceremony, dying in Los Angeles from the smog, and having the military invading Hollywood Boulevard. Finally Alex (Sutherland) goes to see Federico Fellini, his idol, who is working on <u>The Clowns</u>, and tries to pay homage to the Italian moviemaker, but he finds that he cannot communicate with him either. He then encounters Jeanne Moreau in Larry Edmunds' Hollywood bookshop and later meets with an MGM executive who wants him to do an arty film version of a studio-owned property. The film concludes with

bemused Sutherland discussing his problems with a tree in the backyard of his newly-purchased home.

Basically <u>Alex in Wonderland</u> is a mixed-up film about an
equally confused director. The film is more of a Hollywood inside
joke than anything more serious. Apart from its footage lensed on
Hollywood Boulevard and its scenes of Fellini and French actress
Moreau, it provides very little novelty value for Hollywood enthusiasts.

<u>Newsweek</u> magazine observed, "The film wears the clothes of
the hip movie while kidding the old Hollywood--but what is new about
a man with split-level family problems?" <u>Time</u> magazine analyzed,
"The result, although unsuccessful overall, is frequently funny, nasty
and telling. . . . [It] is not the best of the Hollywood-on-Hollywood
movies . . . [but is] an ego trip that is often fun along the way. "

<u>Alex in Wonderland</u> was shot at a time when a foundering
MGM--the remnant of a once-great studio--was attempting to gather
some of the "youth" market by utilizing arty directors. That same
year, 1970, Metro released <u>Zabriskie Point</u>, Italian film director
Michelangelo Antonioni's first American-made feature. Mazursky
had co-scripted and directed Columbia's box-office hit <u>Bob & Carol</u>
<u>& Ted & Alice</u> the previous year, and MGM boss James Aubrey
thought he could bring some tidy profits to money-poor Metro (who
in 1970 auctioned off a vast majority of its studio sets and memora-
bilia). Note that both Mazursky and his daughter Meg appear in the
film.

ALI BABA GOES TO TOWN (20th Century-Fox, 1937) 84 min. [sepia
    sequences]

    Producer, Darryl F. Zanuck; associate producer, Laurence
Schwab; director, David Butler; story, Gene Towne, Graham Baker,
and Gene Fowler; screenplay, Harry Tugend and Jack Yellen; songs,
Mack Gordon, Harry Revel, Raymond Scott; music director, Louis
Silvers; art director, Bernard Herzbrun; set decorator, Thomas
Little; assistant director, Ad Schaumer; costumes, Gwen Wakeley
and Herschel; sound, Alfred Bruzlin; camera, Ernest Palmer; editor,
Irene Morra.

    Eddie Cantor (Ali Baba); Tony Martin (Yusuf); Roland Young
(Sultan); June Lang (Princess Miriam); Louise Hovick [Gypsy Rose
Lee] (Sultana); John Carradine (Ishak); Virginia Field (Dinah); Alan
Dinehart (Boland); Douglass Dumbrille (Omar the Rug Maker); Warren
Hymer and Stanley Fields (Tramps); Ferdinand Gottschalk (Chief
Councilor); Charles Lane (Doctor); the Peters Sisters, Jeni Le Gon,
the Raymond Scott Quintet, and the Pearl Twins (Themselves); Maur-
ice Cass (Omar); John Berkes (Arab Peasant); John George and Mer-
rill McCormick (Tramps); John Bipson (Movie Arab); Sidney Fields
(Assistant Director); George Regas (Bearded Arab); Jim Pierce (Cap-
tain of the Guards); John Rutherford and Herbert Ashley (Sentries);
Sam Hayes (Radio Announcer); Charles Lane (Doctor); Eddie Collins
(Wife-Beating Arab); Marjorie Weaver (Beaten Wife); Francis Mc-
Donald (Peasant Ringleader); Hank Mann (Arab with Cigar/Gas Sta-

Louise Hovick [Gypsy Rose Lee], Roland Young, John Lipson, June Lang, John Carradine, Merrill McCormick and George Regas (plumed turbans), Eddie Cantor, and Douglass Dumbrille in Ali Baba Goes to Town (1937).

---

tion Attendant); Douglas Fairbanks, Lady Sylvia Ashley, the Ritz Brothers, Ann Sothern, Victor McLaglen, Phyllis Brooks, Michael Whalen, Cesar Romero, Tyrone Power, Sonja Henie, Shirley Temple, Dolores Del Rio, and Eddie Cantor (Celebrities in Premiere Newsreel).

Eddie Cantor enjoyed a long career as a star of Broadway, films, radio, and television. Viewing his work today one is immediately struck by the fact that the little guy with the banjo eyes accomplished a great deal with what little talent he had. During the early and mid-thirties he made a series of very popular musicals for Samuel Goldwyn. Today all of them are very dated and survive in interest largely for the Busby Berkeley-created dance sequences. After leaving Goldwyn's tutelege Cantor made only one more feature during the decade, 20th Century-Fox's Ali Baba Goes to Town. It was a mixture of movie-making and fantasy with Cantor thrown into a bygone world, as he had been in the earlier Roman Scandals (1933).

Here Cantor portrays himself working in a desert locale

making an Arabian Nights type of movie. In order to give himself some pep Eddie overdoes his dosage of iron pills. Soon he is dreaming of being in Bagdad as the legendary Ali Baba (complete with turban and cape). In the exotic setting he becomes involved with a corrupt Sultan (Roland Young) who has 365 wives--including Gypsy Rose Lee. Along the way Cantor romances a number of the lovely harem girls but he is outdone in that talent by crooning pal Yusuf (Tony Martin). Eventually the dream ends--after a lot of low-jinks comedy and fine singing--and Eddie wakes up to reality and returns to his desert epic.

"One cannot help wondering if the mass movie audiences will share the pains of wealthy movie folk over high income taxes and 'silly' relief, if so, it would indicate extraordinary sympathy" (New York Post). At best, Ali Baba Goes to Town can only be described as minor-league fun and its inane look at Hollywood is a flimsy one. If nothing else, it really claimed that a sinking film star (Cantor) would much rather dream of movie-like adventures than participate in them as reality.

To be noted: in a film premiere sequence such diverse Fox contract personalities as Dolores Del Rio, Sonja Henie, Tyrone Power, the Ritz Brothers, Ann Sothern, and Shirley Temple appear as themselves. A clip of the chase sequence from Ali Baba would be introduced into Day of the Locust (q. v.), along with Karen Black in footage devised to showing her "with" Cantor.

ALICE IN MOVIELAND see THE SHORT FILMS

THE AMAZING HOWARD HUGHES (CBS-TV, 1977) Color, 186 min.

Producer, Roger Gimbel; director, William A. Graham; based on the book Howard the Amazing Mr. Hughes by Noah Dietrich and Bob Thomas; teleplay, John Gay; production designer, Stan Jolley; music, Laurence Rosenthal; makeup, Mike Westmore; costumes, Frank Novak; aviation coordination, Tallmantz Aviation; camera, Jules Breener; additional camera, Michael Margulies; editor, Aaron Stell.

Tommy Lee Jones (Howard Hughes); Ed Flanders (Noah Dietrich); James Hampton (Wilbur Peterson); Tovah Feldshuh (Katharine Hepburn); Lee Purcell (Billie Dove); Jim Antonio (George); Sorrell Booke (Major La Guardia); Lee Jones-De Broux (Jimmy); Roy Engel (Production Manager); Arthur Franz (Barnes); Denise Galik (Shirley); Howard Hesseman (Jenks); Carol Bagdasarian (Jean Peters); Bart Burns (Robert Maheu); Thayer David (Odlum); Howard Hesseman (Jenks); William Dozier (Senator Ferguson); Barry Atwater (Senator Brewster); Marla Carlis (Jane Russell); Marty Brill (Lewis Milestone); Tannis G. Montgomery (Mrs. Howard Hughes); Gary Walberg (Henry K. Kaiser); Walter O. Miles ("Hap" Arnold); Ben Hammer (Dr. Palmer); Barney Phillips (Saunders); John S. Ragan (Bit); Jim Bacon (Himself).

When Howard Hughes died on April 5, 1976, he was then in

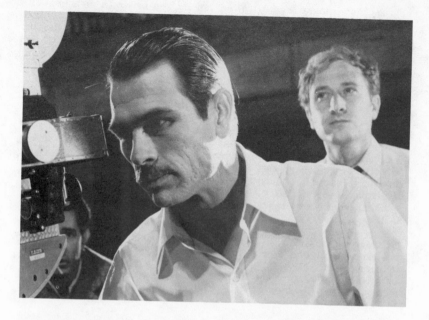

Tommy Lee Jones in <u>The Amazing Howard Hughes</u> (1977).

his seventies. For many decades before that he had been world-
famous as an iconoclastic businessman, later termed the "eccentric
billionaire." Many biographies had been published about the bizarre
industrialist; some were conceived in fact, others on fancy (one such
book falsely claiming to be the authentic account approved by the
subject himself left the author and his wife in jail). From all the
documentation, fabrication, and conjecture to date, it is clear that
this extremely private individual was unique, a man who could con-
struct mighty financial empires, control a movie studio, manipulate
high politics, and generally exercise influence on a grand scale yet
(in his younger years) be at the mercy of his vaguest whims while
absorbed in the conquest of any given female.

In the late twenties and thirties--when Hughes was still visible
to some of the public some of the time--he publically and privately
dated several of Hollywood's most engaging actresses, including Bille
Dove, Katharine Hepburn, and Ginger Rogers. He would make movie
performer Jane Russell the ninth wonder of the forties world, attempt
(unsuccessfully) to do the same with protégée Faith Domergue, and
while courting the likes of Terry Moore, Gina Lollobrigida, et al.,
marry 20th Century-Fox star(let) Jean Peters whom he divorced
years later. He was the man who in the late forties controlled RKO
Pictures--from executive offices <u>away</u> from the lot--the occasional
filmmaker who was responsible for <u>Hell's Angels</u> (1930), <u>The Outlaw</u>
(1943), <u>Jet Pilot</u> (1958), and many others.

In the mid-seventies, when curiosity about Howard Hughes
reached its peak, several filmmakers announced plans to produce
screen biographies of the astounding Texan.   At one point Warren
Beatty was to star in a biopic of Hughes, but he turned down the
million-dollar offer to do so.   To date, The Amazing Howard Hughes,
presented as a two-part CBS-TV (four-hour) video special, is the
only seventies' project to focus on the strange, compelling, compulsive, and frequently revolting man.   It was Hughes who in his final
years became a mentally vague hermit, a victim of his self-made
business empire and his own set of ironclad rules, all of which iso-
lated him from contact with the world at large.
    A good deal of this telefeature focused on Hughes' final years
when he was a straggly-haired, anemic old man, hidden away from
the outside world.   But through flashbacks, sequences dealt with his
building of an airplane empire (ironically one of the TV program's
sponsors was a competing airline), assorted manufacturing combines,
his Las Vegas hotel stakes, the Senate hearings, and, of course,
his years in Hollywood as a suitor of stars, filmmaker, and studio
mogul.
    Several real-life film industry personalities were depicted,
Jane Russell, Jean Peters, Billie Dove, and director Lewis Milestone among them.   Most persuasive of these simulated cameos was
Tovah Feldshuh as the high-powered Katharine Hepburn, the one who
the telescript has saying to Hughes (played effectively by Tommy
Lee Jones), "Every once in a while you get this helpless, little-boy
look.   Charming, but I wonder if it's genuine."
    There are references to such film business figures as Dore
Schary, of whom Hughes says, "That man likes too many war pictures.   I'm through with that."   There are references to Hughes'
upholding of the tenets of the anti-communist witchhunt in Hollywood,
and Hughes' refusal to allow Paul Jericho's credit on a particular
film because he had refused to testify, under Fifth Amendment pro-
tection.   And throughout, there is Hughes' compulsive behavior concerning la belle femme.   One sequence of the long teledrama reveals
Hughes' passion for starlet Elizabeth Taylor and how in the early
fifties he offered her mother $1 million tax free if her daughter
would wed him.   The bid, as is common history, was refused.
    John J. O'Connor reported in the New York Times on this
TV special, based on the book by Bob Thomas and Noah Dietrich (a
leading executive in the Hughes empire for over 32 years), "... this
dramatization has been mounted impressively.   Period details and
special effects, particularly in the flying sequences, are handled very
effectively.   But despite the intelligent manipulation of John Gay's
script, the character of Mr. Hughes remains in headlinelike isolation,
defined largely by well-known incidents, from his air crashes to the
Clifford Irving book caper....   If this long production retains a re-
markably strong level of interest, the performances of Tommy Lee
Jones as Mr. Hughes, and Ed Flanders as Mr. Dietrich constitute
two outstanding reasons."
    The Hollywood Reporter confirmed, "... there is a lack of
insight that has the viewer watching a man in action but never really
understanding what makes him tick.   As a young man he states that
his goals are 'to be the best at whatever I do,' with specific aims

being motion pictures, golf, aviation and gaining the title 'the richest man in the world. ' In this case, the best-laid plans appear to work out but we never really get to meet the internal man. "

ANCHORS AWEIGH (MGM, 1945) Color, 140 min.

Producer, Joe Pasternak; director, George Sidney; story, Natalie Marcin; screenplay, Isobel Lennart; music director, Georgie Stoll; art directors, Cedric Gibbons and Randall Duell; songs, Sammy Cahn and Jule Styne; Ralph Freed and Sammy Fain; music arranger, Axel Stordahl; vocal arranger, Earl Brent; assistant director, George Rheim; art directors, Cedric Gibbons and Randall Duell; set directors, Edwin B. Willis and Richard Pefferle; Technicolor consultants, Natalie Kalmus and Henri Jaffa; sound, Douglas Shearer; camera, Robert Planck and Charles Boyle; editor, Adrienne Fazan.

Gene Kelly (Joseph Brady); Frank Sinatra (Clarence Doolittle); Kathryn Grayson (Susan Abbott); José Iturbi (Himself); Dean Stockwell (Donald Martin); Carlos Ramirez (Carlos); Henry O'Neill (Admiral Hammond); Leon Ames (Commander); Rags Ragland (Police Sergeant); Edgar Kennedy (Police Captain); Pamela Britton (Girl from Brooklyn); Henry Armetta (Hamburger Man); James Burke (Studio Cop); Sharon McManus (Little Girl Beggar); James Flavin (Radio Cop); Sondra Rodgers (Iturbi's Secretary); Peggy Maley (Lana Turner Double); Renie Riano (Waitress); Milton Parsons (Bearded Man); Charles Coleman (Butler); Esther Michelson (Hamburger Woman); William Forrest (Movie Director); Ray Teal (Assistant Movie Director); Milton Kibbee (Bartender).

Anchors Aweigh, while no more than movie fluff of the late World War II years, is memorable because it was the initial screen teaming of Gene Kelly and Frank Sinatra. Kelly's dancing received raves from the critics and moviegoers alike. The film proved to be a very popular item from the Joe Pasternak production unit at Metro.
The delightful musical romp relates the tale of sailors Clarence Doolittle (Sinatra) and Joseph Brady (Kelly) on shore leave in Hollywood where they meet an attractive "movie star" Susan Abbott (Kathryn Grayson) and her precocious nephew, Donald Martin (Dean Stockwell). Grayson is really only an extra, but who cares. Kelly tries to get his girl-shy friend Sinatra into a romance with her. However, after several musical escapades, it becomes evident that it is Grayson and Kelly who are meant for one another. Sinatra, meanwhile, has discovered the charms of a vivacious Brooklyn-born waitress (Pamela Britton). The action resolves with the boys sailing again for Uncle Sam but with the solace of knowing that two lovely girls wait tearfully on shore.
Although the film now does not hold up well under dissection-- its weaknesses attributable mainly to director George Sidney--it is still an entertaining respite from reality. The scenes of film-making are no more credible than MGM's other 1945 excursion into self-dissection, Abbott and Costello in Hollywood (q. v.), but here the production values are far superior. For entertainment contrast there

Advertisement for Anchors Aweigh (1945).

is highbrow pianist José Iturbi going lowbrow, Grayson's warbling, Kelly and Sinatra dueting in song and dance, and Kelly kicking up his heels with two contrasting dance partners: little Sharon McManus and a cleverly interpolated sequence of Kelly hoofing with cartoon mouse "Jerry."

The color feature grossed a whopping $4.5 million in distributors' domestic rentals. Later Kelly and Sinatra would be reteamed at MGM in Take Me Out to the Ball Game and On the Town, both 1949 MGM releases.

ANNABEL TAKES A TOUR (RKO, 1938) 69 min. [See THE AFFAIRS OF ANNABEL.]

Producers, Lee Marcus and Lou Lusty; director, Lew Landers; story, Joe Bigelow and Bert Granet; screenplay, Granet and Olive Cooper; camera, Russell Metty; editor, Harry Marker.

Jack Oakie (Lanny Morgan); Lucille Ball (Annabel Allison); Ruth Donnelly (Josephine); Bradley Page (Howard Webb); Ralph Forbes (Viscount); Frances Mercer (Natalie); Donald MacBride (Thompson); Alice White (Marcella the Manicurist); Chester Clute (Pitcairn); Pepito (Poochy); Jean Rouverol (Laura); Clare Verdera (Viscountess); Edward Gargan (Longshoreman); Mary Jo Desmond (Girl); Wesley Barry (Bellhop); Rafael Storm (Count).

Publicity pose for <u>Annabel Takes a Tour</u> (1938) with Ruth Donnelly,
Lucille Ball, and Bradley Page.

ANOTHER FACE (RKO, 1935) 72 min.

Producer, Cliff Reid; director, Christy Cabanne; story, Ray
Mayer and Thomas Dugan; screenplay, Garrett Graham and John
Twist; camera, Jack MacKenzie; editor, George Hively.

Wallace Ford (Joe Haynes); Brian Donlevy (Broken Nose Dawson [Dutra]); Phyllis Brooks (Sheila); Erik Rhodes (Assistant Director); Molly Lamont (Mary); Alan Hale (Keller); Addison [Jack] Randall (Tex); Paul Stanton (Director); Edward Burns (Cameraman);
Charles Wilson (Captain Spellman); Hattie McDaniel (Maid); Si Jenks
(Janitor); Oscar Apfel (Doctor); Inez Courtney (Mam'e); Emma Dunn
(Sheila's Mother); Ethel Wales (Aunt Hattie); Frank Mills (Muggsie).

"An unusual little picture in that it is both frightening and
funny.... [T]he picture is as lifelike as it is enlightening" (Liberty
magazine).
New York gangster Broken Nose Dawson (Brian Donlevy) has
a facelift and when he realizes what a handsome profile he now enjoys, decides to embark on a Hollywood career.   He is pursued
there by the one person who can identify him, nurse Mary (Molly
Lamont) who was in attendance at his plastic surgery.   It is she who
convinces studio press agent Joe Haynes (Wallace Ford) to bring in
the police on the set of a gangster yarn Donlevy is now emoting in.
The finale finds Donlevy engaged in a spray of real bullets as law
enforcers close in on him and his tenure as a movie player.
Of this comedy, the New York World Telegram decided,
"Satire and melodrama [are] mixed in a reasonably satisfying manner. " Phyllis Brooks appeared as a movie actress and Alan Hale
was on hand as the film producer Keller.

ARE PARENTS PEOPLE?   (Paramount, 1925) 6586 ft.

Presenters, Adolph Zukor and Jesse L. Lasky; director, Malcolm St. Clair; based on the story by Alice Duer Miller; screenplay,
Frances Agnew; camera, Bert Glennon.

Betty Bronson (Lita Hazlitt); Florence Vidor (Mrs. Hazlitt);
Adolphe Menjou (Mr. Hazlitt); Andre Beranger (Maurice Mansfield);
Lawrence Gray (Dr. Dacer); Mary Beth Milford (Aurella Wilton);
Emily Fitzroy (Margaret); William Courtwright (Freebody).

Young Lita Hazlitt (Betty Bronson) is expelled from her boarding school after her roommate types a letter to movie star Maurice
Mansfield (Andre Beranger), asking him to help her break into films.
Since the intercepted letter is unsigned, someone must take the
blame and Bronson has decided to do so.   She has a plan--she hopes
this plight will cause her divorced parents to reconsider their action
and become reunited.   To further her scheme, she goes off in
search of the actor in question, who is on location for his latest
photoplay.   In the course of her efforts, she spends the night--inno-
cently, of course--at the home of young Dr. Dacer (Lawrence Gray),

Paul Stanton, Brian Donlevy, and Wilfred Lucas in Another Face (1935).

---

a handsome surgeon who has intrigued her.   In the morning, Bronson returns home, brings her parents back together, and as a bonus finds that Gray is now entranced by her.

Are Parents People? was one of several light comedies Bronson made for Paramount following her sensational performance in the title role of Peter Pan (1924).   The picture was "a jolly little comedy" and well suited the talents of its lovely star.   Also Menjou and Vidor were quite good as the girl's quarreling parents.   As indicated, the storyline had its fun with the film industry's preoccupation with matinee idols and caddish leading men.

THE BAD AND THE BEAUTIFUL (MGM, 1952) 118 min.

Producer, John Houseman; director, Vincente Minnelli; story,

George Bradshaw; screenplay, Charles Schnee; music, David Raksin; assistant director, Jerry Thorpe; art directors, Cedric Gibbons and Edward Carfagno; set decorators, Edwin B. Willis and Keogh Gleason; costumes, Helen Rose; makeup, William Tuttle; sound, Douglas Shearer; special effects, A. Arnold Gillespie and Warren Newcombe; camera, Robert Surtees; editor, Conrad A. Nervig.

Lana Turner (Georgia Lorrison); Kirk Douglas (Jonathan Shields); Walter Pidgeon (Harry Pebbel); Dick Powell (James Lee Bartlow); Barry Sullivan (Fred Amiel); Gloria Grahame (Rosemary Bartlow); Gilbert Roland (Victor "Gaucho" Ribera); Leo G. Carroll (Henry Whitfield); Vanessa Brown (Kay Amiel); Paul Stewart (Syd Murphy); Sammy White (Gus); Elaine Stewart (Lila); Jonathan Cott (Assistant Director); Ivan Triessault (Von Ellstein); Kathleen Freeman (Miss March); Marietta Canty (Ida); Lucille Knoch (Blonde); Steve Forrest (Leading Man); Perry Sheehan (Secretary); Robert Burton (McDill); Francis X. Bushman (Eulogist); Harold Miller (Man); George Lewis (Lionel Donovan); Madge Blake (Mrs. Rosser); William Tannen, Dabbs Greer, Frank Scannell, and Sara Spencer (Reporters); Stanley Andrews (Sheriff); William "Bill" Phillips (Assistant Director); Karen Verne (Rosa); Barbara Thatcher, Sharon Saunders, and Erin Selwyn (Girls); Peggy King (Singer); Ben Astor (Joe); Bess Flowers (Joe's Friend at Party); Major Sam Harris (Party Guest); Norma Salina, Janet Comeford, and Kathy Qualen (Bobby Soxers); Louis Calhern (Voice on the Recording).

Out of the gloss factory that was MGM in the early fifties came this well-regarded feature which in many respects proved to be one of Hollywood's most devastating looks at itself. While no Norma Desmonds lurk in its compounds, it does tell a rather truthful story of the rise of a movie magnate and of three individuals who both resent his ruthlessness and yet appreciate the chance for fame and wealth he provided them. It well illustrates the Hollywood paradox.

Kirk Douglas starred as the dynamic shoestring producer (some insist the character was patterned after Val Lewton and his days at RKO) who uses a starlet (Lana Turner), a director (Barry Sullivan), and a writer (Dick Powell) as stepping stones in his climb to Hollywood fame. The story is told in flashbacks by each of the three as he/she recounts his/her association with the skunk in question. Turner recalls how she abandoned drink and despair after meeting Douglas who offered her a career and love. Southerner Powell recollects it was Douglas who gave him the gumption and impetus to write commercially, while at the same time it was Douglas' meddling which caused Powell's adulterous wife (Gloria Grahame) to lose her life. Yet it was under Douglas' supervision that Powell would create his best works. Director Sullivan feels used, abused, and discarded by Douglas though it was he who helped to yank him up the ladder of success. At the finale, all three artists again join forces with producer Walter Pidgeon to make a new film for Douglas who needs to engineer a fresh comeback for himself.

When issued, the New York Times judged The Bad and the Beautiful "A superslick, creamily handsome and entertaining saga of

Lana Turner and Sammy White (right) in The Bad and the Beautiful
(1952).

---

a Hollywood heel...." Critic Manny Farber thought it was one of
those pictures that was a "...stunning mixture of mannerism, smooth
construction, and cleverly camouflaged hot air." Interestingly, as
the years have gone by, the movie has grown in stature, becoming
a minor classic that seems destined to rise even higher in estimation
in future generations. After all, considering some of the amateurish
trash distributed today, the facileness of The Bad and the Beautiful
looks very good indeed.

Besides enjoying an excellent screenplay and taut direction by
Vincente Minnelli, the facet that probably made The Bad and the Beautiful
so good was its performances. Dimple-chinned Douglas may have been
a bit staid as the filmmaker, but the other cast members, especially
Pidgeon as a diplomatic studio chieftain and Gilbert Roland as a hot-
blooded film star, were on target. For her interpretation of the "innocent" little wife, Grahame won a Best Supporting Actress Oscar.

THE BANK DICK (Universal, 1940) 74 min.

Director, Edward Cline; story/screenplay, Mahatma Kane

Jeeves [W. C. Fields]; music director, Charles Previn; art director, Jack Otterson; camera, Milton Krasner; editor, Arthur Hilton.

W. C. Fields (Egbert Sousé); Cora Witherspoon (Agatha Sousé); Una Merkel (Myrtle Sousé); Evelyn Del Rio (Elsie Mae Adele Brunch Sousé); Jessie Ralph (Mrs. Hermisillo Brunch); Franklin Pangborn (J. Pinkerton Snoopington); Shemp Howard (Joe Guelpe); Richard Purcell (Mackley Q. Greene); Grady Sutton (Og Oggilby); Russell Hicks (J. Frothingham Waterbury); Pierre Watkin (Mr. Skinner); Al Hill (Filthy McNasty); George Moran (Cozy Cochran); Bill Wolfe (Otis); Jack Norton (A. Pismo Clam); Pat West (Assistant Director); Harlan Briggs (Dr. Stall); Heather Wilde (Miss Plupp); Reed Hadley (Francois); Bill Alston (Mr. Cheek).

The popularity that resulted in the teaming of Mae West and W. C. Fields in My Little Chickadee (1940) convinced Universal that Fields was still a potent box-office factor and the studio gave him a free hand in his following picture, The Bank Dick, which he also wrote. Along with It's a Gift (Paramount, 1934), The Bank Dick ranks as top Fieldsian humor and is one of the best comedies of the period. Adding a great deal to the overall humor of the film is the Great Man's humorous stabs at shoestring film-making.

What little plot The Bank Dick has revolves around Fields and his family's residing in the small town of Lompoc. Fields devotes his energies to answering quiz contests in magazines; much to the consternation of his nagging wife (Cora Witherspoon), slatternly mother-in-law (Jessie Ralph), hair-brained older daughter (Una Merkel), and the mean younger daughter (Evelyn Del Rio).

While drinking one day in Shemp Howard's Black Pussy Cafe and Snack Bar, the Great Man meets Mackley Q. Green (Dick Purcell), a harried front man for a movie company which is filming a short subject in Lompoc. The main problem is the movie director, A. Pismo Clam (Jack Norton), who is on a perpetual drunk. Immediately Fields volunteers (!) to complete the project. After highlighting the good old days when he worked with Fatty Arbuckle, Mack Sennett, and Charlie Chaplin, he announces, "Celluloid is in my blood."

Fields is escorted to the movie location where leading man François (Reed Hadley) is a foot taller than his leading lady (Heather Wilde). Fields states he is changing the romantic drama into a football story, but an altercation with his younger daughter leaves the novice filmmaker a bit the worse for wear. It is not long before Fields abandons his movie career for some refreshment at the Black Pussy Cafe. Later Fields captures, by accident, a bank robber, is then made a bank guard, causes his future son-in-law (Grady Sutton) to embezzle bank funds, becomes involved in a car chase, and ends up a millionaire. It is all a typical Fields fantasy.

What is so striking about the movie sequences within The Bank Dick is the star's obvious low regard of the over-all medium. He depicts movie people as idiocentric clowns and the movie form itself as less than artistic. Fields obviously realized that through the movie medium he could reach a mass audience, but he probably preferred the total control he had enjoyed over his work in the days of his stage triumphs.

W. C. Fields in The Bank Dick (1940).

THE BAREFOOT CONTESSA (United Artists, 1954) Color, 128 min.

Director/screenplay, Joseph L. Mankiewicz; music, Mario Nascimbene; assistant director, Pietro Mussetta; art director, Arrigo Equini; gowns, Fontana; sound, Charles Knott; camera, Jack Cardiff; editor, William Hornbeck.

Humphrey Bogart (Harry Dawes); Ava Gardner (Maria Vargas); Edmond O'Brien (Oscar Muldoon); Marius Goring (Alberto Bravano); Valentina Cortesa (Eleanora Torlato-Favrini); Rossano Brazzi (Vincenzo Torlato-Favrini); Elizabeth Sellars (Jerry); Warren Stevens (Kirk Edwards); Franco Interlenghi (Pedro); Mari Aldon (Myrna); Bessie Love (Mrs. Eubanks); Diana Decker (Drunken Blonde); Bill Fraser (J. Montague Brown); Alberto Rabagliati (Nightclub Proprietor); Enzo

Ava Gardner in The Barefoot Contessa (1954).

Staiola (Busboy); Maria Zanoli and Renato Chiantoni (Maria's Parents);
John Parris (Mr. Black); Jim Gerald (Mr. Blue); Tonio Selwart (The
Pretender); Margaret Anderson (The Pretender's Wife); Gertrude
Flynn (Lulu McGee); Robert Christopher (Eddie Blake); Carlo Dale
(Chauffeur).

The New York Times noted of The Barefoot Contessa, "For
all its arresting spurts and glints of esthetic interest, this caustic
and cynical drama, told in a flashback from the heroine's funeral, is
a grotesque and barren tabloid drama, and beauteous Ava Gardner,
in the important title role, fails to give it plausibility or real appeal. "
But that is not to say that the stark film written and directed by Joseph L. Mankiewicz who had previously dissected stage folk in All
About Eve (1950), did not have its high artistic merits or entertainment values.   Edmond O'Brien as Oscar Muldoon the agent, won a

Best Supporting Actor Academy Award for his efforts in this biting
drama, and the entry remains a striking testament to Humphrey
Bogart's acting acumen.

The film is primarily of intellectual interest as a character
study of two Hollywood types: a once-lofty film director (Bogart) and
a loudmouthed press agent (O'Brien). (For In a Lonely Place, q. v.,
Bogart played a screenwriter involved in ennui, frustration, and murder.) Bogart, in fact, is the true star of this feature, portraying
Harry Dawes, the once-in-demand film director who is hired by an
international playboy (Warren Stevens) to write and helm a screenplay for the latter's amusement. The duo scout for a leading lady
and find Maria Vargas (Gardner) dancing in a cheap Madrid cabaret.
Some spark of her potential genius attracts the two to cast her as
their leading lady; on a personal level they vie with one another for
her romantic attentions. The feature they create is a big success,
helping Bogart to regain his stature and making the girl a star.
The dazzling social whirl which results from her instant fame spells
her doom as a tragic marriage to an impotent Italian count (Rossano
Brazzi) concludes in her murder.

The director, as essayed by Bogart, epitomizes the wise but
passive element of Hollywood characters who are not overly strong
in their own behalf to survive in the movie capitol's cutthroat world--
the cynic with a heart of gold. Did such a type really exist in the
Hollywood environs? If we are to believe this Hollywood-made movie
we must say "yes."

BATTLING HOOFER see SOMETHING TO SING ABOUT

BEHIND THE SCREEN see THE SHORT FILMS

BEHOLD THIS WOMAN (Vitagraph, 1924) 6425 ft.

Presenter, Albert E. Smith; director, J. Stuart Blackton;
based on the novel The Hillman by Edward Phillips Oppenheim;
screenplay, Marian Constance; camera, L. William O'Connell and
Ernest Smith.

Irene Rich (Louise Maurel); Marguerite De La Motte (Sophie);
Charles A. Post (John Strangeway); Harry Myers (Eugene de Seyre);
Rosemary Theby (Calavera); Anders Randolph (Stephen Strangeway).

A young cattleman, John Strangeway (Charles A. Post) falls
in love with screen star Louise Maurel (Irene Rich) after meeting
her at a mountain retreat. But his brother (Anders Randolph) urges
him to find out about her relationship with a playboy. When he confronts the actress about the situation he is disillusioned by her con-
fession and leaves town. Still later, after accepting and then re-
jecting the playboy's marriage proposal, the movie star finds Post
and asks his forgiveness.

This trite melodrama, a starring vehicle for Irene Rich, was
hardly pleasing art and caused more trouble than it should have, or
deserved to. The film was based on Edward Phillips Oppenheimer's

1917 novel The Hillman, but Vitagraph changed the title to Behold
This Woman for the film's release. As a result a lawsuit was
brought against the movie company by T. Everett Haire, the author
of the book Behold the Woman, claiming the new title infringed on
his novel. In the fall of 1924, Vitagraph announced the settlement
of the matter for the sum of $3, 000 and this second-rate celluloid
romance was issued by the declining studio. Unfortunately the film
contained no comparable intrigue.

BELLS OF ROSARITA (Republic, 1945) 68 min.

     Executive producer, Armand Schaefer; associate producer,
Eddy White; director, Frank McDonald; screenplay, Jack Townley;
music director, Morton Scott; music, Joseph Dubin; art director,
Hilyard Brown; set decorator, Earl B. Wooden; choreography, Larry
Ceballos; assistant director, John Grubb; sound, Fred Stahl; camera,
Ernest Miller; editor, Arthur Roberts.

     Roy Rogers (Himself); George "Gabby" Hayes (Gabby Whittaker);
Dale Evans (Sue Farnum); Adela Mara (Patty Phillips); Grant Withers
(William Ripley); Janet Martin (Rosarita); Addison Richards (Slim
Phillips); Roy Barcroft (Maxwell); Sons of the Pioneers, Robert Mit-
chell Boys Choir (Themselves); William "Wild Bill" Elliott, Allan
"Rocky" Lane, Don "Red" Barry, Robert Livingston, Sunset Carson,
and Trigger (Guest Stars).

     The B Western occasionally used the Hollywood-on-Hollywood
motif, especially in the thirties with films like Scarlet River, The
Big Show, Hollywood Cowboy, Hollywood Round-Up, and The Thrill
Hunter (qq. v.). The gimmick, however, came to less use in the
next decade although one of its most spectacular outings in the genre
arose with Republic's Bells of Rosarita. The entry coralled five top
studio cowboy stars to aid the film's hero, Roy Rogers, in punching
out the villains.
     Here Roy Rogers (playing himself as he usually did on screen)
has used Dale Evans' ranch for location shooting for his new feature
film. About to leave, he learns that Dale is being cheated by her
late father's corrupt partner (Grant Withers). The latter has stolen
the mortgage on the ranch and is about to weedle Evans out of her
inheritance, which includes the spread as well as a circus. Several
orphans, wards of Dale ask Roy to stay on to save her property.
He soon realizes he cannot save the situation by himself so he calls
the Republic studio and asks that several of his saddle pals come to
aid him in the trying situation.
     To the timely rescue come "Wild Bill" Elliott and his horse
Thunder, Allan "Rocky" Lane on Feather; Don "Red" Barry and Cy-
clone; Bob Livingstone on Shamrock; and "Sunset" Carson and Silver.
Together the six cowboy film heroes track down Withers and his gang
and put them in jail. At the finale the heroes, aided by Bob Nolan
and the Sons of the Pioneers, put on a big benefit show to earn money
to save Dale's floundering circus.
     While not a particularly overly active entry in the Roy Rogers

Dale Evans and Roy Rogers in <u>Bells of Rosarita</u> (1945).

Republic film series, the picture did excellent business due to the
bonus item of employing guest stars in the finale.   It is intriguing
to observe the Western heroes together and fighting for a joint cause,
especially since it was long rumored that the sextet had little appreciation for one another off the soundstage. (The next year, 1946, Roy
Rogers starred as himself in <u>Rainbow Over Texas</u>.   In this Republic
film he was described as a recording and film star, although no other
evidence of Hollywood was presented.)

BELOVED INFIDEL (20th Century-Fox, 1959) Color, 121 min.

Producer, Jerry Wald; director, Henry King; based on the
book by Sheilah Graham and Gerold Frank; screenplay, Sy Bartlett;
music, Franz Waxman; song, Paul Francis Webster and Waxman;
art directors, Lyle R. Wheeler and Maurice Ransford; camera, Leon
Shamroy; editor, William Reynolds.

Gregory Peck (F. Scott Fitzgerald); Deborah Kerr (Sheilah
Graham); Eddie Albert (Carter); Philip Ober (John Wheeler); Herbert

Rudley (Stan Harris); John Sutton (Lord Donegall); Karin Booth (Janet Pierce); Ken Scott (Robinson); Buck Class (Dion); A. Cameron Grant (Johnson); Cindy Ames (Miss Bull).

The emotional story of the three-year love affair between British-born columnist Sheilah Graham and ragged writing great F. Scott Fitzgerald made fairly engrossing reading. But the best seller did not translate well to the screen. Ms. Graham later claimed the writers at 20th Century-Fox took far too many liberties with her text, completely overlooking her own additions to the scenario, and the result was a film which bore little of the reality of her time with the profligate Fitzgerald. Whatever the cause--and it certainly did not help to cast wooden Gregory Peck as the enigmatic, self-destructive writing genius--the film is a stilted, tame, even vapid affair. It did not explicate the complexities of Fitzgerald (who was pictured as a weakling living off a successful woman) or of Ms. Graham (who appears continually domineering).

Set in the late 1930s and thereafter, the plot revolves about Graham (Deborah Kerr), a successful Hollywood columnist who has risen above her Cockney beginnings. She meets Fitzgerald at the famous Garden of Allah Hotel where the writer is living in his twilight days as a Hollywood scripter. Graham immediately feels sorry for the defeated author who is attempting at this point to earn sufficient money to keep his daughter in boarding school and his mentally unbalanced wife Zelda in a sanitarium. Soon sorrow turns to love and the oddly-matched couple (who continually switch roles as teacher-student) live together for the last three years of his tormented existence. The writer regains enough self-confidence to begin a new novel The Last Tycoon [q. v. , filmed by Paramount in 1976]--on Hollywood--before his sudden death from a heart attack.

Beloved Infidel reflects actual Hollywood in those scenes depicting Graham traipsing about the studios in search of gossip for her column. There is one amusing mini-sequence where Graham visits a soundstage and confronts a temperamental Constance Bennett-like actress. Columnist Graham refers to her as a "witch with a capital B." Too vaguely hinted at is the duality of Fitzgerald's inner nature: he was fascinated by the glamour and luxuries offered by the movie industry but as a true writer he despised the crassness of the production-line scripts turned out by the film factories. Needless to say, it irked him tremendously that he could never adapt himself emotionally or creatively to churning out drivel satisfactory for the celluloid mills. The Hollywood reflected in this film is not a happy one. It is a world where NOW mattered and the once-famous, like Fitzgerald, are of minor worth.

The New York Times labeled this "... a routine, tedious, and luridly-flapping drama.... [T]he picture is neither convincing nor affecting." The proceedings were not helped by veteran director Henry King's having to accommodate the hopefully-intimate tale to the demands of widescreen CinemaScope and the pedestrian appetites which producer Jerry Wald insisted was the basis of decent box-office returns.

Director King would later supervise an overblown screen version of Fitzgerald's Tender Is the Night (1962) starring Jennifer

Deborah Kerr in <u>Beloved Infidel</u> (1959).

Jones and Jason Robards.   Bad as that exercise was, it far better captured the ambiance of bygone eras (in Europe) than did <u>Beloved Infidel</u> reflect the glamourous/hellish peak of Hollywood's Golden Age in the thirties.

BEST FOOT FORWARD (MGM, 1943) Color, 95 min.

Producer, Arthur Freed; director, Edward Buzzell; based on the play by John Cecil Holm, Hugh Martin, and Ralph Blane; screenplay, Irving Brecher, Fred Finklehoffe, and uncredited: Dorothy Kingsley and Virginia Kellogg; music director, Lennie Hayton; songs, Martin and Blane; choreography, Charles Walters and uncredited Jack Donahue; orchestrators, Conrad Salinger, Jack Matthias, LeRoy Holmes, George Bassman, and Leo Arnaud; color consultants, Natalie Kalmus and Henri Jaffa; art directors, Cedric Gibbons and Edward Carfagno; set decorators, Edwin B. Willis and Mildred Griffiths; costumes, Irene; men's costumes, Gile Steele; makeup, Jack Dawn; sound, Douglas Shearer; camera, Leonard Smith; editor, Blanche Sewell.

Lucille Ball (Herself); William Gaxton (Jack O'Riley); Virginia

Weidler (Helen Schlessenger); Tommy Dix (Bud and Eldwood C. Hooper); Nancy Walker (Nancy the Blind Date); June Allyson (Minerva); Kenny Bowers (Dutch); Gloria De Haven (Ethel); Jack Jordan (Hunk); Chill Wills (Chester Short); Beverly Tyler (Miss Delaware Water Gap); Sara Haden (Miss Talbert); Henry O'Neill (Major Reeber); Bobby Stebbins (Greenie); Darwood Kaye (Killer); Morris Ankrum (Colonel Harkrider); Nana Bryant (Mrs. Dalyrimple); Harry James and His Music Makers (Themselves); Bess Flowers (Mrs. Bradd).

John Cecil Holmes' play Best Foot Forward--with a score by Hugh Martin and Ralph Blane--had a 326-performance run on Broadway beginning in the fall of 1941.   Director George Abbott supervised a cast which included Rosemary Lane as the movie star and supporting roles from June Allyson and Nancy Walker.   When MGM purchased the screen rights to the play, Abbott came West with the two female supporting cast members.   Although Lana Turner was selected by Metro for the film's lead, it was soon learned that she was pregnant.   The "Sweater Girl" was replaced by contractee Lucille Ball.
Five years prior, while at RKO, Ball had played a movie star in The Affairs of Annabel and Annabel Takes a Tour (qq. v.). Her role in Best Foot Forward was quite similar to that of Annabel Allison in that she was again a luminary who was ruled by her press agent, this time one Jack Haggerty (William Gaxton).   Gaxton convinces the star that to rebuild her sagging popularity she must accept an invitation from teenage fan Bud Hopper (Tommy Dix) to be his date at his military school prom.   Against her better judgment, Ball goes along with the wild scheme which is ballyhooed in the media by energetic Gaxton.   At the school, though, the star finds that Dix has a jealous girlfriend (Virginia Weidler).   Before the publicity stint is completed, Weidler has attacked the star.   After the melee, Ball loses not only her dignity, but also her formal dress.   All does end happily.
Despite the fact Best Foot Forward was shot in color, it was barely more than a glossy B effort from top-notch MGM.   Newcomers Allyson and Walker shone best in the film, especially the latter in her routine with Harry James and His Orchestra ("Alive and Kicking"). Gaxton was effective as the slippery mouthpiece of the not-so-bright movie personality.   Still the movie was a forced effort and Ball's dubbed performance of the song "You're Lucky" did not help matters. Co-star Weidler, who played the possessive girlfriend, would have more footage to herself in another genre effort of the period, MGM's The Youngest Profession (q. v.).

THE BEST THINGS IN LIFE ARE FREE (20th Century-Fox, 1956)
    Color, 104 min.

Producer, Henry Ephron; director, Michael Curtiz; story, John O'Hara; screenplay, William Bowers and Phoebe Ephron; songs, B. G. DeSylva, Lew Brown, and Ray Henderson; music director, Lionel Newman; assistant director, David Silver; art director, Lyle Wheeler; camera, Leon Shamroy; editor, Dorothy Spencer.

Ernest Borgnine, Gordon MacRae, Sheree North, and Dan Dailey in
The Best Things in Life Are Free (1956).

Gordon MacRae (B. G. DeSylva); Dan Dailey (Ray Henderson);
Ernest Borgnine (Lew Brown); Sheree North (Kitty Kane); Tommy
Noonan (Carl); Murvyn Vye (Manny); Phyllis Avery (Maggie Henderson);
Larry Keating (Sheehan); Tony Galento (Fingers); Norman Brooks (Al
Jolson); Jacques D'Amboise (Specialty Dancer); Roxanne Arlen (Perky
Nichols); Byron Palmer (Hollywood Star); Linda Brace (Jeannie Hen-
derson); Patty Lou Hudson (Susie Henderson); Peter Leeds (Genius);
Barrie Chase (Chorus Girl); Ann B. Davis (Hattie).

The title of this film resulted from one of the songs written
in collaboration by Buddy DeSylva, Lew Brown, and Ray Henderson
in the twenties.   This zesty musical (in CinemaScope and color) included a dozen tunes by the trio of songwriters and benefited by the
slick directing style of Michael Curtiz.   It relayed the breezy account
of the partnership of the creative trio, although many of the situations
pictured were strictly fictional.

The story opens in the twenties with the threesome coming together to write songs for a Broadway musical. They become acclaimed in the field and continue to work for the theatre until the coming of sound films, then transferring their talents to the screen in 1929. They are depicted creating the scores of such features as The Singing Fool and Sunny Side Up before the partnership dissolves; Brown and Henderson return to stage jobs, DeSylva remains in Hollywood and eventually enters the production side of film-making. The movie then (incorrectly) shows the trio reuniting in the forties for collaboration on more songs.

While hardly an earth-shattering experience, the film was well paced and displayed an amazing acting rapport among such disparate screen types as Dan Dailey, Gordon MacRae, and Ernest Borgnine. The songs that were used added much to the proceedings; of special interest to Hollywood buffs were the scenes of the writing of "Sonny Boy" for Al Jolson's The Singing Fool (with the sugary-sad song written as a lark and becoming a surprise hit), as well as the re-staging of the Grauman's Chinese Theatre premiere of Sunny Side Up.

For the record, Sheree North (nearing the end of her Marilyn Monroe-rivalry period) did her own galvanic dancing--in a "jack-knife pas de deux" and as a rambunctious hoodlum's widow in Rod Alexander's ballet on gangsters--but her singing was dubbed by ex-"Your Hit Parade" songstress Eileen Wilson.

BETTER MOVIES see THE SHORT FILMS

THE BIG KNIFE (United Artists, 1955) 111 min.

Producer/director, Robert Aldrich; based on the play by Clifford Odets; screenplay, James Poe; art director, William Glasgow; music director, Frank DeVol; assistant director, Nate Slott; camera, Ernest Laszlo; editor, Michael Luciano.

Jack Palance (Charles Castle); Ida Lupino (Marion Castle); Shelley Winters (Dixie Evans); Wendell Corey (Smiley Coy); Jean Hagen (Connie Bliss); Rod Steiger (Stanley Hoff); Ilka Chase (Patty Benedict); Everett Sloane (Nat Danziger); Wesley Addy (Hank Teagle); Paul Langton (Buddy Bliss); Nick Dennis (Nick); Bill Walker (Russell); Mike Winkelman (Billy Castle); Mel Welles (Bearded Man); Robert Sherman (Bongo Player); Strother Martin (Stillman); Ralph Volkie (Referee); Michael Fox (Announcer).

Not overly successful at the time of its issuance, The Big Knife has since acquired a cult following. Today it is considered one of the best of producer-director Robert Aldrich's early efforts if for no other reason than it "... impales the Zanuck-Goldwyn bigshot in Hollywood" (Manny Farber in Commentary). Probably the most ironic thing about the film today is that it made the all-possessive and ruthless studio head its main villain, this at a time when the likes of Harry Cohn and Darryl F. Zanuck were still very much in

Wendell Corey, Ida Lupino, Jean Hagen, Ilka Chase, Jack Palance, Everett Sloane, and Rod Steiger in a publicity pose for The Big Knife (1955).

power (which is one good reason why the film was produced and released through United Artists, a haven for independent moviemakers).

Based on Clifford Odets' 1949 Broadway play, The Big Knife
presented the mental conflict between a big-time popular movie star
(played by Jack Palance) and his growing antipathy with the Hollywood system, which feeds and nurtures him like a prize animal.
The main source of his unhappiness is the tyrannical studio boss (Rod
Steiger). As long as the star brings revenue into the studio coffers
the tycoon demands him to be constantly employed, no matter how
unhappy he may be with the company scheme of life. Finally the
actor can no longer tolerate the situation and insists on being released
from his contract. Then an old "skeleton" is yanked from the closet.
It seems years before the luminary was responsible for the death of
a girl and the film company boss had had a studio underling sent to
jail for the crime. Still the desperate star attempts the final break
and the result is tragedy.

Albeit engulfed in a "method acting" approach Palance offered
one of his best performances as the distraught star and Steiger presented the first of his Harry Cohn impersonations here (the second
came in the telefeature, The Movie Maker, q. v.). Others in the
stellar cast included Wendell Corey as Steiger's hypercritical, de-
ceitful hatchetman, Ida Lupino as Palance's shallow (was this intended?) spouse, Wesley Addy as an integrity-soaked writer, Everett
Sloane as an intense agent, and two trollops, Shelley Winters and Jean
Hagen (who had scored in MGM's Singin' in the Rain, q. v. , an entirely different type of "indictment" of Hollywood).

There were few superlatives offered for this study of the
effect of Hollywood on its workers. Bosley Crowther (New York
Times) noted, "Actually, it looks as though The Big Knife originally
was written and aimed as an angry, vituperative incident of the personal and professional morals of Hollywood. This is the clear impli-
cation of what is presented on the screen. ... [T]he simple fact is
that Mr. Odets--and James Poe, who wrote the screen adaptation--
were more disposed to extreme emotionalism than to actuality and
good sense. They picture a group of sordid people jawing at one
another violently. But their drama arrives at a defeatist climax. "

THE BIG SHOW (Republic, 1936) 70 min.

Producer, Nat Levine; director, Mark V. Wright; story/screen-
play, Dorrell and Stuart McGowan; songs, Sam H. Stept, Ned Washington, and Ted Koehler; camera, William Nobles and Edgar Lyons;
editor, Robert Johns.

Gene Autry (Gene Autry/Tom Ford); Smiley Burnette (Frog);
Kay Hughes (Marion Hill); Sally Payne (Toodles); William Newell
(Wilson); Max Terhune (Max); Charles Judels (Swartz); Rex King
(Collins); Harry Worth (Rico); Mary Russell (Mary); Christine Maple
(Elizabeth); The Sons of the Pioneers with Roy Rogers (Themselves).

Cowboy film star Tom Ford is snobbish and incompetent in
action sequences, the latter being accomplished by his stunt double,

who receives no credit for his hazardous work.   When Mammoth
Studios pressure Ford to appear in person at Dallas' Texas Centennial, the star refuses and the studio officials hastily decide to use
his look-alike double.   The replacement, it turns out, is not only a
nice fellow, but he can also sing and he proves his real-life heroics
when he stops crooks from stealing the profits from the centennial
show.   By the picture's end, it is Ford who ends up working as the
double for the new star.

Gene Autry played the dual roles of both Ford and the likeable
stuntman, but the action work in the feature was actually accomplished
by Yakima Canutt, since Autry himself could barely stay astride a
horse.   The Big Show (which refers to the Texas festivities) was a
big, colorful production and one that incorporated much actual footage
from the Texas Centennial to add authenticity as well as spectacular
(low-cost) action.   Bob Nolan and the Sons of the Pioneers (including
Roy Rogers) were in the cast to back up Autry with musical interludes.   Some intriguing footage (from earlier Republic and Mascot
films) were blended into the proceedings to display the complexities
and dangers of assorted stunt work.

"It looked classy, and was" is how Don Miller summed up the
film in Hollywood Corral (1976) and there can be little doubt that
this was one of the films which helped to place Gene Autry on the
top of the heap as the most popular cowboy film star, a position he
would maintain until the coming of World War II when he voluntarily
and temporarily retired from films.

Interestingly, Autry would again be cast as a cinema stunt
man in another Hollywood-oriented Western, Shooting High (q. v.).
In Gaucho Serenade (1940), also starring Autry, Smith Ballew played
a cowpoke who gives up the girl to Autry so he can depart for Hollywood and star in Western sagas.

BIG TIME (Fox 1929) 7815 ft.

Presenter, William Fox; associate producer, Chandler Sprague;
director, Kenneth Hawks; stage director, A. H. Van Buren; based on
the story "Little Ledna" by William Wallace Smith; adaptor, Sidney
Lanfield; dialogue, Lanfield and William K. Wells; songs, Lanfield;
assistant director, Max Gold; costumes, Sophie Wachner; camera, L.
William O'Connell; editor, Al De Gaetano.

Lee Tracy (Eddie Burns); Mae Clarke (Lily Clark); Daphne
Pollard (Sybil); Josephine Dunn (Gloria); Stepin Fetchit (Eli); John
Ford (Himself).

This early talkie was one of the first sound films to delve
into the breakup of a show business family with the movies as a
background.   Its chief interest today, however, is a guest appearance
by triple Oscar-winning director John Ford as himself on the Fox
lot (where he was then employed).

Lee Tracy (in his film debut) starred as Eddie Dunn, a big-
headed, conceited song-and-dance man comedian who teams with
pretty Lily Clark (Mae Clarke--also debuting) to appear in a small-

time theatre act. Tracy's character is convinced he is destined for the big time. Later he and Clarke wed and enjoy show business success until she becomes pregnant and has a child. Thereafter he hires a new partner, Gloria (Josephine Dunn), with whom he has an affair. When Clarke learns of this philandering she leaves him; his act with Gloria then flops and they split apart.

Tracy is unable to find stage work and is told repeatedly that Clarke was the secret of his former success, both domestically and professionally. Tracy then drifts from job to job until he winds up working at a lunch counter. Finally he hops a train to Hollywood where he earns his passage by trying to make a train conductor laugh. In the movie capital he finds that Mae Clarke is a big success in talking films. The only work he can find in the industry is as an extra. Eventually he is cast in one of her starring vehicles which brings them back together romantically.

The New York Times said that this feature, directed by Howard Hawks' brother Kenneth, "... is so cleverly produced, in the matter of humor, its incidents / and telling atmosphere, and so glibly acted by Lee Tracy, that it affords a most agreement entertainment." Photoplay magazine weighed it "darned good."

THE BLACK CAMEL (Fox, 1931) 71 min.

Director, Hamilton MacFadden; based on the novel by Earl Derr Biggers; screenplay, Hugh Stange, Barry Conners, and Philip Klein; camera, Joe August and Dan Clark; editor, Al De Gaetano.

Warner Oland (Charlie Chan); Sally Eilers (Julie O'Neil); Bela Lugosi (Tarneverro); Dorothy Revier (Shelah Fane); Victor Varconi (Robert Fyfe); Robert Young (Jimmy Bradshaw); Marjorie White (Rita Ballou); Richard Tucker (Wilkie Ballou); J. M. Kerrigan (Thomas MacMaster); Mary Gordon (Mrs. MacMaster); C. Henry Gordon (Van Horn); Violet Dunn (Anna); William Post, Jr. (Alan Jaynes); Dwight Frye (Jessop); Murray Kinnell (Smith); Otto Yamaoka (Kashimo); Rita Roselle (Luana); Robert Homans (Chief of Police); Louise Mackintosh (Housekeeper).

The Black Camel (referring to death) was one of the six Charlie Chan novels written by Earl Derr Biggers. Fox brought it to the screen in mid-1931 with Warner Oland as Chan, a role he had initially popularized a year earlier. Teamed with Oland was Bela Lugosi who played a major red-herring in the proceedings. (Fox sent The Black Camel company to Hawaii for location work. Lugosi had planned to wed Lillian Arch aboard the ship carrying the group to Hawaii, however the 19-year-old's parents learned of the scheme and Bela went alone; the couple did wed in 1933.) Lugosi's marquee value (Dracula had been issued six months earlier) greatly helped the film's popularity. Today, The Black Camel is the earliest of the Chan features to be available for television viewing.

Despite the deletion of a great deal of the overall content of the book in the 71-minute feature, the basic plot line remained in-

Warner Oland and Sally Eilers in The Black Camel (1931).

tact.   A movie company is filming in location in Honolulu and Chan
is called in to solve the murder of the star Shelah Fane (Dorothy
Revier).   The Oriental sleuth, however, has his task cut out for him,
for the situation is loaded with suspects, including an ex-husband and
a spiritualist (Lugosi) who had been preying on the star who had a
past to hide.   There is also a house-full of suspicious domestics,
including the butler Jessop (played by Dwight Frye, who was seen
as Renfield of Lugosi's Dracula).   Eventually Chan deduces who
is the murderer; it turns out to be a member of the household staff
who has taken drastic revenge on the actress for a past misdeed.
        Although a bit creeky by today's standards, this early talkie
was quite a successful entry in the blooming Charlie Chan series.
The picture was well-produced and quite entertaining, especially in
the dialogue exchanges between Oland's Charlie Chan and Lugosi's
Tarneverro.   For some the repartee between the two verge on "camp, "
as for example when the mystic confides to Chan, "Shelah was killed
because she knew too much!"   Although Robert Young was under contract to MGM at the time of The Black Camel, he was being loaned
out by his home lot to give the fledgling screen player needed on-
camera experience.

BLACK EYE (Warner Bros. , 1974) Color, 98 min.

        Executive producer, Jack Reeves; associate producer, Larry
Noble; producer, Pat Rooney; assistant producer, Anne Reeves;

director, Jack Arnold; based on the novel <u>Murder on the Wild Side</u> by Jeff Jacks; screenplay, Mark Haggard and Jim Martin; set decorators, Chuck Pierce and John Rozman; assistant directors, Clark Paylow and David Hamburger; music, Mort Garson; wardrobe, Tony S. Scarano; makeup, Harry Ray; sound, Bud Alper, Gene Ashbrook, and A. Gilmore; camera, Ralph Woolsey; editor, Gene Ruggiero.

Fred Williamson (Shep Stone); Rosemary Forsyth (Miss Francis); Teresa Graves (Cynthia); Floy Dean (Diane Davis); Richard Anderson (Raymond Dole [Nick Masetti]); Cyril Delevanti (Talbot T. Talbot); Richard X. Slattery (Lieutenant Bill Bowen); Larry Mann (Reverend Avery); Bret Morrison (Max Majors); Susan Arnold (Amy Dole); Frank Stell (Harry Chess); Nancy Fisher (Vera Brownmiller); Joann Bruno (Moms); Edmund Penny (Marcus Rollo); Gene Elman (Lou Siegel); William O'Connell (Minister); Bob Minor (Black Hench).

This low-calibre thriller, which depicts operations on the very fringes of the movie industry, was directed by Jack Arnold, a technician highly-regarded in the fifties.

Its protagonist is Shep Stone (Fred Williamson), a black former police lieutenant suspended from his job for killing a dope pusher. He committed the deed to avenge his sister's death from an overdose. Now he is a private eye in a tacky California beach resort town. After finding the dead body of a hooker, he is attacked by her killer, Harry Chess (Frank Stell), with a fancy cane the dead girl had stolen from a recently-deceased film star. When the attacker escapes, Williamson is assigned by the local police to work on the case. The trail leads to a porno filmmaker, but the lead is a false one.

Later he is approached by Raymond Dole (Richard Anderson) who hires him to trace his missing daughter Amy (Susan Arnold). The detective discovers she has become a Jesus freak and lives with a group run by a guru named Reverend Avery (Larry Mann). Her special lover turns out to be none other than Stell. When Stell is killed for not giving up the cane, Williamson uncovers that the instrument is hollow and was used to smuggle drugs. Still later, at a party, the blue movie producer and his thugs corner Williamson. He escapes and takes Anderson to a meeting of Mann's flock. Anderson shoots the religious leader and is about to kill Arnold, who has heroin taped to her body, when the girl is saved by Williamson. The police arrive and the true story comes out. It seems that Arnold is not Anderson's daughter, but a pusher who worked for him until she had turned against him and has stolen a consignment of dope.

Tying this thriller into the Hollywood ambiance is a brief sequence in which Williamson visits a porno movie set. He appears to be the only one there interested in the titillating action being filmed.

BLAZING SADDLES (Warner Bros., 1974) Color, 93 min.

Producer, Michael Hertzberg; director, Mel Brooks; story, Andrew Bergman; screenplay, Brooks, Norman Steinberg, Bergman,

Dom DeLuise (right) in <u>Blazing Saddles</u> finale (1974).

Richard Pryor, and Alan Uger; production designer, Peter Wooley; set decorator, Morey Hoffman; music/music director, John Morris; orchestrators, Jonathan Tunick and Morris; songs, Morris and Brooks; costumes, Nino Novarese; choreography, Alan Johnson; sound, Gene S. Cantamessa; special effects, Douglas Pettibone; camera, Joseph Biroc; editors, John C. Howard and Danford Greene.

Cleavon Little (Bart); Gene Wilder (Jim [Waco Kid]); Slim Pickens (Taggart); Harvey Korman (Hedley Lamarr); Madeline Kahn (Lily Von Shtupp); Mel Brooks (Governor William J. Lepetomane/Indian Chief); Burton Gilliam (Lyle); Alex Karras (Mongo); David Huddleston (Olson Johnson); Liam Dunn (Reverend Johnson); John Hillerman (Howard Johnson); George Furth (Van Johnson); Claude Ennis Starrett, Jr. (Gabby Johnson); Carol Arthur (Harriett Johnson); Richard Collier (Dr. Sam Johnson); Charles McGregor (Charlie); Robyn Hilton (Miss Stein); Don Megowan (Gum Chewer); Dom DeLuise (Buddy Bizarre); Count Basie (Himself).

Besides contributing to the genre of the Western film, this

movie also makes a minor addition to the realm of the Hollywood-on-
Hollywood picture.   Unfortunately this aspect of the storyline emerges
at the finale and is considered by some to be a jarring dissonance
to the excellent harmony of theme that had preceded it.
        Black sheriff Bart (Cleavon Little) is called upon to battle all
manners of odds and a wide assortment of villains--including the
oversized Mongo (Alex Karras)--in his efforts to clean up a Western
town.   The climax of Blazing Saddles almost appears to have been
grafted onto the main plot.   It has the film stars leaving the old
West and running rampant through the Warner Bros. studios in a
madcap race to reach the theatre screening the premiere of Blazing
Saddles.   In the ensuing mayhem, chaos reigns supreme on a soundstage where Buddy Bizarre (Dom DeLuise) is leading a chorus line
through their paces a la Busby Berkeley.   At the end, Harvey Korman is shot down in the cement in front of Grauman's Chinese
Theatre, with Little and Gene Wilder later buying tickets to see a
showing of the film and learn how it concludes.
        Iconoclastic filmmaker Mel Brooks expanded his kidding of
Hollywood to much better advantage in the later Silent Movie (q. v.).

BLONDE BOMBSHELL   see   BOMBSHELL

BLUEBEARD'S SEVEN WIVES (First National, 1926) 7774 ft.

        Presenter, Robert Kane; director, Alfred Santell; story,
Blanche Merrill and Paul Schofield; titles, Randolph Bartlett; art
director, Robert M. Haas; camera, Robert Haller.

        Ben Lyon (John Hart/Don Juan Hartez); Lois Wilson (Mary
Kelly); Blanche Sweet (Juliet); Dorothy Sebastian (Gilda La Bray);
Diana Kane (Kathra Granni); Sam Hardy (Gindelheim); Dick Bernard
and Andrew Mack (Film Magnates); B. C. Duval (Dan Pennell); Wilfred Lytell (Paris); Dorothy Sebastian, Katherine Ray, Ruby Blaine,
Lucy Fox, Muriel Spring, Kathleen Martyn, and Diana Kane (Bluebeard's Seven Wives).

        This popular comedy was a cute satire on Hollywood, especial-
ly about oft-married film stars and their over-active press agents.
"Let the gas out and use the quarter to see this," was Photoplay
magazine's way of heartily recommending this romp.   "You'd never
believe Ben Lyon could be so funny, with Lois Wilson in the role
of a flapjack flipper at Childs," the magazine continued.
        John Hart (Lyon), a none-too-efficient bank clerk, messes up
his accounts after his girl, Mary Kelly (Wilson) announces she will
not wed him unless he grows a moustache.   He loses his bank post
and finding no other work is forced to become a movie extra.   On
the set of a feature to which he is assigned, the temperamental star
quits and the angy director claims he can make anyone a star out of
the part.   He selects Lyon and soon the young man has become a big
cinema celebrity.   However, he is at the mercy of his studio and
its publicity department which churns up romance after romance for

him and finally arranges seven marriages in seven weeks. Disgusted
with movie life, Lyon returns to Wilson and they wed. They retire
to a farm and exist happily ever after, Lyon refusing to return to
movie chores.

BOMBSHELL (aka BLONDE BOMBSHELL) (MGM, 1933) 91 min.

    Associate producer, Hunt Stromberg; director, Victor Fleming;
based on the play by Caroline Francke and Mack Crane; screenplay,
Jules Furthman and John Lee Mahin; art director, Merrill Pye; set
decorator, Edwin B. Willis; gowns, Adrian; camera, Chester Lyons
and Harold G. Rosson; editor, Margaret Booth.

    Jean Harlow (Lola Burns); Lee Tracy (Space Hanlon); Frank
Morgan (Pop Burns); Franchot Tone (Gifford Middleton); Pat O'Brien
(Jim Brogan); Una Merkel (Miss Mac); Ted Healy (Junior Burns); Ivan
Lebedeff (Marquis di Binelli); Isabel Jewell (Junior's Girl); Louise
Beavers (Loretta); Leonard Carey (Winters); Mary Forbes (Mrs. Mid-
dleton); C. Aubrey Smith (Mr. Middleton); June Brewster (Alice Cole).

    Movie star Lola Burns (Jean Harlow) tires of her sexy film
roles and all of the attendant publicity. She craves more dramatic
parts and a happier life. To achieve domestic bliss, she becomes
engaged to a marquis (Ivan Lebedeff), but her press agent (Lee
Tracy) has him arrested as an illegal alien. Film director Jim
Brogan (Pat O'Brien) wants to marry her and have her continue in
films, but she refuses. Instead she tries to adopt a baby. Her
zany father (Frank Morgan) and brother (Ted Healy), however, ruin
this chance when adoption officials visit her mansion and declare
the environs unfit for a child.
    So a distraught Harlow departs for Palm Springs to think over
her future and there meets a handsome and seemingly rich young
man (Franchot Tone). His snobbish family (Mary Forbes and C.
Aubrey Smith), however, dislike her and her brother and father,
and she breaks the engagement.
    Back at the studio she again sees Tone and his family and
learns they are actors hired by Tracy to insure that she will return
to work. He convinces the still skeptical Harlow that she truly belongs in films. At the same time, she realizes he cares for her
romantically.
    Director Victor Fleming guided this sugary gloss through its
paces in zesty form. The end result is an entertaining exercise
with Harlow deliciously rambunctious as the fickle Lola Burns. In
the course of the 91 minutes, Harlow projects some hearty dialogue.
At one point when she is being courted by Tone, she gasps, "Not
even Norma Shearer or Helen Hayes in their nicest pictures were
spoken to like this!" At another juncture when she is in the midst
of an interview with a determined gossip columnist, Harlow remarks
about her outrageous publicity, "I ask you as one lady to another
... isn't that a load of clams?"
    The supporting cast was almost as good as the star, especial-
ly Tracy as the crafty publicity agent, Morgan as the addled father,

Jean Harlow and Lee Tracy in a publicity pose for Bombshell [also,
Blonde Bombshell] (1973).

O'Brien as the stern director, and Tone as the pretender.   Tone and
Harlow made quite a romantic duo on screen and were reteamed for
MGM's The Girl from Missouri (1934), Reckless (1935), and Suzy
(1936).
      "This farce comedy ... enjoys itself at Hollywood's expense,
and as it spins its slangy but mirthful yarn, it has some unexpected
and adroitly conceived turns..." wrote Mordaunt Hall of the New York
Times.   Many reviewers, however, did not regard the film on its
sturdy face value, but instead regarded it as just another stepping
stone in the soaring career of sex goddess Harlow.
      This Metro release was also issued as Blonde Bombshell, be-
cause the studio feared the public would think the film's title referred
to the war movie genre.

BOSTON BLACKIE GOES HOLLYWOOD (Columbia, 1942) 68 min.

Producer, Wallace MacDonald; director, Michael Gordon; screenplay, Paul Yawitz; music director, Morris Stoloff; camera, Henry Freulich; editor, Arthur Seid.

Chester Morris (Boston Blackie); George E. Stone (The Runt); Richard Lane (Inspector Farraday); Forrest Tucker (Whipper); William Wright (Slick Barton); Lloyd Corrigan (Arthur Manleder); John Tyrrell (Steve); Walter Sand (Sergeant Mathews); Constance Worth (Gloria Lane); Shirley Patterson (Stewardess); Ralph Dunn (Sergeant); Charles Sullivan and Al Herman (Cab Drivers); Jessie Arnold (Tenant); Cy Ring (Hotel Manager).

Made as the fourth entry in Columbia's long-running Boston Blackie series, this programmer used the motion picture capital in its title to stimulate box-office revenues. (Even as late as the forties filmgoers were relatively unjaded about soundstage stories.) Although the caper supposedly took place in and about Hollywood, it was strictly backlot all the way and the double-bill item provided minimum information about film-making or its array of workers.
Blackie (Chester Morris) and his pal The Runt (George E. Stone) become involved in the theft of the fabulous Monterey diamond. The film opens as Morris receives an urgent call from a California pal who requests that the former jewel thief extract $60,000 from the man's Manhattan safe and bring it to Hollywood as fast as possible. Morris carries out the mission, but Inspector Faraday (Richard Lane) and the boys from the New York police department arrive on the scene and discover Morris with the bundle of cash. After a good deal of explanation Morris is allowed to head West. Actually the police chief intends to follow the amateur sleuth there for he is convinced the one-time thief is somehow entangled in the diamond robbery. Once in Hollywood Morris naturally captures the robbers and restores the diamond to its proper owners by the film's fade-out.
A much better effort in the low-budget detective genre "going Hollywood" was found two years later in RKO's The Falcon in Hollywood (q. v.).

BOTH ENDS OF THE CANDLE   see   THE HELEN MORGAN STORY

BOTTOMS UP (Fox, 1934) 85 min.

Producer, B. G. DeSylva; director, David Butler; story/screenplay, DeSylva, Butler, and Sid Silvers; music director, C. Bakaleinikoff; orchestrator, Howard Jackson; songs, Harold Adamson and Burton Lane, Richard Whiting and Gus Kahn; choreography, H. Hecht; art director, Gordon Wiles; dance sets/costumes, Russell Patterson; sound, Joseph Aiken; camera, Arthur Miller; editor, Irene Morra.

Spencer Tracy (Smoothie King); John Boles (Hal Reed); Pat Paterson (Wanda Gale); Herbert Mundin (Limey Brook); Sid Silvers

(Spud Mosco); Harry Green (Louis Baer); Thelma Todd (Judith Marlowe); Robert Emmet O'Connor (Detective Rooney); Dell Henderson
(Lane Worthing); Suzanne Kaaren (Secretary); Douglas Wood (Baldwin).

A Canadian beauty contest winner (Pat Paterson) heads to
Hollywood to try her luck in pictures. But she runs out of money
and meets up with a trio (Spencer Tracy, Herbert Mundin, and Sid
Silvers) of out-of-work fellows who take her to live with them in an
abandoned hut on a miniature golf course. Tracy is a one-time news
agent and to get himself and his pals back in the dough he launches
a phony publicity campaign about Paterson, stating that she is the
daughter of a British nobleman visiting in the film capital. Mundin,
a forger recently released from prison, poses as the titled gentleman.
Tracy later manages to get Paterson an invitation to a party hosted
by Hal Reed (John Boles), a heavy-drinking film star. Tracy then
manufactures a romance between Boles and Paterson.
      By now Tracy has fallen in love with his client, but he is bent
on getting her ahead in the film business. He wangles a part for her
in Boles' latest musical. Paterson proves adept in the film role and
she gains fame, even when her true parentage is discovered.
      At the finale she and Boles plan to wed while Tracy gallantly
steps aside and seeks new suckers to fleece.
      "If the film Bottoms Up ... fires darts and daggers at Holly-
wood in a less subtle fashion than was done in Once in a Lifetime
[q. v.], this current attraction has its full share of honest humor and
also several tuneful songs. It is a neat, carefree piece of work"
(New York Times). The film represents a typical mid-thirties Tracy
film with the star portraying a wise-cracking crook with a heart of
gold. Britisher Paterson (who would wed Charles Boyer in 1934)
made her U.S. film debut as the aspiring actress who succumbs to
the charms of screen crooner Boles. Boles, always an underrated
actor, actually held the film together and made the most of his two
songs, "Little Did I Dream" and "Waiting at the Gate for Katie"
(the latter a production number complete with mixed chorus).

BOY MEETS GIRL (Warner Bros., 1938) 80 min.

      Producer, George Abbott; director, Lloyd Bacon; based on the
play by Bella and Sam Spewack; screenplay, the Spewacks; music director, Leo F. Forbstein; song, Jack Scholl and M. K. Jerome; makeup, Perc Westmore; costumes, Milo Anderson; sound, Dolph Thomas;
camera, Sol Polito; editor, William Holmes.

      James Cagney (Robert Law); Pat O'Brien (J. C. Benson);
Marie Wilson (Susie); Ralph Bellamy (C. Elliott Friday); Frank Mc-
Hugh (Rossetti); Dick Foran (Larry Toms); Bruce Lester (Rodney
Bevan); Ronald Reagan (Announcer); Paul Clark (Happy); Penny Single-
ton (Peggy); Dennie Moore (Miss Crews); Harry Seymour and Bert
Hanlon (Songwriters); James Stephenson (Major Thompson); Pierre
Watkin (B. K.); John Ridgely (Cutter); George Hickman (Office Boy);
Cliff Saum (Smitty); Carole Landis (Commissary Cashier); Curt Bois
(Dance Director); Hal K. Dawson (Wardrobe Attendant); Bert Howland

(Director); Vera Lewis (Cleaning Woman); Peggy Moran (New York Telephone Operator).

Boy Meets Girl has a history which is perhaps just as captivating as the film itself. Warner Bros. acquired the screen rights to the play in 1935, intending for producer George Abbott to handle a cast including Marion Davies and the comedy team of Olsen and Johnson. (The stage version starred Allyn Joslyn and Jerome Cowan as the writers, Joyce Arling as the waitress, and Charles McClelland as the cowboy star.) Miss Davies, however, did not like the script and decided to retire from films. Eventually the property became James Cagney's first film back at Warners after breaking his contract in 1936 and starring in two projects for Grand National, including Something to Sing About (q. v.). Cagney would always have an ambivalent attitude toward this film; he once remarked the feature should never have been made.

In the story, set at Warner Bros., Cagney and Pat O'Brien are teamed as two daffy scenarists who continually use the theme of "boy meets girl" in their pictures. Their practical jokes on the lot do not make them overly popular with the studio heads, despite the success of their writing. Moreover, they are always at odds with the lot's pompous cowboy star Larry Toms (Dick Foran). To upset Foran, the over-aged boys write a part in his new film for the yet unborn child of a studio commissary waitress (Marie Wilson). When the baby is born the writers become its godfathers and promise to sponsor the infant in pictures. The baby is named Happy and he soon steals the limelight from the distraught cowboy star.

Understandably, not many films have poked fun at the breed of screen writers, a group perhaps most responsible for some of the cinema's most literate material as well as some of its most puerile of pap. According to some theories, Sam and Bella Spewack, who wrote the Broadway hit and adapted it for the screen, based their prototypes on Ben Hecht and Charles MacArthur, although they never would acknowledge the fact.

Boy Meets Girl was a solid box-office success; its slick pacing and the screwball performances of the leads carried the film very well. The production was helped immeasurably by Wilson's dumb blonde performance as the waitress, by Foran* as the witless cowboy star, by Ralph Bellamy as the loutish producer (nearly always a chief villain or figure of abuse in movies on moviemaking), Frank McHugh as the pugnacious talent agent, and in a bit, by Ronald Reagan as a radio announcer. Reagan is seen at the Carthay Circle Theatre reporting on the opening of Errol Flynn's latest picture, The White Rajah; which was an "inside" joke since the swashbuckling star had sold his studio, Warner Bros., a story by this title, which they never produced.

---

*In the late thirties, Dick Foran was making a series of B Westerns for Warner Bros., which were above average for that market. The possessor of a good singing voice, he frequently vocalized in his films and often made recordings for Bluebird Records.

Although many who had seen the biting Broadway version of
Boy Meets Girl were disappointed that Hollywood had diluted its in-
dustry parody, the film had its adherents. The New York Herald-
Tribune labeled it "an extremely amusing screen comedy," while
Time magazine said it "goes like a house afire...."
     Cagney and O'Brien who had already teamed on screen in
Here Comes the Navy (1934), Devil Dogs of the Air (1935), The Irish
In Us (1935), and Ceiling Zero (1935), would be rematched in Angels
with Dirty Faces (1938), The Fighting 69th (1940), and Torrid Zone
(1940), the latter two directed by William Keighley who supervised
Boy Meets Girl. Also in 1938, Keighley had directed for Warner
Bros. , Secrets of an Actress, a lacklustre Kay Francis-George
Brent mini-vehicle which dealt very tangently with another performing
medium, the theatre.

BROADWAY BROKE (Selznick Distributing Corp. , 1923) 5923 ft.

     Director, J. Searle Dawley; based on the story by Earl Derr
Biggers; screenplay, John Lynch; camera, Bert Dawley.

     Mary Carr (Nellie Wayne); Percy Marmont (Tom Kerrigan);
Gladys Leslie (Mary Karger); Dore Davidson (Lou Gorman); MacKlyn
Arbuckle (P. T. Barnum); Macey Harlam (Claude Benson); Edward
Earle (Charles Farrin); Pierre Gendron (Jack Graham); Billy Quirk
(Joe Karger); Henrietta Crosman (Madge Foster); Sally Crute (Augusta
Karger); Leslie King (Mark Twain); Albert Phillips (General Grant);
Frederick Burton (Augustin Daly); Lassie Bronte (Chum the Dog).

     Actress Mary Carr tended to make a professional living play-
ing older women, many of these characters being two or three times
her real age. Here she interpreted Nellie Wayne who becomes a
movie star late in life. It is intriguing that this early twenties'
silent should depict an older woman become a film success when the
genre--especially after Sunset Boulevard (q. v.)--would more usually
concentrate on has-beens. (This trend had begun as early as Show
Girl in Hollywood, q. v. , with Blanche Sweet as a faded movie queen.)
     This minor outing, derived from an Earl Derr Biggers' story,
focued on retired stage star Nellie Wayne who supported herself and
her family by the earnings of "Chum" their aging vaudeville canine.
When the dog dies the family is without a steady income. Carr's
Nellie digs up some of her old stage plays which she had written as
starring vehicles. She then sells the properties to movie producers
who are eager for screen material. Finally one big mogul sees potential in Carr as a screen actress and soon she is rediscovered for
the "flickers. "
     It should be noted that a good deal of the film's footage focus-
es on theatre life and not on film activities.

BROADWAY TO HOLLYWOOD (MGM, 1933) 90 min.

     Associate producer, Harry Rapf; director, Willard Mack;

screenplay, Mack and Edgar Allan Woolf; art director, Stanwood
Rogers; songs, Al Goodhart; Howard Johnson and Gus Edwards; Edgar
Smith and John Stromberg; Robert B. Smith and Stromberg; camera,
William Daniels and Norbert Brodine.

Alice Brady (Lulu Hackett); Frank Morgan (Ted Hackett);
Madge Evans (Anne Ainslee); Russell Hardie (Ted Hackett, Jr.);
Jackie Cooper (Ted Hackett, Jr. as a Child); Eddie Quillan (Ted
Hackett III); Mickey Rooney (Ted Hackett III as a Child); Edward
Brophy (Joe Mannion); Tad Alexander (David); Ruth Channing (Wanda);
Jean Howard (Grace); Jimmy Durante, Fay Templeton, May Robson,
Claire DuBrey, Muriel Evans, Claudelle Kaye, Nelson Eddy, Una
Merkel, Albertina Rasch Dancers (Guest Bits).

The tracing of the history of performers in show business,
usually progressing from the stage to films, has been a popular
slant in motion pictures.   It has especially been a favorite device
for screen musicals such as Broadway to Hollywood.   Unfortunately
this entry was a minor effort, a glossy B film which is practically
forgotten today, except for the work of a few guest-star performers.
The 90-minute feature relates the tale of three generations of
the Hackett family from their days in vaudeville on through their
years in films.   Frank Morgan and Alice Brady appeared as the
grandparents who had been stars in the vaudeville circuit and who--
in the last third of the feature--guide the career of their grandson
Ted (played by Eddie Quillan).   Quillan soon becomes a big picture
star, but he has none of the needed integrity and sense of responsi-
bility to cope with the fame.   It is only the advice of his wise grandfather that keeps him from sinking in the quicksand of stardom.   At
the finale, while the young man is doing a family-worn routine for
the cameras, Morgan collapses and dies in his wife's arms, happy
to know that Quillan is carrying on the family tradition.
The New York American enthusiastically and generously reported, "All the heartbreak and all the happiness, the tragedy as
well as the comedy of life behind the footlights is portrayed in gra-
phic fashion. "   For viewers even then, much of the narrative seemed
already worn with clichés.
The history behind Broadway to Hollywood is more interesting
than the film itself.   In 1929 material was filmed for a super lavish
MGM musical, but when that vogue died out in 1930 the footage was
junked.   Its producers, however, continued to search for a framework in which to use the shelved sequences.   Eventually some of
the scrapped footage (including bits with Jimmy Durante and Fay
Templeton) wound up in this release.   Also to be noted is that Nelson Eddy made his feature film debut in this picture.

BROKEN HEARTS OF HOLLYWOOD (Warner Bros., 1926) 7770 ft.

Director, Lloyd Bacon; story, Raymond L. Schrock and Edward Clark; screenplay, C. Graham Baker; assistant director, Ted
Stevens; camera, Virgil Miller; assistant camera, Walter Robinson;
editor, Clarence Kolster.

Patsy Ruth Miller (Betty Anne Bolton); Louise Dresser (Virginia Perry); Douglas Fairbanks, Jr. (Hal Terwilliger); Jerry Miley (Marshall); Stuart Holmes (McLain); Barbara Worth (Molly); Dick Sutherland (Sheriff); Emile Chautard (Director); Anders Randolf (District Attorney); George Nicholls (Chief of Detectives); Sam De Grasse (Defense Attorney).

This low budget fare offered a popular cast, a maudlin story of filmland and little else, resulting in Photoplay magazine's judgment, "It's just as bad as it sounds."

Louise Dresser was featured as a faded film star who has become an alcoholic. It seems she was once a popular player who retired to marry and become a mother. She was, however, lured back to the cameras and in the process deserted her family. Older and now no longer beautiful, she finds work only on poverty row.

Meanwhile, her grown daughter Betty Anne Bolton (Patsy Ruth Miller) wins a beauty contest and comes to Hollywood. She fails her screen test and becomes involved with a pseudo-acting school. She falls in love with a stuntman who is later badly injured in a fall. To earn money to help him, she resorts to prostitution. A matinee idol picks her up, takes a paternal interest in her, and she / moves in with his family. He gives her the expense money for her boyfriend's hospitalization as well as the lead in his next film which happens to have her mother in a supporting role.

Dresser does not allow Miller to suspect who she is. When she discovers the crooked owner of the acting school has lecherous plans for her offspring, Dresser, while drunk, shoots him. She is put on trial, but is saved by her daughter's testimony. Thereafter the two enjoy a happy reunion.

THE BUSTER KEATON STORY (Paramount, 1957) 91 min.

Producers, Robert Smith and Sidney Sheldon; director, Sheldon; screenplay, Sheldon and Smith; assistant director, Francisco Day; costumes, Edith Head; music, Victor Young; camera, Loyal Griggs; editor, Archie Marshek.

Donald O'Connor (Buster Keaton); Ann Blyth (Gloria); Rhonda Fleming (Peggy Courtney); Peter Lorre (Kurt Bergner); Larry Keating (Larry Winters); Richard Anderson (Tom McAfee); Dave Willock (Joe Keaton); Claire Carleton (Myra Keaton); Larry White (Buster Keaton at Age Seven); Jackie Coogan (Elmer Case); Dan Seymour (Cannibal Chief); Nan Martin (Mr. Winters' Secretary); Ralph Dumke (Mr. Jennings); Robert Christopher (Nick); Richard Aherne (Butler); Ivan Triesault (Duke Alexander); Liz Slifer (Mrs. Anderson); Guy Wilkerson (Boarder); Dick Ryan (Susan's Father); Keith Richards (Leading Man); Pamela Jayson (Leading Woman); Constance Cavendish (Guest).

One of the sorriest of all cinema biographies of famous stars is The Buster Keaton Story. Paramount paid the financially-bereft Keaton $50,000 for the screen rights to his life and for publicity purposes hired the once-illustrious clown as technical advisor on the

Donald O'Connor and Peter Lorre in The Buster Keaton Story (1957).

film.   Other than coaching star Donald O'Connor in the recreation of
some of his funnier screen bits, the silent star was given little opportunity to contribute to the overall film which was nothing more
than a fictional piece headdressed with the name of Buster Keaton.
     The trite narrative tells of Keaton's birth into a family of
vaudevillians and of how his father was killed in a circus accident
when Buster was a small boy (in actuality Keaton never worked in
a circus).   Thereafter Buster goes to work as a comedian in vaudeville until he begins working in silent films and he develops a winning
screen style which launches his stardom during the Roaring Twenties.
This fame, however, is ended with the coming of sound and the end
of his marriage.   Later he is shown drifting about in search of employment.   Dejected, he becomes an alcoholic until he meets a pretty
casting studio director (Ann Blyth) at Famous Studios who helps him
to find himself and builds a new career.   The two also marry.
     Ironically, this black-and-white feature, filmed in widescreen
VistaVision, seems more falacious today than when released two
decades ago.   (In 1962 Keaton wrote his autobiography, My Wonderful
World of Slapstick.   Three years earlier he had received a special
Academy Award for his "... unique talents which brought immortal

comedies to the screen." Born in 1895, he died in 1966, having enjoyed a professional renaissance in his final years (with such films
as How to Stuff a Wild Bikini, 1965, and A Funny Thing Happened
on the Way to the Forum, 1966). In recent years, there have not
only been several in-depth studies of the great sad-faced screen comic
published, but a representative selection of his short and full-length
silent film work has enjoyed constant revival at art houses.

On the plus side, underrated O'Connor, who was limber enough
to duplicate some of Keaton's gymnastic visuals, was quite good in
creating some of the famous scenes from the movie comedian's silents like The Balloonatic, The Boat, and The Frozen North.

The New York Times reported, "Donald O'Connor's grand
imitation of the beloved deadpan comic who was one of the titans of
the silent screen, performed under the guidance of Keaton himself
(unseen, naturally) ... is the sole, steadying brightness of this otherwise rags-to-riches saga...." One might have added that the bulk
of personal events used to pad out the chronicle were fictitious; either
from carelessness on the scripter's part, or from the desire not to offend still living participants. What emerged was a clichéd account of a
great entertainer who had made millions laugh but could find little
consolement from others when he was down on his luck.

CACCIA ALLA VOLPE see AFTER THE FOX

CALLAWAY WENT THATAWAY (MGM, 1951) 81 min.

        Producers/directors/story/screenplay, Norman Panama and
Melvin Frank; art directors, Cedric Gibbons and Eddie Imazu; music,
Marlin Skiles; camera, Ray June; editor, Cotton Warburton.

        Fred MacMurray (Mike Frye); Dorothy McGuire (Deborah
Patterson); Howard Keel (Stretch Barnes/Smoky Callaway); Jesse
White (Georgia Markham); Fay Roope (Tom Lorrison); Natalie Schafer
(Martha Lorrison); Douglas Kennedy (Drunk); Elisabeth Fraser (Marie);
Johnny Indrisane (Johnny Tarranto); Stan Freberg (Marvin); Don Hag-
gerty (Director); Clark Gable, Elizabeth Taylor, and Esther Williams
(Guest Stars); Dorothy Andre (Girl); Kay Scott and Margie Liszt
(Phone Girls); Glenn Strange (Black Norton); Mae Clarke (Mother);
Hugh Beaumont (Mr. Adkins); Earle Hodgins (Doorman).

        Two advertising agents (Fred MacMurray and Dorothy McGuire)
have utilized all their funds to acquire the TV rights to old films
starring "Smoky" Callaway. When shown on the small screen, the
films are an enormous success and the duo decide that if they can
find the real "Smoky," who has long since left Hollywood for a life
of women and drink, they can make more films, have personal appearance tours, and gather a fortune. They set the star's old agent
on his trail and in the meantime find a lookalike in the person of
real-life cowboy "Stretch" Barnes (Howard Keel). Work begins with
Stretch but Smoky (also played by Keel) arrives on the scene and
wants a financial stake in the action. When he learns, however, that

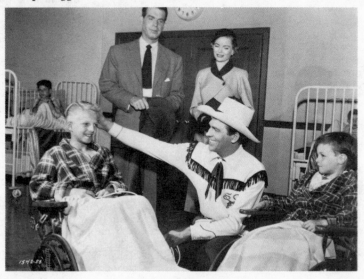

B. G. Norman, Fred MacMurray, Dorothy McGuire, Howard Keel, and Mickey Little in Callaway Went Thataway (1951).

Stretch has agreed to turn over his earnings to a boys' home, Smoky heads for South America, while McGuire and Stretch fall in love.

An obvious satire on Hopalong Cassidy and TV Westerns, Callaway Went Thataway was one of the first Hollywood films from a major studio to accept the popularity of the rival medium, television, as well as to kid the budding medium. The picture did well at previews but brought few filmgoers to theatres, despite the presence of the likes of Clark Gable, Elizabeth Taylor, and Esther Williams in cameo bits as themselves. Cameos featuring Dick Powell and June Allyson had also been filmed for the picture, but were deleted from the release print. The simple fact was that TV was stealing so much of the theatrical audience at the time. Also TV Westerns, especially Hopalong Cassidy, were extremely popular and a feature kidding the genre was just too far ahead of its time.

Callaway Went Thataway contains an excellent performance by Howard Keel in the dual role of Stretch and Smoky; it proved that his success in MGM's Annie Get Your Gun (1950) and Show Boat (1951) were not flukes. Not to be overlooked was adroit MacMurray at his underplaying best as promoter Mike Frye. The film really had all the ingredients requisite for commercial success, excepting for its poor timing in release.

THE CARPETBAGGERS (Paramount, 1964) Color, 150 min.

Producer, Joseph E. Levine; director, Edward Dmytryk;

based on the novel by Harold Robbins; screenplay, John Michael
Hayes; art directors, Hal Pereira and Walter Tyler; music, Elmer
Bernstein; assistant director, D. Michael Moore; costumes, Edith
Head; special effects, Paul K. Lerpae; camera, Joseph MacDonald;
editor, Frank Bracht.

George Peppard (Jonas Cord, Jr.); Alan Ladd (Nevada Smith);
Bob Cummings (Dan Pierce); Martha Hyer (Jennie Denton); Elizabeth
Ashley (Monica); Lew Ayres (McAllister); Martin Balsam (Bernard
Norman); Ralph Taeger (Buzz Dalton); Archie Moore (Jedediah); Leif
Erickson (Jonas Cord, Sr.); Carroll Baker (Rina Marlowe Cord);
Audrey Totter (Woman); Arthur Franz (Morrissey); Tom Tully (Amos
Winthrop); Charles Lane (Denby); Anthony Warde (Moroni); Tom Lo-
well (David Woolf); Vaughn Taylor (Doctor); Francesca Bellini (Cyn-
thia Randall); Victoria Jean (Jo-Ann Cord); Frankie Darro (Bellboy);
Ann Doran (Reporter); Donald "Red" Barry (Sound Man); Peter Dur-
yea (Assistant Director).

Young Jonas Cord, Jr. (George Peppard) detests his industrialist father (Leif Erickson) and after that cold, unloving man dies,
Peppard inherits a chemical plant and a yen for the man's pretty,
young widow, Rina (Carroll Baker). With profits from the plant
Peppard enters the aviation field with great success. Thereafter he
purchases a Hollywood studio and makes a star of his stepmother,
now dubbed Rina Marlowe. The latter's meteoric career rise, however, meets its finale when she falls from a chandelier, on which
she is swinging, at a wild Hollywood party. Next Peppard, who already has a lovely but ignored young wife (Elizabeth Ashley), becomes
involved with prostitute Jennie Denton (Martha Hyer) whom he also
transforms into a film star. Hyer succumbs to trouble when her
agent (Robert Cummings), needing money, threatens to blackmail her
concerning a pornographic film she once made. Meanwhile, Peppard
has been making features starring Nevada Smith (Alan Ladd), a cowpoke who wandered into the film capital and becomes a big star. It
is Ladd, through the use of his fists, who shakes sense into Peppard,
returning him back to his estranged wife and to a hopeful future.
Harold Robbins' best-selling (five million copies) novel, from
which the film derived, was allegedly based on the life of Howard
Hughes with the Rina Marlowe character a take-off on Jean Harlow,
and Nevada Smith patterned after Ken Maynard. Whatever its origin,
the color picture was flawed at best and presented a most distorted
view of Hollywood and its inhabitants. A long (150 minutes!) garish
soap opera, The Carpetbaggers--thanks to the promotional acumen
of producer Joseph E. Levine--did exceptionally well at the box-office
(with $15.5 grosses in distributors' domestic rentals). However,
over the years the film has been justly neglected.
About the only redeeming aspect of the offering was its array
of performances. While phlegmatic Peppard left much to be desired
in the lead, Ladd (who died January 29, 1964, just after the com-
pletion of the picture) was superb as Nevada Smith. It had been
contemplated to star him in the spin-off film, Nevada Smith (1966),
a role which eventually went to Steve McQueen. The Carpetbaggers
launched one-time method actress Carroll Baker into her sex symbol

Francesca Bellini, Alan Ladd, and Don "Red" Barry (right front) in
The Carpetbaggers (1963).

period, and was considered by many to be her warm-up assignment
for starring in Levine's version of Harlow (q. v.). Cummings was surprisingly adept and unmannered as the unscrupulous agent and Hyer
proved outstanding as the mercenary Jennie.

When the much-ballyhooed feature was released, Time magazine informed its readers, "... [it] is the kind of movie that you
cannot put down. Like the book, it scores its cheap success as a
swift, irresistibly vulgar compilation of all the racy stories anyone
has ever heard about wicked old Hollywood of the '20's and '30's....
Actress Baker seems uncertain about which actress living or dead
she is not supposed to resemble. Although her widely publicized
nude scene has been denuded, she wears costumes that thinly conceal
the loss.... Director Edward Dmytryk keeps a narrator warmed up
to respond to the question, 'How did it all happen?' with quick sum-
maries of Robbins' lip-smacking prose.... The only Carpetbagger
exhaling unpolluted air is Broadway Actress Elizabeth Ashley [then
wed in real-life to Peppard]. Given an insipid role as the cast-off
wife who keeps stumbling over platinum blondes in Peppard's hotel
suites, she turns her rough-velvet charm to advantage in a performance that bleach cannot beat. "

The New York Times was equally damning in its report on
the film, "Each successive episode is manufactured claptrap, super-

ficial and two-dimensional.... Mr. Dmytryk has gone at this film,
which might have been trenchant in the manner of Citizen Kane, with
a baseball bat. He has beaten it down to a square, flat surface,
without cinematic lift or style. "

In the early seventies where there developed a vogue about
Howard Hughes, the eccentric billionaire, books, articles, and stories
on the allegedly peculiar industrialist/filmmaker poured forth with
amazing speed. Also there appeared such (television) film accounts
as The Amazing Howard Hughes (q. v.), a narrative focusing a good
deal on the last years of the peculiar rich man who died on April
5, 1976.

CITIZEN KANE (RKO, 1941) 119 min.

Producer/director, Orson Welles; screenplay, Herman J. Man-
kewicz and Welles; art directors, Van Nest Polglase and Perry Ferguson; gowns, Edward Stevenson; music, Bernard Herrmann; special
effects, Vernon L. Walker; camera, Gregg Toland; editors, Robert
Wise and Mark Robson.

Orson Welles (Charles Foster Kane); Joseph Cotten (Jedediah
Leland); Dorothy Comingore (Susan Alexander); Agnes Moorehead
(Kane's Mother); Ruth Warrick (Emily); Ray Collins (Jim Gettys);
Erskine Sanford (Carter); Everett Sloane (Bernstein); William Alland
(Thompson the Reporter); Paul Stewart (Raymond); George Coulouris
(Thatcher); Fortunio Bonanova (Matiste); Gus Schilling (Headwaiter);
Philip Van Zandt (Rawlston); Georgia Backus (Miss Anderson); Harry
Shannon (Kane's Father); Sonny Bupp (Kane's Son); Buddy Swan (Kane
at the Age of Eight); Al Eben (Mike); Charles Bennett (Entertainer);
Lew Harvey (Newspaper Man); Bruce Sidney (Newsman); Tom Curran
(Teddy Roosevelt); Ed Peil and Charles Meakin (Civic Leaders); Ir-
ving Mitchell (Dr. Corey); Tudor Williams (Chorus Master); Herbert
Corthell (City Editor); Alan Ladd, Louise Currie, Eddie Coke, Walter
Sande, Arthur O'Connell, Richard Wilson, and Katherine Trosper
(Reporters); Philip Morris (Politician); Myrtle Mischell (Governess);
Joe North (Secretary).

While Citizen Kane has no Hollywood reflections directly within its plotline, the classic cinema production certainly fits into the
category discussed in this book. The picture is told as a movie-
within-a-movie. The newsreel format, telling of the death of Charles
Foster Kane (Orson Welles), opens the film and its plot has a group
of newsreel reporters assigned to find out the meaning of the man's
last word, "Rosebud. "

Much of the picture is devoted to the relationship of Kane with
Susan Alexander (Dorothy Comingore), an aspiring opera singer. Of
course, it is widely claimed that Kane was really a disguise of newspaper tycoon/film producer William Randolph Hearst while Miss Alexander was the celluloid counterpart of Marion Davies, whose lengthy
film career had concluded four years before the release of Citizen
Kane.

Orson Welles in <u>Citizen Kane</u> (1941).

The character of Susan Alexander so reflected Miss Davies that it was claimed that both Hearst and his mistress were more upset by that characterization and how it was played on screen than by Welles' work as Kane.   As interpreted by Comingore, Susan Alexander emerged as a none-too-bright young lady who becomes Kane's mistress and the latter spares no expense to make her a star of the opera, discarding the fact that she has little talent for that professional field.   Later, the revelation of their affair ruins Kane's political chances and her true lack of ability as a singer eventually brings about her career downfall.   Interviewed for the newsreel story, she is found as a drunken singer in a third-rate roadhouse; it is a rainy night and there are no patrons.

For The Times We Had (1975), the memoir of the late Marion Davies, Welles provided the foreword and stated, "As one who shares much of the blame for casting another shadow--the shadow of Susan Alexander Kane--I rejoice in this opportunity to record something which today is all but forgotten except for those lucky enough to have seen a few of her pictures: Marion Davies was one of the most delightfully accomplished comediennes in the whole history of screen. She would have been a star if Hearst had never happened.   She was also a delightful and very considerable person. "

CITY OF ILLUSION   see   HOLLYWOOD, CIUDAD DE ENSUEÑO

CLOTHES MAKE THE WOMAN (Tiffany-Stahl, 1928) 5209 ft.

Director/screenplay, Tom Terriss; titles, Lesley Mason; art director, Hervey Libbert; set decorator, George Sawley; camera, Chester Lyons; editor, Desmond O'Brien.

Eve Southern (Princess Anastasia); Walter Pidgeon (Victor Trent); Charles Byer (The Director); George E. Stone (Assistant Director); Adolph Millar (Bolshevik Leader); and: Duncan Renaldo, Gordon Begg, Catherine Wallace, Corliss Palmer, Margaret Selby, and H. D. Pennell.

In Russia during the Bolshevik Revolution, the czar's daughter, Princess Anastasia (Eve Southern), is ordered shot by a firing squad. However, she is rescued by a young revolutionary (Walter Pidgeon) who risks his life to do so.   He manages to have her smuggled out of the country to safety.   Years later they meet again in California. Now known as Victor Trent (Pidgeon), he is a popular movie idol while the former princess works in the ranks of extras.   She is however, hired to portray herself in a drama on the Russian Revolution.   When the scene of her rescue is re-enacted, Pidgeon accidentally shoots her.   The injury is not a serious one, however, and when she recovers they get married.

This poverty-row quickie was obviously inspired by the high class The Last Command (q. v.), issued earlier in the year.   Only here the roles have been switched so that the Russian revolutionary is now a star (instead of a director as in The Last Command) and

Eddie Kane, Luis Alberni, unknown, Dorothy Christy, Emma Dunn, George Sidney, Charlie Murray, June Clyde, Esther Howard, Edwin Maxwell, and John Roche in The Cohens and Kellys in Hollywood (1932).

the crux of the story is focused on a dethroned Russian princess, instead of the czar's cousin, an army officer.

If one were confused by the film's title, which has little relevance to the storyline, there is equal dismay at the liberties taken with historical reality as to the ill-fated czar's daughter (consider the "facts" as offered in the play and movie entitled Anastasia). The New York Times alerted its readers, "... there is too much dispute about the [real] Princess Anastasia at the present time to make the Tiffany solution anything but bathos. If the theme had been drawn from the imagination rather than from disputed history it would have been a good picture. As it is there are scenes which are above the average. The acting of Eve Southern and Walter Pidgeon is acceptable if taken apart from some of the situations they encounter."

For film historians there are some shots of the Tiffany-Stahl Studios in Hollywood, a much more valid reason for viewing the film than the specious attempt to cash in on the whatever-really-happened-to-Anastasia vogue.

THE COHENS AND KELLYS IN HOLLYWOOD (Universal, 1932) 73 min.

Director, John Francis Dillon; story/screenplay, Howard Greene; dialogue, James Mulhouser; camera, Jerry Ash; editor, Harry W. Lieb.

George Sidney (Moe Cohen); Charles Murray (Michael Kelly); June Clyde (Kitty Kelly); Norman Foster (Maurice Cohen); Emma Dunn (Mrs. Cohen); Esther Howard (Mrs. Kelly); Eileen Percy (Magazine Writer); Edwin Maxwell (Chauncey Chadwick); Luis Alberni (Solarsky); John Roche (Gregory Gordon); Robert Greig (Chesterfield); Tom Mix, Sidney Fox, Genevieve Tobin, Boris Karloff, Lew Ayres, Harry Barris (Themselves).

Aaron Hoffman's play Two Blocks Away was the basis for Universal's Cohens and Kellys film series which produced seven films bridging the silent and sound eras. This entry was the next-to-the-last and it resulted in "... still nothing new in thought, gesture, motion or mannerism ..." (Variety).

Herein the two contrasting families live in the small Midwestern town of Hillsboro. The Cohens run a small cinema and their son Maurice (Norman Foster) is developing his talents as a songwriter. Foster loves pretty Kitty Kelly (June Clyde), who has star aspirations, and he helps her win a screen test with Continental Productions. After she is given a contract she takes her family to Hollywood and soon becomes a star, living in a mansion and snubbing her former friends, the Cohens. The arrival of sound films, however, puts an end to Clyde's career; but Foster is soon earning money writing theme songs for musical pictures. Now the situation is reversed, with the Cohens well-to-do and the Kellys poor. However, when the fad of screen musicals ends and Foster is out of work, the two families return to Hillsboro. They are wiser from their Hollywood sojourn.

The forerunner of various series pictures centering a segment on Hollywood, this film is pretty tame material by today's standards. Its main point of interest is a scene with the two ethnic families visiting the famed Cocoanut Grove Club and observing such Universal contract stars as Tom Mix, Sidney Fox, Genevieve Tobin, Boris Karloff, Lew Ayres, and crooner Harry Barris. Midst the stereotyped gosh-gee-we're-in-Hollywood storyline, there is a rather wild presentation of a Soviet film director, played in outlandish style by Luis Alberni.

For director John Francis Dillon, who had spent most of the late twenties at First National Pictures, this was his only sound picture for Universal (where he worked in the teens). After four other directorial assignments, he died in 1934. For veterans George Sidney, Charles Murray, Emma Dunn, and Esther Howard--as well as Clyde and Foster--there would be one final Cohens and Kellys appearance, In Trouble (1933).

THE COMEBACK see A MANIAC IN LOVE

THE COMIC (Columbia, 1969) Color, 95 min.

Producers/directors/screenplay, Carl Reiner and Aaron Ruben; production designer, Walter Simonds; assistant director, Rusty Meek; music, Jack Elliott; costumes, Guy Verhille; sound, Charles J. Rice, Les Freshotz, and Arthur Piantadosi; camera, W. Wallace Kelley; editor, Adrienne Fazan.

Dick Van Dyke (Billy Bright); Michele Lee (Mary Gibson); Mickey Rooney (Cockeye); Cornel Wilde (Frank Powers); Nina Wayne (Sybil); Pert Kelton (Mama); Steve Allen (Himself); Barbara Heller (Ginger); Ed Peck (Edwin C. Englehardt); Jeannine Riley (Lorraine); Gavin MacLeod (First Director); Jay Novello (Miguel); Craig Huebing (Doctor); Paulene Myers (Phoebe); Fritz Feld (Armand); Jerome Cowan (Lawrence); Isabel Sanford (Woman); Jeff Donnell (Nurse); Carl Reiner (Al Schilling).

No type of performer is as quickly forgotten by the public as the comedian whose humor does not adapt to changing times. Few comics have routines or charisma to withstand the onslaught of a change in mores and thus many of them have been cast aside by Hollywood when their box-office appeal has withered. It has not been uncommon to witness once-famous comics (for instance Snub Pollard, Billy Bevan, and Billy West) reduced to playing bits or even extra roles in pictures just a few years after the spectacular decline of their screen careers. Even big names like Harold Lloyd, Buster Keaton, and Laurel and Hardy had difficulty in obtaining movie work in later years, even if their finances were "stable" enough to keep them from doing bits. This near-total disregard for the laughmakers that made the movies a national pastime is the basis of The Comic. In particular, The Comic was inspired by the fate of Stan Laurel who lived out the latter part of his life most modestly in a small Santa

Dick Van Dyke and Isabel Sanford in The Comic (1969).

Monica, California apartment, always watching televised revivals of
his films.   Carl Reiner and Dick Van Dyke (the latter delivering the
eulogy at Laurel's funeral in 1965) fashioned this film after the poi-
gnancy of Laurel's situation.
        The film opens at the funeral of once-famous comedy star
Billy Bright (Dick Van Dyke) and it (à la Sunset Boulevard, q. v.) has
the dead man's voice tell the story of his life.   The comic began in
show business in vaudeville and broke into the movies doing two-
reelers which made him famous.   He later marries his pert, pretty
co-star, Mary Gibson (Michele Lee).   They are happy until he dallies
with a producer's wife.   Lee leaves him and takes their young son
with her.   With the arrival of talkies, Van Dyke's style becomes
dated, but he refuses to change.   Soon he is unemployed.   He spends
many bitter, lonely years bemoaning his fate.   A close pal is another
has-been comic star, Cockeye (Mickey Rooney).   Finally, with the
arrival of TV, Van Dyke appears with Steve Allen and from that
outing does a few commercials.   However, he is now an embittered
and broken man.   At his funeral he complains about the poor turnout
and the overall cheapness of the affair.
        Van Dyke was outstanding as Billy, while Lee reminded many
viewers of Mabel Normand in her characterization of Mary.   Also
adding nostalgia to the proceedings was Rooney as Cockeye, a character patterned obviously after Ben Turpin.   Sadly, Columbia Pictures

did not have much faith in the venture and refused to promote this offbeat feature.   Actually it is one of the best illustrations of what really happened to a Hollywood great when his term of popularity expired.   Variety judged it an "... amusing, loosely-constructed yarn.... " For modest marquee alure, there was Cornel Wilde as Frank Powers, a big-time movie director who has his share of problems with his on-camera actors.

THE COWBOY AND THE BLONDE (20th Century-Fox, 1941) 68 min.

Associate producers, Ralph Dietrich and Walter Morosco; director, Ray McCarey; story, Walter Bullock and William Brent; screenplay, Bullock; art directors, Richard Day and Lewis Creber; music director, Cyril J. Mockridge; camera, Charles Larke; editor, Harry Reynolds.

Mary Beth Hughes (Crystal Wayne); George Montgomery (Lank Garrett); Alan Mowbray (Phineas Johnson); Robert Conway (Don Courtney); John Miljan (Bob Roycroft); Richard Lane (Gilbert); Robert Emmett Keane (Mr. Gregory); Minerva Urecal (Camille); Fuzzy Knight (Skeeter); George O'Hara (Melwyn).

After appearing in films in the late thirties under the name of George Letz, George Montgomery finally earned a stardom build-up when he signed at 20th Century-Fox and underwent a name change. Professionally the situation improved for the young, handsome actor and that year he starred in a genre picture, Star Dust (q. v.).   Mainly, though, Fox utilized Montgomery in outdoor epics and Westerns. However, since he had been good as the football hero-turned-leading man in Star Dust, the studio combined the Hollywood motif with his Western footing.   The end result was a passive little B picture called The Cowboy and the Blonde.
Perhaps the title of this entry was meant intentionally to remind audiences of the Gary Cooper-Merle Oberon teaming in Samuel Goldwyn's The Cowboy and the Lady (1938).   But even that poorly-received comedy was above this vague effort.   (On the other hand, sources such as the Cleveland Press pointed out the title was so nondescript that it might keep away viewers, and insisted that the film was "... not exactly so dull as it sounds. ")   Here Montgomery portrayed cowpoke Lank Garrett who wins a screen test with Consolidated Pictures after becoming a rodeo circuit hero.   Montgomery's Lank is not much of a thespian, however, and he fails to win a studio contract until it becomes known by the lot's bosses that he is romancing temperamental star Crystal Wayne (Mary Beth Hughes). Because the hateful girl has become good-humored due to Montgomery's romancing, the studio places him under contract--only because it will save production time on her pictures.   Montgomery eventually discovers the subterfuge and returns to the range, but with Hughes in hot pursuit.   Much to the chagrin of the film executives, the girl remains on the wide-open prairies with her man.   They wed and settle down to domestic bliss.

THE COWBOY STAR (Columbia, 1936) 56 min.

Director, David Selman; based on the story by Peter B. Kyne; adaptors, Frank Melford and Cornelius Reece; screenplay, Frances Guihan; camera, Allen G. Siegler; editor, William Lyon.

Charles Starrett (Spencer Yorke/George Weston); Iris Meredith (Mary Baker); Si Jenks (Buckshot); Marc Lawrence (Johnny Sampson); Ed Piel, Sr. (Sheriff Clem Baker); Wally Albright (Jimmy); Ralph McCullough (Pretty Boy Hogan); Richard Jerry (Midget); Landers Stevens (John Kingwell); Dick Terry (Midget); and: Winifred Hari, Nick Copeland, and Lew Meehan.

Charles Starrett achieved his niche in Hollywood as Columbia Pictures' most enduring Western star. Having played leading men roles in both A and B productions for various studios, he settled down at Columbia in the mid-thirties. For nearly two decades he churned out Western thrillers--totaling over 120. One of the better of these, and definitely one of the most offbeat was The Cowboy Star, with Starrett naturally playing the title role. The ad line for this feature boasted, "He Rode out of the Movies into an Avalanche of Action.... Gangsters invade the West but a Hollywood Hero Blasts a Barrage of Blazing Death!"

Supposedly based on a Peter B. Kyne story, the film was scripted by Frances Guiham, who had created many of Buck Jones' actionful scenarios. Like Jones' forays into kidding moviemaking, this film never took itself too seriously. In fact, Starrett was not above poking a little fun at his newly-established cinema image. In the opening sequence, for example, he is shown in a hard-riding contest with a bucking bronc, that is until the camera pulls back showing him on a riding machine used to accomplish such sequences in close-up. There is also a scene where he is joshed by other cast members for affecting makeup.

The plot of The Cowboy Star has movie hero Spencer Yorke (Starrett) tiring of the glamourous life but low pay of making Westerns. He and his pal Buckshot (Si Jenks) head to a small Western town for relaxation. There he calls himself George Weston and meets and romances realtor Mary Baker (Iris Meredith) who sells him a ranch. The girl's young brother, Jimmy (Wally Albright) recognizes Starrett, a man he has always idolized. The youngster is sure of his identification once Starrett and Jenks ride into town and stop a runaway wagon, saving the lives of a woman and her child. Albright has a yen to visit a nearby ghost town where it develops three bandits are hiding. When he goes to the locale, against his father's wishes, he is captured. Meanwhile the outlaws plan to kill both the sheriff (Ed Piel, Sr.) and Starrett, believing the latter is a G-Man. Piel is later shot as he follows the youth to the deserted town, but the boy manages to latch onto the lawbreakers' machine gun. Starrett soon arrives, kills two of the hoodlums with the gun, and knocks out the other man in a fight. As a result, he is acclaimed a hero. Later he and Meredith leave for Hollywood where he has signed a new acting contract at a much larger salary.

CRASHING HOLLYWOOD (RKO, 1938) 61 min.

Producer, Cliff Reid; director, Lew Landers; based on the play by Paul Dickey and Mann Page; screenplay, Paul Yawitz and Gladys Atwater; special effects, Vernon L. Walker; camera, Nicholas Musuraca; editor, Harry Marker.

Lee Tracy (Michael); Joan Woodbury (Barbara); Paul Guilfoyle (Herman); Lee Patrick (Goldie); Richard Lane (Wells); Bradley Page (Darcy-Hawk); George Irving (Peyton); Tom Kennedy (Al); Frank M. Thomas (Decker); Jack Carson (Dickson); Alec Craig (Receptionist); James Conlin (Crisby).

In 1929 Lee Tracy had starred in Big Time (q. v.), one of the first sound films with a Hollywood theme. Eight years later he was back in the genre with this B product which was a remake of the silent feature, Lights Out (q. v.). The end result of this quickie was "... a silly little picture about Hollywood, or what passes for it in the lotus world of fan-magazines and autograph albums ... " (New York Times). The more generous Brooklyn Daily Eagle, in contrast, noted "It offers variety in staging and there's a freshness about its action. There are a few novel camera angles too, and a few minutes of photo montage that are striking. "

Here Tracy is cast as Michael, a big-shot newspaper writer who arrives in Hollywood to do screen work. He manages to collaborate with a hoodlum on a gangster yarn. The racketeer tells Tracy how he accomplished a bank robbery and then was implicated by his two-timing cohorts. Although Tracy's character is a novice at script-writing, he puts the facts and fancy together and sells it to a studio which transforms it into a hit picture. Unfortunately the gangster has exposed too much about the hold-up and his ex-underworld pals and the police reopen the case, eventually closing in on the culprits. The gangsters then come to Hollywood to get even with Tracy and nearly do him in before he is saved by the law and the love of Barbara (Joan Woodbury), the girl he met on the initial train ride to California.

CRAZY HOUSE (Universal, 1943) 81 min.

Associate producer, Erle C. Kenton; director, Edward F. Cline; screenplay, Robert Lees and Frederic I. Rinaldo; art directors, John B. Goodman and Harold H. MacArthur; set decorators, Russell A. Gausman and A. Gilmore; assistant director, Howard Christie; music productions devised and staged by George Hale; music director, Charles Previn; music supervisor, Ted Cain; orchestrators, Frank Skinner, Larry Russell, and Jim Mundy; songs, Gus Kahn and Isham Jones; Rudolf Friml, Herbert Stohart, Bob Wright, and Chet Forrest; Irving Bibo and Al Piantadosi; Frank Signorelli, Matt Malneck, and Mitchell Parish; Allie Wrubel; Don Raye and Gene de Paul; Eddie Cherkose and Milton Rosen; Frank Steininger; Don Shapiro; Jerry Seelen, Lester Lee; Cohn and Chaplin; Vernon Duke and John Latouche; Glenn Miller; Jack Little; Warfield and Williams; sound,

Lee Patrick, Paul Guilfoyle, and Lee Tracy in <u>Crashing Hollywood</u>
(1938).

Bernard B. Brown and Paul Neal; special camera, John P. Fulton;
camera, Charles Van Enger; editor, Arthur Hilton.

Ole Olsen and Chic Johnson (Themselves); Martha O'Driscoll
(Margie); Patric Knowles (Eddie MacLean); Cass Daley (Sadie Silver-
fish/Herself); Percy Kilbride (Colonel Merriweather); Leighton Noble
(Himself); Thomas Gomez (Colonel Wagstaff); Edgar Kennedy (Judge);
Ray Walker (Announcer); Robert Emmett Keane (Lawyer); Franklin
Pangborn (Hotel Manager); Chester Clute (Fud); Billy Gilbert, Richard
Lane, Allan Jones, Alan Curtis, Hans Conried, Shemp Howard, Fred
Sanborn, Leo Carrillo, Grace MacDonald, Lon Chaney, Jr. and Andy
Devine (Guest Bits); Glenn Miller Singers, the DeMarcos, Chandra
Kaly Dancers, Laison Brothers, The Five Hertzogs, Bobby Brooks,
Ward and Van, Terry Sheldon, Harry Powers, Billy Reed, and Count
Basie & His Band (Specialty Routines). Basil Rathbone and Nigel
Bruce (Unbilled Guest Appearance).

The zany comedy team of Ole Olsen and Chic Johnson followed
the initial screen adaptation of their hit Broadway show <u>Hellzapoppin'</u>

Ole Olsen and Chic Johnson in <u>Crazy House</u> (1943).

(q. v.), with <u>Crazy House.</u> In some ways it was a bit difficult to detect where one left off and the other began as the comedy team continued their wild antics and endless patter through this entry as well as the first. In <u>Crazy House,</u> however, Universal assigned nearly every name contract player on the lot to make an appearance to strengthen the box-office appeal of the project. As a result, <u>Crazy House</u> was not only effective crazy comedy but a welcome potpourri of familiar movie faces and good music.

    <u>Crazy House</u> opens with Olsen and Johnson returning to Universal Pictures to star in a follow-up to <u>Hellzapoppin'.</u> But studio chief Colonel Wagstaff (Thomas Gomez) has no script for them and he wants no part of the madcap duo. (In fact studio employers barricade the studio gates against them.) The zanies then decide to underwrite their own screen epic, to be called <u>Crazy House.</u> They obtain financial "backing" from Colonel Merriweather (Percy Kilbride), a well-meaning but impoverished braggart. Ex-film editor Eddie MacLean (Patric Knowles) is hired to direct the picture and the boys select pretty car-hop Margie (Martha O'Driscoll) to play the feminine lead. The film is eventually made but the creditor forecloses on the comics. At the last minute the screen team persuades a judge (Edgar Kennedy) to give them permission to premiere the feature and to sell it to the highest bidder. By accident Universal acquires the picture.

By this point Knowles and O'Driscoll have fallen in love but Chic
shoots them and tells the audience, "This is one film that's not going
to have a happy ending. "

CRIMSON CANYON (Universal, 1928) 4201 ft.

Supervisor, William Lord Wright; director, Ray Taylor;
story/continuity, Hugh Nagrom; titles, Val Cleveland; camera, Joseph
Brotherton; editor, Gene Havlick.

Ted Wells (Phil "Six Gun" Lang); Lotus Thompson (Daisy Lanning); Wilbur Mack (Sam Slade); Buck Connors ("Dad" Packard);
George Atkinson (Abner Slade); and: Henri De Velois.

In the mid-twenties Ted Wells had a brief starring period as
a Western actor in a series for Universal. In one of the entries
made near the end of his contract term, he touched briefly on an introspective look at Western moviemaking. The Crimson Canyon, besides Hoot Gibson's The Texas Streak (q. v.), was one of the few
Westerns of the decade to use the making of a motion picture in its
plot background.
Wells starred as Phil "Six Gun" Lang, a cowpoke who helps
a man pay off a $1000 debt to crooked Abner Slade (George Atkinson).
Riding out of town he observes a girl (Lotus Thompson) on a runaway
wagon and rescues her only to find that he has just spoiled a scene
being shot by a motion picture studio on location for a sagebrush entry. Later he escorts Thompson to a dance but is attacked by Atkinson's son, Sam (Wilbur Mack), who knocks out Wells and abducts
the heroine. When he revives, the hero gives chase and rescues the
young lady. He later reunites her with her uncle, who turns out to
be the individual he had helped previously.

DANCING IN THE DARK (20th Century-Fox, 1949) Color, 93 min.

Producer, George Jessel; director, Irving Reis; based on the
play The Bandwagon by George S. Kaufman; adaptor, Marion Turk;
screenplay, Marcy C. McCall; additional dialogue, Jay Dratler; art
directors, Lyle Wheeler and George W. Davis; set decorators, Thomas Little and Paul S. Fox; vocal director, Ken Darby; orchestrators,
Herbert Spencer and Earle Hagen; music director, Alfred Newman;
songs, Howard Dietz and Arthur Schwartz; assistant director, Henry
Weinberger; makeup, Ben Nye, Thomas Tuttle, and Bill Riddle;
choreography, Seymour Felix; costumes, William Travilla; sound,
Bernard Freericks and Roger Heman; special effects, Fred Sersen;
camera, Harry Jackson and Louis Loeffler.

William Powell (Emery Slade); Mark Stevens (Bill Davis);
Betsy Drake (Julie); Adolphe Menjou (Grossman); Randy Stuart (Rosalie Brooks); Lloyd Corrigan (Barker); Hope Emerson (Mrs. Schlag-
hammer); Walter Catlett (Joe Brooks); Don Beddoe (Barney Basset);

Jean Hersholt (Himself); Sid Grauman (Himself); Prince Michael Romanoff (Himself); Louis Bacigalupi (Rubber); Syd Saylor (Projectionist); Milton Parsons (Butler); Byron Foulger (Makeup Man); Bob Adler (Officer); Ann Corcoran, Phyllis Planchard, and Claire Richards (Women); Elaine Edwards (Girl); Frank Ferguson (Sharkey); Edward Clark (Costumer); Jean "Babe" London (Hula Girl); Sally Forrest (Secretary); Belle Daube, Larry Keating, Claire Whitney, John Davidson, and Joseph Crehan (Board Members); George E. Stone (Cutter).

Although 20th Century-Fox purchased the screen rights to the 1931 stage musical The Band Wagon and adapted it for this comedy, the end result used only a quartet of songs from the play.   Moreover, much of the plotline was adapted from the studio's earlier Star Dust (q. v.).   The latter film was improved upon, however, by the addition of the character of the debonair, arrogant, drunken, fallen movie matinee idol Emory Slade, played to the hilt by sophisticated picture veteran William Powell.

In the Hollywood of the post-World War II years, onetime movie idol Emory Slade (Powell) is down on his luck.   Due to his arrogance in the days when he was a top-ranking name, he now cannot find work.   Besides having spent all his income, he is behind in his rent for the small furnished apartment he inhabits in a very unpretentious section of Hollywood.   Finally the Motion Picture Relief Fund (headed by Jean Hersholt as himself) offers Powell charity, but he gallantly refuses.   With no place to turn, and about to be evicted from his digs, a change of fate puts the actor on the Fox studio payroll.   It seems that he has the power to persuade movie-shy stage star Rosalie Brooks (Randy Stuart) to make a film version of The Band Wagon.   However, in the meantime, Powell meets a pretty newcomer, Julie (Betsy Drake), and campaigns to win her the part.   In his effort to accomplish this feat, he is aided by press agent Bill Davis (Mark Stevens), who has fallen in love with the ingenue.   Finally Drake is assigned the coveted role and it is then that Powell discovers the girl is actually his daughter.   Dancing in the Dark is one of those unjustly neglected films which is all the better for its kidding but still realistic look at Hollywood.   Besides Powell's superb performance as Emory Slade, the feature offers Adolphe Menjou in an excellent take-off on mogul Darryl F. Zanuck, along with Sid Grauman and Prince Michael Romanoff in their true-life roles as leaders of the Hollywood social scene.   Although basically a comedy, the film rather aptly presents the muddled world of a fallen film star.   The character of Emory Slade was no doubt a conglomerate of many of the once big names of the twenties and thirties, now fallen on leaner times.

In 1953 MGM presented a musical screen version of The Band Wagon, produced by Arthur Freed, directed by Vincente Minnelli, and starring Fred Astaire, Nanette Fabray, Jack Buchanan, Oscar Levant, and Cyd Charisse.

A DAY IN THE VITAGRAPH STUDIO   see   THE FILM SHORTS

THE DAY OF THE LOCUST (Paramount, 1975) Color, 144 min.

Producer, Jerome Hellman; associate producer, Sheldon Schrager; director, John Schlesinger; based on the novel by Nathaniel West; screenplay, Waldo Salt; production designer, Richard MacDonald; art director, John Lloyd; set decorator, George Hopkins; music, Arnie Schmidt; music director, John Barry; choreography, Marge Champion; costumes, assistant directors, Tim Zinnemann, Charles Ziarcho, Barry Stern, and Ann Roth; makeup, Del Armstrong; sound, Tommy Overton; special effects, Tim Smyth; special camera effects, Albert Whitlock; camera, Conrad Hall; editor, Jim Clark.

Donald Sutherland (Homer Simpson); Karen Black (Faye Greener); Burgess Meredith (Harry Greener); William Atherton (Tod Hackett); Geraldine Page (Big Sister); Richard A. Dysart (Claude Estee); Bo Hopkins (Earle Shoop); Pepe Serna (Miguel); Lelia Goldoni (Mary Dove); Billy Barty (Abe); Jackie Lee Haley (Adore); Gloria Le Roy (Mrs. Loomis); Jane Hoffman (Mrs. Odlesh); Norm Leavitt (Mr. Odlesh); Madge Kennedy (Mrs. Johnson); Ina Gould and Florence Lake (Lee Sisters); Margaret Willey and John War Eagle (The Gingos); Natalie Schafer (Audrey Jennings); Gloria Stroock (Alice Estee); Nita Talbot (Joan); Nicholas Cortland (Projectionist); Alvin Childress (Butler); Paul Stewart (Helverston); John Hillerman (Ned Grote); William Castle (Director); DeForest Covan (Shoeshine Boy); Michael Quinn (Major Domo); Jonathan Kidd (Undertaker); Margaret Jenkins (Choral Director); Queenie Smith (Palsied Lady); Dick Powell, Jr. (Dick Powell); Billy Baldwin (Announcer at Premiere).

The Day of the Locust culminates in a brutal extras' riot at the Hollywood premiere of Cecil B. DeMille's The Buccaneer (1938). The macabre event did not occur in actuality, although extras rioting supposedly did happen in the thirties. It is ironic that in this fashion screenwriter/novelist Nathanael West envisioned the fall of Hollywood rather than by the decay from within which eventually did practically destroy the industry. In any event, the riot is a fitting finale to a story packed with the insecurity and ambitions of those trying to climb to the top of success in the movie business.
West had been a screenwriter at RKO and was killed in an auto accident in 1940, at the age of 36, four months after this book was published. The story is a bitter, cynical appraisal of the film industry. British director John Schlesinger maintained this concept in his screen adaptation although various plotline ingredients were altered. The final product appeared to be more of a fantasy-nightmare than a realistic look at the life of an extra in the bygone days of Hollywood's glory.
The narrative is recounted through the eyes of Tod Hackett (William Atherton), a young set designer who is employed by a big studio and who falls in love with Faye Greener (Karen Black), a struggling extra who lives in the same apartment complex as Atherton--her roommate is her faded vaudevillian father (Burgess Meredith), a dying man who is forced to peddle from door to door to eek out a living.

Karen Black in <u>The Day of the Locust</u> (1975).

On one of these selling jaunts, Meredith meets repressed
bookkeeper Homer Simpson (Donald Sutherland) and presses his daughter's attentions on the man, who obviously desires her. In deference
to Atherton, who has a strong sexual attraction for Black, she moves
in with Sutherland after her father's death, although the relationship
is platonic.

At the studio Atherton is involved in the filming of The Battle
of Waterloo and he warns the producers of a potential accident on the
soundstage--it happens and some extras are killed and many injured.
The studio pays Atherton to forget the nightmare. He becomes even
more jaded with California life after finding Black in bed with Miguel
(Pepe Serna), a Hollywood stud. Atherton cuts off his relationship
with Black, but they meet again at a Hollywood premiere where Sutherland, driven to insanity by Black's cold treatment of him, kills
an annoying child. This causes the crowd of extras to kill him and
sets into motion the chaos which ends with Atherton being injured.
At the finale Black comes back to the bungalow to find that Atherton,
disgusted with it all, has left the film capital.

Running way overlong at 144 minutes, The Day of the Locust
was beautifully filmed and finely acted (Meredith was nominated for
a Best Supporting Actor's Oscar). However, in retrospect, the film
is remembered for individual scenes rather than as a cohesive whole.
Among the more remarkable portions of the picture are the sequences
with Sutherland seated in his garden as the leaves blow around him
and he wishes to possess Black; the scene where Atherton prepares
to attend a Hollywood party, leaving Black eating ice cream as Nick
Lucas intones "I Wished on the Moon" over the radio; the violent
rooster fight in Sutherland's garage followed by the battle between the
cowboy player (Bo Hopkins) and pal Pepe Serna over Black after the
latter is discovered in bed with Serna by both the stunned Sutherland
and the irate Hopkins. Of course, the climactic riot and the literal
crucifixion of Sutherland is gripping, but it is too broadly and grotesquely staged to match up properly with the remainder of the low-
keyed film. Also of interest is the scene where Meredith attends
church to be healed by Big Sister (Geraldine Page), an obvious satire
of the various extreme religious sects flourishing in Hollywood of the
period.

Film enthusiasts found their special moments of interest in The
Day of the Locust. Sequences of The Battle of Waterloo are pre-
sided over by a director played by producer-director William Castle.
There is the scene where Atherton attends a party at a high-class
brothel where he sees French stag movies. Throughout, the sights
and sounds of Hollywood are aptly presented. There is even a bit
with Karen Black shown to be in the film Ali Baba Goes to Town
(q. v.), with footage of the actress interpolated into a riding scene
with that picture's star, Eddie Cantor.

Despite its multi-million dollar trappings and themes of sex
and violence in Hollywood, it was not a success. One reason may
be that it was not properly exploited. When released, there were
many people who thought the film's title indicated the picture was a
science fiction thriller about bugs. Others, however, claimed that
the movie's commercial weakness belonged to Schlesinger. Dr. Joan
Zlotnick noted in an article in Filmograph, "It can be said that all

of the important flaws in the film are related either to the director's misconceptions of the novel or to his deliberate attempts to alter the material, undoubtedly, one should think, to insure success at the box office. "

DEATH AT LOVE HOUSE (ABC-TV, 1976) Color, 75 min.

Executive producers, Aaron Spelling and Leonard Goldberg; producer, Hal Sitowitz; director, E. W. Swackhamer; teleplay, Jim Barnett; music, Laurence Rosenthal; art director, Paul Sylos; camera, Dennis Dalzell; editor, John Woodcock.

Robert Wagner (Joel Gregory Jr./Joel Gregory, Sr.); Kate Jackson (Donna Gregory); Sylvia Sidney (Mrs. Josephs); Marianna Hill (Lorna Love); Joan Blondell (Marcella Geffenhart); John Carradine (Conan Carroll); Dorothy Lamour (Denise Christian); Bill Macy (Oscar); Joe Bernard (Bus Driver); John A. Zee (Eric Herman); Robert Gibbons (Director); Al Hansen (Policeman); Croften Hardester (Actor in Film).

A screenwriter (Robert Wagner) becomes obsessed with the relationship between his father and thirties' glamour film star Lorna Love (Marianna Hill). He and his wife (Kate Jackson) then accept an offer to stay in the late actress' home in order to study the atmosphere and write a script concerning her life. The house is cared for by Mrs. Josephs (Sylvia Sidney), the celebrity's former housekeeper. After Wagner and Jackson take up residence at the mansion, several strange events occur. Conan Carroll (John Carradine), the director of Lorna Love's greatest triumphs, is murdered and an attempt is made on the life of Jackson.
Wagner, himself, has dreams of making love with the late star. A subsequent interview with Denise Christian (Dorothy Lamour), a one-time rival of Lorna's, reveals that Love stole the affections of his father (also played by Wagner) from Lamour. In the present Wagner and Jackson also meet Marcella Geffenhart (Joan Blondell), a strange woman who supervises a fan club devoted to Lorna's memory. Eventually it becomes clear that Lorna's spirit--her body is enshrined at the estate--is seeking to murder Jackson and to claim Wagner for herself. Jackson, however, uncovers the fact that the film legend never died. Actually she was badly scarred in a satanic ritual years before and everyone had been made to believe that she died. She turns out to be the housekeeper in disguise. However, a sudden fire engulfs her as she tries to kill Jackson. Instead she dies.
The young couple leave the mansion, deciding to abandon the script and to allow Lorna Love's legend to remain intact.
Considering it was grist for the telefeature market, Death at Love House was a better-made entry than could be expected. Providing the picture with authentic flavor was the fact that it was filmed at Harold Lloyd's 16-acre Beverly Hills estate, Greenacres, and in his 44-room mansion. After the movie was made, the mansion's treasures were auctioned off and the estate was sold to a business

syndicate despite the fact that the late comedy great had hoped his
home would be utilized for a movie museum.

THE DEATH KISS (World Wide, 1932) 75 min.

Director, Edwin L. Marin; based on the novel by Madelon St.
Dennis; adaptors/dialogue, Barry Barringer and Gordon Kahn; sound,
Hans Weeren; camera, Norbert Brodine; editor, Rose Loewinger.

David Manners (Franklyn Drew); Adrienne Ames (Marcia Lane);
Bela Lugosi (Joseph Steiner); John Wray (Detective Sheehan); Vince
Barnett (Officer Gulliver); Alexander Carr (Leon Grossmith); Edward
Van Sloan (Tom Avery); Harold Minjir (Howell); Wade Boteler (Hilli-
ker); Al Hill (Assistant Director); Barbara Bedford (Script Girl); Alan
Roscoe (Chalmers); Mona Maris (Mrs. Avery); Edmund Burns (Brent);
Jimmy Donlin (Hill); Harold Waldridge (Clerk); Lee Moran (Todd);
George O'Hanlon (Extra in Studio).

"... [It] represents neither very original planning nor the
most thrilling of murder mystery drama elements. It is nicely paced,
however, and (miracle of miracles) most of its comic relief actually
succeeds in being comical" (Brooklyn Daily Eagle).
    The Death Kiss opens with a girl (Adrienne Ames) stepping
out of a car containing two men and then kissing a man who has just
left a nightclub. The surprised man tells the doorman he does not
know the girl and is immediately thereafter shot down by gangsters.
At that moment the director (Edward Van Sloan) says "cut" and calls
for a re-take declaring the scene was not realistic enough. At that
point it is suddenly realized that the "murdered" actor is actually dead.
The police are called in and suspicion falls on the actress as the
murdered man was her ex-husband. Scenario writer Franklyn Drew,
however, loves Ames and he tries to solve the crime himself. Eventually he accomplishes his mission--the police, headed by not-too-
bright Detective Shannon (John Wray) are not of much help--but not
before two other murders occur.
    Obviously made on the cheap to cash-in on the popularity of
Dracula (1931), The Death Kiss boasted three of the stars from that
well-remembered feature: Bela Lugosi (as a red-herring film supervisor), Manners, and Van Sloan. With most of the action taking place
in a movie studio, the picture had a more authentic flavor than did
the average poverty-row quickie.
    The Death Kiss has another reason for surviving as a bit of
cinema history. It was the vehicle used to reopen the Rox Theatre
in January 1933 after that flagship emporium had been forced to
close for several months. Tickets for the film (which included a
full-length stage show) were 25¢ before 6 P.M. and 35¢ thereafter.
The critics were so happy to see the showcase theatre back in business that they were kinder than need be to the feature attraction,
which "... proves to be entertainment more expert than might be
guessed from the lurid title" (New York Herald-Tribune). "Perhaps
the most ingenious element in the film is that which makes Bela
Lugosi a leading suspect up to the very end. Mr. Lugosi's reputa-

Adrienne Ames and Bela Lugosi in a publicity pose for <u>The Death Kiss</u> (1932).

---

tion in these cinema crimes makes it almost impossible for the amateur sleuths out front to dismiss him from suspicion. As a smoke screen, Mr. Lugosi is rather more effective than he has been recently in the more showy roles of ghoulish madmen. David Manners is pleasing as the scenario writer who solves the crime" (<u>New York Times</u>).

DEEP IN MY HEART (MGM, 1954) Color, 132 min.

Producer, Roger Edens; director, Stanley Donen; based on the book by Elliott Arnold; screenplay, Leonard Spigelgass; assistant director, Robert Vreeland; choreography, Eugene Loring; orchestrators, Hugo Friedhofer and Alexander Courage; art directors, Cedric Gibbons and Edward Carfagno; set decorators, Edwin B. Willis and Arthur Krams; music conductor, Adolph Deutsch; choral arranger, Robert Tucker; makeup, William Tuttle; special effects, Warren Newcombe; camera, George Folsey; editor, Adrienne Fazan.

Jose Ferrer, Merle Oberon, and Doe Avedon in Deep in My Heart (1954).

Jose Ferrer (Sigmund Romberg); Merle Oberon (Dorothy Donnelly); Helen Traubel (Anna Mueller); Doe Avedon (Lillian Harris Romberg); Walter Pidgeon (J. J. Shubert); Paul Henreid (Florenz Ziegfeld); Tamara Toumanova (Gaby Deslys); Paul Stewart (Bert Townsend); Isobel Elsom (Mrs. Harris); David Burns (Berrison, Sr.); Jim Backus (Ben Judson); Rosemary Clooney, Gene and Fred Kelly, Jane Powell, Vic Damone, Ann Miller, William Olvis, Cyd Charisse, James Mitchell, Howard Keel, Tony Martin, and Joan Weldon (Guest Stars); Douglas Fowley (Harold Butterfield); Robert Easton (Cumberly); Suzanne Luckey (Arabella Bell); Russ Tamblyn (Berrison, Jr.); Ludwig Stossel (Mr. Novak); Else Neft (Mrs. Novak); Norbert Schiller and Torben Meyer (Card Players); Reuben Wendorff and Franz Roehn (Men); Laiola Wendorff (Woman); John Alvin (Mr. Mulvaney); Jean Vander Pyl (Miss Zimmerman); Mary Alan Hokanson (Miss Cranbrook); Henry Sylvester (Judge); Gail Bonney and Jean Dante (Women Guests).

This color presentation from Metro-Goldwyn-Mayer was one in a series of movie musical biographies of big-name composers that contained little plot but a huge number of popular entertainers performing the composer's more famous songs. While Till the Clouds

Jean Harlow and Wallace Beery in <u>Dinner at Eight</u> (1933).

Roll By (about Jerome Kern), Rhapsody in Blue (George Gershwin),
The Best Things in Life Are Free (Brown-DeSylva-Henderson), Three
Little Words (Bert Kalmar and Harry Ruby) (qq. v.), and others were
fairly entertaining as well as melodic, Deep in my Heart, the musical
biopic of Sigmund Romberg (1887-1951), had only its music and multitude of guest stars to bolster a most mundane scenario.

Although the composer of dozens of beautiful melodies for
many of Broadway's finest shows (e. g. Maytime, The Desert Song,
The Student Prince, The New Moon, and Up in Central Park), Hun-
garian-born Romberg did not lead a life that was overly romantic or
particularly filmatic. Besides a few minor setbacks in his career
and a thwarted romance, his life was his music--fortunately the expensively-mounted color feature contains a great deal of that.

Making it a part of the "Hollywood on Hollywood" genre, the
picture recounts his brief composing chores for the cinema in the
early days of talkies.

Among the fine vocals in the movie are Tony Martin singing
"Lover Come Back to Me, " a quartet of songs by former Metropolitan opera singer Helen Traubel, Howard Keel doing "Your Land and
My Land, " Vic Damone and Jane Powell dueting on "Will You Remember?" and Gene and Fred Kelly's delightful rendition of "I Love
to Go Swimmin' with Women. " These interludes, along with the chic
presence of Merle Oberon as composer-romanticist Dorothy Donnelly,
helped one to overlook the stiffness of Jose Ferrer's interpretation
of the lead character. Walter Pidgeon as J. J. Shubert and Paul
Henreid as Florenz Ziegfeld offered authority to their characterizations, if lacking in sufficient dash. The picture would gross $4. 1
million in distributors' domestic rentals.

DINNER AT EIGHT (MGM, 1933) 113 min.

Producer, David O. Selznick; director, George Cukor; based
on the play by George S. Kaufman and Edna Ferber; adaptors, Frances Marion and Herman J. Mankiewicz; camera, William Daniels;
editor, Ben Lewis.

Marie Dressler (Carlotta Vance); John Barrymore (Larry Re-
nault); Wallace Beery (Dan Packard); Jean Harlow (Kitty Packard);
Lionel Barrymore (Oliver Jordan); Lee Tracy (Max Kane); Edmund
Lowe (Dr. Wayne Talbot); Billie Burke (Millicent Jordan); Madge
Evans (Paula Jordan); Jean Hersholt (Jo Stengel); Karen Morley (Lucy
Talbot); Louise Closser Hale (Hattie Loomis); Phillips Holmes (Er-
nest De Graff); May Robson (Mrs. Wendel the Cook); Grant Mitchell
(Ed Loomis); Phoebe Foster (Miss Alden); Elizabeth Patterson (Miss
Copeland); Hilda Vaughn (Tina, Kitty's Maid); Harry Beresford (Fos-
dick); John Davidson (Assistant Manager); Edward Woods (Eddie);
George Baxter (Gustave the Butler); Anna Duncan (Dora the Maid);
Herman Bing (The Waiter).

Although Dinner at Eight is set entirely in New York City
and revolves around the lives of several people invited to a plush
dinner party given by members of the Park Avenue set, it does

contain several biting scenes about Hollywood and in particular about
the downfall of a once-famous movie star. Dinner at Eight, one of
the few features of its vintage still to be revived theatrically, stands
the test of time quite well. Its plotline, humor, pathos, and performances are still (almost) as fresh today as when the film was issued during the heart of the Depression.

Two aspects of show business at its twilight are exemplified
by this feature. Marie Dressler is top-billed as Carlotta Vance, a
dinosaur of the stage who has survived into another time, being wealthy and full of memories of the past but still firmly implanted in the
present. On the other hand, John Barrymore's Larry Renault is
nothing more than a ghost of the past. He is highly representative
of how quickly Hollywood, but not the general public, forgets the
performers who once brought revenue to the filmmakers.

At one point in Dinner at Eight, Louise Closser Hale rattles
off a few of the stars her movie buff husband (Grant Mitchell) could
recall. Names like Francis X. Bushman and Mae Marsh are tossed
about, people who were still active in films at the time and whose
days of stardom were less than a decade old. Hollywood--probably
more than any other industry--buries its dead long before the corpse
heaves its last breath.

In the course of this grade A drama, Barrymore's Larry Renault (a one-time top film idol who cannot even get extra work in
Hollywood but who is still good for a big feature story in the New
York newspapers) recounts his climb to fame to his secret mistress
(Madge Evans), the daughter of the hostess (Billie Burke) of the
swank party he will not live to attend. He talks of the old days--
of "fried egg sandwiches" and the three wives who used him, the
most recent now "on top of the heap" (no doubt reminiscent of the
fall of John Gilbert and the rise of two of his wives, Ina Claire and
Virginia Bruce). At the finale, Barrymore's character commits suicide (careful to leave his profile showing), predating Norman Maine
in A Star Is Born (q. v.) by four years.

DOUBLING FOR ROMEO (Goldwyn, 1922) 5304 ft.

Director, Clarence Badger; story, Elmer Rice; screenplay,
Bernard McConville; camera, Marcel Le Picard.

Will Rogers (Sam [Romeo]); Sylvia Breamer (Lulu [Juliet]);
Raymond Hatton (Steve Woods [Paris]); Sydney Ainsworth (Endleton
[Mercutio]); Al Hart (Big Alec [Tybalt]); John Cossar (Foster [Capu-
let]); C. E. Thurston (Duffy Saunders [Benvolio]); Cordelia Callahan
(Maggie [Maid]); Roland Rushton (Minister [Friar]); Jimmy Rogers
(Jimmie Jones); William Orlamond (Movie Director); Guinn "Big Boy"
Williams (Bit).

While Will Rogers was under contract to producer Samuel
Goldwyn he turned out a number of film comedies including this
feature which joshed the movies, especially silver screen cowboys
and swashbucklers. Even Elizabethan playwright William Shakespeare
received his share of friendly "digs. " Photoplay magazine wrote,

"Will Rogers collaborating with Will Shakespeare ... both of the talented authors deserve credit. " Unfortunately for its box-office potential, the photoplay also teased the Will Rogers image which annoyed the distaff side of filmgoing audiences.

Rogers portrayed Sam, an Arizona cowboy who falls in love with Lulu (Sylvia Breamer) who is enamoured of the cinema.   When he tells her of his romantic intentions she decides that to win her heart he must court her in the tradition of screen suitors.   To obtain a firsthand look at the technique the cowpoke travels to Hollywood and obtains a job as a double/stuntman at the Goldwyn Studios.   There he is badly shaken up performing a stunt in a Western and refuses to work when a retake is requested.   Next he gains a chance to test for the role of a celluloid lover, but his audition is a flop.   He returns home without learning the movies' techniques of lovemaking. However, he then has a dream in which he is cast as Romeo and from the fantasy he acquires the expertise required to properly woo the damsel of his choice.

Two years later Rogers would again kid the films, but this time in a short subject, Uncensored Movies (1923).

DOWN MEMORY LANE (Eagle Lion, 1949) 70 min.

Producer, Aubrey Schenck; director of new sequences, Phil Karlson; screenplay, Steve Allen; additional music, Sol Kaplan; music director, Irving Friedman; camera, Walter Strenge; editor, Fred Allen.

Steve Allen (TV Host/narrator); Mack Sennett and Franklin Pangborn (Themselves); Frank Nelson (Mr. Jeffers); Yvonne Peattie (Miss Ryan); Rennie McEvoy (Technician); Jo Ann Joyce (Girl in Bed); Rowland McCracken (Bald Headed Man); Irving Bacon (Bit).

This compilation feature, with new footage shot by director Phil Karlson, was one of the first films to use television as a background and at the same time it reprised much cinema history--drawing on films from the Keystone Studios of Mack Sennett. As a bridge format for the reshowing of these old clips, TV star Steve Allen decides (within the thin storyline) to unreel old movie scenes of his video program and invites Mack Sennett, Frank Nelson, and Franklin Pangborn to view the vintage pictures with him.   Thus the format for Down Memory Lane was conceived and the resulting 72 minutes was delightful fodder for most nostalgic viewers.   It was a forerunner of the type of cinema made popular in the sixties by compiler/ producer Robert Youngson.

Down Memory Lane offered prime Mack Sennett films dating from the early silent days up through the premier years of the talkies.   Besides showcasing such teens' and twenties' cinema greats as Gloria Swanson, Ben Turpin, Mabel Normand and many others, the picture also spotlighted W. C. Fields in The Dentist and Bing Crosby in Blue of the Night.   These latter two entries, shown almost in their entirety, were early sound shorts made by Sennett.

In 1940 a number of Sennett's early sound two-reelers had been interpolated into the feature Road to Hollywood. But Down Memory Lane was the first such motion picture to include the pioneer producer-director himself in the proceedings. More importantly, this is the first American feature to accept the small screen on its own level, as an ally and not an enemy to the cinema.

DOWN MEXICO WAY (Republic, 1941) 77 min.

Producer, Harry Grey; director, Joseph Santley; story, Dorrell and Stuart McGowan; screenplay, Olive Cooper and Albert Duffy; song, Eddie Cherkose and Jule Styne; camera, Jack Marta; editor, Howard O'Neill.

Gene Autry (Gene); Smiley Burnette (Frog Millhouse); Fay McKenzie (Maria Elena); Harold Huber (Pancho Grande); Sidney Blackmer (Gibson); Joe Sawyer (Allen); Andrew Tombes (Mayor Tubbs); Murray Alper (Flood); Arthur Loft (Gerard); Duncan Renaldo (Juan); Paul Fix (Davis); Julian Rivero (Don Alvarado); Ruth Robinson (Mercedes); Thornton Edwards (Captain Rodriguez); The Herrera Sisters (Themselves); Eddie Dean (Rider).

After a solo sojourn at 20th Century-Fox for Shooting High (q. v.), Gene Autry was back making Westerns at Republic Pictures. In Down Mexico Way he returned to the theme of moviemaking. This time, though, Autry was not in the film business but on the trail of fly-by-night producers bilking locals of money on the pretext they would produce a film in whatever town they were then inhabiting.
The crooks pull this con game in the town of Sage City and victims Gene Autry, Frog Millhouse (Smiley Burnette), and Pancho Grande (Harold Huber)--the latter a reformed outlaw--take after the cheating duo and chase them south-of-the-border. In a small town they learn the two swindlers are attempting to wheedle money from landowner Don Alvarado (Julian Rivero), claiming they will produce a feature starring the gentleman's daughter Maria Elena (Fay McKenzie).
When Autry et al. catch up with the scoundrels, however, they prove not to be the ones who had swindled Gene and the boys. But Autry recognizes the car that the culprits are using as the one driven by the men who cheated the people of Sage City. It develops the latter crooks had been cohorts of the former but had been put out of the way for overuse of the make-a-movie scheme. Meanwhile Rivero agrees to back the film, but Gene and his pals kidnap McKenzie and convince her to persuade Dad to demand the producers provide a goodly portion of the production costs themselves.
Not having the ready money, the crooks plan to rob the bank car bringing in Rivero's money from Mexico City and then place the blame for the crime on Autry, Burnette, and Huber. The scheme fails and the local folk aid the heroes in rounding up the wrongdoers and retrieving the money for the citizens of Sage City.
"Story carries along at a good pace, neatly intermingling action, romance, comedy and song for solid audience attention" was

the verdict of Variety. Down Mexico Way boasted a well-staged fight finale. But its real highlight was an assortment of beautiful songs which brightened the proceedings. Gene sings "Maria Elena," "Down Mexico Way," "South of the Border," and "Beer Barrel Polka."

Also of note within the film is the use of the character name of Don Alvarado, a character played herein by Julian Rivero. There actually was a Hollywood film star in the late twenties and early thirties with this name. Also in the cast, in a bit as a cowhand, is future singing cowboy movie star Eddie Dean.

DOWN MISSOURI WAY (Producers Releasing Corporation, 1946) 73 min.

Producer/director, Josef Berne; screenplay, Sam Neuman; songs, Kim Gannon and Walter Kent; music, Karl Hajos; camera, Vincent J. Farrar; editor, W. Donn Hayes.

Martha O'Driscoll (Jane Colwell); John Carradine (Thorndyke P. Dunning); Eddie Dean (Mortimer); William Wright (Mike Burton); Roscoe Ates (Pappy); Renee Godfrey (Gloria Baxter); Mabel Todd (Cindy); Eddie Craven (Sam); Chester Clute (Professor Shaw); Will Wright (Professor Morris); Paul Scardon (Professor Lewis).

Long winded, but low-grade Hollywood film director, Thorndyke P. Dunning (John Carradine) is planning to make an epic to end all epics: a hillbilly movie operetta. For his star he scouts around for a bright mule (this was before Francis the Talking Mule). Finally he locates one who happens to be enrolled as an experimental student at a Missouri agricultural college. Carradine then collects his cast and crew and sets off for the campus where they shoot their backwoods musical.

Conceived on a minuscule budget, this minor PRC release was on the same level as the brand of picture it sought to portray. Down Missouri Way was mostly dull going. All of the characters were pat stereotypes, with Martha O'Driscoll as the ingenue of the picture, Eddie Dean as the young singer, and Carradine (on reprieve from his horror movie assignments) as a gabby director. O'Driscoll had definitely seen better days at Universal, and Dean, who was allowed to sing the majority of the eight songs in this film, was better showcased at the studio in his musical Westerns. The only saving grace of the entry was Carradine's hammy part. Variety noted that his "... performance is a perfect facsimile of the Armour brand of thesping made famous by John Barrymore [who had been a real-life friend of Carradine's] during the latter's more flamboyant moods."

DREAMBOAT (20th Century-Fox, 1952) 83 min.

Producer, Sol C. Siegel; director, Claude Binyon; based on the story by John Weaver; screenplay, Binyon; music, Cyril J. Mockridge; orchestrator, Bernard Mayers; art directors, Lyle Wheeler and Maurice Ransford; set decorators, Thomas Little and Fred J. Rode; camera, Milton Krasner; editor, James B. Clark.

Ginger Rogers, Anne Francis, and Jeffrey Hunter in <u>Dreamboat</u> (1952).

Clifton Webb (Thornton Sayre [Bruce Blair]); Ginger Rogers (Gloria Marbowe); Anne Francis (Carol Sayre); Jeffrey Hunter (Bill Ainslee); Elsa Lanchester (Dr. Coffey); Fred Clark (Sam Levitt); Paul Harvey (Harrington); Ray Collins (Timothy Stone); Helene Stanley (Mimi); Richard Garrick (Judge Bowles); George Barrows (Commandant); Jay Adler (Desk Clerk); Marietta Canty (Lavinia); Emory Parnell (Used Car Salesman); Laura Brooks (Mrs. Gunther); Gwen Verdon, Matt Mattox, and Frank Radcliffe (Performers in Commercial); May Wynn (Cigarette Girl); Victoria Horne (Waitress); Alphonse Martel (Maitre D'); Mary Treen (Wife); Fred Graham (Bartender).

In the wake of Sunset Boulevard (q. v.), with its rather morbid account of Hollywood's past and lost stardom, 20th Century-Fox went to the opposite end of the spectrum and made a delicious spoof of silent pictures and what "really" happened to their stars with the advent of sound and the passing years. (Fox did however also offer its own dour account of the fate of an ex-movie great in its 1952 The Star, q. v. , with Bette Davis.) In Dreamboat Bruce Blair (Clifton Webb) and Gloria Marlowe (Ginger Rogers), the famous silent film love duo are certainly not of Norma Desmond's tragic ilk. Webb wants to forget the "folly" of his movie days while career-minded Rogers is seeking another chance at fame and, more importantly, money.

Herein the old pictures of silent idols Webb and Rogers are being revived on television with great popularity; Rogers hosts the program. A nationwide hunt then begins for her old co-star who is finally discovered teaching in a small college under an assumed name. Sickened by the new publicity surrounding the reissue of his primitive flickers, Webb hastens to New York to take legal action against any further showing of the movies. Rogers, once his love and the reason he made the features initially, objects; she sees a chance for new popularity and big salaries from fresh Webb-Rogers features.

In the courtroom, Webb proves that TV has no cultural value and that he has a right to his own privacy. He wins his case and the old movies are barred from TV showings. Back home, however, he loses his job when the old-maid president of the college where he teaches fires him because of her insatiable lust for the screen image of Bruce Blair. The veteran star is then saved by a new offer from Hollywood which he accepts. At the premiere of his new picture (a clip from Clifton Webb's Sitting Pretty, 1948, is shown) he is acclaimed as a rediscovered screen personality. His happiness is short-lived, however, as he discovers that Rogers has purchased his contract.

Both Webb and Rogers provided the right light touch in interpreting their roles of the former movie luminaries. The recreation of some of their silent pictures was well handled, especially the take-offs on Douglas Fairbanks' swashbuckling pictures and the popular World War I action films. Dreamboat also sallied a few good jabs at TV, then still a very sore point with Hollywood producers trying to recover from the effects of the "boob tube. "

DRUG STORE COWBOY (Independent Pictures, 1925) 4356 ft.

Director, Park Frame.

Franklyn Farnum (Marmaduke Grandon); Robert Walker (Gentleman Jack); Jean Arthur (Jean); Malcolm Denny (Wilton); Ronald Goetz (Director); Dick La Reno (Sheriff).

One of the most ingratiating of Western film heroes was Franklyn Farnum, an actor who made hundreds of pictures but whose starring career never rose above the level of poverty row. Besides being a rugged personality, Farnum often injected levity into his oaters, making them much lighter than the heavy-handed counterparts of many of his contemporaries. Occasionally the star would step off the range for a present-day comedy. Drug Store Cowboy is an example of this; within its telling are several barbs at the "art" of film-making.

Marmaduke Grandon (Farnum), a drugstore clerk, wants desperately to become a movie star. Finally he has the opportunity to appear in a film when an actor dies suddenly during a shooting schedule and a quick replacement is essential. Farnum is hired but he never reaches the studio. He is walking to the set in his cowboy garb, when a bandit captures him, forces the fledgling performer to exchange clothes with him, and then ties up the hapless victim. The robber then joins the movie company in the guise of Farnum. Later the store clerk arrives and runs the culprit off the set, ruining the leading lady's big scene. Still later, during a bank robbery sequence, the real bandit uses the acting troupe and the staged scene as a front and tries to hold up the bank for real. But Farnum stops him, again ruining the filming. But this time he wins the love of leading lady Jean (Jean Arthur).

Drug Store Cowboy is best remembered today as one of the earliest features to star Jean Arthur.

EASY GO   see   FREE AND EASY

THE EDDIE CANTOR STORY (Warner Bros. , 1953) Color, 116 min.

Producer, Sidney Skolsky; director, Afred E. Green; story, Skolsky; screenplay, Jerome Wiedman, Ted Sherdeman, and Skolsky; music numbers staged by LeRoy Prinz; assistant director, Al Alleborn; camera, Edwin DuPar; editor, William Ziegler.

Keefe Brasselle (Eddie Cantor); Marilyn Erskine (Ida Cantor); Aline MacMahon (Grandma Esther); Arthur Franz (Harry Harris); Alex Gerry (David Tobias); Greta Granstedt (Rachel Tobias); Gerald Mohr (Rocky); William Forrest (Ziegfeld); Jackie Barnett (Durante); Richard Monda (Eddie Cantor at Age Thirteen); Marie Windsor (Cleo Abbott); Ann Doran (Lillian Edwards); Hal March (Gus Edwards); Douglas Evans (Leo Raymond); Susan Odin (Ida at Age Eleven); and: Will Rogers, Jr. (Will Rogers); Eddie Cantor and Ida Cantor (Themselves in Prologue and Epilogue).

Keefe Brasselle (in blackface) in The Eddie Cantor Story (1953).

This proved to be a very minor movie biography, produced by Hollywood columnist Sidney Skolsky who had helped to bring The Jolson Story and Jolson Sings Again (qq.v.) to the screen. Alfred E. Green, who directed The Jolson Story, helmed The Eddie Cantor Story. Cantor himself made many films with the Hollywood motif (for instance Ali Baba Goes to Town and Thank Your Lucky Stars [qq. v.]) and he was also associated with a goodly number of standard tunes through his years in vaudeville, radio, recordings, and films. The latter aspect of his half-century career, however, was hardly touched upon in this bland screen portrayal.

The Eddie Cantor Story unfolds the typical and timeworn tale of the rise of a young boy from a poor family on Manhattan's Lower East Side. It traces his beginning in vaudeville and how he becomes a Broadway celebrity. From there come movies, radio, and eventually television. Through it all he is supported by his understanding wife Ida (Marilyn Erskine) and their five daughters, although he is frequently depicted as having neglected his family due to his constant professional activities. The 115-minute excursion begins and ends with the real-life Eddie and Ida Cantor attending a private showing of the motion picture.

Perhaps the biggest drawback to the film, besides its two-dimensional script, was the casting of toothy Keefe Brasselle in the title role. The actor was too tall for the part, totally lacked the charisma of Cantor, and was only able to exude an outlandish parody

of the "banjo-eyed" comedian.   Fortunately, Cantor himself provided
the dubbing of the numerous songs ("If You Knew Susie, " "Ida, " etc.)
mouthed and pantomimed by Brasselle in the picture.

The New York Times branded this exercise ". . . tedious,
treacly and titanically tame. " One of the few participants to receive
good reviews was Aline MacMahon as Grandma Esther.   The combination of her sheer presence and her capacity to draw credibility
from hackneyed situations and dialogue made some of the screen offering palatable.

Cantor, who had negotiated for the film being produced--even
arranging to finance the drafting of the scenario--would say years
later of this celluloid account, "If that was my life, I didn't live. "

ELLA CINDERS (First National, 1926) 6540 ft.

Presenter, John McCormick; director, Alfred E. Green; based
on the comic strip "Cinderella in the Movies" by William Conselman
and Charles Plumb; screenplay, Frank Griffin and Mervyn LeRoy;
titles, George Marion, Jr.; art director, E. J. Shulter; camera,
Arthur Martinelli; editor, Robert J. Kern.

Colleen Moore (Ella Cinders); Lloyd Hughes (Waite Lifter);
Vera Lewis (Ma Cinders); Doris Baker (Lotta Pill); Emily Gerdes
(Prissy Pill); Mike Donlin (Film Studio Gateman); Jed Prouty (The
Mayor); Jack Duffy (The Fire Chief); Harry Allen (The Photographer);
D'Arcy Corrigan (The Editor); Alfred E. Green (The Director); Harry
Langdon (Himself); E. H. Calvert, Chief Yowlache, and Russell Hop-
ton (Bits).

Ella Cinders was based on the popular comic strip by Bill
Conselman and Charles Plumb and this film version was a fair recreation of it.   However, several of the strip characters, including
Ella's father and the iceman, were deleted; a new one--the boy-
friend--was added.   Overall, it evolved into a well-made and funny
film which Photoplay magazine judged an "enjoyable Cinderella story"
and added "Take the children. "

Colleen Moore had one of her most popular screen assignments
in the title part as the small town girl who slaves so that her mother
and evil half-sisters can live in comfort.   In an effort to break away
from her family she enters a movie contest which she wins.   The
prize is a free trip to Hollywood.   There, however, she realizes
she has been the victim of a hoax and she can find no employment.
Eventually she makes her entry into the film studio and onto a set
where a fire sequence is being lensed.   She believes the blaze is
real and attempts to save the actors, ruining the set and the scene.
But she does emerge from the embarrassing situation with a contract, a reward for her realistic performance in the seemingly hazardous predicament.

The studio then sets about making an actress out of the non-
professional.   During her screen audition an escaped lion causes her
to react with real fear, further solidifying her "acting" talent in the
eyes of the studio heads.   Later she is called upon to imitate such

Hollywood greats of the day as Jackie Coogan, Lillian Gish, and Charles Chaplin. Eventually she earns fame as a movie player and finds love with Waite Lifter (Lloyd Hughes).

Ella Cinders was a big financial success for First National Pictures and presenter/producer John McCormick, then the husband of the exceedingly popular Miss Moore. This silent photoplay still holds its inherent humor. It is especially appealing to movie lovers today because of the guest appearance of screen great Harry Langdon in a too short cameo. Among others appearing in the filming-within-the-filming is the picture's director Alfred E. Green who had two years earlier supervised two moviemaking-oriented features for First National Pictures: In Hollywood with Potash and Perlmutter and Inez from Hollywood (qq. v.). Far later in his lengthy career Green would direct film biographies of two stars, The Jolson Story and The Eddie Cantor Story (qq. v.), each depicting scenes of how movies were "actually" made.

THE ERRAND BOY (Paramount, 1961) 92 min.

Producer, Ernest D. Glucksman; associate producer, Arthur Schmidt; director, Jerry Lewis; screenplay, Lewis and Bill Richmond; songs, Lou Y. Brown, Richmond, and Lewis; costumes, Edith Head; music, Walter Scharf; choreography, Nick Castle; assistant director, Ralph Axness; art directors, Hal Pereira and Arthur Lonergan; set decorators, Sam Comer and James Payne; sound, Hugo and Charles Grenzbach; camera, W. Wallace Kelley; editor, Stanley E. Johnson.

Jerry Lewis (Morty S. Tashman); Brian Donlevy (Mr. T. P.); Dick Wesson (The A. D.); Howard McNear (Dexter Sneak); Felicia Atkins (Serina); Pat Dahl (Miss Carson); Kathleen Freeman (Mrs. T. P.); Mary and Paul Ritts (Themselves); Isobel Elsom (Irma Paramutual); Fritz Feld (Foreign Director); Iris Adrian (Great Actress); Renee Taylor (Miss Giles); Sig Rumann (Exasperated Film Director); Dan Blocker, Lorne Green, Michael Landon, and Pernell Roberts (Guest Bits); Donald Barry, Sue Casey, Harry Cheshire, Quinn O'Hara, Benny Rubin, Doodles Weaver, Milton Frome, Hal Rand, Mary Treen, Bill Wellman, Jr. (Bits).

While still teamed with Dean Martin, Jerry Lewis had appeared in Hollywood or Bust (q. v.). After the team went their separate ways, Lewis returned to the genre in Rock-a-Bye-Baby (1958) in which he was a bachelor babysitting for movie star Marilyn Maxwell's triplets, and in Ladies' Man (1961) he was the handyman at a Hollywood actresses' hotel: these slim threads were the only connections those two Paramount features had with film-making. However, Lewis did make two pictures in the early sixties for Paramount with a distinct Hollywood theme: The Errand Boy and The Patsy (q. v.).

The Errand Boy opens with a voice-over stating "This is Hollywood. The land of the real and the unreal...." Morty S. Tashman (Lewis) is a bumbling young man employed at Paramutual

Jerry Lewis in a publicity shot for The Errand Boy (1961).

Studios in a most minor capacity.   He is hired by arrogant studio
head Mr. T. P. (Brian Donlevy--himself a Paramount star in the
forties) to spy on the employees to insure their efficiency.   At Paramutual, Jerry wreaks havoc while attempting to fulfill his comprehensive mission.   He upsets two directors, one of them when he wrecks
a set after becoming infatuated with a pretty actress.   In the sound
dubbing department, he messes up the work on a new film, and later
causes a scramble in scripts at the secretarial pool.   On another
occasion he ruins a birthday gala for a self-centered star (Iris Adrian) and causes the studio head's portly wife (Kathleen Freeman) to
get dunked in a car-washing sequence.   All in all, the hapless boob
causes more damage and costs to the studio than he could possibly
have saved by his efficiency spying.
        Most critics, and fans alike, found the film quite amusing in
its first half, but from there on the picture seemed to become labored
and run out of creative juice.   The idea of lunatic Lewis wrecking
a movie studio was a viable concept, but too quickly the farce became repetitious.   Perhaps the best bits occur at the picture's start
where a variety of genres are shown on the screen and then the
camera pulls back to reveal how the illusion has been created on the
soundstage.   Since this entry was shot at Paramount's Marathon

Street studio, it was a natural promotional gimmick for the company's
television branch, to have the stars of "Bonanza" (Lorne Green,
Michael Landon, Dan Blocker, and Pernell Roberts) appear in guest
bits.

When the film debuted in England, the British Monthly Film
Bulletin reported, "Vague continuity and the disorientation of many
of the gags would matter less if Lewis were as disciplined and con-
sistent a comedian as, say W. C. Fields.   But he is at times in-
tolerably smug.   The best moments come from Lewis's team of
veteran small-part players: Iris Adrian as the talentless star, all
dripping mascara and sluttish rage, Sig Rumann as a white-gloved director (Sternberg? Dieterle?) reduced to tearful hysteria on finding
the day's rushes ruined by Morty's presence among the extras; and
from a sustained mime sequence which says all there is to say about
the terrors of a sardine-packed lift. "

EXCESS BAGGAGE (MGM, 1928) 7182 ft.

     Director, James Cruze; based on the play by John Wesley
McGowan; dialogue/titles, Ralph Spence; continuity, Frances Marion;
sets, Cedric Gibbons; wardrobe, David Cox; camera, Ira Morgan;
editor, George Hively.

     William Haines (Eddie Kane); Josephine Dunn (Elsa McCoy);
Neely Edwards (Jimmy Dunn); Kathleen Clifford (Mabel Ford); Greta
Granstedt (Betty Ford); Ricardo Cortez (Val D'Errico); Cyril Chad-
wick (Crammon).

     Eddie Kane (William Haines), a small-time vaudeville juggler
and acrobat, falls in love with Elsa McCoy (Josephine Dunn), a dancer.   The two marry but as time passes Dunn wins her big chance
in the movies and develops into a big star while Haines remains on
the stage, making no professional headway.   Because of his wife's
success and his failures, Haines begins to believe Dunn has been
unfaithful.   With his morale at a low ebb, he slips and falls from a
wire during his act and is seriously injured.   As time passes Haines
recovers and attempts a comeback, but his nerve fails him until
Dunn returns to reassure him of her enduring love.

This eight-reeler was issued in the fall of 1928 with sound
effects and a musical score, but with no dialogue.   Director James
Cruze effectively handled this project and he elicited an underplayed
performance from star Haines, previously noted for his brash over-
playing of comedy.   While having a minimum of the Hollywood-on-
Hollywood theme in its plot, the photoplay did effectively exploit the
too-often real life situation of one member of a show business team
becoming a sensation while the other is nothing more than "excess
baggage. "

The next year, Haines and Dunn--who were something of a
screen team in the silent era--would appear for MGM and for director James Cruze in A Man's Man (q. v.).

William Haines and Josephine Dunn in <u>Excess Baggage</u> (1928).

THE EXTRA GIRL (Associated Exhibitors, 1923) 7 reels

Producer, Mack Sennett; director, F. Richard Jones; story, Sennett; screenplay, Bernard McConville; camera, Homer Scott and Eric Crockett.

Mabel Normand (Sue Graham); Ralph Graves (Dave Giddings); George Nichols (Pa Graham); Anna Hernandez (Ma Graham); Vernon Dent (Aaron Applejohn); Ramsey Wallace (Phillip Hackett); Charlotte Mineau (Belle Brown); and: Mary Mason, Max Davidson, Louise Carver, William Desmond, Carl Stockdale, Harry Gribbon, Billy Bevan, and Andre Beranger.

This slapstick farce detailed the plight of thousands of young girls who came to California each year only to wind up as cinema extras at best and generally going back home as Hollywood failures.

Sue Graham (Mabel Normand) wins a beauty contest by accident in her Illinois home town. As a result she earns a trip to Hollywood. In the film capital she can find no screen work and must be satisfied with a job as an assistant in a wardrobe department. Disgusted with the elusive search for stardom, she returns home after many comic misadventures in tinsel town. (At one point in her misadventures on the film lot, Normand's Sue Graham thinks she is leading a Great Dane dog around the lot but is dismayed to discover that the animal turns out to be a lion.)

Photoplay magazine printed that the film was "... chiefly notable because Mabel Normand heads the cast and her pictures are always worthwhile." No doubt the presence of the very talented comedienne gave this rather thin offering the box-office push it needed. Still by 1923 her career was on the decline after her involvement in the headlined William Desmond Taylor murder case two years prior.

F. SCOTT FITZGERALD IN HOLLYWOOD (ABC-TV, 1976) Color, 100 min.

Executive producer, Herbert Brodkin; producer, Robert Verger; director, Anthony Page; teleplay, James Costigan; music, Morton Gould; production designer, Brian Eatwell; art director, Jack Degovia; consultant, Sheilah Graham; camera, James Crabe; editor, Sidney Katz.

Jason Miller (F. Scott Fitzgerald); Tuesday Weld (Zelda); Julia Foster (Sheilah Graham); Dolores Sutton (Dorothy Parker); Susanne Benton (The Starlet); Michael Lerner (Marvin Margulies); Tom Ligon (Alan Campbell); John Randolph (Rupert Wahler); Tom Rosqui (Edwin Knopf); Audrey Christie (The Hostess); Jacque Lynn Colton (Waitress in Schwab's); Norma Connolly (Zelda's Nurse); Sarah Cunningham (Mrs. Taft); Hilda Haynes (The Maid); Paul Lambert (Lucius Krieger); Joseph Stern (Detmar); James Woods (Lenny Schoenfield).

F. Scott Fitzgerald (1896-1940) and Hollywood have always interested writers and the public alike. Most insist that Fitzgerald

Ralph Graves and Mabel Normand in The Extra Girl (1923).

was badly misused by the film capital and that it traded on his once-famous name while suffocating whatever talent he may have had left at the twilight of his see-sawing creative career. His lover, Sheilah Graham's, version of the story covered several tomes and was filmed in part as Beloved Infidel (q. v.). Later, less-biased versions of the Fitzgerald-Hollywood love/hate relationships appeared. Today the pendulum seems to be swinging the other way--to the premise that Hollywood provided a near has-been writer with a chance to work and out of that opportunity emerged his final (unfinished) novel, The Last Tycoon (q. v.).

F. Scott Fitzgerald in Hollywood is a telefeature which nobly attempts to recapture the writer's wasted years in the cinema colony-- both at the time he was an acclaimed writer and in the later years when alcohol ruled his pathetic existence. The teledrama opens in 1927 when Fitzgerald (Jason Miller) and his accomplished wife Zelda (Tuesday Weld) come to California, sparkling with the success of his novels, including The Great Gatsby. The celebrated couple are the toast of the town and they quickly captivate the impressed film community. A decade then elapses and Fitzgerald returns to Hollywood, but under far different circumstances. Zelda has been committed to a sanatorium for mental illness. In order to meet the mounting expenses, the writer, now sickly and nearly broke, accepts a job to do screenwriting. Besides coping with the autocratic control of the film moguls over his "creative" output, he must deal with the fact that he is an alcoholic. An affair with rising Hollywood columnist, British-born Sheilah Graham (Julia Foster) brings some respite into his troubled life and he begins a new novel before his sudden death.

While Jason Miller was by no means a vividly memorable Fitzgerald--Richard Chamberlain had been far more appropriate in an earlier TV drama which blended a Fitzgerald portrait with the writer's fiction--his interpretation was an improvement on Gregory Peck's stolid work in Beloved Infidel. Weld supplied a surprisingly deft and dramatic interpretation of the tortured, brilliant Zelda with Dolores Sutton a standout in the supporting cast as witty, creative Dorothy Parker. It is she who ends the film by eulogizing over Fitzgerald's corpse the famous literary line from The Great Gatsby, "The poor son-of-a-bitch."

The film trade papers were not enthusiastic about this exercise. The Hollywood Reporter termed it "a devastating, if familiar view of the town that has little use for a literary genius, but is willing to buy one when he's up for sale." Daily Variety wondered, "Just why the tormented, overexposed spirits of F. Scott and Zelda Fitzgerald have again been trotted out to perform in James Costigan's teleplay other than for exploitation is a mystery.... The Fitzgerald story ... is far better told in his own books and short stories. Now, perhaps, the Fitzgeralds can rest in peace."

An engrossing, meticulous study of Fitzgerald in Hollywood was written by Aaron Latham in Crazy Sundays (1971) tracing the renowned author's fumbles in working on a film project in 1927 for Constance Talmadge, but Lipstick, as it was to be called, would later be abandoned; of Fitzgerald's participation in several MGM projects in the late thirties including A Yank at Oxford (1938), Three Comrades (1938), The Women (1939), and what evolved as 1943's Madame Curie. Budd Schulberg, who worked with Fitzgerald on United Artists' Winter Carnival (1939), would two decades later write a thinly-veiled account of this traumatic endeavor. The book, The Disenchanted, would be turned into a compelling Broadway drama starring Jason Robards as Fitzgerald, Rosemary Harris as Zelda, and Robert Morse as the young Schulberg-type figure.

THE FALCON IN HOLLYWOOD (RKO, 1944) 67 min.

Producer, Maurice Geraghty; director, Gordon Douglas; based

Walter Soderling, Barbara Hale, Veda Ann Borg, and Tom Conway
in The Falcon in Hollywood (1944).

on a character created by Michael Arlen; screenplay, Gerald Geraghty; art directors, Albert S. D'Agostino and L. O. Croxton; music
director, C. Bakaleinikoff; choreography, Theodore Rand; camera,
Nicholas Musuraca; editor, Gene Milford.

Tom Conway (Tom Lawrence the Falcon); Barbara Hale (Peggy
Calahan); Veda Ann Borg (Billie Atkins); John Abbott (Martin S.
Dwyer); Sheldon Leonard (Louis Buchanan); Konstantin Shayne (Alex
Hoffman); Emory Parnell (Inspector McBride); Frank Jenks (Higgins);
Jean Brooks (Roxana Miles); Rita Corday (Lilli D'Allio); Walter So-
derling (Ed Johnson); Usaf Ali (Nagari); Robert Clarke (Perc Saun-
ders); Patti Brill (Secretary); Bryant Washburn and Sammy Blum
(Actors' Agents); Jimmy Jordan (Operator); Wheaton Chambers and
Bert Moorhouse (Bits); Chili Williams (Beautiful Blonde).

This entry in the RKO detective property was one of only two
(the other was Boston Blackie in Hollywood, q. v.) of the forties'

sleuth series which employed the Hollywood background. This double-bill entry marked the final Falcon series production by Maurice Geraghty, who had done the previous half-dozen episodes, while his brother, Gerald Geraghty, wrote the scenario. Gordon Douglas spiritedly directed this film, budgeted for $131,000 on an 18-day shooting schedule.

The plot finds actor Tom Conway as Tom Lawrence, the Falcon, vacationing on the West Coast and enjoying an afternoon at the Santa Anita racetrack in the company of film stars Peggy Calahan (Barbara Hale) and Lilli D'Allio (Rita Corday). As they are leaving Conway notes the former stealing the latter's handbag and he follows her back to Sunset Studios (actually RKO). On a soundstage he finds the corpse of the actor-husband of studio designer Roxana Miles (Jean Brooks).

Meanwhile Inspector McBride (Emory Parnell) and Higgins (Frank Jenks) appear on the scene and immediately, because of his unsavory reputation, suspect Conway of the crime. The Falcon decides he had better solve the crime quickly and is aided in his mission by garrulous female cab driver Billie Atkins (Veda Ann Borg).

The duo, however, tumble onto a school of red herrings, which includes the film's director (Konstantin Shayne), who was seen hiding the murder weapon and who carried on affairs with both Brooks and Corday. Also there is the Shakespeare-quoting producer (John Abbott) who owned the murder weapon, and in addition, gangster Louis Buchanan (Sheldon Leonard), who is Corday's current beau. When Leonard is also murdered, the Falcon narrows down his list of suspects and finally he pins the crime on ... ! who had hoped to halt the production of the picture in order to salvage the money for a feature with his own backers.

While hardly an in-depth look into the Hollywood scene of the World War II years, The Falcon in Hollywood was an entertaining effort that provided a pleasant outing on the RKO backlot.

THE FARMER IN THE DELL (RKO, 1936) 67 min.

Director, Ben Holmes; based on the novel by Phil Strong; screenplay, Sam Mintz and John Grey; camera, Nick Musuraca; editor, George Hively.

Fred Stone (Pa Boyer); Jean Parker (Adie Boyer); Esther Dale (Ma Boyer); Moroni Olsen (Chester Hart); Frank Albertson (Davy Davenport); Maxine Jennings (Maud Durant); Ray Mayer (Spike); Lucille Ball (Gloria); Rafael Corlo (Nicky Ranovitch); Frank Jenks (Crosby); Spencer Charters (Milkman).

Part of the accepted American dream of the thirties was that heaven on earth was undoubtedly to be found by living in Hollywood. Thus Ma Boyer (Esther Dale) persuades her obliging farmer husband (Fred Stone) to abandon their Midwestern spread and move with their daughter (Jean Parker) to the mecca of happiness in California. Dale's plans also include launching Parker in the film world.

Once there, however, it is rustic Stone who is grabbed by the filmmakers and he soon finds himself working for director Chester Hart (Moroni Olsen). Before long, Dale has "gone Hollywood" complete with Beverly Hills manse, chauffeur, and snooty attitudes. The change in ambiance also has its toll on Parker. Her hometown beau (Frank Albertson) has followed her westward, but their conflicting goals almost lead to their breaking apart.

As many reviewers of the day noted, this was the type of bucolic fare that was the special province of the late Will Rogers. Stone, who had abandoned the Broadway musical comedy stage (after suffering leg injuries in a plane crash), had come to Hollywood in 1935, where he scored in RKO's Alice Adams (1935) as Katharine Hepburn's Pa.

This modest production found greater reception in England, where the critics were far kinder to it than had been their American counterparts. One London trade paper noted, "There are some sly digs at production, while authentic Hollywood exteriors and studio shots lend colour to the action. Sympathetic direction imparts considerable conviction to the development, and the farmer's trouncing of wife and daughter is excellently staged."

Note RKO contractee Lucille Ball as Gloria, a wise-mouthed script girl. Two years later she would be starring in her own genre vehicles, The Affairs of Annabel and Annabel Takes a Tour (qq. v.).

THE FEMALE ANIMAL (Universal, 1958) 84 min.

Producer, Albert Zugsmith; director, Harry Keller; story, Zugsmith; screenplay, Robert Hill; gowns, Bill Thomas; music, Hans J. Salter; assistant director, Gordon McLean; art directors, Alexander Golitzen and Robert Clatworthy; sound, Leslie I. Carey and Frank Wilkinson; camera, Russell Metty; editor, Milton Carruth.

Hedy Lamarr (Vanessa Windsor); Jane Powell (Penny Windsor); Jan Sterling (Lily Frayne); George Nader (Chris Farley); Jerry Paris (Hank Lopez); Gregg Palmer (Piggy); Mabel Albertson (Irma Jones); James Gleason (Tom Maloney); Richard Cutting (Dr. John Ramsay); Ann Doran (Nurse); Yvonne Peattie (Hairdresser); Casey Adams (Charlie Grant); Douglas Evans (The Director); Aram Katcher (Mischa Boroff).

Whenever Universal latched onto another studio's big star, even a fading one, they usually provided the individual with the trappings of his or her former glory, including a color mounting for the opus. This did not occur, however, in the case of Hedy Lamarr, MGM's one-time exotic beauty who came to Universal for the programmer The Female Animal. It was a highly mixed-up affair, shot in CinemaScope, which did benefit from an unusually solid performance from its Hungarian star, and a far less creditable one from another younger ex-MGM luminary, Jane Powell.

In a rather cruel ploy, Universal cast Lamarr as a faltering movie queen who has less control over her emotionally troubled teenaged daughter (Powell) than she does over her fast-slipping

Jane Powell, Hedy Lamarr, and George Nader in <u>The Female Ani-</u>
<u>mal</u> (1958).

career.   On the set of her latest picture the star encounters handsome young film extra Chris Farley (George Nader) to whom she is
immediately attracted.   She hires him to be the caretaker of her
beach estate, although there is obviously more passion than gardening
in her scheme.   While working there Nader meets Powell and despite
the fact he is having an affair with Lamarr, he and Powell succumb to
love.

Lamarr, realizing she is losing the man she adores to her
alienated offspring, decides to fight for him even if it means grabbing
away her daughter's happiness.   Another screen actress, Lily Frayne
(Jan Sterling), once a sex symbol but now a boozer, advises Lamarr
to forget the younger man and to act her age before she ends up like
her.   Realizing Sterling is right (after an aborted suicide attempt),
Lamarr abandons Nader and vows to face her uncertain future grace-
fully.

"Far and away the best thing about Mr. Zugsmith's production
(again) is the jaded ugliness and brisk carnality of the chatter.   The
talk, supplied by scenarist Robert Hill and Mr. Zugsmith, who surely
must know, seems so authentic it hurts.

"Furthermore, this verbal ice-cold buckshot blends neatly with some extremely glossy interiors of various bars, homes and even bungalow courts.   (One studio set is visited briefly.)   Atmospherically the picture is solid, and this includes a fine portrait of a tawdry has-been actress by Jan Sterling.

"The real trouble is nobody matters--none of them.   Mr. Nader's iron gentility is unconvincing in a notorious career arena. As for the two ladies, who finally turn Stella Dallas and Little Orphan Annie, respectively, Miss Powell alone does the acting.   But oh boy, that atmosphere!" (New York Times).

FILM FAVORITES   see   THE SHORT FILMS

FILM FAVORITES' FINISH   see   THE SHORT FILMS

A FILM JOHNNIE   see   THE SHORT FILMS

THE FIRST NUDIE MUSICAL (Northal Film Distributor, 1976) Color, 100 min.

Executive producers, Stuart W. Phelps and Peter S. Brown; producer, Jack Reeves; directors, Mark Haggard and Bruce Kimmel; screenplay/music and lyrics by Kimmel; music arranger/conductor, René Hall; music supervisor, Murray Cohen; art director/costumes, Tom Rassmussen; assistant directors, Edwin T. Morgan, Alan Iezman, and Bonnie MacBird; choreography, Lloyd Gordon; set decorator, Timothy J. Block; makeup, Dodie Warren; production artist/title designer, Nancy Lee; camera, Douglas H. Knapp; editor, Allen Peluso.

Stephen Nathan (Harry Schechter); Cindy Williams (Rosie Brady); Bruce Kimmel (John Smithee); Leslie Ackerman (Susie Jones); Alan Abelew (George Brenner); Diana Canova (Juanita Juanita); Alexandra Morgan (Mary La Rue); Frank Doubleday (Arvin ["Riff"]); Kathleen Hietala (Eunice); Art Marino (Eddie); Hy Pyke (Benny Smirnoff); Greg Finley (Jimmy); Herb Graham (Frankie); René Hall (Dick Davis); Susan Stewart (Joy Full); Artie Shafer (Actor); Jerry Hoffman (Harry Schlong); Wade Crookham (Mr. "Orgasm"); Nancy Chadwick (Lesbian); John Kirby (Bad Actor); Ian Praise (Clark the Cameraman); Kathryn Kimmel (The Hand); Chris Corso (Pervert); Jane Ralston (Buck & Wing Girl).

The idea of kidding both the genres of the musical and porno films was combined in this forced effort which advertised itself as "... an all-singing, all-dancing, all-nude musical extravaganza." What it was, however, was a rather sleazy R-rated effort which Paramount Pictures had abandoned after keeping it on the distribution shelf for some time (fearing that its release might spoil the charisma of performer Cindy Williams who had gone on to stardom in Paramount TV's "Laverne and Shirley" program).   (Paramount had opened

the film in a few test engagements in the U.S. in 1976 and then withdrew it. The picture had been shot in 18 days in 1974 on a $150,000
budget in Los Angeles.) The feature was acquired for distribution
by Northal Films, receiving mixed reviews from the critics.

Surprisingly, Judith Crist (New York Post) was rather enthusiastic about this offering, which carries the old Judy Garland-Mickey
Rooney let's-put-on-the-show to a far different level: "... if you
have a sense of humor about porno, an appreciation of spoofery of
traditional Hollywood and a liking for talented young people, you'll
enjoy yourself very much indeed." Crist was particularly impressed
by "... the inspirational first number, a nudie chorus-line song-and-
dance routine promising 'the biggest grosser since the word "gross"';
a backer's insistence that his near-idiot nephew be made director;
the typical casting call and session, with both porno vets and cuties
fresh from Indiana responding; the looming deadline; the ultimate
disaster--the defection of the stars, and guess who steps in to replace them?; the glorious it's-a-hit premiere, and true love for the
fadeout."

On the other hand, the New York Times found the proceedings
looked too "fly-by-night" and that Bruce Kimmel who codirected,
wrote the screenplay, and acted in the film had provided a "tuneless
score."

The story relates how Harry Schechter (Stephen Nathan), the
son of the aged owner of Schecter Studios, is forced to turn out porno
films in order to keep the studio out of receivership, all of this unknown to his Dad. A series of flops, however, causes Nathan's in-
vestors to balk at financing any more of his ventures. Then his
secretary-girlfriend Rosie Brady (Williams) suggests he make a nude
musical.

The backers are enthusiastic by the concept but he must hire
the naive nephew of one of them to direct the epic. A conglomerate
of people arrive for the casting call, but the young director (Kimmel)
quickly proves he knows nothing about the art of directing and Nathan
takes over the position. Trouble, however, develops at every turn
as Nathan has only two weeks to make the picture or suffer the loss
of his studio. The leading lady later makes a play for Nathan, but
Williams comes to his rescue. When the movie leads are in-
capacitated, Nathan and Williams must perform the finale number
(dealing with the joy of oral sex). The picture is previewed and
turns out to be a hit. Nathan's studio is saved. Now he plans
to make only class A films and he and Williams set their wedding date.

The First Nudie Musical contained a "flick-within-a-film"
which was made at Producers Studio in Hollywood and on location
along Hollywood Boulevard. The picture also contained the title song
and nine other second-rate tunes ("Gotta sing, gotta dance; While
I'm takin' off my pants"). One critic termed the overall production
"a sleazy Singin' in the Rain." About the only real asset the film
had was Williams as Rosie, who seemed to have fallen on hard times
after her successful work in American Graffiti (1974), and before her
hit "Laverne and Shirley" series developed.

THE FLYING MARINE (Columbia, 1929) 5951 ft.

Producer, Harry Cohn; director, Albert Rogell; story/continuity, John Francis Natteford; titles, Weldon Melick; art director, Harrison Wiley; assistant director, Tenny Wright; camera, Ted Tetzlaff; editor, William Hamilton.

Ben Lyon (Steve Moran); Shirley Mason (Sally); Jason Robards, Sr. (Mitch Moran).

Before movie stunting films became popular with fare like The Lost Squadron and Lucky Devils (qq. v.), producer Harry Cohn made this modest B entry which depicted the dangers of doing stunt flying for the movies.   Actually the film was more of a conventional melodrama than a true accounting of the hazardous existence of movie stunt pilots.
Mitch Moran (Jason Robards, Sr.), a commercial flyer, takes his younger brother Steve (Ben Lyon) into his business, and it is not long before Lyon falls in love with Robards' fiancée, Sally (Shirley Mason).   Mason is thrown into a whirl by the overly active life which Lyon leads--he had been a stunt pilot--and she is quickly attracted to him in preference to her beau.   Finally she accepts Lyon's marriage proposal but is soon sorry because she discovers he is irresponsible.   Later she returns to Robards.
When Lyon is injured later performing a movie stunt, he loses his hearing.   Robards and Mason do not tell him about their reconciliation but instead raise the funds necessary for an operation which will restore Lyon's hearing.   After the surgery he finds out what the two have done for him.   He returns to stunting to earn the money to repay them.   Thereafter he is killed in an aerial accident.
Actor Lyon soon began work after The Flying Marine on another aviation adventure: Howard Hughes' Hell's Angels (1930).

FOLLOW THE BOYS (Universal, 1944) 122 min.

Producer, Charles K. Feldman; associate producer, Albert L. Rockett; director, Eddie Sutherland; screenplay, Lou Breslow and Gertrude Purcell; art directors, John B. Goodman and Harold H. MacArthur; set decorators, Russell A. Gausman and Ira S. Webb; music director, Leigh Harline; music production numbers devised and staged by George Hale and Joe Schoenfeld; songs, Sammy Cahn and Jule Styne; Kermit Goell and Walter Donaldson; Billy Austin and Louis Jordan; Dorothy Fields and Jimmy McHugh; Shelton Brooks; Inez James and Buddy Pepper; Phil Moore; Leo Robin, W. Franke Harling, and Richard Whiting; Roy Turk and Fred Ahlert; Dick Charles and Larry Markes; assistant director, Howard Christie; sound, Robert Pritchard; special camera, John P. Fulton; camera, David Abel; editor, Fred R. Feitshans, Jr.

George Raft (Tony West); Vera Zorina (Gloria Vance--formerly Bertha Lindquist); Charles Grapewin (Nick West); Grace McDonald (Kitty West); Charles Butterworth (Louis Fairweather); George Macready (Walter Bruce); Elizabeth Patterson (Annie); Theodore Von Eltz

Maxine, Patty, and LaVerne Andrews in Follow the Boys (1944).

(William Barrett); Regis Toomey (Dr. Jim Henderson); Ramsey Ames
(Laura); Spooks (Junior); Jeanette MacDonald, Orson Welles, Marlene
Dietrich, Dinah Shore, Donald O'Connor, Peggy Ryan, W. C. Fields,
The Andrews Sisters, Artur Rubinstein, Carmen Amaya and Company,
Sophie Tucker, Delta Rhythm Roys, Leonard Gautier's Bricklayers,
Agustin Castellon Sabicas, Ted Lewis & His Band, Freddie Slack &
His Orchestra (Guest Stars); Louise Beavers, Clarence Muse, Maxie
Rosenbloom, Maria Montez, Susanna Foster, Louise Allbritton, Rob-
ert Paige, Alan Curtis, Lon Chaney, Jr., Gloria Jean, Andy Devine,
Turhan Bey, Evelyn Ankers, Noah Beery, Jr., Gale Sondergaard,
Peter Coe, Nigel Bruce, Thomas Gomez, Lois Collier, Samuel S.
Hinds, Randolph Scott, Martha O'Driscoll, Elyse Knox, and Philo
McCullough (Hollywood Victory Committee Members); Mack Gray
(Lieutenant Reynolds); John Estes (Patient); Doris Lloyd (Nurse); Ad-
dison Richards (MacDermott the Life editor); Stanley Andrews (Aus-
tralian Officer); Frank Jenks (Chick Doyle); Billy Benedict (Joe, a
Soldier); Howard Hickman (Dr. Wood); George "Shorty" Chirello (Or-
son Welles' Magic Show Assistant); Bill Wolfe (Man in Zoot Suit in
W. C. Fields' Number).

This was Universal's two-hour tribute to the celebrities who
entertained the soldiers during World War II. It was packed with
specialty acts surrounded by a sticky-thin plot about a performer
who dies in the entertainment service. Still, movie audiences savored the opportunity to view dozens of their favorites in one celluloid
package. This opus proved profitable if not critically acceptable.

George Raft starred as Tony West, a vaudevillian who has a
stage act with his sister (Grace McDonald) and his father (Charles
Grapewin) a la the Cohans. He transfers to Hollywood when the
three-a-day circuit expires and secures a job as a chorus boy in
Hollywood musicals. From there he quickly becomes the dancing
partner of star Gloria Vance (Vera Zorina) a la Fred Astaire-Ginger
Rogers, and the couple soon wed. They continue to turn out a series
of popular screen musicals.

But with the coming of World War II they split; Raft is rejected for military service because of a bad knee. His failure to
explain to Zorina about the situation leads her to believe he is a
coward. Soon, however, Raft is requested to package an entertainment show for the servicemen abroad and he invites Zorina to join
him. She refuses, not revealing she is pregnant with his child, and
she waits at home while he entertains the G. I. s abroad. On a ship
to Australia which is torpedoed by the Japanese, Raft is the only person not rescued, thereby not surviving to see his new-born son.

As pap entertainment Follow the Boys was A-1. It was highlighted by many contrasting performers' best routines: W. C. Fields'
pool hall antics, Jeanette MacDonald's vocals, Orson Welles' magic
act (with Marlene Dietrich); the Andrews Sisters' harmonizing, and
so on, and benefitted from some sincere emoting by Raft in the lead.
He also had the chance to do a little hoofing in the film; one sequence
had him dancing to the rhythm of the rain, predating Gene Kelly's
famous number in Singin' in the Rain (q. v.). "For show business
it's a timely salute. For the fans, it smacks of authentic inside
stuff" (Variety).

45 MINUTES TO HOLLYWOOD   see   THE SHORT FILMS

FOUR GIRLS IN TOWN (Universal, 1956) Color, 85 min.

Producer, Aaron Rosenberg; director/screenplay, Jack Sher; art directors, Alexander Golitzen and Ted Haworth; music, Joseph Gershenson; "Rhapsody" by Alex North; assistant directors, Dick Mayberry and Wilbur Mosier; gowns, Rosemary Odell; special camera effects, Clifford Stine; camera, Irving Glassberg; editor, Frederick Y. Smith.

George Nader (Mike Snowden); Julie Adams (Kathy Conway); Marianne Cook (Ina Schiller); Elsa Martinelli (Maria Antonelli); Gia Scala (Vicki Dauray); Sydney Chaplin (Johnny Pryor); Rock Hudson (Guest Bit); Grant Williams (Spencer Farrington, Jr.); John Gavin (Tom Grant); Herbert Anderson (Ted Larabee); Hy Averback (Bob Trapp); Ainslie Pryor (James Manning); Judson Pratt (William Purdy); James Bell (Walter Conway); Mabel Albertson (Mrs. Conway); Dave Barry (Vince); Maurice Marsac (Henri); Helene Stanton (Rita Holloway); Irene Corlett (Mildred Purdy); Eugene Mazzola (Paul); Phil Harvey (Assistant Director); Cynthia Patrick (Girl); Charles Tannen (Hotel Manager); Jack Mather (Gaffer); Helen Andrews and Rodney Bell (Couple at Pool); Voltaire Perkins (Business Man); Robert Hoy (Indian); George Nardelli (Bit); Evelyn Ford and Kitty Muldoon (American Girls); Hubie Kerns (Casting Man); George Calliga (Frenchman).

Blonde star Rita Holloway (Helene Stanton) refuses the title role in The Story of Esther to be produced by Manning National Films. Immediately a talent hunt is initiated to locate a substitute. Newcomer director Mike Snowden (George Nader) is set to direct all the girls in their auditions.
    Several candidates are selected for tests; both their private and professional lives are altered drastically as a result of the chance. There is off-Broadway actress Kathy Conway (Julie Adams) who is drawn to Nader romantically; Italian actress Maria Antonelli (Elsa Martinelli) who is attracted to playboy Spencer Farrington, Jr. (Grant Williams); Vicki Dauray (Gia Scala), who longs for her husband and baby in France; and Austrian Ina Schiller (Marianne Cook), who tries to dismiss memories of a brief, unhappy marriage and becomes romantically entangled with composer Johnny Pryor (Sydney Chaplin).
    After a good deal of amorous complications--and sequences shot inside the studio (at Universal)--none of the quartet wins the coveted screen assignment. It seems Stanton has changed her mind and now accepts the lead. However, Nader is selected to direct the pending epic and he finds love with Adams.
    Shot in color and CinemaScope, Four Girls in Town was a minor offering which still managed to provide viewers with a good dose of Hollywood. In its unpretentious if contrived manner, it turned out to be one of the better introspective films in the genre, pointing out the ambitions, fears, and complications that accost newcomers to the medium. The New York Times said "... he [Sher]

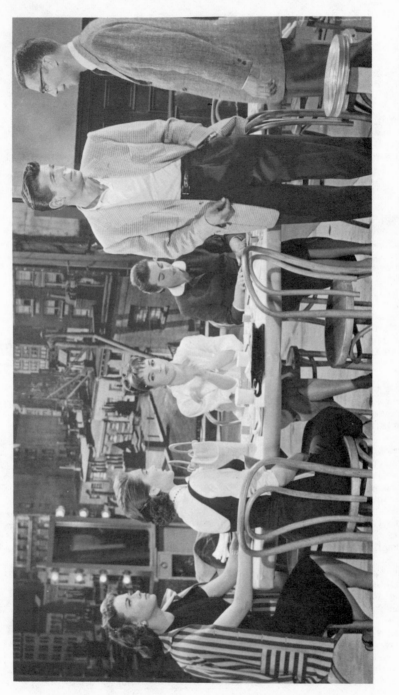

Gia Scala, Julie Adams, Elsa Martinelli, Marianne Cook, George Nader, and Herbert (Guy) Anderson in Four Girls in Town (1957).

is offering a thoughtful, engaging and deceptively casual plea for ad-
herence to basic values in a town he obviously knows. " Universal's
own Rock Hudson made a brief guest appearance as himself in the
film.

FREE AND EASY (MGM, 1930) 75 min. [TV title: EASY GO]

    Director, Edward Sedgwick; screenplay, Richard Schayer; dia-
logue, Al Boasberg; adaptor, Paul Dickey; art director, Cedric Gibbons; songs, Fred E. Ahlert; William Kernell; choreography, Sammy
Lee; wardrobe, David Cox; sound, Karl E. Zint and Douglas Shearer;
camera, Leonard Smith; editors, William Levanway and George Todd.

    Buster Keaton (Elmer Butts); Anita Page (Elvira); Trixie Frig-
anza (Ma); Robert Montgomery (Larry); Fred Niblo (Director); Edgar
Dearing (Officer); Gwen Lee, John Miljan, and Lionel Barrymore (Bed-
room Scene--Themselves); William Haines (Guest); William Collier,
Sr. (Master of Ceremonies); Dorothy Sebastian and Karl Dane (Cave
Scene--Themselves); David Burton (Director); Cecil B. DeMille,
Jackie Coogan, Joe Farnham, and Arthur Lange (Themselves).

    After making his sound film debut in the all-star Hollywood
Revue of 1929 (q. v.), Buster Keaton launched his initial starring
talkie with Free and Easy. As the decade proceeded, Metro thereafter teamed him with their "new" comedy star Jimmy Durante, and
before the thirties were over, Keaton wound up the way he broke into
films--in two-reelers.
    Free and Easy is infrequently revived today. It displays the
difficulty Keaton had in adapting to the sound medium. The plot has
Buster as Elmer Butts, a young Kansas man who journeys to Hollywood with Elvira (Anita Page), his protégée, who has just won a beauty contest. He intends to make her a movie star. In the film capital he meets pal Larry (Robert Montgomery) who is now a leading
man, and the "friend" proceeds to steal Buster's girl from him.
Keaton then travels throughout the MGM studio looking for her. In
the process he disrupts and makes a shambles of several films-in-
the-making. At the finale Keaton loses his darling to Montgomery
but as a result of his comic activities on the sets he is offered a
contract to star in screen comedies.
    At the time of its release, Photoplay magazine labeled Free
and Easy "a whizzing comedy" but today it is more of "an interesting
oddity" (Film Fan Monthly). What attracts film students is Buster's
forays on the soundstages. During the course of the picture he accidentally ruins the efforts of directors Lionel Barrymore, David Burton, and Fred Niblo (all playing themselves as did such stars as William Haines, Jackie Coogan, Karl Dane, Dorothy Sebastian, John
Miljan, and producer-director Cecil B. DeMille). One of the films-
within-a-film finds Montgomery performing in the musical comedy
genre, actually singing "It Must Be You. " Bits of this sequence
would be utilized in MGM's compilation feature, That's Entertainment! (q. v.).

FUGITIVES FOR A NIGHT (RKO, 1938) 63 min.

Producer, Lou Lusty; director, Leslie Goodwins; story, Richard Wormser; screenplay, Dalton Trumbo; music director, Russell Bennett; camera, Frank Redmond; editor, Desmond Marquette.

Frank Albertson (Matt Ryan); Eleanor Lynn (Ann Wray); Allan Lane (Nelson); Bradley Page (Dennis Poole); Adrienne Ames (Eileen Baker); Jonathan Hale (Captain); Russell Hicks (Tenwright); Paul Guilfoyle (Monks); Ward Bond (Tough).

Dalton Trumbo wrote this pleasant murder mystery involving Matt Ryan (Frank Albertson) who travels to Hollywood to be an actor but who ends up as an assistant and all-around stooge to fading matinee idol Dennis Poole (Bradley Page).   Albertson's girl, Ann Wray (Eleanor Lynn), badgers him to quit working for the self-centered star and to abandon the competitive film business.   She suggests he turn to the real world and make a living operating, for example, a hamburger stand.   At the opening of a swank nightclub, a producer, Tenwright (Russell Hicks), is murdered and suspicion falls on Albertson.   He leaves the scene with Lynn and spends the night piecing together the clues, meanwhile trying to elude the law.   The next day, however, he and Lynn return to the club and accuse the real killer of the homicide, proving the man's guilt.

This compact thriller even received solid reviews from big-city newspapers such as the New York Times.   "The lines are engaging, the tone is breezy and the players in fine fettle. "   In retrospect, Don Miller discussed the picture in his book B Movies (1973) stating it "proved to be well above the norm for a low-budget film" and that Trumbo "surrounded his threadbare plot with a fresh, accurate, insider's view of Hollywood, its denizens, and film-making. "

THE FUZZY PINK NIGHTGOWN (United Artists, 1957) 87 min.

Producer, Robert Waterfield; director, Norman Taurog; based on the novel by Sylvia Tate; screenplay, Richard Alan Simmons; music, Billy May; assistant director, Stanley H. Goldsmith; costumes, Travilla; art director, Serge Kruzman; camera, Joseph LaShelle; editor, Archie Marshek.

Jane Russell (Laurel Stevens); Keenan Wynn (Dandy); Ralph Meeker (Mike Valla); Fred Clark (Sergeant McBride); Una Merkel (Bertha); Adolphe Menjou (Arthur Martin); Benay Venuta (Daisy Parker); Robert H. Harris (Barney Baylies); Bob Kelley (TV Announcer); Dick Haynes (Disc Jockey); John Truax (Flack); Milton Frome (Lieutenant Dempsey).

As the fifties waned, so did the screen career of forties' buxom sex symbol Jane Russell.   The decade had given the star her ups and downs in the cinema but by the time she made this effort (produced by her husband Robert Waterfield for their production company)

her career was virtually at a standstill.   This quickie was played off in
theatres even faster than it was made.

The wispy plot premise casts Russell as blonde film doll
Laurel Stevens who has just completed a feature entitled The Kidnapped Bride.   For publicity her agent, Adolphe Menjou, insists it
would be great promotion if she were actually wisked away.   He hires
two rather good-natured criminals (Keenan Wynn and Ralph Meeker)
to accomplish the foul deed.   Unfortunately Russell is not made aware
of the situation and takes none too kindly to the abduction until she
is attracted romantically to Meeker.   When the police finally apprehend the duo, who actually had plans to extort money for Russell's
release until Meeker changes his mind, all is forgiven.   It seems
the law enforcers believe the caper was merely a sappy publicity
gimmick.   At the fade-out Russell and Meeker are happily in love.

Hardly anyone who saw the witless film liked it and it was soon
relegated to late night TV showings.   As uninspired as the performances were the stereotypes of the film industry, from the unintellectual
sex symbol to the grasping agent.

GABLE AND LOMBARD (Universal, 1976) Color, 131 min.

Producer, Harry Korshak; director, Sidney J. Furie; screen-
play, Barry Sandler; music, Michel Legrand; production designer,
Edward C. Carfagno; set decorator, Hal Gausman; costumes, Edith
Head; assistant directors, James A. Westman, [Mike Messinger, and
Jon Triesault;] sound, Robert L. Hoyt and Don Sharpless; camera,
Jordan S. Cronenweth; editor, Argyle Nelson.

James Brolin (Clark Gable); Jill Clayburgh (Carole Lombard);
Allen Garfield (Louis B. Mayer); Red Buttons (Ivan Cooper); Melanie
Mayron (Dixie); Carol McGinnis (Noreen); S. John Launer (Judge);
William Bryant (Colonel); Joanne Linville (Ria Gable); Noah Keen (A.
Broderick); Alice Backes (Hedda Hopper); Morgan Brittany (Vivien
Leigh); Jodean Russo, Drew Michaels, Aron Kincaid, Richard Gittings,
and Sally Kemp (Party Guests); Army Archerd (Emcee); Frank Stell
(Ragland); Jack Griffin (Gate Guard); Andy Albin (Forest Ranger);
Ivan Bonar (Brogan).

What an opportunity Hollywood wasted in presenting Gable and
Lombard!   This true-life love story could have been a tasty bill of
fare if offered as close to historical accuracy as literary license and
a two-hour time limit would have allowed.   Hollywood of the thirties
and forties could have been depicted with the joie de vivre that really
existed at the time.   But Gable and Lombard, as Richard Schickel
in Time magazine lamented, "presents morally realistic (that is,
morally relative) Hollywood fighting off armies of blue-haired ladies
who want to impose their outmoded behavioral codes.   This is an
example of Hollywood paranoia at its most ludicrous, a fundamental
mis-reading of both its former audiences and the gullibility of its
present one. "

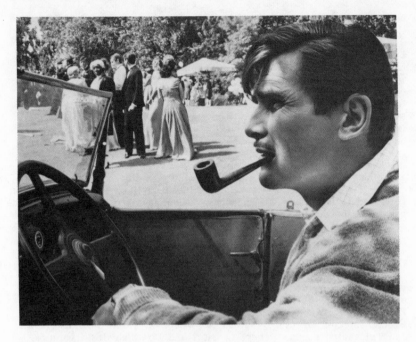

James Brolin in <u>Gable and Lombard</u> (1975).

The specious film begins at the site of the Lombard plane
crash in 1942 with Gable (James Brolin) awaiting news of possible
survivors.   In flashbacks he recalls their zany, loving life together--
either his memory is terribly faulty or the scriptwriters felt that
this was to be an entirely fabricated account.   According to this non-
sensical version, the duo met in 1936 when Gable crashed his car
into a tree in order to avoid an ambulance that was carrying madcap
Carole Lombard (Jill Clayburgh) to a daytime costume party.   She
is shown as a popular movie star while he is shown only on the way up.
In reality he had already won an Oscar (for <u>It Happened One Night,</u>
1934) by 1936 and the two had truly met in 1932 when they had filmed
<u>No Man of Her Own</u> together at Paramount.   When Carole drops him
with an uppercut, the two fall madly in love.   They want to get married but cannot due to legal proceedings arising from his second marriage and an involvement in a paternity suit with a waitress.   Finally
all is settled, they are wed and very happy (despite Lombard's outbursts of jealousy over his leading ladies) until she is tragically
killed in the plane crash.   The finale has Gable departing the wreck-
age site, trying to hold back tears and recalling a joke once told him
by his now-deceased wife.
          Brolin and Clayburgh as Gable and Lombard respectively were
out of their league.   As Vincent Canby (<u>New York Times</u>) summed it

up, "... there are always problems when small performers try to
portray the kind of giant legends that Gable and Lombard were. " On
the plus side of this film were recreation scenes from Gone with the
Wind with Morgan Brittany as Vivien Leigh and Allen Garfield as
Louis B. Mayer.

When Gable and Lombard was initially released, it carried
the adline, "They had more than love--they had fun. " When this
campaign failed to counterbalance the critical press and bad word-of-
mouth, the slogan was altered to "They had more than love--they
had romance. " Nothing seemed to matter. The public would not buy
this balderdash.

The following year Gable and Lombard was shunted to television. Judith Crist in TV Guide warned her readers, "Clark Gable
and Carole Lombard are posthumously defamed in ... [this film]
which reduces the relationship of two top stars to a 131-minute history of fornication between a department-store dummy (James Brolin
with putty ears) and a foulmouthed floozy (Jill Clayburgh without her
usual talent). Anyone interested in these stars can study their biographies and learn that the truth was far more dramatic and entertaining than the cheap fiction contained herein. " For television, the
ad-line became "He was the King of the movies ... she was the
Queen of comedy ... and off-screen, they were Hollywood's greatest
love affair!"

THE GEORGE RAFT STORY (Allied Artists, 1961) 105 min.

Producer, Ben Schwalb; director, Joseph M. Newman; based
upon the life of George Raft; screenplay, Crane Wilbur; art director,
David Milton; set decorator, Joseph Kish; music, Jeff Alexander;
assistant director, Lindsley Parsons, Jr. ; wardrobe, Roger W. Wein-
berg, Norah Sharpe; makeup, Norman Pringle; sound, Monty Pearce
and Ralph Butler; camera, Carl Guthrie; editor, George White.

Ray Danton (George Raft); Jayne Mansfield (Lisa Lang); Julie
London (Sheila Patton); Barrie Chase (June); Barbara Nichols (Texas
Guinan); Frank Gorshin (Moxie Cusack); Margo Moore (Ruth Harris);
Brad Dexter (Benny Siegel); Neville Brand (Al Capone); Robert Strauss
(Frenchie); Herschel Bernardi (Sam); Joe De Santis (Frankie Dona-
tella); Jack Lambert (Jerry Fitzpatrick); Argentina Brunetti (Mrs.
Raft); Robert H. Harris (Harvey); Jack Albertson (Milton); Pepper
Davis and Tony Reese (Comedy Team); Tol Avery (Mizner the Wit);
Murvyn Vye (Johnny); Cecile Rogers (Charleston Dancer).

George Raft's life to date has been an intriguing one, with
enough career ups and downs to fill a half-dozen exciting films. (In
the early 1950s the internationally-known celebrity offered some details of his life in a Saturday Evening Post magazine series; in 1974
two biographies of the gangster movie personality were published.)
It is thus a shame that The George Raft Story emerged as nothing
more than a glossy and very superficial look at Hollywood's epitome
of a gangster player. Obviously cheaply shot with an eye on a quick
playoff, the black-and-white feature proved to be neither titillating

Ray Danton, Barrie Chase, and Jayne Mansfield in The George Raft Story (1961).

nor a tribute to the tenacity and staying power of Raft the personality.   The actor who rose to prominence in 1930s' Hollywood certainly deserved better than this complicated and untruthful "homage. "
   In the tried-and-true tradition of American biography-pictures, this rendering relates the story of young George's rise from poverty to riches and back to semi-obscurity.   It starts with his early life in New York City's Hell's Kitchen, from which he escapes as a dancer and as an underling involved with the racketeers.   Later he is shown being hired as an advisor on the film Scarface (1932) and also given a small role which, it turns out, makes him a silver screen notable.   Thereafter he spends years in California as a big-name performer and a romancer of assorted flashy women, all of whom he eventually deserts.   Bad times eventually befall Raft as his career disintegrates; after an unsuccessful gambling venture in Cuba he returns to Hollywood and further professional disappointment.   The chronicle ends on an upbeat note, however, with his agent offering him a featured role in the movie Some Like It Hot (1958).
   Ray Danton--who years later would become a film director-- did the best he could with the shallow central role, but he had none of the Raft appeal or dancing skill.   Jayne Mansfield (in a flimsy takeoff of Betty Grable, a real-life flame of Raft's), Barrie Chase,

and Julie London provided the love interest, while Herschel Bernardi is seen as the actor's faithful agent. More colorful were others in the supporting cast: Barbara Nichols as Texas Guinan, the hostess with the mostest, and Neville Brand as infamous hoodlum Al Capone (a role he was then playing on TV's "The Untouchables").

Although the New York Times found the film "a blithely glossy and entertaining little biographical drama," the movie was not overly successful even on the action distribution market. It would be issued in Great Britain as Spin of a Coin, that title coming from one of Raft's famous screen mannerisms. The British Monthly Film Bulletin decided, "... this film is necessarily scrappy in design and disjointed in effect, oscillating as it does between the underworld and show business backgrounds.... Because of its subject the whole thing has a certain clinical interest."

As with most biographies of individuals who gained prominence in the cinema, The George Raft Story, falls into the familiar pitfall. It assumes the public is not interested in the actual dynamics of filmmaking (which often encompasses very boring stretches of preproduction and actual shooting and constant retakes), so what emerges is an unconvincing portrait of a person's craft told in the sketchiest of details. And as with The Jolson Story, The Eddie Cantor Story (qq. v.), and many others, there are usually too many actual participants still alive, so the "truth" must be disguised/diluted, leading to a very wishy-washy representation of the situations and personality traits which combined to make the person's life so engaging in the first place. Truth is really stranger and more entertaining than fiction, but for the above reasons, it so rarely occurs in dealing with the public and private lives of screen figures.

THE GIRL ON THE LATE, LATE SHOW (NBC-TV, 1974) Color, 75 min.

Executive producer, David Gerber; producer, Christopher Morgan; director, Gary Nelson; teleplay, Mark Rodgers; music, Richard Markowitz; camera, Robert Morrison; editor, Richard C. Meyer.

Don Murray (William Martin); Bert Convy (F. J. Allen); Yvonne De Carlo (Lorraine); Gloria Grahame (Carolyn Parker); Van Johnson (Johnny Leverett); Ralph Meeker (Inspector DeBiesse); Cameron Mitchell (Norman Wilder); Mary Ann Mobley (Librarian); Joe Santos (Sergeant Scott); Laraine Stephens (Paula); John Ireland (Bruno Walters); Walter Pidgeon (John Pahlman); Sherry Jackson (Pat Clauson); Frankie Darro (Studio Guard).

This telefeature was originally conceived as the pilot entry for a series to star Don Murray as a TV producer and talk show host and encompass his interaction with assorted guest subjects. When the plot premise failed to sell as a series, however, NBC-TV slotted this Screen Gems production into a double feature in the spring of 1974. It received little notice, which is a shame since the film has an outstanding cast of veterans and a rather captivating story premise. Ironically, although the TV film revolved around the character of Carolyn Parker (as played by Gloria Grahame), she only appears on screen in the closing seconds of the narrative.

Murray is seen as William Martin--a conglomerate of Joe Pyne and Merv Griffin--who sets out to locate fifties' film star Carolyn Parker. Due to video exposure of her films, she has a resurgence in popularity. In order to track her down for his Manhattan daytime TV gab fest, Murray flies to Hollywood and begins a tough search for the reclusive once-star. He meets with many of the actress' past associates but none of them claim to know her current whereabouts. Among those contacted is restaurant owner Lorraine (Yvonne De Carlo), formerly the manager of the studio club where Carolyn was under contract. She tells Murray that "life" went wrong for the ex-star. Eventually Murray learns that Grahame had been involved in murder and blackmail; a situation which necessitated her vanishing at the height of her stardom. When he does encounter Grahame, she displays manifestations of insanity.

The Girl on the Late, Late Show interpolated clips from Grahame's own past features to represent the screen work of Carolyn Parker. Among the scenes shown were ones from In a Lonely Place (q. v.), Human Cargo, and Fatal Desire (all Columbia Pictures). Despite its nostalgia value, Variety reported that it "wasn't much as a movie and was even less as a pilot. "

A GIRL'S FOLLY (Paragon-World, 1917) 5 reels

Director, Maurice Tourneur; based on the story "A Movie Romance" by Frances Marion and Tourneur; screenplay, Marion and Tourneur.

Doris Kenyon (Mary Baker); Robert Warwick (Kenneth Driscoll); June Elvidge (Vivian Carleton); Johnny Hines (Hank); Chester Barnett (Johnny Applebloom); Jane Adair (Mrs. Baker).

While photographing a Western in the wilds of New Jersey, movie idol Ken Driscoll (Robert Warwick) meets pretty young Mary Baker (Doris Kenyon) and takes an immediate romantic, albeit sexual, interest in her. He has grown tired of his costar-lover Vivian Carleton (June Elvidge) and decides this new girl will be good for him. In order to manipulate her interest in accompanying him to Fort Lee, he tells the young lady--who is obviously smitten with the star--that she would be ideal for the motion pictures. At the World Studios he arranges a test for her, but it proves disappointing. Nevertheless, Kenyon decides to remain with Warwick--as his mistress. He then escorts her to a wild party but her mother (Jane Adair) arrives on the scene and begs her to return home. Later she weds her original boyfriend, while Warwick returns to Elvidge.

Despite its rather maudlin plotline, A Girl's Folly holds interest today--as it did six decades ago--for its candid look at moviemaking. As its current distributor, Grigg's Moviedrome Films, reports, it is "remarkable for its shots of how a movie was made in the early silent days on the East Coast. There are many behind-the-scene shots showing how the sets were put up, the swimming pool that was used as a tank in the water scenes, how the cameramen worked and even the film processing equipment--clearly the best film that has survived showing the operation of an early movie studio. "

Filmed at Fort Lee, New Jersey, at the World Studios (where the bulk of the action occurs) the film was initially titled A Movie Romance.

GIRL'S TOWN (Producers Releasing Corp. , 1942) 69 min.

Producers, Lou Brock and Jack Schwartz; director, Victor Helperin; camera, Arthur Reed; editor, Martin Cohn.

Edith Fellows (Sue); June Storey (Myra); Kenneth Howell (Kenny); Alice White (Nicky); Anna Q. Nilsson (Mother); Warren Hymer (Joe); Vince Barnett (Dimitri); Paul Dubov (Fontaine); Peggy Ryan (Penny); Dolores Diane (Sally); Helen McCloud (Mayor); Bernice Kay [Cara Williams] (Ethyl); Charlie Williams (Coffer).

Variety had little enthusiasm for this poverty-row effort. "... [It] constitutes an awkward screen test for many comparative newcomers. "

This "featherweight yarn" focused on the boarding house run by a crippled, old ex-actress (Anna Q. Nilsson), whose boarders are would-be actresses. When these Hollywood newcomers find work, then they can pay back any old debts to Nilsson and/or help out their less fortunate housemates. Sue (Edith Fellows) is the less-comely sister of beauty contest winner (June Storey) who accompanies her sibling to Hollywood. Nasty Storey sets out to bash her way into the cinema, double-crossing anyone (from her sister to Nilsson) to engineer her screen break. As fate (and justice) would have it, it is Fellows who makes her bow in films, while Storey is left on the sidelines.

Of passing interest to film enthusiasts are the appearances of screen veteran Nilsson, Alice White (as a stunt girl), Vince Barnett (as comedy relief), Warren Hymer, and others.

The now fast-maturing Fellows had appeared in her "salad days" in Columbia's Little Miss Roughneck (q. v.), an equally unsuccessful excursion into the world of Hollywood-on-Hollywood.

GLAMOUR BOY (Paramount, 1941) 81 min.

Producer, Sol C. Siegel; associate producer, Colbert Clark; director, Ralph Murphy; screenplay, Bradford Ropes and Val Burton; art directors, Hans Dreier and Haldane Douglas; camera, Dan Fapp; editor, William Shea.

Jackie Cooper (Tiny Barlow); Susanna Foster (Joan Winslow); Walter Abel (A. J. Colder); Darryl Hickman (Billy Doran); Ann Gillis (Brenda Lee); William Demarest (Papa Doran); William Wright (Hank Landon); Katherine [Karin] Booth (Helen Trent); Jackie Searle (Georgie Clemons).

Jackie Cooper and Susanna Foster in Glamour Boy (1941).

"... [Y]oung Cooper is now playing a few pages from his own personal history. It's a neat trick if you can work it, this projecting Hollywood itself on the screen. It's been tried and found wanting in many instances, but this isn't one of them" (Dallas Morning News).

Glamour Boy made no pretentions about being an A picture, it was simply entertaining double-bill fodder which had intriguing sidelights. As Variety rejoiced, "This is one of the happiest idea films turned out by Hollywood in a long time. "

Eighteen-year-old Tiny Barlow is an ex-child star now employed as a soda jerk in a Hollywood drug store. Marathon Studio, where he once was a star, has new tot Billy Doran (Darryl Hickman) under contract, but needs a property to showcase his potential. Cooper suggests to studio production head A. J. Colder (Walter Abel) that a remake of Skippy (Cooper had played the lead in this 1931 Paramount feature) would be sensible. Cooper is hired to coach Hickman and this provides an excuse to screen sizeable segments from the 1931 feature.

The cast included Susanna Foster as a pert young player on the Marathon lot; Jackie Searle (who had been the heavy in Skippy) as the heavy in the contemporary scene, and William Demarest as Hickman's pop who is astounded by his son's intellect.

Years later Cooper would attempt to package a Skippy pilot
for a TV series.

GO WEST, YOUNG MAN (Paramount, 1936) 82 min.

Producer, Emanuel R. Cohen; director, Henry Hathaway; based
on the play Personal Appearance by Lawrence Riley; adaptor, Mae
West; songs, Arthur Johnson and John Burke; music director, George
Stoll; gowns, Irene Jones; art director, Wiard Ihnen; sound, Hugo
Grenzbach; camera, Karl Struss; editor, Ray Curtiss.

Mae West (Mavis Arden); Warren William (Morgan); Randolph
Scott (Bud Norton); Alice Brady (Mrs. Struthers); Elizabeth Patterson
(Aunt Kate); Lyle Talbot (Francis X. Harrigan); Isabel Jewell (Gladys);
Margaret Perry (Joyce); Etienne Girardot (Professor Rigby); Maynard
Holmes (Clyde); John Indrisano (Chauffeur); Alice Ardell (Maid); Nico-
demus Stewart (Nicodemus); Charles Irwin (Master of Ceremonies);
Walter Walker (Andy Kelton); scene within Drifting Lady: Jack LaRue
(Rico); Robert Baikoffy (Officer); G. P. Huntley, Jr. (Philip the Em-
bassy Officer); Xavier Cugat & Orchestra (Themselves); Eddie Dunn
(Extra); Dick Elliott (Reporter); Si Jenks (Bumpkin).

By the mid-thirties, the film industry censors and various
church and civic groups had so thoroughly laundered Mae West's
screen characters and dialogue that a great deal of the verve and
zest (and one would imagine her own interest) in her movie work diminished.   Such is the case with Go West, Young Man. While it turned
out to be a mildly entertaining opus, it obviously would have been far
superior had Mae had her "wicked" way with the dialogue and situations.   Although she is credited with the scenario, the zesty edge
that made her prior films so zingy is gone, and this must be rated
as one of her lesser Paramount efforts.   Nevertheless, along with
Klondike Annie (her other 1936 release), this feature kept Mae West
a top box-office attraction and the studio's highest paid female star.
Although Mae West interpreted show business types in nearly
all of her features, this is the only picture in which she played a
film star (the next closest is as the actors' agent in Myra Breckinridge, q. v.).   As Mavis Arden, "the talk of the talkies," Mae is
first seen in a segment from her latest epic Drifting Lady costarring
Jack LaRue as Rico. She is on a personal appearance tour and tells
the movie theatre audience that although she is the glamourous star
of Super Fine Pictures, she longs for the simple life and, oh, if the
public could only visit her at her "Eye-talian" villa in the Hollywood
Hills, they would know the real Mavis Arden.   She then bids the
audience farewell, "Tell all of your friends, I said goodnight," in a
take-off on the kiss-throwing Gloria Swanson.
Although West's character has a yen for handsome politician
Francis X. Harrigan (Lyle Talbot), her slick press agent, Morgan
(Warren William), steers her clear of an entanglement with the dupli-
citous voter-grabber.   William, who secretly loves Mae, warns her
that her contract forbids her to marry, and therefore she must continue with her promotional tour.   On the road, car trouble causes

Mae West and Randolph Scott in Go West, Young Man (1936).

her to stop over at Mrs. Struthers' boarding house where she has eyes for Bud Norton (Randolph Scott) the beau of Joyce (Margaret Perry). William again breaks up the romance but Talbot, believing William has kidnapped West to keep her away from him, arrives on the scene with the police and has the agent arrested. West then reveals her true love for William and rescues him from the law. Together they resume the tour.

The critics were not enthusiastic about the film. The New York Herald-Tribune, like other reviewing sources, recalled the movie's source (the Broadway hit Personal Appearance) and the stage

play's leading lady (Gladys George) all too vividly.   It labeled the
Paramount release a "slipshod and tedious offering" while the Christian Science Monitor declared it was "not very funny. " Variety, on
the other hand, found it "earthy, erotic, pungent. " Perhaps Jon
Tuska in The Films of Mae West (1973) best weighed the situation:
". . . her humor [here] suffers from the limitations placed upon it.
She enjoyed a fine supporting cast, technical and otherwise, but comedy at her expense, as opposed to being at the expense of others,
and particularly comedy which did not reflect her in a sympathetic
light, hurt her more than it helped. "
      Within the 82 minutes there were several potshots taken at
moviemaking.   The sequences from Drifting Lady were a delightful
parody of the tearjerking woman's story so popular in the early thirties; Isabell Jewell does a wonderful send-up of West's Paramount
rival Marlene Dietrich; and throughout the storyline there are references to filmgoers being "morons" and the fact that most glamour
queens are emotionally and intellectually vapid.
      Not to be overlooked are an array of Westian zingers: "A
thrill a day keeps the chill away"; "No man can support a wife an'
me at the same time"; "I can't tell ya the number of men I've helped
to realize themselves, " etc.   In the course of the film she sings "I
Was Saying to the Moon, " "On a Typical Tropical Night, " and "Go
West, Young Man. "

THE GOAT (Paramount, 1918) 5 reels

     Director, Donald Crisp; story/screenplay, Frances Marion.

     Fred Stone ("Chuck" McCarthy); Rhea Mitchell (Bijou Lamour);
Sylvia Ashton (Baby Vampire); Noah Beery (Griffin the Director);
Raymond Hatton (Jimmy Quicksilver); Charles Ogle (Graham the Director); Ernest Joy (Studio Manager); Clarence Geldert (Casting Director); Winifred Greenwood (Molly O'Connor); Charles McHugh (Mr.
McCarthy); Fannie Midgely (Mrs. McCarthy); Philo McCullough (Marmaduke X. Caruthers); Ramon Novarro (Bit).

     In early movie jargon a "goat" was the company stuntman who
took all the risks in the making of a movie.   This early Paramount
feature, penned by Frances Marion, is one of the initial studies of
stunt work in films and it rather comprehensively points out the hardships of the practitioner, the one who risks his life and limb for very
little money, glory, or appreciation.   When the picture was released
various trade magazines, including the Motion Picture News and Motion Picture Magazine, chided the production for giving its audience
too much of an inside view of studio life.   Today, however, the production remains a historical record of the trials of the pathfinding
movie stunt workers.
     Famous stage star Fred Stone starred as Chuck McCarthy, an
ironworker who deserts the boring aspects of his existence by visiting his neighborhood theatre where he is enthralled by the magic of
the movies.   Assigned to work on the construction of a new studio
lot, Stone rescues the pet monkey of star Bijou Lamour (Rhea Mitch-

Kim Stanley and Lloyd Bridges in The Goddess (1958).

ell). Because of the athletics he displayed in the feat he is hired to double the company's lead actor in his action films. He thus becomes "the goat" of the lot.

Soon Stone finds himself quite infatuated with Mitchell and with movie life until he is thrown from a horse while performing in one of her thrillers. For publicity the studio bandages the film's costar, Marmaduke X. Caruthers (Philo McCullough), and has him sent to the hospital amidst a flood of news stories while Stone is paid off and quietly dismissed from his job.

Realizing he has made a mistake, Stone returns to his girl Molly O'Connor (Winifred Greenwood) and goes back to the simple life he had known before his brush with the glamourous world of moviemaking.

THE GODDESS (Columbia, 1958) 105 min.

Producer, Milton Perlman; director, John Cromwell; screenplay, Paddy Chayevsky; assistant director, Charles H. Maguire; music, Virgil Thompson; costumes, Frank L. Thompson; special supervisor, George Justin; art director, Edward Haworth; camera, Arthur J. Ornitz; editor, Carl Lerner.

Kim Stanley (Rita Shawn [Emily Ann Faulkner]); Betty Lou Holland (The Mother); Joan Copeland (The Aunt); Gerald Hiken (The Uncle); Burt Brinckerhoff (The Boy); Steven Hill (John Tower); Gerald Petrarca (The Minister); Linda Soma (Bridesmaid); Curt Conway (The Writer); Joan Linville (Joanna); Joyce Van Patten (Hillary); Lloyd Bridges (Dutch Seymour); Bert Freed (Lester Brackman); Donald McKee (R. M. Lucas); Louise Beavers (The Cook); Elizabeth Wilson (Secretary); David White (Burt Harris); Roy Shuman and John Lawrence (G. I. s); Chris Flanagan (Emily Ann at age 4); Patty Duke (Emily at age 8); Mike O'Dowd and Sid Raymond (Men); Margaret Brayton (Mrs. Woolsy); Werner Klemperer (Mr. Woolsy); Fred Herrick (The Elder); Gail Haworth (Emily's Daughter).

The Goddess is a highly-praised accounting of the life of a neurotic movie star; for many then and now it seems to be based heavily on the life of Marilyn Monroe. Kim Stanley in the lead as Emily Ann Faulkner gave a bravura performance as the poor girl who strove mightily for success without ever really comprehending the meaning of the word, or how to cope with it. Unfortunately the rest of the film seems bland in contrast to Stanley's captivating interpretation, and the production sank into a morass of self-pity and vapidity long before the end credits flashed on the screen.

Paddy Chayefsky's screenplay (divided into three sections: Portrait of a Child, Portrait of a Girl, and Portrait of a Goddess) follows the life of Emily Ann Faulkner (Stanley). She is a small-town girl whose father committed suicide when she was a small child and whose mother (Betty Lou Holland) never wanted her. As a teenager in Maryland, the would-be actress dreams of becoming a film star, but is also an easy mark for the sex-hungry boys in her high school class. When the son (Steven Hill) of a Hollywood film star arrives in town, crafty Hunter gets him drunk and they end up married.   They later have a child and he goes to war while Hunter remains in Hollywood.

Giving her daughter to her mother to care for, Hunter divorces her spouse and changes her name to Rita Shawn.   She begins to rise in the world of the movies via the casting couch and after making a good impression in a small role in a film.   Along the way she marries a world-weary ex-boxing champ (Lloyd Bridges), but the relationship is brief.   Eventually Hunter has all the success and money she has ever dreamed of, but she is unable to adjust to her lofty status.   After a bout with religion, she turns to the bottle and pills, and then attempts suicide.   At the film's finale she is existing in a hazy world of alcohol and dope.

In short, as Chayefsky's narrative points out, success as a goddess can be hellish.   More importantly, the scenarist is demonstrating his belief that there was a new generation who had lived through the Depression and who sought financial success as an end-all, most of them never coming to terms with human emotions, especially love.

Gordon Gow in Hollywood in the Fifties (1971) said, "The screenplay by Paddy Chayefsky was a distinct advance upon the average run of movies about the movie queen who arrives from nowhere.... Given Chayefsky's dialogue and a notable interior performance by Kim Stanley, the grains of truth that lurk in every cliché seemed grittier than usual....   [The] core of the theme: the display of status, the keeping up of appearances, became too great a burden for a small personality that had been inflated by the cinema's publicity machine, and the lure of the bitch-goddess--'Success'. "

GOING HOLLYWOOD (MGM, 1933) 80 min.

Producer, Walter Wanger; director, Raoul Walsh; story, Frances Marion; screenplay, Donald Ogden Stewart; art director, Merrill Pye; set decorator, Edwin B. Willis; gowns, Adrian; songs, Nacio Herb Brown and Arthur Freed; camera, George Folsey; editor, Frank Sullivan.

Marion Davies (Sylvia Bruce); Bing Crosby (Bill Williams); Fifi D'Orsay (Lili Yvonne); Stuart Erwin (Ernest B. Baker); Ned Sparks (Bert Conroy); Patsy Kelly (Jill Barker); Bobby Watson (Jack Thompson); the Three Radio Rogues (Themselves); Sterling Holloway (Recording Boy).

Going Hollywood was a luxurious and easy-going musical which teased the world of moviemaking.   It starred Marion Davies in a song-and-dance role and made recording and radio star Bing Crosby, under contract to Paramount Pictures, a name to reckon with as a screen actor.   Almost needless to say, William Randolph Hearst backed the venture which took a leisurely six months to film and which, despite its heavy production costs, earned a profit for MGM. Action director Raoul Walsh helmed this mirthful effort which introduced the famous standard tune "Temptation. "

Frances Marion concocted the story of a girl named Sylvia Bruce (Davies) who abandons her career as a schoolteacher to pursue her idol, crooning movie idol Bill Williams (Crosby) to Hollywood. There she meets his frequent costar and jealous girlfriend Lili Yvonne (Fifi D'Orsay). Crosby, meanwhile, is making a film, but Fifi decides to take him to Mexico to get him away from Davies who nonetheless follows and persuades the crooner to return to the movie--minus his costar. Davies is then assigned to replace D'Orsay and executes all the musical numbers in addition to winning the vocalist's affection.

Going Hollywood was produced by Davies' long-time pal Walter Anger and in it she enjoyed a big production number, "We'll Make Hay While the Sun Shines." Despite her top billing she was subordinated to costar Crosby, who sang such tunes as "Going Hollywood" (which was shown in the course of the compilation feature That's Entertainment!, q. v.). Walsh allegedly spent much of the half year of genteel filming practicing golf.

Although there was much on-the-surface satire to be enjoyed in this entry, especially in the deliberate spoofing of exotic film types by Fifi D'Orsay and the tongue-in-cheek performing of Davies, Variety felt obliged to warn its readers, "Pretentious musical with class in every department but one. It has names, girls and good music, but its story is weak from hunger and the script will prevent a big click. "

THE GOLDWYN FOLLIES (United Artists, 1938) Color, 120 min.

Producer, Samuel Goldwyn; associate producer, George Haight; director, George Marshall; story/screenplay, Ben Hecht; additional material, The Ritz Brothers, Sam Perrin, and Arthur Phillips; music director, Alfred Newman; songs, George and Ira Gershwin; ballet sequence directed by George Balanchine; ballet music, Vernon Duke; orchestrator, Edward Powell; assistant director, Eddie Bernoudy; art director, Richard Day; camera, Gregg Toland; editor, Sherman Todd.

Adolphe Menjou (Oliver Merlin); Zorina (Olga Samara); Andrea Leeds (Hazel Dawes); Kenny Baker (Danny Beecher); Helen Jepson (Leona Jerome); Phil Baker (Michael Day); Ella Logan (Glory Wood); Bobby Clark (A. Basil Crane, Jr.); Jerome Cowan (Lawrence); Nydia Westman (Ada); Charles Kullmann (Alfredo); and: American Ballet of the Metropolitan Opera, Edgar Bergen & Charlie McCarthy, the Ritz Brothers (Themselves); Roland Drew (Roland); Alan Ladd (Auditioning Singer).

Producer Samuel Goldwyn spent over $2 million on this lavish color musical, sparing no expense. He hired George and Ira Gershwin to write the score, although George would die during the production and only three of their songs were used. Vernon Duke was contracted as a replacement, while George Balanchine created the choreography for ballerina Vera Zorina and the corps de ballet of the Metropolitan Opera. Opera singer Helen Jepson was also featured

Edgar Bergen and Charlie McCarthy in The Goldwyn Follies (1938).

in the conglomeration of talent corralled for the revue-style feature, along with Ella Logan, Phil Baker, the Ritz Brothers, Kenny Baker, Bobby Clark, and Edgar Bergen & Charlie McCarthy. (This was the first film to showcase Edgar Bergen & Charlie McCarthy, with extensive footage devoted to their flip humor--e. g. , when Menjou gives a studio pass to Bergen to take a look around in attempts to woo him to a contract, Charlie quips, "Shall we go slumming?" Bergen had received a special 1937 Oscar for his radio show and his freshly begun screen work with Charlie McCarthy.) Despite all the trimmings, the outing proved to be a folly.

In a theme that would be used to much better advantage by Preston Sturges in 1941's Sullivan's Travels (q. v.), Adolphe Menjou starred as a famous film producer who feels he is losing contact with the public taste after his last few films have flopped. He encounters a sweet young girl (Andrea Leeds) who has just arrived in Hollywood from her rural home and he hires her to advise him on

Opposite: Pugilistes Marion Davies (left) and Fifi D'Orsay, with Patsy Kelly (seated, behind Davies) in Going Hollywood (1933).

making movies with the common touch of life.   He dubs her "Miss
Humanity" and his next project is a success.   The producer then
falls in love with the girl and he plans to announce his engagement
to her at a cast party for the picture.   But he learns she really loves
a struggling singer (Kenny Baker) who is employed at a local hamburger stand.   Menjou gallantly steps aside so that the young couple can
find happiness.

In Movie Comedy Teams (1970) Leonard Maltin opined that the
helter-skelter film "turned out to be one of the producer's (Goldwyn)
biggest bombs, with an incredibly jumbled cast sinking in a sea of
cliches and uninspired musical numbers. "   For all its shortcomings--
and there are many--The Goldwyn Follies did have a few good moments.   Adolphe Menjou did the best he could with the stilted role of
the producer and the film provided Kenny Baker with his lifelong song
theme, "Love Walked In. "   The Ritz Brothers offered their zaniness,
especially in a sketch filled with animals, and for highbrow tastes
there was the ballet work of Vera Zorina, a performer never used
properly by the movies.

For the average filmgoer, The Goldwyn Follies, with its alleged look at the lunacy behind the scenes, only convinced the lay
person that Hollywood was run by imbeciles.

GOOD TIMES (Columbia, 1967) Color, 91 min.

Executive producer, Steve Broidy; producer, Lindsley Par-
sons; director, William Friedkin; story, Nicholas Hyams; screenplay,
Tony Barrett; music/songs/music conductor, Sonny Bono; music ar-
ranger, Harold R. Battliste, Jr. ; costumes, Leah Rhodes; wardrobe,
Forrest T. Butler; makeup, Ed Butterworth; choreography, Andre
Tayir; assistant director, David Salven; sound, Ray Cossar and Rich-
ard Spelker; special effects, Bob Peterson; process camera, Farciot
Edouart; camera, Robert Wyckoff; editor, Melvin Shapiro.

Sonny and Cher (Themselves); George Sanders (Mordicus);
Norman Alden (Warren); Larry Duran (Smith); Kelly Thordsen (Tough
Hombre); Lennie Weinrib (Garth); Peter Robbins (Brandon); Edy Wil-
liams, China Lee, and Diane Haggerty (Mordicus' Girls); James Fla-
vin (Lieutenant); Phil Arnold (Solly); Hank Worden (Kid); John Cliff
(Gangster); Richard Collier (Peddler); Howard Wright (Old Timer);
Joe Devlin (Bartender); Mike Kopach (Deputy); Herk Reardon and
Bruce Tegner (Wrestlers).

Columbia Pictures sought to make a viable film commodity of
the popular singing duo Sonny and Cher Bono in this fantasy-musical.
But the studio succeeded only in creating a slick entry directed in a
brisk manner by William Friedkin.   (He would later turn out such
big-budgeted features as The French Connection and The Exorcist.)
"There are lovely little bits of fun sprinkled throughout the reels,
a ridiculous Western number, a ludicrous Tarzan take-off and a
Mickey Spillane spoof, all of them evidence that Sonny does not have
to rely on music for a living.   Good Times is part-time tongue-in-

cheek, part-time beguiling foot-in-mouth ... a tasty tidbit of entertainment" (New York Times).

Film tycoon Mordicus (smartly played by droll George Sanders) attempts to induce Sonny and Cher (as themselves) into making
a film for him.   He offers the team adequate compensation but the
project he outlines is a dud.   Bowing to their creative demands, he
gives the duo a short time to come up with a better story suggestion.
It leads them into dreaming about the type of motion picture they actually would like to make.   They germinate three plot ideas: a detective thriller, a Western, and a jungle epic.   The last one, a Tarzan and Jane parody, has them as the Jungle Man and his woman
with Sanders as the leader of the safari which is tracking the ele-
phants' burial ground.   Finally Sonny and Cher return to reality.   In
a moment of rationality they decide to forego possible Hollywood stardom to return to the world of music.

The moral of the film is obviously geared to the public's long-
standing conception that the picture industry is the corruptor of cultural integrity and the distorter of creative talent.

GOODBYE CHARLIE (20th Century-Fox, 1964) Color, 117 min.

Producer, David Weisbart; director, Vincente Minnelli; based
on the play by George Axelrod; screenplay, Harry Kurnitz; music,
Andre Previn; song, Previn and Dory Langdon; orchestrator, Al Wood-
bury; art directors, Jack Martin Smith and Richard Day; set decora-
tors, Walter M. Scott and Keogh Gleason; makeup, Ben Nye; costumes,
Helen Rose; assistant director, David Hall; sound, W. D. Flick and
Elmer Raguse; special camera effects, L. B. Abbott and Emil Kosa,
Jr.; camera, Milton Krasner; editor, John W. Holmes.

Tony Curtis (George Tracy); Debbie Reynolds (Charlie Sorel--
the Woman); Pat Boone (Bruce Minton); Walter Matthau (Sir Leopold
Sartori); Joanna Barnes (Janie); Laura Devon (Rusty); Ellen MacRae
[Burstyn] (Franny); Martin Gabel (Morton Craft); Roger Carmel (In-
spector); Harry Madden (Charlie Sorel--the Man); Myrna Hansen (Star-
let); Michael Romanoff (Patron); Michael Jackson (Himself); Antony
Eustrel (Butler); Donna Michelle (Guest on Yacht); Jerry Dunphy (TV
Newscaster); Carmen Nisbet and Sydney Guilaroff (Patrons at Beauty
Saloon); Jack Richardson (Party Guest); Natalie Martinelli (Italian
Girl).

Although partially dealing with films, much of the action of
this picture takes place in Malibu Beach, California and it just so
happens that some of the characters are in the movie business.   The
basic plot, however, could readily have been transferred to any large-
scale profession and the end result would still have been the same.

In late 1959, George Axelrod's play Goodbye Charlie opened
on Broadway, starring Lauren Bacall, Sydney Chaplin, and Sarah
Marshall.   What had been a semi-amusing exercise in smut humor
on the stage, emerged as formula-laden trivia when cleaned up for
the screen.

Tony Curtis and Debbie Reynolds in Goodbye Charlie (1964).

Wildly jealous Hungarian film producer Sir Leopold Sartori (Walter Matthau) kills a reckless playboy after catching him in a flirtatious position with the filmmaker's wife.   Once the playboy settles into a watery grave he is reincarnated in the person of a very beautiful girl (Debbie Reynolds) who sets out to take revenge for the murder.

Reynolds moves into the beach home of her former self and confronts her earthly best friend, George Tracy (Tony Curtis), who is trying to salvage what is left of the dead man's jumbled estate. When Curtis learns the full story, he does not know how to handle the situation but agrees to go along with the revenge scheme.   First Reynolds begins to take advantage of the former affairs her once self had with various Hollywood wives claiming to be the dead man's widow.   In doing so she becomes the romance object of wealthy man-about-town Bruce Minton (Pat Boone).   Later she finds herself pursued by arch culprit Matthau.   From there Reynolds takes out her planned revenge.

The New York Times noted, "Goodbye Charlie was bad enough on the stage.   On the screen, it is a ... conglomeration of outrageous whimsies and stupidities. "   Time magazine added, "Public apathy is apt to send Charlie off to the boneyard reserved for classic Hollywood fumbles. "   What probably turned mass audiences off this would-be sex farce was the casting of such "wholesome" types as Reynolds, Curtis, and Boone.   It was hard to imagine that Vincente Minnelli who had directed such incisive studies of Hollywood as The Bad and the Beautiful and Two Weeks in Another Town (qq. v.), could have supervised this lugubrious mess.   If anything, this box-office turkey reconfirmed for the few patrons who saw it that one, the Hollywood film industry was filled with sex-hungry egotists and, two, movies were worse than ever.

GOODBYE, NORMA JEAN (A. Stirling Gold, 1976) Color, 95 min.

Executive producer, Amadeo C. Curcio; producer, Larry Buchanan; associate producer, Lynn Shubert; director, Buchanan; assistant director, John S. Curran; inspired by the life of Marilyn Monroe; screenplay, Shubert and Buchanan; music/music director, Joe Beck; song, Johnny Cunningham; costumes, Alexis Seepo; art director, John Carter; makeup, Zoltan Elek; special makeup for Miss Rowe, Marie Carter; sound, Henri Price; camera, Robert B. Sherry; editors, Curran and Buchanan.

Misty Rowe (Norma Jean Baker); Terrence Locke (Ralph Johnson); Patch Mackenzie (Ruth Latimer); Preston Hanson (Hal James); Marty Zagon (Irving Olbach); Andre Philippe (Sam Dunn); Ivey Bethune (Ruby Kirshner); Steve Brown (Master of Ceremonies); Adele Claire (Beverly); Sal Ponti (Randy Palmer); Frank Curcio (Mel); Lilyan McBride (House Mother); Burr Middleton (Sleazy Photographer); Paula Mitchell (Cynthia); Garth Pillsbury (Police Officer); Jean Sarah Frost (Ethel); Stuart Lancaster (George); Anthony Gigor (Sid); Darla Leroy (Receptionist); Duncan McLeod and Edward Ansara (Doctors); Debbie Daniels and Sherry Kay Campbell (Girls in Snuff Movie); Charles

Misty Rowe in Goodbye, Norma Jean (1976).

Aidikoff (Director); Don Brodie (Projectionist); Harry Woolman (Wino in Snuff Movie); Sheila Sisco (Aspiring Actress).

This R-rated cheapie purported to tell of the early years of Marilyn Monroe (1926-1962) when she was known as Norma Jean Baker. All the tawdry aspects of a starlet's attempted rise to fame are exploited in this misguided film, which surprisingly contains a fine interpretation by Misty Rowe in the title assignment. The feature claims to recapture many of the locales of the sex goddess' early years as well as to report all the little-known "facts" of her pre-stardom days. If so, then the late actress went from pillar to post, and always to bed, to attain the foundation and framework of her exalted Hollywood legend.

Beginning at the start of World War II, Goodbye, Norma Jean relates how her guardian's lover first attempted to molest the girl and how she is later raped by a motorcycle cop in lieu of being given a speeding ticket. Also detailed is her coming under the guidance of an Army photographer (Terrence Locke) who maneuvers her into a beauty contest--which she wins--while she is employed in a munitions factory.

Once in Hollywood (at least according to this salacious account) she is forced to submit to the sexual desires of assorted film personnel, including a lady agent (Patch Mackenzie), and in one scene

she is depicted visiting a shabby hotel on the pretext of posing for
a magazine photo layout.   There she is raped by two men who film
the event.   Finally an ailing producer, Hal James (Preston Hanson),
makes her his protégée and develops her into a potential star although
he dies after a night of making love to her.   The celluloid biography
concludes with the cocoon of little Norma Jean Baker shed to reveal
hard, ambitious Marilyn Monroe, on her way to her destiny as a
Hollywood superstar and tragedy.

As a composite picture of the low life of Hollywood and the
tribulations of a pretty girl in the film capital, the release is more
than adequate.   Its production values, however, are amiss; this is
perhaps due to producer-director-cowriter Larry Buchanan who has
been responsible for such negligible items as Zontar: The Thing from
Venus, Curse of the Swamp Creature, and Creatures of Destruction
although Misty Rowe more than makes up for such deficiencies with
"a fine and sensitive performance ... " (Variety).

In the usual gambit employed with such bare-all-the-facts excursions, the only character who is morally held up to (possible) ri-
dicule is the Monroe figure.   All the other participants in the soft-
core porno melodrama are carefully disguised/telescoped versions of
people once supposedly associated with the late star.   According to
promotional material, filmmaker Buchanan claims to have once known
Monroe.   The pity is she is not alive to tell her side of the story
in a more responsible and less male-chauvinistic format.

GRAND CANYON (Screen Guild, 1949) 69 min.

Executive producer, Robert L. Lippert; producer, Carl Hittleman; director, Paul Landres; story, Hittleman; screenplay, Jack Harvey and Milton Luban; assistant director, Frank Fox; music director,
Albert Glasser; art director, F. Paul Sylos; sound, Carry Harris;
camera, Ernest Miller; editor, Landres.

Richard Arlen (Mike Adams); Mary Beth Hughes (Terry Lee);
Reed Hadley (Mitch Bennett); James Millican (Tex Hartford); Olin
Howlin (Windy); Grady Sutton (Halfnote); Joyce Compton (Mabel); Char-
lie Williams (Bert); Margia Dean (Script Girl); Anna May Slaughter
(Little Girl); Stanley Price (Makeup Man); Holly Bane [Mike Regan]
(Rocky).

Grand Fun!
Grand Feudin'!
Grand Fightin'!
Grand Lovin'!
... where the laffs begin!

So read the advertisement of this grade C effort supposedly
shot on location in the Grand Canyon region.   But it is filled with
obvious stock footage (supposedly, adverse weather forced the filmmakers to abandon the natural locale) of the area and a storyline so
trite that the only residue of the 69 minutes of screen fare is tedium.
Cinematically the only interest this entry holds (besides witnessing
star Richard Arlen attempt to make something credible out of the

Olin Howlin, Grady Sutton, and Joyce Compton in a publicity pose
for Grand Canyon (1949).

mish-mash of the script) is its continual references to Robert Lippert Productions, the outfit which actually manufactured this clinker.
It is a shame the producers did not strive harder to instill a more
satisfactory look at film-making into the storyline, thus giving the
picture a worthwhile documentary flavor. It would have enhanced the
end product tremendously.

Director Mitch Bennett (Reed Hadley) connives to persuade the
boss of Lippert Productions to make a film on location about the
Grand Canyon. Finally winning out, Hadley takes his crew and cast
to the famous gorge where the operator of a mule team, Mike Adams
(Arlen), is hired for the duration of picture shooting. Arlen quickly
becomes enamored of the unit's leading lady, Terry Lee (Mary Beth
Hughes). Later he is given a chance to co-star with her when the
movie's prissy leading man fortuitously breaks his leg while on location. To add zest to the film, Hadley clandestinely films Arlen's
courting of Hughes in their off hours; when Arlen learns that his
wooing will be on the final product, he disgustedly deserts the project and his new-found love. Hadley, though, tries to convince the
wholesome outdoorsman that the whole scheme was his idea and he
contrives a situation in which Arlen rescues Hughes from an alleged
peril. The plan works and Arlen and Hughes are reunited. As for

Hadley he is happy--he has a Western love story set in the Grand
Canyon, and if things go well, a new star for his future ventures
in the person of Arlen.

The film was shot in Sepia; the overabundance of comedy relief was provided by Grady Sutton (Halfnote) and Joyce Compton
(Mabel), among others.

THE GREAT WALDO PEPPER (Universal, 1975) Color, 107 min.

Producer, George Roy Hill; associate producer, Robert L.
Crawford; director/story, Hill; screenplay, William Goldman; assist-
ant directors, Ray Gosnell and Jerry Ballew; art director, Henry
Bumstead; set decorator, James Payne; costumes, Edith Head; music,
Henry Mancini; air work, Tallmantz Aviation; air sequences super-
visor, Frank Tallman; sound, Bob Miller and Ronald Pierce; spe-
cial effects, Ben McMahon; camera, Robert Surtees; editor, William
Reynolds.

Robert Redford (Waldo Pepper); Bo Svenson (Alex Olsson); Bo
Brundin (Ernst Kessler); Susan Sarandon (Mary Beth); Geoffrey Lewis
(Newton Potts); Edward Herrmann (Ezra Stiles); Philip Bruns (Doc
Dillhoefer); Roderick Cook (Werfel); Kelly Jean Peters (Patsy); Mar-
got Kidder (Maude); Scott Newman (Duke); James S. Appleby (Ace);
Patrick W. Henderson, Jr. (Scooter); James Harrell (Farmer); Elma
Aicklen (Farmer's Wife); Deborah Knapp (Farmer's Daughter); John
A. Zee (Director on Western Set); John Reilly (Western Star); Jack
Manning (Director on Spanish Set); Joe Billings (Policeman); Lawrence
Casey (German Star); Greg Martin (Assistant Director).

During World War I, Waldo Pepper (Robert Redford) had been
a flying ace, continually in a rivalry with German ace counterpart
Ernst Kessler (Bo Brundin).   After the Great War, Redford continues
to fly but as a barnstormer in the U.S. who travels from town to
town doing aerial stunts and charging $5 for a five-minute plane ride.
At one of the stopovers, Redford encounters Captain Alex Olsson (Bo
Svenson) and an intense rivalry develops between the two.   They engage in acts of mutual sabotage but finally realize they would be better off as a team.

As a result they join forces to develop an act for a traveling
circus.   Mary Beth (Susan Sarandon) who is a part of their group,
becomes nervous about wing walking and during a performance plunges to her death.   Redford and Svenson then dissolve their partnership.   Redford then heads for Hollywood where he finds employment
as a stunt pilot.   While participating in a World War I film, he
again meets the German, Brundin.   The latter is now debt-plagued
and is serving as technical advisor on a film speciously covering his
career.   The two of them continue their flying rivalry but this time
for the movie cameras.   As if the war were still on, the two compete again in the air.   When Redford realizes that Brundin has acknowledged defeat, the two aviators head their badly-damaged crafts
into a cloud bank.

Bo Svenson and Robert Redford in The Great Waldo Pepper (1975).

In many ways The Great Waldo Pepper is a modern-day counterpart of RKO's The Lost Squadron and Lucky Devils (qq. v.), both
from the thirties.   These films also told of World War I pilots reduced to doing dangerous stunts for the movies.   Here the story focuses on one pilot, rather than a group, and it adds in for good
measure a continuing rivalry between the Allied ace and his German
opposite number.   In its meandering way, this feature did present
a good study of the hazardous profession of stunt flying for the movies and the circumstances which led some of America's war heroes
to that ill-paying, unglorious profession when their dashing combat
days were over.
    Thanks to the popularity of star Redford, the George Roy Hill
production achieved decent box-office proportions, but it was a minor-
league film, containing few thrills in its anemic storyline.   Noted
Films in Review, "Aviation buffs will enjoy the expert flying sequences, for which a dozen people receive credit; but most filmgoers
will be disappointed despite superior direction, good production values, and uniformly fine performances. "

HARLOW (Paramount, 1965) Color, 126 min.

    Producer, Joseph E. Levine; director, Gordon Douglas; based
on the book by Irving Shulman in collaboration with Arthur Landau;
screenplay, John Michael Hayes; color consultant, Richard Mueller;
art directors, Hal Pereira and Roland Anderson; set decorator,
James Payne; music/music director, Neal Hefti; song, Jay Livingston
and Ray Evans; costumes, Edith Head; sound, Stan Jones; camera,
Joseph Ruttenberg; editor, Frank Bracht.

    Carroll Baker (Jean Harlow); Red Buttons (Arthur Landau);
Angela Lansbury (Mama Jean Bello); Raf Vallone (Marino Bello);
Martin Balsam (Everett Redman); Peter Lawford (Paul Bern); Michael
Connors (Jack Harrison); Hanna Landy (Mrs. Arthur Landau); Leslie
Neilsen (Richard Manley); Mary Murphy (Studio Secretary); Peter
Hansen (Assistant Director); Peter Leeds (Director of Thirties' Scene);
Edy Williams (Mail Room Girl); Myron Healey (Rex Chambers); Kipp
Hamilton (Girl at Pool).

HARLOW (Magna, 1965) 107 min.

    Executive producer, Brandon Chase; producer, Lee Savin;
director, Alex Segal; screenplay, Karl Tunberg; music, Al Ham and
Nelson Riddle; assistant directors, Greg Peters, Johnny Wilson, and
Dick Bennett; art director, Duncan Cramer; set decorator, Harry
Gordon; camera, Jim Kilgore.

    Carol Lynley (Jean Harlow); Efrem Zimbalist, Jr. (William
Mansfield); Ginger Rogers (Mama Jean); Barry Sullivan (Marino Bello); Hurd Hatfield (Paul Bern); Lloyd Bochner (Marc Peters); Hermione Baddeley (Marie Dressler); Audrey Totter (Marilyn); John Williams (Jonathan Martin); Audrey Christie (Thelma); Michael Dante
(Ed); Jack Kruschen (Louis B. Mayer); Celia Lovsky (Maria Ouspen-

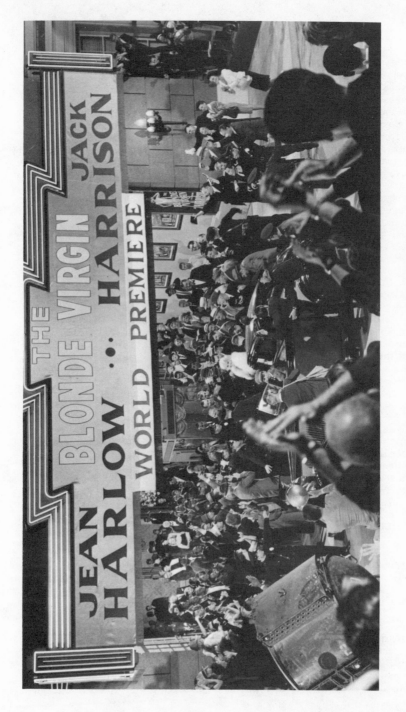

Carroll Baker as <u>Harlow</u> (Paramount 1965).

Barry Sullivan, Ginger Rogers, and Carol Lynley in Harlow (Magna 1965).

skaya); Robert Strauss (Hank); James Dobson (Counterman); Sonny Liston and Nick Demitri (Fighters); Cliff Norton (Billy); Paulle Clarke (Waitress); Jim Plunkett (Stan Laurel); John "Red" Fox (Oliver Hardy); Christopher West (Bern's Secretary); Fred Conte (Photographer); Catherine Ross (Wardrobe Woman); Maureene Gaffney (Miss Larsen); Lola Fisher (Nurse); Fred Klein (Himself).

In his "intimate biography" Harlow (1964), novelist Irving Shulman offered a very commercialized rendering of the life and times of the legendary Jean Harlow (1911-1937), focusing on her sexual forays. It was inevitable that a Hollywood version of the tome would appear. As it developed, not one but two biopics based on the tragic life of Harlow were announced--each proved to be an ugly distortion of the sensational but pathetic career of the "Blonde Bombshell. "
The "official" celluloid version of Shulman's fancy, Harlow, was produced by Joseph E. Levine for Paramount Pictures, with Carroll Baker (fresh from her fatal chandelier ride of The Carpetbaggers, q. v.) in the title role. A surprisingly solid cast allowed

themselves to be exploited: Angela Lansbury and Raf Vallone as
Harlow's money-lusting parents, Peter Lawford as MGM producer
Paul Bern, whose notoriety as the blonde's impotent, suicidal husband
supplied the more scandalous details of the book/movie; Michael Connors as Gable-ish star "Jack Harrison"; Leslie Nielsen as Howard
Hughes-ish "Richard Manley" (who tries to rape his starlet); and
Red Buttons as Arthur Landau, Harlow's agent. (It was the real-life
Landau who, ill and financially wasted, "revealed" the story of Harlow's life to Shulman--only to confess later that the Jean Harlow of
the best-seller was little more than a gorgon of the author's imagination.)

Within Levine's 126-minute version, there was color, sex,
flamboyantly dissipated episodes such as Harlow stumbling half-naked
along the Santa Monica beach with booze in hand, coughing from fatal
pneumonia (Harlow actually died of uremic poisoning), a Bobby Vinton
theme song ("Lonely Girl"), and enough audience interest to secure
a domestic gross of $3 million.

Levine's picture cast its lot on sensationalistic distortion and
a huge promotional campaign. Bill Sargent's rival version for Magna was no better. It was filmed in "Electronovision" (eight days of
filming with TV-style cameras on a $600,000 budget). It belched in-
to theatres to beat the arrival of Levine's big-budget production. The
nearly sacrilegious mess cast Carol Lynley in the title role. As
she tried hopelessly to perfect a pout and to sashay about (both with
ludicrous results), some good actors performing yeoman work sought
to achieve credible characterizations. Ginger Rogers (replacing Judy
Garland) was a moving "Mama Jean, " Barry Sullivan a smoothly lecherous stepfather "Marino, " Efrem Zimbalist Jr. a respectful composite of William Powell (who had vowed a lawsuit if his name and
status as Harlow's last deep love were dragged into the mire) and
Gable, and Hurd Hatfield as an extravagantly piteous Paul Bern. Less
can be said for Jack Kruschen, who even managed to malign the
not-benign memory of Louis B. Mayer. With a bevy of laughable
distortions of Harlow's life and times--including her employment of
male whores and her running away from Hollywood to study drama
with Maria Ouspenskaya, Sargent's Harlow died in the theatres.

As a footnote, it should be mentioned that in the late fifties,
20th Century-Fox had projected a Harlow biopic to star Marilyn Monroe. She certainly would have suggested the heart and sensuality of
Harlow more closely than either of the "sexpots" who drew the eventual honors.

HEARTS OF THE WEST (MGM/United Artists, 1975) 102 min.

Producer, Tony Bill; director, Howard Zieff; screenplay, Bob
Thompson; art director, Robert Luthardt; music, Ken Lauber; camera, Mario Tosi; editor, Edward Warschilka.

Jeff Bridges (Lewis Tater); Andy Griffith (Howard Pike); Don-
ald Pleasence (A. J. Nietz); Blythe Danner (Miss Trout); Alan Arkin
(Kessler); Richard B. Shull (Fat Man); Herbert Edelman (Polo); Alex
Rocco (Earl); Frank Cady (Pa Tater); Anthony James (Lean Man);

Jeff Bridges in <u>Hearts of the West</u> (1975).

Burton Gilliam (Lester); Matt Clark (Jackson); Candy Azzara (Waitress); Thayer David (Bank Manager); Wayne Storm (Lyle); Marie Windsor (Woman in Nevada).

          In 1975 MGM-United Artists gave the big promotional push to
The Sunshine Boys for the Oscars and in doing so bypassed one of
the most enjoyable films ever to examine the Hollywood scene.
Hearts of the West focused on the real Hollywood of Poverty Row of
the thirties.   For the first time on camera, the fly-by-night outfits
which churned out low-grade Westerns were aptly depicted on the
screen.   It resulted in a comedy which "steals its way into your
heart" (New York Daily News).
          Lewis Tater (Jeff Bridges), an Iowa boy, goes West hoping
to nurture his ambitions to write Western pulp fiction.   After accidentally becoming involved with two con artists in Nevada he later
flees from them into the desert and is thereafter rescued by a low-
budget movie company and befriended by Howard Pike (Andy Griffith),
an extra.   Bridges joins the troupe as a stuntman.   When the star
quits, he is briefly elevated to the lead for director Kessler's (Alan
Arkin) next picture.   Along the way he finds himself smitten with
screenwriter Miss Trout (Blythe Danner).   The ambitious if naive
Bridges also composes a novel entitled Hearts of the West.   He
makes the error of showing the scenario to Griffith who doublecross-
es him and sells the property to a big studio.
          Everything then goes bad for Bridges.   The crooks catch up
to him--thinking he has stolen their loot--and simultaneously his
screen career dissolves.   Just as he is about to be liquidated by the
con men, Griffith and Danner appear on the scene and save him.
The injured Bridges is carted off to the hospital, but he is content
now, for his future looks bright.   His novel is to be published, Danner has confirmed her love for him, and Griffith has made amends.
          Hearts of the West admirably captured the feel of the era and
in particular, the sleazy quality of Hollywood's Gower Gulch: the
cowboy extras lounging around awaiting a work call, the harried director trying to accomplish his filming in one take, the shabby build-
ings, and so on.   Also adding authenticity to the feature is Nick Lucas singing vintage songs on the soundtrack.   Several of the other
performances are quite telling, especially Griffith as screen extra
Howard Pike, once a star of the genre and now reduced to bits (as
were so many grade B Western stars in real life).
          As a purveyor of a portion of bygone Hollywood as it really
existed Hearts of the West has no equal to date.
          In England the feature was retitled Hollywood Cowboy.   When
it premiered there, the British Monthly Film Bulletin reported, "What
keeps the film happy and hopeful through ... rough spots--apart from
a successfully muted sense of period decor--are its quieter virtues,
all geared round cheerful connections between characters and performances: a rusty old-timer sporting his 'true' Western profile in a
flush of bashful vanity; a campy barber protesting when Lewis orders
his hair to be cut exactly like Zane Grey's; Alan Arkin, as the ex-
citable director, jerking the chair he's seated on across an office
floor in a kind of prolonged manic stutter.   But more essentially,
the movie belongs to its two stars ... Jeff Bridges, mouthing his

cowboy cliches with a relish that makes them indelible; and Blythe Danner, triumphing over a conventional Girl Friday part...."

HEAT (Warhol Films, 1972) Color, 100 min.

Producer, Andy Warhol; associate producer, Jed Johnson; director, Paul Morrissey; screen idea, John Hallowell; screenplay, Morrissey; music, John Cale; camera, Morrissey; editors, Lana Jokel and Jed Johnson.

Joe Dallesandro (Joey); Sylvia Miles (Sally); Andrea Feldman (Jessica); Pat Ast (Motel Owner); Ray Vestal (Movie Producer); P. J. Lester (Sally's Former Husband); Harold Child (His Roommate); Eric Emerson (Mute); Gary Koznocha (Mute's Brother); John Hallowell (Hollywood Columnist); Bonnie Glick (Jessica's Friend); Pat Parlemon (Girl by Pool).

In this minor, but exploitable Paul Morrissey effort, Andy Warhol regular Joe Dallesandro appears as a former child movie star who decides to attempt a comeback. The young man lacks ambitions to the point that the only way he will "work" is through hustling various women. He maintains his living quarters by making love to a fat landlady (Pat Ast) at the motel, but moves out when he becomes the lust object of a one-time big film actress named Sally (Sylvia Miles). Problems develop here too as Miles has a young daughter (Andrea Feldman) who is bisexual and has an illegitimate child. The girl, in acts of psychological warfare with her mother, attempts to win Dallesandro away from Miles, but this gambit fails. Finally the apathetic once-actor leaves Miles, looking for more fertile territory to captivate. Miles attempts to kill him with an unloaded gun, symbol of their empty emotional/sexual relationship.
Similar to many films of this ilk, Heat has little to recommend it, beyond the stumbling ambiance of the "improvisational" cast. Miles who portrays the has-been star a bit more sharply and energetically than required, would graduate to the big leagues of filmdom, even receiving an Oscar nomination for her supporting part in Farewell, My Lovely (1975). For those gluttons of visions of Hollywood past-present-and-fictional, Heat does provide a fantasy view of the seedier side of the lives of some moviemakers, those who fulfill the public image of moral and emotional instability.
A few critics noted that Heat was a "vague send-up" of Sunset Boulevard (q. v.), but one has to search hard to find more than surface comparisons in plot or character execution. Of this film shot in two weeks at a $70,000 cost, Time magazine snarled, "What is despicable about Heat is the way it both flaunts and mocks the grotesqueries of its cast, who seem generally neither to notice nor greatly care. "

THE HELEN MORGAN STORY (Warner Bros. , 1957) 118 min.

Producer, Martin Rackin; director, Michael Curtiz; screen-

Ann Blyth in The Helen Morgan Story (1957).

---

play, Oscar Saul, Dean Reisner, Stephen Longstreet, and Nelson Giddings; music numbers staged by LeRoy Prinz; costumes, Howard Shoup; assistant director, Paul Helmick; art director, John Beckman; set decorator, Howard Bristol; vocal arranger, Charles Henderson; sound, Francis J. Scheid and Dolph Thomas; camera, Ted McCord; editor, Frank Bracht.

Ann Blyth (Helen Morgan); Paul Newman (Larry); Richard Carlson (Wade); Gene Evans (Whitey Krause); Alan King (Ben); Cara Williams (Dolly); Virginia Vincent (Sue); Walter Woolf King (Ziegfeld); Dorothy Green (Mrs. Wade); Ed Platt (Haggerty); Warren Douglas (Hellinger); Sammy White (Sammy); The DeCastro Sisters, Jimmy McHugh, Rudy Vallee, and Walter Winchell (Themselves); Gogi Grant (Singing Voice of Helen Morgan).

In the mid-fifties musical biographies of several Jazz Age female singers, for instance Ruth Etting in Love Me or Leave Me and Lillian Roth's I'll Cry Tomorrow (q. v.), proved to be very commercial fare. The same year Polly Bergen starred in The Helen Morgan Story on television ("Playhouse 90"--April 16, 1957, CBS-TV), Warner Bros. was involved in preparing a feature on the life and hard times of the torch singer. Unfortunately Bergen did not repeat her heralded TV rendition; instead the lead was assigned to Ann Blyth, with her songs dubbed by Gogi Grant. What resulted was an inaccurate and too glossy picture of the famed songstress. The entry did recapture some of the Roaring Twenties' flavor as well as that of the Depression, relying on a myriad of colorful songs to create most of the illusion.

Like many similar pictures, The Helen Morgan Story had an anemic plotline, leading publications such as the Toronto Globe and Mail to complain, "The minutes between the songs are almost universally soggy...." The all-too-common tale has struggling vocalist Morgan (Blyth) becoming sidetracked romantically, first with a married lawyer (Richard Carlson) and then by a punk-hoodlum (Paul Newman). The latter has such an emotional hold on her that he drives the woman to drink, debilitating a very talented performer who, despite everything, is rising in show business. Her success as Julie in Show Boat is recounted, as are dozens of the songs associated with the singer. Her movie career, however, is almost totally ignored, as are most of the actual facts in the life of the performer whose career was devastated by alcohol.

Blyth made an adequate Helen Morgan, aided immeasurably by Grant's offscreen singing. Today the film is chiefly revived because of the casting of handsome Newman as the tough, cold gangster, the one who tells his woman, "In my own way, Helen, I love you." (In a rather glamourized finale, he reforms.) There are interesting cameos offered by songwriter Jimmy McHugh, columnist Walter Winchell, and crooner Rudy Vallee (singing "My Time Is Your Time").

Douglas McVay reported in The Musical Film (1967), "... the Prohibition era is capably evoked ... and the finale of the ex-alcoholic Helen reacting in tearful gratitude to a surprise welcome by all her old fans at her night-club has the moviegoers in tears too."

Although the film's veteran director, Michael Curtiz, was at Warner Bros. -First National the same time (mid-thirties) as Morgan, he never directed her at the Burbank facilities.

In England the film was retitled Both Ends of the Candle, with approximately 30 minutes chopped from its running time.

HELLZAPOPPIN' (Universal, 1941) 84 min.

Producer, Jules Levey; associate producers, Glenn Tryon and Alex Gottlieb; director, H. C. Potter; based on the play by Nat Perrin; screenplay, Perrin and Warren Wilson; songs, Gene DePaul and Don Raye; special effects, John Fulton; camera, Woody Bredell; editor, Milton Carruth.

Ole Olsen (Ole); Chic Johnson (Chic); Robert Paige (Jeff Hunter); Jane Frazee (Kitty Rand); Lewis Howard (Woody Tyler); Martha Raye (Betty Johnson); Clarence Kolb (Mr. Rand); Nella Walker (Mrs. Rand); Mischa Auer (Pepi); Richard Lane (Director); Elisha Cook, Jr. (Assistant Director); Hugh Herbert (Detective Quimby); Olive Hatch and Harlem Congeroo Dancers (Specialties); Shemp Howard (Louie); Jody Gilbert (Blonde); Andrew Tombes (Producer); George Davis (Butler); Harry Monti (Midget); Don Brodie (Theatre Manager); Dale Van Sickel (Man Who Falls into Pool); Bert Roach (Man in Audience);

The Six Hits and Slim and Sam (Specialties); Eddie Parker (Frankenstein Monster).

Comics Olsen and Johnson had appeared in Hellzapoppin' on Broadway for three years before Universal transferred the hit show into a feature film.   Unfortunately too much of the zest and punch of the outrageous stage production was lost on the Hollywood soundstage.   At least the initial portion of the screen outing took a number of delightful potshots at Hollywood film-making in general.   The offbeat film, which had little plotline and little conventional presentation, was a financial success and permitted the comedy team to make more of their zany efforts on films, including another genre outing, Crazy House (q. v.).   (Because Universal was so heavily promoting its starring comedy team of Abbott and Costello, the equally funny and rambunctious Olsen and Johnson duo never had a real chance to succeed on a long-term basis at the studio.)

Hellzapoppin' opens in Hades where devils torture their victims in various manners.   Then Olsen and Johnson arrive in a taxi. They have an argument with the Devil and then order a projectionist to roll the film again--suddenly it is revealed they are actually making a movie.   Unhappy about the progress of Hellzapoppin' on film, the boys talk to the director (Richard Lane) who informs them the picture needs a strong love element.   When they respond that their hit Broadway version did NOT, he retorts, "We change everything here-- we've got to."   From there, the feature focuses on a romantic triangle involving a producer (Robert Paige) who is attempting to put on a show and who in turn becomes involved with vocalist Kitty Rand (Jane Frazee) and her fiancé.   Hugh Herbert plays Detective Quimby who continually pops in and out of the proceedings (always in a different costume), and Martha Raye as man-hungry Betty Johnson in pursuit of an eccentric count (Mischa Auer).   She zigzagged frantically in and out of the storyline (what there was of it) and sang, "What Kind of Love Is This?"   "Watch the Birdie," "Robert E. Lee," and "Conga Beso."   The finale is the actual production which Paige is trying to stage.   At the end director Lane shoots the scriptwriter who is wearing a bulletproof vest which turns out not to be waterproof-- a pity.

Hellzapoppin' did have some cute thrusts to make at the film industry.   (For example, on one Alaskan soundstage the boys pass a snow sled with the name "Rosebud" on it.)   Still the feature was disappointing to loyal fans of the comedy team and to those who enjoyed the show during its 1100-performance run on Broadway (or during its subsequent road tour).   Ironically Universal actually enacted the satirical thrust of the movie: it altered a good stage presentation into a typical Hollywood marshmallow.   Thus it made fun of itself in the process!

HER DRAMATIC DEBUT _see THE SHORT FILMS

Opposite: Ole Olsen, Martha Raye, and Chic Johnson in Hellzapoppin' (1941).

HER BIG NIGHT (Universal, 1926) 7603 ft.

Presenter, Carl Laemmle; director, Melville W. Brown; based on the story "Doubling for Lora" by Peggy Gaddis; screenplay, Nita O'Neil and Rex Taylor; camera, Arthur Todd.

Laura La Plante (Frances Norcross/Daphne Dix); Einar Hansen (Johnny Young); ZaSu Pitts (Gladys Smith); Tully Marshall (J. Q. Adams the Reporter); Lee Moran (Tom Barrett); Mack Swain (Myers); John Roche (Allan Dix); William Austin (Harold Crosby); Nat Carr (Mr. Harmon); Cissy Fitzgerald (Mrs. Harmon).

The old comedy ploy of look-a-likes leading to romantic complications was dusted off and rerouted for a movie atmosphere in this Universal comedy, a vehicle for the talented Laura La Plante (in a dual role). The result was a most pleasing little comedy that provided an insight into the movie world as an added bonus.
La Plante portrays a big-time movie lead who is exhausted from her work schedule. She departs on a long-anticipated vacation, to join a millionaire on his yacht. Her harried producer (Mack Swain) and slightly dishonest publicist (Lee Moran) implore the star to return to Hollywood for the premiere of her latest endeavor. But she refuses. At wit's end, the two men seek a double for the star and find her in the person of a salesgirl (also La Plante) who agrees to make the personal appearance. Approaching the festive occasion, the sales clerk panics and further complications arise when the star's husband (John Roche) believes she IS his wife. Then the millionaire's spouse arrives to accuse the stand-in of alienating the affections of her husband. To make matters worse, the girl's own boyfriend (Einer Hansen) becomes upset over the complications. Finally, a nosey newspaperman (Tully Marshall) uncovers the plot.
"It is a picture that catches your interest the minute after you have taken your seat, and yet the plot is relatively thin," observed the New York Times' Mordaunt Hall. "As this feature is unfurled," he added, "one does not often hear loud outbursts of laughter. The amusement is more genuine, the sort of picture in which there is fun every scene. There are, toward the end, some clever double exposures, in which Laura La Plante is seen as Frances Norcross [the sales girl] and Miss Dix, a screen star."

HER FACE VALUE (Paramount, 1921) 4718 ft.

Director, Thomas N. Heffron; based on the story "The Girl Who Paid Dividends" by Earl Derr Biggers; screenplay, Percy Heath; camera, William E. Collins.

Wanda Hawley (Peggy Malone); Lincoln Plummer (Pop Malone); Dick Rosson (Eddie Malone); T. Roy Barnes (Jimmy Parsons); Winifred Bryson (Laurette); Donald MacDonald (Martin Fox); Harvey Clark (F. B. Sturgeon); George Periolat (James R. Greenwood); Eugene Burr (Jack Darian); Ah Wing (Chinese man).

Earl Derr Biggers, the creator of <u>Charlie Chan</u> and the author of the perennially popular <u>Seven Keys to Baldpate</u>, sometimes
used movie themes in his works and <u>Her Face Value</u> was the first film
to be based on one of his stories.   It was followed by <u>Broadway
Broke</u> (q. v.), and <u>The Black Camel</u> (q. v.), the latter adapted from
one of his Charlie Chan novels.

Wanda Hawley, a leading player of <u>We Can't Have Everything</u>
(q. v.), starred here as a chorus girl, Peggy, who is the support of
her lazy father (Lincoln Plummer) and brother (Dick Rosson).   She
marries a press agent, Jimmy Parsons (T. Roy Barnes), and the
two loafers move in with them, forcing Hawley to return to the stage.
Not in good health, Barnes is forced to move to Arizona for the cli-
mate.   Meanwhile, Hawley travels to Hollywood where she breaks
into the movies and promptly becomes a big star.   When she is injured while working on location, Barnes rushes to her side and she
choses him over the advances of a wealthy suitor.   Barnes then develops into a successful screen writer and the couple find renewed
happiness.

HIGH HAT (First National, 1927) 6161 ft.

Presenter Robert Kane; director, James Ashmore Creelman;
story/screenplay, Creelman and Melville Baker; camera, William
Schurr.

Ben Lyon (Jerry); Mary Brian (Millie); Sam Hardy (Tony);
Lucien Prival (The Director); Osgood Perkins (The Assistant Direc-
tor); Jack Ackroyd (The Property Man); Iris Gray and Ione Holmes
(The Stars).

Jerry (Ben Lyon), a lazy extra for Superba-Prettygood Pictures, tumbles romantically for wardrobe mistress Millie (Mary
Brian), who is also courted by another extra, Tony (Sam Hardy).
A temperamental German director, von Strogoff (Lucien Prival), is
making a film on the Russian revolution and Brian gets Lyon a close-
up, which is the dream of every extra.

Lyon, however, falls asleep on the set and is fired.   Meanwhile Hardy steals some jewelry entrusted to Brian as they were to
be worn in the movie.   Hardy sells the stones to some crooks and
Lyon follows in pursuit.   However, the hoodlums capture him.   He
later escapes and gives chase to Hardy who returns to the studio.
There the two men battle, creating a scene which is filmed by Prival.
When the jewels are later recovered, it is discovered they are paste.
Still the fight scene remains in the film with Lyon getting his close-
up and winning Brian's affections.

<u>Photoplay</u> magazine dubbed the film "Life among the movie
extras--which might have been more interesting than the film would
have you believe."   Lyon would go on to star in <u>The Flying Marine</u>
(q. v.), having already made <u>Bluebeard's Seven Wives</u> (q. v.).   As for
Lucien Prival, who enjoyably interpreted von Strogoff, he would again
be provided a chance to perform his broad impersonation of the flamboyant Erich von Stroheim in the sound film, <u>Hollywood Speaks</u> (q. v.).

HIS NEW JOB   see   THE SHORT FILMS

THE HISTORY OF THE BLUE MOVIE (Screening Room, 1970) 140
   min.

        Director, Alex de Renzy; assistant director, Paul Gerber;
editor, Jack Kerpan.

        With the coming of the seventies and the end (?) of stringent
movie censorship, old pornographic films began to appear in legitimate theatres, usually in the form of compilation features, and often
with an encompassing storyline which claimed that the new viewing
of the titillating material was purely for scholarly and sociological
reasons.   The first of this type film was A History of the Blue
Movie.   The picture offered an entertaining compilation of stag films
from circa 1915 to the present.   In the book Sinema (1972), Kenneth
Turan and Stephen F. Zito called it, "The first, best and most popular of these [porno compilation] films...." In Contemporary Erotic
Cinema (1973), William Rotsler labeled it, "The definitive study of
early porn."
        The 140-minute showcase includes A Free Ride (1915), stripper
Candy Barr's Smart Alec, and such other tid-bits as The Janitor,
Buried Treasure, The Nun's Story, and On the Beach.
        Addison Verrill reported in Variety, "To de Renzy's credit
... the most erotic section of the film is a cheapie short made by
him in which a stunning girl (in tight closeup) describes some of her
sexual fantasies--minus any pictorial graphics.   It's a knockout....
Pic on the whole is as rough as the subject matter indicates, but
most of it is so brimful of nostalgic that 'erotic' seems an inappro-
priate term for the total effect."   Verrill describes the film's format
as, "He's put them [the clips] all together with rinkytink music track
and a sober narration which attempts to report the changes in American attitudes towards sex as reflected in the stages, including the
naive peepshows of the '40s and early '50s.   Pic is often funny and
surprisingly informative...."   It is Verrill's contention that "stag
pix are as American as the proverbial apple pie, and many U.S.
males have had that grandly 'degenerate' experience of straining
their eyes at grainy old prints of fairly unattractive people making
it, ofttimes still wearing spike heels and drooping socks.   From
suburban garages to bachelor parties and hale-fellow smokers, the
blue movie is part and parcel of the American experience, one now
rapidly fading away as urban skin houses begin unspooling slick color
versions of the old forbidden fruit."
        After the critical and financial success of A History of the
Blue Movie, it was to be expected that several (inferior) imitations
would crop up in release.   The first of these was Bill Osco's Hollywood Blue (1971).   Like the earlier compilation, the successor utilized old stag film shorts (including one allegedly starring Marilyn
Monroe; the actress is actually Arline Hunter), and it incorporated
such items as censored clips from King Kong (where the beast re-
moves a portion of Fay Wray's dress) and Hedy Lamarr's nude bathing

scene from Ecstasy. Hollywood Blue also utilized interviews with
Jayne Mansfield, June Wilkinson, and Mickey Rooney, and it even
dragged in old newsreel clips of Shirley Temple and Ronald Reagan.
The picture's loose structure was supposed to expose several Hollywood stars' indiscretions before they became famous.   However, authors Turan and Zito observed in Sinema that the entry "is known
primarily for the tacky audacity with which it exploits and possibly
defames several revered Hollywood stars.... "
       Other follow-ups using the same premise included Making the
Blue Movie (1973), which had old porno clips interpolated with more
recent material, as well as interviews with such genre "stars" as
Harry Reems and Tina and Jason Russell. It Happened in Hollywood
(q. v.) was issued about the same time (circa 1973) as was John Kirk-
land's Pornography in Hollywood.   The latter effort analyzed the pornography business in the film capital but did NOT really touch on the
movie business per se.   Rotsier in Contemporary Erotic Cinema
judged it a "sloppy, uninteresting film. "
       Finally, in 1974, another of these compilations emerged, this
one called Panorama Blue. The film was basically a soft-core paste-
up of various stag shorts, including a few vintage entries from the
teens, twenties, and thirties.   It did have some engaging sequences
purporting to demonstrate how "blue" movies are made.   Of more
interest to the history of the genre was Old Stag Movies (1974), another compilation of vintage skin flicks, mostly dating back to the
silent era.   It was played for laughs and proved genuinely entertaining.

HOBOKEN TO HOLLYWOOD see THE SHORT FILMS

HOLD BACK THE DAWN (Paramount, 1941) 115 min.

       Producer, Arthur Hornblow, Jr. ; director, Mitchell Leisen;
story, Ketti Frings; screenplay, Charles Brackett and Billy Wilder;
art directors, Hans Dreier and Robert Usher; song, Fred Loesser,
Jimmy Berg, Fred Spielman, and Fred Jacobson; camera, Leo Tover;
editor, Doane Harrison.

       Charles Boyer (Georges Iscovescu); Olivia de Havilland (Emmy
Brown); Paulette Goddard (Anita Dixon); Victor Francen (Van Den
Luecken); Walter Abel (Inspector Hammock); Curt Bois (Bonbois);
Rosemary De Camp (Berta Kurz); Eric Feldary (Josef Kurz); Nestor
Paiva (Flores); Eva Puig (Lupita); Micheline Cheirel (Christine); Mad-
eleine LeBeau (Anni); Billy Lee (Tony); Mikhail Rasumny (Mechanic);
Mitchell Leisen (Mr. Saxon); Brian Donlevy and Richard Webb (Ac-
tors); Veronica Lake (Actress); Sonny Boy Williams (Sam); Edward
Fielding (American Consul); Don Douglas (Joe); Gertrude Astor (Young
Woman at Climax Bar); Carlos Villarias (Mexican Judge); Arthur Loft
(Hollander); Charles Arnt (Mr. MacAdams); Ella Neal (Bride); Ray
Mala (Young Mexican Bridegroom); June Wilkins (Miss Vivienne Wor-
thington); Leon Belasco (Mr. Spitzer); Chester Clute (Man at Climax
Bar).

European dancer/gigolo Georges Iscovescu (Charles Boyer) decides to come to America at the start of World War II, but he finds he cannot get into the U. S. because of immigration quotas. Stuck in a small Mexican border town he meets a former flame, Anita Dixon (Paulette Goddard), who advises him that if he marries an American he will be able to enter the country very easily. Soon he meets a naive young American schoolteacher named Emmy Brown (Olivia de Havilland). He woos her and they are soon wed.

The young bride returns home, and the gigolo prepares to move to the U. S. However, the girl returns and meets Goddard who tells her the truth about her husband's past and present. Nevertheless, de Havilland still testifies in her husband's behalf before the immigration authorities. Later she deserts him and is badly injured in an auto accident while returning to the States.

Despite a possible jail sentence, Boyer illegally crosses the border to be with his bride and provide her with the will to live. At the finale he is still domiciled in Mexico but the authorities agree to overlook his violation as his loyal wife announces she will wait for him to cross the border legally.

All of this high-class melodrama hardly sounds like a Hollywood-insider film except for the fact that the entire story is told by gigolo Boyer to director Mitchell Leisen (the actual director of Hold Back the Dawn) on a Paramount soundstage after Leisen has finished a scene with Veronica Lake, Brian Donlevy, and Richard Webb from I Wanted Wings (1941). Only the finale of the picture--with the bride awaiting her husband--is depicted after the gigolo finishes talking with the director.

As is revealed in the soundstage-within-the-soundstage scene, the reason Boyer's character comes to Leisen is he hopes his offbeat story is sufficiently interesting that Leisen's studio will purchase the screen rights. This belief depicted the concept held by most filmgoers: that a movie studio will grab at any story idea no matter what the source, and that the truth is stranger and more entertaining than fiction.

HOLLYWOOD (Paramount, 1923) 8100 ft.

Presenter, Jesse L. Lasky; director, James Cruze; story, Frank Condon; adaptor, Tom Geraghty; camera, Karl Brown.

Hope Drown (Angela Whitaker); Luke Cosgrave (Joel Whitaker); George K. Arthur (Lem Lefferts); Ruby Lafayette (Grandmother Whitaker); Harris Gordon (Dr. Luke Morrison); Bess Flowers (Hortense Towers); Eleanor Lawson (Margaret Whitaker); King Zany (Horace Pringle); Roscoe Arbuckle (Fat Man in Casting Director's Office); Gertrude Astor, Mary Astor, Agnes Ayres, Baby Peggy Montgomery, T. Roy Barnes, Noah Beery, William Boyd, Clarence Burton, Robert Cain, Edythe Chapman, Betty Compson, Ricardo Cortez, Viola Dana, Cecl B. DeMille, William De Mille, Charles De Roche, Dinky Dean, Helen Dunbar, Snitz Edwards, George Fawcett, Julia Fayne, James Finlayson, Alec B. Francis, Jack Gardner, Sid Grauman, Alfred E.

Green, Alan Hale, Lloyd Hamilton, Hope Hampton, William S. Hart, Gale Henry, Walter Hiers, Mrs. Walter Hiers, Stuart Holmes, Sigrid Holmquist, Jack Holt, Leatrice Joy, Mayme Kelso, J. Warren Kerrigan, Theodore Kosloff, Kosloff Dancers, Lila Lee, Lillian Leighton, Jacqueline Logan, May McAvoy, Robert McKim, Jeanie Macpherson, Hank Mann, Joe Martin, Thomas Meighan, Bull Montana, Owen Moore, Nita Naldi, Pola Negri, Anna Q. Nilsson, Charles Ogle, Guy Oliver, Kalla Pasha, Eileen Percy, Carmen Phillips, Jack Pickford, Chuck Reisner, Fritzi Ridgeway, Will Rogers, Sennett Girls, Ford Sterling, Anita Stewart, George Stewart, Gloria Swanson, Estelle Taylor, Ben Turpin, Bryant Washburn, Maude Wayne, Claire West, Laurence Wheat, and Lois Wilson (Guest Stars and Celebrities).

Hollywood is an amusing account of a young woman, Angela Whitaker (Hope Drown), who dreams of making it big in the movies, but who, despite all the chances anyone could reasonably ask for, never makes her fantasy come true.   This was one of the first American features to begin the fad of using dozens of cinema luminaries in cameos as themselves as a box-office gimmick.
   The tale concerned starry-eyed Drown, who arrives in Hollywood with her grandfather (Luke Cosgrave), the latter having traveled westward for his health.   In the film mecca she searches for employment and meets many stars who could help her but she inexplicably recognizes NONE of these celebrities.   Cosgrave, however, whose health improves on the West Coast, is discovered by William De Mille and he becomes a movie notable.   As if this is not enough to heighten Drown's chagrin, all of her family become movie successes when they move West--even her boyfriend (George K. Arthur).   After her marriage to him, their twins, and even the family parrott--get into the movies--but not Drown.
   Besides the brief on-camera appearances of an assortment of name players, the film boasted location filming at Pickfair (to include shots of Douglas Fairbanks and Mary Pickford).   Despite the fact the photoplay was a comedy it also included a certain amount of pathos and jabs at the coldness that existed toward those ostracized by the industry as a whole.   One scene has the heroine waiting in line at the Christie Studios to see if work is available and being given a place before the employment office window by a fat man.   After she leaves jobless, the rotund soul steps up for his turn and beholds a "closed" sign.   The man turns to depart and it is Roscoe "Fatty" Arbuckle who (in the post-scandal period of his life) could not get work as an actor in Hollywood.
   Photoplay magazine reported, "Dozens of the picture stars shown unconventionally to prove they are just humans after all.   A rattling good picture with lots of laughs and interest."

HOLLYWOOD AND VINE (Producers Releasing Corp. , 1945) 66 min.

   Director, Alexis Thurn-Taxis; story, Edith Watkins, Charles Williams, and Robert Wilmot; screenplay, Watkins and Williams; art director, George Van Marter; set decorator, Glenn T. Thompson;

Karin Lang, Leon Belasco, James Ellison, Wanda McKay, and Emmett Lynn in <u>Hollywood and Vine</u> (1945).

assistant director, Edward Davis; dialogue director, Watkins; sound, Ferol Redd; camera, Ira Morgan; editor, Donn Hayes.

James Ellison (Larry); Wanda McKay (Martha); June Clyde (Gloria); Ralph Morgan (B. B. Benton); Franklin Pangborn (Reggie); Leon Belasco (Cedric); Emmett Lynn (Pop); Vera Lewis (Fanny); Karin Lang (Ann); Robert Greig (Jenkins); Charlie Williams (Chick); Ray Whitley (Tex); Dewey Robinson (Mug); Cy Ring (Attorney Hudson); Grandon Rhodes (Attorney Wilson); Billy Benedict (Joe the Newsboy); Donald Kerr (Assistant Director); Lillian Bronson (Abigail); John Elliott (Judge); Jack Raymond (Gateman); Charles Jordan (Cop); Lou Crocker (Doctor); Hal Taggart (Casting Director).

Poverty row's Producers Releasing Corporation (PRC) was never noted for making even low-budget classic films. However, this modest B effort was not only effective, but it took particular pleasure in poking fun at the moguls who ran Hollywood's big studios. In an era when a film tycoon was all powerful and accepted no kidding, it required a small outfit like PRC to have the courage to produce such a self-deprecating satire as this one. <u>Variety</u> labeled it "a well produced comedy on an adult level...."

James Ellison headed the cast as Larry, a scriptwriter fresh from New York. Once in Hollywood he is assigned to write a film that will be a showcase for a dog under contract to the company. Ellison is befriended by a young hopeful, Martha (Wanda McKay), who thinks that he is really a sodajerk working for hamburger stand operator Pop (Emmett Lynn). The latter soon becomes rich in Hollywood real estate while studio head B. B. Benton (Ralph Morgan) shows more interest in keeping all his relatives on the payroll than in his actual productions. Also the picture pungently points up the fact that with enough publicity, anyone can become a film star, even a dog!

HOLLYWOOD BARN DANCE (Screen Guild, 1947) 72 min.

Producer, Jack Schwarz; director/story, B. B. Ray; adaptor/ screenplay, Dorothy Knox Martin; assistant director, Mack V. Wright; art director, Frank Paul Sylos; music, Walter Greene; sound, Ferel Redd; camera, Jack Greenhalgh; editor, Robert Crandall.

Ernest Tubb (Himself); Lori Talbott (Agent's Daughter); Helen Royce (Chaperone); Earle Hodgins (Agent); Frank McGlynn (Mr. Tubb); Dotti Hackett (Herself); Pat Combs (Ernest Tubb As a Boy); Jack Gutherie (Himself); and: Phil Arnold, Larry Reed, Red Herron, Anne Kunde, Betty Mudge, Cy Ring, Frank Bristow, and Albin Robeling.

This country-music film outing, billed as a Western-musical, uses the "Hollywood" title since much of its action is situated in movieland. It does not, however, concern film-making but instead treats the world of country music. Mainly this Screen Guild release is a musical revue which highlights the talents of Ernest Tubb and his Texas Troubadours, a group that had been quite successful in the recording field on Decca Records and who had supported Charles Starrett in his Westerns at Columbia Pictures.
The picture opens with Tubb as a musically-interested small boy on his father's farm. As he grows up, he forms a group and they practice at the local church. One day they accidentally burn down the house of worship so they go on the road to earn sufficient money to rebuild the structure. Along the way they get involved with a crooked promoter (Earle Hodgins) who has a pretty daughter (Lori Talbott) to whom Tubb (playing himself) is attracted. It turns out Talbott can also sing, as she proves in a show presented in Hollywood. From the proceeds, which Hodgins finally turns over to the performers, the boys return home and rebuild the country church.
Eighteen songs were employed in the film; 13 of them were sung by Tubb. The film also included a number of novelty acts from the country music circuit. The reviewer for Daily Variety noted that "Performances are very stilted and unconvincing when cast is not in the midst of song."

HOLLYWOOD BLUE (Sherpix, 1970) Color, 90 min.

Producer-director-camera, Bill Osco; editors, Mike Light and Howard Ziehm. With: Mickey Rooney and June Wilkinson; clips of: Arline Hunter, Hedy Lamarr, Fay Wray, Evelyn West, and Jayne Mansfield.

See THE HISTORY OF THE BLUE MOVIE

HOLLYWOOD BOULEVARD (Paramount, 1936) 75 min.

Producer, A. M. Botsford; director, Robert Florey; story, Faith Thomas; screenplay, Marguerite Roberts; music, Gregory Stone; art directors, Hans Dreier and Earl Hedrick; sound, Walter H. Oberst; camera, Karl Struss; editor, Harvey Johnston.

John Halliday (John Blakeford); Marsha Hunt (Patricia Blakeford); Robert Cummings (Jay Wallace); C. Henry Gordon (Jordan Winslow); Frieda Inescort (Alice Winslow); Esther Ralston (Flora Moore); Esther Dale (Martha); Betty Compson (Betty); Albert Conti (Sanford); Richard Powell (Moran); Rita La Roy (Nella); Oscar Apfel (Dr. Inslow); Purnell Pratt (Mr. Steinman); Irving Bacon (Gus the Bartender); Lois Kent (Little Girl); Gregory Gay (Russian Writer); Eleanore Whitney (Herself); Tom Kennedy (Bouncer); Francis X. Bushman (Director of Desert Scene); Maurice Costello (Director); Charles Ray (Charlie Smith the Assistant Director); Mae Marsh (Carlotta Blakeford); Herbert Rawlinson (Manager of Grauman's Chinese Theatre); Jane Novak (Mrs. Steinman); Kathryn "Kitty" McHugh (Secretary); Bryant Washburn (Robert Martin); William Desmond (Guest); Bert Roach (Scenarist); Mabel Forrest (Mother); Roy D'Arcy (The Sheik); Jack Mulhall, Creighton Hale, and Gary Cooper (Men at Bar); Harry Myers, and Frank Mayo (Themselves); Gertrude Simpson (Gossip); Jack Mower (Frank Stucky); Pat O'Malley (Dance Extra).

Fallen film star John Blakeford (John Halliday) is finished in pictures. As a result, his family has alienated themselves from him, except for daughter Patricia (Marsha Hunt). A money-minded and dishonest magazine publisher, however, sees interest in Halliday and offers him $25,000 for a serialization of his life story. The former star reluctantly accepts, but his narrative is altered to throw unflattering light on his family. After his daughter pleads with him, Halliday hastens to the publisher and begs that the serialization be stopped. The publisher refuses and further threatens to have Halliday removed from a comeback film he is making. A fight ensues between the two men and Halliday is killed. The crafty publisher places the blame on Hunt. Her fiancé (Robert Cummings), outwits the killer by playing back a dictaphone recording of the conversation that occurred just before Halliday was murdered.

Director Robert Florey made excellent use of the Paramount backlot in creating this B effort. It held a strong nostalgic flavor due to its wise use of many star names from the past. Florey also

induced pal Gary Cooper to perform a cameo as himself in a bar sequence, which further heightened the reality and the box-office take.
Although a minor effort, Hollywood Boulevard actually is the precursor of such films as Dancing in the Dark and Sunset Boulevard (qq. v.),
relating the torments of passé film stars in a fast-moving town that
used and casually discarded them.   That the story more than had its
roots in reality was proved by its supporting cast.

HOLLYWOOD BOULEVARD (New World, 1976) Color, 83 min.

        Producer, Jon Davison; associate producer, Terri Schwartz;
directors, Joe Dante and Allan Arkush; screenplay, Patrick Hobby;
music, Andrew Stein; costumes, Jane Rum; masks, Don Post Studios;
art director, Jack DeWolfe; sound, Bob Haddonfield; special effects,
Roger George; camera, Jamie Anderson; editors, Amy Jones, Arkush,
and Dante.

        Candice Rialson (Candy Wednesday); Mary Woronov (Mary Mc-
Queen); Rita George (Bobbi Quackenbush); Jeffrey Kramer (Patrick
Hobby); Dick Miller (Walter Paisley); Richard Doran (P. G.); Tara
Strohmeier (Jill McBain); Paul Bartel (Erich Von Leppe); John Kra-
mer (Duke Mantee); Jonathan Kaplan (Scotty); George Wagner (Cam-
eraman); W. L. Luckey (Rico Bandello); David Boyle (Obnoxious Kid);
Glen Shimada (Ubiquitous Filipino); Joe McBride (Drive-in Rapist);
Barbara Pieters (Drive-in Mother); Sean Pieters (Drive-in Kid); Sue
Veneer (Drive-in Dyke); Charles B. Griffith (Mark Dentine); Miller
Drake (Mutant); Roberta Dean and Milt Kahn (Reporters); Todd Mc-
Carthy (Author); Godzina (Herself); Commander Cody & The Lost
Planet Airmen (Themselves).

        Using the same title as Paramount's fondly-remembered B
film of the thirties, this crafty send-up of low-budget features (porno-
flicks, three-day-wonders, and so forth) billed itself as "a fast-and-
furious and slightly fantastic action comedy. " On the exploitation
market it had a brisk playoff; its future as a TV entry remains slim
because of the abundance of (senseless) violence.
        Miracle Pictures is on the bottom strata of poverty row.
Mary McQueen (Mary Woronov) is the star of its shoe-string productions while P. G. (Richard Doran) is the sex-maniac producer who
"tests" all the actresses for their roles.   Erich Von Leppe (Paul
Bartel) is their third-rate director and Patrick Hobby (Jeffrey Kramer) is the untalented scripter of the company.   Onto this unpromising
scene arrives Candy Wednesday (Candice Rialson), fresh from Indiana.
The naive young thing accidentally becomes involved in a real bank
heist and lands a part in a Miracle film as a stunt driver after she
eludes the law.
        Also on the scene arrives Bobbi Quackenbush (Rita George)
a roller derby queen, and she is teamed with Rialson and Woronov
for an on-location war movie in the Phillippines in which the trio
massacre 300 soldiers.   In the process, another starlet Jill McBain
(Tara Strohmeier) is shot.   The picture is previewed at a Los Angeles drive-in theatre where the projectionist nearly rapes Rialson.

Dick Miller and Robby the Robot (of Forbidden Planet fame) in Hollywood Boulevard (1976).

Next the actress trio star in a futuristic cop epic and George is murdered doing retakes in the middle of the night. Ready to leave Hollywood, Rialson discovers that Woronov is the insane killer. On the hillside overlooking Tinsel Town, Kramer and Rialson do battle with Woronov, who is killed when one of the huge letters spelling out "HOLLYWOOD" falls on the girl. Kramer then concocts a script about the event and it turns into a hit film; Rialson becomes a star sensation.

For anyone with an appreciation for low-budget movies of the fifties onward (especially by Roger Corman, whose New World Pictures released this effort), Hollywood Boulevard--1976 style--has its share of burlesque delights and amusing "in" jokes.

HOLLYWOOD CANTEEN (Warner Bros. , 1944) 124 min.

Producer, Alex Gottlieb; director/screenplay, Delmer Daves; music director, Leo F. Forbstein; music adaptor, Ray Heindorf; songs, E. Y. Harburg and Burton Lane; Ted Koehler and Lane; Harold Adamson and Vernon Duke; Koehler and M. K. Jerome; Marian Sunshine, Julio Blanco, and Obdulio Morales; Larry Neal and Jimmy Mundy; Bob Nolan; Ray Heindorf; Koehler, Heindorf, and Jerome; Jean Barry, Leah Worth, and Dick Charles; music numbers staged by LeRoy Prinz; art director, Leo Kuter; set decorator, Casey Rob-

Eddie Cantor serving soldier and Nora Martin in <u>Hollywood Canteen</u> (1944).

erts; assistant director, Art Lueker; makeup, Perc Westmore, Milo Anderson; sound, Oliver S. Garretson and Charles David Forrest; camera, Bert Glennon; editor, Christian Nyby.

Joan Leslie (Herself); Robert Hutton (Slim); Dane Clark (Sergeant); Janis Paige (Angela); The Andrews Sisters, Jack Benny, Joe E. Brown, Eddie Cantor, Kitty Carlisle, Jack Carson, Joan Crawford, Helmut Dantine, Bette Davis, Faye Emerson, Victor Francen, John Garfield, Sydney Greenstreet, Alan Hale, Paul Henreid, Andrea King, Peter Lorre, Ida Lupino, Irene Manning, Nora Martin, Joan McCracken, Dolores Moran, Dennis Morgan, Eleanor Parker, William Prince, Joyce Reynolds, John Ridgely, Roy Rogers & Trigger, S. Z. Sakall, Alexis Smith, Zachary Scott, Barbara Stanwyck, Craig Stevens, Joseph Szigeti, Donald Woods, Jane Wyman, Jimmy Dorsey & His Band, Carmen Cavallaro & His Orchestra, the Golden Gate Quartet, Rosario & Antonio, Sons of the Pioneers, Virginia Patton, Lynne Baggett, Betty Alexander, Julie Bishop, Robert Shayne, Johnny Mitchell, John Sheridan, Colleen Townsend, Angela Green, Paul Brooke, Marianne O'Brien, Dorothy Malone, Bill Kennedy, Mary Gordon, and Chef Joseph Milani (Themselves); Jonathan Hale (Mr. Brodel); Barbara Brown (Mrs. Brodel); Betty Brodel (Herself); Mark Stevens (Soldier on Deck); Rudolph Friml, Jr. (Orchestra Leader); George Turner (Tough Marine); Theodore Von Eltz (Director); Ray Teal (Captain); Eddie Marr (Dance Director).

Two soldiers, Slim (Robert Hutton) and Sergeant (Dane Clark), are on sick leave before returning to active duty in New Guinea during World War II. They choose to spend an evening at the Hollywood Canteen, an entertainment center for soldiers founded by Bette Davis and John Garfield and supervised by Hollywood personalities. (The real Canteen opened on October 17, 1942, at 1451 La Cahuenga, not far from Sunset Boulevard.) Hutton turns out to be the one-millionth G. I. to enter the Canteen; as a result he wins a date with Joan Leslie, while Clark has the opportunity to dance with Joan Crawford. Love quickly develops between Hutton and Leslie, and at the finale she promises to wait for him upon his return from the battle front.

Between the thick and contrived (many found it offensive) plotline, dozen of name stars (mostly Warner Bros. folk) appeared in the picture. Canteen President Davis and Vice-President Garfield provide a background of the Canteen's history. All of this is interspersed with a myriad of music and comedy ranging from the Andrews Sisters singing "Hollywood Canteen, " "Don't Fence Me In, " and "Corns for My Country, " to Jack Carson and Jane Wyman dueting "What Are You Doing the Rest of Your Life, " to Eddie Cantor and Nora Martin performing "We're Having a Baby. " There was Jimmy Dorsey and His Orchestra performing "One O'Clock Jump, " Carmen Cavallaro and His Orchestra playing "Voodoo Moon, " Kitty Carlisle singing "Sweet Dreams Sweetheart, " Roy Rogers and the Sons of the Pioneers rendering "Don't Fence Me In, " Dennis Morgan and Joe E. Brown in "You Can Always Tella Yank, " Joan McCracken dancing to "Ballet in Jive. " Perhaps the best of the routines was a comic violin duet of "The Bee" by Jack Benny and Joseph Szigeti.

Like the previous Thank Your Lucky Stars (q. v.), Hollywood Canteen was a rather insubstantial film offering. But it was entertaining; what better escapism than to see celebrities in allegedly candid moments doing things they supposedly did in everyday life? "Call the whole thing a great big scrambled vaudeville show with enough talent to have made a dozen fine movies" (New York Herald-Tribune).

In many respects Hollywood Canteen was an imitation of United Artists' Stage Door Canteen (1943) in which a soldier falls in love with the hostess of Broadway's answer to the West Coast Canteen. Despite the similarity of plots and the use of scads of V. I. P. s by both films, Hollywood Canteen turned out to be the (slightly) better of the two movies. More importantly it recorded Hollywood's efforts to entertain the soldiers in-the-flesh on the home front.

HOLLYWOOD CAVALCADE (20th Century-Fox, 1939) Color, 96 min.

Producer, Darryl F. Zanuck; associate producer, Harry Joe Brown; director, Irving Cummings; screen idea, Lou Breslow; story, Hilary Lynn and Brown Holmes; screenplay, Irving Pascal; color consultants, Natalie Kalmus and Henri Jaffa; silent picture sequences director, Malcolm St. Clair; silent picture sequences supervisor, Mack Sennett; art directors, Richard Day and Wiard B. Ihnen; set decorator, Thomas Little; music director, Louis Silvers; costumes, Herschel; sound, Eugene Grossman and Roger Heman; camera, Ernest Palmer and Allen M. Davey; editor, Walter Thompson.

Don Ameche, Chick Chandler, Alice Faye, Stuart Erwin, and Donald
Meek in Hollywood Cavalcade (1939).

Alice Faye (Molly Adair); Don Ameche (Michael Linnett Con-
nors); J. Edward Bromberg (Dave Spingold); Alan Curtis (Nicky Hay-
den); Stuart Erwin (Pete Tinney); Jed Prouty (Chief of Police); Buster
Keaton (Himself); Donald Meek (Lyle P. Stout); George Givot (Claude);
Eddie Collins, Hank Mann, Heinie Conklin, James Finlayson, and
Snub Pollard (Keystone Cops); Chick Chandler (Chick the Assistant
Director); Russell Hicks (Roberts); Willie Fung (Willie); Ben Turpin
(Bartender in Western Scene); Chester Conklin (Sheriff in Western
Scene); Al Jolson and Mack Sennett (Themselves); Robert Lowery
(Henry Potter); Ben Welden (Agent); Mary Forbes (Mrs. Gaynes); Ir-
ving Bacon (Bakery Clerk); Lee Duncan (Himself); Lynn Bari (Trixie
Farrell); Victor Potel and Marjorie Beebe (Bits).

The year 1939 is considered by many to be the apex season
of the American cinema.   Not only did some of the great classics of
the Hollywood screen (e. g. , Gone With the Wind, Stagecoach, and Of
Mice and Men) appear then, one of the finest tributes made by Hollywood to its past was issued also.   While Hollywood Cavalcade did
not adhere strictly to history, the feature contained a relatively accurate and--more importantly--loving account of the rise of the movie
industry from its fledgling flicker days to the debut of the talkies.

What is so surprising about the expensively-mounted color feature is that it was released at a time when there was relatively little interest in the movie industry's past.   Today it remains as fresh and original as when first issued four decades ago.

The inherent interest and continued popularity of the film can be attributed also to the fact that its characters are loosely based on dynamic real-life people.   Director Michael Linnett Connors (charmingly played by Don Ameche) is a blend of D. W. Griffith and Mack Sennett, while Alice Faye's Molly Adair is strongly reminiscent of Mabel Normand and Mary Pickford.   Of special interest to devout filmgoers, both in 1939 and today, is the casting of many old timers (Buster Keaton, Ben Turpin, Mack Sennett and Al Jolson among them) as themselves.

The narrative begins in 1913 when pals Michael Linnett Connors (Ameche) and Dave Spingold (J. Edward Bromberg) sign stage star Molly Adair (Faye) to a motion picture contract at $100 weekly. Her first film, a slapstick farce with Buster Keaton, is a sensation and together with the two film-makers she helps stimulate the growth of the fledgling industry.   Years pass and Faye falls in love with Ameche, who remains too busy to notice her strong affection.   She finally marries leading man Nicky Hayden (Alan Curtis).   Ameche later fires them both.   They sign with the Metro company and become the biggest attractions of the Roaring Twenties while Ameche's career fades into near oblivion.   While the husband-and-wife team are making Common Clay, the sound film comes into commercial reality.   Meanwhile Curtis is killed in a car crash and Faye is also injured.   The studio wants to shelve Common Clay.   Ameche, however, steals the negative and shoots sound sequences when Faye recovers.   The film, issued as a part-talkie, becomes an instant success.   Thus at the dawning of the talkie film era, Faye, Ameche, and Bromberg are reunited and look at their past with satisfaction and ahead to their future with anticipation.

Irving Cummings directed the bulk of Hollywood Cavalcade, but the early film-within-a-film slapstick portions were helmed by Malcolm St. Clair and supervised by Mack Sennett (who later appears in the feature as himself at a testimonial dinner for Molly and Nicky). Their expertise, along with Keaton as the costar of the slapstick portions, added the right touch for the recreation of the beginnings of the silent screen's action comedy.

HOLLYWOOD, CIUDAD DE ENSUEÑO (aka CITY OF ILLUSIONS)
    (Super-Joya-Hispano-Universal, 1934)

        Director, George Crane; story, José Bohr; screenplay, Miguel de Zarraga; supervisor, Bohr.

        With: José Bohr, Lia Tora, Donald Reed, Nancy Drexel, Enrique Acosta, Elena Landeros, and Cesar Vanoni.

        In this Spanish-language feature shot in Hollywood, a young man (José Bohr) from South America comes to California where he learns he bears a strong resemblance to film favorite Donald Reed.

The lovely head (Lia Tors) of a big movie company intervenes on the
man's behalf as he has been unable to get movie work due to his too-
familiar profile. She obtains a job for him with her studio and soon
finds herself falling in love with him. She later tries to woo him
away from pretty blonde actress Nancy Drexel and even learns Spanish in order to court him properly. But in the finale, she loses her
dream-love.

   This effort was churned out at a time when the major companies were making foreign-language films for various world markets.
The Spanish-language versions were good grossers not only in Spain
but also in Central and South America. This particular production is
a rather telling account of the thirties' Hollywood scene and its realistic ending heightened the effect of the story it unfolded. The picture was made in 1934, but did not receive much U. S. release (and
then only in large cities with a Spanish-speaking population) until after
the successful distribution of La Ciudad de Carton.

HOLLYWOOD COWBOY (aka WINGS OVER WYOMING) (RKO, 1937)
   65 min.

   Producer, George A. Hirliman; director, Ewing Scott; screenplay, Dan Jarrett and Scott; camera, Frank B. Wood.

   George O'Brien (Jeffrey Carson); Cecilia Parker (Joyce But-
ler); Maude Eburne (Violet Butler); Joe Caits (G. Gadsby Holmes);
Frank Milan (Westbrook Courtney); Charles Middleton (Doc Kramer);
Lee Shumway (Benson); Walter De Palma (Rolfe Metzger); Al Hill
(Camby); William Royle (Klinker); Al Herman (Steger); Frank Hagney
(Gillie); Dan Wolheim (Morey); Slim Balch (Slim); Sid Jordan (Mor-
gan); Lester Dorr (Joe Garvey); Harold Daniels (Hotel Clerk).

   Moving from extra work to stardom in The Iron Horse (Fox,
1925), George O'Brien became one of Fox Studio's top stars of the
twenties and he always excelled in athletic, rugged roles. With the
coming of sound, he began a series of high-grade B Westerns for
the studio. As the thirties progressed his films were still issued
by Fox, but produced by Sol Lesser's independent low-budget unit.
In 1936, however, O'Brien left both Lesser and Fox and switched to
working for producer George Hirliman who issued his films through
RKO. The standard which the actor had set in his earlier screen
work continued. Hollywood Cowboy was the second of the new series,
the first being the excellent historical drama, Daniel Boone (1936).

   In Hollywood Cowboy, O'Brien was cast as Western film star
Jeffrey Carson who longs for a rest. With a writer friend suffering
from eternal indigestion, he leaves Tinsel Town and resettles in a
small town under an assumed name. There he begins to romance
the daughter (Cecilia Parker) of a rich rancher and soon becomes
aware that the local ranchers are being cheated by a cattlemen's protective association. The latter has been diverting some of the live-
stock shipments, causing cattle to stampede with the use of planes,
and creating unrest among the ranch hands over wages. Finally
O'Brien delves to the crux of the situation. He breaks up the crooked

alliance and wins the heart of Parker--all before his true identity is discovered.

O'Brien's Westerns often appealed to adults as well as to youngsters; he always kept a high level of production values, story-line, and acting in his movies.   Often, as in this entry, he employed both comedy and romance, two factors that did not show up very much in series B Westerns, where the small fans preferred action above everything.

HOLLYWOOD COWBOY [1975] see HEARTS OF THE WEST

HOLLYWOOD DAREDEVILS see THE SHORT FILMS

HOLLYWOOD EXTRA GIRL see THE SHORT FILMS

A HOLLYWOOD HERO see THE SHORT FILMS

HOLLYWOOD HOODLUM (aka HOLLYWOOD MYSTERY) (Regal, 1934)
    53 min.

        Director, Reaves Eason; story, William Bloecher; screenplay, John Thomas Neville; art director, Paul Palmentola; sound, Terry Kellum; camera, Ernest Miller; editor, Jeanne Spencer.

        June Clyde (Doris Dawn); Frank Albertson (Dan Ryan); Jose Crespo (Tony Capello); Tenen Holtz (Benjamin Vogel); John Davidson (Siegfried Sonoff); Stanley Price (Romano); Cyril Ring (Duke); Edith Terry Preuss (Mabel).

        Just as he would in Fugitives for a Night (q. v.), Frank Al-bertson plays here a publicity specialist who becomes involved in a murder caper.

        Dan Ryan (Albertson) is fired from the studio just as he plans a buildup for Doris Dawn (June Clyde), who happens to be his girl-friend.   The only way Albertson can be reinstated on the lot is if he finds a way to maneuver high-priced, temperamental foreign dir-ector Benjamin Vogel (Tenen Holtz) off the lot.   Albertson's scheme is to plant a fake villain (Jose Crespo) to be selected for Holtz' up-coming gangster yarn and start confusion on the set.

        "Something might have been made of this idea, but stilted writing and poor casting put this one out of the running.   Wise Holly-wood press agents are a bit stale and here another one has to carry all the weight" (Variety).

HOLLYWOOD HORROR HOUSE (aka THE COMEBACK) (Avco Embassy
    1975) Color, 90 min.

        Producer, Donald H. Wolfe; associate producer, Ann May; director/screenplay, Wolfe; music, Stu Phillips; production designer, Norm Houle; assistant director, Don May; makeup, Lou Lane; wardrobe, Ruth Foster; Miss Hopkins' gowns by Treva; sound, Rod Sutton and Jim Contreras; camera, John A. Morrill; editor, Hartwig Deeb.

Miriam Hopkins (Katharine Packard); John David Garfield (Vic Valence); Gale Sondergaard (Leslie); Virginia Wing (Greta); Florence Lake (Mildred); Lester Mathews (Ira Jaffe); Riza Royce (Mrs. Jaffe); Joe Besser (Movie Tour Busdriver); Minta Durfee (Dinner Party Guest).

A series of killings baffle police in the region of the Hollywood Hills where former movie star Katharine Packard (Miriam Hopkins), now a reclusive alcoholic, lives in her mansion under the domination of her private secretary Leslie (Gale Sondergaard). The latter hires a young man, Vic Valence (John David Garfield), to be the ex-star's male nurse, but soon Hopkins is having an affair with him. He soon turns her against Sondergaard and takes charge of her business. When a young housemaid is later murdered, Sondergaard begins to suspect that Garfield may be the killer the police are seeking. She further fears that he may have already murdered Hopkins. Eventually she discovers the truth, but not before the insane killer turns the house into a mansion of death.

This minor-league mystery--coming very late in the What Ever Happened to Baby Jane? (q. v.), cycle--has a most interesting history. It was shot on the cheap in 1972 as The Comeback but not issued. Its star, Miriam Hopkins, died in 1973, and the film lay dormant until 1975 when Avco Embassy gave the color shocker a brief theatrical release. The following year, New Line Cinema reissued the picture as A Maniac Is Loose.

For Hopkins, this outing provided her with the meatiest film assignment she had enjoyed in years. Her interaction with Sondergaard reminded many of the screen chemistry that existed between Hopkins and Bette Davis in their two famous Warner Bros. excursions, The Old Maid (1939) and Old Acquaintances (1943). Since the picture was made, two other cast members have died: Lester Mathews and Minta Durfee. The latter was a one-time Mack Sennett star and was once wed to Roscoe "Fatty" Arbuckle. John David Garfield is the son of the late Warner Bros. star, John Garfield.

HOLLYWOOD HOTEL (Warner Bros. , 1938) 109 min.

Producer, Hal B. Wallis; associate producer, Sam Bischoff; director, Busby Berkeley; story, Jerry Wald and Maurice Leo; screenplay, Wald, Leo, and Richard Macaulay; dialogue director, Gene Lewis; art director, Robert Haas; songs, Richard Whiting and Johnny Mercer; orchestrator, Ray Heindorf; music director, Leo F. Forbstein; camera, Charles Rosher and George Barnes.

Dick Powell (Henry Bowers); Rosemary Lane (Virginia Stanton); Lola Lane (Mona Marshall); Hugh Herbert (Chester Marshall); Ted Healy (Fuzzy); Glenda Farrell (Jonesey); Johnnie Davis (Georgia); Frances Langford (Alice); Benny Goodman & His Orchestra, Louella

Benny Goodman, Frances Langford, Johnnie Davis, Dick Powell, and
Ted Healy in Hollywood Hotel (1938).

Parsons, Ken Niles, Jerry Cooper, Duane Thompson, Raymond Paige
& His Orchestra (Themselves); Alan Mowbray (Alexander Dupre);
Mabel Todd (Dot Marshall); Allyn Joslyn (Bernie Walton); Grant Mitch-
ell (B. K. Faulken); Edgar Kennedy (Callaghan); Fritz Feld (The Rus-
sian); Curt Bois (Dress Designer); Eddie Acuff (Cameraman); Sarah
Edwards (Mrs. Marshall); William B. Davidson (Director Melton);
Wally Maher (Drew the Assistant Director); Clinton Rosemond and
Pearl Adams (Black Couple); Ronald Reagan (Master of Ceremonies);
Susan Hayward (Starlet at Table).

Hollywood Hotel was the eleventh and last teaming of director
Busby Berkeley and crooner Dick Powell. The idea and title for the
feature derived from the popular radio program of the same name
with Louella O. Parsons, who briefly appeared in the film as herself. Richard Whiting and Johnny Mercer wrote "Hooray for Hollywood" (which has become a standard). Of special interest to music
buffs are production numbers by Benny Goodman and his Orchestra;
at the time he was the most popular musician in the U.S.
      The film, which was dated even at the time of its release,
unfolds the story of Henry Bowers (Powell), a saxophonist with the
Goodman band, who wins a talent contest and a contract with All Star
Pictures. He is assigned to accompany nasty star Mona Marshall
(Lola Lane) to a premiere but he ends up escorting and falling in

love with her twin sister and stand-in Virginia (Rosemary Lane).
When Lola Lane finds out, she has Powell fired and he ends up working in a drive-in restaurant where a producer hears him singing on
the job.   Powell is then hired to dub a non-talent ham in a Civil War
film which also stars Lola Lane.   The dubbing is so good that Powell
is asked by Louella Parsons to appear on her radio show.   He de-
clines, but Rosemary Lane works to get him on the show, where he
is a big success.
     Except for the Goodman musical interludes, Hollywood Hotel
is stilted.   It is obvious from this picture that both Berkeley and
Powell had long since lost their interest in screen musicals of this
type.   The storyline did manage to poke some fun at hammy and no-
talent performers, a commodity all too prevalent in the film-making
of any decade.

THE HOLLYWOOD KID   see   THE SHORT FILMS

HOLLYWOOD MYSTERY   see   HOLLYWOOD HOODLUM

HOLLYWOOD ON PARADE   see   THE SHORT FILMS

HOLLYWOOD ON TRIAL (October Films, 1976) 100 min.

     Producer, James C. Gutman; director, David Helpern, Jr.;
screenplay, Arnie Reisman; camera, Barry Abrams.

     John Huston (narrator); with: Dalton Trumbo, Alvah Bessie,
Edward Dmytryk, Albert Maltz, Gale Sondergaard, Zero Mostel,
Martin Ritt, and Ring Lardner, Jr.

     This documentary attempted to relate the account of the black-
listing of the famous Hollywood Ten after members of the group refused to testify before the House UnAmerican Activities Committee
(HUAC).   There is little doubt from those involved (John Huston, for
example, is the narrator) that the film favors the stand taken by the
"Unfriendly Ten. "   Since all the events discussed here happened 25
years ago (or earlier), it is unlikely that this effort or any other
dealing with the group's eventual vindication, will have much influence
with the general public other than causing minor interest as to which
individuals were once actually blacklisted.   (The entire section of
The Way We Were (q. v.), dealing with the blacklisting of people in
Hollywood, proved to be the least effective to present-day audiences,
who for the most part could not understand or care what all the
characters--Viveca Lindfors, Barbra Streisand, e. g. --were shouting
about.)
     Hollywood on Trial   employs its first twenty minutes to delve
into the social conditions of the thirties and forties which spawned
leftist leanings in the entertainment industry and elsewhere.   Then
footage of the actual HUAC hearings is interpolated with shots of
those pertinently involved in the proceedings (including the late script-

er Dalton Trumbo, director Edward Dmytryk, and actress Gale Sondergaard). Also interviewed are director Martin Ritt and actor Zero
Mostel, both of whom were photographed while on location with The
Front (1976), Woody Allen sombre comedy dealing with blacklisting
mainly in the TV industry of the day. Hollywood on Trial makes
the point that the "Unfriendly Ten" took the Fifth Amendment rather
than testify because they believed the Supreme Court would overturn
their convictions. Such did not occur and some of the individuals
went to jail.

Critic Arthur Knight perceptively noted in the Hollywood Reporter, "What is so disturbing about this film ... is that the same
kind of picture could be made--maybe 20 years from now--about Ehr-
lichman, Haldeman, Mitchell and company. Hollywood On Trial is
laudable for what it shows, culpable for what it doesn't. This same
criticism might well be leveled--maybe 20 years from now--against
a venturesome 'Watergate on Trial'. "

HOLLYWOOD OR BUST (Paramount, 1956) Color, 95 min.

Producer, Hal B. Wallis; associate producer, Paul Nathan;
director, Frank Tashlin; based on the story "Beginner's Luck" by
Erna Lazarus; screenplay, Lazarus; assistant director, James Rosen-
berger; costumes, Edith Head; music numbers created and staged by
Charles O'Curran; new songs, Sammy Fain and Paul Francis Webster;
art directors, Hal Pereira and Henry Bumstead; camera, Daniel
Fapp; editor, Howard Smith.

Dean Martin (Steve Wiley); Jerry Lewis (Malcolm Smith);
Anita Ekberg (Herself); Pat Crowley (Terry); Maxie Rosenbloom
(Bookie Benny); Willard Waterman (Neville the Manager); Jack Mc-
Elroy (Stupid Man); Mike Ross (Guard); Wendell Niles (Master of
Ceremonies); Frank Wilcox (Director); Kathryn Card (Old Lady);
Richard Karlan (Sammy Ross); Tracey Roberts (Redhead); Ben Welden
(Boss); Rose Westlake (Sheep Woman); Gretchen Houser (Specialty
Dancer); Sandra White, Adele August, and Valerie Allen (Girls).

Hollywood or Bust proved to be the 17th and final film pairing
of comic Jerry Lewis and crooner Dean Martin. It was hardly an
auspicious finale to their teaming. Yet it was a pleasant comedy in
which both stars were roundly upstaged by a huge Great Dane who
stole every piece of footage in which he trotted. This entry also
provided Lewis with his first on-camera opportunity to single-handed-
ly destroy the Paramount studios, which he would do again in The
Errand Boy (q. v.).

Movie fan extraordinaire Malcolm Smith (Lewis) has more enthusiasm than intellect. He has a great yen to meet his idol Anita
Ekberg. Gambler Steve Wiley (Martin) needs to vacate New York
City before some unpleasant bookies locate him. As luck would have
it, the bizarre duo win a bright red convertible and begin a cross-
country trip at the George Washington Bridge, accompanied by Lewis'
pet dog, Mr. Bascomb.

Along the way they pick up Terry (Pat Crowley) a lovely traveling companion who yearns to be a Las Vegas showgirl. In the gambling capitol Martin wins $10,000 which supplies the trio with funds to reach California. Once in Hollywood, it is Mr. Bascomb who is the show business success as he is immediately signed by Paramount which Jerry nearly crumbles in his search for statuesque Miss Ekberg. When they finally meet it is love at first sight--not for Jerry and Anita, but for Mr. Bascomb and the star's pet poodle.

HOLLYWOOD PARTY (MGM, 1934) 68 min. [color sequence]

Directors Roy Rowland and Richard Boleslawski; story/screenplay, Howard Dietz and Arthur Kober; songs, Gus Kahn and Walter Donaldson; Dietz and Donaldson; Arthur Freed and Nacio Herb Brown; cartoon sequence, Walt Disney Productions; camera, James Wong Howe; editor, George Boemler.

Jimmy Durante (Jimmy [Schnarzan the Ape Man]); Lupe Velez (Lupe); Laurel and Hardy (Themselves); Polly Moran (Henrietta); Jack Pearl (Baron Munchausen); George Givot (Liondora); Eddie Quillan (Bob); June Clyde (Linda); Ben Bard (Sharley); Richard Carle (Knapp); Tom Kennedy (Beavers); Frances Williams, Charles Butterworth, Mickey Mouse, and Ted Healy (Specialties); Arthur Jarrett (Singer); Shirley Ross Quartet, Harry Barris, the Three Stooges, Robert Young (Themselves); Jed Prouty (Theatre Manager); Arthur Treacher (Butler).

Jungle film star Schnarzan (Jimmy Durante) is told by his manager that his pictures are slipping in popularity because his lions are anemic. He then hires explorer Baron Munchausen (Jack Pearl) to go to Africa to corral new lions but these beasts are also sought by rival jungle star Liondora (George Givot). Durante throws a big party for the Baron and most of Hollywood's elite make an appearance. The real owners of the lions, however, arrive and accidentally allow one of the animals to escape, causing a stampede among the guests. A rich Oklahoman then purchases the lions and sells them to Givot. But when his wife is promised the lead in Durante's next film, the Oklahoman is forced to return the lions to Durante.

Hollywood Party had been conceived in 1933 and it was to star the biggest names on the MGM lot, including Marie Dressler, Jean Harlow, and Joan Crawford. When the film was finally issued it had little to offer and was so bad that no director would take credit for it. Jimmy Durante made a most tiring burlesque Tarzan and only scenes with Lupe Velez (wed to real Tarzan actor, Johnny Weissmuller) had any zest. The best scene comes at the film's end, when the lions' owners, Laurel and Hardy, appear and wage an egg fight with Velez.

The Technicolor animated footage made for the feature by Walt Disney no longer exists, but the Laurel and Hardy scenes were later used in the Robert Youngson compilation, M-G-M's Big Parade of Comedy (1964). Their material from Hollywood Party was also

reworked into a starring film for the comedy duo, 20th Century-Fox's The Bullfighters (1945).

After the film was completed, Allan Dwan was called in to see if he could patch it together. It was his idea to have Durante dream the whole affair while waiting for his wife to dress. Dwan shot a few extra scenes for this sequence and the film was tacked together and hurriedly released (and forgotten). As expected, it was a lamentable box-office bomb.

HOLLYWOOD REVUE OF 1929 (MGM, 1929) 116 min.   (color sequences)

   Producer, Harry Rapf; director, Charles Reisner; skit, Joe Farnham; dialogue, Al Boasberg and Robert E. Hopkins; art direc-tors, Cedric Gibbons and Richard Day; choreography, Sammy Lee and George Cunningham; assistant directors, Jack Cummings, Sandy Roth, and Al Shenberg; costumes, David Cox, Henrietta Frazer, and Joe Rapf; music arrangers, Arthur Lange, Ernest Klapholtz, and Ray Heindorf; songs, Arthur Freed and Nacio Herb Brown; Raymond Klages and Jesse Greer; Andy Rice and Martin Broones; Joe Trent and Louis Alter; Fred Fisher; Joe Goodwin and Gus Edwards; sound, Douglas Shearer; camera, John Arnold, Irving Ries, Maxmililan Fabian, and John M. Nicholaus; editors, William S. Gray and Cameron K. Wood.

   Conrad Nagel and Jack Benny (Masters of Ceremonies); and: John Gilbert, Norma Shearer, Joan Crawford, Bessie Love, Lionel Barrymore, Cliff Edwards, Stan Laurel, Oliver Hardy, Anita Page, Nils Asther, The Brox Sisters, Natacha Natova and Company, Marion Davies, William Haines, Buster Keaton, Marie Dressler, Charles King, Polly Moran, Gus Edwards, Karl Dane, George K. Arthur, Ann Dvorak, Gwen Lee, Albertina Rasch Ballet, The Rounders, The Biltmore Quartet, Angela, Claudine and Claudette Mawby, Beth Laem-mle, Myrtle McLaughlin, Nacio Herb Brown, and Ernest Belcher's Dancing Tots (Themselves).

   When full sound came to films, all the major studios jumped on the bandwagon with all-star revues which provided plenty of stars (with a chance to try their skills at talkies), but little true enter-tainment. One of the most empty and surprisingly dull of the lot was MGM's Hollywood Revue. It sported a huge galaxy of the studio's stars, most of whom were cast into parts they were not capable of filling. Outside of hosts Conrad Nagel and Jack Benny and the de-lightful appearance of Stan Laurel and Oliver Hardy in a very funny segment (in which they play bungling magicians), the film was dull going.

   There was John Gilbert and Norma Shearer performing the balcony scene from Romeo and Juliet, both as the Bard had written it, and in a slangy send-up. (After finishing the Shakespearean scene,

Opposite: Lupe Velez with Oliver Hardy and Stan Laurel in Hollywood Party (1934).

the camera pulls back to show Lionel Barrymore directing the scene
as a movie and there is a minute or two of the trio discussing the
sequence.) As would be demonstrated when the clip was utilized for
That's Entertainment! (q. v.), Joan Crawford's singing and dancing
to "Gotta Feelin' for You" displayed more enthusiasm than skill.
Camera magic allowed Bessie Love to pop out of Jack Benny's pocket
in miniature and with a chorus sing "I Could Never Do a Thing Like
That. " Marie Dressler and Polly Moran were amusing--in spots--in
the rendition of "For I'm the Queen, " while Buster Keaton had little
screen opportunity with his "The Dance of the Sea" act. Throughout
the 116 minutes, there was a good deal (too much, in fact) of "singing"
often by those not really equipped for it. One rousing number was
Cliff Edwards' reprise-production number of "Singin' in the Rain. "
The film concluded with a Technicolor finale segment of Charles King
singing "Orange Blossom Time" and another offering of the principals
harmonizing to "Singin' in the Rain. "
    If one regards this film (which was nominated for a Best Pic-
ture Oscar) as a commercial screen test for a huge group of name
celebrities, then the film has historical value.

HOLLYWOOD ROUND UP (Columbia, 1937) 63 min.

    Producer, L. G. Leonard; director, Ewing Scott; screenplay,
Joseph Hoffman and Monroe Shaff; assistant director, Harve Foster;
art director, F. Paul Sylos; dialogue director, Ethel LaBlanche;
music supervisor, Morris Stoloff; sound, Thomas A. Carman; camera, Allen G. Thompson; editor, Robert Crandall.

    Buck Jones (Buck Kennedy); Helen Twelvetrees (Carol Stephens);
Grant Withers (Grant Drexel); Shemp Howard (Oscar); Dickie Jones
(Dickie Stephens); Eddie Kane (Henry Westcott); Monty Collins (Fred-
die Foster); Warren Jackson (Perry King); Lester Dorr (Louis Law-
son); Lee Shumway (Carl Dunning); Edward Keane (Lew Wallach);
George Beranger (Hotel Clerk).

    "Hollywood's Hardest Ridin' ... Toughest Fightin' ... Warmest
Lovin' Buckaroo!" So read the ad for this Columbia release.
    After the success of The Thrill Hunter (q. v.), which found him
as a fast-talking cowpoke transformed into a cowboy star, Buck Jones
returned to the light-hearted kidding of the movie industry in Hollywood Round Up. The Hollywood motif was an added plus for the film.
Unlike The Thrill Hunter, in which Jones was cast as a kindly
but over-talkative hero, he is true blue in this one. As stuntman
Buck Kennedy he earns the admiration of star Carol Stephens (Helen
Twelvetrees) and is a hero to her small brother Dickie (Dickie Jones)
as well as the friend of all those working on the movie set. His one
enemy is movie lead Grant Drexel (Grant Withers), for whom he

---

Opposite: Jack Benny, Karl Dane, George K. Arthur, and Ann Dvorak
(middle row, third from right) in Hollywood Review of 1929.

doubles.   Withers resents Jones' athletic ability and popularity, especially with Twelvetrees who has spurned Withers.

While on location in Cornville, Jones and Withers have a fight
and the director, against his better judgment, fires Buck.   The latter
then finds a job with another movie company on location in that town,
but that outfit turns out to be bank robbers pretending to make a
film while they actually rob the local bank.   Jones ends up as their
fall guy and as a result of the robbery he is put in jail.

Dickie Jones learns that the gangsters are hiding out at Echo
Canyon and he helps Buck to escape.   Dickie follows Jones who sees
the gangsters about to take off in a plane.   He ropes the craft and
prevents their escape.   Meanwhile Dickie is filming the action with
a movie camera his sister had given him, but accidentally he gets
in the way of the plane and is hurt.   Jones comes to the youth's aid
just as Withers arrives with a posse which rounds up the outlaws.
Withers takes credit for the capture.   However, back in Hollywood
at a dinner for Withers' heroism, Dickie shows the film he took,
proving Buck the real hero.

The New York Daily News noted in its two-star review, "Some
of the early scenes hold an imaginary mirror up to a Western star
at such an acute angle that his vanities and foibles are cruelly exposed to public view, without benefit of spiritual make-up. "

Three years later Gene Autry would appear in Shooting High
(q. v.)--very similar to this entry.   Therein Autry would be the nice
guy stuntman for snob action star Robert Lowery.   Unfortunately
Autry possessed none of Jones' ability to handle such an action role,
especially when it came to performing stunt feats.

HOLLYWOOD SCOUT   see   THE SHORT FILMS

HOLLYWOOD SCREEN TEST   see   THE SHORT FILMS

HOLLYWOOD SPEAKS (Columbia, 1932) 72 min.

Director, Eddie Buzzell; story, Norman Krasna; screenplay,
Krasna and Jo Swerling; sound, Edward Bernds; camera, Ted Tetzalff;
editor, Gene Havlick.

Genevieve Tobin (Gertrude Smith); Pat O'Brien (Jimmie Reed);
Lucien Prival (Frederick Landau); Ralf Harolde (Carp); Rita La Roy
(Millie Coreen); Leni Stengel (Mrs. Landau); Anderson Lawler (Joe
Hammond).

A young woman, Gertrude Smith (Genevieve Tobin), watches
the excitement of a premiere at Hollywood's Chinese Theatre and
then places her feet in the various famous cement prints there.   Depressed, she is about to take poison in the lobby but is stopped by
newspaperman Jimmy Reed (Pat O'Brien), who agrees to help her in
her quest for film stardom.

The would-be actress creates for herself the new name of

Pat O'Brien and Genevieve Tobin in Hollywood Speaks (1932).

Greta Swan, and O'Brien introduces her to the right industry people. She meets the famous director Frederick Landau (Lucien Prival), a philanderer, and she wants to work in one of his prestigious productions. A subordinate director wins her a screen test and then takes her to a party hosted by Prival. There O'Brien saves her from the director's too-constant attentions.

Nevertheless, Tobin wins a role in Prival's upcoming picture and when it is released, she is acclaimed a success. Later the filmmaker's wife (Leni Stengel) commits suicide and in a note found by the authorities she blames Tobin for her actions. Gangsters move in and attempt to blackmail Tobin. The scandal is aired in the press and it ruins her promising career. O'Brien proclaims his continuing love for her and they wed. Now Tobin puts her struggles for success in Hollywood behind her.

Mordaunt Hall observed for New York Times readers, "There are some interesting sidelights on life in the film capital in Hollywood Speaks.... What the picture needs is a stronger and less melodramatic story, for the natures of the characters are well defined." It is interesting to ponder how such a storyline would be handled today, when for many women marriage is not the right alternative/substitute for a career gone wrong.

A HOLLYWOOD STAR see THE SHORT FILMS

HOLLYWOOD STORY (Universal, 1951) 77 min.

Producer, Leonard Goldstein; associate producer, Billy Grady, Jr.; director, William Castle; story/screenplay, Frederick Kohner and Fred Brady; art directors, Bernard Herzbrun and Richard H. Riedel; set decorators, Russell A. Gausman and Julia Heron; music director, Joseph Gershenson; gowns, Rosemary O'Dell; camera, Carl Guthrie; editor, Virgil Vogel.

Richard Conte (Larry O'Brien); Julia Adams (Sally Rousseau); Richard Egan (Lieutenant Lennox); Henry Hull (Vincent St. Clair); Fred Clark (Sam Collyer); Jim Backus (Mitch Davis); Houseley Stevenson (Mr. Miller); Paul Cavanagh (Roland Paul); Katherine Meskill (Mary); Louis Lettieri (Jimmy); Joel McCrea, Richard Neill, "Baby" Marie Osborne, William Farnum, Betty Blythe, Francis X. Bushman, Helen Gibson, Cleo Ridgely, Elmo Lincoln, Dorothy Vernon, Spec O'Donnell, Arline Pretty, Stuart Holmes, and Babe Kane (Guest Bits).

A young producer (Richard Conte) arrives in Hollywood intent on making an independent film and rents space at an old studio facility which has not been used since the advent of sound. It was here that director Franklin Ferrara was murdered in 1929 and the young producer becomes intrigued with the case. Against the advice of others, he begins a script based on the unsolved crime.

A girl (Julia Adams), the daughter of a silent film actress who was Ferrara's lover, tries to stop the project, but Conte proceeds and uncovers the late director's scriptwriter (Henry Hull) living in poverty in a beach shack. He hires the man to write a scenario about Ferrara and he soon discovers that his financial backer (Fred Clark) was once Ferrara's business manager. He also uncovers faded actor Roland Paul (Paul Cavanagh), now a bit player, who was the secret husband of Ferrara's mistress. Finally Conte uncovers a long-kept secret which solves the 25-year-old murder caper.

Director William Castle did the best he could to capture the ambiance of Hollywood. He did location shooting in downtown Hollywood, at the Motion Picture Country House, the Hollywood Roosevelt Hotel, and at the Universal studio itself. Further, Castle rounded up old-time favorites such as Francis X. Bushman, Helen Gibson, Betty Blythe, William Farnum, and Elmo Lincoln for walk-on appearances, as well as a cameo by Joel McCrea. However, Castle could not surmount the hackneyed script, which had its hazy origins in the William Desmond Taylor murder case of the twenties. There was some effective acting work, especially from Julia Adams as both the silent star and her daughter.

Richard Conte and Richard Egan in Hollywood Story (1951).

HOLLYWOOD THRILL-MAKERS (Lippert, 1954) 59 min.

Producer, Maurice Kosloff; director/story, Bernard Ray; screenplay, Janet Clark; music director, Michael Terr; music, Gene Garf; camera, Elmer Dyer; editor, Robert Jahns.

James Gleason (Risky Russell); Bill Henry (Dave Wilson); Theila Darin (Marion Russell); Joan Holcombe (Jean Cummings); James Macklin (Bill Cummings).

Movies dealing with stuntmen have been on-and-off affairs, ranging from The Goat in 1918 to The Great Waldo Pepper in 1975 (qq. v.). Several films like Lucky Devils (q. v.) have been superior, but most have been only run-of-the-mill, like Fade-In (1969), starring Burt Reynolds. Perhaps none attained the rock-bottom stature of Hollywood Thrill-Makers, a cheap production which used quarter-century-old stock footage of Richard Talmadge to beef up its spotty action. Around these "borrowed" stunts was strung a plot that was "a hashed-up affair which holds little interest" (Variety).

The frail story revolved around stuntman Dave Wilson (Bill Henry), who makes a living doing hazardous stunts for action movies. He marries Marion Russell (Theila Darin), the daughter of old-time stunter Risky Russell (James Gleason).   After being injured in an airplane accident and upon the constant urging of his wife, Henry retires.   Later a close stuntman buddy, Bill Cummings (James Macklin), is goaded into a dangerous stunt by a tyrannical director and as a result he is killed.   In order to earn $5000 for Macklin's widow, Henry agrees to carry out the stunt in his buddy's plane.   He succeeds, and then retires from the profession for good.

Running less than an hour, Hollywood Thrill-Makers contains all the plot ingredients long used in this brand of film: good buddies working together, worried wives, and of course, overdemanding directors who care more for their films than the personnel.

HOME MADE MOVIES   see   THE SHORT FILMS

HONOLULU (MGM, 1939) 83 min.

Producer, Jack Cummings; director, Edward Buzzell; story/screenplay, Herbert Fields and Frank Partos; art director, Cedric Gibbons; songs, Gus Kahn and Harry Warren; camera, Ray June; editor, Conrad Nervig.

Eleanor Powell (Dorothy March); George Burns (Joe Duffy); Gracie Allen (Millie DeGrasse); Robert Young (Brooks Mason/George Smith); Rita Johnson (Cecelia Grayson); Clarence Kolb (Mr. Grayson); Willie Fung (Wong); Ruth Hussey (Gale Brewster); Cliff Clark (Carter); Edward Gargan (Burton); Eddie "Rochester" Anderson (Washington); Hal K. Dawson (Wally); Edgar Dearing (Jailer); Jo Ann Sayers (Vera); Sig Rumann (Professor Timmer); Mary Treen (Gwen); Tom Neal (Interne); Edward Earle, Bess Flowers, and Bert Roach (Guests).

Screen star Brooks Mason (Robert Young) becomes tired of all the adulation from his legion of fans and longs for a more quiet and secluded life.   He finds out that he has a look-alike in George Smith (also played by Young), an Hawaiian pineapple farmer.   He convinces the man to exchange places with him for a time.   Brooks sneaks away to Hawaii to tend the pineapple plantation while the farmer remains in the continental U. S. making a personal appearance tour in the star's stead.   On the ship to Hawaii, Brooks meets dancer Dorothy March (Eleanor Powell) whom he saves from an unhappy romance in Hawaii.

This bit of screen trifle did provide Robert Young an occasion to play amusing dual roles, but the black-and-white feature was mainly an MGM vehicle for ace studio dancer Eleanor Powell who performed an extravagant hula.   For comedy relief there was George Burns and Gracie Allen in their final joint screen appearance; Burns did not make another picture until 1975 (The Sunshine Boys).   The versatile Miss Allen not only provided her usual ration of droll double talk, but she danced in tandem with Powell (proving no slouch in the hoofing department) and even vocalized a bit.

Perhaps the most interesting part of the film, and its look at the film industry, came in its peculiar foreword, which read, "The motion picture studios and all personalities herein shown to be connected with such motion picture studios and all the events and characters portrayed herein, are fictional.   Any similarity to actual persons, events or studios is purely coincidental. "   Aboard the Hawaii-bound vessel, the passengers enjoy a costume ball; among the many MGM figures represented are several Marx Brothers and Laurel and Hardy, among others.

Honolulu propounds the theory that basically movie stars would love to shed their glamour, and all the responsibilities of being a celebrity, in exchange for the simple life.

THE HOUSE OF SEVEN CORPSES (International Amusements Corporation, 1973) Color, 90 min.

Executive producer, Dayton A. Smith; producers, Paul Lewis and Paul Harrison; director, Harrison; screenplay, Harrison and Thomas J. Kelly; art director, Ron Garcia; camera, Don Jones; editor, Peter Parasheles.

John Ireland (Eric Hartman); Faith Domergue (Gail); John Carradine (Price); Carole Wells (Ann); Charles McCaulay (Christopher); Jerry Stricklen (David); with: Ron Foreman, Charles Baice, and Marty Hornstein.

In an eerie mansion, a woman chants a satanic ritual which brings forth a monster, leading the woman to commit suicide.   Immediately a director yells "cut" and the next scene is set up in the Beal mansion as the caretaker, Price (John Carradine), protests that it was not the way the woman died in real life.   On a tour of the house, Carradine relates how the entire family met terrible deaths--which is the plotline director Eric Hartman (John Ireland) is using to make his latest horror film entry for his poverty-row company. Starring in the picture is one-time star Gail (Faith Domergue), the director's ex-love; and newcomer Ann (Carole Wells).   The latter is in love with David (Jerry Stricklen), the production assistant who spotted the Beal home as a location site.

As the filming continues, dialogue is used from the Tibetan Book of the Dead and the incantation actually causes the resurrection of the corpse of one of the dead Beals.   The monster begins murdering members of the company until Ireland finally discovers that one of his crew is really a dead Beal responsible for the rash of homicides.

Given only scant theatrical release, The House of Seven Corpses is a fairly entertaining quickie which holds audience interest in its creepy-horror angles.   For movie buffs, though, there are some engrossing sequences depicting such facets of poverty-row film-making as camera loading and set-ups, lighting, sound equipment, and the actual shooting of scenes for "one take" to save money. After a long day of shooting, director Ireland thanks his cast and crew for a "good day's work." One-time star Domergue retorts, "At Metro that would have been a week's work."

HOW MOTION PICTURES ARE MADE AND SHOWN see THE SHORT FILMS

HOW TO MAKE A MONSTER (American-International, 1958) 75 min. (color sequence)

Producer, Herman Cohen; director, Herbert L. Strock; story/ screenplay, Kenneth Langtry and Cohen; art director, Leslie Thomas; set decorator, Morris Hoffman; makeup, Philip Scheer; assistant director, Herb Mendelson; wardrobe, Oscar Rodriguez; music/music conductor, Paul Dunlap; song, Dunlap and Skip Redwine; sound, Herman Lewis; camera, Maury Gertzman; editor, Jerry Young.

Robert H. Harris (Pete Drummond); Paul Brinegar (Rivero); Gary Conway (Tony Mantell); Gary Clarke (Larry Drake); Malcolm Atterbury (Richards); Dennis Cross (Monahan); Morris Ankrum (Captain Hancock); Walter Reed (Detective Thompson); Paul Maxwell (Jeff Clayton); Eddie Marr (John Nixon); Heather Ames (Arlene Dow); Robert Shayne (Gary Droz); Rod Dana (Lab Technician); Jacqueline Ebeier (Jane); Joan Chandler (Marilyn); Thomas B. Henry (Martin Brace); John Phillips (Detective Jones); Pauline Myers (Millie the Maid); John Ashley (Guest Star).

Makeup man Pete Drummond (Robert H. Harris), an expert in creating monster disguises, is fired by American-International Pictures after working there for a quarter of a century (actually the studio had been in existence at that time for only three or four years). He is, however, allowed to complete work on his current epic, The Werewolf Meets Frankenstein, before the studio embarks on its new cycle--musicals. The mad artist plans revenge on his "oppressors." He places a formula in the facial makeup of two actors playing the Frankenstein monster and the Wolfman which causes them to become deranged and to kill the two studio moguls who made the decision to fire Harris. After the effects of the drug wear off, the two actors-turned-killers are unaware of their crimes. Later they attend a farewell party at Harris' home where all the heads of his movie monster creations hang on the walls. When the makeup man announces he plans to add the two actors' heads to his "trophy" collection, one of them upsets a candelabra which causes the house to catch on fire. Harris is killed in the blaze trying to salvage his precious makeup creations.

Producer Herman Cohen turned out this film in an obvious attempt to utilize the monster makeup that AIP had been employing in its cheapie horror offerings for the drive-in circuit in the late fifties. Despite its inexpensive aura, the picture comes off rather

well--mostly tongue-in-cheek--and provides a tour of the inside operations of AIP in its salad days, much as <u>The Death Kiss</u> (q. v.) had
done at World Wide two decades earlier.   Producer Cohen and director Herbert L. Strock had recently completed the moneymaking <u>I</u>
<u>Was a Teenage Frankenstein</u> (1957) for the company and here Gary
Clarke, who played the title role in that film, is seen as an actor
assigned to be the Frankenstein monster.   Among the props and monsters dredged up from past AIP mini-epics were the teenage Frankenstein and Werewolf, the She Creature, a three-eyed mutant, and
a cat girl.

I'LL CRY TOMORROW (MGM, 1955) 117 min.

     Producer, Lawrence Weingarten; director, Daniel Mann; based
on the biography by Lillian Roth, Mike Connolly, and Gerold Frank;
screenplay, Helen Deutsch and Jay Richard Kennedy; music director,
Charles Henderson; background music, Alex North; assistant director,
Al Jennings; costumes, Helen Rose; art directors, Cedric Gibbons
and Malcolm Brown; camera, Arthur E. Arling; editor, Harold F.
Kress.

     Susan Hayward (Lillian Roth); Richard Conte (Tony Bardeman);
Eddie Albert (Burt McGuire); Jo Van Fleet (Katie); Don Taylor (Wal-
lie); Ray Danton (David Tredman); Margo (Selma); Virginia Gregg
(Ellen); Don Barry (Jerry); David Kasday (David as a Child); Carole
Ann Campbell (Lillian as a Child); Peter Leeds (Richard); Tol Avery
(Fat Man); Ralph Edwards (Himself); Charles Tannen and Harlan
Warde (Stage Managers); Ken Patterson and Stanley Farrar (Direc-
tors); Voltaire Perkins (Mr. Byrd); George Lloyd (Messenger); Nora
Marlowe (Nurse); Peter Brocco (Doctor); Bob Dix (Henry); Anthony
Jochim (Paul the Butler); Veda Ann Borg (Waitress); Jack Gargan
(Drug Clerk); Gail Ganley (Lillian at Age Fifteen); Ruth Storey (Marge
Belney); James Ogg (Usher); Bernadette Withers and Kathy Garner
(Girls).

     "Filmed on location ... inside a woman's soul," the ads pro-
claimed for <u>I'll Cry Tomorrow</u>, the film version of singer Lillian
Roth's autobiography of the years she went from star of stage and
screen to skid-row alcoholic.   The book (written with Mike Connolly
and Gerold Frank) was a number one best seller and Roth's return
from inside the bottle served as a model for millions the world over.
Roth had always promoted Susan Hayward for the title role in the
film and MGM gave her the part, although both June Allyson and
Jane Russell were considered initially.   Much to Roth's chagrin,
however, star Hayward sang the songs in the picture, thus depriving
the author of the chance to sing on the soundtrack of her life story,
a la Al Jolson and others.
     Actually <u>I'll Cry Tomorrow</u> had relatively little to do with the
Hollywood ambiance other than by its recreation of some of the musical numbers from Roth's early talkies (made at Paramount).   Basically the tear-jerking narrative related how the ambitious young

Susan Hayward in I'll Cry Tomorrow (1955).

woman rose to stardom on the stage and then in film, guided by her
dominating mother (Jo Van Fleet), and of her two unhappy marriages,
the latter to a sadist (Richard Conte).   She turns to drink and eventually becomes a lush.   From there she becomes interested in the
Alcoholics Anonymous movement and finds peace and security with
a third spouse, Burt McGuire (Eddie Albert).

   I'll Cry Tomorrow grossed $6 million in distributors domestic
rentals.   Hayward won awards at the Cannes and Cork Film Festivals
and was nominated for a Best Actress Oscar (losing the prize to
Anna Magnani of Paramount's The Rose Tatoo).

I'M STILL ALIVE (RKO, 1940) 72 min.

   Producer, Frederic Ullman, Jr. ; director, Irving Reis; story/
screenplay, Edmund North; camera, J. Roy Hunt; editor, Theron
Warth.

Kent Taylor (Steve Bennett); Linda Hayes (Laura Marley); Howard da Silva (Red Garvey); Ralph Morgan (Walter Blake); Don Dillaway (Tommy Briggs); Clay Clement and Fred Niblo (Directors).

"Risking your life for a movie isn't as silly as starving to death" is the philosophy of stuntman Steve Bennett (Kent Taylor), much to the chagrin of his movie-star wife, Laura Marley (Linda Hayes). Hayes wants Taylor to quit his hazardous job as a stunt flyer and he does so after she finds him acting assignments. He then refrains from performing a stunt which later misfires and costs the life of a buddy.

Gravely upset, Taylor barnstorms the country in his plane which results in injury of his eyes. Later though, when another friend cannot perform a dangerous crack-up flying trick, Taylor steps in and does the job. He thereafter retires from stunting for good. He and Hayes remain together.

The New York Daily News called it a "tribute to the stunt-fliers and car-wreckers," adding, "It's a nice thought, but the story that is worked around it is forced and hard to believe. Certainly this modest programmer was not in the same league with earlier films about stuntmen, such as The Lost Squadron and Lucky Devils (qq. v.), but its intentions were honorable. To be noted is the casting of veteran director Fred Niblo in the small role of a movie director in the proceedings.

IN A LONELY PLACE (Columbia, 1950) 94 min.

Producer, Robert Lord; associate producer, Henry S. Kesler; director, Nicholas Ray; based on the novel by Dorothy B. Hughes; adaptor, Edmund H. North; screenplay, Andrew Solt; music, George Antheil; music director, Morris Stoloff; orchestrator, Ernest Gold; assistant director, Earl Bellamy; art director, Robert Peterson; set decorator, William Kiernan; technical adviser, Rodney Amateau; makeup, Clay Campbell; sound, Howard Fogetti; camera, Burnett Guffey; editor, Viola Lawrence.

Humphrey Bogart (Dixon Steele); Gloria Grahame (Laurel Gray); Frank Lovejoy (Brub Nicolai); Carl Benton Reid (Captain Lochner); Art Smith (Mel Lippman); Jeff Donnell (Sylvia Nicolai); Martha Stewart (Mildred Atkinson); Robert Warwick (Charlie Waterman); Morris Ankrum (Lloyd Barnes); William Ching (Ted Barton); Steven Geray (Paul); Hadda Brooks (Singer); Alix Talton (Frances Randolph); Jack Reynolds (Henry Kesler); Ruth Warren (Effie); Ruth Gillette (Martha); Lewis Howard (Junior); Guy Beach (Swan).

One of Hollywood's most intelligent self-analytical efforts is Nicholas Ray's In a Lonely Place. This somber and too-often realistic feature revolves around a brief and bittersweet love affair between a neurotic screenwriter (Humphrey Bogart) and his attractive neighbor (Gloria Grahame). Woven around the love theme is the depiction of the general emptiness of life in the film world--a way of life that has its main interest in profit, not art nor feeling.

Morris Ankrum, Humphrey Bogart, Art Smith, and Billy Gray in In a Lonely Place (1950).

Scenarist Bogart is assigned to adapt a low-class novel for the screen and he asks a hat-check girl (Martha Stewart) to read it to him in his apartment. Later she is found murdered and Bogart is a chief suspect until a neighbor (Grahame) provides him with an alibi. In short order he and the friend-indeed become amorous and she helps him with his screen adaptation. Soon they plan to marry, despite the combination of the unsolved murder of the girl, Bogart's sudden proclivity for violence, and the urging of his friends that Grahame not involve herself with such an unstable individual.

Bogart's bad temper flares several times (including the savage beating of a teenager who runs his car off the road). Finally Grahame decides she must leave him, especially after he slugs his agent (Art Smith) for having taken his unfinished script. Bogart pursues Grahame, learns of her plans, and in a rage starts choking her. The phone suddenly rings and it is the police who inform Bogart that the hat-check girl was murdered by her boyfriend, who has confessed to the crime. But by this time, Bogart and Grahame realize their affair has run its course and they impassively part.

Manny Farber, in the introduction to his book Negative Space
(1971), states that this film "... is a Hollywood scene at its most
lackluster, toned down, limpid, with [director] Ray's keynote strange-
ness: a sprawling, unbent composition with somewhat dwarfed characters, each going his own way. A convention studio movie but very
nice: Ray stages everything, in scenes heavily involved with rules
of behavior, like a bridge game amongst good friends, no apparent
sweat. "

Besides Ray's crisp direction of a taut script, the picture
benefitted greatly from the screen chemistry of Bogart and Grahame,
and superior supporting work from Art Smith as the ten-percenter
and by Robert Warwick as an alcoholic, faded movie star.

IN HOLLYWOOD WITH POTASH AND PERLMUTTER (Associated First
    National, 1924) 6685 ft.

Presenter/producer, Samuel Goldwyn; director, Alfred Green;
based on the play Business Before Pleasure by Montague Glass and
Jules Eckert Goodman; adaptor, Frances Marion; titles, Glass; art
director, Ben Carré; camera, Arthur Miller and Harry Hallenberger;
editor, Stuart Heisler.

Alexander Carr (Morris Perlmutter); George Sidney (Abe Po-
tash); Vera Gordon (Rosie Potash); Betty Blythe (Rita Sismondi); Belle
Bennett (Mrs. Perlmutter); Anders Randolph (Blanchard); Peggy Shaw
(Irma Potash); Charles Meredith (Sam Pemberton); Lillian Hackett
(Miss O'Ryan); David Butler (Crabbe); Sidney Franklin and Joseph W.
Girard (Film Buyers); Norma Talmadge and Constance Talmadge
(Guest Stars).

First National initially brought Alexander Carr and Barney
Bernard to the screen in 1923 in Potash and Perlmutter which was
based on the 1917 play Business Before Pleasure. The film was so
well received that a follow-up, written by Frances Marion and again
based on the play, was filmed. This time around, George Sidney replaced Barney Bernard. Photoplay magazine evaluated In Hollywood
with Potash and Perlmutter as "a corking good comedy with a laugh
in every sub-title. "

This episode found the two overgrown boys relinquishing their
textile business to become movie producers. Their first cinematic
fling, however, is a big flop. But they finally convince a banker to
finance their second production and to star in it they hire famous
vamp Rita Sismondi (Betty Blythe). The on-camera temptress, however, quickly breaks up their homes with her antics. Eventually all
is restored to normal. The film proves to be a big success and
Blythe begins a romance with the picture's director.

Of interest to movie buffs are scenes interpolated into the
movie showing Norma and Constance Talmadge being directed in two
separate features: Norma by Sidney Franklin and Constance by David
Butler. It should be remembered that Betty Blythe a few years before had been a sensation as Fox's The Queen of Sheba (1921).

IN PERSON (RKO, 1935) 85 min.

Producer, Pandro S. Berman; director, William A. Seiter;
based on the novel by Samuel Hopkins Adams; screenplay, Allan
Scott; songs, Dorothy Fields and Oscar Levant; choreography, Hermes Pan; camera, Edward Cronjager; editor, Arthur Schmidt.

Ginger Rogers (Carol Corliss); George Brent (Emory Muir);
Alan Mowbray (Jay Holmes); Grant Mitchell (Judge Thaddeus Parks);
Samuel S. Hinds (Dr. Aaron Sylvester); Joan Breslau (Minna); Louis
Mason (Sheriff Twing); Spencer Charters ("Parson" Lunk); Bob Mc-
Kenzie (Theatre Manager); Lee Shumway (Studio Representative); Lew
Kelly (Man Giving Directions); William B. Davidson (Bill Sumner,
the Director).

Following the success of Top Hat (1935), RKO moguls starred
Ginger Rogers in this comedy programmer which details the trials
of a movie star who cannot abide her adoring public.   Teamed with
Rogers was Warner Bros. fast-developing leading man George Brent,
but the duo produced none of the spark that was evident on-camera
with Ginger and Fred Astaire, or between Brent and Bette Davis at
Warner Bros.   For the two stars, this turned out to be just another
assignment, and one mostly forgotten today.

The plot revolved about glamourous movie idol Carol Corliss
(Rogers), who develops a phobia about being recognized after she is
manhandled by her demanding fans at a movie premiere.   The star
then takes to wearing a wig, glasses, and false teeth while in public,
but finally the situation becomes so impossible she makes a retreat
to the country.   There she encounters handsome Emory Muir (Brent)
at a mountain retreat.   The two promptly fall in love, with Brent
not knowing who Rogers really is; when he learns the truth he is not
impressed.   Later when she embarks on some of her famous stardom
tantrums, Brent pays little attention to her childish ways.   She realizes he is just the kind of solid man she requires in the high-strung
world of moviemaking.

In Person was merely another B romp of the thirties which
pictured chic movie stars as spoiled but essentially honest girls who
only require a little honest loving and a lot of discipline to make
them happy.   Andre Sennwald observed in the New York Times that
the film "works up some laborious fun out of the situation, prolonging
it far beyond its normal life-span." Helping along the fluff were the
Dorothy Fields-Oscar Levant songs: "Don't Mention Love to Me,"
"Got a New Lease on Life," and "Out of Sight, Out of Mind."

A decade later Rogers again played a movie celebrity in MGM's
Week-End at the Waldorf (1945).   This film, however, had very little
to do with the picture industry other than showcasing Ginger as top-
level movie queen Irene Malvern, a level-headed celebrity who stops
at the Waldorf in New York and shields a war correspondent (Walter
Pidgeon) who has stolen into her suite for business rather than amorous intentions.   The whole thing was a revamp of Grand Hotel (1932),
with Ginger's role having originally been a fading ballerina, played
by Greta Garbo.

Mary Astor and Lewis Stone in Inez from Hollywood (1924).

IN THE MOVIES see THE SHORT FILMS

INEZ FROM HOLLYWOOD (First National Pictures, 1924) 6919 ft.

Director, Alfred E. Green; based on the story "The Worst Woman in Hollywood" by Adela Rogers St. John; adaptor, J. G. Hawks; sets, Jack Okey; assistant director, Jack Boland; camera, Arthur Edeson; editor, Dorothy Arzner.

Anna Q. Nilsson (Inez Laranetta); Lewis S. Stone (Stewart Cuyler); Mary Astor (Fay Bartholdi); Laurence Wheat (Pat Summerfield); Rose Dione (Marie d'Albrecht); Snitz Edwards (The Old Sport); Harry Depp (Scoop Smith); Ray Hallor (Freddie); E. H. Calvert (Gardner).

This simple little screen variation was primarily a starring vehicle for then top star, Swedish-born Anna Q. Nilsson. In the course of the story, there was some joshing of the Hollywood scene, especially of the vamp image (which had faded greatly since the heyday of Theda Bara in the late Teens).

Here Nilsson portrayed Inez Laranatta, a big Hollywood favorite known for her vamping roles, who is out to protect the interests of her younger sister (Mary Astor) from the soundrels of the film capitol, only to find the girl is enamored of prominent New Yorker Stewart Cuyler (Lewis S. Stone). The star fights to protect her sister from this man with a lengthy past of conquests, only to find that his intentions are honorable. Nilsson is consoled by her manager (Laurence Wheat).

Photoplay magazine reported, "Title will attract, but this story of a screen vamp ... who isn't really what she's painted is a trifle overdone...." That fan magazine, however, was enchanted with the picture's star, the woman of "the quivering exquisite mouth, the deep-blue eyes and the ever-present sense of humor." Nilsson would later play a cameo as herself in one of the genre's classics, Sunset Boulevard (q. v.).

INSERTS (United Artists, 1976) Color, 99 min.

Producers, Davina Belling and Clive Parsons; director/screenplay, John Byrum; costume designer, Shirley Russell; art director, John Clark; camera, John Harris; editor, Mike Bradsell.

Richard Dreyfuss (Boy Wonder); Jessica Harper (Cathy Cake); Bob Hoskins (Big Mac); Veronica Cartwright (Harlene); Stephen Davies (Rex).

Set some decades ago, a one-time child star (Richard Dreyfuss), once known as the Boy Wonder, has become a hopeless alcoholic and will not leave his spacious but gloomy Hollywood home. To make a living these days he films porno movies there with young

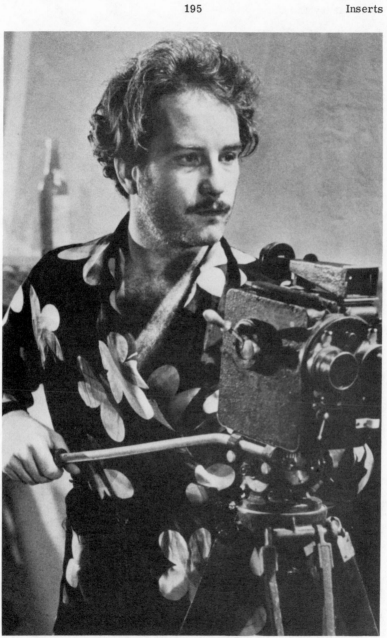

Richard Dreyfuss in <u>Inserts</u> (1976).

women who are seeking a quick buck in California. This basic synopsis sums up the premise of Inserts, the title referring to shots that are "inserted" into the overall action scenes, usually after the main portion of the movie has been completed.

Although the setting of Inserts is Hollywood, it was filmed in London for around $300, 000 from director John Byrum's screenplay. It was anticipated that any film starring Dreyfuss--one of the costars of the ultra-popular Jaws (1975)--would do well at the box office. But this X-rated feature died a quick death.   Few critics endorsed the film: the New York Daily News dismissed it as a "dreary witless movie" while the New York Post regarded it as "two hours of tedious bombast. "

The period costumes were designed by Shirley Russell, the wife of filmmaker Ken Russell.

INSIDE DAISY CLOVER (Warner Bros. , 1965) Color, 128 min.

Producer, Alan J. Pakula; director, Robert Mulligan; based on the novel by Gavin Lambert; screenplay, Lambert; art director, Robert Clatworthy; set decorator, George James Hopkins; music, Andre Previn; songs, Andre and Dory Previn; choreography, Herbert Ross; montage sequences, John Hoffman; sound, M. A. Merrick; camera, Charles Lang, Jr. ; editor, Aaron Stell.

Natalie Wood (Daisy Clover); Christopher Plummer (Raymond Swan); Robert Redford (Wade Lewis); Ruth Gordon ("The Dealer"); Katharine Bard (Melora Swan); Roddy McDowall (Baines); Peter Helm (Milton Hopwood); Betty Harford (Gloria Goslett); John Hale (Harry Gaslett); Harold Gould (Cop); Ottola Nesmith (Old Lady in Hospital); Edna Holland (Cynara);   Jackie Ward (Singing Voice of Daisy Clover).

Gavin Lambert's well-regarded novel about the rise and fall of a young Hollywood actress was adapted to the screen as a meandering hodgepodge about a neurotic girl who was neither talented nor ingratiating.

Natalie Wood was given the almost hopeless task of portraying the title character, a 15-year-old beachcomber who makes her living selling movie postcards and who associates only with her bizarre mother (Ruth Gordon).   The latter is known as "The Dealer" a woman locked into her own private memories.   One day Wood records her voice and sends it to a movie studio and the head of the company offers her a screen test.   As a result she soon becomes known as "America's Little Valentine, " a toast of the cinema industry.   Thrown into the Hollywood social swing she falls in love with movie idol Wade Lewis (Robert Redford) and they have a brief affair, but he deserts her.

Eventually they are reunited after Wood has become a big star.   They wed but he soon departs again.   Later the wife of the studio head informs the perplexed girl that her disappearing spouse is a homosexual.   Wood then tries to rebuild her life.   She has "The

Dealer" removed from a mental hospital and together they move into
a beach house, where the mother soon dies.   Wood herself then becomes a recluse.   Pleadings from the studio and even from Redford
fail to bring her back to reality, let alone soundstage work.   She
later attempts suicide with gas, but leaves the house only to witness
it explode.   Thereafter, in a moment of perspicacity, Wood realizes
that although she is a screen has-been at 19, she still has a life
ahead of her.

Overlong and tedious, Inside Daisy Clover is perhaps best
summed up by Donald Reed, who in his book Robert Redford (1975),
called it "an odd, disjointed reworking of the Hollywood success myth.
For all its lush production values, some superior camera work, and
an occasional effective sequence ... the film remains vague, remote
and ultimately pointless."

Ruth Gordon was Oscar-nominated for Inside Daisy Clover but
she lost the Best Supporting Actress prize to Shelley Winters (A
Patch of Blue).   Jackie Ward dubbed the off-camera singing soundtrack for Natalie Wood.

IRVING BERLIN'S SECOND FIDDLE (20th Century-Fox, 1939) 86 min.

Producer, Gene Markey; director, Sidney Lanfield; screenplay,
Harry Tugend; songs, Irving Berlin; music director, Louis Silvers;
camera, Leon Shamroy; editor, Robert Simpson.

Sonja Henie (Trudi Hovland); Tyrone Power (Jimmy Sutton);
Rudy Vallee (Roger Maxwell); Edna May Oliver (Aunt Phoebe Hovland);
Mary Healy (Jean Varick); Lyle Talbot (Willie Hogger); Alan Dinehart
(George Whitney); Minna Gombell (Jenny); Stewart Reburn (Skating
Partner); Spencer Charters (Joe Clayton); Brian Sisters (Themselves);
George Chandler (Justice of the Peace); Maurice Cass (Alex Blank);
Robert Lowery (Orchestra Leader); Lillian Porter (Jimmy's Girl);
Edward Earle (Greg); Leyland Hodgson (Maitre d'Hotel); Purnell
Pratt (Abbott).

By the late thirties, 20th Century-Fox was finding it difficult
to dream up suitable "original" vehicles for its dimpled Scandinavian
skating star, Sonja Henie.   This outing had leading men Tyrone Power and Rudy Vallee definitely playing "second fiddle" to Sonja, although the scenario structure was so gossamer, and its quartet of
Irving Berlin tunes so mild, the whole affair turned out to be nothing
more than a deluxe programmer.

Basically a spoof on the David O. Selznick hunt for Scarlett
O'Hara for Gone with the Wind, the film tells of Consolidated Pictures' efforts to locate a leading lady for Girl of the North.   Over
400 candidates are tested; but none are suitable.   A young man in
Minnesota then sends his girl's photo to the studio where the publicity
head, under pressure from the media to make a selection soon, dispatches an underling (Tyrone Power) to find the girl and see if she
is at all suitable for the part.   The girl, Trudi Hovland (Henie) happens to teach school and although she thinks her chances of winning

Rudy Vallee, Sonja Henie, and Tyrone Power in a publicity pose for
<u>Irving Berlin's Second Fiddle</u> (1939).

---

the part are near zero, she agrees to make the audition. Her Aunt
Phoebe (Edna May Oliver) accompanies her on the trip and she winds
up with the role opposite popular crooner Roger Maxwell (Rudy Vallee), much to the chagrin of Vallee's fiancée, Jean Varick (Mary
Healy), who also coveted the part. Power then concocts a romance
between Vallee and Henie and she falls in love with Vallee, not knowing it is Power who is writing the love letters. When she learns the
truth, she returns home. But by now Power realizes he loves her.
He pursues her and proposes. She accepts, much to the surprise
of her waiting boyfriend (Lyle Talbot).

IT HAPPENED IN HOLLYWOOD (Columbia, 1937) 67 min.

Director, Harry Lachman; based on the story "Once a Hero"
by Myles Connolly; screenplay, Ethel Hill, Harvey Fergusson, and
Samuel Fuller; camera, Joseph Walker.

Richard Dix (Tim Bart); Fay Wray (Gloria Gay); Victor Kilian
(Slim); Franklin Pangborn (Mr. Forsythe); Charlie Arnt (Jed Reed);

Granville Bates (Sam Bennett); William B. Davidson (Al Howard); Arthur Loft (Pete); Edgar Dearing (Stevens); James Donlan (Shorty); Billy Burrud (Billy); Zeffie Tilbury (Miss Gordon); Harold Goodwin (Buck); Charles Brinley (Pappy).

Myles Connolly's story, "Once a Hero" was used as the basis of this 1937 film in which future director Samuel Fuller has co-adaptation credits.   In it Richard Dix starred as Tim Bart, a has-been comedy film idol who could not adapt properly to dialogue with the coming of the sound era.   After refusing to do villain roles in talkies (out of deference to his fans), he dropped out of pictures.   Also he became estranged from Gloria Gay (Fay Wray) the girl he adored, who was also his costar, but whose movie status skyrocketed with the new era.

Years later, Dix is lonely and forgotten when he comes to the aid of a crippled boy, a loyal fan, and again meets Wray.   Soon Dix accidentally comes upon an actual holdup and shoots the trio of robbers in their escape attempt.   This action makes Dix a front-page hero and brings back his old pictures to the theatres.   He is asked to make new films, again with Wray as his costar.   This time the two actors stay together and in love.

Since so many Hollywood cowboy stars had suffered a similar plight to the one delineated in this film, the picture bore the ring of truth.   With stalwart Dix, that square-jawed leading man of integrity and conviction, playing the key role, the double-bill entry proved to be an engrossing study, all the more engaging because it did not sink into a mire of tears.

IT HAPPENED IN HOLLYWOOD (Bulo Productions, 1973) Color, 74 min.

Producers, Jim Buckley and Peter Locke; director/screenplay, Locke; music, Ron Frangipane and Al Steckler; production designer, Peter Bramley; camera, Steven Bower; editor, Wes Craven.

With: Felicity Split, Mark Stevens, Al Levitsky, Alan Spitz, Al Goldstein, Richard Sternberger, Jim Buckley, Liz Torres.

In 1973 the crew of Screw newspaper produced a triple-X-rated feature which won praise in its genre for its technical achievements, although its contents rated it no higher than most other films of its ilk. Here a young woman becomes bored with her telephone operator's job and sets out to become a movie star via the casting couch.   After more than sufficient such tests she finally makes it to the lead in a version of Samson and Delilah.   The lensing of this "epic" occupies the last half of the feature and provides the excuse for an extended orgy-on-celluloid.   In Contemporary Erotic Cinema (1973), William Rotsler judges it, "A spoof film that is not very erotic, but fast."

IT HAPPENED IN NEW YORK (Universal, 1935) 65 min.

Associate producer, Edmund Grainger; director, Alan Crosland; based on the story "Bagdad on the Hudson" by Ward Morehouse and Jean Dalrymple; screenplay, Rian James and Seton I. Miller; camera, George Robinson.

Lyle Talbot (Charley Barnes); Gertrude Michael (Vania Nardi); Heather Angel (Chris Edwards); Hugh O'Connell (Haywood); Robert Gleckler (Venetti); Rafael Storm (The Prince); Adrienne D'Ambricourt (Fleurette); Huntley Gordon (Hotel Manager); Phil Tead (Radio Announcer); Wallis Clark (Joe Blake); Dick Elliott (Publicity Man); Bess Stafford (Landlady).

Just as in RKO's In Person (q. v.), released the same year, It Happened in New York dealt with the ploy of the movie queen who must get away from her over-adoring public and enjoy being a normal, everyday person. Herein Vania Nardi (Gertrude Michael), the idol of millions of fans, cannot abide the patent-leather-hair set in Hollywood any more and comes to Manhattan for a rest. However, she has not counted on her overindustrious press agent, Haywood (Hugh O'Connell), who follows her and arranges a series of public appearances. Meanwhile, the star encounters a very proletarian taxi driver, Charley Barnes (Lyle Talbot), who persists in calling the regal personality "Toots. " Talbot is seeking $200 to buy a partnership in a garage and to pave the way for marrying his girlfriend (Heather Angel). Adding to the madcap mixture are a group of jewel thieves who wish to acquire Michael's prize collection.
The New York Times endorsed this well-conceived entry as "a gay and rollicking comedy ... with a cast in the best of spirits, a merry script and a director with a nice sense of pace.... " It might be noted that director Alan Crosland had helmed two of Warner Bros. ' pathleading pictures, which helped to bring about the commercial talkie era: Don Juan (1926) which had a musical score track synchronized with the picture, and The Jazz Singer (1927), which contained those famous talking scenes by Al Jolson.

IT'S A GREAT FEELING (Warner Bros. , 1949) Color, 84 min.

Producer, Alex Gottlieb; director, David Butler; story, I. A. L. Diamond; screenplay, Jack Rose and Melville Shavelson; art director, Stanley Fleischer; set decorator, Lyle B. Reifsnider; assistant director, Phil Quinn; music numbers staged by LeRoy Prinz; music director, Ray Heindorf; music, Jule Styne; songs, Styne and Sammy Cahn; makeup, Perc Westmore and Mickey Marcellino; costumes, Milo Anderson; Technicolor consultants, Natalie Kalmus and Mitchell Kovaleski; sound, Dolf Thomas and David Forrest; special effects, William McGann and H. F. Koenekamp; camera, Wilfred M. Cline; editor, Irene Morra.

Dennis Morgan and Jack Carson (Themselves); Doris Day (Judy Adams); Bill Goodwin (Arthur Trent); Irving Bacon (Information

Dennis Morgan, Doris Day, and Jack Carson in It's a Great Feeling (1949).

Clerk); Claire Carleton (Grace); Harlan Warde (Publicity Man); Jacqueline de Wit (Trent's Secretary); David Butler, Michael Curtiz, King Vidor, Raoul Walsh, Gary Cooper, Joan Crawford, Sydney Greenstreet, Danny Kaye, Patricia Neal, Eleanor Parker, Ronald Reagan, Edward G. Robinson, Jane Wyman, and Maureen Reagan (Themselves); Errol Flynn (Jeffrey Bushdinkel).

A substantial look at the Warner Bros. lot and brief glimpses of many of its then stars were afforded by It's a Great Feeling. As an introspective look at the motion picture profession, however, this zany outing had very little fresh to offer. It was too intent on being cute in its plotline, and in the star cameos. Each of the celebrities was showcased to highlight his/her trademark characteristics (rather than displaying off-camera traits). Still it was a year away from Sunset Boulevard (q. v.), and audiences were looking for comedy entertainment, not truth or history, from the Hollywood scene.

Dennis Morgan and Jack Carson (playing themselves) have a script for a new feature, but no director will take it--Carson's reputation for hamming and having a too-strong ego has preceded him. Then plucky Carson decides to direct the project himself; but the team is still in a quandary to locate a leading lady. Finally they decide on one of the studio commissary waitresses, star-struck Judy Adams (Doris Day). She readily agrees to do the picture. She proves to be a good choice but before long she is satiated with the antics of Carson and Morgan and the motion picture business in general. She finds herself longing to go home to Wisconsin and to wed her fiancê. Finally she can tolerate no more and she departs California. The finale has her marrying Jeffrey Bushdinkel who--in the film's most amusing sequence--turns out to be none other than Errol Flynn.

Of the other guest stars, Joan Crawford's turn--spoofing her dramatic genre of filmmaking--was the most engaging.

JACQUELINE SUSANN'S ONCE IS NOT ENOUGH (Paramount, 1975) Color, 122 min.

Executive producer, Irving Mansfield; producer, Howard W. Koch; director, Guy Green; based on the novel by Jacqueline Susann; screenplay, Julius J. Epstein; production designer, John De Cuir; art director, David Marshall; set decorator, Ruby Levitt; music, Henry Mancini; songs, Mancini and Larry Kusik; titles, Dan Perri; sound, Larry Jost; camera, John A. Alonzo; editor, Rita Roland.

Kirk Douglas (Mike Wayne); Alexis Smith (Deidre Milford Granger); David Janssen (Tom Colt); George Hamilton (David Milford); Melina Mercouri (Karla); Gary Conway (Hugh Robertson); Brenda Vaccaro (Linda Riggs); Deborah Raffin (January Wayne); Lillian Randolph (Mabel); Renata Vanni (Maria); Mark Roberts (Rheingold); John Roper (Franco); Leonard Sachs (Dr. Peterson); Jim Boles (Scotty); Ann Marie Moelders (Girl at El Morocco ; Trudy Marshall (Myrna); Eddie Garrett (Maitre d' in Polo Lounge); Sid Frohlich (Waiter); Kelly Lange (Weather Lady); Maureen McCluskey, Harley Farber, Michael Millius, and Tony Ferrara (Beautiful People).

This nonsense soaper version of the Jacqueline Susann bestseller focuses on movie producer Mike Wayne (Kirk Douglas) who is apparently a broad caricature of the late bon vivant packager Mike Todd. The filmmaker's professional life is a success, but his personal one is a shambles: his estranged, elegant wife, Deidre (Alexis Smith) is a lesbian who loves a legendary screen actress (Melina Mercouri); his daughter January (Deborah Raffin) prefers an older, impotent writer (David Janssen) to a wealthy, handsome playboy (George Hamilton). Laced around this hot-bed of never-ending family problems is Douglas' activities in the movie and magazine publishing industries and amidst the jet-set crowd.

With its casual attitude to facts and/or reality, the picture it presents of the film business is surface-deep at best: one has no sense of the genius that allegedly lies behind the clef chin of Douglas' character.

Director Guy Green reportedly preferred Dick Van Dyke for the role of Mike Wayne and by the time the scripters were through adapting the late Ms. Susann's novel, there was little left of the original plotline but the title. (Allegedly, some four different endings

Kirk Douglas and Alexis Smith in <u>Jacqueline Susann's Once Is Not Enough</u> (1975).

were filmed to the story--each one wilder than the next.)   Unlike the screen versions of Susann's earlier <u>Valley of the Dolls</u>, (q. v.), or <u>The Love Machine</u> (1971)--dealing with the television industry--this entry was not a financial success.   It was a toss-up whether the dialogue was cornier than the plotline, and as to which veteran performer provided the more embarrassing performance.

JAM SESSION (Columbia, 1944) 74 min.

Producer, Irving Briskin; director, Charles Barton; story, Harlan Ware and Patterson McNutt; screenplay, Manny Seff; art directors, Lionel Banks and Paul Murphy; set decorator, William Kiernan; assistant director, Earl Bellamy; music director, Morris Stoloff; songs, Ray Noble; Sammy Cahn and Jule Styne; Frank Loesser and Jimmy McHugh; S. K. Russell and Ary Barroso; Glen Gray; W. C. Handy; Spud Murphy; Dorothy Fields and McHugh; camera, L. W. O'Connell; editor, Richard Frantl.

Ann Miller (Terry Baxter); Jess Barker (George Carter Haven); Charles D. Brown (Raymond Stuart); Eddie Kane (Lloyd Marley); George Eldredge (Berkley Bell); Renie Riano (Miss Tobin); Clarence Muse (Henry); Pauline Drake (Evelyn); Charles La Torre (Coletti);

Anne Loos (Neva Cavendish); Ray Walker (Fred Wylie); Nan Wynn, the
Pied Pipers & Charlie Barnet, Louis Armstrong, Alvino Rey & His
Orchestra, Jan Garber & His Orchestra, Glen Gray & His Orchestra,
and Teddy Powell & His Orchestra (Themselves).

This minor B musical (part of Ann Miller's campy Columbia
canon of the forties) was highlighted by guest appearances from some
of the jitterbugger's favorite musical stars. Because of this gimmick,
the picture was more than successful and today is still worth viewing
as a mirror of the musical styles of the World War II era. The
New York Times stated of the 1944 release that it "rolls evenly and
amusingly along on an entertaining if somewhat pre-ration story. "
The threads of narrative on which the multitude of musical
numbers were strung concerned a pretty, young small-town contest
winner, Terry Baxter (Ann Miller), who earns a trip to Hollywood
and an entree into a film studio. Her dancing ability impresses young
screenwriter George Carter Haven (Jess Barker) and the two soon
admit their love for one another. Through Barker's instigations, she
finally wins the lead in his new film; off-screen they enjoy their romantic bliss.
Among the musical highlights were Charlie Barnett's classic
"Cherokee, " Louis Armstrong's rendition of "I Can't Give You Anything But Love, Baby, " and Jan Garber performing "I Lost My Sugar. "

JAMES DEAN (NBC-TV, 1976) Color, 94 min.

Executive producers, Gerald Isenberg and Gerry Abrams; producers, William Bast and John Forbes; director, Robert Butler; teleplay, Bast; art director, Perry Ferguson III; set decorator, Sam
Jones; music, Billy Goldenberg; camera, Frank Stanley; editor, John
A. Martinelli.

Stephen McHattie (James Dean); Michael Brandon (Bill Bast);
Candy Clark (Chris White); Meg Foster (Dizzy Sheridan); Jayne Mead-
ows (Reva Randall); Dane Clark (James Whitmore); Katherine Helmond
(Claire Folger); Heather Menzies (Barbara); Leland Palmer (Arlene);
Amy Irving (Norma); Robert Foxworth (Psychiatrist); Chris White
(Receptionist); and: Rita Taggart, Wes Parker, Julian Burton, and
Vahan Moosekian.

Actor James Dean (1931-1955) has had a huge cult following
since his death in a motorcycle accident on September 30, 1955. At
the time he was on the rise as a star-rebel in a trio of box-office
hits, Rebel Without a Cause (1954), and East of Eden and Giant (both
1955). Not long after his demise, a documentary-like feature was
issued to theatres called The James Dean Story and in recent years
a series of books have revived interest in the teenage idol of two
decades ago. As a result of these tomes, NBC-TV produced the
telefeature James Dean which purported to relate the factual account
of the iconoclastic star's early life.
William Bast wrote the teleplay, and the narrative is related

Stephen McHattie and Michael Brandon in <u>James Dean</u> (1976).

through his eyes (as played by actor Michael Brandon), reliving the
early years of his friendship with James Dean (played by Stephen
McHattie), before Dean became a Hollywood name and a cultural symbol of restless youth.

The account begins in New York City as the two youths are
drawn together in their struggle for success. It is there that Dean
first pursues an acting career which initially earns him a few minor
roles on television and on stage. It is during this period that he
has brief romances with actress Chris White (Candy Clark) [the real-
life Chris White plays a secretary in the Actors Studio scenes] and
dancer Dizzy Sheridan (Meg Foster), with the teleplay giving impli-
cations that Dean's sexuality was not always oriented towards women.
Later Dean and Bast travel to Hollywood where the former wins a
few bit roles in pictures before eventually securing the lead in <u>Rebel
Without a Cause</u> at Warner Bros. The stardom he had sought was
cut short by his tragic death at the age of 24.

Bast, who also coproduced the memory excursion, called it
"one man's recollection of James Dean, an image of the actor as
seen through the eyes of a friend." McHattie in the difficult assignment of Dean was more effective in capturing the star's look and
mannerisms than in conveying any of the inner turmoil that allegedly
beset the rebel celebrity. More successful was Brandon in the role
of his very loyal friend.

Jeff Chandler, Kim Novak, and Richard Gaines in <u>Jeanne Eagels</u> (1957).

The definite study of Dean has yet to be produced; hopefully
it will cope with how a magnetizing loner bucked the establishment
system of Hollywood as few had done before him in the star system
decades.

JEANNE EAGELS (Columbia, 1957) 109 min.

Producer/director, George Sidney; story, Daniel Fuchs; screenplay, Fuchs, Sonya Levien, and John Fante; art director, Ross Bellah; music director, Morris Stoloff; music, George Duning; orchestrator, Arthur Morton; assistant director, Charles S. Gould; gowns,
Jean Louis; camera, Robert Planck; editors, Viola Lawrence and Jerome Thoms.

Kim Novak (Jeanne Eagels); Jeff Chandler (Sal Satori); Agnes
Moorehead (Mme. Neilson); Charles Drake (John Donahue); Larry
Gates (Al Brooks); Virginia Grey (Elsie Desmond); Gene Lockhart
(Equity Board President); Joe de Santis (Frank Satori); Murray Ham-
ilton (Chick O'Hara); Will Wright (Marshal); Sheridan Comerate (Ac-
tor - Confederate Officer); Lowell Gilmore (Reverend Dr. Davidson);
Juney Ellis (Mrs. Davidson); Beulah Archuletta (Mrs. Horn); Jules
Davis (Mr. Horn); Florence MacAfee (Mrs. McPhail); Snub Pollard
(Quartermaster Bates); Joseph Novak (Patron); Johnny Tarangelo (Pri-
vate Griggs); Bert Spencer (Dr. McPhail); Richard Harrison (Corpor-
al Hodgson); Ward Wood (Stage Manager); Myrtle Anderson (Jeanne's
Maid); Michael Dante (Sergeant O'Hara); Joseph Turkel (Eddie); Rich-
ard Gaines (Judge); John Celentano and Tommy Nolan (Satori's Sons);
Raymond Greenleaf (Elderly Lawyer); Doris Lloyd (Mrs. Corliss);
Frank Borzage (Director); Lou Borzage (Assistant Director); Jack Ano
(Extra).

Actress Jeanne Eagels (1894-1929) was a sensation on Broadway in the late twenties in Rain and she appeared in a few early
talkies (Deception and The Letter--both 1929) before coming under the
strong influence of alcohol and drugs, which brought about a tragically early demise. Following her death, she became something of a
legend and in 1957 Columbia Pictures used its bright new glamour
star, Kim Novak, to play the role of the actress in a biography in
which all events "are based on fact and fiction."
The specious chronicle has Eagels growing up in the Midwest
and working as a honkytonk dancer in a carnival whose owner, Sal
Satori (Jeff Chandler), falls desperately in love with her. Realizing
her career must come first, they part and she travels to New York
and comes under the control of iron-willed drama coach Mme. Neilson (Agnes Moorehead). When an aging actress (Virginia Grey) later
asks Eagels to recommend the play Rain to a producer as a vehicle
for Grey, it is Jeanne who reads the part and gains the coveted role.
On opening night the drunken overlooked actress kills herself. Despite Eagel's professional triumph in the show she is shackled with
personal guilt and seeks escape in drink and drugs. She then weds
playboy Jack Donahue (Charles Drake) but continues to imbibe and
rely on drugs. Later the Actors Equity Association prohibits her

from further stage work. Still further on in the account, she encounters her old flame Chandler, now owner of a concession on the Board-
walk in Atlantic City. He persuades her to work in vaudeville. However, her mental state is poor and eventually the drugs kill her.

Outside of Eagel's having performed in Rain there is little
truth to the banal production. (Perhaps its only saving grace was
the matching on-camera of two such handsome creatures as Novak
and Chandler.) The picture hardly touched on the famed actress'
screen work; there is an episode in which Chandler visits a movie
theatre and watches a posthumously released film in which his late
love warbles "I'll Take Romance" (dubbed by Eileen Wilson).

The New York Times queried, "Whatever possessed Columbia
to cast this comparative fledgling, with her nice light comedy flair,
as one of Broadway's immortals, remains a studio secret." Mrs.
Elaine Eagels Nicklas sued the studio for $950,000, claiming that
the costly feature depicted her relative as a "dissolute and immoral
person" and as a "woman of low character." The case was settled
out of court.

JOEY AND HIS TROMBONE see THE SHORT FILMS

JOLSON SINGS AGAIN (Columbia, 1949) Color, 96 min.

Producer, Sidney Buchman; director, Henry Levin; screenplay,
Buchman; art director, Walter Holscher; set decorator, William Kier-
nan; music, George Duning; music advisor, Saul Chaplin; orchestra-
tor, Larry Russell; music director, Morris Stoloff; song stager, Au-
drene Brier; songs, Al Dubin and Harry Warren; Noble Sissle and
Eubie Blake; Edgar Smith and John Stromberg; B. G. De Sylva and
Louis Silvers; Irving Caesar and George Gershwin; Mort Dixon and
Harry M. Woods; De Sylva, Al Jolson, and Joseph Meyer; Joe Young,
Sam Lewis, and Jean Schwartz; Gus Kahn and Walter Donaldson; Kahn,
Tony Jackson, and Egbert Van Alstyne; Benny Davis and Harry Akst;
assistant director, Milton Feldman; makeup, Clay Campbell; costumes,
Jean Louis; sound, George Cooper and Philip Faulkner; camera, Wil-
liam Snyder; editor, William Lyon.

Larry Parks (Al Jolson/Himself); Barbara Hale (Ellen Clark);
William Demarest (Steve Martin); Ludwig Donath (Cantor Yoelson);
Bill Goodwin (Tom Baron); Myron McCormick (Ralph Bryant); Tamara
Shayne (Mama Yoelson); Eric Wilton (Henry); Robert Emmett Keane
(Charlie); Frank McLure and Jock Mahoney (Men); Betty Hill (Woman);
Charles Regan, Charles Perry, Richard Gordon, David Newell, Joe
Gilbert, David Horsley, Wanda Perry, Louise Illington, Gertrude Astor,
Steve Benton, and Eleanor Marvak (Bits); Margie Stapp (Nurse); Nelson
Leigh (Theatre Manager); Morris Stoloff (Orchestra Leader); Peter Broc-
co (Captain of Waiters). Al Jolson (Singing Voice of Al Jolson).

THE JOLSON STORY (Columbia, 1946) Color, 128 min.

Producer, Sidney Skilsky; associate producer, Gordon Griffith;

Top: Major Sam Harris (second from left), Larry Parks (center), and Bess Flowers (second from right) in Jolson Sings Again (1949). Bottom: (from left) Erick Wilton, William Forrest, William Demarest, Elinor Vandiveer; (at right) Larry Parks and Evelyn Keyes in The Jolson Story (1946).

director, Alfred E. Green; screenplay, Stephen Longstreet; adaptors, Harry Chandlee and Andrew Solt; assistant director, Wilbur McGaugh; montage director, Lawrence W. Butler; choreography, Jack Cole; production numbers staged by Joseph H. Lewis; music director, Morris Stoloff; vocal arranger, Saul Chaplin; orchestrator, Martin Fried; music recording, Edwin Wetzel; re-recording, Richard Olson; songs, Edward Madden and Gus Edwards; Joseph McCarthy and Jimmy Monaco; Sam Lewis, Joe Young, and Ray Henderson; Al Jolson, Billy Rose, and Dave Dreyer; Lewis, Young, and Walter Donaldson; Lewis, Young, and Jean Schwartz; Ira and George Gershwin; L. Wolfe Gilbert and Lewis E. Muir; B. G. De Sylva and Louis Silvers; Al Dubin and Harry Warren; Will Dillon and Harry Von Tilzer; Jolson; Billy Merson; art directors, Stephen Goosson and Walter Holscher; set decorators, William Kiernan and Louis Diage; Technicolor consultants, Natalie Kalmus and Morgan Padelford; gowns, Jean Louis; makeup, Clay Campbell; camera, Joseph Walker; editor, William Lyon.

Larry Parks (Al Jolson); Evelyn Keyes (Julie Benson); William Demarest (Steve Martin); Bill Goodwin (Tom Baron); Ludwig Donath (Cantor Yoelson); Tamara Shayne (Mrs. Yoelson); John Alexander (Lew Dockstader); Joe-Carroll Dennison (Ann Murray); Ernest Cossart (Father McGee); Scotty Beckett (Al Jolson as a Boy); Ann E. Todd (Ann Murray as a Girl); Emmett Vogan (Jonsey); Edwin Maxwell (Oscar Hammerstein); Eddie Kane (Florenz Ziegfeld); Jimmy Lloyd (Roy Anderson); Adele Roberts (Ingenue); Bob Stevens (Henry); Harry Shannon (Policeman Riley); Bud Gorman (Call Boy); Charles Jordan (Assistant Stage Manager); Helen O'Hara (Dancer/Actress); Donna Dax (Girl Publicist); Fred Sears (Cutter); Eric Wilton (Harry the Butler); Elinor Vandiveer (Maid); Major Sam Harris (Nightclubber); Franklyn Farnum (Extra in Audience); Al Jolson (the Singing Voice of Al Jolson).

Al Jolson launched the era of the commercial sound film in America with The Jazz Singer for Warner Bros. in 1927. However, that studio declined to do a film based on the entertainer's life when columnist Sidney Skolsky approached them with the concept in the early forties. They had had their share of the temperamental Mr. Jolson, a contract star a decade before; and considered him washed up in pictures. Finally Columbia Pictures' mogul Harry Cohn, a long-standing Jolson fan, set the project as a plushy Bouting, with contract player Larry Parks playing the title role and Jolson dubbing his trademark songs. (At one point in the mid-forties, Cohn had Jolson under Columbia contract as a "producer.")

The film proved to be a somewhat accurate account of Jolson's career, his struggling days, the years as the king of Broadway, and his important role in making talkies a Hollywood reality. The Jolson Story, however, left out more of the entertainer's hectic life than it included, especially in regard to the women involved with him, in marriage or otherwise. Ex-spouse Ruby Keeler refused to have her name associated with the project and thus the fictitious Julie Benson was created, with Evelyn Keyes portraying an amalgam of Jolson's three wives to that point in his life. The screen biography also carefully avoided depicting Jolson's renowned characteristics of ego-centricity and thoughtlessness.

Not given much of a chance at the box-office, the color fea-ture developed into a "sleeper" and went on to gross $7.6 million in distributors' domestic rentals. As a result of the bonanza biography, Jolson's own career was completely rejuvenated and Larry Parks be-came a movie star.

It was almost inevitable for Columbia to package another Jol-son story, using footage not employed in the original film plus some material that was. The new entry picks up its storyline where its predecessor left off, with Jolson having separated from his actress wife in 1939 and returning to the New York stage to distract himself from his marital woes. The 96-minute feature traces how Jolson made a comeback in the early forties entertaining troops during World War II, and tells of his marriage to nurse Ellen Clark (Barbara Hale). The last portion of Jolson Sings Again deals with the filming of The Jolson Story. This plot device led to the bizarre situation of seeing actor Parks appearing as the aging Jolson watching Parks the screen performer do his stuff in front of the camera in the movie-within-a-movie.

Despite being turned out on a smaller budget than the original, Jolson Sings Again proved a box-office champion, grossing $5 million in distributors' domestic rentals. It was not up to the initial film in quality or entertainment value, however.

As was typical of most screen biographies of the decade, the two Jolson films were mostly pegs upon which to hang a host of fam-ous songs aped by Parks in the Jolie style and with the real super-star performing the off-screen singing.

KATHY O' (Universal, 1958) Color, 99 min.

Producer, Sy Gomberg; director, Jack Sher; based on the story "Memo on Kathy O'Rourke" by Sher; screenplay, Sher and Gom-berg; music, Frank Skinner; song, Charles Tobias, Ray Joseph, and Sher; assistant director, Frank Shaw; gowns, Bill Thomas; art dir-ectors, Alexander Golitzen and Bill Newberry; sound, Leslie I. Car-ey and Joe Lapin; camera, Arthur E. Arling; editor, George Gittens.

Dan Duryea (Harry Johnson); Jan Sterling (Celeste); Patty Mc-Cormack (Kathy O'Rourke); Mary Fickett (Helen Johnson); Sam Le-vene (Ben Melnick); Mary Jane Croft (Harriet Burton); Rickey Kelman (Robert "Bo" Johnson); Terry Kelman (Tommy Johnson).

In the late fifties Universal produced a rash of features dealing with the film industry. These films (including Four Girls in Town, Slim Carter, The Female Animal, qq. v., and Kathy O'), allowed for occasional on-the-set scenes, the inclusion sometimes of guest stars, and always the box-office bait of treating the public to some of the "secrets" of the glamourous industry.

Kathy O' turned out to be a "sleeper" for Universal who had released the CinemaScope color entry with little fanfare. Patty Mc-

Dan Duryea and Patty McCormack in <u>Kathy O'</u> (1958).

Cormack starred as a pint-sized child star of the movies who is badly neglected by her guardian-aunt (Mary Jane Croft), who thought of
her as no more than a financial investment. As a result the unloved
child is self-centered and hard to handle, the bane of her director
(Tristram Coffin) and fellow performers.

Publicity man Harry Johnson (Dan Duryea) is hired to handle
the difficult tyke in her various public relations outings, one of which
includes being interviewed by a noted magazine writer (Jan Sterling),
who just happens to be Duryea's former wife. Later when McCormack becomes disgusted with being used/abused by the film world,
she runs away. Everyone at the studio thinks she has been kidnapped.
Having nowhere else to turn, the lonely girl goes to Duryea's home
where she observes warmth, love, and family ties for the first time.
After relinquishing her initial brattish ways, she is fully accepted
into the family. For the first time in her young life, she finds personal happiness. Eventually she returns to the film lot, but her
guardianship is given over to the publicist who promises to provide
a happy home environment for the contented little actress.

In its appealing, unpreachy way, <u>Kathy O'</u> makes a strong
statement against the commercialization of youngsters as show business breadwinners, especially when there is no love to compensate
for the strain of having to inhabit an adult world at too early an age.

KEEP SMILING (20th Century-Fox, 1938) 77 min.

Producer, John Stone; director, Herbert I. Leeds; screen

idea, Frank Fenton and Lynn Root; screenplay, Frances Hyland and Albert Ray; camera, Edward Cronjager; editor, Harry Reynolds.

Jane Withers (Jane Rand); Gloria Stuart (Carol Walters); Henry Wilcoxon (Jonathan Rand); Helen Westley (Mrs. Willoughby); Jed Prouty (Jerome Lawson); Douglas Fowley (Cedric Hunt); Robert Allen (Stanley Harper); Pedro de Cordoba (J. Howard Travers); Claudia Coleman (Mrs. Bowman); Paula Rae Wright (Bettina Bowman); The Three Nelsons (Themselves); Etta McDaniel (Violet); Carmencitta Johnson (Brutus); Mary McCarty (Froggy); Hal K. Dawson (Casting Director).

At 20th Century-Fox, Jane Withers was to B movies what Shirley Temple was to top-drawer productions. This outing had the second-string moppet star performing a first-class impersonation of Bobby Breen (then a popular RKO child star).

Jane Rand (Withers) is the orphaned niece of once-famous film director Jonathan Rand (Henry Wilcoxon), whose screen work has deteriorated because of his drinking. His addiction has cost him not only his professional standing but also the affection of Carol Walters (Gloria Stuart), the girl he loves who was once his secretary. Little Jane steps in and rectifies the situation with the help of Stuart. Soon Wilcoxon is back on the road to redemption and is directing a new film, starring none other than his helpful young niece.

Although Keep Smiling did decent business at the box-office as a double-bill entry, Withers would have a much more popular entry in the Hollywood genre film when she was teamed with Gene Autry for Shooting High (q. v.) two years later.

KID 'N HOLLYWOOD see THE SHORT FILMS

KING KONG (RKO, 1933) 110 min.

Executive producer, David O. Selznick; directors/screen idea, Merian C. Cooper and Ernest B. Schoedsack; story, Edgar Wallace and Cooper; adaptors, James Creelman and Ruth Rose; chief technician, Willis O'Brien; technical staff, E. B. Gibson, Marcel Delgado, Fred Reefe, Orville Goldner, and Carol Shepphird; art directors, Carroll Clark and Al Herman; art technicians, Mario Larrinaga and Byron L. Crabbe; production assistants, Archie Marshek and Walter Daniels; music, Max Steiner; sound, E. A. Wolcott; sound effects, Murray Spivak; camera, Edward Linden, Verne Walker, and J. O. Taylor; editor, Ted Cheeseman.

Fay Wray (Ann Darrow); Robert Armstrong (Carl Denham); Bruce Cabot (John Driscoll); Frank Reicher (Captain Englehorn); Sam Hardy (Weston); Noble Johnson (Native Chief); James Flavin (Briggs the Second Mate); Steve Clemento (Witch King); Victor Long (Lumpy); Ethan Laidlow (Mate); Dick Curtis and Charlie Sullivan (Sailors); Vera Lewis and LeRoy Mason (Theatre Patrons); Paul Porcasi (Apple Vendor); Lynton Brent and Frank Mills (Reporters); and King Kong, the Eighth Wonder of the World.

The 1933 King Kong is a classic that can fit into many genre
categories: horror, science fiction, fantasy, adventure, and cinema.
After all, it was the challenge of making a movie that inspired Carl
Denham (Robert Armstrong) to invade Skull Island with beast-killing
beauty Ann Darrow (Fay Wray) as his leading lady. RKO's King
Kong can be included in this volume for its good-natured sallies at
the on-location adventure travelogues that were so popular in the
early thirties and which still have a foothold on today's television.

The character of Carl Denham obviously is a takeoff on Frank
Buck, who made a number of popular features for RKO in the thirties during his wild animal treks throughout the world. The type of
fare offered by Buck, and earlier in such pictures as Trader Horn
(MGM, 1930), presented intriguing escape for Depression-weary audiences and proved to be consistently popular amusement.

Of course, the plotline of King Kong is too familiar to be re-
told here; but it should be noted that the entire crux of the film is
based on the plan by Denham to shoot a movie. Of course, he had
no idea of the true size of the legendary Kong when he embarked on
the voyage to Skull Island, but like Frank Buck, he was intent on
bringing home a film that would excite and astound his paying audience. Instead he brought home Kong in captivity and nearly joined
the brigade of corpses pummeled by Kong before his Empire State
Building tumble. It should be observed that the story/conception of
the Kong scenario derived from the prolific British thriller writer
Edgar Wallace who some years earlier had written a novel which included an intelligent simian. The book was The Hairy Arm (1924)
and its background was concerned with the on-location shooting of a
B movie in England.

King Kong's follow-up, Son of Kong was released by RKO in
1933. It also included the character of Denham (again played by
Armstrong), but this time the director had deserted movies. He returned to Skull Island intent on finding a rumored treasure there,
hoping to acquire enough loot to pay off the law suits brought against
him for damages done by the Great Ape during his brief New York
City romp.

LADY KILLER (Warner Bros. , 1933) 76 min.

Production supervisor, Henry Blanke; director, Roy Del Ruth;
based on the story "The Finger Man" by Rosalind Keating Shaffer;
adaptors, Ben Markson and Lillie Hayward; screenplay, Markson;
assistant director, Chuck Hansen; costumes, Orr-Kelly; music director, Leo F. Forbstein; makeup, Perc Westmore; art director,
Robert Haas; camera, Tony Gaudio; editor, George Amy.

James Cagney (Dan Quigley); Mae Clark (Myra Gale); Leslie
Fenton (Duke); Margaret Lindsay (Lois Underwood); Henry O'Neill
(Ramick); Willard Robertson (Conroy); Douglas Cosgrove (Jones); Raymond Hatton (Pete); Russell Hopton (Smiley); William Davidson (Williams); Marjorie Gateson (Mrs. Wilbur Marley); Robert Elliott (Brannigan); John Marston (Kendall); Douglass Dumbrille (Spade Maddock);

George Chandler (Thompson); George Blackwood (The Escort); Jack Don Wong (The Oriental); Frank Sheridan (Los Angeles Police Chief); Edwin Maxwell (Jeffries the Theatre Manager); Phil Tead (Usher Sargeant Seymour); Dewey Robinson (The Movie Fan); H. C. Bradley (Man with Purse); Harry Holman (J. B. Roland); Harry Beresford (Dr. Crane); Olaf Hytten (Butler); Harry Strang (Ambulance Attendant); Al Hill (Casino Cashier); Dennis O'Keefe (Man in Casino); James Burke (Handout); Robert Homans (Jailer); Sam McDaniel (Porter); Herman Bing (Western Director); Spencer Charters (Los Angeles Cop); Luis Alberni (Director); Sam Ash (Hood); Ray Cooke (Property Man); Harold Waldridge (Letter Handler).

As a young man Dan Quigley (James Cagney) worked as an usher in a movie theatre, but as he matures in the big city he becomes involved in a life of crime and rises to become a top gangster. To avoid an encircling police dragnet, he departs for Hollywood where he earns a bit in a movie as an Indian and proves to be a screen sensation. Soon he becomes a top Hollywood personality and all is going smoothly until his old gang and his moll (Mae Clarke) show up on the scene; his mob hopes to persuade him to help them in robbing the homes of celebrities. Cagney refuses, finds love with the reformed Clarke, and when the gang is eventually captured, he is cleared of all connection with them. He is free to pursue his career and to enjoy a happy home life with Clarke.

Lady Killer was produced to take advantage of the popularity of the team of Cagney and his grapefruit recipient, Mae Clarke, of The Public Enemy (1931). This time, Cagney drags Clarke around a room by her hair and tosses her down a hallway. As the New York Evening Post observed, "The reason for the picture's existence seems to have been due to a desire to give the versatile and gifted Mr. Cagney a chance to show himself in an all-around way, and Lady Killer is therefore a kind of resume of everything he has done to date in the movies." One very amusing scene has gangster-turned-movie actor Cagney confronting a critic who had given him a bad film review. The pugnacious star forces the erring aisle-sitter to eat the critique!

THE LAST COMMAND (Paramount, 1928) 8154 ft.

Presenters, Adolph Zukor and Jesse L. Lasky; supervisor, J. G. Bachmann; associate producer, B. P. Schulberg; director, Josef von Sternberg; story, Lajos Biro; adaptor/screenplay, John F. Goodrich; titles, Herman J. Mankiewicz; makeup, Fred C. Ryle; technical director, Nicholas Kobyliansky; set designer, Hans Dreier; camera, Bert Glennon; editor, William Shea.

Emil Jannings [General Dolgorucki (Grand Duke Sergius Alexander)]; Evelyn Brent (Natascha Dobrowa); William Powell (Leo Andreiev); Nicholas Soussanin (Adjutant); Michael Visaroff (Serge the Valet); Jack Raymond (Assistant Director); Viacheslav Savitsky (A Private); Fritz Feld (A Revolutionist); Harry Semels (Soldier Extra); Alexander Ikonnikov and Nicholas Kobyliansky (Drill Masters).

The movies have often been a drawing place for erstwhile aristocrats and many such European refugees came to the film capitol in the twenties. In the early days of film, it should be remembered, Leon Trotsky worked as an extra for Vitagraph and by the twenties many once-wealthy Russian nobles populated Hollywood, some of them drawing out a living as extras. It is claimed that Ernst Lubitsch evolved the idea for The Last Command, based in part on a General Lodijenski of the Imperial Russian Army who then operated a Russian restaurant in Hollywood and performed occasional extra work. Still he was far from the only such person with an illustrious past from the Continent who did the same; this study could have been conceived about many an individual.

Grand Duke Sergius Alexander (Emil Jannings) had been a commander in the Russian Army, being a cousin of the Czar. A decade later he is chosen from the ranks of Hollywood extras to play the small role of a general in a feature about the Russian Revolution. The man who selects him is the film's director, Leo Andreiev (William Powell), a onetime Russian revolutionary and former director of the Kiev Imperial Theatre. In a flashback it is related how Powell once was brought before Jannings who put him in jail and took his mistress (Evelyn Brent) as his own. When the Revolution occurs, it is Jannings who is jailed, but Brent is freed and leaves the country. Powell puts Jannings in charge of a battle scene after informing him that Brent has died (in reality she has changed her name and is working in Hollywood). Caught up in the scene, the old man believes he really is back in Russia leading his army. After giving a command, he collapses and dies.

Photoplay magazine noted, "Thanks to the magnificent acting of Emil Jannings, this film is the most popular crying-fest of the season. " Mordaunt Hall of the New York Times stated, "The motion picture end of this feature is wonderfully good, even to the selection of the players. There are the 'yes men, ' the light experts, the electric wires like eels around the studio floor. The instructions are done to a T, without anything being too extravagant. The story opens up with the choosing of a General for the battle scene, and Dolgorucki's photograph is brought out. It results in his selection and soon the casting director's assistant is on the wire calling Dolgorucki on the telephone at his shabby abode. He is told to report at 6:30 the next morning. "

THE LAST MOVIE (Universal, 1971) Color, 108 min.

Executive producer, Michael Gruskoff; producer, Paul Lewis; associate producer, David Hopper; director, Dennis Hopper; story, Stewart Stern and Dennis Hopper; screenplay, Stern; music, Kris Kristofferson; songs, John Buck Wilkin, Chabuca Granda, Severn Darden, and the Villagers of Chinchero, Peru; camera, Laszlo Kovacs; editors, David Bertalsky and Antranig Makakian.

Opposite: Evelyn Brent and Emil Jannings in The Last Command (1928).

Julie Adams (Mrs. Anderson); Daniel Ades (Tomas Mercado); John Alderman (Jonathan); Michael Anderson, Jr. (Mayor's Son); Rich Aguilar (Gaffer); Donna Baccala (Miss Anderson); Tom Baker (Member of Billy's Gang); Toni Basil (Rose); Poupee Bocar (Singer); Anna Lynn Brown (Dancehall Girl); Rod Cameron (Pat); Bernard Casselman (Doctor); James Contreras (Boom Man); Eddie Donno (Stunt Man); Severn Darden (Mayor); Lou Donelan (Prop Man); Roy Engel (Harry Anderson); Peter Fonda (Sheriff); Fritz Ford (Citizen); Samuel Fuller (Director); Michael Green (Hired Gun); Samya Greene (Baby); Dennis Hopper (Kansas); George Hill (Key Grip); Kris Kristofferson (Minstrel Wrangler); John Phillip Law (Little Brother); Ted Markland (Big Brother); Tomas Milian (Priest); Sylvia Miles (Script Girl); Jim Mitchum (Art); Michelle Phillips (Banker's Daughter); Robert Rothwell (Citizen); Dean Stockwell (Billy); Russ Tamblyn (Man in Gang); Alan Warnick (Assistant Director); Dennis Stock (Still Man); Warren Finnerty (Banker); Stella Garcia (Maria); William Gray and Bud Hassink (Gang Members); Don Gordon (Neville); Al Hopson (Sheriff); Henry Jaglom (Minister's Son); Gray Johnson (Stunt Man); Clint Kimbrough (Minister); Jorge Montero (Jorge); John Stevens (Cameraman); John Buck Wilkin (Minstrel Wrangler); Al Montroe (Citizen); Cynthia McAdams and Toni Stern (Dance Hall Girls).

Following the success of Easy Rider (1969), Peter Fonda and Dennis Hopper were riding high on the pop cinema scene. Then Hopper, long a minor player in the movies, decided to make an anti-violent Western, insisting he was prompted by the violence in his brief scenes in True Grit (1969). He took a film crew to an out-of-the-way place in Peru where he made The Last Movie, a heavy-handed allegorical film that seemed to fulfill all that Hopper had to say about cinema. Unfortunately for him, his message was incomprehensible to the vast bulk of moviegoers.

Hopper--besides writing and directing the feature--starred himself as Kansas, a wrangler who is now a stuntman in the movies and who enjoys wanton violence for its own sake. He arrives at a small village in the Peruvian Andes to shoot a violent Western for director Samuel Fuller. After the company has departed, Hopper remains in this beautiful region, hoping to buy up the real estate. He is convinced the village and the surrounding area would be an ideal place to shoot Westerns (in the manner of what thirties' Western film hero Ray "Crash" Corrigan did when he developed his Corriganville in California). Unfortunately for Hopper, who relives much of his past experiences in flashbacks, the local natives consider filmmaking a religious experience and the stuntman is eventually sacrificed in one of their ceremonies.

Despite its more than adequate cast (with some "names" present) and its well-conceived cinematography, The Last Movie received scant bookings when it premiered. Charles Champlin (Los Angeles Times) took occasion to lambast the film for its negative effect on the entire picture industry. "As a piece of film-making it is inchoate, amateurish, self-indulgent, tedious, superficial, unfocused, and a precious waste not only of money, but, more importantly, of a significant and conspicuous opportunity. The cause of

the adventurous young filmmaker and the cause of complete control
for any filmmaker working in Hollywood have been damaged. "

THE LAST OF SHEILA (Warner Bros. , 1973) Color, 123 min.

Executive producer, Stanley O'Toole; producer/director, Herbert Ross; screenplay, Stephen Sondheim and Anthony Perkins; assistant directors, William C. Gerrity and Michael Cheyko; production
designer, Ken Adam; art director, Tony Roman; set decorator, John
Jarvis; music, Billy Goldenberg; sound, Cyril Swern; sound re-recording, David Dockendorf; camera, Gerry Turpin; editor, Edward Warschilka.

Richard Benjamin (Tom); Dyan Cannon (Christine); James Co-
burn (Clinton Greene); Joan Hackett (Lee); James Mason (Philip); Ian
McShane (Anthony); Raquel Welch (Alice); Yvonne Romaine (Sheila
Greene); Pierro Rosso (Vittorio); Serge Citon (Guido); Robert Rossi
(Captain); Elaine Geisinger and Elliott Geisinger (American Couple);
Jack Pugeat (Silver Salesman); Maurice Crosnier (Concierge).

The Last of Sheila had a lot going for it at the box-office. It
boasted a large and well-known cast all integrated into a mystery
setting, glamour abounded, and it appeared to be a ready-made success. The opposite resulted, however, since its performers seemed
ill-at-ease (sometimes hostile) with one another, the mystery element
emerged more like the plot of a dullish daytime soap opera, and
what little chic the picture enveloped appeared strained and at times
gaudy. The Last of Sheila had only a very brief theatrical run before being demoted to prime-time television where it enjoyed no more
impact that it had on the big screen.
Like many other films dealing with people in the movie industry, The Last of Sheila (based on a script by Broadway composer
Stephen Sondheim and actor/pal Tony Perkins) really dealt very little
with movie making. Its mystery format could just as easily have
been attached to any profession, from sports to big business. The
movie derives its title from two sources: the name of the luxury
yacht on which the story takes place, and from the name of the dead
wife of the film producer (James Coburn) who invited a half-dozen
people--all close friends of the deceased woman--for a week's cruise
on the Riviera.
Those aboard are Sheila's director (James Mason), who has
a difficult time these days finding work; a rival Hollywood glamour
girl (Raquel Welch) and her business-manager husband (Ian MacShane),
a screenwriter (Richard Benjamin) and his rich wife (Joan Hackett),
and a talent agent (Dyan Cannon). On the ship the passengers are
prepared for a pleasant jaunt when their host suggests a game in
which every person is given a card with a secret about another voy-
ager. One of the cards reports that a passenger is a murderer and
the hit-and-run driver who killed Sheila. At a stopover at old island
fortress, one of the passengers kills the host, and the remaining
members are forced to reveal deeply hidden secrets about themselves
before the real criminal is brought to light.

James Mason, Joan Hackett, and Richard Benjamin in The Last of Sheila (1973).

The British Monthly Film Bulletin weighed, "It's ultimately the kind of film that must have been more amusing to plot and shoot than it is to watch; and the most teasing riddles for an audience are likely to be the real identities of the Hollywood personalities being satirised. "

THE LAST TYCOON (Paramount, 1976) Color, 122 min.

Producer, Sam Spiegel; director, Elia Kazan; based on the unfinished novel by F. Scott Fitzgerald; screenplay, Harold Pinter; music, Maurice Jarre; production designer, Gene Callahan; art director, Jack Collis; set decorators, Bill Smith and Jerry Wunderlich; costumes/wardrobe, Anna Hill Johnstone, Anthea Sylbert, Thalia Phillips, and Richard Bruno; assistant director, Danny McCauley; sound, Dick Vorisek and Larry Jost; camera, Victor Kemper; editor, Richard Marks.

Robert DeNiro (Monroe Stahr); Tony Curtis (Rodriguez); Robert Mitchum (Pat Brady); Jeanne Moreau (Didi); Jack Nicholson (Brimmer); Donald Pleasence (Boxley); Ingrid Boulting (Kathleen Moore); Ray Milland (Fleishacker); Dana Andrews (Red Ridingwood); Theresa Russell (Cecilia Brady); Peter Strauss (Wylie); Tige Andrews (Popolos); Morgan Farley (Marcus); John Carradine (Guide); Jeff Corey (Doctor); Angelica Huston (Edna); Don Brodie (Assistant); Seymour Cassell (Seal Trainer); Leslie Curtis (Mrs. Rodriguez); Lloyd Kino (Butler); Peggy Feury (Hairdresser); Betsy Jones-Moreland (Lady Writer).

Although the critics were negative about Paramount's production of F. Scott Fitzgerald's The Great Gatsby (1973), the film did tremendous box-office business (helped immensely by the presence of star Robert Redford), which stimulated the studio to produce the writer's last unfinished work, The Last Tycoon. In his twilight years, Fitzgerald had worked for MGM as a scriptwriter and there he saw the single-handed power that Irving Thalberg had over that studio's production. Many scholars insist the character of Monroe Stahr in the novel The Last Tycoon is based upon Thalberg, while others find it a conglomeration of that high-powered individual and the author himself. Whatever the combination, it took nearly four decades for the work (which was published in 1941) to reach the screen.

The wispy plotline for The Last Tycoon relates the life of Stahr (Robert DeNiro), a New York City Jew who migrates to Holly- wood to rise and take control of a large production company. It depicts how he controls virtually every aspect of the dozens of films made by the studio each year, how he deals with neurotic performers and craftsmen, how he fuses politics and entertainment, and fights to maintain his position against overly ambitious rivals. The film details his mental collapse after meeting a lovely young girl (Ingrid Boulting) who greatly reminds him of his late actress-wife whom he loved dearly. After his spouse's demise, his life had become his work. But he deserts that protective surrounding to give pursuit

Ray Milland, Robert Mitchum, Jeanne Moreau, and Robert DeNiro in The Last Tycoon (1976).

to the young lady who teases but does not succumb to his advances. The result of her rejection is eventual mental collapse.

DeNiro carries the bulk of the load of the film, but he constantly is hampered by a too-sketchy scenario characterization of Stahr. The lovely Boulting--in her first major assignment--is miscast as the Lilith of the story, although cameos by Robert Mitchum (as a studio executive rival), Tony Curtis (as a macho movie star), Jeanne Moreau (as an aging great actress), Dana Andrews (as a B movie director) and Ray Milland (as an East Coast lawyer) were particularly effective.   Less can be said for Jack Nicholson's performance as a strike leader involved in leftist activities.

"Written by Harold Pinter, and directed by Elia Kazan, the movie attempts to take Hollywood seriously, without hoopla and gro-tesqueries, and especially to take Thalberg-Stahr seriously. ... The movie is full of echoes. We watch it as if at a far remove from what's happening, but that too is appropriate; Fitzgerald was writing history as it happened. " Such was Vincent Canby's verdict in the

august New York Times. The usually more indulgent Variety carped,
"In its relentless focus on the Monroe Stahr character, the script
provides too much form and not enough substance. Kazan & Co. deliver all the superficials and precious little of the inner person. Who
knows? Maybe there isn't much beneath the surface, but as is, who
cares? ... Whether in the script, direction or editing, there's one
pervasive strain to the entire 112-minutes: Everyone spends a lot of
time staring and reacting in some kind of puzzlement, as though Allen Funt has just emerged from behind the camera in every take explaining that it's all a 'Candid Camera' stunt. Nobody deliberately
makes a film of reaction shots, so there must have been more, at
one time. "

Frank Rich (New York Post) was generally pleased with the
results, especially as to the finale of the uncompleted book original.
"Rather than use Fitzgerald's baroque notes for his books' conclusion,
they've simply taken a minor anecdote from one of the novel's early
chapters and used it to sew the whole work together: As Stahr ad-
dresses us to expound his philosophy of 'making pictures, ' we simultaneously see that the hero is a part of another movie, of his own
life, that's beyond his control. With this one masterstroke, Kazan
and Pinter bring home almost every level of The Last Tycoon's
meaning - and while their daring film isn't likely to enrich Fitzgerald's
estate too much, it profoundly enriches our understanding of his art. "

While Peter Cowie (reviewing in Focus on Film magazine)
found "incidental pleasures" within The Last Tycoon, he does view
"as unforgivable ... the persistent suggestion of the 'rushes' in The
Last Tycoon, that during the Thirties Metro--or even all of Holly-
wood--was turning out a series of schmaltzy melodramas, when retrospective after retrospective has proved otherwise. Perhaps the
final irony is that those vintage movies of Thalberg's will long out-
live Sam Spiegel's Last Tycoon. "

THE LEGEND OF HOLLYWOOD (Producers Distributing Corp. , 1924)
    5414 ft.

    Presenter, Charles R. Rogers; director, Renaud Hoffman; based
on the article by Frank Condon; screenplay/titles, Alfred A. Cohn;
camera, Karl Struss; editor, Glenn Wheeler.

    Percy Marmont (John Smith); ZaSu Pitts (Mary Brown); Alice
Davenport (Mrs. Rooney); Dorothy Dorr (Blondie); Cameo (Himself).

    Frank Condon's Photoplay piece was the basis for this minor
yarn about an idealistic young scenario writer, John Smith (Percy
Marmont), who comes to Hollywood in search of fame and fortune.
He lodges at the modest boarding house of Mrs. Rooney (Alice Davenport) and there meets movie-struck Mary Brown (ZaSu Pitts), who
secretly falls in love with him. When various companies reject his
scripts, Marmont becomes depressed and chooses to commit suicide.
He fills seven glasses with wine and puts poison in one and then mixes
the glasses and drinks one each day for a week. Finally he consumes
the last glassful and waits to die. Only then does he learn that Pitts

has removed the poisoned glass and replaced it.   He then understands
that her love is more important than movie success and they plan to
wed.

THE LEGEND OF LYLAH CLARE (MGM, 1968) Color, 130 min.

Producer, Robert Aldrich; associate producer, Walter Blanke;
director, Aldrich; based on the teleplay by Robert Thom and Edward
De Blasio; screenplay, Hugo Butler and Jean Rouverol; music, Frank
De Vol; song, De Vol and Sibylle Siegfried; art directors, George W.
Davis and William Glasgow; set decorators, Henry Grace and Keogh
Gleason; makeup, William Tuttle and Robert Schiffer; assistant dir-
ector, Cliff C. Coleman; costumes, Renie; sound, Franklin Milton;
camera, Joseph Biroc; editor, Michael Luciano.

Kim Novak (Lylah Clare/Elsa Brinkmann); Peter Finch (Lewis
Zarkan); Ernest Borgnine (Barney Sheean); Milton Selzer (Bart Lang-
ner); Rossella Falk (Rossella); Gabriele Tinti (Paolo); Coral Browne
(Molly Luther); Valentina Cortese (Countess Bozo Bedoni); Jean Car-
roll (Becky Langner); Michael Murphy (Mark Peter Sheean); George
Kennedy (Matt Burke in Anna Christie scene); Lee Meriwether (Young
Girl); James Lanphier and Hal Maguire (Legmen); Robert Ellenstein
(Mike); Nick Dennis (Nick); Dave Willock (Cameraman); Peter Bravos
(Butler); Ellen Corby (Script Woman); Michael Fox (Announcer); Ver-
non Scott (Himself); Queenie Smith (Hairdresser); Barbara Ann Wark-
meister and Mel Warkmeister (Aerialists); Sidney Skolsky (Himself).

Producer-director Robert Aldrich turned out two of the best
of the Hollywood-looks-at-itself films, The Big Knife and What Ever
Happened to Baby Jane? (qq. v.), but he turned sour with The Legend
of Lylah Clare, a ludicrous, boring venture.   In retrospect it seems
more a horror film gone astray than a tale of Hollywood revealing
any of its dark secrets.
Young actress Elsa Brinkmann (Kim Novak) is discovered by
director Lewis Zarkan (Peter Finch) and given the chance to portray
Lylah Clare, a famous screen goddess who died mysteriously years
before on her wedding night with Finch.   Novak is soon emotionally
caught up in the part as Finch literally transforms her into Lylah,
so much so that the dead woman's spirit seems to have taken possession of her body.   Finch, a has-been seeking a comeback with
this new film, finds himself falling in love with the fresh image of
Lylah.   Through this discovery a horrible secret is revealed.   Finch
had killed the real Lylah by pushing her down a staircase after he
discovered she was a lesbian.   Tragically, Novak becomes so involved
in her new role as Lylah, that she too meets a violent death in a
fall.
Obviously impressed by Novak's similar dual role in Alfred
Hitchcock's Vertigo (1958), Aldrich sought to repeat the scene here.
But Novak seemed too ill-at-ease (and too old) for the part; it would
have been far more ideal for Elke Sommer to play the Teutonic, icy
beauty.   Neither Ernest Borgnine in a Harry Cohn-like part nor Coral

Ernest Borgnine, Peter Finch, Kim Novak, and Michael Murphy in
The Legend of Lylah Clare (1968).

Browne as the gossip columnist amalgam (Hedda Hopper-Louella Par-
sons-et al.) were sufficiently sharp enough in their portrayals to give
any flavor of the Hollywood scene. (One bit of true-life casting was
to have character actress Ellen Corby as a script woman in the story;
that is how she began her Hollywood career.)

    The film was trounced by the critics and ignored by the pub-
lic. Saturday Review dismissed it as "unpalatable" and Newsweek
magazine scoffed that it "fights cliches with cliches." There were
only a few members of the press who found a subtle enjoyment in
distilling parallels from the film to Hollywood's past: i.e. the assumption that the Finch-Novak relationship was a reworking of the
special rapport that existed between Josef von Sternberg and Marlene
Dietrich during her early Paramount years.

For the record, in the brief <u>Anna Christie</u> film-within-the-film scene, that is George Kennedy trying to be Matt Burke.

THE LEGEND OF VALENTINO (ABC-TV, 1975) Color, 100 min.

Producers, Aaron Spelling and Leonard Goldberg; director, Melville Shavelson; teleplay, Shavelson; music, Charles Fox; art director, Tracy Bousman; wardrobe designer, Nolan Miller; choreography, Anita Mann; camera, Arch Dalzell; editor, John Woodcock.

Suzanne Pleshette (June Mathis); Franco Nero (Rudolph Valentino); Judd Hirsch (Jake Auerbach); Lesley Warren (Laura Lorraine); Milton Berle (Jesse Lasky); Yvette Mimieux (Natacha Rambova); Harold J. Stone (Sam Baldwin); Alicia Bond (Nazimova); Michael Thoma (Rex Ingram); Connie Forslund (Silent Star); Brenda Venus (Constance Carr); Ruben Moreno (Mexican Mayor); Penny Santon (Madame Tullio); Jane Alice Brandon (Teenager).

After a dismal attempt to bring the life of silent movie idol Rudolph Valentino (1895-1926) to the screen in 1951 in <u>Valentino</u> (q. v.), interest waned cinematically in the star until the late sixties. Then Irving Shulman's book on the actor was published and its titillating account became a best seller. By the mid-seventies the interest in the legendary screen lead had risen to the point that several film projects were in the works. In Italy there had been <u>Ciao Rudy</u>, a musical about Valentino. There was talk in the mid-seventies of Elvis Presley's recreating the stage role at Radio City Music Hall for a limited engagement; it remained just talk. ABC-TV got off to an early start with the telefeature, <u>The Legend of Valentino,</u> aired late in 1975.

The play opens in 1920 when screenwriter June Mathis (Suzanne Pleshette) discovers Rudolph Valentino (Franco Nero), a struggling Italian immigrant, and discerns potential in him as a future film star. With the help of press agent Jake Auerbach (Judd Hirsch), Mathis wins Valentino the lead in <u>The Four Horsemen of the Apocalypse</u> which in short order elevates him to stardom. Unfortunately the star's private life is far less happy, engulfed with unpleasant marital unions. His marriage to Natacha Rambova (Yvette Mimieux), a protégée of screen star Nazimova (Alicia Bond) is a severe strain. Natacha rules Rudy with an iron hand and assumes control over his career, leading her husband into artistic chaos. Buckling under the strain of living up to his screen image (and combatting the press' scorn that he is a powderpuff star) Valentino's health begins to fail. He dies suddenly in New York City on the eve of the premiere of his latest film, <u>Son of the Shiek</u>.

Outside of the use of actual character names, the telefeature had little relation to truth. Morna Murphy in <u>The Hollywood Reporter</u> panned this obvious lack of regard for the facts thusly, "Screenwriter Melville Shavelson excuses this slander by claiming 'I found that the easiest way to write the script was to work from his image and not from reality!' But since he obviously made no attempt to use even well-known facts of Valentino's life this is a poor excuse. "

Yvette Mimieux and Franco Nero in The Legend of Valentino (1975).

Franco Nero did what he could with the shallowly-conceived title role, although he was a bit too mature for the assignment, and Suzanne Pleshette was too beautiful and slick for the Mathis part.   Milton Berle played Jesse Lasky with no regard for the original Lasky and Yvette Mimieux seemed at a loss as how best to portray the complicated Natacha Rambova role.

In short, The Legend of Valentino did nothing to clarify the legend or the facts, it only repeated that the controversial personality was a tortured and misunderstood man.   That assumption, however, had been apparent since the time of his death, a half-century ago!   The film did try, however, to enlighten its audience about the Hollywood of the period--at least as the movie colony was conceived by writer-director Shavelson.   His view was rather bleak, as noted by John O'Connor in the New York Times: "What emerges is a portrait of the innocent against the corrupting forces of commerce and vulgarity.   As someone snarls, 'This is Hollywood--we all eat dirt out here--it pays well. '"

LET'S FALL IN LOVE (Columbia, 1934) 64 min.

Director, David Burton; screenplay, Herbert Fields; songs,

Ann Sothern, Edmund Lowe, and Tala Birell in Let's Fall in Love (1934).

Harold Arlen and Ted Koehler; music director, Constantin Bakaleini-koff; camera, Benjamin Kline; editor, Gene Melford.

Edmund Lowe (Ken); Ann Sothern (Jean); Miriam Jordan (Gerry); Gregory Ratoff (Max); Greta Meyer (Lisa); Tala Birell (Forsell); Arthur Jarrett (Composer); Marjorie Gateson (Agatha); Betty Furness (Linda).

Celebrated film director Ken (Edmund Lowe) must quickly find a replacement for a temperamental, but popular, movie queen who has returned home to Sweden. He scouts around and finally locates a Brooklyn girl (Ann Sothern) working at a carnival and signs her to an acting contract. After six weeks of training he introduces her as his latest European discovery. During the tutelage, the girl comes to adore Lowe, much to the chagrin of his fiancée, Gerry (Miriam Jordan). Finally the jealous Jordan reveals Sothern's true background. But by now she has been fully accepted by the public and she finds happiness with the man she loves, along with a successful film career.
Let's Fall in Love is a first for several reasons. It was the first to star Ann Sothern, who had previously been known as Harriett Lake. It also introduced Harold Arlen to writing movie music and

he penned a trio of tunes for the film, including the very popular title song. Also the film provided Gregory Ratoff with yet another opportunity to enlarge upon his harried producer role. Finally, Let's Fall in Love, is one of the few Hollywood-on-Hollywood entries which has been re-made--as Slightly French (q. v.) in 1949 with Dorothy Lamour.
    The New York Times evaluated it as "a nimble-witted romantic comedy which trips along so lightly that the fade-out brings the spectator out of a mood. "

LET'S GO PLACES (Fox, 1930) 6442 ft.

    Presenter, William Fox; director, Frank Strayer; story, Andrew Bennison; screenplay/dialogue, William K. Wells; songs, Con Conrad, Sidney Mitchell, and Archie Gottler; James Hanley and James Brockman; George A. Little and John Burke; Joseph McCarthy and Jimmy Monaco; Cliff Friend and Monaco; choreography, Danny Dare; assistant director, William Tummell; sound, Frank MacKenzie; camera, Conrad Wells; editor, Al De Gaetano.

    Joseph Wagstaff (Paul Adams); Lola Lane (Marjorie Lorraine); Sharon Lynn (Virginia Gordon); Frank Richardson (J. Speed Quinn); Walter Catlett (Rex Wardell); Dixie Lee (Dixie); Charles Judels (Du Bonnet); Ilka Chase (Mrs. Du Bonnet); Larry Steers (Ben King).

    The old show business cliché about mistaken identity was given still another airing in this early talkie musical comedy. Despite the hackneyed posture of the plot, the ploy worked sufficiently well under the direction of Frank Strayer.
    Here Joseph Wagstaff portrayed Paul Adams, an energetic young singer who arrives in Hollywood intent on a screen career. While there he is accidentally mistaken for an important performer with a similar name and he takes advantage of this error in identity to open the "doors" necessary to becoming a success. When the ruse is finally discovered, it is too late as the young man is already an established star. The happy ending is complete as along the way Wagstaff has met and fallen in love with Marjorie Lorraine (Lola Lane), the girl of his dreams.
    An interesting aspect of the production--especially for the early sound era--was the depiction of actual filming of the musical numbers which were a part of the film-within-the-film situation.

LIGHTS OUT (Film Booking Offices of America, 1923) 6938 ft.

    Director, Al Santell; based on the play by Paul Dickey and Mann Page; adaptor, Rex Taylor; camera, William Marshall.

    Ruth Stonehouse (Hairpin Annie); Walter McGrail (Sea Bass); Marie Astaire (Barbara); Theodore von Eltz [Eggs (Egbert Winslow)]; Ben Deely (High-Shine Joe); Hank Mann (Ben); Ben Hewlett (Keith Forbes); Mabel Van Buren (Mrs. Gallant); Fred Kelsey (Decker); Harry Fenwick (Peyton); Chester Bishop (Bangs the Film Director); Max Ascher (Wellabach the Film Producer).

Joseph Wagstaff (top), Lola Lane, and Frank Richardson in a publicity shot for Let's Go Places (1930).

This film, based on the 1922 play of the same name, commences when crooks Hairpin Annie (Ruth Stonehouse) and Sea Bass (Walter McGrail) steal a suitcase on a train and find it is loaded with movie scenarios.   They are pursued by the suitcase's owner, Egbert Winslow (Theodore von Eltz) who agrees to write a script about the underworld based on McGrail's recollections.   The latter wants to get even with an ex-pal for double-crossing him on a job and thus bases his remembrances on that criminal.

The script is later purchased by a studio and filmed.   Everyone is basking in the success of the project until the crook-in-question sees the photoplay in a South American cinema and realizes he has been exploited.   Immediately he hurries back to the U. S. , intent on killing McGrail.   Later, the president of a bank, once robbed by the crook, recognizes the culprit as he searches for McGrail and saves the writer by bringing the police onto the scene just in time.

The film would be remade in 1937 by RKO as Crashing Hollywood (q. v.).

LITTLE MISS ROUGHNECK (Columbia, 1938) 64 min.

Director, Aubrey Scotto; screenplay, Fred Niblo, Jr. , Grace Neville, and Michael L. Simmons; songs, Milton Drake, George Jessel, and Ben Oakland; sound, George Cooper; camera, Benjamin Kline; editor, James Sweeney.

Edith Fellows (Foxine LaRue); Leo Carrillo (Pascual); Scott Colton (Partridge); Jacqueline Wells [Julie Bishop] (Mary); Margaret Irving (Gert); Inez Palange (Mercedes); George McKay (Edward); Thurston Hall (Crowley); Frank C. Wilson (DeWilde); John Gallaudet (Larkin); Walter Stahl (Von Hammer); Ivan Miller (Yerkes); Al Bridge (Sheriff); Wade Boteler (Carr); Guy Usher (Dorn).

For some unknown reason, the few films dealing with youngsters seeking a screen career proved flat and unmemorable.   Little Miss Roughneck was no exception.   It starred Edith Fellows, Columbia Pictures' response to the box-office magic of Judy Garland and Deanna Durbin.   Variety complained of the film that it was "light fare, paced stodgily, with little if any b. o. future. "

Gert (Margaret Irving) is a determined stage mother with a singing child (Fellows) and a non-pro offspring, Mary (Jacqueline Wells--later Julie Bishop).   Because talent scout Partridge (Scott Colton) has a yen for Wells, he agrees to represent Fellows.   Nothing gells in her career until the youngster dreams up an enterprising kidnapping scheme--involving Leo Carrillo--and she becomes the center of newspaper headlines.   As a result she is given a seven-year contract.

Fellows would also star in another genre entry, Girl's Town (q. v.).

THE LOST SQUADRON (RKO, 1932) 79 min.

Director, George Archainbaud; story, Dick Grace; screenplay,

Wallace Smith; dialogue, Smith and Herman Mankiewicz; sound, Hugh
McDowell; aerial camera, Roy Robison and Elmer Dyer; camera,
Leo Tover and Edward Cronjager; editor, William Hamilton.

Richard Dix (Captain Gibson); Mary Astor (Follette Marsh);
Erich von Stroheim (Erich Von Furst); Dorothy Jordan (The Pest);
Joel McCrea (Red); Robert Armstrong (Woody); Hugh Herbert (Fritz);
Ralph Ince (Detective); Dick Grace, Art Gobel, Leo Nomis, and
Frank Clark (Flyers).

The plight of World War I flying aces, reduced to performing
dangerous and underpaid work as stunt pilots for the movies in the
twenties and the thirties, is presented herein. The Lost Squadron
displays the story of a quartet of such pilots making a World War I
flying epic for a half-mad, tyrannical German director. Unfortunately this RKO release contains too much soap elements and not enough
reality to make it an accurate reflection of the lives of the men it
sought to portray.

Captain Gibson (Richard Dix) is the leader of the flight group--
with Fritz (Hugh Herbert) as their mechanic--who is forced to fly
overly-dangerous stunts for demanding director Erich von Furst (well-
played by Erich von Stroheim) in a war movie. This genre of cinema was still popular at the time, as exemplified by Hell's Angels,
Cock of the Air, The Dawn Patrol and others. When members of
the squadron begin to die in the course of the moviemaking effort,
Dix becomes more at odds with the heartless director but is soothed
in amorous ways by the love of actress Follette Marsh (Mary Astor).
Eventually the deaths of the pilots causes the disgrace of the director, thus making The Lost Squadron an early plea for safety pre-
cautions for both stuntmen and stunt fliers.

Although Dix and the rest of the cast (including a young Joel
McCrea) were solid in their roles and von Stroheim magnificent, the
film is badly dated today.

There was enough footage left over from this aerial excursion
to provide RKO with stock scenes for Lucky Devils (q.v.), issued
the next year. Surprisingly this re-hash of The Lost Squadron was
far superior to the melodramatic original.

When released, The Lost Squadron was advertised as "Not
Just an Air Picture ... But an Air Picture in the Making! ... Re-
vealing the Sights, Thrills, Drama of the Studio the Public Never
Sees!"

THE LOVE GODDESSES (Walter Reade-Sterling, 1965) 87 min.

Producers/script, Saul J. Turell and Graeme Ferguson; technical supervisor, Ray Angus; music, Percy Faith; consultants, William K. Everson, Paul Killiam, and James A. Lebenthal; researchers, George Labrousse and Gideon Bachmann; editors, Nat Greene
and Howard Kuperman.

Opposite: Mary Astor and Richard Dix in The Lost Squadron (1932).

Carl King (Narrator).

Scenes include: Blonde Venus (1932) and Morocco (1930) with
Marlene Dietrich; True Heart Susie (1919) with Lillian Gish; Leopard
Woman (1920) with Louise Glaum; Cleopatra (1917) with Theda Bara;
Intolerance (1916) with Mae Marsh; The Cheat (1915) with Fannie
Ward and Sessue Hayakawa; The Sheik (1921) with Agnes Ayres and
Rudolph Valentino; Hula (1927) with Clara Bow; Blood and Sand (1922)
with Nita Naldi; Woman of the World (1925) with Pola Negri; The Sor-
rows of Satan (1926) with Lya De Putti; The Loves of Sunya (1927)
with Gloria Swanson; The Diary of a Lost Girl (1929) with Louise
Brooks; Ecstasy (1933) with Hedy Lamarr; L'Atlantide (1932) with
Brigitte Helm; Peter the Tramp (1922) with Greta Garbo; Platinum
Blonde (1931) with Jean Harlow; Cabin in the Cotton (1932) with Bette
Davis; Gold Diggers of 1933 (1933) with Ruby Keeler and Dick Powell;
No Man of Her Own (1932) with Carole Lombard and Clark Gable;
Professional Sweetheart (1933) with Ginger Rogers and Norman Fos-
ter; Love Me Tonight (1932) with Jeanette MacDonald, Myrna Loy,
Maurice Chevalier, and Charlie Ruggles; I'm No Angel (1933) with
Mae West; Baby Face (1933) with Barbara Stanwyck; Now and For-
ever (1934) with Shirley Temple; They Won't Forget (1937) with Lana
Turner; College Swing (1938) with Betty Grable; Her Jungle Love
(1938) with Dorothy Lamour and Ray Milland; Gilda (1946) with Rita
Hayworth; A Place in the Sun (1951) with Elizabeth Taylor and Montgomery Clift; Some Like It Hot (1959) with Marilyn Monroe; It Started
in Naples (1960) with Sophia Loren and Clark Gable; Tiger Bay (1959)
with Hayley Mills and Horst Buchholz; Roman Holiday (1953) with Audrey Hepburn and Gregory Peck; Room at the Top (1958) with Heather
Sears and Simone Signoret; Love Is My Profession (1958) with Brigitte Bardot; Expresso Bongo (1959) with Sylvia Syms; The American
Venus (1926) with Esther Ralston; and Cleopatra (1934) with Claudette
Colbert.

In the mid-sixties, some years before the beginning of the
nostalgia craze, Walter Reade-Sterling issued this documentary which
traced the origin and progress of the Hollywood female sex symbol.
Naturally the then-current availability of material greatly influenced
the content, as well as the overall gist and slant of the film's thesis.
Still, many of the clips included were rarely seen. Overall the 87-
minute offering was a diverting (if not very historical) accounting of
Hollywood's various distaff stars.
The film's clips begin in the teens with scenes of such World
War I-era stars as Fannie Ward and Theda Bara and then progresses
into the Roaring Twenties to show Lillian Gish, Gloria Swanson, Nita
Naldi, Clara Bow, et al. The main emphasis of the documentary,
and obviously where more footage was available, was the thirties.
The best sequences from the decade involve scenes of Mae West,
Marlene Dietrich, and Hedy Lamarr. The forties are represented
by Rita Hayworth, while the fifties bring Elizabeth Taylor, Marilyn
Monroe, and Brigitte Bardot to the fore.
Of real interest to film enthusiasts were excerpts from such
little-seen items as Peter the Tramp which introduced Greta Garbo,
Theda Bara's Cleopatra, and Brigitte Helm in L'Atlantide.

James Coburn and Robert Morse in <u>The Loved One</u> (1965).

THE LOVED ONE (MGM, 1965) 119 min.

Executive producer, Martin Ransohoff; producers, John Calley and Haskell Wexler; associate producer, Neil Hartley; director, Tony Richardson; based on the novel by Evelyn Waugh; screenplay, Terry Southern and Christopher Isherwood; assistant director, Kurt Neumann; production designer/costumes, Rouben Ter-Arutunian; set decorator, Jim Payne; music/music director, John Addison; makeup supervisor, Emil La Vigne; sound, Stan Fiferman; special effects, G. G. Gaspar; camera, Wexler; supervising editor, Anthony Gibbs; editors, Hal Ashby and Brian Smedley-Aston.

Robert Morse (Dennis Barlow); Jonathan Winters (Wilbur Glenworthy/Harry Glenworthy); Anjanette Comer (Aimee Thanatogenos); Rod Steiger (Mr. Joyboy); Dana Andrews (General Brinkman); Milton Berle (Mr. Kenton); James Coburn (Immigration Officer); John Gielgud (Sir Francis Hinsley); Tab Hunter (Guide); Margaret Leighton (Mrs. Kenton); Liberace (Mr. Starker); Roddy McDowall (D. J., Jr.); Robert Morley (Sir Ambrose Abercrombie); Lionel Stander (The Guru Brahmin); Ayllene Gibbons (Joyboy's Mother); Bernie Kopell (Assis-

tant to the Guru Brahmin); Asa Maynor (Secretary to D. J. , Jr.);
Alan Napier (English Club Official); Barbara Nichols (The Widow).

"Now that we've had The Loved One, " wrote critic Judith
Crist, "can black comedy get any blacker?" Indeed, Evelyn Waugh's
1948 novel, described by its English satirist author as "a little nightmare produced by the unaccustomed high living of a brief visit to
Hollywood, " was proudly presented by its director Tony Richardson
as "the movie with something to offend everybody. " It was chock
full of thumb-nosing at the American dream and centered its heartless
lampoon on the Hollywood funeral industry a la Forest Lawn. The
result, in the words of critic Shana Alexander, suggested "a sort of
mad Marx Brothers adventure in necrophilia. "

A parade of grotesques comprise the cast of characters of
The Loved One: a worthless English poet (Robert Morse) who decides to visit Hollywood to prey on the wealth of his script writer
uncle (Sir John Gielgud); Mr. Joyboy (Rod Steiger), the repulsive top
mortician of Whispering Glades Memorial Park who tends to Gielgud's
corpse after the latter hangs himself; tender Aimee Thanatogenos
(Anjanette Comer), a dedicated fledgling mortician who commits suicide by embalming herself after suffering romantic disillusionment;
Jonathan Winters as Whispering Glades' director who creates a chapel
with pornographic stained-glass windows; and others.

While Richardson cast numerous offbeat unknowns (including
obese Ayllene Gibbons as Joyboy's viciously hungry mother--who de-
vours a roast pig, eyes and all--and a young Paul Williams as a
rocket-launching punk), he also employed a host of stars in cameo
assignments, including Liberace as an unctuous coffin salesman, Lionel Stander as a drunken guru, and Dana Andrews as a military man
whose staff has sex with fishnet-stockinged whores in caskets (a
"special treat" of the Whispering Glades establishment). A book
could be written about the various sequences deleted from The Loved
One. In The Unkindest Cuts (1972), Doug McClelland details how
scenes featuring Ruth Gordon, Keenan Wynn, Jayne Mansfield (as a
traveler's aid worker) were deleted, and how Barbara Nichols' role
as the stripteaser widow of America's first astronaut was reduced
to a mere walk-on. (Back in 1957, agent Ingo Preminger (brother
of Otto) planned to film The Loved One, with a script by Luis Buñuel
and Philip Roll, with Buñuel directing and Alec Guinness starring.
At one point in that period, Shirley MacLaine was being considered
to play the Aimee Thanatogenos role.)

As is perhaps obvious by the plot discussion, The Loved One,
in the words of the Saturday Review "is gallows humor, which may
not be to everyone's taste. But it is certainly the longest and boldest
step up from conventional film fare ever to come from a major American studio. That faint whirring heard on the soundtrack from time
to time is probably old Louis B. Mayer slowly revolving in his
grave. "

Though MGM harbored high hopes for the offbeat film because
of the American public's then topical interest in black humor, the
picture was simply too sick (and too broadly conceived) for most
general audiences. Filmgoers could accept Dr. Strangelove (1964)
but were repelled by the grizzly morbidities of The Loved One.

LUCKY DEVILS (RKO 1933) 64 min.

Executive producer, David O. Selznick; associate producer,
Merian C. Cooper; director, Ralph Ince; story, Casey Robinson and
Bob Rose; adaptors, Agnes Christine Johnson and Ben Markson; art
director, Van Nest Polglase; sound, Earl A. Walcott; camera, J.
Roy Hunt; editor, Jack Kitchin.

William Boyd (Skipper); Dorothy Wilson (Fran); William Gargan
(Bob); Rosco Ates (Gabby); William Bakewell (Slugger); Bruce Cabot
(Happy); Creighton Chaney [Lon Chaney, Jr.] (Frankie); Bob Rose
(Rusty); Julie Haydon (Doris); Betty Furness (Ginger); Phyllis Fraser
(Midget); Sylvia Picker (Toots); Edwin Stanley (Spence); Charles Gil-
lette (Cameraman); Gladden James (Neville); Alan Roscoe (Director).

A group of daredevil Hollywood stuntmen, led by Skipper (William Boyd) and Bob (William Gargan) sit at their favorite speakeasy, the
Angel's Nest, picking glass off of their clothes after performing
stunts for a bank robbery epic.   One of their number, Slugger (William Bakewell), accidentally breaks a bottle--a bad omen--and announces he is going to get married, which means he will turn soft
and do no more dangerous stunts.
Later Boyd and Gargan save Fran (Dorothy Wilson) from committing suicide and they find her work at the studio; meanwhile both
daredevils fall in love with her.   When Gargan dies in the line of
work, Boyd feels a greater need for security and he and Wilson wed.
After three months of "bliss," Wilson can no longer tolerate
the worries of having a stuntman husband and she forces Boyd to
quit the daredevil racket after he is badly burned doing a stunt on a
movie.   Thereafter when he learns Wilson is pregnant, he volunteers
to accomplish a deadly stunt for $200.   He comes out of the harrow-
ing episode alive and rushes to his wife's bedside to learn he is the
father of a son.
This modest B motion picture was packaged to take advantage
of leftover footage from The Lost Squadron (q. v.).   Amazingly, it
evolved as a more satisfying production than its predecessor; being
far more realistic in its presentation.   It was not populated by glamourous Hollywood types nor by tyrannical directors.   Instead it concerned real people in real stunting situations--it focused on the lack
of security, both financial and healthwise, that was a part of every
stuntman's existence.   The picture was based on a story coauthored
by stuntman Bob Rose, who once doubled for such players as William
Desmond, Ruth Roland, Elmo Lincoln, and Eddie Polo.   Rose had a
part in Lucky Devils, playing Rusty.
Harrison's Reports judged it "good entertainment for the masses"; the Hollywood Reporter acknowledged that its "production and
photography are first rate"; and Variety noted it was "the type of
entertainment that sets solidly with an audience. "

LUKE'S MOVIE MUDDLE see THE SHORT FILMS

Gladden James, Alan Roscoe, and William Boyd in Lucky Devils (1932).

MABEL'S DRAMATIC CAREER   see   THE SHORT FILMS

MADHOUSE (American International, 1974) Color, 89 min.

Executive producer, Samuel Z. Arkoff; producers, Max J.
Rosenberg and Milton Subotsky; associate producer, John Dark; director, Jim Clark; based on the novel Devilday by Angus Hall; adaptor, Ken Levison; screenplay, Greg Morrison; art director, Tony
Curtis; assistant director, Allan James; music, Douglas Gamley;
song, Gordon Clyde; makeup, George Blackler; wardrobe, Dulcie
Midwinter; sound, Danny Daniel and Gerry Humphreys; special effects, Kerss and Spencer; camera, Ray Parslow; editor, Clive Smith.

Vincent Price (Paul Toombes); Peter Cushing (Herbert Flay);
Robert Quarry (Oliver Quayle); Adrienne Corri (Faye); Natasha Pyne
(Julia); Michael Parkinson (TV Interviewer); Linda Hayden (Elizabeth);
Barry Dennen (Blout); Ellis Dayle (Alfred); Catherine Willmer (Louise);
John Garrie (Harper); Ian Thompson (Bradshaw); Jenny Lee Wright
(Carol); Julie Crosthwaite (Ellen); Peter Halliday (Psychiatrist).

For years actor Paul Toombes (Vincent Price) has made a
successful career of starring in films as Dr. Death, a mad killer
who employs various disguises to carry out his dastardly deeds.
When he learns that his fiancée is an ex-porno star, it causes Price
to have a nervous breakdown. When his girlfriend is later found the
victim of a grizzly death, Price is not sure whether he was responsible for the crime. Unable to work thereafter for years, Price
finally accepts an offer to go to London and star in a television program based on the Dr. Death movies to be written by old pal
Herbert Flay (Peter Cushing).
At the video studio, however, he is at odds with cruel producer Oliver Quayle (Robert Quarry) and further distraught by a
series of ghastly murders, all accomplished in the Dr. Death tradition. At first Price believes he is insane and responsible for the
rash of homicides, but then he begins to investigate the crimes. He
learns that Cushing is the actual killer, a situation brought about
because the writer has long harbored a deep hatred for the star.
Finally Price and Cushing clash and in the confrontation Cushing is
killed. Because the latter was in disguise the corpse is identified
as that of the movie star. Now Price plans a comeback--permanently
in new makeup: that of the deceased scripter.
Filmed in London, this macabre set piece was a horror film
variation of Sunset Boulevard (q. v.). Vincent Price as Toombes provided a bravura performance and contributed several engaging makeups in the course of the story. Veteran genre players Cushing and
Quarry added zest to the proceedings, which proved to be a genre
fan's delight. Adding to the enjoyment and the atmosphere was the
employment of old AIP film clips with Boris Karloff and Basil Rathbone serving as examples of Dr. Death movies.

MAID IN HOLLYWOOD   see   THE SHORT FILMS

Vincent Price and Adrienne Corri in Madhouse (1974).

MAKE ME A STAR (Paramount, 1932) 68 min.

Director, William Beaudine; based on the novel Merton of the Movies by Harry Leon Wilson and the play by George S. Kaufman and Mark Connelly; adaptors, Sam Wintz, Walter De Leon, and Arthur Kober; sound, Earle S. Hayman; camera, Allen Siegler; editor, Leroy Stone.

Stuart Erwin (Merton Gill); Joan Blondell (Flips Montague); ZaSu Pitts (Mrs. Scudder); Ben Turpin (Ben); Charles Sellon (Mr. Gashwiler); Florence Roberts (Mrs. Gashwiler); Helen Jerome Eddy (Tessie Kearns); Arthur Hoyt (Hardy Powell); Dink Templeton (Buck Benson); Ruth Donnelly (The Countess); Sam Hardy (Jeff Baird); Oscar Apfel (Henshaw); Frank Mills (Chuck Collins); Polly Walters (Doris Randall); Victor Potel, Bobby Vernon, Snub Pollard, Billy Bletcher, Nick Thompson, and Bud Jamison (Actors); Tallulah Bankhead, Clive Brook, Maurice Chevalier, Claudette Colbert, Gary Cooper, Phillips Holmes, Jack Oakie, Charlie Ruggles, and Sylvia Sidney (Guest Stars).

Stuart Erwin and ZaSu Pitts in Make Me a Star (1932).

Merton Gill (Stuart Erwin) is a country grocery clerk who dreams constantly of becoming a movie star. He takes a trip to Hollywood where, by a ruse, he ends up in a film studio. There he meets vivacious extra player Flips Montague (Joan Blondell). Almost at once, Blondell becomes infatuated with Erwin and works to get him into films, eventually winning him the lead in a picture which burlesques Westerns. Not knowing that the production is a comedy, Erwin plays his cowboy role straight, making the line delivery even funnier. At the preview he realizes what has happened and he believes he had been ill-used by both the movies and Blondell.

As he is about to pack and return home, Blondell arrives and persuades him that he does have a future in the cinema--as a comedian. She convinces him of her love for him. With that, Erwin decides to remain in the business and fulfill his dream.

Make Me a Star drew its inspiration from Harry Leon Wilson's 1922 novel, Merton of the Movies, which became a hit play on Broadway as adapted by George S. Kaufman and Marc Connelly. In 1924 Glenn Hunter starred in the film version of Merton of the Movies (q. v.). For this Paramount sound remake, the storyline was updated to the thirties. Erwin was admirably cast as the bumbling yokel

Merton and director William Beaudine added much authenticity to the
project, shooting on the sets of other current studio films like Dr.
Jekyll and Mr. Hyde and Madame Racketeer.   A number of stars
then on the Paramount lot were used in cameo assignments.   Beaudine made use of veteran comedian Ben Turpin to highlight some
slapstick sequences.   The adept actress Blondell was borrowed from
Warner Bros. for this film.

Abel Green wrote in Variety, "It's the forerunner of the latest
Hollywood production cycle dealing with insights of filmland ... [and]
it conveys to the muggs the general futility of busting into the movies
and at the same time holds the dramatic interest, nicely mixing up
pathos and buffoonery.   The laugh punctuations are at times robustly
hilarious, although the general background of pathos is sustained
throughout. "

This enjoyable feature is not presently available for TV as
MGM bought the screen rights to it in 1947 when it remade the
property for Red Skelton, again reverting back to the original title,
Merton of the Movies (q. v.).

MAKING MOTION PICTURES: A DAY IN THE VITAGRAPH STUDIO
    see THE SHORT FILMS

MAN OF A THOUSAND FACES (Universal, 1957) 122 min.

Producer, Robert Arthur; director, Joseph Pevney; story,
Ralph Wheelwright; screenplay, R. Wright Campbell, Ivan Goff, and
Ben Roberts; art directors, Alexander Golitzen and Eric Orbom;
music, Frank Skinner; orchestrator, Joseph Gershenson; costumes,
Bill Thomas; makeup, Bud Westmore and Jack Kevan; assistant dir-
ector, Phil Bowles; sound, Leslie I. Carey and Robert Pritchard;
special effects, Clifford Stine; camera, Russell Metty; editor, Ted
J. Kent.

James Cagney (Lon Chaney); Dorothy Malone (Cleva Creighton
Chaney); Jane Greer (Hazel Bennett); Marjorie Rambeau (Gert); Jim
Backus (Clarence Logan); Robert J. Evans (Irving Thalberg); Celia
Lovsky (Mrs. Chaney); Jeanne Cagney (Carrie Chaney); Jack Albert-
son (Dr. J. Wilson Shields); Nolan Leary (Pa Chaney); Roger Smith
(Creighton Chaney at Age 21); Robert Lyden (Creighton Chaney at
Age 13); Rickie Sorensen (Creighton Chaney at Age 8); Dennis Rush
(Creighton Chaney at Age 4); Simon Scott (Carl Hastings); Clarence
Kolb (Himself); Danny Beck (Max Dill); Phil Van Zandt (George
Loane Tucker); Hank Mann and Snub Pollard (Comedy Waiters).

One of the most notably unglamourous of screen biographies
was the story of Lon Chaney (1883-1930), Man of a Thousand Faces.
James Cagney's very literate portrayal of the famous actor lent
great dignity to the production as did the work of the supporting cast.
Rather shoddy recreations of Chaney's monster makeups, however,
detracted from the project as did the over-compactness of the facts

Dennis Rush and James Cagney in <u>Man of a Thousand Faces</u> (1957).

of his life. The actor's son, Lon Chaney, Jr., wrote the original
screen synopsis, which Universal purchased. The next day five
writers were put to work on the project by the studio and the younger
Chaney was not pleased with the final scenario. Chaney, Jr., did,
though, share the overwhelming critical consensus that Cagney performed a masterful portrayal of his father.
    The narrative revolves around Chaney (Cagney) the son of
deaf-mute parents, who enters show business and later marries his
vaudeville partner Cleva Creighton (Dorothy Malone). They have a
son but jealousies on the part of Malone cause the marriage to dissolve; the boy goes with his father. After a long struggle they mi-
grate to Hollywood where Chaney becomes a movie extra and eventually works his way up to being the top character actor in the industry during the Roaring Twenties. His astounding disguises caused
the following to be coined, "Don't step on it, it might be Lon Chaney."

A second marriage--to the compassionate Hazel Bennett (Jane Greer) --is successful for the screen star, but his growing son (Roger Smith) learns his mother is still alive. Loyalty to her causes him and his father to be alienated for a period. Eventually they are reunited but Chaney, Sr. , contracts throat concer. As he dies he writes the word "Jr. " after "Lon Chaney" on his battered makeup box and gives it to his son.

In reality, Lon Chaney never desired his son to be in show business and only the hard times of the Depression drove the younger Chaney to take up the craft, in which he would perform until his death from cancer in 1973.

Since Universal made the picture, it naturally focused on the period Chaney was under contract to that studio, devoting several screen minutes to the making of such classics as The Hunchback of Notre Dame and The Phantom of the Opera. It would be in these segments of the 122-minute, black-and-white feature that Cagney was at his more vulnerable, unable to compete with the startling and unmatchable original characterizations offered by the real-life Chaney. But on the whole, the star provided "a tender salute to a fine artist and troubled man" (Life magazine). Many thought he would be nominated for an Oscar for his effective interpretation, but he was not. (That year Alec Guinness won the Best Actor award for his role in The Bridge on the River Kwai.) Not to be overlooked in the proceedings were some long-stanging stage/screen veterans: Marjorie Rambeau, who played a colorful has-been, and Clarence Kolb, who appeared as himself. Experienced silent screen comics Hank Mann and Snub Pollard were on tap as comedy waiters, Cagney's sister Jeanne was cast as Chaney's sister Carrie, and Robert Evans (who later would run Paramount Pictures and then become a successful independent producer) appeared as a very slick, handsome, young Irving Thalberg, Chaney's mentor at Universal and later at MGM.

THE MAN WHO UNDERSTOOD WOMEN (20th Century-Fox, 1959)
    Color, 135 min.

Producer/director, Nunnally Johnson; based on the novel The Colors of the Day by Romain Gary; screenplay, Johnson; music, Robert Emmett Dolan; song, Paul Francis Webster and Dolan; wardrobe designer, Charles LeMaire; art directors, Lyle Wheeler and Maurice Ransford; set decorators, Walter M. Scott and Paul S. Fox; sound, Charles Peck and Harry M. Leonard; special effects, L. B. Abbott; camera, Milton Krasner; editor, Marjorie Fowler.

Leslie Caron (Ann Garantier); Henry Fonda (Willie Bauche); Cesare Danova (Marco Ranieri); Myron McCormick (Preacher); Marcel Dalio (Le Marne); Conrad Nagel (G. K.); Edwin Jerome (The Baron); Bern Hoffman (Soprano); Harry Elberle (Kress); Frank Cady (Milstead); Ben Astar (French Doctor).

Willie Bauche (Henry Fonda), a Hollywood movie mogul courts and marries much younger Anne Garantier (Leslie Caron) and hastily

models her into an international cinema star.   After three years of
marriage, however, he is devoting more time to work than to their
domestic situation--their union remains unconsummated.

For her next picture assignment, Fonda escorts Caron to Nice
on the French Riviera, still not comprehending that she cares more
for him than a career.   As his cold attitude persists, Caron on the
rebound meets an officer named Marco Ranieri (Cesare Danova), who
has carried a cheesecake shot of her throughout his various battle-
front campaigns.   When Danova confesses this to her and tells the
actress he adores her, they gravitate to his clifftop villa.

When Fonda learns of the romances he impulsively hires as-
sassins to eliminate Danova, but they are bunglers and one kills the
other.   Later, after a blackmailer is thwarted by Fonda, he assumes
the role of a clown and heads to the villa to reclaim his wife and to
finally demonstrate his love for her.

Nunnally Johnson adapted and directed this comedy-drama.
Newsweek said the end result was "only moderately successful ...
the approach is adult, the adultery is dull...."   With Fonda as
Willie Bauche sporting a goatee and wearing a lot of flashy clothes
and playing the Hollywood director very broadly indeed, the film concept was a bit hard to swallow.   Still Myron McCormick as Fonda's
aid was quite good with his various bits of philosophy, and it was
nice to have veteran Conrad Nagel on hand (even if in a smallish
role).

With its first half set in Hollywood and the finale on the
French Riviera, the picture had a difficult time placing its plot as
well as its location.   Certainly it provided no fresh insights into the
world of film-making or filmmakers.

A MANIAC IS LOOSE see HOLLYWOOD HORROR HOUSE

A MAN'S MAN (MGM, 1929) 6683 ft.

        Director, James Cruze; based on the play by Patrick Kearney;
screenplay, Forrest Halsey; titles, Joe Farnham; art director, Cedric Gibbons; song, Al Bryan and Monte Wilhitt; wardrobe, David Cox;
camera, Merritt B. Gerstad; editor, George Hively.

        William Haines (Mel); Josephine Dunn (Peggy); Sam Hardy
(Charlie); Mae Busch (Violet); John Gilbert and Greta Garbo (Themselves); and: Gloria Davenport.

        Following the solid reviews which resulted from the teaming
of star William Haines and director James Cruze in films like Excess Baggage (q. v.) and The Duke Steps Out (1929), MGM reteamed
the duo (along with Josephine Dunn who had been in Excess Baggage)
for another Hollywood-looks-at-itself-film.   Haines later stated that
this was one of his favorite credits and that he was very pleased
with his work in the movie.   Despite good reviews, though, the entry was not a success.   One reason was that it was released in the

spring of 1929 when talkies were the rage of the country. Despite
some last-minute-added sound effects and music (but no dialogue),
the public, eager to hear its stars speak, was disappointed.
    Peggy (Dunn) arrives in Hollywood, determined to make good
in films. She meets and falls in love with a sodajerk named Mel
(Haines) and they wed. Later a swindler sells Haines some worthless stock and he also promises to make Dunn a cinema celebrity.
Eventually the couple realize they are being cheated, and they collect
evidence on the crook. They also come to the conclusion that the
intricate world of Hollywood is not for two rural souls and they leave
the cinema haven in quest of a simple future together--elsewhere.
    Dunn's character made herself a Greta Garbo look-alike in her
efforts to crash the walls of Hollywood. In order to generate interest
in the film, MGM included a shot of Garbo and John Gilbert together
at a premiere. However, this bonus of the screen team together
only served to remind the public that A Man's Man had been sitting
on the shelf a spell. For by the time of its release, Garbo and
Gilbert had each gone separate ways romantically.
    Photoplay magazine printed of this release, "Lively satire on
Hollywood as it isn't. But funny. "

MARRIED IN HOLLYWOOD (Fox, 1929) 9700 ft. (color sequences)

    Presenter, William Fox; director, Marcel Silver; director of
musical numbers, Edward Royce; based on the play by Leopold Jacob-
son and Bruno Hardt-Warden and the operetta Ein Waltzertraum by
Oskar Straus; adaptor/dialogue, Harlan Thompson; songs, Harlan
Thompson and Dave Stamper; Thompson and Straus; Thompson and
Arthur Kay; assistant directors, Virgil Hart and Sid Bower; wardrobe,
Sophie Wachner and Alice O'Neill; camera, Charles Van Enger and
Sol Halperin; editor, Dorothy Spencer.

    J. Harold Murray (Prince Nicholai); Norma Terris (Mary Lou
Hopkins/Mitzi Hofman); Walter Catlett (Joe Glitner); Irene Palasty
(Annushka); Lennox Pawle (King Alexander); Tom Patricola (Mahai);
Evelyn Hall (Queen Louise); John Garrick (Stage Prince); Douglas
Gilmore (Adjutant Octavian); Gloria Grey (Charlotte); Jack Stambaugh
(Captain Jacobi); Bert Sprotte (Herr von Herzen); Lelia Karnelly
(Frau von Herzen); Herman Bing (German Director); Paul Ralli (Na-
mari); Carey Harrison and Roy Seegar (Detectives); Donald Gallaher
(Movie Director).

    This antiquated early talkie was a first in several area, but
today it is virtually forgotten. The techniques of early sound films--
especially musicals--left them as curiosity items only a few short
years after their release. Combined with its puerile storyline,
little-known movie leads, and crude recording techniques, Married
in Hollywood is rarely seen today.
    As for the precedents it did set: Oskar Straus wrote the
music for this operetta; it was the first operetta to be written directly for films and the first Viennese-style operetta to be photographed

Norma Terris and J. Harold Murray in <u>Married in Hollywood</u> (1929).

(with color sequences as a bonus). The movie's stars, Norma Terris and J. Harold Murray, each had a solid stage success behind
them (Terris had been in <u>Show Boat</u> while Murray had appeared in
<u>Rio Rita</u>). The combination of these leads (at least in 1929) plus the
highly-publicized Straus music, and the fact the venture was an all-
talkie, no doubt accounted for the film's box-office popularity.

In Vienna a young American girl Mary Lou Hopkins (Terris)
is trying for a singing career. She is romanced by Prince Nicholai
(Murray), leading to the couple's realization that their contrasting
social strata will always keep them apart. They separate and she
returns to America. On the boat across the Atlantic, she performs
a concert and impresses a film producer who awards her a film contract. In Hollywood she is a huge success and is asked to compose
her next screen vehicle. She decides to retell the story of her Aus-
trian love affair but ends the account with her killing the woman of

royal blood whom the prince plans to wed. The monarch, deposed
by a revolution at home, turns up in Hollywood and the film and
their love life has a new happy ending.

The New York Times said that director Marcel Silver "keeps
a check rein on his comedy, with the consequence that the fun is
never spoiled by a too generous dose of one idea. True, his conception of the happiness of two lovers by showing them cavorting under trees in the Springtime is not conspicuously original, but before
that sequence reaches the screen Mr. Silver has already captured the
hearts of the audience by his Barriesque depiction of Mary Lou's
(Miss Terris) dream. "

When the film debuted at the Roxy Theatre in New York, it
was accompanied by a Fox Movietone newsreel, Viennesse Caprice.

MARY OF THE MOVIES (Columbia, 1923) 6500 ft.

Conceived and supervised by Louis Lewyn and Jack Cohn;
director, John McDermott; screenplay, Louis Lewyn; titles, Joseph
W. Farnham; camera, George Meehan and Vernon Walker.

Marion Mack (Mary); Florence Lee (Her Mother); Mary Kane
(Her Sister); Harry Cornelli ("Lait" Mayle the Postman); John Geough
(Reel S. Tate the Squire); Raymond Cannon (Oswald Tate--His Son);
Rosemary Cooper (Jane the Extra Girl); Creighton Hale (Himself);
Francis McDonald (James Seiler); Henry Burrows (The Producer);
John McDermotty (Himself--the Director); Jack Perrin (Jack--Mary's
Brother); Ray Harford (The Old Man); Barbara La Marr, Douglas
MacLean, Bryant Washburn, Johnnie Walker, J. Warren Kerrigan,
Herbert Rawlinson, Alec B. Francis, Richard Travers, David Butler,
Louise Fazenda, Anita Stewart, Estelle Taylor, Rosemary Theby,
Bessie Love, Marjorie Daw, Tom Moore, Elliott Dexter, ZaSu Pitts,
Carmel Myers, Rex Ingram, Maurice Tourneur, Edward J. Le Saint,
and Wanda Hawley (Celebrities).

A young girl, Mary (Marion Mack) needs to obtain money in
order to support her family, so she goes to Hollywood--then considered a mecca where any gamble might pay off with a miracle--to try
to break into movies. She is not successful despite the fact she
meets many movie personalities in her quest. Finally she is fright-
ened by a "boulevard sheik" and takes a job as a studio restaurant
waitress where it is noted she bears a strong resemblance to a star
who has become ill. It is in this manner that she obtains the lead
in a photoplay and "overnight" becomes a screen star.

Mary of the Movies interpolated the theme of the young country person seeking movie fame, a plot device used so engagingly in
Merton of the Movies (q. v.). Other films had employed the gambit
of stars in candid cameos--(e. g. , Hollywood, Night Life in Hollywood,
and Souls for Sale (qq. v.). This time around, though, neither gimmick worked to advantage. Photoplay confirmed, "Again the Hollywood stars trailing in a story of a screen-struck girl. That is the
only interest. The story is weak. "

Florence Lee and Marion Mack in <u>Mary of the Movies</u> (1923).

THE MASQUERADERS   see   THE SHORT FILMS

MEL BROOKS' SILENT MOVIE   see   SILENT MOVIE

MERTON OF THE MOVIES (Paramount, 1924) 7655 ft.

     Presenters, Adolph Zukor and Jesse L. Lasky; producer/director, James Cruze; based on the novel by Harry Leon Wilson and the play by George S. Kaufman and Marc Connelly; screenplay, Walter Woods; camera, Karl Brown.

     Glenn Hunter (Merton Gill); Charles Sellon (Pete Gashwiler); Sadie Gordon (Mrs. Gashwiler); Gale Henry (Tessie Kearns); Luke Cosgrave (Lowell Hardy); Viola Dana (Sally "Flips" Montague); De Witt Jennings (Jeff Baird); Elliott Roth (Harold Parmalee); Charles Ogle (Mr. Montague); Ethel Wales (Mrs. Montague); Frank Jonasson (Henshaw); Eleanor Lawson (Mrs. Patterson).

MERTON OF THE MOVIES (MGM, 1947) 82 min.

     Producer, Albert Lewis; director, Robert Alton; based on the

novel by Harry Leon Wilson and the play by George S. Kaufman and
Marc Connelly; screenplay, George Wells and Lou Breslow; art directors, Cedric Gibbons and Howard Campbell; set decorators, Edwin
B. Willis and Joseph W. Holland; music, David Snell; assistant director, Al Raboch; sound, Douglas Shearer; camera, Paul C. Vogel;
editor, Frank E. Hull.

Red Skelton (Merton Gill); Virginia O'Brien (Phyllis Montague);
Gloria Grahame (Beulah Baxter); Leon Ames (Lawrence Rupert); Alan
Mowbray (Frank Mulvaney); Charles D. Brown (Jeff Baird); Hugo Haas
(Von Strutt); Harry Hayden (Mr. Gashwiler); Tom Trout (Marty);
Douglas Fowley (Phil); Dick Wessell (Chick).

Harry Leon Wilson's novel Merton of the Movies had been a
great success when published in 1922; its plot of a small-town individual seeking for the "glamour" life of the movie gave substance to
several films, Mary of the Movies and Polly of the Movies (qq. v.)
among them.   Before the popular story was made into a film, George
S. Kaufman and Marc Connelly had already transformed the plot into
a hit Broadway play starring Glenn Hunter.   Ironically by the time
the Paramount Picture was released, the spinoff versions had drained
a great deal of life from the plot concept, thus cheating the fine
property from the tremendous screen success it deserved.
     The by-now hackneyed scenario starred Hunter again (later to
become a director) as Merton Gill, an Illinois grocery clerk, who
dreams of becoming a famous motion picture player--after all, it
looks so easy what the people do in front of the camera.   Young Hunter takes a correspondence course in becoming a "experienced" movie
actor and then quits his job.   He boards a train for Hollywood where
he meets film extra girl Sally "Flips" Montague (Viola Dana); it is
she who arranges for him to get inside a studio.   Hunter, however,
is snobbish about his proposed screen fare and longs to be an important dramatic actor, but the only employment he can manage is in a
Western comedy.   Hunter nevertheless plays the role straight and
when he is finished with the film he feels he is a decided failure and
plans to return to the midwest.   But, due to his "serious" emoting
in the sagebrush tale, he lands a studio contract and he and Dana
wed.
     The New York Times enthusiastically reported, "... it is only
too rare that one sees a celluloid gem as well-nigh perfect as this
one, for in it the acting is performed by all the players with an obvious comprehension of the characters and of the narrative as a
whole. ...   In every adaptation of a play there are spots where the
picture can atone for what it lacks in color and sound. ...   The in-
troductory sequences shows a scene of the 'great open spaces where
men are men, ' and one sees Merton as a cowboy, high on a cliff,
espying a bewigged beauty about to become the victim of bandits. ...
This scene dissolves into reality, showing Merton in a rear room of
the town grocery shop with his arm around the neck of a store dummy.   'You cur, ' he hisses at a male effigy.   His various dreams of
success as an actor are cleverly illustrated. ... "
     The initial sound version of the property would be Make Me

a Star (q. v.), and this 1932 Paramount remake would emerge the
best of the trio of films made from this Harry Leon Wilson work.
   One would have thought that by the forties a great deal of the
lustre of dreaming of a Hollywood career would have rubbed off--
World War II had changed the public's tastes, standards, and ambitions, in so many other areas.   However, moviegoers retained that
mystical fascination for the cinema and the allegedly golden life of
those who walked in its supposedly sparkling midst.   MGM picked up
the property for Red Skelton in 1947 for a film that is little seen today.   Basically this version covered the same territory as the first
renditions, and it reverted back to its original title.   In this outing,
however, Merton is a movie usher who arrives in Hollywood to crash
the cinema, with Virginia O'Brien (she of the deadpan style) assuming
the role of Flips.   Borrowing a page from stunt movies like The
Lost Squadron (q. v.), Hugo Haas was cast as a wild-man Teutonic
director called "von Strutt. "
   This picture was no more (nor much less) than a typical Skelton vehicle, though it was one of his least successful pictures in that
decade.   There was a good deal of slapstick added to the storyline,
which retained the twenties' setting.   Buster Keaton, way down on
his luck, was used by MGM to instruct Skelton in the ways of silent
film comedy and to keep a generally authentic flavor to the overall
picture.   The New York Times bemoaned, "Mr. Skelton's true comic
personality never comes to the surface, chiefly because the script is
unashamedly inane when a smooth blending of comedy and pathos was
required. ...   This world is still crowded with counterparts of Mer-
ton--that is, the Merton whom Mr. Wilson created years back.   Let's
hope there are not any around who remotely resemble this latest
Metro reincarnation of Merton Gill, for he's pretty hopeless. "

MICKEY'S MOVIES   see   THE SHORT FILMS

MILLION DOLLAR JOB   see   THE SHORT FILMS

MIRACLE OF THE BELLS (RKO, 1948) 120 min.

   Producers, Jesse L. Lasky and Walter MacEwen; director,
Irving Pichel; based on the novel by Russell Janney; screenplay, Ben
Hecht and Quentin Reynolds; art director, Ralph Berger; music, Leigh
Harline; music director, C. Bakaleinikoff; choreography, Charles
O'Curran; costumes, Renie; makeup, Karl H. Herlinger; assistant
director, Harry D'Arcy; sound, Philip N. Mitchell; camera, Robert
de Grasse; editor, Elmo Williams.

   Fred MacMurray (Bill Dunnigan); Alida Valli (Olga Treskovna);
Frank Sinatra (Father Paul); Lee J. Cobb (Marcus Harris); Harold
Vermilyea (Nick Orloff); Charles Meredith (Father Spinsky); Jim No-
lan (Ted Jones); Veronica Pataky (Anna Klovna); Philip Ahn (Ming
Gow); Frank Ferguson (Dolan the Director); Frank Wilcox (Dr. Jen-
nings); Ray Teal (Koslick); Dorothy Sebastian (Katie); Billy Wayne

Alida Valli and Fred MacMurray in <u>Miracle of the Bells</u> (1948).

(Tom Elmore); Syd Saylor (Freddy Evans); Thayer Roberts (Earl of Warwick); Herbert Evans (Nobleman); Franz Roehn (Cauchon); Pat Davis (Assistant Director); Ned Davenport and Charles Miller (Priests); Franklyn Farnum, Snub Pollard, and Beth Taylor (Worshippers); Jim Pierce and Roger Creed (Soldiers); George Chandler (Max the Telegraph Operator); Oliver Blake (Slenzka).

Press agent Bill Dunnigan (Fred MacMurray) arrives in a small Pennsylvania mining town to fulfill a promise he made to his client--to bury her beside her coal miner father.   MacMurray relates to the local priest, Father Paul (Frank Sinatra), how he had made the vow to the girl (Alida Valli) on her death bed as she succumbed to tuberculosis.   He then cites the story--shown in flashbacks --of just how he met Valli while she was in burlesque, and his attempts to nurture her burning ambition to be a great dramatic actress.   Finally he maneuvers the lead for her in a Hollywood superproduction dealing with Joan of Arc.

Now that she is deceased, the film's producer (Lee J. Cobb)

wants to shelve the film, insisting the public will not come to see a movie starring a deceased personality. The press agent seeks to win publicity by having the town's church bells toll for four days, but the producer still remains adamant in his decree. Then it is noticed that two religious statues at St. Michael's Church have "moved" and are now facing the girl's coffin. MacMurray labels the act a miracle and it convinces Cobb to distribute Valli's feature.

Photoplay magazine was nice enough to call this well-meaning project "a sentimental story with an inspirational message. " That, however, was about the best that could be stated for the slow-moving feature. None of the leads were right for their roles, except for Cobb as film producer Marcus Harris. Sinatra seemed rather ill-at-ease in his priest's characterization (he did sing the song "Ever Homeward"), unlike rival Bing Crosby who had made such a hit in Going My Way (1944) and The Bells of St. Mary's (1945). It took a bit of daring to accept European exotic Alida Valli (under contract to David O. Selznick) as a stripper from a Pennsylvania coal town.

About the only real Hollywood touch in the offering was the old taboo about the public's not accepting a recently-deceased star's film (something disproven after the deaths of James Dean, Clark Gable, et al.). Today Miracle of the Bells is mostly played off to unsuspecting TV viewers as a Christmas-time holiday "treat. "

MISS BREWSTER'S MILLIONS (Paramount, 1926) 6457 ft.

Presenters, Adolph Zukor and Jesse L. Lasky; director, Clarence Badger; suggested by the novel by George Barr McCutcheon and the play by Winchell Smith, and Byron Ongley; adaptor, Monty Brice; screenplay, Lloyd Corrigan and Harold Shumate; camera, H. Kinley Martin.

Bebe Daniels (Polly Brewster); Warner Baxter (Thomas Barrington Hancock, Jr.); Ford Sterling (Ned Brewster); Andre de Beranger (Mr. Brent); Miss Beresford (Landlady).

Longtime comedy director Clarence Gadger, who seemed at his best when dealing with female comics, supervised Bebe Daniels in this vehicle which was a pleasant throwback to the old days of slap-dash comedy. Using the inheritance-must-be-spent plot gimmick of the novel-play (of Brewster's Millions, which has been frequently filmed on its own terms), the movie proved more satisfying to the younger set than to adults. It briefly touches on the Hollywood medium and does so without deprecating the film industry--which in itself is something of an oddity.

Daniels is seen as Polly Brewster, who struggles to make a scant living as a movie extra, without much success. Upon her father's death, she inherits $1 million, but his will stipulates she cannot spend the money. She, instead, must invest every penny of it. When her uncle learns of this situation, he comes West to advise Daniels that he will provide her with $5 million if she spends her father's inheritance within one month. Daniels agrees and she and her Boston-bred lawyer (Warner Baxter) begin to distribute her

Bebe Daniels and Warner Baxter in Miss Brewster's Millions (1926).

assets to every conceivable source. (The sign over her investment
office reads, "You furnish the idea, and we furnish the money.")
After the month is up, Daniels sadly learns that Uncle is actually
bankrupt. Still a happy ending prevails when she learns that the
money she invested in a movie company has paid off handsome dividends.

The New York Times chided, "The whirlwind start, in which
is incorporated the stunt of a tea tray to fall on the landlady, is
dangerously near to the antiquated custard pie throwing.... Miss
Daniels displays no little ability as the energetic girl with $1,000,000.
This actress really ought to be cast in a vehicle that would serve
her better than such a rambunctious picture."

MONDO HOLLYWOOD (Emerson Film Enterprises, 1967) Color, 91
    min.

        Executive producers, Howard I. Cogan and Arthur Gilbert;
associate producers, Gerald Alcan and Helene K. Cohen; producer/
director/screenplay, Robert Carl Cohen; music director, Mike Curb;
aerial camera, Doyle E. Fields; camera/editor, Robert Carl Cohen.

        Lewis Beach Marvin (Creator of "Moonfire"); Dale Davis (Sur-
fing Film Producer); Jim Arender (Sky Diver/Actor); Vito (Art and
Dance Instructor); Theodore Charack (Night Stalker); Sheryl Carson
(Psychedelic Body Painter); Bobby Jameson (Folksinger); Richard Alpert Ph D. (Clinical Psychologist); Valerie Porter (Sculptress); Jennie Lee ("Bazoom Girl"); Jack Gerard (Hollywood Agent); Jay Sebring
(Men's Hair Stylist); Hope Chest (Exotic Dancer); Carazine ("The
Cigarette Comic"); Mrs. Herbert White (Silent Film Star); Rudi Gernreich (Designer); Peanuts (Transvestite); Mary Ewaldt (Artist); Mur-
ry Schurmmer (Pan); Dee Dee Cartier and Helen Frank (Models);
Gypsy Boots (Bit).

        This mishmash of a feature was obviously strung together to
cash in on the documentary-type fad begun in the mid-sixties by the
likes of Mondo Cane. Variety reported, "Said to be 18 months in
preparation and edited from more than 120,000 feet of color film,
what comes out is series of clips wrapped up with specially-shot
footage. Occasionally dull, it nevertheless probably will be exploitable for okay returns...." Documentary producer Robert Carl Cohen,
who had been responsible for such fine TV documentaries as "Inside
Red China" and "Inside Castro's Cuba," was in charge of this production as director, photographer, and editor.
        Mondo Hollywood seeks to display aspects of the film capitol
(rather than film-making) which are not generally known to the public at large. It focuses on the freak types and the hangers-on, rather
than the successful lot of Hollywood workers. A number of well-
known screen figures, such as Jayne Mansfield, are glimpsed in the
footage, but no "names" took part in the actual production of this
entry. Among its episodes are chats with Dr. Richard Alpert, who
had been dismissed from Harvard College for LSD experiments;

sculptress Valerie Porter "doing her thing"; sky diver Jim Arender, who leaps from a plane in a free fall; and Rudi Gernreich, the inventor of the topless fad, at work.   There are also scanning shots of assorted Tinsel Town premieres with a gaggle of celebrities clumped into the footage.

Mondo Hollywood is more of a travelogue of the nightlife and the "other side" of existence in the California metropolis.   Unfortunately by the time this picture was packaged, Hollywood no longer possessed the glamour or prestige of yore.

THE MOON'S OUR HOME (Paramount, 1936) 80 min.

Producer, Walter Wanger; director, William A. Seiter; based on the story by Faith Baldwin; screenplay, Isabel Dawn, Boyce De-Gaw, Dorothy Parker, and Alan Campbell; song, Leo Robin and Fredrick Hollander; camera, Joseph Valentine.

Margaret Sullavan (Cherry Chester [Sarah Brown]); Henry Fonda (Anthony Amberton); Beulah Bondi (Boyce Medfore); Henrietta Crosman (Lucy Van Steedan); Lucien Littlefield (Ogden Holbrook); Charles Butterworth (Horace Van Steedan); Walter Brennan (Lem); Brandon Hurst (Babson); Spencer Charters (Abner Simpson); Margaret Hamilton (Mitty Simpson); Dorothy Stickney (Hilda); Margaret Fielding (Miss Manning); Grace Hale (Miss Hambridge); Monte Vandergrift (Brakeman); Richard Powell (Candy Butcher); Lorna Dunn, Eva Dennison, Betty Farrington, and Helen Dickson (Women); Harry Bowen and Harry Harvey (Reporters); Corbet Morris (Secretary); Georgie Cooper (Maid); Bobby Bolder (Butler); Thelma White and Andrea Leeds (Salesgirls); Jack Norton (Drunk); Estelle Ettere (Stewardess).

Wealthy heiress and headstrong screen star Cherry Chester (Margaret Sullavan) and travel writer Anthony Amberton (Henry Fonda) detest one another by reputation although they have never met. When both of them arrive at a winter resort to get away from their respective public, they meet, not realizing one another's identity. While they are skiing, Fonda bets Sullavan she cannot stand on her skis unaided and she accepts the wager.   So sure is she of her skill that she agrees to wed Fonda if she fails.

To her surprise she loses the test and the duo wind up getting married, the ceremony being performed by a deaf judge while the two are constantly arguing.   On their wedding night, Sullavan's perfume makes Fonda violently ill, as he is allergic to her brand and the two are soon separated.   Eventually they both realize they are in love. But they cannot locate one another because they do not know the other's true identity or profession.   Finally they are happily reunited.

It was one of the vagaries of Hollywood to costar a former real-life couple, Sullavan and Fonda (who had married in 1931, divorced in 1933), in a wacky screwball comedy about an incompatible couple who eventually adjust to one another.

In Lovers and Lunatics (1974), Ted Sennett notes of this agreeable entry, "Despite the screenplay's conspicuous lack of sense or reason, <u>The Moon's Our Home</u> succeeds in being genuinely amusing. The early scenes offer a lightly malicious look at the headstrong movie star in full bloom--Cherry gives an interview to a Hedda Hopperish reporter in which she describes marriage as a ski-jump, 'swift, reckless!' (Her companion, Beulah Bondi, comments that she would settle for 'a nice job as a night nurse in a psychiatric ward.') And Sullavan and Fonda are extremely likeable as 'two free people with the world behind them' who somehow manage to quarrel incessantly at the same time that they confess their love for each other."

Films such as this entry managed to reinforce the widely held theory that most movie stars were overgrown wilful children who have not a sensible care in the world.

MOVIE CRAZY (Paramount, 1932) 81 min.

Director, Clyde Bruckman; story, Agnes Christine Johnston, John Grey, and Felix Adler; screenplay, Vincent Lawrence; camera, Walter Lundin; editor, Bernard Burton.

Harold Lloyd (Harold Hall); Constance Cummings (The Girl); Kenneth Thomson (The Gentleman Heavy); Sidney Jarvis (The Director); Eddie Fetherstone (The Assistant Director); Robert McWade (Mr. Kitterman the Producer); Louise Closser Hale (Mrs. Kitterman).

This flick "makes no pretenses about being anything but a good old-fashioned slap-stick comedy" (<u>New York World-Telegram</u>).

Young Kansas college boy Harold Hall (Harold Lloyd) longs to be in the movies and he writes to a movie company requesting work. He accidentally encloses a photograph of a handsome young man, instead of a snapshot of himself. Soon the studio wires him to come to the Coast. When he steps off the train he finds he is in the midst of a movie set-up. He finds employment as an extra but bungles the scenes, ruins the straw hat of the producer (Robert McWade), and makes life miserable for the director (Sidney Jarvis). The leading lady (Constance Cummings), though, takes a shine to him; but her alcoholic leading man (Kenneth Thomson) does not. Later director Jarvis makes a screen test of Lloyd, but it is a failure.

Determined, romantic Lloyd still continues to pursue Cummings who, for fun, dresses up in a Spanish outfit and flirts with him, snaring his college pin. Then as herself, Cummings claims to be angry with Lloyd and when he tries to reacquire his pin from the "Spanish dancer" she refuses to part with it. Cummings then sends him a farewell note on the back of a party invitation. Lloyd ends up at the social gathering where he accidentally puts on a magician's tail coat while in the washroom and soon is causing a great deal of havoc.

Still later, at the studio, the rival actor knocks out Lloyd who comes to and finds the man attacking his lady love. Lloyd jumps to the rescue, not realizing the whole affair is part of a film. Eventually he winds up with a picture contract after the studio moguls view the footage.

Kenneth Thomson, Constance Cummings, and Harold Lloyd in Movie Crazy (1932).

Movie Crazy was not too far removed from Merton of the Movies (q. v.), with the theme of a young rube hoping for Hollywood success and eventually winning it--only through a series of accidents (which says something about the state of the American dream). For many, this Lloyd vehicle was a visual treat, full of wonderful sight gags and sequences; the party segment about the mistaken magician's prop coat ran for ten hilarious minutes. Movie Crazy proved to be one of the more mirthful looks at Hollywood of the thirties. Aiding the venture greatly, was genteel, attractive Constance Cummings, forced to cope with a ridiculous plotline dual assignment.

When Movie Crazy premiered in England, the London Times took the occasion to editorialize, in a rather harsh manner, "In form, though not in substance, all Mr. Harold Lloyd's films are alike. His personality is engaging rather than humourous, and we laugh less often at him than at the tricks he plays. For a time each of his films is content to live in dependence on these tricks; but always there comes a time when it sets out to win that cumulative laughter which mere studio 'business', however fresh and ingenious, seldom wins. ... Movie Crazy, his latest film, tries for this effect with a long drawn out fight in a flooded film studio. This fight has many amusing moments, but it remains a collection of tricks.... Mr.

Lloyd, then, has failed once more to make a film that generates a
comic energy of its own. After every novel prank laughter sinks to
sleep and must be wakened anew. "
    At any rate, on the American side of the Atlantic, Movie Crazy
remained a popular item. It was reissued in the U.S. (as well as
overseas) in 1950 and a portion of it was included in the compilation
Harold Lloyd's World of Comedy (1962).

MOVIE DAZE see THE SHORT FILMS

MOVIE FANS see THE SHORT FILMS

MOVIE MAD see THE SHORT FILMS

THE MOVIE MAKER (NBC-TV, 1967) Color, 91 min.

    Producer, Harry Tatelman; director, Josef Leytes; teleplay,
Rod Serling and Steven Boscho; music, Benny Carter; costumes, Helen
Colvig; makeup, Bud Westmore; set decorator, Fred Arrigo; sound,
Waldon O. Watson; camera, John F. Warren; editor, Gene Palmer.

    Rod Steiger (Michael Kirsch); Robert Culp (Peter Furgash);
James Dunn (Russell Landers); Sally Kellerman (Gerry Kirsch); Anna
Lee (Paula Kirsch); Norman Fell (Bert Miller); Michael Pataki (Young
Mike Kirsch); Laraine Stephens (Young Paula); Jim Begg (Young Russ
Landers); Edward Binns (Victor Green); Sharon Farrell (Melissa);
Bob Hope and Rod Serling (Bits); and: Leon Belasco, Woodrow Par-
frey, Marian Moses, and Simon Scott.

    In March of 1964, "Bob Hope Chrysler Theatre" presented a
two-part drama on NBC-TV entitled A Slow Fade to Black. Three
years later it would be edited into a "feature" film and released to
local TV stations as The Movie Maker. The teleplay was written
by Rod Serling who has a bit in the film, as did the TV series' host,
Bob Hope.
    Michael Kirsch (Rod Steiger) is a dying breed in the NEW Hol-
lywood. Times have changed but he remains the same dictatorial
mogul who refuses to cope with altering situations. "I'm going to live
to see it like the old times, " he screams. ... Fade-out and flashback to 1910's New York where young Mike Kirsch (Michael Pataki)
operates a Second Avenue nickelodeon. He sells his business to try
Hollywood with the hope of becoming a producer. His motto is "I
don't want little by little ... I want a lot now. " He wins a job in
the publicity department of Globe Pictures; his big opportunity comes
when he revamps a potential dud The Queen's Pirates into a hit,
merely by re-editing and changing the emphasis of the film from
drama to comedy. "Nothing is old hat, " he explains, "if you do it
right. "
    As time passes, he climbs the ladder of success at the studio,
eventually becoming its head. For years he is one of Hollywood's

great rulers; neither beloved on the lot (he is called a "movie Mussolini") or at home by his wife (Anna Lee) or their daughter Gerry
(Sally Kellerman).   The latter is thrice-wed, and a tramp now living
in San Francisco.
          After a power struggle with Peter Furgash (Robert Culp) Stei-
ger is deposed from power.   As the disloyal Culp explains to Steiger,
"You're the kind of man that has to get knifed; you never step aside. "
At the 37th Annual Academy Award, Steiger accepts the producer-of-
the-year prize ("it's my turn, " he says) and then informs the industry audience, "A funny thing happened to me on the way over from
the studio.   I lost it. "
          The film concludes with Steiger in a viewing room watching
the pictures he helped to promote into success.
          The more captivating segments of the Hollywood story told
herein are those clips of pictures made by mogul Steiger, especially
from the days of slapstick comedy.   Much of the dialogue has a ring
of authenticity or hackneyed philosophy (depending on one's point of
view).
          Keller: "Who did you have for lunch today that didn't agree
with you?" Steiger: "I had two aspirins and one agent for lunch. "
          At one point, a film worker says of nostalgia, "You can't eat
memories. "   Lee, who offers a wonderfully modulated performance
as the neglected wife states, "Talent is like an arm or leg.   If you
don't use it for a long time, it atrophies. "
          Earlier Steiger had portrayed a studio chieftain in The Big
Knife (q. v.).   His performance in The Movie Maker as a combination
Harry Cohn-Louis B. Mayer is equally oversized, but a bit more
shaded.

MOVIE MANICS see THE SHORT FILMS

MOVIE NIGHT see THE SHORT FILMS

MOVIE NUT see THE SHORT FILMS

THE MOVIE PEOPLE see THE SHORT FILMS

MOVIE PESTS see THE SHORT FILMS

A MOVIE ROMANCE see A GIRL'S FOLLY

THE MOVIE STAR see THE SHORT FILMS

MOVIE STAR, AMERICAN STYLE; OR, LSD, I HATE YOU! (Famous
     Players Corp. , 1966) 99 min.   (color sequence)

          Executive producer, Arnold Stoltz; producer, Robert Caramico;
director, Albert Zugsmith; screenplay, Zugsmith and Graham Lee
Mahin; dialogue, Lulu Talmadge; music, Joe Greene; camera, Cara-
mico; editor, Herman Freedman.

Robert Strauss (Joe Horner); Del Moore (Dr. Horatio); T. C. Jones (Skippy Roper); Steve Drexel (Dr. Oscar Roscoe); Steven Rogers (Barry James); Richard Clair (David Erickson); Jill Darling (Miranda Song); Cara Garnett (Movie Queen); Sandra Lynn (Countess); Peter Van Boom (Harvey Homantash); Ned York (Crash Dramm); Frank Delfino (Photographer Midget); Juliet Picaud (Miss Bee); Paula Lane (Honey Bunny); Albert Zugsmith (Director).

This color presentation is yet another offering from the production mill of writer-producer-director Albert Zugsmith, who has made some of the lowest-quality films to come out of Hollywood. This time around, he devotes his efforts to the movies and to a then-topical LSD sequence.

Honey Bunny (Paula Lane) is a Marilyn Monroe-type who suffers a nervous breakdown. Her studio boss Joe Horner (Robert Strauss) orders her to recuperate at a bizarre mental hospital run by the daffy Dr. Horatio (Del Moore). At the sanatorium, Lane encounters a gamut of odd characters, including an effeminate designer (played by T. C. Jones, the female impersonator), a stereotyped leading man (Steven Rogers), an overly intellectual author (Richard Clair), and a vamp (Cara Garnett) with a penchant to overeat. When all attempts fail to elevate Lane from her doldrums and back to work, LSD is administered. The "trip" which ensues is the supposed highlight of the film. This storyline facet consumes the last quarter of the picture and is lensed in various hues to heighten the visual effect of the mental excursion.

Clearly shot on the cheap, the film may have been the first to include an LSD sequence, but it did not help much at the box-office. Variety reported, "Occasionally sophisticated and also relying on some inside gags that would register only in Hollywood, the Albert Zugsmith film is basically an okay slapstick satire on contemporary sex symbols and psychiatry heightened by optical and musical gimmicks."

MOVIE STRUCK   see   PICK A STAR

MOVIE TOWN   see   THE SHORT FILMS

MOVIELAND MAGIC   see   THE SHORT FILMS

MOVIN' PITCHERS   see   THE SHORT FILMS

THE MOVING PICTURE COWBOY   see   THE SHORT FILMS

THE MOVING PICTURE GIRL   see   THE SHORT FILMS

MY GEISHA (Paramount, 1962) Color, 120 min.

Producer, Steve Parker; director, Jack Cardiff; screenplay, Norman Krasna; assistant director, Harry Kratz; music, Franz Waxman; song, Waxman and Hal Davis; art directors, Hal Perreira, Arthur Lonegan, and Makoto Kikuchi; costumes, Edith Head; sound, Harold Lewis and Charles Grenzbach; camera, Shunichiro Nakao; second unit camera, Stanley Sayer; editor, Archie Marshek.

Shirley MacLaine (Lucy Dell [Yoko Mori]); Yves Montand (Paul Robaix); Edward G. Robinson (Sam Lewis); Bob Cummings (Bob Moore); Yoko Tani (Kazumi Ito); Tatsuo Saito (Kenichi Takata); Alex Gerry (Leonard Lewis); Nobuo Chiba (Shig); Ichiro Hayakawa (Hisako Amatsu); George Furness (George).

Continental Paul Robiax (Yves Montand), a talented film director, is known mainly for supervising the films of his popular actress wife Lucy Dell (Shirley MacLaine). Finally he decides to break the professional mold and departs for Japan to do a screen version of Madama Butterfly with an unknown Japanese girl in the lead. MacLaine and producer Sam Lewis (Edward G. Robinson) follow him to the Orient with MacLaine wanting--demanding--but not getting, the film lead. She then disguises herself as a geisha for a party and her husband fails to recognize her.

Thereafter she decides to use the name of Yoko Mori and tests for the role, which she wins. A problem develops, however, when her costar, Bob Moore (Bob Cummings) becomes romantically involved with her and asks Montand to help him win her love. During the filming Montand begins to realize that Yoko is actually his wife, but he says nothing. Instead he begins to romance her himself.

Finally the studio decides to release the fact that Yoko is really MacLaine, convinced it will bolster the box-office appeal of the production. But MacLaine refuses the gambit, not wishing to divert attention from Montand's opportunity to show his directing mettle. At a press party, MacLaine announces that Yoko has withdrawn to a convent which ends the search for the mysterious Oriental actress. Later Montand confesses to MacLaine that he actually knew the truth about her identity.

My Geisha is one of the few American-produced films on moviemaking that left the confines of Hollywood to unfold its story, although it did little to enlighten its audience on Japanese moviemaking procedures. Still MacLaine did take geisha lessons for her assignment (one of the first Americans ever allowed to do so) and her then real-life spouse Steve Parker produced the comedy. The New York Herald-Tribune noted, "Much of it reminds you of television situation comedy, which is endurable only to those fascinated by the personalities of the players." The British Monthly Film Bulletin admitted, "It is perhaps a tribute to the cast that the film often appears less crass and vulgar than it might have been...." As always Robinson was a delight; that same year he would play in another genre entry, Two Weeks in Another Town (q.v.).

MY NEIGHBOR'S WIFE (Davis Distributing Division, 1925) 6 reels

Producer, Clifford S. Elfelt; director, Clarence Geldert; based on the story "The Other Man's Wife" by James Oliver Curwood; camera, Joseph Walker.

E. K. Lincoln (Jack Newberry); Helen Ferguson (Florence Keaton); Edward Davis (Mr. Keaton); Herbert Rawlinson (Allen Albright); William Russell (Eric von Greed); William Bailey (Greed's Assistant); Chester Conklin (Cameraman); Tom Santschi (Inventor); Mildred Harris (Inventor's Wife); Douglas Gerard (Bertie); Margaret Loomis (Kathlyn Jordan); Ralph Faulkner (William Jordan); Philippe De Lacy (William Jordan, Jr.).

Jack Newberry (E. K. Lincoln), the son of a millionaire, seeks to make himself a business success on his own by producing a motion picture. After spending all of his own funds on the project, he borrows $40,000 from Mr. Keaton (Edward Davis), the father of his fiancée (Helen Ferguson). He then hires a famous but temperamental German director, Eric von Greed (a takeoff on Erich von Stroheim, played very broadly by Western film hero William Russell), to direct the picture. To the surprise of everyone, the picture turns out to be a success. Completing his happiness, Lincoln marries his girlfriend.

Not much can be said for this quickly churned out melodrama, other than its producers, the Davis Distributing Company, obviously savored the chance to spoof the major companies with their wild lampoon of creative but outrageous von Stroheim.

MYRA BRECKINRIDGE (20th Century-Fox, 1970) Color, 95 min.

Producer, Robert Fryer; director, Michael Sarne; based on the novel by Gore Vidal; screenplay, Sarne and David Giler; additional material, Mae West; music supervisor/conductor, Lionel Newman; song, John Phillips; choreography, Ralph Beaumont; orchestrators, Jack Elliott, Jeff Alexander, Allyn Ferguson, and Lyn Murray; costumes, Theodora Van Runkle; Miss West's costumes, Edith Head; art directors, Jack Martin Smith and Fred Harpman; set decorators, Walter M. Scott and Reg Allen; makeup supervisor, Dan Striepeke; makeup, Del Acevedo; assistant director, Dick Glassman; sound, Don Bassman and Dave Dockendorf; special camera effects, L. B. Abbott and Art Cruickshank; camera, Richard Moore; editor, Danford B. Greene.

Mae West (Leticia Van Allen); John Huston (Buck Loner); Raquel Welch (Myra Breckinridge); Rex Reed (Myron Breckinridge); Farrah Fawcett (Mary-Ann); Roger C. Carmel (Dr. Montag); Roger Herren (Rusty); George Furth (Charlie Flager, Jr.); Calvin Lockhart (Irving Amadeus); Jim Backus (Doctor); John Carradine (Surgeon); Andy Devine (Coyote Bill); Grady Sutton (Kid Barlow); Robert Lieb (Charlie Flager, Sr.); Skip Ward (Chance); Kathleen Freeman (Bobbie Dean Loner); B. S. Pully (Tex); Buck Kartalian (Jeff); Monty Landis (Vince); Tom Selleck (Leticia's Secretary); Peter Ireland (Student); Nelson Sardelli (Mario); William Hopper (Judge); Genevieve Waite (Girl in Dentist Chair); Michael Sarne (Man in Posture Class).

John Huston and Mae West in <u>Myra Breckinridge</u> (1970).

This is a sad example of the overindulgence that pervaded
Hollywood after the demise of censorship in the late sixties.   Based
on Gore Vidal's best seller (he later wrote a follow-up, <u>Myron</u>
<u>Breckinridge</u>), the resulting film is one of the more outrageously
tasteless entries ever produced by a major Hollywood lot.   Little of
the plotline or ambiance of the Vidal work remained intact in the
screen rendering; instead it was a pastiche of old film clips interpolated into new footage, which frequently made little sense and held
even less interest.   The film's only bright moments were supplied
by Mae West's in-and-out appearance as Leticia Van Allen.   Unfortunately (but fortunately for West who altered the character from a
passive to domineering woman), her characterization did not fit into
the overall scheme of the project and the lively moments with West
were lost amidst the sticky sickness of the overall project.
        Raquel Welch has the focal role of the sex-change character
(Rex Reed is the alter-ego Myron) who appears in Hollywood to leech
off of her gross uncle, Buck Loner (John Huston), a one-time cowboy
star who now runs an acting studio attended by the more talentless
and most degenerate characters on the California scene.   Besides

bilking Uncle Huston for his money, Welch's greatest desire is to
sexually humiliate a male, which she does to dim-witted Rusty (Roger
Herron). At the same time Welch becomes attracted to Herron's
girlfriend, Mary-Ann (Farrah Fawcett) and desires a return to mas-
culinity to fulfill her love for the girl. Meanwhile, sexually insatiable agent Leticia (West) woos Herron away from both Welch and
Fawcett.

In no quarter did the X-rated Myra Breckinridge receive good
critical reaction--except for Mae West's scenes. Many mature filmgoers were annoyed, not pacified, by the array of clips from old Fox
films, inserted with little logic and even less regard for the performers' image. (There was also a clip of Marlene Dietrich in her naval
drag, singing a number within Universal's 1940 Seven Sinners.) A
clip of Shirley Temple from Heidi (1937) was excised from the Rex
Reed sex scene (allegedly on orders from the White House who thought
it would have bad connotations for the then United Nations representative). Loretta Young objected to (and threatened suit about) clips showing her with Clark Gable in Call of the Wild (1935) and with Don
Ameche in The Story of Alexander Graham Bell (1939), and they were
deleted from release prints.

West's two songs, "You've Gotta Taste All the Fruit" and
"Hard to Handle" were issued as a 45 r. p. m. recording.

NEVER GIVE A SUCKER AN EVEN BREAK (Universal, 1941) 70 min.

Director, Edward Cline; associate director, Ralph Ceder;
story, Otis Criblecoblis [W. C. Fields]; screenplay, John T. Neville
and Prescott Chaplin; music director, Charles Previn; music, Frank
Skinner; art directors, Jack Otterson and Richard H. Riedel; set
decorator, Russell A. Gausman; costumes, Vera West; sound, Bernard B. Brown; camera, Jerome Ash; editor, Arthur Hilton.

W. C. Fields (The Great Man); Gloria Jean (His Niece); Billy
Lenhart (Butch); Kenneth Brown (Buddy); Anne Nagel (Madame Gor-
geous); Franklin Pangborn (The Producer); Mona Barrie (The Pro-
ducer's Wife); Leon Errol (The Rival); Margaret Dumont (Mrs. Hemo-
globen); Susan Miller (Ouliotta Hemogloben); Charles Lang (Peter
Carson); Irving Bacon (Soda Jerk); Leon Belasco (Pianist); Minerva
Urecal (Cleaning Woman); Jody Gilbert (Waitress); Michael Visaroff
(Russian Peddler); Carlotta Monti (Receptionist); James "Brick" Sullivan (Fire Truck Driver); Claud Allister (Englishman), and: Jack
Lipson, Emmett Vogan, Lloyd Ingraham, Eddie Bruce, Kay Deslys,
Kathryn Sheldon, Frances Morris, Frank Austin, Jack Roper, Ar-
mand "Curley" Wright, Irene Colman, William Alston, Emma Tansey,
and Charles McMurphy.

After a successful trio of starring vehicles (You Can't Cheat
an Honest Man, My Little Chickadee, and The Bank Dick, qq. v.),
W. C. Fields made this engaging hodgepodge for Universal. The
comedy made little sense--a habit with Fields' films--but it was a
biting satire on Hollywood and film-making in general, especially

censorship. All of the usual Fields traits (child hating, lechery,
dishonesty, drunkeness, etc.) are commingled in the plot. In spite
of the lack of coherence, Never Give a Sucker rates as one of the
star's better features. It is a fitting swan song to his stardom days
in the movies.

The film opens with the Great Man venturing to Esoteric Studios to sell latest screen idea. Along the way he is set upon by two
nasty children, knocked down by a man who is unhappy about Fields'
overtures to his girl, and pestered by Bill Woolf who wants a job in
Fields' next film. "Go away or I'll kill ya," Fields advises Woolf.

At the studio Fields describes a most inane story to the Producer (Franklin Pangborn) and is sent on his way. Later he comes
across his niece (Gloria Jean) playing in a shooting gallery. After
Gloria's mother is killed while making a circus picture (this sequence
has been deleted from the release print), the girl becomes Fields'
ward and the two set forth by plane to Mexico where W. C. plans to
sell wooden nutmeg to the Russian colony.

Along the way Fields loses a bottle from the plane and dives
after it, landing on a mountaintop where he plays a kissing game with
a pretty young thing (Susan Miller), before being accosted by her
man-hungry mama (Margaret Dumont). After a run-in with a gorilla,
W. C. escapes back to civilization but learns the matron is rich and
returns to romance her.

It develops that the entire wild account is the screenplay Fields
wants to have filmed and it is at this point that the Producer runs
him out of his office. While awaiting his niece outside a department
store, a woman climbs into the back of Fields' car and he thinks she
is pregnant and about to have a baby. So he rushes her to the hospital; along the way he manages to demolish his car.

Fields intended calling the film The Great Man--after the nick-
name he gave himself in the picture--but Universal chose the release
title instead. Fields claimed the title would be shortened for mar-
quees and would read "Fields-Sucker." Still Fields managed a bit
in the proceedings for his real-life mistress, Carlotta Monti. She
is seen as Franklin Pangborn's secretary and as Fields enters the
producer's office, she yells, "You'll drown in a vat of whiskey."
Fields then mutters aloud (to himself), "To drown in a vat of whiskey. Death where is thy sting?" It turns out the gal is actually
talking to her boyfriend on the telephone.

James Agee noted in Time magazine, "Largely as a result of
bickering, Sucker is far from being the kind of picture that only
W. C. Fields would turn out. His unique talent needs intelligent
direction. It does not need all the props that its owner thinks are
a necessity for his performance. The great comedian can play
straight better and more firmly than anyone in the business."

In Never Give a Sucker an Even Break, Fields hits hardest
at the studio system (which he hated) and his generally biting look
at the picture industry (and the way it treated him) gives an interesting outlook of the movies, through the jaded eyes of one of its great
comedians.

Stella Stevens, Ryan O'Neal (blaring), and Tatum O'Neal in Nickelodeon (1976).

NICKELODEON (Columbia, 1976) 122 min.

Producers, Irwin Winkler and Robert Chartoff; director, Peter Bogdanovich; screenplay, W. D. Richter and Bogdanovich; music, Richard Hazard; choreography, Rita Abrams; art director, Richard Berger; set decorator, Darrell Silvers; costumes/wardrobe, Theadora Van Runkle, Norman Salling, and Sandra Berke; assistant director, Jack Sanders; stunt coordinator, Hal Needham; sound, Arthur Piantadosi, Les Fresholtz, and Michael Minkler; special effects, Cliff Wenger; special camera effects, Howard A. Anderson Company; camera, Laszlo Kovacs; editor, William Carruth.

Ryan O'Neal (Leo Harrigan); Burt Reynolds (Buck Greenway); Tatum O'Neal (Alice Forsyte); Brian Keith (H. H. Cobb); Stella Stevens (Marty Reeves); John Ritter (Franklin Frank); Jane Hitchcock (Kathleen Cooke); Jack Perkins (Michael Gilhooley); Brion James (Bailiff); Sidney Armus (Judge); Joe Warfield (Defense Attorney); Tamar Cooper (Edna Mae Gilhooley); Alan Gibbs (Patents Holligan); Mathew Anden (Hecky); Lorenzo Music and Arnold Soboloff (Cobb's Writers); Jeffrey Byron (Steve); Andrew Winner (Stage Manager); Mark Dennis (Cobb's Cutter); Rita Abrams, Sara Jane Gould, and Mary Beth Bell (Dutch Damsels); Griffin O'Neal (Bicycle Boy); Patricia O'Neal, Morgan Farley, Anna Thea, Elaine Partnow, Joseph G. Medalis, Billy Beck, and Roger Hampton (Movie Fanatics); Thomas

Murphy (Hollywood Realtor); Chief Elmer Tugsmith (Elmer); Rude
Frimel (Orchestra Conductor).

Following the critical and commercial failures of Daisy Miller
(1974) and At Long Last Love (1975), writer/director Peter Bogdanovich returned to the movie genre where he first won acclaim for Targets (q. v.), and co-wrote/directed Nickelodeon. The picture was allegedly based on incidents told to the youngish director by veterans
Allan Dwan and Raoul Walsh. Bogdanovich is one of the few directors
today in the U. S. who has an affectionate regard for cinema history;
besides writing numerous essays on film (some of which were combined in the book Pieces of Time, 1974), he has also written studies
on directors Dwan, John Ford, and Orson Welles.

Nickelodeon is a slapstick comedy/drama which harks back
to the fly-by-night days of the cinema's infancy and deals with industry mogul H. H. Cobb (Brian Keith) who is producing two-reelers for
his Kinegraph Studios in 1912 Chicago. He is fighting the onslaughts
of the big conglomerate, the Patents Company, which often wrecks
his operations. Later he drafts struggling lawyer Leo Harrigan (Ryan
O'Neal) into becoming a movie director and the latter is thereafter
taught the trade by cameraman Franklin Frank (John Ritter) in the
wilds of California (where the crew hopes to be safe from the vin-
dictive patents combine.)

The company then hires seedy hobo Buck Greenway (Burt Reynolds) as its leading man and they encounter Alice Forsyte (Tatum
O'Neal), an enterprising young lady who rents them equipment and
thinks up ideas for their "impromptu" comedies. Myopic chorus girl
Kathleen Cooke (Jane Hitchcock) is hired as the troupe's leading lady
and both O'Neal and Reynolds fall in love with the lovely gal and
eventually have a falling out over her.

Finally O'Neal attends a screening of D. W. Griffith's The
Birth of a Nation and he realizes that the movie business is far more
than a profit-making con game, it is an art form. At the finale he
sets out to make motion pictures of lasting importance.

With its "special thanks to Allan Dwan and Raoul Walsh, "
Nickelodeon is founded on a good deal of actual movie history. But
its uneven combination of both slapstick and drama was confusing to
most audiences, especially when the rather flippant first portion of
the feature gave way to the dramatic second half and then closed
with an upbeat finale.

Jonathan Rosenbaum in the British Monthly Film Bulletin pin-
pointed Nickelodeon's problem when he observed, "... the virtually
total rejection by Bogdanovich of anything that exists beyond the boundaries of certified (and ossified) movie myth may help to explain the
curious sterility of Nickelodeon in relation to its fascinating subject
and sources. " Richard Eder (New York Times) said, "Mr. Bogdanovich mistreats his love for the vitality of American movie-making
by proclaiming it so breathily. He mistreats his love for the tricks
of the trade, especially the slapstick comic trade, by virtually itali-
cizing each trick as he trots it out.... " Summing it all up, Variety
decided, "Making a film about films is ever tricky, and the failure
rate is abnormally high. Nickelodeon lands in a never-never land
between achievement and abortion. "

Despite its commercial failure, there is no doubt that Bogdanovich was attempting a tribute to the bygone days of the cinema.
That he reveres the art form is clear when he has Keith's character
state near the end (paraphrasing part of a speech actually made recently by actor James Stewart), "Think of it.   All those people going
to see the pictures.   And a lot of them can't even talk American.
They don't have to because pictures are a language that everyone
understands. . . .   And if you're good, if you're really good, then maybe what you're doin' is you're giving 'em little tiny pieces of time
. . . that they never forget. "

A NIGHT AT THE MOVIES see THE SHORT FILMS

NIGHT LIFE IN HOLLYWOOD (Arrow Film Corp. , 1922) 6059 ft.

Presenter, Mrs. A. B. Maescher; director/story, Fred Cald-
well.   (Possible co-director, Jack Pratt.)

J. Frank Glendon (Joe); Josephine Hill (Leonore Baxter); Gale
Henry (Carrie); J. L. McComas (Pa Powell); Elizabeth Rhodes (Ma
Powell); Jack Connolly (Elkins); Delores Hall (Amy); Wallace Reid
and Family, Theodore Roberts, Sessue Hayakawa and Tsuru Aoki,
William Desmond, Bryant Washburn and Family, Bessie Love, J.
Warren Kerrigan and Mother, Johnny Jones, Denishawn Dancers
(Themselves).

Following the scandals that rocked Hollywood in the early
twenties, several films were produced glorifying life in the movie
capital, suggesting that actually work and play there was no different
from anywhere else in America.   To add authenticity to this theory,
many stars and technicians appeared as themselves on camera, ex-
emplifying the "normal" lives they led way out West.   While Hollywood and Souls for Sale (qq. v.) were each big-budgeted productions
promoting this concept, it was the inexpensive Arrow production,
Night Life in Hollywood, which beat them to the box-office punch.
The release appeared in March, while Souls for Sale came out the
next month, and Hollywood followed in the summer of 1922.
The silly story has Joe (J. Frank Glendon) and Carrie (Gale
Henry), brother and sister from rural Arkansas, descending on Hollywood, convinced the town is a modern Babylon.   Instead they discover that its residents lead private lives no stranger than elsewhere
in the U. S. and that actually Hollywood is a relatively quiet little community.   Eventually Glendon falls in love with actress Leonore Baxter (Josephine Hill) and secures his parents' approval to marry her.
To illustrate the "homey" nature of moviedom's then head-
quarters this film had several stars appearing in domestic scenes,
along with a view of Will Rogers' home and an Easter Service at the
Hollywood Bowl.   One can only wonder why the title Night Life in
Hollywood--which immediately conjures visions of wild parties and
madcap abandon--was selected for a feature which purported to exem-
plify the simple virtues of filmdom.

NOCTURNE (RKO 1946) 88 min.

Executive producer, Jack Gross; producer, Joan Harrison;
director, Edwin L. Marin; story, Frank Fenton and Rowland Brown;
screenplay, Jonathan Latimer; art directors, Albert D'Agostino and
Robert Boyle; set decorators, Darrell Silvera and James Altwies;
technical advisor, Lieutenant Barney Ruditsky; music, Leigh Harline;
songs, Harline and Mort Greene; Eleanor Rudolph; music director,
C. Bakaleinikoff; assistant director, James Anderson; sound, Jean
Speak; special effects, Russell A. Cully; camera, Harry J. Wild;
editor, Elmo Williams.

George Raft (Lieutenant Joe Warne); Lynn Bari (Frances Ran-
som); Virginia Huston (Carol Page); Joseph Pevney (Fingers); Myrna
Dell (Susan); Edward Ashley (Paul Vincent); Walter Sande (Halberson);
Mabel Paige (Mrs. Warne); Bernard Hoffman (Torp); Queenie Smith
(Queenie); Mack Gray (Gratz); Pat Flaherty (Cop with Susan); Lorin
Raker (Police Chemist); William Challee (Police Photographer); Greta
Grandstedt (Clara); Lilian Bond (Mrs. Billings); Carol Forman (Re-
ceptionist); Robert Malcolm (Earn); Jim Pierce, William Bloom, Ed
Dearing, and Roger Creed (Cops); Janet Shaw (Grace); Will Wright
(Mr. Billings); James Carlisle (Elderly Man); Jack Norton (Drunk);
Betty Farrington, Connie Evans, Doris Stone, Monya Andre, Norma
Brown, and Eleanor Counts (Women); Al Hill (Cop at Brown Derby);
Lillian Bronson (Cashier at Gotham); Matt McHugh (Coffee Attendant);
Donald Kerr (Gaffer); Bert Moorhouse (Director) Dick Rush (Studio
Cop).

Nocturne is a dark, brooding, and sadly neglected small detective film highlighted by George Raft's low-key work as a police
lieutenant turned hunter.   Not to be overlooked is the impressive
title theme by Leigh Harline.   Furthermore, the art direction (Albert D'Agostino and Robert Boyle) and cinematography (Harry J.
Wild) are superior and effectively heighten the picture's sense of
suspense and intrigue.   A small portion of the film takes place on the
set of another RKO film, Douglas Fairbanks Jr. 's Sinbad the Sailor
(1947).
     In Hollywood, a famous movieland composer, Paul Vincent
(Edward Ashley) is found murdered.   On the wall of his home, where
the crime took place, hang ten photographs of various women.   The
police believe the clue to his killing is in those photos, one of which
may reveal his murderer.
     The upper echelon in the police department, however, wants
the case closed and declare the composer's death a suicide.   But
Lieutenant Joe Warne (Raft) insists the man was murdered, pointing
out there were powder burns on the victim.   For continuing to work
on the case, Raft is suspended from the force--but he pursues his
probe anyway.   Later he meets a nightclub singer (Virginia Huston)
and another woman, Frances Ransom (Lynn Bari), both of whom were
close to the deceased.   Then there is a piano player named Fingers

---

Opposite: George Raft in Nocturne (1946).

(played by Joseph Pevney who later became a film director).   In his
travels, Raft is beaten up by a man named Torp (Bernard Hoffman)
and he finds another suspect has been murdered.   Finally the detective uncovers a new composition written by Ashley just before his
death.   As Fingers plays the song, the clue emerges as to the true
killer of the first victim.

In reassessing this sombre study of the unglamorous work-a-
day ambiance of forties' Hollywood, Allen Eyles recently wrote in
Focus on Film.   "From the beginning, Nocturne displays authority
as a piece of filmcraft.   A smooth succession of urban nightscapes,
drawing further and further back, occur behind the main titles until
the movement is reversed on the director's credit and the camera
plunges down on a chic hillside bungalow passing through a large
scenic window to approach a pianist seated in the middle of a large
room, gliding round his shoulder to focus on a woman seated motion-
less in the shadowy background.   The transition from model bungalow
with matted-in view of the interior to the interior set itself is barely
perceptible and fully upholds the standards established by RKO for
such special effects in Citizen Kane.... "

OH, FOR A MAN! see WILL SUCCESS SPOIL ROCK HUNTER?

OLD STAG MOVIES see THE HISTORY OF THE BLUE MOVIE

ON AN ISLAND WITH YOU (MGM, 1948) Color, 107 min.

Producer, Joe Pasternak; director, Richard Thorpe; story,
Charles Martin and Hans Wilhelm; screenplay, Dorothy Kingsley,
Dorothy Cooper, Martin, and Wilhelm; Technicolor consultants, Nata-
lie Kalmus and Henri Jaffa; art directors, Cedric Gibbons and Ed-
ward Carfagno; set decorators, Edwin B. Willis and Richard A.
Pefferle; music director, George Stoll; songs, Nacio Herb Brown and
Edward Heyman; choreography, Jack Donahue; assistant director, Al
Jennings; makeup, Jack Dawn; costumes, Irene; sound, Douglas Shear-
er and James K. Brock; special effects, Arnold Gillespie; camera,
Charles Rosher; editors, Douglas Biggs and Ferris Webster.

Esther Williams (Rosalind Reynolds); Peter Lawford (Lieuten-
ant Lawrence Y. Kingslee); Ricardo Montalban (Ricardo Montez); Jim-
my Durante (Buckley); Cyd Charisse (Yvonne Torro); Xavier Cugat
(Himself); Leon Ames (Commander Harrison); Kathryn Beaumont
(Penelope Peabody); Dick Simmons (George Blaine); Marie Windsor
(Jane); Arthur Walsh (Second Assistant Director); Betty Reilly (Vocal-
ist); Kay Norton (Martha the Hairdresser); Chester Clute (Tommy the
Waiter); Uluao Letuli (Sword Dancer).

Movie star Rosalind Reynolds (Esther Williams) is dispatched
with a movie company on location to Honolulu to make a motion picture.   There she is romanced by a young naval aviator (Peter Lawford) whom she had met earlier on one of the Hawaiian islands where

Esther Williams and Ricardo Montalban in <u>On an Island with You</u>
(1948).

she entertained troops during World War II. She is rather cold to
the flyer's romantic advances so he abducts her and rushes her off
to the isle where they first met. He claims a dance with her, melts
her resistance, and she succumbs to him. Ricardo Montalban is
Ricardo Montez, her screen fiancé, who turns to Cyd Charisse for
consolation and for a partner to perform the flamboyantly effective
"Apache" dance.

     This Technicolor confection--one of a long string of success-
ful Esther Williams musical-aquatic melees--boasted location filming
in Hawaii, the antics of Jimmy Durante (performing his "Strutaway"
routine), and the Latin American beat of Xavier Cugat and his orchestra. Requisite of any Williams screen fare was her cavorting above
and beneath the water, and this film was no exception.

     Viewers were treated to bits of filming-within-filming as Wil-
liams performed aquatic numbers on the soundstage. Segments from
this would appear in <u>That's Entertainment!</u> (q. v.). If anything, Williams' performance as a genuine moo-vee star only confirmed the
public's long-held belief that screen actors were amorous infants
without too many serious cares in the world.

ONCE IN A LIFETIME (Universal, 1932) 75 min.

Director, Russell Mack; based on the play by Moss Hart and George S. Kaufman; screenplay, Seton I. Miller; camera, George Robinson.

Jack Oakie (George Lewis); Sidney Fox (Susan Walker); Aline MacMahon (May Daniels); Russell Hopton (Jerry Hyland); ZaSu Pitts (Miss Leighton); Louise Fazenda (Helen Hobart); Gregory Ratoff (Herman Glogauer); Onslow Stevens (Lawrence Vail); Robert McWade (Mr. Walker); Jobyna Howland (Mrs. Walker); Claudia Morgan (Miss Chasen); Gregory Gaye (Rudolph Kammerling); Edward Kane (Meterstein); Johnnie Morris (Weisskopf); Mona Maris (Phyllis Fontaine); Carol Tevis (Florabel Leigh); Frank LaRue (Sign Painter).

With vaudeville dying with the advent of radio, talking pictures, and the Depression, three none-too-talented stage folk (Jack Oakie, Aline MacMahon, and Russell Hopton) plan to invade Hollywood as "experts" on voice culture, a subject on which they are practically ignorant. Aboard the westward-bound train, they meet an influential movie columnist (Louise Fazenda) and from this creature they wangle the necessary professional introductions.

Once in California they confer with studio mogul Herman Glogauer (Gregory Ratoff). Among the typical Hollywood types they encounter on the lot are a writer (Onslow Stevens) who has been on full salary for six months without ever seeing the studio boss, let alone work; some feather-headed actresses (Carol Tevis and Mona Maris); a deadpan receptionist (ZaSu Pitts) who cannot remember anything, and others. It is Stevens who tells Oakie, the leader of the bogus trio, that Hollywood is run by a batch of fools. Nitwit Oakie repeats the words to the tycoon, but instead of being fired, he is made supervising producer on the lot.

Oakie soon bungles his new task, remaking a 1910 Biograph one-reeler into something called Gingham and Orchids on which he forgets to light part of the sets and accidentally adds sound effects by his continual nut-cracking during shooting. The critics, however, hail the film as a masterpiece and Oakie is assigned to make a war picture. He orders 200 planes (which seems financial folly), until it develops that he has cornered the market, and now these crafts can be rented to other studios for big fees. Next Oakie orders the studio razed. When the workmen arrive the mogul gives the word to go ahead as everything always seems to turn out all right for Oakie.

This incisive, fast-paced, entertaining look at the Hollywood power structure and production system was written by Moss Hart and George S. Kaufman in 1930 for the Broadway stage. The original comedy was Hart's (Kaufman revised it) and at the time Hart had never been to California; he had assembled his notion from movies he had seen and from constant reading of Variety newspaper. What resulted was one of the most brilliant satires ever devised about the movie world. Universal filmed the storyline intact, deleting none of the punch of the theatre original. Oakie was at his cinematic best as the jovial fool George while MacMahon added her wry humor as his partner. Gregory Ratoff as the bombastic mogul fitted the image very well, as did Maris as an exotic, unintellectual movie star.

In 1971 the feature was revived on public broadcasting television, winning new praise and gaining fresh adherents.

ONCE IS NOT ENOUGH see JACQUELINE SUSANN'S ONCE IS NOT ENOUGH

THE OSCAR (Embassy, 1966) Color, 119 min.

Executive producer, Joseph E. Levine; producer, Clarence Greene; director, Russell Rouse; based on the novel by Richard Sale; screenplay, Harlan Ellison, Rouse, and Greene; songs, Leo Robin and Ralph Rainger; Sammy Cahn and James Van Heusen; music supervisor, Irving Friedman; orchestrators, Leo Shuken and Jack Hayes; music, Percy Faith; art directors, Hal Pereira and Arthur Lonergan; set decorators, Robert Benton and James Payne; gowns, Edith Head; women's wardrobe, Glenita Dinneen; Mr. Boyd's wardrobe, Robert Magahay; assistant director, Dick Moder; dialogue coach, Leon Charles; choreography, Steven Peck; sound, Harry Lindgren and John Wilkinson; camera, Joseph Ruttenberg; editor, Chester W. Schaeffer.

Stephen Boyd (Frank Fane); Elke Sommer (Kay Bergdahl); Milton Berle (Kappy Kapstetter); Eleanor Parker (Sophie Cantaro); Joseph Cotten (Kenneth H. Regan); Jill St. John (Laurel Scott); Tony Bennett (Hymie Kelly); Edie Adams (Trina Yale); Ernest Borgnine (Barney Yale); Ed Begley (Grobard); Walter Brennan (Orrin C. Quentin); Broderick Crawford (Sheriff); James Dunn (Network Executive); Peter Lawford (Steve Marks); Jack Soo (Sam); Jean Hale (Cheryl Barker); Edith Head, Hedda Hopper, Frank Sinatra, Bob Hope, Merle Oberon, and Nancy Sinatra (Themselves).

One of Hollywood's most unflattering, deprecating looks at itself occurred in The Oscar, one of the trilogy of Hollywood-oriented pictures by filmmaker Joseph E. Levine (The Carpetbaggers and Harlow, qq. v., being the other two.) The Oscar claimed to depict the inside workings of the selection of those winning the coveted Academy Awards; instead, it emerged a sleazy soap opera with only offbeat casting to create mild interest. Saddled with unspectacular production values and inept performances (especially Tony Bennett's as Stephen Boyd's pal), the feature was a box-office turkey. Discriminating moviegoers preferred to watch the real thing--the Oscarcast--on television--and hypothecate themselves as to the behind-the-scenes chaos involved.

The Oscar opens (where else but?) on the night of the Academy Award presentations and it centers on egocentric star Frankie Fane (Boyd) who, while waiting to be named Best Actor, recounts his life in flashbacks. It all started when he and a pal (Bennett) were working as announcers in a strip joint and they decided to make a fresh start in California. Then drama coach Sophie Cantaro

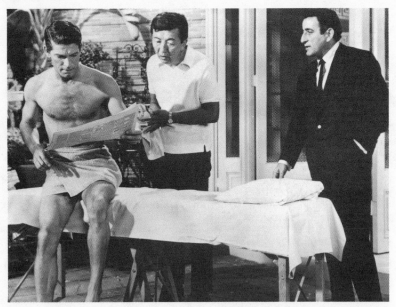

Stephen Boyd, Jack Soo, and Tony Bennett in The Oscar (1966).

(Eleanor Parker) takes a liking to Boyd and she helps him to make an entree into pictures in return for amorous favors.   Once established in films, Boyd drops Parker and weds glamourous star Kay Bergdahl (Elke Sommer).   He also takes advantage of her and she leaves him, as does his friend-factotum Bennett.   Rounding out the picture is Milton Berle as Boyd's one-time agent.   Now that he is approaching death Berle no longer has to suffer Boyd's arrogance and he redeems his pride in a confrontation with the temperamental celebrity.

Returning to the present, Boyd is prepared to accept the Oscar.   After all, he has spent a good deal of money currying publicity and hopefully votes for the big prize.   When the Award is announced, he stands up to accept it, only to discover it is for Frank, but Frank Sinatra.

Populated with characters with names like Kappy Kapstetter (Berle the agent), Hymie Kelly (Bennett the pal), and Trina Yale (Edie Adams, an actress), the film suffered from some of the tritest dialogue ever to waterlog a film.   Repeatedly Bennett's character utters such clichés as, "If you lie down with garbage, you come up smelling like a pig."   The only redeeming moments to the 119-minutes of embarrassment were the scenes of the Oscar award ceremony; especially the guest appearances by Merle Oberon and Frank Sinatra.

Richard Shickel wrote in Life magazine, "... this is that true movie rarity--a picture that attains a perfection of ineptitude quite beyond the power of words to describe.   You have to see it to dis-

believe it and still you will come away wondering what possible excuse there is for it--beyond obvious commercialism. " Bosley Crowther exorted in the New York Times, "Another distressing example
of Hollywood fouling its nest--professionally, socially, commercially
and especially artistically--. ... Obviously the community doesn't
need enemies so long as it has itself. "

THE OTHER WOMAN (20th Century-Fox, 1954) 81 min.

Producer/director/screenplay, Hugo Haas; music, Ernest Gold;
camera, Eddie Fitzgerald; editor, Robert S. Eisen.

Hugo Haas (Darman); Cleo Moore (Sherry); Lance Fuller (Ronnie); Lucille Barkley (Mrs. Darman); Jack Macy (Lester); John Qualen
(Papasha); Jan Arvan (Collins); Carolee Kelly (Marion); Steve Mitchell
and Mark Lowell (Assistant Directors); Melinda Markey (Actress).

Multi-faceted Hugo Haas created this low-budget pot-boiler
about a second-rate film director who is blackmailed by a low-class
actress.   The end result was a typical brooding Haas project, short
on production values, thin on scripting, full of high-pitched acting,
and reflective of the "dark mood" style of cinema-making that Haas
had acquired in the thirties while directing in his native Hungary.
Haas was top-billed as Darman, a foreign film director who
has solidified himself in Hollywood by marrying the daughter (Lucille
Barkley) of a film studio president (Jack Macy).   He rejects extra
Sherry (Cleo Moore) for a bit role in his latest cinema project and
the girl schemes to win revenge.   She lures the director to her
apartment, drugs him, and later blackmails him for $50,000, insist-
ing there was an affair (which never took place).   The effect on Haas
is to drive him to near insanity, especially after Moore is mysteriously strangled to death.   A meek man from the girl's past gets the
blame for the killing but eventually the police apprehend Haas and he
is sentenced to life in prison.
Perhaps The Other Woman is a reflective look at Haas' own
film-making; if so, it reveals the director certainly never set his
cinematic sights very high.   He did, however, portray the lead assignment convincingly and his then-protégée, Cleo Moore, was both
physically and professionally acceptable as the doomed, scheming
extra.   Overall though, the picture was a study of the sleazier side
of film-making and one that was not popular with audiences.   Haas
would again direct a Hollywood-oriented film and again cast himself
as a director in Stars in Your Backyard (q. v.).
Variety determined that The Other Woman "has enough sex
and drama for lesser situations" while the Hollywood Reporter found
it to be "just another movie ... laid in Hollywood.... "

OUT CALIFORNIA WAY (Republic, 1946) Color, 67 min.

Associate producer, Louis Gray; director, Lesley Selander;

Monte Hale and Tom London in <u>Out California Way</u> (1946).

story, Barry Shipman; screenplay, Betty Burbridge; art director, Hilyard Brown; set decorators, John McCarthy, Jr. and Otto Siegel; music, Nathan G. Scott; songs, Jack Meakin and Foster Carling; assistant director, George Webster; sound, Ferol Redd; camera, Budd Thackery; editor, Charles Craft.

Monte Hale (Monte); Adrian Booth (Gloria McCoy); Bobby Blake (Danny McCoy); John Dehner (Rod Mason); Nolan Leary (George Sheridan) Fred Graham (Ace Carter); Tom London (Johnny Archer); Jimmy Starr (Himself); Edward Keane (E. J. Pearson); Bob Wilke (Assistant Director); Brooks Benedict (Cameraman); Roy Rogers and Trigger, Dale Evans, Don "Red" Barry, Allan "Rocky" Lane, St. Luke's Choristers, Foy Willing & The Riders of the Purple Sage (Themselves).

After Gene Autry departed Republic Pictures following his service in World War II, that studio's head, Herbert J. Yates, was continually seeking a new talent to bolster the performer ranks for B cowboy features. He found likeable singer Monte Hale and the actor's third starring picture in his Republic Western series was

filmed in Trucolor and entitled Out California Way. Like earlier
Gene Autry entries (The Big Show and Down Mexico Way, qq. v.), it
utilized moviemaking as a backdrop.

Monte is a cowpoke with a tremendous desire to follow the
great American twentieth-century tradition--become a movie hero.
He reaches Hollywood where Global Studios gives him a test and signs
him to appear in a string of Westerns. A fading cowboy star (well
played by John Dehner), however, attempts to make life rough for
the newcomer. The rookie eventually fails, in part because of the
sudden arrival of (and help from) Roy Rogers and Trigger, Dale
Evans, Don "Red" Barry, Allan "Rocky" Lane, and Foy Willing and
the Riders of the Purple Sage.

The gimmick of having assorted studio cowboy stars in cameo
roles had been used to good advantage in Bells of Rosarita (q. v.), and
it worked fine here as did Hale's well-modulated vocalizing. Variety
reported, "With the swooner firmly in the saddle these days, the
wild and woolly sagas of the western plains are becoming as rare as
buffalos, and this picture is definitely part of the latter day trend. "
Hale would make 11 more entries in his Republic series.

PANORAMA BLUE (Ellman Film Enterprises, 1974) Color, 85 min.

Executive producer, Richard Ellman; producer/director, Alan
Roberts; screenplay/music, Steve Michaels; set decorator, Don Mul-
derick; sound, Phil Brandon; camera, Bob Brownell; editor, James
Walters.

With: Carona Faoro, Stephen Nave, Sue Moses, Dennis
Zlamal, Rene Bond, Sandy Dempsey, John Paul Jones, Rich Loots,
Linda York, Charlotte Ruse, Bob Taylor, Reg Bartram, Con Covert,
Johna Lee, Cyndee Summers, Rich Cassidy, Richard S. Ellman,
Uschi Digart, and John Holmes.

See THE HISTORY OF THE BLUE MOVIE.

PARADISE ALLEY (aka STARS IN YOUR BACKYARD) (Astor 1961)
    81 min.

Producer, Hugo Haas; associate producer, Robert Erlik;
director/screenplay, Haas; music, Franz Steininger; assistant director, Marty Moss.

Hugo Haas (The Director); Marie Windsor (The Prostitute);
Corinne Griffith (The Mother); Billy Gilbert (The Father); Carol
Morris (The Daughter); and: Don Sullivan, Chester Conklin, Mar-
garet Hamilton, William Forrest, Tom Fadden, Jesslyn Fox, Almira
Sessions, Jan Englund, Tom Duggan, William Schallart, Clegg Hoyt,
Tim Johnson, Bob Dennis, James Canino, and Skipper McNally.

During the fifties, Hungarian actor/writer/producer/director
Hugo Haas contributed a number of interesting B melodramas to the

American cinema; they were decidedly on the sombre side, heavily dramatic, mildly erotic, and somewhat turgid examples of the "European style" film-making. Of his movies accomplished during the decade, two dealt with Hollywood-oriented themes, The Other Woman (q. v.) and Paradise Alley (made under the working title of Stars in Your Backyard).

Made in 1957 but not released until 1962, the film is primarily of interest for its cast, rather than for its simplistic and not very picturesque storyline.

A once-famous film director (Haas) attempts to produce a movie in a slum where everyone hates each other. The end result is not only the discovery of a lovely girl (skating star Carol Morris) to star in the picture, but also the healing of old emotional wounds and a rebirth of respect and friendship in the neighborhood. Among those in the production were ex-silent film star Corinne Griffith as the mother, comedian Billy Gilbert as the father, Almira Sessions as a local gossip.

Without violence or the usual pseudo-sex associated with Haas' movies, this film failed to obtain a distributor and lay dormant until 1961 when Astor Pictures acquired the rights to the film and sold it to TV.

PARAMOUNT ON PARADE (Paramount, 1930) 128 min.   (color sequences)

Producer, Albert S. Kaufman; production supervisor, Elsie Janis; directors, Dorothy Arzner, Otto Brower, Edmund Goulding, Victor Heerman, Edwin H. Knopf, Rowland V. Lee, Ernst Lubitsch, Lothar Mendes, Victor Schertzinger, A. Edward Sutherland, Frank Tuttle; songs, Janis and Jack King; Ballard MacDonald and Dave Dreyer; Ernesto De Curtis; L. Wolfe Gilbert and Abel Baer; Richard A. Whiting and Raymond B. Eagan; Whiting and Leo Robin; David Franklin; Sam Coslow; choreography, David Bennett; set designer, John Wenger; sound, Harry M. Lindgren; camera, Harry Fischbeck and Victor Milner.

Iris Adrian, Richard Arlen, Jean Arthur, Mischa Auer, William Austin, George Bancroft, Clara Bow, Evelyn Brent, Mary Brian, Clive Brook, Virginia Bruce, Nancy Carroll, Ruth Chatterton, Maurice Chevalier, Gary Cooper, Cecil Cunningham, Leon Errol, Stuart Erwin, Henry Fink, Kay Francis, Skeets Gallagher, Edmund Goulding, Harry Green, Mitzi Green, James Hall, Phillips Holmes, Helen Kane, Dennis King, Abe Lyman & His Band, Fredric March, Nino Martini, Mitzi Mayfair, Marion Morgan Dancers, David Newell, Jack Oakie, Warner Oland, Zelma O'Neal, Eugene Pallette, Joan Peers, Jack Pennick, Russ Powell, William Powell, Charles "Buddy" Rogers, Lillian Roth, Rolfe Sedan, Stanley Smith, Fay Wray (Guest Performers).

Just when it was thought that the all-star, all-talking musical revue had run its course, Paramount presented what was probably the

Evelyn Brent and Maurice Chevalier in <u>Paramount on Parade</u> (1930).

best of the batch, Paramount on Parade.   More than three dozen
studio stars emblazoned this 128-minute spectacular, which had some
of its sequences in color.   Under the general supervision of Elsie
Janis and helmed by 11 directors, the film survives as one of the
best of Hollywood's introspective revues.   For once, the personalities on-camera tended to be cast into sequences to which they could
relate and perform with zest.

Plotless, the picture opens with a group of chorus girls and
ushers singing the title theme song; Jack Oakie, Skeets Gallagher,
and Leon Errol offer "We're the Masters of Ceremony," then Charles
"Buddy" Rogers and Lillian Roth sing "Any Time's the Time to Fall
in Love" (on a cuckoo clock set).   In the sketch "Murder Will Out,"
a take-off on the popular detective film genre, Oakie and rotund Eugene Pallette assist William Powell (as Philo Vance), Clive Brook (as
Sherlock Holmes), and Warner Oland (as Dr. Fu Manchu) in solving
a crime.   Next, Maurice Chevalier and Evelyn Brent exhibit the origin of the Apache dance.   Nino Martini sings "Torna a Sorrento,"
and in the sketch "In a Hospital" Errol, Helen Kane, and David Newell are featured.   Oakie and Zelma O'Neal engage in shenanigans
in "In a Girl's Gym."   Harry Greer is a toreador and Kay Francis
is Carmen in a comic turn, and then Ruth Chatterton performs a
torch version of "My Marine," joined by Stuart Erwin, Stanley Smith,
and Fredric March.   After Chevalier croons "All I Want Is Just One
Girl," little Mitzi Green offers her impersonations of the French
singer.   Helen Kane learns that in "The Schoolroom" her pupils know
all about "Boop Boopa Doop."   Dennis King renders "Nichavo" and
then to the accompaniment of Abe Lyman's band, Nancy Carroll sings
and dances to "Dancing to Save Your Sole."   In the romantic sketch,
"Dream Girl," Richard Arlen, Gary Cooper, James Hall, David Newell, Phillips Holmes, Fay Wray, Mary Brian, Jean Arthur, Virginia
Bruce, and Joan Peers are involved in a contemporary and period
setting.   Clara Bow then sings "I'm True to the Navy Now" to a
chorus of 42 sailors.   In "Impulses" burly George Bancroft lampoons
the society film dramas, aided by Kay Francis, William Austin, et
al.   The finale has Chevalier and a girls' chorus singing "Sweeping
the Clouds Away."

Photoplay magazine called it "Glorified vaudeville that brings
in virtually everybody on the Paramount lot....   Unceasing speed,
beauty of sound and picture--these are outstanding characteristics."
Variety reported, "Real entertainment incorporating everything on
the schedule into its twenty numbers, [the film] witnesses the first
production of this kind linking together with almost incredible smooth-
ness achievements from the smallest technical detail to the greatest
artistic endeavor."

Spotted in the opening segment of the revue film are shots of
Paramount and some of its soundstage activities.   There were several
foreign language versions made of this picture; in the Spanish edition,
Jeanette MacDonald served as a hostess/participant.

PARIS WHEN IT SIZZLES (Paramount, 1964) Color, 110 min.

Producers, Richard Quine and George Axelrod; associate pro-

Audrey Hepburn in Paris When It Sizzles (1964).

ducers, Carter De Haven and John R. Coonan; director, Quine; story, Julien Duvivier and Henri Jeanson; screenplay, Axelrod; art director, Jean D'Eaubonne; set decorator, Gabriel Bechir; music, Nelson Riddle; orchestrator, Arthur Morton; Miss Hepburn's wardrobe and perfume, Hubert de Givenchy; makeup, Frank McCoy; assistant director, Paul Feyder; sound, Jo De Bretagne and Charles Grenzbach; special camera effects, Paul K. Lerpae; camera, Charles Lang, Jr.; editor, Archie Marshek.

William Holden (Richard Benson); Audrey Hepburn (Gabrielle Simpson); Gregoire Aslan (Police Inspector); Noël Coward (Alexander Meyerheimer); Raymond Bussieres (Gangster); Christian Duvallex (Maitre d'Hotel); Marlene Dietrich, Tony Curtis, and Mel Ferrer (Guest Stars); Fred Astaire and Frank Sinatra (Singing Voices).

A self-centered and semi-alcoholic screenwriter luxuriates in a roof-top suite at a Paris hotel. Badly in need of fresh funds, Richard Benson (William Holden) agrees to hack out an espionage yarn, The Girl Who Stole the Eiffel Tower, for Alexander Meyerheimer (Noël Coward), head of his own film production company. He hires pretty secretary Gabrielle Simpson (Audrey Hepburn) as his typist and she agrees to stay with him in the apartment to help him meet the 48-hour deadline he has for completing the scenario. Together they concoct outlandish spy situations and imagine themselves in various super agent guises until they have not only finished the script but have fallen in love.   Holden emerges from the experience a rehabilitated person.

This bland comedy, from George Axelrod's screenplay (he wrote the play Will Success Spoil Rock Hunter?, q. v.), was a complete miss and instead of "sizzle" it "fizzled" at the box-office. Both Holden as the scripter and Hepburn as the functionary seemed lost in the maze of foolish situations into which they were thrown by the incoherent script.   Even fleeting guest appearances by Marlene Dietrich, Tony Curtis, and Mel Ferrer (as well as special soundtrack vocals by Frank Sinatra and Fred Astaire) did not alleviate the tedium of this Paris lensed clinker.   (The film had been shot in 1962, but shelved; obviously aging in the storage vault did not improve the product.)

Variety best summed up the film, judging it to be "contrived, utterly preposterous and totally unmotivated. " For many who remembered the charming screen teaming of Holden and Hepburn in 1954's Sabrina, Paris When It Sizzles was a sharp let-down.

THE PARTY (United Artists, 1968) Color, 98 min.

Producer, Blake Edwards; associate producer, Ken Wales; director/story, Edwards; screenplay, Edwards, Tom Waldman, and Frank Waldman; production designer, Fernando Carrere; set decorators, Reg Allen and Jack Stevens; music, Henry Mancini; song, Mancini and Don Black; assistant director, Mickey McCardle; sound, Robert Martin; special effects, Norman Breedlove; camera, Lucien Ballard; editor, Ralph Winters.

Peter Sellers (Hrundi V. Bakshi); Claudine Longet (Michele Monet); Marge Champion (Rosalind Dunphy); J. Edward McKinley (Fred Clutterbuck); Fay McKenzie (Mrs. Clutterbuck); Steve Franken (Levinson the Waiter); Gavin MacLeod (C. S. Divot); Denny Miller (Wyoming Bill Kelso); Sharron Kimberly (Princess Helena); Buddy Lester (Davey Kane); Corinne Cole (Janice Kane); Kathe Green (Molly Clutterbuck); Carol Wayne (June Warren); Tom Quine (Congressman Dunphy); Timothy Scott (Gore Pontoon); Elianne Nadeau (Wiggy); Al Checco (Bernard Stein); James Lanphier (Harry); Danielle De Metz (Stella D'Angelo); Jerry Martin (Bradford); Dick Crockett (Wells); Frances Davis (Maid); Allen Jung (Cook); Herb Ellis (Film Director).

A bungling actor from India, Hrundi V. Bakshi (Peter Sellers) is brought to Hollywood to appear in a remake of Gunga Din.   He wreaks havoc on the picture while on location by becoming too caught up in the action.   At one point he accidentally sets off a charge which blows up the fortress set before the production is ready to film the expensive event.   He is promptly fired but by accident is invited to a party at the mansion of a studio executive where he continues his unconscious reign of havoc.

At the fete, he loses his shoe, spots it on a food tray, and travels around the room causing mayhem until he recovers it.   Later

Peter Sellers crouches near Timothy Scott and Carol Wayne in The
Party (1968).

---

he disrupts a musicians' reefer conclave, then spoils the muscle-man
butler's exercises, and becomes involved with a dumb blonde.   By
the time the gala is over, the Indian has made a worse shambles of
the plush home that he did of the movie set.
       Sellers, as the British-accented Indian, certainly was the life
and focal point of The Party, with the script requiring him to accomplish a great deal of visual comedy.   Coming on the heels of his
successful work in After the Fox (q. v.), the entry proved to be disappointing to all but the more ardent Sellers fans.   At the box-office
it emerged a throw-away item, failing to generate the strong business
of his previous starring vehicle.   It was one of the causes for the
decline of his career, which did not recover until 1975's Return of
the Pink Panther, also directed by Blake Edwards.
       Variety chided, "All the charm of two-reel comedy, as well
as all the resulting tedium when the concept is distended to 10 reels,
is evident in The Party.   The one-joke script, told in a laudable, if
unsuccessful, attempt to emulate silent pix technique, is dotted with

The Patsy   286

comedy ranging from drawing room repartee to literally, bathroom
vulgarity. "

However, if one can see through the crude visual slapstick,
the vehicle does offer its own commentary on the film industry caste
system, in which the world of extras, executives, and stars should
NEVER mingle socially.

THE PATSY (Paramount, 1964) Color, 101 min.

Producer, Ernest D. Glucksman; associate producer, Arthur
Schmidt; director, Jerry Lewis; screenplay, Lewis and Bill Richmond;
assistant directors, Ralph Axness and Howard Roessell; art directors,
Hal Pereira and Cary O'Dell; costumes, Edith Head; music, David
Raksin; sound, Ray Cossar; camera, Wallace Kelley; editor, John
Woodcock.

Jerry Lewis (Stanley Belt); Ina Balin (Ellen Betz); Everett
Sloane (Caryl Fergusson); Keenan Wynn (Harry Silver); Peter Lorre
(Morgan Heywood); John Carradine (Bruce Alden); Phil Harris (Chic
Wymore); Hans Conreid (Dr. Mule-rrr); Phil Foster (Mayo Sloan);
Richard Deacon (Sy Devore) Scatman Crothers (Shoeshine Man); Fritz
Feld (Maitre d'); Del Moore (Policeman); Nancy Kulp (Theatregoer);
Rhonda Fleming, Hedda Hopper, George Raft, Ed Sullivan, Mel Torme,
and Ed Wynn (Guest Stars); Jerome Cowan (Executive); Ned Wynn
(Page); Jerry Dumphy (TV Newscaster); Jerry Dexter (Radio News-
caster); Benny Rubin (Waiter).

When a famous film star is killed in a plane crash his movie
production unit is desperate to find a quick replacement to complete
a feature they have begun.   They latch onto Stanley Belt (Jerry Lewis), a bumbling bellboy at the Beverly Hilton Hotel.   The team,
hoping not to lose their jobs, set about to remodel the silly young
man into a presentable movie star.   They hire a vocal coach, try
to dress him properly and make a gentleman out of him--but it is
all to no avail.   Only Ellen Betz (Ina Balin), the group's secretary,
fathoms any hope in Lewis and she remains loyal to him as they fall
in love.

In disgust, the rest of the troupe abandon the bellboy, but by
a ruse he earns a spot on Ed Sullivan's TV variety show.   His insane comedy proves a hit with viewers so the star-making team re-
hire him for the film and he and Balin find happiness.

Lewis co-wrote and directed himself in this farce which was
"essentially a rerun of the same movie Jerry has been making over
and over for the past eight years" (Time magazine).   Outside of the
plot gimmick and a cast of veterans supporting the star, the meandering film holds little interest.   Most of the activity within the picture,
including its supposed comedy, is pretty threadbare.   The inane
yelling and brainless actions of the on-screen Lewis soon become
irritating.

One bright but brief spot occurs when Lewis is being fitted
with elegant new clothes.   The young man informs the tailor (Richard

Jerry Lewis and Ina Balin in The Patsy (1964).

Deacon) that he wants to be dressed in such a fashion as to look like George Raft.   After putting on a dapper suit he surveys himself in the mirror; the reflection he sees is not of himself but of Raft.

Lewis let slip through his production grasp a good opportunity to penetrate the not-so-rare occurence of a talent task force shaping an unknown into a commodity the public will accept and elevate to stardom.   The studios did it all the time and in recent years it has been a frequent ploy within the music field.

PEG O' THE MOVIES   see   THE SHORT FILMS

THE PERILS OF PAULINE (Paramount, 1947) 98 min.

Producer, Sol. C. Siegel; director, George Marshall; story, J. P. Wolfson; music score, Robert Emmett Dolan; art director, Hans Dreier and Roland Anderson; songs, Frank Loesser, Raymond Walker and Charles McCarron; camera, Ray Rennahan; editor, Arthur Schmidt.

Betty Hutton (Pearl White); John Lund (Michael Farrington);

Billy De Wolfe (Timmy); William Demarest (Chuck McManus); Constance Collier (Julia Gibbs); Frank Faylen (Joe Gurt); William Farnum (Hero--Western Saloon Set); Paul Panzer (Gent--Interior Drawing Room); Snub Pollard (Propman--Western Saloon); Creighton Hale (Marcelled Leading Man); Chester Conklin, James Finlayson, Hank Mann (Chef Comics); Bert Roach (Bartender--Western Saloon); Francis MacDonald (Heavy--Western Saloon); Heinie Conklin (Studio Cop); Franklyn Farnum (Friar John); Eric Alden (Officer); Ethel Clayton (Lady Montague); Harry Hayden (Stage Manager); Julia Faye (Nurse); Chester Clute ("Willie" Millick); Myrtle Anderson (Maid); Frank Ferguson (Theatre Owner); Rex Lease, Stanley Blystone, Sidney D'Albrook (Reporters); John "Skins" Miller (Cameraman--Drawing Room Set); Bess Flowers, Paula Ray (Reporters); Tom Dugan (Balloonist); Eugene Borden (French Doctor); Byron Poindexter (Man); Raymond de Ravenne (Call Boy); Jack Shea (Workman).

This action entry borrowed its title from the famous silent film serial of 1914, but in reality it was a biopic of that cliffhanger's star, Pearl White (1889-1938). Like most Hollywood-conceived screen biographies, though, it was a misrepresentation of the star's private and public life. The producers did take surprising care to reconstruct the serial days of the silent movies with the famous stunts and action routines which thrilled early movie audiences. As an added bonus, George Marshall, who himself had supervised silent chapterplays, helmed this feature and used such serial personalities from bygone years as Creighton Hale and Paul Panzer. In addition the cast of this Paramount release boasted film veterans William Farnum, Snub Pollard, Chester Conklin, Hank Mann, Jimmy Finlayson, Heinie Conklin, Franklyn Farnum, Ethel Clayton, Julia Faye, Bert Roach, and Rex Lease. On the soundtrack there was Frank Loesser's "I Wish I Didn't Love You More" and best of all, there was the shrewd casting of the forties' "blonde bombshell" Betty Hutton as Pearl White. It was a good followup to her portrayal of Texas Guinan (who had also made silent action films) in Paramount's Incendiary Blonde (1945).

Unfortunately the plot of The Perils of Pauline falls far short of its cast and high-class production values. The narrative purports to relate how Pearl White (Hutton), a seamstress in a sewing shop, delivers costumes to a Shakespearean stage company and is promptly attracted to the acting game. Performing a crazy, energetic song for the director (William Demarest) she is hired to do bits, but fails. The director, however, realizes she will be great for action movies and serials and her screen career begins leading her to the heights as the queen of the silent chapterplays. After her love affair with her arrogant costar (John Lund) comes to naught, Pearl deserts the movies for a theatre tour. She is badly injured in a stage accident and realizes she does not have long to live.

Most of the incidents utilized in this film are not true, although the recreation of the Pearl White serials is well done and entertaining. Thankfully Hutton is bombastic enough to fill the role well, supported by the many silent film veterans. All in all the picture does contain the flavor of good oldtime movie-making.

In 1967 Universal released a feature entitled The Perils of Pauline, but it concerned the wild misadventures of a young girl (Pamela Austin) and had nothing to do with the cinema art form.

THE PHANTOM OF HOLLYWOOD (CBS-TV, 1974) Color, 75 min.

Executive producer, Burt Nodell; producer/director, Gene Levitt; story, George Shenk; teleplay, Robert Thom and Shenk; music, Leonard Rosenman; art director, Edward Carfagno; phantom makeup, William Tuttle; camera, Gene Polito; editor, Henry Berman.

Skye Aubrey (Randy Cross); Jack Cassidy (Otto Vonner/Karl Vonner); Jackie Coogan (Jonathan); Broderick Crawford (Captain O'Neal); Peter Haskell (Ray Burns); John Ireland (Lieutenant Gifford); Peter Lawford (Roger Cross); Kent Taylor (Wickes); Bill Williams (Fogel); Corinne Calvet (Mrs. Wickes); Regis Toomey (Joe); Billy Halop (Studio Engineer); Gary Barton (Duke); John Lupton (Al); Fredd Wayne (Clyde); Carl Byrd (Cameraman); Edward Cross (Clint); Bill Stout (Commentator); Damon Douglas (Andy); George Nolan (Pilot).

In order to make use of the deserted Lot #2 at Culver City, MGM borrowed the old premise of The Phantom of the Opera (which itself had been recently reworked into the rock music scene in The Phantom of the Paradise film) and changed the Paris Opera House locale to a deserted movie lot, with the star being of the celluloid variety.   Here the phantom resides in the place of former splendor but emerges to embark on a reign of terror when it appears his habitat is going to be demolished.
     Roger Cross (Peter Lawford), the owner of Worldwide Studios, decides to sell off Lot #2, including its Western town and plaster castles sets, in order to stave off financial losses engendered by mounting operating overhead.   He plans to turn the property over to real-estate developers.   But when the news is issued by his press agent, Ray Burns (Peter Haskell), he receives a mysterious warning not to negotiate the sale.   Not heeding the threat, Lawford finds that several strange deaths and disappearances suddenly happen on the property in question.   The situation is climaxed by the kidnapping of his daughter Randy (Skye Aubrey) and the murder of a real-estate executive who plans to make the purchase.   ("Coincidentally," Skye's father, Jim Aubrey, was head of MGM "production" at one point in the early seventies; her mother, actress Phyllis Thaxter, was a MGM contractee in the forties.)   Finally it is learned that an old actor, once the star of the lot but long ago scarred in a freak accident and thought dead, had been hiding out at the facilities.   It is he who is the culprit of all the bizarre occurrences.   The police decide to permit the razing of the buildings.   In the meanwhile, the phantom is found and killed, and Aubrey is saved.
     With its reliance on the MGM backlot for location, and the inclusion of a veteran cast, The Phantom of Hollywood turned out to be a joy for movie enthusiasts.   Not much favorable could be said for the creaky plotline, but the cast carried it off with finesse, and the use of actual vintage sets made the proceedings atmospheric.

John Ireland and Broderick Crawford in The Phantom of Hollywood (1974).

PICK A STAR (MGM, 1937) 76 min.

Presenter, Hal Roach; director, Edward Sedgwick; story/ screenplay, Richard Flournoy, Arthur Vernon Jones, and Thomas J. Dugan; songs, Fred Stryker and Johnny Lange; R. Alex Anderson; music directors, Arthur Morton and Marvin Hatley; camera, Norbert Brodine; editor, William Terhune.

Patsy Kelly (Nellie Moore); Jack Haley (Joe Jenkins); Rosina Lawrence (Cecilia Moore); Mischa Auer (Rinaldo Lopez); Lyda Roberti (Dagmar); Charles Halton (Mr. Klawheimer); Tom Dugan (Dimitri Hogan); Russell Hicks (Mr. Stone); Cully Richards (Nightclub M. C.); Spencer Charters (Judge); Sam Adams (Sheriff); Robert Gleckler (Headwaiter); Joyce Compton and Johnny Arthur (Newlyweds); James Finlayson (Director); Walter Long (Bandit); Wesley Barry (Assistant Director); Johnny Hyams (Mr. McGregor); Leila McIntyre (Mrs. Mc- Gregor); Benny Burt (Tony); Laurel and Hardy (Themselves).

In 1937, Hal Roach-MGM remade Free and Easy (q. v.) as Pick a Star and in it, Rosina Lawrence played a country girl who em- barked for Hollywood seeking fame and fortune. Through her publicity man (Jack Haley), she reaches stardom. Along the way she encounters various pitfalls, typical of those befalling any aspiring starlet.

While not pretending to be more than it was, a pleasant B film, Pick a Star turned out to be an entertaining effort which won more than its usual share of playdates due to the inclusion of Stan Laurel and Oliver Hardy in two long sequences.

There were some who felt the ration of the absurd which permeated this offering went a bit too far. "You simply have to have a sense of the ridiculous to enjoy it. A mere sense of humor won't do" (New York Daily News). The film was later reissued as Movie Struck.

PLAY IT AS IT LAYS (Universal, 1972) Color, 99 min.

Producer, Frank Perry; co-producer, Dominick Dunne; director, Perry; based on the novel by Joan Didion; screenplay, Didion and John Gregory Dunne; assistant director, Edward Teets; clothes, Joel Schumacher; production designer, Pato Guzman; camera, Jordan Cronenweth; editor, Sidney Katz.

Tuesday Weld (Maria Wyeth); Anthony Perkins (B. Z.); Tammy Grimes (Helene); Adam Roarke (Carter); Ruth Ford (Carlotta); Eddie Firestone (Benny Austin); Diana Ewing (Susannah); Paul Lambert (Larry Kulik); Chuck McCann (Abortionist's Assistant); Severn Darden (Hypnotist); Tony Young (Johnny Waters); Richard Anderson (Les Goodwin); Elizabeth Claman (The Chickie); Mitzi Hoag (Patsy); Tyne Daly (Journalist); Roger Ewing (Nelson); Richard Ryal (Apartment Manager); John Finnegan (Frank); Tracy Morgan (Jeanelle); Darlene Conley (Kate's Nurse); Arthur Knight and Albert Johnson (Themselves); Alan Warnick (TV Panelist).

As she drives down a California freeway, diminished movie star Maria Wyeth (Tuesday Weld) relives her traumatic life in her mind. She is completely disgusted with Hollywood; she has no faith in love after countless affairs; she trusts no one in the film capital after having been used by so many people; she has a retarded child; her parents, whom she did not see for years, have died; her famous director husband (Adam Roarke), who became an industry success guiding her through Angel Beach, does not care about her now; and her only friend, a gay producer named B. Z. (Anthony Perkins), decided to give it all up and took an overdose of pills, dying in her arms. Maria later finds herself a patient in a mental sanatorium.

To say the least, Maria Wyeth's view of Hollywood is a deeply depressing one--its denizens are pictured as grasping low-life, while the actress (since it is told from her point of view) is depicted as the victim rather than the culprit of the affair. Only Tuesday Weld's performance held much interest in the lugubrious, ponderous feature, which, despite a huge pre-release campaign, proved to be a box-office dud. Weld won the Venice Film Festival Best Actress Award for her performance as Maria, a victory which caused Thomas Meehan of the Saturday Review to sneer, "Next year, I suppose, the Nobel Prize for Literature will go to Jacqueline Susann."

Vincent Canby reported in the New York Times that the film "is so chic and elegant looking that it reminds me of a charity ball for mental health. The cause is a good one, but it seems to be the last thing on anybody's mind at the moment. Unlike the novel, which evokes pity, the film is more likely to evoke pure unadulterated envy. "

Charles Champlin observed for the Los Angeles Times that Weld's character is "drawn from a sub-sub-subculture. She is from a rarefied part of Hollywood, which is rare enough to begin with and distinct from Southern California, which is in turn distinct from anywhere else. "

PLAYMATES (RKO, 1941) 96 min.

Producer, Cliff Reid; director, David Butler; story, Butler, James V. Kern, M. M. Musselman; screenplay, Kern; additional dialogue, Artie Phillips; choreography, Jack Crosby; songs, James Van Heusen and Johnny Burke; camera, Frank Redman; editor, Irene Morra.

Kay Kyser (Himself); John Barrymore (Himself); Lupe Velez (Carmen del Torre); Ginny Simms (Ginny); May Robson (Grandma); Patsy Kelly (Lulu Monahan); Peter Lind Hayes (Peter Lindsey); George Cleveland (Mr. Pennypacker); Alice Fleming (Mrs. Pennypacker); Kay Kyser's Orchestra featuring Harry Babbitt, Ish Kabibble, and Sully Mason (Themselves); Joe Bernard (Thomas); Ray Cooke (Bellhop); Hobart Cavanaugh (Tremble); Jacques Vanaire (Alphonse); Sally Cairns (Manicurist); Fred Trowbridge (Hotel Clerk); Leon Belasco (Prince Maharoohu); Sally Payne (Gloria); Billy Chaney (Call Boy); Wally Walker and Marshall Ruth (Comedy Bull Team); The Guardsmen (Themselves).

Popular bandleader and radio favorite Kay Kyser was a hopeful for film stardom. But despite the best efforts of RKO Pictures he never developed into a top-notch film commodity. That studio starred him in several (relatively) expensive features, surrounded him with competent casts, and attempted to experiment with various genres to determine which best suited the Kyser personality. First RKO presented him in That's Right, You're Wrong (q. v.), and then in 1940 they showcased him in the spook-spoof, You'll Find Out with Bela Lugosi, Boris Karloff, and Peter Lorre. Then the company ordained that he be teamed with John Barrymore (in his final film) and Lupe "Mexican Spitfire" Velez for Playmates. Unfortunately it proved to be one of the more dismal entries of the season.

John Barrymore agrees to coach Kyser in the writings of William Shakespeare and to appear with him in a festival of the Bard's works, all in an effort to pay off back taxes. A lot of activity takes place in this limp affair, but about the only bits worth

Opposite: Mischa Auer, Rosina Lawrence, Charles Halton, and Tom Dugan in Pick a Star (1937).

Patsy Kelly, John Barrymore, and Lupe Velez in Playmates (1941).

remembering are Barrymore's recital of the "To Be or Not to Be" soliloquy from Hamlet and Velez's rendering of a hot number entitled "Chiquita" with Kyser's band.

With a chance of utilizing its cast to real advantage, Playmates missed its mark entirely. It might have taken a serious look at the emotional repercussions of a once famous star, now down on his luck and forced to work with a non-talent in a dismal B movie.

POLLY OF THE MOVIES (First Division, 1927) 6900 ft.

Director, Scott Pembroke; story, Arthur Hoerl; screenplay, George Dromgold and Jean Plannette; special effects, Robert Stevens; camera, Ted Tetzlaff.

Jason Robards (Angus Whitcomb); Gertrude Short (Polly Primrose); Mary Foy (Mrs. Beardsley); Corliss Palmer (Liza Smith); Stuart Holmes (Benjamin Wellington Fairmount); Jack Richardson (Rolland Harrison); Rose Dione (Lulu Fairmount).

A rather plain girl from Hohokus, Polly Primrose (Gertrude Short) has dreams of becoming a grand movie star. When she inherits $25,000, she gravitates promptly to the movie capital and invests her funds in a feature starring, of course, herself. She shoots the picture as a melodrama, but it and she are so inept that it proves funny, much to her dismay and embarrassment. Finding the photoplay to be an amusing comedy, a movie mogul pays her a handsome profit for releasing the entry. As a result, Short is established not only as a new comedy star, but also as a smart business woman.

A fast-buck take-off of Merton of the Movies (q. v.), this First Division release was able to rise above its poverty-row origins and emerged an enjoyable caper. Perhaps someday a scholarly study will be done encompassing the fractured American dream about becoming a glamourous show business success, especially that facet dealing with an ugly duckling whose misguided visions of achievement as a dramatic artiste backfire, leaving her a celebrity--but at the price of being laughed at on the screen.

PORNOGRAPHY IN HOLLYWOOD see THE HISTORY OF THE BLUE MOVIE

THE PREVIEW MURDER MYSTERY (Paramount, 1936) 62 min.

Producer, Harold Hurley; director, Robert Florey; story, Garnett Weston; screenplay, Brian Marlow and Robert Yost; camera, Karl Struss; editor, James Smith.

Reginald Denny (Johnny Morgan); Frances Drake (Peggy Madison); Gail Patrick (Claire Woodward); Rod La Rocque (Neil DuBeck); Ian Keith (E. Gordon Smith); George Barbier (Jerome Hewitt); Conway Tearle (Edwin Strange); Thomas Jackson (Lieutenant McKane); Jack Raymond (Tyson); Eddie Dunn (Tub Wilson); Bryant Washburn (Jennings); Lee Shumway (Police Chief); Jack Mulhall (Screen Heavy); Chester Conklin (Himself); Henry Kleinbach [Brandon] (Screen Actor-The Bat Man); John George (Dwarf); Charlie Ruggles (Himself); Jack Norton (Comedy Director); Wilfred Lucas (Director).

A famed movie star (Rod La Roque), already fearing for his life, is mysteriously murdered in his seat at the lavish premiere of his latest motion picture. At the same time his director (Ian Keith) is killed at the actor's home lot. The police are summoned to investigate the homicides and to determine if they are linked together. Meanwhile the film's producer (George Barbier), now fearing --with good reason--for his safety, hires the studio publicity director (Reginald Denny) and his secretary (Frances Drake) to solve the crimes. All of the suspects are kept inside the studio confines and finally the publicity wizard corners Edwin Strange (Conway Tearle), a one-time movie idol, long thought dead. He admits to the killings, explaining he believed the murdered men were responsible for intentionally ruining his career.

This zesty little B effort is not only a well-acted and finely made whodunit, but it also offers a good study of the workings of a

Reginald Denny and Frances Drake in The Preview Murder Mystery (1936).

---

movie studio, the people involved, and the all-important film preview.

Like director Robert Florey's earlier Hollywood Boulevard (q. v.), this Paramount entry was loaded with film veterans, enough to lure any seasoned patron to the theatre unreeling it.

THE PROJECTIONIST (Maron, 1971) Color, 85 min.

Producer, Harry Hurwitz; associate producer, David Wolfson; director/screenplay, Hurwitz; assistant director, Roy Frumkes; music, Igo Kantor and Erma E. Levin; camera, Victor Petrashevic.

Chuck McCann (Projectionist/Flash); Ina Balin (The Girl); Rodney Dangerfield (Renaldi/The Bat); Jara Kohout (Candy Man/Scientist); Harry Hurwitz (Friendly Usher); Robert Staats (TV Pitchman); Robert King (Premiere Announcer); David Holiday (Fat Man/Henchman); Stephen Phillips (Minister); Clara Rosenthal (Crazy Lady); Jacqueline Glenn (Nude on Bearskin); Morocco (Belly Dancer); Mike Gentry, Lucky Kargo, Sam Stewart, Robert Lee, and Alex Stevens (Ushers/Henchmen).

This underground camp entry supposedly took five years to complete.   Although hardly a genre classic, the satire on the old movie serials and on movie buffs in general earned it respectable reviews.
Chuck McCann was the overweight, easy-going New York City projectionist who thrusts himself into the fantasy world of the movies he is showing.   In this state he becomes superhero Captain Flash, who protects a worthy scientist (Jara Kohout) and his lovely daughter (Ina Balin) from a villain known as The Bat (Rodney Dangerfield), who has a real-life counterpart in the theatre owner for whom he works.
For film enthusiasts, this picture not only provided amusing take-offs on the cliffhangers of yesteryears, but also a myriad of stock footage from dozens of vintage films, plus an interesting "coming attraction" showing the end of the world.   In the course of the feature, McCann performs his impersonations of Humphrey Bogart, Wallace Beery, and Oliver Hardy.

RAINBOW 'ROUND MY SHOULDER (Columbia, 1952) Color, 76 min.

Producer, Jonie Taps; director, Richard Quine; screenplay, Blake Edwards and Quine; music director, George Duning; new songs, Hal David and Don Rodney; Neal Stuart and Terry Gilkyson; Robert Wright and George Forrest; choreography, Lee Scott; camera, Ellis W. Carter; editor, Richard Fantl.

Frankie Laine (Himself); Billy Daniels (Himself); Charlotte Austin (Cathy Blake); Arthur Franz (Phil Young); Ida Moore (Martha Blake); Lloyd Corrigan (Tobias); Barbara Whiting (Suzy Milligan); Ross Ford (Elliot Livermore); Arthur Space (Joe Brady); Frank Wilcox (Sidney Gordon); Diane Garrett (Lane Lamarr); Chester Marshall (Red); Helen Wallace (Mrs. Toomey); Eleanore Davis (Lucie Evans); Eugene Baxter (Bob); Ken Garcia (Roger Stevens); Mira McKinney (Mrs. Abernathy); Edythe Elliott (Mrs. Gilmore); Jean Andren (Mrs. Riley).

A beautiful young girl (Charlotte Austin) from Pasadena, California, the daughter of well-to-do parents, wants to break into the entertainment business and takes a position as a messenger girl at Columbia Pictures.   By accident she auditions a song for an upcoming musical starring Frankie Laine and the director (Arthur Franz) likes her work sufficiently well to hire her for the project.   Her family, however, has no respect for the movies and takes actions to put a stop to her plans.   To save her budding career, Frankie Laine, Billy Daniels, and other performers give a concert for her family's favorite charity, thus winning them over to her being a film personality.   In the meantime, Austin and Franz have fallen in love.
This was the best of a series of musicals Columbia produced in the fifties starring Frankie Laine.   The entries usually had dull plots, serving as weak bridges between the zesty musical numbers by Laine and various other singers.   Here Laine had a best-selling

Arthur Franz and Charlotte Austin in a publicity pose for Rainbow 'Round My Shoulder (1952).

recording of the title song (an old standard) for Columbia Records at the time of the picture's release.   The real star of this venture, though, was Charlotte Austin as the aspiring songstress-actress. The pert and lovely ingenue (daughter of crooner Gene "My Blue Heaven" Austin) added a great deal of vitality to this rather threadbare musical.

An intriguing aspect of the film was its inclusion of a great many shots of the old Columbia lot, which has since been razed. The film also included glimpses (mainly through stock footage) of assorted studio contract stars, such as Broderick Crawford.

THE RELUCTANT DRAGON (RKO, 1941) Color, 72 min.

Producer, Walt Disney; live action director, Alfred I. Werker; cartoon directors, Hamilton Luske, Jam Handley, Ford Beebe, Erwin Verity, and Jasper Blystone; screenplay, Ted Sears, Al Perkins, Larry Clemmons, and Bill Cottrell; Technicolor consultant, Natalie

Kalmus; cartoon art directors, Ken Anderson, Hugh Hennesy, and
Charles Philippi; songs, Frank Churchill and Larry Morey; Charles
Wolcott and Larry Morey; animators, Ward Kimball, Fred Moore,
Milt Neil, Wolfgang Reitherman, Bud Swift, Walt Kelly, Jack Camp-
bell, Claude Smith, and Harvey Toombs; special effects, Ub Iwerks
and Joshua Meador; live action camera, Bert Glennon and Winton
Hoch; editors, Paul Weatherwax and Earl Rettig.

Robert Benchley (Himself); Frances Gifford (Studio Artist);
Nana Bryant (Mrs. Benchley); Buddy Pepper (Studio Guide); Florence
Gill and Clarence Nash (Themselves); Frank Faylen (Orchestra Lead-
er); Truman Woodworth, Hamilton McFadden, Maurice Murphy, Jeff
Corey, and Henry Hall (Studio Cops); Lester Dorr (Slim); Gerald
Mohr (Guard); Walt Disney, Ward Kimball, Norman Ferguson (Them-
selves); the voices of: Barnett Parker (The Dragon); Claud Allister
(Sir Giles); Billy Lee (The Boy); The Rhythmaires, Clarence Nash
(Donald Duck); Pinto Colvig (Goofy); Gerald Mohr (Baby Weems nar-
rator); Alan Ladd (Bit).

Robert Benchley's wife nags him until he agrees to speak with
Walt Disney about a forthcoming film version of The Reluctant Dragon. Arriving at the Disney facilities he is given a V. I. P. tour of
the complex, but he gets away from his guide and explores the studio
for himself. In a story conference he interupts some writers discussing the shooting of an upcoming cartoon Baby Weems and he then
encounters a girl in a recording studio who explains about sound dubbing. Later he is shown how cartoons are animated and filmed and
then he inspects all of the various work departments, such as the
model shop, the art class, and the painting room. At last he has
the opportunity to meet Disney about the subject at hand. But he
finds himself in a screening room to see his latest completed product, The Reluctant Dragon. On the way home Benchley gives his
wife the "rasberry" via a Donald Duck squawk.
Made for approximately $600,000, this 72-minute color pro-
duction provided a documentary-like tour of the Disney studio in an
entertaining format, informing its audience on the making of cartoons.
Besides the showcasing of the Disney plant, there is the inclusion of
the delightful Baby Weems cartoon about an infant who is a mental
giant, a Goofy short called How to Ride a Horse, and, of course,
The Reluctant Dragon animated film. The full-length production was
only moderately successful in release, and it is one of the few Disney features never to be reissued theatrically, although portions of
it have been shown on the Disney TV program.
In The Disney Films (1973), Leonard Maltin pointed out, "In
its attempt to tell a mass audience how cartoons are made, it white-
washes much of the technique and omits most of the detail. It gives
the erroneous impression that the sound track is matched to the cartoon, instead of vice versa. It uses actors in the roles of animators,
musicians, cameramen, and never lets us in on the real creative process that produces Disney's cartoon. It's certainly a far cry from
the cinema-verite technique that has more recently been used to show
filmmakers at work!"

SATURDAY NIGHT IN APPLE VALLEY (Emerson, 1965) 89 min.

Director/screenplay, John Myhers; music, Foster Wakefield; camera, Alan Stensvold; editor, Myhers.

Phil Ford (Big Man); Mimi Hines (Mimi Madison); Cliff Arquette (Charley Weaver/Mama Coot); Stanton Granger (Beau Coot); Joan Benedict (Poopsie Patate); Anthony Dexter (Matador).

A rather obscure and minor film, Satuday Night in Apple Valley was the brainchild of John Myhers who wrote/directed/edited this little-seen feature.   The picture toplines popular TV and nightclub performers Phil Ford, Mimi Hines, and Cliff Arquette.   Variety found the end results to be an "extremely self-conscious attempt to satirize Hollywood and foreign films. "
Basically it is 89 minutes of sight gags, set in the small community of Apple Valley.   There Big Man (Ford), a hoodlum, comes and tries to woo local school teacher, Mimi Madison (Hines).   Also inhabiting the quaint town are Charley Weaver and Mama Coot (both roles played by Arquette, the former his trademark) and her son, Beau Coot (Stanton Granger).   Eventually right triumphs over wrong and Ford wins Hines' affection.
While not precisely concerned with films and filming, Saturday Night in Apple Valley is a complete take-off on the "new wave" of moviemaking, especially in its situations and technical aspects.   Such auteurs as Federico Fellini and Ingmar Bergman are spoofed as is the medium of television.   Toward the finale, Anthony Dexter (the star of Valentino, q. v.) plays a matador trying to skewer a bull. Finally his aged mother runs into the arena to help; the angry Dexter turns on her and shouts, "Please mother, I'd rather do it myself!" This punchline derives from a once-popular TV commercial which had long since losts its amusement when this mediocre feature was in production.

SCANDAL SHEET (Arrow, 1925) 6750 ft.

Director, Whitman Bennett; story, Frank R. Adams; sound, Eugene Merritt; camera, Edward Paul.

Niles Welch (Neil Keenly/Harrison Halliday); Madge Kennedy (Sheila Kane); Ewin August (Howard Manning); Coit Albertson (Julian Lewis); Louise Carter (Cora Forman); J. Moy Bennett (Pat O'Malley).

During the filming of a feature, movie idol Neil Keenly (Niles Welch) is killed in an auto crash.   Harrison Halliday (also played by Welch), a look-alike for the star, takes his place and the film is completed.   The deception succeeds and the public is not made aware of the star's demise.   Welch then falls in love with the dead man's widow (Madge Kennedy), also a film star.   However, their happiness is threatened by Cora Forman (Louise Carter), an extra on the movie, who knew of the star's death and who now blackmails the substitute and Kennedy. Finally, Forman is outwitted, leaving Welch and Kennedy to pursue their happiness.

Photoplay magazine thought this an "interesting movie because of movie studio atmosphere." Probably the most beguiling aspect of the film is its treatment of the moral issue of the look-alike becoming enamored of his late double's widow and she, in turn, more than reciprocating--and all of this happening in 1925!

SCARLET RIVER (RKO, 1933) 62 min.

Producer, David O. Selznick; associate producer, David Lewis; director, Otto Brower; story/adaptor, Harold Shumate; art director, Al Sherman; sound, Clem Portman and Hugh McDowell; camera, Nicolas Musuraca; editor, Fred Knudtson.

Tom Keene (Tom Baxter); Dorothy Wilson (Judy); Rosco Ates (Ulysses); Betty Furness (Babe); Billy Butts (Buck); Edgar Kennedy (Sam Gilroy); Creighton Chaney [Lon Chaney, Jr.] (Jeff Todd); Hooper Atchley (Clint McPherson); John Barrymore, Lionel Barrymore, Myrna Loy, Joel McCrea, Robert Armstrong, Bruce Cabot, Phoebe Foster, Rochelle Hudson, and Hugh Sinclair (Actors in Studio Cafeteria).

During the thirties, RKO made very few Westerns, although the studio did keep at least one "resident" Western star working during the decade and in the forties. The first of these sagebrush cavaliers was Tom Keene. He was a fine actor, although a bit too energetic at times. RKO gave him good scripts and sufficiently well-mounted vehicles. In fact, some of his entries were among the best B films of the period. Another unusual aspect of this series was that none of the films was accomplished in a set formula; all were different. _Scarlet River_ is of special note because of its use of the Hollywood motif in its plotline.

The film opens at the RKO studio where a number of contract stars (Joel McCrea and Myrna Loy among them) are shown at the cafeteria. The plot then heads out West where screen cowboy Tom Baxter (Keene) is making a film on a ranch belonging to a young woman named Judy (Dorothy Wilson). Wilson is about to lose the property to crook Clint McPherson (Hooper Atchley) who threatens to foreclose her bank loan. Meanwhile, Wilson is about to wed her foreman, Jeff Todd (Creighton Chaney), who works secretly for Atchley to sabotage the ranch so she will not have the funds to pay off the mortgage. Film star Keene, meanwhile, learns of the nefarious goings-on and puts a stop to the situation. He saves Wilson's ranch and--naturally--wins her undying love.

RKO promoted the film with the tag lines, "But what is danger when a man's in love?" "The movie cowboy showed the western 'bad men' speed and class when they got funny with the girl he loved."

SCATTERBRAIN (Republic, 1940) 73 min.

Associate producer/director, Gus Meins; screenplay, Jack

Townley and Val Burton; additional dialogue, Paul Conlon; music director, Cy Feuer; art director, John Victor Mackay; songs, Hy Heath, Johnny Lange, and Lew Porter; camera, Ernest Miller; editor, Ernest Nims.

Judy Canova (Judy Hall); Alan Mowbray (J. R. Russell); Ruth Donnelly (Miss Stevens); Eddie Foy, Jr. (Eddie MacIntyre); Joseph Cawthorn (Nicholas Raptis); Wallace Ford (Sam Maxwell); Isabel Jewell (Esther Harrington); Luis Alberni (Professor DeLemma); Billy Gilbert (Hoffman); Emmett Lynn (Pappy Hull); Jimmy Starr (Joe Kelton); Cal Shrum's Gang (Themselves); Matty Malneck and Orchestra (Themselves).

As her first starring vehicle for Republic Pictures, Judy Canova was showcased in a simple-minded but entertaining diversion which derived many of its guffaws from filmgoers' generalizations about the cinema, how stars are made, and what studio executives are "really" like.

J. R. Russell (Alan Mowbray), producer-director at Perfection Pictures, approves of press agent Eddie MacIntyre's plan to have his girlfriend (Isabel Jewell) "planted" with an Ozark family so she can later be "discovered" and play a hillbilly heroine, Ruthybelle, in the studio's upcoming property, Thunder Over the Ozarks. Jewell is dispatched to the Ozarks to live with Judy Hall (Canova) and her one-of-a-kind Pappy (Emmett Lynn). Before long, fate plays its hand and Canova is signed to a film contract by error and arrives in Hollywood. A distraught Mowbray, realizing the mistake seeks to have his new employee fired--his idea is to trick her into marrying so she will be in violation of her studio pact. It is Foy who is selected as the stimulus to turn Canova marriage-conscious.

Meanwhile, Canova does make the film, she and it prove to be hits, and she decides to remain in Hollywood under the tutelage of Mowbray and Foy.

One of the film's "highlights" is the music lesson given Canova by tongue-twisting, exasperated music instructor Hoffman (Billy Gilbert). Canova sang, in her famous hillbilly style, "Benny the Beaver (You Better Be Like That, Yeah, Yeah)."

This entry was so popular with rural mass audiences that Herbert J. Yates, head of Republic, promptly signed Canova to a five-year contract, elevating her to stardom along with such other studio leads as Gene Autry, Roy Rogers, and John Wayne.

Two years later, Canova was scheduled by Republic to star in Yokel Boy (q. v.), based on her 1939 Broadway hit. But the actress was feuding with her studio and it would be Joan Davis who would be teamed with Alan Mowbray, Eddie Foy, Jr., and Albert Dekker in another wild, wooley, and countrified tale of a bucolic miss who disrupts life at a Hollywood film studio.

SCREEN SNAPSHOTS   see   THE SHORT FILMS

SECOND FIDDLE   see   IRVING BERLIN'S SECOND FIDDLE

SECRETS OF HOLLYWOOD (States Rights, 1933) 58 min.

Producer, Lester F. Scott; directors, George M. Merrick and Holbrook Todd; story/dialogue, Betty Burbridge; sound, Earl Crain; camera, Jules Cronjager; editors, Merrick and Todd.

Mae Busch (Herself); Wally Wales (Himself); June Walters (Starlet); George Cowl (Director); Norbert Nyles (Makeup Man); David Cellis, Tom Francis, and Ernie Adams (Writers).

This poverty-row effort is one of the few attempts by Hollywood in the thirties to look nostalgically at the silent-film era. Unfortunately the review of past decades was instituted more by the necessity to use old footage from the Thomas H. Ince library to bolster the film's running time than for scholarly purposes. Nevertheless, the film did use quite a few movie clips of major stars of the silent era and these stock shots were tied into a story which purported to show how Hollywood films were actually made--as seen from the production end of movie making.
    Among the silent film clips used are: Barbara Fritchie (PDC, 1924) with Edmund Lowe and Florence Vidor; Soul of the Beast (Metro, 1923) with Madge Bellamy, Noah Beery, and Cullen Landis; The Marriage Cheat (First National, 1924) with Leatrice Joy, Adolphe Menjou, and Percy Marmont; Hairpins (Paramount, 1920) with Enid Bennett and Matt Moore; Rookie's Return (Paramount, 1921) with Wallace Beery; and Busher (Paramount, 1919) with Charles Ray, Colleen More, and John Gilbert.
    Despite its title promise of rather lurid goings-on, Secrets of Hollywood finds Mae Busch (as herself) showing starlet June Walters the "ropes" of film-making, and between shots on their melodramatic film being lensed--which also stars Wally Wales (as himself)--Busch recounts her days as a silent picture star, using vintage footage to illustrate her tales. Secrets of Hollywood also depicts soundmen, cameramen, directors, assistants, writers, et al., performing their jobs to make a motion picture. Obviously producer Lester F. Scott (best known for grinding out low-grade Westerns in the twenties and thirties) had a scant budget to work with, and his employing a studio background plus accessible old footage saved him quite a bit on the cost of turning out this quickie.
    One (unintentionally) amusing scene of this entry has Wales entering a restaurant where two onlookers see him and one exclaims, "There's Wally Wales, the movie star!" Unlike many cheapies of the time, this film used quite an elaborate film score, mostly classical selections with a long visual sequence being backed up by the fine "Storm and War."

THE SEX SYMBOL (ABC-TV, 1974) Color, 110 min.

Producer, Douglas S. Cramer; director, David Lowell Rich; based on the novel The Symbol by Alvah Bessie; teleplay, Bessie; art director, Ross Bellah; set decorators, Audrey Blasdel and John France, Jr.; music, Jeff Alexander; title music, Francis Lai; title

Shelley Winters and Connie Stevens in The Sex Symbol (1975).

music conductor, Henry Mancini; assistant director, Tom McCrory; camera, J. J. Jones; editor, Byron Brandt.

Connie Stevens (Kelly Williams); Shelley Winters (Agatha Murphy); Jack Carter (Manny Fox); William Castle (J. P. Harper); Don Murray (Grant O'Neal); James Olson (Calvin Bernard); Nehemiah Persoff (Nick Fortis); Madlyn Rhue (Joy Hudson); Milton Selzer (Phil Bamberger); William Smith (Buck Wischnewski); Albert Able, Herb Graham, Henry Slate, and Burr Smidt (Reporters); Rand Brooks (Edward Kelly); Jack Collins (Ted Brown); Eduard Franz (Voice of Dr. Litzky); Frank Loverde (Investigator); Bill McGovern (Helmut); Dennis Rucker (Tom); Bing Russell (P. R. Man); Joe Turkel (Director); Tony Young (Rick Roman).

Broken and depressed and near death from alcohol and pills, fading screen sex symbol Kelly Williams (Connie Stevens) tries to telephone the people who were important to her in her past. She finds herself telling the story of her life to her psychiatrist.
It all began in her efforts to find employment in Hollywood; the impact of her first one-line role, and her subsequent disillusionment with the studio system. The encouragement of her agent Phil

Bamberger (Milton Selzer) leads to an eventual contract with J. P.
Harper (William Castle), a hard-hearted studio mogul. Along the
path to stardom she meets a pro football player (William Smith) and
they wed. But she is also involved with politician Grant O'Neal
(Don Murray); he later drops her when it appears she might jeopar-
dize his career. After divorcing the athlete, she weds a famous artist (James Olson), who tries to manage and guide her career, but
they eventually part. Through it all, each of her personal failures
is dragged into lurid print by arch gossip columnist Agatha Murphy
(Shelley Winters). The finale finds the sex legend tottering between
life and death, a victim of her own glamour and lack of emotional
direction.

Obviously culled from the lives of Marilyn Monroe and Jayne
Mansfield, The Sex Symbol was based on Alvah Bessie's 1966 novel,
The Symbol. Its transition to the television screen, however, was
poorly conceived and accomplished. The characters and performances are nothing more than worn clichés. All of the expected stereotypes are paraded forth: Selzer's kindly agent, Castle's lecherous
studio mogul, Nehemiah Persoff as a hard-nosed movie maker, and
so on. In the title role, Connie Stevens added no depth, zest or
life to the tattered image of the screen goddess who was used for
sex and publicity in order to make truckloads of money for her studio while finding no personal fulfillment. Only Shelley Winters in
her oversized performance as a combination Louella Parsons-Hedda
Hopper offered an engaging characterization. But her screen time
was limited and her part extraneous to the dull proceedings in which
it was involved.

This TV movie generated tremendous pre-release coverage,
due to the behind-the-scenes efforts to prune a good deal of the segment involving Marilyn Monroe-ish Connie Stevens and JFK-ish Don
Murray. Stevens felt she had the acting role of a lifetime, and when
an Emmy nomination did not materialize, she invited the nominating
committee to see an uncut version of the teleplay: still no Emmy
nomination for her overwhelmingly panned performance.

THE SHEIK OF HOLLYWOOD see THE SHORT FILMS

SHOOTING HIGH (20th Century-Fox, 1940) 65 min.

Director, Alfred E. Green; screenplay, Lou Breslow and Owen
Francis; songs, Gene Autry and Harry Tobias; Autry and Johnny Mar-
vin; Sidney Clare and Harry Akst; camera, Ernest Palmer; editor,
Nick De Maggio.

Jane Withers (Jane Pritchard); Gene Autry (Will Carson); Mar-
jorie Weaver (Marjorie Pritchard); Frank M. Thomas (Calvin Pritch-
ard); Robert Lowery (Bob Meritt); Katherine [Kay] Aldridge (Evelyn
Trent); Hobart Cavanaugh (Clem Perkle); Jack Carson (Gabby Cross);
Hamilton MacFadden (J. Wallace Rutledge); Charles Middleton (Hod
Carson); Ed Brady (Mort Carson); Tom London (Eph Carson); Eddie

Acuff (Andy Carson); Pat O'Malley (Sam Pritchard); George Chandler (Charles Pritchard).

In 1940 the 20th Century-Fox studio borrowed the screen's most popular cowboy star, Gene Autry, and teamed him with fading moppet lead Jane Withers in a send-up of Western film-making entitled Shooting High. It was somewhat similar to an earlier Autry film made for Republic entitled The Big Show (q. v.). In both films he played a stunt double elevated to stardom.

Here Gene was cast as Will Carson (one of the few times he did not use his own name on screen), a resident of a small Western town and the grandson of famous lawman-hero, Wild Bill Carson. Autry is in love with Marjorie Pritchard (Marjorie Weaver), who is a member of a family having a feud with his own. But he has an ally in her younger sister Jane (Jane Withers) who wants to see the two lovebirds wed. A movie outfit arrives in town to do location work on a film about the life and times of Wild Bill Carson starring a snobbish actor (Robert Lowery).

No one in town likes Lowery and Jane finally tells him that her family is planning to hang him because he is portraying a rival Carson. With that, the actor high-tails it out of town, leaving the leading role vacant. The publicity people quickly come up with the scheme of starring Autry as his grandfather. During the shooting, a group of bank robbers plan to use such a scene in the movie to disguise their actual holdup. But Autry becomes aware of their plan and later captures the bandits, saving the rival family's savings. As a result he is given Marjorie's hand in marriage. He rejects a movie contract to stay home with the woman he loves.

"Mighty pleasant little 'hoss opera'" was how the New York Daily Mirror judged this production. Due to Autry's legion of fans, the film made a profit. Perhaps the most amusing aspect of the feature was the fact that Autry was supposed to be doubling another actor in fight scenes; in reality, he himself was doubled for the actual action.

SHOOTING UP THE MOVIES see THE SHORT FILMS

THE SHORT FILMS

Even before the inception of feature-length motion pictures (four or more reels) in the United States, the American film industry--then in its infancy--was taking a look at itself. During the early years of the flickers a few films were produced which revealed to audiences exactly how movies were made. As the 1910s saw the technical and visual improvements of the medium, more and more films poked fun at themselves. By the twenties, a variety of film comics were turning out short subjects kidding their "bread and butter. " Although Hollywood continued to turn a mirror to itself in the thirties, forties, and fifties, fewer and fewer one-and two-reelers did so. By the fifties the theatrical short subject became a victim of competing TV.

Perhaps the movies' first mirror study of itself occurred in 1908 when Vitagraph produced MAKING MOTION PICTURES: A DAY IN THE VITAGRAPH STUDIO. This one-reeler was a swift visual account of just how films were turned out by Vitagraph, from pre-production to the filming in Brooklyn's Flatbush area to the final product, which was shown as the last part of the film and called Love Is Better Than Riches. This modest effort satisfied the public's growing curiosity for professional knowledge about the entertainment form, for it apparently spawned no imitators for several years thereafter.

In 1912 the Edison Company released HOW MOTION PICTURES ARE MADE AND SHOWN and the New York Dramatic Mirror said the 15-minute film "is the most comprehensive motion picture description of the way films are produced."

Probably the first entry to wholeheartedly look at the film industry in an entertainment-dramatic format was A VITAGRAPH ROMANCE, a one-reeler of 1912. Here a young woman (Clara Kimball Young) weds a writer (James Morrison) against the wishes of her Senator father (Edward Kimball). Morrison begins to write for the movies and a director (James Young) hires the couple to work for Vitagraph. After seeing his daughter in a film, the senator journeys to the Brooklyn studio and meets its corporate heads (played by J. Stuart Blackton, William T. Rock, and Albert E. Smith--all as themselves) and is reunited with his offspring.

The next year, 1913, offered what is suggested as the first real comic look at the movies: Mack Sennett's MABEL'S DRAMATIC CAREER. This one-reel comedy, which Sennett wrote and directed, presented Mabel Normand as a kitchen maid who is forced to leave the farm because of jealousy over her beau (Sennett). She makes her way to Hollywood and wins a job at Keystone Films. Sennett then realizes he loves Mabel. When he watches her in a film at the local nickelodeon (the scene shows her being pursued by villain Ford Sterling), he heads west to rescue Normand. But once there he discovers she is really married to Sterling and is the mother of his children. For all his troubles, the suitor is rewarded with a basketful of water at the picture's finale. The comedy short would be reissued by W. H. Productions as Her Dramatic Debut.

The year 1913 witnessed a trio of other films dealing with movies. Excelsior's THE MOVING PICTURE GIRL was a maudlin tale of a woman who takes her small daughter and leaves her husband. Years later the child grows up to become a film star and while filming in front of a mansion is recognized by the owner as his long-lost daughter. The joyful relations are happily reconciled. Edison's two-reeler, PEG O' THE MOVIES, has the heroine deserted by her lover and joining the Edison Company. Later the hero pursues her when she travels west with the movie troupe. He locates her and takes her home, thus putting a finish to her budding career in the flickers. MOVIN' PITCHERS (Selig) was an early short which predated the Our Gang-type of film in that it concerned a gang of children who watch a movie being filmed and then dream about the scenes with themselves now in the lead roles.

At Keystone in 1914 Charlie Chaplin made two entries which

joshed the movies.   In A FILM JOHNNIE, Charlie tumbles for a heroine who he sees on the screen in a nickelodeon.   He visits the Keystone studio to locate her and there he follows a film crew to an actual fire but he winds up ruining the negative.   This was the first
film in which Chaplin used a movie studio for plot background and
in it Fatty Arbuckle played a film star.   The film also featured Minta Durfee and Virginia Kirtley; it was variously known also as Movie
Nut and Million Dollar Job.   Chaplin thereafter directed himself in
the title role of THE MASQUERADER, another Keystone one-reeler.
Here he portrayed an actor fired for ruining a scene in a film.
Later he returns dressed as a woman but is discovered causing even
more havoc on the movie set.   In the supporting cast were Arbuckle
and Chester Conklin as rival performers and Charlie Murray as the
harried director.
        In 1914 Tom Mix appeared in the first of several shorts he
made lampooning films.   In Selig's two-reeler, THE MOVING PIC-
TURE COWBOY, he not only starred, but wrote and produced the
effort.   He was a celluloid cowpoke who intends to rest at his uncle's
ranch.   There he brags about his adventures and prowess in "Western" life.   He is proved to be a braggart, though, as the second
reel of the entry reveals him failing at the deeds he describes so
grandly in the first portion.
        The year 1914 also saw two popular movie queens in cinema-
oriented roles.   Former Vitagraph star Florence Turner journeyed
to Great Britain for FILM FAVORITES, a Gaumont-British release,
while Virginia Forde had the title role in Nestor's SOPHIE OF THE
MOVIES.   In the latter, a girl leaves home to become a film notable
and joins the "Uneeda Feature Film Company" and becomes its leading lady when the star quits.   Forde muffs the opportunity though,
and returns home to her job as a laundress.   The film was advertised as "The first of a series of comedies set in and around a motion picture studio. "
        Another 1914 cinema look at the movies came in Warner Bros. '
THE MOVIE QUEEN, a three-reeler.   Here a seamstress is aided
by a wealthy woman in obtaining the lead in a screen production of
Cinderella.   At the mansion where the film is being shot, the director tries to seduce the heroine and she departs, forgetting her slip-
per.   The nobleman who owns the house finds the shoe and sets out
to woo the girl who has gone back to her trade.   Naturally he eventually locates her and all ends happily.
        A MOVIE NUT (Banner, 1915) was a two-reel entry which told
of a young man who yearns to become a movie legend but who ruins
his big chance by trying to direct the film as well.   Later he dreams
of rivaling Charlie Chaplin as comedy's king only to be awakened by
his landlady who demands the overdue rent money.   The same year
Edison released a one-reeler entitled JOEY AND HIS TROMBONE,
which starred Gladys Hulette and used the Bronx Edison studio for
its background.
        MOVIE FANS (Falstaff, 1915) was a bittersweet tale of a
young couple who meet in a cinema after visualizing themselves as
the film's author and star.   The duo fall in love and tell each other
of their dream ambition.   While they fail to obtain their goal, they

do have their domestic happiness. On a more frivolous note was
FILM FAVORITES' FINISH (Mutual, 1915), which concerned a self-
centered matinee idol, the star of the Climax Film Company. The
snobbish star would have nothing to do with the other performers,
cared only about his scenes and eventually attempts to seduce the
leading lady before rightfully suffering a downfall at the film's finale.

     Charlie Chaplin made two additional short films dealing with
the movies, the first being HIS NEW JOB (Essanay, 1915). This two-
reeler was the comedian's first assignment for Essanay and in it he
portrayed a jaunty actor who wins a part in a film, bungles it, and
is quickly reduced to being prop man. Later he is elevated to being
an extra and winds up in an on-camera pie fight. Besides being a
very funny film in itself, His New Job boasted Ben Turpin as a rival
actor and Gloria Swanson and Agnes Ayres as extras.

     By 1916 Chaplin had moved to Mutual where he starred in
BEHIND THE SCREEN. Here he was an overworked stagehand who
is promoted to the lead part with disastrous results. The story ends
with custard pies flying in all directions, mostly aimed at Chaplin's
sadistic prop boss, Eric Campbell, while Chaplin romances sweet
Edna Purviance. In the plot, she had masqueraded as a boy to break
into the movies; it was Chaplin who discovered her true gender.

     The year 1916 also witnessed three other entries released in
the U. S. which kidded the motion pictures, two with Tom Mix starring. In Selig's two-reeler, SHOOTING UP THE MOVIES, Mix played
an outlaw who chances upon a movie unit and rescues the heroine
(Virginia Forde) not knowing her troubles were all cinematic. He becomes enamored of her and soon she converts him to a good guy. He
later becomes the deputy sheriff. In A MIX-UP IN MOVIES (Selig),
Tom was a cowhand who plans to rob a bank and who comes across
a movie company doing the same deed for a film. He decides to join
them and carry out the robbery but is thwarted in his attempt by the
love of the company's leading lady (Babe Christian). The same year
also saw huge, walrus-faced Mack Swain in the title role as THE
MOVIE STAR, a Keystone/Triangle comedy directed by Fred Fishback.

     As the War years came to a close so did the number of short
subjects which teased the cinema. The genre seemed to fade out with
MOVIE MAD, a 1918 Al Christie comedy with Neal Burns as a movie
star. With the coming of the Roaring Twenties, however, a new
batch of entries would emerge in the short film field, giving the public a fresh look at the film business, practically all of them on the
humorous side.

     In the twenties, a variety of comics, mostly those working
with Mack Sennett and Hal Roach, made pictures which burlesqued the
movies. Roach had begun making such films as early as 1917, when
he produced and directed Harold Lloyd in the Pathé one-reeler LUKE'S
MOVIE MUDDLE and Sennett continued what he had begun with Mabel's
Dramatic Career, by starring Slim Summerville as VILLA OF THE
MOVIES (1917), a two-reeler from Keystone directed by Eddie Cline.

     These films led directly to such twenties' farces as HOBOKEN
TO HOLLYWOOD, a 1926 Keystone two-reeler directed by Del Lord
with Billy Bevan as the lead player; and Ben Turpin in a trio of
comedies for Keystone: HOME MADE MOVIES (1923; directed by Ray

Grey and Gus Meins), THE HOLLYWOOD KID (1924; directed by Del
Lord), and A HOLLYWOOD HERO (1926; directed by Harry Edwards).
Sennett closed out the decade with an early talkie two-reeler entitled
A HOLLYWOOD STAR, which Mack helmed for a 1929 release. In
this comedy Harry Gribbon was a pompous and goofy cowboy star who
appears at a small town theatre, run by Andy Clyde, for the premiere of his first talkie and the end results leave the theatre in a
shambles.

Roach produced a number of movie spoofs in the twenties for
Pathé release. Among these two-reelers were Snub Pollard in IN
THE MOVIES (1922; directed by Charles Parrott) and Our Gang in
BETTER MOVIES (1925; directed by Robert McGowan). In 1926
Roach wrote and produced 45 MINUTES TO HOLLYWOOD, an entry
in the Glenn Tryon short series. Here Tryon was a country rube
who comes with his family to Hollywood, hoping to find a way to pay
an overdue mortgage. They embark on a sightseeing tour of the
Roach lot and see a film being made. Later they become involved
in an actual holdup, with Glenn concluding a lengthy chase at the
Hollywood Hotel. The short boasted Theda Bara and Our Gang as
tourist attractions at the Roach lot and in the supporting cast was
Oliver Hardy as a hotel detective and Stan Laurel as a starving actor.

One of the last silent films to be made by Roach was Charlie
Chase in MOVIE NIGHT (1929), which Kalton Lahue in World of
Laughter (1966) dubbed as "one of Charlie's best." This hilarious
ribbing told of the trials and tribulations of the Chase family on their
weekly sojourn to the cinema. In the cast was future moppet/juvenile
star Edith Fellows, herein playing Charlie's little daughter.

Other twenties' films dealing with take-offs on the world of
movies were THE SHEIK OF HOLLYWOOD (1923). Will Rogers
aimed his satire at the films the same year in UNCENSORED MOVIES,
and 1928's MICKEY'S MOVIES starred Mickey McGuire (aka Mickey
Rooney) in a send-up of the medium.

The Depression years brought another plethora of entries dealing with movie-life topics. An early 1930 Hal Roach comedy called
MOVIE DAZE starred Billy Gilbert as the famed director Mr. Schmaltz
and in 1931 Sennett starred himself in his two-reeler MOVIE TOWN,
a "special" made in Natural Color. Also that year Roscoe "Fatty"
Arbuckle, under a pseudonym, directed the two-reeler, WINDY RILEY
GOES TO HOLLYWOOD, for Warner Bros., with Louise Brooks in
the cast. Little Shirley Temple in her salad days, was promoted
from extra to movie star in KID 'n HOLLYWOOD, an Educational
"Baby Burlesk" one-reeler of 1933 which had Shirley becoming a film
heroine when Freda Snoboo is "too tired" to go on. Unfortunately
the on-camera Shirley is a flop, but she ends up in domestic bliss
with a little man her own size. On more of an adult level was
Roach's MAID IN HOLLYWOOD, a 1934 MGM two-reeler, directed
by Gus Meins. It detailed how Patsy Kelly accidentally wrecks pal
Thelma Todd's screen audition.

One of the most revealing of movie shorts dealing with the
ways of the cinema world was HOLLYWOOD EXTRA GIRL (Paramount, 193-; directed by Herbert Moulton). The film was a sugary
story of the behind-the-scenes life of an extra girl. The short was

set against the making of Cecil B. DeMille's The Crusades and interpolated scenes from this historical feature. DeMille also appeared
as himself, giving advice to an extra girl on how to work for stardom. Of interest in the short was the showing of how extras are
numbered and herded about in their on-camera duties and the long
odds against rising above the status of extra. Appearing in this entry were Ann Sheridan on the way to stardom, and Clara Kimball
Young, a has-been by the time this quickie was ground out for Paramount.

The Three Stooges played a trio of loonies mistaken for New
York City "brains" who have come West to run a movie studio in
MOVIE MANICS, a two-reeler from 1936 which Del Lord supervised
for Columbia, while Robert Benchley's A NIGHT AT THE MOVIES
(MGM, 1937; directed by Roy Rowland) was nominated for an Academy
Award in the short subject field.

No discussion of thirties' short films would be complete without mention of a certain trio of series shorts. The most ludicrous
of the bunch was THE VOICE OF HOLLYWOOD, released by Tiffany
Pictures in the early part of the decade. This group of shorts used
a radio format from Hollywood to introduce many stars in a variety
of settings, most of them phony and uninteresting. Still the short-
lived segments did present a number of silent idols such as Tom
Mix in their "sound" debuts, while also featuring rising newcomers
like John Wayne.

Louis Lewyn produced HOLLYWOOD ON PARADE for Paramount during the decade and the segments were quite lavish by the
genre's standards, using top names in each short and each season
introducing the newest batch of Wampas Baby Stars. Also of high
grade, and with a much longer run, was Columbia's SCREEN SNAP-
SHOTS series, which were produced from the late teens--when conceived by Jack Cohn--until the fifties. From the thirties onward,
the entries were the pet project of Ralph Staub, who turned it into
the most entertaining batch ever of miniature documentaries looking
at Hollywood from the inside out.

Other studios produced entries dealing with Hollywood during
the thirties. For example, Universal turned out HOLLYWOOD SCREEN
TEST in 1937, directed by S. Sylvan Simon. Kay Hughes is seen as
a Hollywood hopeful who Simon (as himself) guides through a movie
test. She performs a scene from a then-current release, She's
Dangerous, playing the Tala Birell role, with Cesar Romero repeating
his part from the Universal feature opposite her.

The forties was the final decade to present theatrical short
films depicting movies, outside the realm of the documentary short.
In this period Warner Bros. made ALICE IN MOVIELAND (1940),
featuring young Joan Leslie as a movie hopeful. The same studio
also turned out SWINGTIME IN THE MOVIES (1941), a musical about
a looney director (Fritz Feld) who drives everyone mad by being too
much of a perfectionist. Feld repeated the role in another short
called QUIET PLEASE (Warner Bros. , 1940) which used much footage
from the earlier film. The newer entry, however, dealt with a day
in the life of a young actress. Another Warners' short, MOVIELAND
MAGIC (1945; directed by James V. Kern) was lensed in color and

featured Mel Torme conducting a musical tour of the studio facilities.
Unfortunately it was packed with footage from earlier shorts.

In 1940 Edward L. Chan directed Our Gang in THE BIG PRE-
MIERE for MGM. Here the kids get expelled from a local movie
premiere so they decide to make their own movie and exhibit it to
the neighborhood youths. MGM also issued a trio of one-reel PETE
SMITH SPECIALITIES during the World War II years; these centered
on Hollywood themes. Louis Lewyn directed HOLLYWOOD DARE-
DEVILS (1943), which concerned a day in the hazardous life of a stuntman (Harry Woolmen). MOVIE PESTS, nominated for an Academy
Award as Best One-Reel Short Subject of 1944, was directed by Will
Jason and told the account of various annoyances one may face at the
movies: e. g. , a lady with a large hat, a peanut cracker, and a man
with his long legs stretched in the aisle. The film also depicted how
to take revenge. HOLLYWOOD SCOUT (1945; directed by Phil Anderson) revealed a "typical day" in the life of a Hollywood talent hunter,
this one with animals for clients.

Closing out the forties--and the genre of movie-oriented short
subjects--was SO YOU WANT TO BE IN PICTURES, a 1947 Warner
Bros. one-reeler, nominated for an Academy Award in the short film
field. Narrated by Art Gilmore and directed by Richard L. Bare,
this was an entry in the Joe McDoakes comedy series featuring George
O'Hanlon. This segment related the troubles one average man en-
dures to crash the world of movies.

With the coming of commercial television in America and the
transfer of the short subject to the small screen, as half-hour programs, the theme of Hollywood as portrayed by Hollywood moved to
the new medium, to return to the large screen on only a very occasional basis.

During the past quarter of a century there have been a few
television shows which have taken a look inside Hollywood. Among
them have been Mary Astor portraying Norma Desmond in Sunset
Boulevard on "Robert Montgomery Presents" in 1956 on NBC. Gloria
Swanson essayed the role of a faded movie queen in A Toast to Yesterday in 1961 on ABC's "Straightaway" show, and five years later
she portrayed herself on an installment of CBS-TV's "The Beverly
Hillbillies" which dealt with the Clampett family's attempt to make
a movie. (In a 1968 episode of CBS's "The Lucy Show" zany Lucille Ball would mistakenly assume that cinema queen Joan Crawford
was down on her luck and try to get her a break again in the movies;
previously on the "I Love Lucy" shows of the early fifties, many
segments were devoted to Ball, Desi Arnaz, Vivian Vance, and William Frawley running amok in Hollywood at MGM, at the Brown Derby Restaurant, at Grauman's Chinese Theatre, etc.) Just as Swanson was typecast as a silent movie queen by TV, so screen veteran
Francis X. Bushman more than once played the has-been movie idol
on the small screen. He essayed the part in All Our Yesterdays in
1958 on ABC's "77 Sunset Strip" and in the same program John Carradine was cast as a director fallen on hard times. In 1961 Bushman also played a faded movie star in The Last Resort on ABC's
"Peter Gunn".

Another TV show which examined Hollywood's past was The

Silent Partner, an episode of the NBC "Screen Directors Playhouse" series, directed by George Marshall. The show opens at the Academy Award ceremonies with Bob Hope presenting a famous director (Joe E. Brown) with a special Oscar. Brown then reveals how his success was due to his directing a once-famous, but now forgotten silent film comic. A segment of one of their joint films is shown and in a bar the comic (Buster Keaton) watches the picture and is recognized by movie buff ZaSu Pitts. Besides Keaton, the segment featured Evelyn Ankers as a movie heroine, Jack Elam as a hammy movie leading man, and Jack Kruschen as a bully in the bar.

Another engaging look at the Hollywood mystique was seen on the Death Scene episode of "Alfred Hitchcock Theatre" over NBC in 1965. Here Vera Miles portrayed the daughter of a once-famous movie queen with John Carradine as her director father. The climax of the segment has Miles revealed as the movie queen herself, the "daughter" role being a masquerade, her youth preserved by a face mask.

The above are only a small part of the TV shows that have dealt with aspects of Hollywood, a subject which continues to intrigue video scripters, as for example, the 1977 episode of "Charlie's Angels" which featured Ida Lupino as a prominent film star now in retirement who wants to make a comeback but is fearful of a mysterious assailant out to kill her.

While many of the motion picture studios gave in to the competition of television by entering the field in the mid-fifties, their shows ("Warner Bros. Presents," "The Twentieth Century-Fox Hour," "The MGM Parade", etc.) were frequently either rehashes of old theatrical vehicles refilmed for the small screen, or else expensive trailers for upcoming theatrical releases. On the other hand, "Hollywood and the Stars" programs, narrated by Joseph Cotten and seen during the 1963-1964 season, were half-hour shows devoted to either a genre of film, a particular star, or a way of life in the industry. None of the segments delved too deeply into truth or the unpleasant reality of breaking into or staying on top in the industry. However, it did provide viewers with some glimpses of veteran top personalities in the business. Even with all its glossiness, it was still a more discerning study of the motion picture business than such live interview shows as the mid-fifties "Hollywood Today" with gossip reporter Sheila Graham over NBC or the more recent syndication "news" shots of columnist Rona Barrett.

Mention should be made of a 26-minute color film called THE MOVIE PEOPLE, made in 1972 as a pilot for a syndicated TV series. It was directed by Steve Barkett and photographed by Emmy-winner Jerry Sims. I offered an examination/interview of John Cassavetes in his offices at Universal City. The entry had some theatrical release and is now available for sale to private collectors.

In the fall of 1977 20th Century-Fox-TV distributed a half-hour video series entitled "That's Hollywood" narrated by Tom Bosley, which utilized studio footage to provide mini-documentaries on a variety of screen genres and themes.

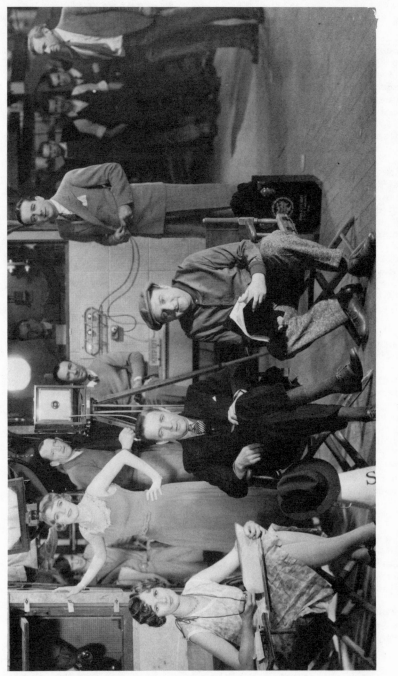

Blanche Sweet (standing), Lee Shumway, Herman Bing, and Jack Mulhall in Show Girl in Hollywood (1930).

SHOW GIRL IN HOLLYWOOD (First National, 1930) 80 min. (color sequences)

Producer, Robert North; director, Mervyn LeRoy; based on the novel Hollywood Girl by J. P. McEvoy; screenplay, Harvey Thew and James A. Starr; art director, Jack Okey; songs, Bud Green and Sammy Stept; choreography, Jack Haskell; music director, Leo F. Forbstein; camera, Sol Polito; editor, Peter Fritch.

Alice White (Dixie Dugan); Jack Mulhall (Jimmy Doyle); Blanche Sweet (Donna Harris); Ford Sterling (Sam Otis); John Miljan (Frank Buelow); Virginia Sale (Otis' Secretary); Lee Shumway (Kramer); Herman Bing (Bing); Walter Pidgeon (Guest Star).

Entertainer Dixie Dugan (Alice White) is seen in her nightclub act by a famous movie director who thinks she suits for the lead of a new musical he is making. Brought to Hollywood, White becomes friendly with a has-been female film star (Blanche Sweet) who gives her a heart-to-heart talk on the realities of life in the film capital. In return, White maneuvers a comeback role for Sweet in her picture.
It is not long before White has "gone Hollywood," becoming very temperamental, demanding story changes, a new director, etc. As a result she is fired and the production is halted. Seeing her opportunity for a film comeback evaporate, Sweet commits suicide. The death of her friend makes White realize the error of her new ways. She asks for and is given a second chance.
Show Girl in Hollywood was a sequel to Show Girl (First National, 1928) in which Alice White also played the part of Dixie Dugan. Here her performance is rather tepid and the overall musical with a film setting is dull despite some color sequences. The supporting cast, however, was quite superior, with Jack Mulhall as the leading man, John Miljan as the director, and Blanche Sweet as the trouble-plagued older star. It is the latter who has the highlight of the picture as she sings "There's a Tear for Every Smile in Hollywood." First National contractee Walter Pidgeon makes a brief guest appearance as a studio star.
Paul d'Estournelle de Constant scripted a French-language version of Show Girl in Hollywood; it was directed by Clarence Badger and Jean Daumery, and starred Suzy Vernon, Geymond Vital, Rolla Norman, Helen Darly, Leon Lanve, and Roland Caillaux. It was filmed in Hollywood by First National.

SHOW PEOPLE (MGM, 1928) 7453 ft.

Director, King Vidor; screen treatment, Agnes Christine Johnston and Laurence Stallings; continuity, Wanda Tuchock; titles, Ralph Spence; song, William Axt and David Mendoza; wardrobe, Henrietta Frazer; sets, Cedric Gibbons; camera, John Arnold; editor, Hugh Wynn.

Marion Davies (Peggy Pepper); William Haines (Billy Boone);

William Haines, Marion Davies, and Charlie Chaplin in Show People
(1928).

Dell Henderson (Colonel Pepper); Paul Ralli (Andre); Tenen Holtz
(Casting Director); Polly Moran (Maid); Harry Gribbon (Comedy Dir-
ector); Sidney Bracy (Dramatic Director); Albert Conti (Producer);
John Gilbert, Mae Murray, Charles Chaplin, Douglas Fairbanks,
Elinor Glyn, Dorothy Sebastian, Louella O. Parsons, Estelle Taylor,
Claire Windsor, Aileen Pringle, Karl Dane, George K. Arthur, Lea-
trice Joy, Renee Adoree, Rod La Rocque, Norma Talmadge, Marion
Davies, and William S. Hart (Themselves).

   This delightful comedy satire was LOOSELY based on the
early career of Gloria Swanson, according to director King Vidor.
Another comic note had star Marion Davies seeing her real-life
counterpart on the set of a film (via double exposure) and commenting
(via title card), "She's too much." Finally, director Vidor managed
to corral a large number of big-name stars to perform cameos in
the picture. It provided a chance to see Charlie Chaplin as himself,
as well as William S. Hart in his next-to-last screen appearance.
   The narrative tells of Southern belle Peggy Pepper (Davies),

a movie-struck lass, who comes to Hollywood hoping to become a
star.   But she can only find employment as the foil of Billy Boone
(William Haines) in unprestigious slapstick comedies.   Haines teaches
the newcomer the tricks of the trade and eventually she begins to
earn opportunities in dramatic films, and in turn, she becomes a
success.   With stardom, however, Davies changes her name to Patricia Pepoire and forgets her former slapstick comedy pals, including
Haines.   She almost winds up marrying her phony leading man (Paul
Ralli), until Haines, who still adores her, comes to the rescue and
teaches her a lesson in humility.   Davies, realizing the error of her
ways, marries Haines and settles down to a life of contentment.

Show People, which was issued with a musical score and sound
effects but no dialogue, was an immediate success, and earned solid
reviews, especially for stars Davies and Haines.   Interestingly,
Davies' mentor/lover William Randolph Hearst would not allow the
actress to exploit her full range of comedy talent.   In the course of
her picture making he forbids her to be hit in the face with custard
pies, etc. , although he did allow her to be squirted in the face with
seltzer water.   Regarding her performance, David Robinson said, in
Hollywood in the Twenties (1968), that "she brilliantly caricatures
the affectation of twenties divas, down to the primped lips and pro-
truded front teeth which were de rigueur in glamour photographs of
the time. "

SILENT MOVIE (20th Century-Fox, 1976) Color, 86 min.

Producer, Michael Hertzberg; director, Mel Brooks; story,
Ron Clark; screenplay, Brooks, Clark, Rudy DeLuca, and Barry
Levinson; music, John Morris; choreography, Rob Iscove; orchestrators, Bill Byers and Morris; costumes, Pat Norris; assistant directors, Ed Teets and Richard Wells; production designer, Al Brenner; set decorator, Rick Simpson; makeup, William Tuttle; men's
wardrobe, Wally Harton and Jay Caplan; ladies' wardrobe, Nancy
Martinelli; special effects, Ira Anderson, Jr. ; camera, Paul Lohmann;
editors, John C. Howard and Stanford C. Allen; assistant editor,
David Blangsted.

Mel Brooks (Mel Funn); Marty Feldman (Marty Eggs); Dom
DeLuise (Dom Bell); Bernadette Peters (Vilma Kaplan); Sid Ceasar
(Studio Chief); Harold Gould (Engulf); Ron Carey (Devour); Carol Arthur (Pregnant Lady); Liam Dunn (Newsvendor); Fritz Feld (Maitre
d'); Chuck McCann (Studio Gate Guard); Valerie Curtin (Intensive
Care Nurse); Yvonne Wilder (Studio Chief's Secretary); Arnold Sobo-
loff (Acupuncture Man); Patrick Campbell (Motel Bellhop); Harry
Ritz (Man Leaving Tailor Shop); Charlie Callas (Blind Man); Eddie
Ryder (British Officer); Henny Youngman (Fly-in-Soup Man); Al Hop-
son, Rudy DeLuca, Barry Levinson, Howard Hesseman, Lee Delano,
and Jack Riley (Executives); Inga Neilsen, Sivi Aberg, and Erica
Hagen (Blondes); Robert Lussier (Projectionist); Marcel Marceau,
Liza Minnelli, James Caan, Paul Newman, Anne Bancroft and Burt
Reynolds (Guest Stars).

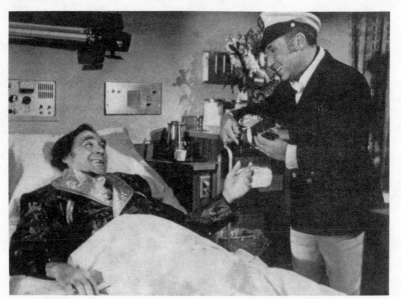

Sid Caesar and Mel Brooks in Silent Movie (1976).

     After having successfully kidded Westerns in Blazing Saddles
(q. v.), and horror films in Young Frankenstein (1975), Mel Brooks
and company turned to a parody of the movies in Silent Movie. This
slapstick farce has so far grossed $20, 311, 000 in distributors' do-
mestic rentals.
     The crazy tale has Brooks as has-been movie director Mel
Funn.   He is an alcoholic who has his drinking problem in check and
now wants to make a Hollywood comeback.   Working with him are
pals Marty Eggs (Marty Feldman) and Dom Bell (Dom DeLuise), who
more than hamper his attempts with their looney ideas.   Finally the
trio convince a Studio Chief (Sid Caesar) to make a silent movie under Brooks' direction.   This outrageous concept just might be the
box-office gimmick to save Caesar's studio from a takeover by the
conglomerate headed by Engulf (Harold Gould) and Devour (Ron Carey).
     Having achieved this step toward making the film, the madcap
trio set out to sign a group of movie stars to appear in the picture.
They have a series of misadventures with James Caan, Anne Bancroft, Paul Newman, Liza Minnelli, and Burt Reynolds, all of whom
agree to do the film.   Only Marcel Marceau says "no" (the only
spoken word of dialogue in the film) to the proposition.
     In order to stop Brooks' plan, Gould hires Vilma Kaplan (Bern-
adette Peters) to romance and cripple the director's will to work.
She accomplishes her nefarious deed and the love-stricken director
seeks consolation in liquor.   Later, ashamed of herself, Peters joins

with DeLuise and Feldman to restore Brooks' confidence and to wean
him from the bottle.   Eventually the film is completed.   Brooks and
company have a rowdy chase to get the reels to the theatre (while
Peters entertains the audience) with Gould and his hoodlums in pursuit.   The film is shown and is a hit.   The studio is saved, Brooks
is re-established, and he and Peters can now relax and enjoy their
romance.

A fine visual comedy and a solid satire of Hollywood, Silent
Movie has many good bits.   Brooks and troupe's coke-machine battle
with Gould and his punks is a comedy classic as are bits by Harry
Ritz as the man coming out of the tailor shop, Charlie Manna as the
blind man walking his dog, and Henny Youngman as the diner with a
fly in his soup.   In retrospect, Silent Movie may well be the funniest
film ever to kid the movie industry.   Most interestingly, it displayed
the universal appeal of silent film-making, nearly a half-century
after the medium ceased to exist commercially.

SINGIN' IN THE RAIN (MGM, 1952) Color, 103 min.

Producer, Arthur Freed; directors, Gene Kelly and Stanley
Donen; story/screenplay, Adolph Green and Betty Comden; music
director, Lennie Hayton; songs, Freed and Nacio Herb Brown; Comden, Green, and Roger Edens; art directors, Cedric Gibbons and
Randall Duell; camera, Harold Rosson; editor, Adrienne Fazan.

Gene Kelly (Don Lockwood); Donald O'Connor (Cosmo Brown);
Debbie Reynolds (Kathy Selden); Jean Hagen (Lina Lamont); Millard
Mitchell (R. F. Simpson); Rita Moreno (Zelda Zanders); Douglas
Fowley (Roscoe Dexter); Cyd Charisse (Dancer); Madge Blake (Dora
Bailey); King Donovan (Rod); Kathleen Freeman (Phoebe Dinsmore
the Diction Coach); Bobby Watson (Diction Coach); Tommy Farrell
(Sid Phillips the Assistant Director); Dan Foster (Jimmie Thompson
the Assistant Director); John Dodsworth (Baron de la May de la Toulon);
Judy Landon (Olga Mara); Stuart Holmes (J. C. Spendrill III); Dennis
Ross (Don Lockwood as a Boy); Richard Emory ("Phil" the Cowboy
Hero); Julius Tannen (Man on Screen); Bill Lewin (Bert the Western
Villian); Dawn Addams and Elaine Stewart (Ladies in Waiting); Doro-
thy Patrick, William Lester, Charles Evans, and Joi Lansing (Audi-
ence); Dave Sharpe and Russ Saunders (Fencers).

Long acknowledged as a classic and generally recognized as
the most delightful film ever to satirize the advent of cinema sound,
MGM's perenially popular Singin' in the Rain boasts a great deal of
authentic technical Hollywoodiana.   Studio research recreated everything from flapper costumes to primitive camera microphone equipment to a glass soundstage, all serving as perfect background for the
zestiest of Hollywood's self-spoofs.   In addition there are irresistible
star performances and a joyous Arthur Freed-Nacio Herb Brown
score.

The story begins at a movie premiere where silent film idol
Don Lockwood (played with a fine mixture of spice and restraint by

Gene Kelly) and his unspeakable screen vis-à-vis Lina Lamont (a classic camp unforgettably portrayed by the late Jean Hagen) relate the road to glory with a Hollywood columnist.

The action picks up as Kelly, in a mad rush to escape pursuing female fans, drops from the top of a bus into the open-topped car of young Kathy Sheldon (blandly personified by inexperienced Debbie Reynolds), who has singing and acting aspirations. She insists he is "above" the pictures. Later at a party, Kelly discovers Reynolds leaping out of a cake to perform a wild Charleston dance-- so much for her unimpeachable standards.

As Kelly and Reynolds form a romance, Kelly and Hagen begin work on their latest romantic effort--a talkie--entitled The Duelling Cavalier. The film evolves as dated, laughable claptrap, principally sabotaged by Hagen's atrocious vocality. To salvage the picture, Kelly's pal (arguably Donald O'Connor's finest performance) persuades the studio to re-shoot the film as a musical comedy, with Reynolds dubbing Hagen's voice.

The ruse works, and nasty Hagen demands that Reynolds become her permanent "voice," restricting the girl's chances for true cinema stardom. However, at the premiere, the cheering audience demands that Hagen sing! Reynolds is rushed behind the curtain to provide the voice, but Hagen's career is scuttled and Reynolds' is launched when Kelly and O'Connor pull up the curtain--and reveal the true star of the film.

In The Musical Film (1967), Douglas McVay writes that Singin' in the Rain "... has a witty, satirical and farcical script ... a funny and tuneful score ... imaginative decors ... a splendid dumb-movie-star cameo from Jean Hagen ... [and] Kelly's famous song-and-dance of the title number is certainly immaculately conceived and executed...."

SITTING PRETTY (Paramount, 1933) 85 min.

Producer, Charles R. Rogers; director, Harry Joe Brown; story suggested by Nina Wilcox Putnam; screenplay, Jack McGowan, S. J. Perelman, and Lou Breslow; choreography, Larry Ceballos; songs, Mack Gordon and Harry Revel; camera, Milton Krasner.

Jack Oakie (Chick Parker); Jack Haley (Pete Pendleton); Ginger Rogers (Dorothy); Thelma Todd (Gloria Duval); Gregory Ratoff (Tannenbaum); Lew Cody (Jules Clark); Harry Revel (Harry the Pianist); Jerry Tucker (Buzz); Mack Gordon (Meyers the Song Publisher); Hale Hamilton (Vinton); Walter Walker (George Wilson); Kenneth Thomson (Norman Lubin); William B. Davidson (Director); Lee Moran (Assistant Director); The Pickens Sisters, Arthur Jarrett, and Virginia Sale (Guest Performers); Irving Bacon and Stuart Holmes (Dice Players); Fuzzy Knight (Stock Clerk); Lee Phelps (Studio Aide); Harry C. Bradley (Set Designer); Dave O'Brien (Assistant Cameraman); James

---

Opposite: Donald O'Connor, Debbie Reynolds, and Gene Kelly in Singin' in the Rain (1952).

Burtis (Foreman of Movers); Charles Coleman (Butler); Frank La
Rue (Studio Gateman); Wade Boteler (Jackson--Aide to Wilson).

The title of this spunky musical comedy is frequently confused
with the more famous Sitting Pretty (1948) with Clifton Webb.   This
entry, however, did have several firsts to make it memorable: it
contained Jack Haley's feature film debut; it was the movie that established Ginger Rogers as a leading lady of the first rank (and led
to her screen teaming with Fred Astaire at RKO); and it introduced
the now standard tune, "Did You Ever See a Dream Walking?"
Its plot revolved about two famous Broadway composers,
Chick Parker (Jack Oakie) and Pete Pendleton (Haley) who are per-
suaded by their pals to take a stab at Hollywood where musicals are
the fad.   Low on money, the duo begin hitchhiking across the country
and along the way they meet a pretty and talented lunch-wagon owner
(Rogers) who falls in love with Haley.   With her savings she gets
the boys to their destination where they become successes, but Oakie
is entranced by glamourous movie star Gloria Duval (Thelma Todd).
When she drops him, he realizes that he was played for a sap and
returns to his work.   Later Haley and Rogers wed and the song
writing duo become the best in the film capitol.
Note the guest appearances by the film's composers Mack
Gordon and Harry Revel, and Gregory Ratoff portraying his usual
movie colony stereotype--the outlandish producer.

THE SKYROCKET (Associated Exhibitors, 1926) 7350 ft.

Director, Marshall Neilan; based on the short story and novel
by Adela Rogers St. John; screenplay, Benjamin Glazer; camera,
David Kesson.

Prologue: Gladys Brockwell (Rose Kimm); Charles West (Edward Kimm); Muriel McCormac (Sharon Kimm); Junior Coghlan (Mickey).

Story: Peggy Hopkins Joyce (Sharon Kimm); Owen Moore
(Mickey Reid); Gladys Hulette (Lucia Morgan); Paulette Duval (Mildred
Rideout); Lilyan Tashman (Ruby Wright); Earle Williams (William
Dvorak); Bernard Randall (Sam Hertzfelt); Sammy Cohen (Morris
Pincus); Bull Montana (Film Comedian); Arnold Gregg (Stanley Craig);
Ben Hall (Peter Stanton); Nick Dandau (Vladmir Strogin); Eddie Dillon
(Comedy Director); Hank Mann (Comedy Producer); Joan Standing
(Sharon's Secretary); Eugenie Besserer (Wardrobe Mistress).

The romance between director Marshall Neilan and oft-married
personality Peggy Hopkins Joyce had completely cooled by the time
he chose her to play the title role of Sharon Kimm in The Skyrocket.
It was an independent project financed by Joseph P. Kennedy and P.

Opposite: Fan dancers Sitting (and Standing) Pretty (1933).

A. Powers. The result was an excellent film but production delays (mainly due to disagreements between the director and star) burdened the project with a hefty financial cost, a sum hardly covered by its poor distribution.

Based on a short story and (later) novel by Adela Rogers St. John, the film tells the tale of a young girl (Joyce) from the wrong side of the tracks who rises to become one of Hollywood's greatest stars thanks to all-powerful film director William Dvorak (Earle Williams), who lusts after both power and women.

Sharon Kimm's meteoric rise is said to be based on Gloria Swanson's while the director could well have been Neilan or any of a half-dozen other top helmsmen of the day. As a representation of Hollywood and its power structure, the entry depicted Hollywood as a cruel place where only the most ruthless survive and prosper.

Photoplay magazine evaluated it as "the best picture about motion picture people so far...."

SLIGHTLY FRENCH (Columbia, 1949) 81 min.

Producer, Irving Starr; director, Douglas Sirk; story, Herbert Fields; screenplay, Karen DeWolf; art director, Carl Anderson; set decorator, James Crowe; music, George Duning; music director, Morris Stoloff; songs, Allan Roberts and Lester Lee; assistant director, Paul Donnelly; choreography, Robert Sidney; costumes, Jean Louis; camera, Charles Lawton; editor, Al Clark.

Dorothy Lamour (Mary O'Leary); Don Ameche (John Gayle); Janis Carter (Louisa Gayle); Willard Parker (Douglas Hyde); Adele Jergens (Yvonne LaTour); Jeanne Manet (Nicolette); Frank Ferguson (Marty Freeman); Myron Healey (Stevens); Leonard Carey (Wilson); Earle Hodgins (Barker); William Bishop (Voice of J. B. the Producer); Patricia Barry (Hilda); Jimmy Lloyd and Michael Towne (Assistants); Fred Sears (Cameraman); Frank Mayo (Sound Man); Fred Howard and Robert B. Williams (News Men); Charles Jordan (Studio Policeman); Hal K. Dawson (Director); Frank Wilcox (Starr the Playwright); Will Stanton (Cockney Barker); Al Hill (Brazilian Barker); Pierre Watkin (Publicity Man).

This programmer was an amusing remake of Let's Fall in Love (q. v.).

Fading film director John Gayle (Don Ameche) is stuck with a half-completed picture after alienating his female star, who has quit in anger. Needing to complete the project to re-establish himself in Hollywood, Ameche tries to find a proper replacement. He comes across Mary O'Leary (Dorothy Lamour), a carnival dancer who specializes in Brazilian, French, and China doll impersonations. Ameche decides to present the girl as a French heiress with acting ambitions in order to obtain the lead in his film for her. He then tutors the willing pupil in her new life's role. During the instructional period she falls in love with him. However, it is not until after the charade is blown sky-high that the seemingly obtuse Ameche realizes that he loves her as well.

The film was aimed at "a modest level of entertainment" (New York Times) and in it, Lamour did not wear her traditional sarong, although she did have a sultry scene in a bathing suit.

SLIM CARTER (Universal, 1957) Color, 82 min.

Producer, Howie Horwitz; director, Richard Bartlett; story, David Bramson and Mary C. McCall, Jr.; screenplay, Montgomery Pittman; gowns, Bill Thomas; assistant director, William Holland; music, Herman Stein; songs, Ralph Freed and Beasley Smith; Jimmy Wakely and Joseph Gershenson; art directors, Alexander Golitzen and Eric Orbon; music director, Gershenson; special camera effects, Clifford Stine; camera, Ellis W. Carter; editor, Fred MacDowell.

Jock Mahoney (Slim Carter [Hughie Nash]); Julie Adams (Clover Doyle); Tim Hovey (Leo Gallagher); William Hopper (Joe Brewster); Ben Johnson (Montana Burriss); Joanna Moore (Charlene Carroll); Walter Reed (Richard L. Howard); Bill Williams (Frank Hanneman); Barbara Hale (Allie Hanneman); Maggie Mahoney (Hatcheck Girl); Roxanne Arlen (Cigarette Girl); Jean Moorhead (Mary); Donald Kerr (Assistant); Jim Healy (M. C.).

A studio publicity girl, Clover Doyle (Julie Adams), discovers handsome Hughie Nash (Jock Mahoney) working in a nightclub and she takes him to her movie studio and begins promoting him as a new Western star. Finally the company agrees to gamble on his future and his name is changed to Slim Carter. He is given roping lessons from a top stuntman and is generally doubled in all his action scenes. His film proves a big success and Mahoney becomes a star. But all of this fanfare feeds his already over-egotistical nature and he soon becomes a pain to his coworkers and even Adams, who secretly loves him (but is convinced he would not make a good husband).

Finally the studio drums up a "Visit Slim Carter" contest with the lucky child winner getting to spend a month with the star. The recipient is orphan Leo Gallagher (Tim Hovey), a nice young fellow, and the folk at the studio do nothing which might dispel his belief in the screen image of Mahoney. After a month with the boy, however, it is Mahoney who has altered. His ego has deflated and he takes a new appraisal of himself and his situation. As a result, Mahoney and Adams wed and they adopt Hovey.

Although a modest B film, the ingratiating performances of Mahoney, Adams, and Hovey made all the difference. Also of interest was the casting in cameo roles of real life husband-and-wife Bill Williams and Barbara Hale as a Hollywood husband-and-wife acting team.

A SMALL TOWN IDOL (Associated Producers, 1921) 7 reels

Presenter/supervisor, Mack Sennett; director, Erle Kenton;

screenplay, Sennett; special camera effects, Fred Jackman; camera, Perry Evans and J. R. Lockwood.

Ben Turpin (Sam Smith [Samuel X. Smythe]); James Finlayson (J. Wellington Jones); Phyllis Haver (Mary Brown); Bert Roach (Martin Brown); Al Cooke (Joe Barnum); Charles Murray (Sheriff Sparks); Marie Prevost (Marcelle Mansfield); Dot Farley (Mrs. Smith); Eddie Gribbon (Bandit Chief); Kalla Pasha (Bandit Chief's Rival); Billy Bevan (Director); George O'Hara (Cameraman); Ramon Novarro (Dancer).

Since the earliest days of his Keystone comedies, Mack Sennett spoofed the movies. He loved to poke fun at the industry that made him rich and famous; one of his best (and lengthier) outings in this regard was the hour-long, A Small Town Idol. For this slapstick affair, Sennett rounded up most of the name performers on the Keystone lot and centered the action around his then most popular star, cross-eyed Ben Turpin. The film is also notable in that it provided Ramon Novarro with one of his earliest screen roles as a dancer.

Turpin played the sexton of a small-town church who is engaged to his childhood sweetheart until he is run out of town after being falsely accused of thievery. He winds up in Hollywood where he is soon at the end of his emotional rope and contemplates suicide. By accident he happens to be on the set of a Western film which calls for the star to jump from a high bridge. The star, not caring for the risky situation, refuses and Turpin, with nothing to lose, agrees to accomplish the stunt. He does the feat, but is then asked to do it again, as the director's cap accidentally covered the camera lens. After completing the death-defying task a second time, Ben is given the leading role in the movie. He soon becomes a picture star and the idol of the small town which had dispossessed him.

Turpin was at his crazy best as the star of this madcap satire. Billy Bevan, a famous comic in his own right, was the bumbling director, and other veteran stars to appear in the feature included Jimmy Finlayson, Bert Roach, Charles Murray, Dot Farley, and Eddie Gribbon, with Phyllis Haver as the leading lady of the Western that makes Ben a celebrity.

SO THIS IS LOVE (Warner Bros., 1953) Color, 101 min.

Producer, Henry Blanke; director, Gordon Douglas; based on the autobiography of Grace Moore; screenplay, John Monks, Jr.; choreography, LeRoy Prinz; music adaptor, Max Steiner; music director, Ray Heindorf; camera, Robert Burks; editor, Folmar Blangsted.

Kathryn Grayson (Grace Moore); Merv Griffin (Buddy Nash);

Opposite: Jock Mahoney (extreme left), Julie Adams, Bill Williams, and William Hopper; right foreground: Barbara Hale and Donald Kerr in Slim Carter (1957).

Kathryn Grayson and Merv Griffin in So This is Love (1953).

Joan Weldon (Ruth Obre); Walter Abel (Colonel Moore); Rosemary De Camp (Aunt Laura Stokley); Jeff Donnell (Henrietta Van Dyke); Douglas Dick (Bryan Curtis); Ann Doran (Mrs. Moore); Margaret Field [Maggie Mahoney] (Edna Wallace); Mabel Albertson (Mary Garden); Fortunio Bonanova (Dr. Marafioti); Noreen Corcoran (Grace Moore at Age Eight); Marie Windsor (Marilyn Montgomery); The Szonys (Dance Specialty); Lillian Bronson (Mrs. Wilson Green); Ray Kellogg (John McCormack); Roy Gordon (Otto Kahn); Moroni Olsen (Arnold Reuben); Mario Siletti (Gatti Casazza); Charles Meredith (Arthur Bodansky); William Boyett (George Gershwin).

Lost among the shuffle of mid-fifties biopics of famous actresses and singers was So This Is Love, the supposed story of opera star Grace Moore (1901-1947), who had a brief movie career in the thirties, first at MGM (unsuccessful) and then at Columbia (very successful). Although shot in color, starring Kathryn Grayson, and filled with lovely songs, the film collapsed at the box-office. It is chiefly known today as the only major screen vehicle to costar talk show host Merv Griffin.

The feature followed the tried-and-true format of the musical celluloid biography: small-town Tennessee girl Grace Moore (Gray-

son) rises to become the star of the Metropolitan Opera in New York
City, overcoming obstacles at every turn of the way. Along the way
she experiences a slight brush with the movies and an even deeper
one with love but spurns the latter in deference to her blossoming
career. The finale has her killed in a plane crash while still at the
height of her popularity.

Thanks to lovely Grayson, who handled both the acting and
singing chores quite competently, the picture does have substance.
But for those unappreciative of the world of opera or the traditional
turns of screen biographies, it can be sluggish going.

SO YOU WANT TO BE IN PICTURES see THE SHORT FILMS

SOMETHING TO SING ABOUT (Grand National, 1937) 84 min.

Producer, Zion Myers; director/story, Victor Schertzinger;
art directors, Robert Lee and Paul Murphy; music director, C. Bakaleinikoff; songs, Schertzinger; music arranger, Myrl Alderman; choreography, Harlan Dixon; assistant director, John Sherwood; camera,
John Stumar; editor, Gene Milford.

James Cagney (Terry Rooney); Evelyn Daw (Rita Wyatt); Wil-
liam Frawley (Hank Meyers); Mona Barrie (Stephanie Hajos); Gene
Lockhart (Bennett O. Regan); James Newill (Orchestra Soloist); Harry
Barris (Pinky); Candy Candido (Candy); Cully Richards (Soloist); Wil-
liam B. Davidson (Cafe Manager); Richard Tucker (Blaine); Marek
Windheim (Farney); Dwight Frye (Easton); John Arthur (Daviani);
Philip Ahn (Ito); Kathleen Lockhart (Miss Robbins); Kenneth Harlan
(Transportation Manager); Herbert Rawlinson (Studio Attorney); Ernest
Wood (Edward Burns); Chick Collins (The Man Terry Fights); Duke
Green (Other Man); Harlan Dixon, Johnny Boyle, Johnny "Skins" Mil-
ler, Pat Moran, Joe Bennett, Buck Mack, and Eddie Allen (Dancers);
The Vagabonds (Specialty); Dottie Messmer, Virginia Lee Irwin, and
Dolly Waldorf (Three Shades of Blue).

By the mid-thirties, James Cagney had become increasingly
aggitated at his treatment (especially financial) by the brothers Warner. He broke his contract with the studio and signed with a small
outfit called Grand National. There he made a gangster film, Great
Guy (1936), and a musical which loosely kidded the Hollywood scene.
Although both features proved popular, Warner Bros. came up with
an improved contract and Cagney was soon back at the Burbank lot,
where in 1938 he made another Hollywood-oriented picture, entitled
Boy Meets Girl (q. v.).

Still at Grand National, the 1937 Something to Sing About offered Cagney as bandleader Terry Rooney who abandons his Manhattan bandstand to come to Hollywood to make a musical. A scheming
producer (Gene Lockhart), however, advises the novice that his career is doomed after the film seems a flop. The bandleader marries
his former soloist, Rita Wyatt (Evelyn Daw), and the couple embarks

on a honeymoon to the South Seas. Meanwhile, the picture in question turns out belatedly to be a success. Cagney returns to Hollywood and signs a seven-year contract which requires him to remain
a bachelor. Daw goes along with it for a spell. But after the sti-
pulation begins to cause a rift in their marriage, the lovers return
to Manhattan and resume their club musical careers.

Despite some rather bland numbers, the musical score for
this film was nominated for an Academy Award. It did not win.
Against Hollywood tradition (but probably to cut corners on the budget), director Victor Schertzinger shot this film in continuity. Something to Sing About provided Cagney with ample opportunity to perform some good hoofing.

In 1947, the film was reissued by Screencraft as Battling
Hoofer.

SONS OF ADVENTURE (Republic, 1948) 68 min.

Associate producer, Franklin Adreon; director, Yakima Canutt;
screenplay, Adreon and Sol Shor; art director, James Sullivan; set
decorators, John McCarthy, Jr. and James Redd; music director,
Morton Scott; assistant director, Bob Shannon; makeup, Bob Marks;
sound, Earl Crain, Sr.; special effects, Howard and Theodore Ly-
decker; camera, John MacBurnie; editor, Harold Minter.

Lynne Roberts (Jean); Russell Hayden (Steve); Gordon Jones
(Andy); Grant Withers (Sterling); George Chandler (Billy Wilkes); Roy
Barcroft (Bennett); John Newland (Peter Winslow); Stephanie Bachelor
(Laura); John Holland (Paul Kenyon); Gilbert Frye (Sam Hodges);
Richard Irving (Eddie); Joan Blair (Glenda); John Crawford (Norton);
Keith Richards (Harry); James Dale (Whitey).

Stunt director/performer Yakima Canutt supervised this Republic film which featured action sequences by many professional
stunt men. As Variety noted, "Production helming takes full advantage of the studio to give color to physical values."

During World War II, while serving in the South Pacific,
Steve (Russell Hayden) and Andy (Gordon Jones) become friends.
Years later and back in Hollywood, stunt man Hayden obtains a job
for Jones on a Western film. When the picture's star is killed, the
chief suspect seems to be Jones. Hayden sets out to capture the
culprit, who, it develops, is assistant director Billy Wilkes (George
Chandler).

SOPHIE OF THE MOVIES see THE SHORT FILMS

SOULS FOR SALE (Goldwyn Pictures, 1923) 7864 ft.

Producer/director, Rupert Hughes; based on the novel by
Hughes; camera, John Mescall.

Eleanor Boardman (Remember Steddon); Mae Busch (Robina
Teele); Barbara La Marr (Leva Lemaire); Richard Dix (Frank Clay-
more); Frank Mayo (Tom Holby); Lew Cody (Owen Scudder); Arthur
Hoyt (Jimmy Leland); David Imboden (Caxton); Roy Atwell (Arthur
Tirrey); William Orlamond (Lord Fryingham); Forrest Robinson (Rev-
erend John Steddon); Edith Yorke (Mrs. Steddon); Dale Fuller (Abi-
gail Tweedy); Snitz Edwards (Hank Kale); Jack Richardson (Motion
Picture Heavy); Aileen Pringle (Lady Jane); Eve Southern (Velma
Slade); May Milloy (Mrs. Sturges); Sylvia Ashton (Mrs. Kate); Mar-
garet Bourne (Leva Lemaire's Mother); Fred Kelsey (Quinn); Jed
Prouty (Magnus); Yale Boss (Prop Man); William Haines (Pinkey);
George Morgan (Spofford); Auld Thomas (Assistant Cameraman); Leo
Willis (Electrician); Walter Perry (Grip); Sam Damen (Violin Player);
R. H. Johnson (Melodeon player); Rush Hughes (Another Cameraman);
L. J. O'Connor (Doyle); Charles Murphy (Boss Cameraman); Hugo
Ballin, Mabel Ballin, T. Roy Barnes, Barbara Bedford, Hobart Bos-
worth, Charles Chaplin, Chester Conklin, William H. Crane, Elliott
Dexter, Robert Edeson, Claude Gillingwater, Dagmar Godowsky, Ray-
mond Griffith, Elaine Hammerstein, Jean Haskell, K. C. B., Alice
Lake, Bessie Love, June Mathis, Patsy Ruth Miller, Marshall Neilan,
Fred Niblo, Anna Q. Nilsson, ZaSu Pitts, John Sainpolis, Milton
Sills, Anita Stewart, Erich von Stroheim, Blanche Sweet, Florence
Vidor, King Vidor, Johnny Walker, George Walsh, Kathlyn Williams,
Claire Windsor (Celebrities).

Made at a time when Hollywood was coming under fire for
various scandals, Souls for Sale was writer Rupert Hughes' vindication of the film capital of any essential wrong-doing. Hughes scripted
his novel for the feature which was made by Samuel Goldwyn. Besides depicting industry craftsmen as likeable, hardworking, and dedicated folk, the photoplay also included a host of guest appearances
by many of the biggest film names in town.
    A small-town lass named Remember Staddon (Eleanor Board-
man), a minister's daughter, weds Owen Scudder (Lew Cody), a
stranger. On their honeymoon trip West she realizes she has made
a bad mistake and disembarks at a whistle stop. Later she learns her
husband is a wife-killer who marries girls and then murders them
for their insurance. Stranded in a small town, Boardman finds a
job as an extra on a desert-sands film being made on location there.
    Both the leading man Tom Holby (Frank Mayo) and the direc-
tor Frank Claymore (Richard Dix) take her under their wing and once
back in Hollywood, they try to get her to make a career in films.
But she refuses, having heard too many evil things about the film
business. Finally she begins to make the rounds of the studios;
eventually going to work for Dix and Mayo. It is not long before she
becomes a top-notch screen performer.
    Then her husband menacingly arrives on the scene. During
the making of a circus picture, a big wind rips through the tent.
As the husband tries to start a large plane, planning to kill the director, he himself is killed by the propeller, which had been used as
a wind machine. Boardman then selects Dix for her new husband
and they embark on a life of happiness.

Photoplay magazine noted the film was "A Cook's Tour of the
Hollywood studios.   A false and trivial story, but it takes you behind
the camera and is very entertaining. "
Only an abridged version of Souls for Sale survives today, but
it does contain some fascinating scenes of the early studios plus
glimpses of such items as Charles Chaplin directing A Woman of
Paris, Erich von Stroheim at the helm of Greed, and Fred Niblo
supervising The Famous Mrs. Fair.

THE SPEED GIRL (Paramount, 1921) 5792 ft.

Director, Maurice Campbell; story, Elmer Harris; screenplay, Douglas Doty; camera, H. Kinley Martin.

Bebe Daniels (Betty Lee); Theodore von Eltz (Tom Manley);
Frank Elliott (Carl D'Arcy); Walter Hiers (Soapy Taylor); Norris
Johnson (Hilda); Truly Shattuck (Mrs. Lee); William Courtright (Judge
Ketcham); Barbara Maier (Little Girl).

Bebe Daniels had a deservedly long and esteemed career in
films and in the talkie era she exemplified the portrait of the stage
has-been in 42nd Street (Warner Bros. 1933), and a similar role in
Alice Faye's Music Is Magic (q. v.).   The Speed Girl was a vehicle
for the actress that proved overly topical.   It was issued following
her real-life arrest and jail sentence for speeding.
Daniels was seen to advantage as 20-year-old Betty Lee, who
is famous as a movie stunt girl because of her acrobatics in planes
and fast roadsters.   At one point she allows Ensign Tom
Manley (Theodore von Eltz) to think he has saved her on a runaway
horse.   But later at the studio she introduces him to her suitor,
Carol D'Arcy (Frank Elliott).   She then turns down Elliott's proposal
of marriage in order to go to lunch with von Eltz.   They linger too
long with their meal and he is late for his ship, but Daniels drives
him in her fast car.   She is arrested for speeding and is sentenced
to jail for ten days.   Von Eltz has returned to his ship and is unaware of her situation.
Meanwhile Elliott is pursued by revenue agents who have followed up clues linking him to various crimes.   Then a press agent
concocts a story having Daniels and Elliott wed while she is still in
jail.   Von Eltz, however, arrives on the scene in time to expose
Elliott and to declare his love for the movie worker.

SPIN OF A COIN   see   THE GEORGE RAFT STORY

STAND-IN (United Artists, 1937) 90 min.

Producer, Walter Wanger; director, Tay Garnett; based on the
serialized novel by Clarence Budington Kelland; screenplay, Gene
Towne and Graham Baker; music, Heinz Roemheld; music director,

Leslie Howard and Joan Blondell in <u>Stand-In</u> (1937).

Rox Rommel; art directors, Alexander Toluboff and Wade Rubottom; costumes, Helen Taylor; assistant director, Charles Kerr; sound, Paul Neal; camera, Charles Clarke; editors, Otho Lovering and Dorothy Spencer.

Leslie Howard (Atterbury Dodd); Joan Blondell (Lester Plum); Humphrey Bogart (Douglas Quintain); Alan Mowbray (Koslofski); Marla Shelton (Thelma Cheri); C. Henry Gordon (Ivor Nassau); Jack Carson (Potts); Tully Marshall (Pennypacker, Sr.); J. C. Nugent (Pennypacker, Jr.); William V. Mong (Pennypacker).

Warner Bros. loaned three of its bigger names (Leslie Howard, Joan Blondell, and Humphrey Bogart) to producer Walter Wanger for this production, which poked fun at film-making and the corporate aspects of the cinema. <u>Stand-In</u> is mainly noted today, however, for its offbeat casting of Bogart as the comic alcoholic producer Douglas Quintain, a role obtained for him by director Tay Garnett, over the objections of Wanger and United Artists.

Britisher Howard starred as Atterbury Dodd, an egghead who works for a New York bank, which dispatches him to the West Coast to learn whether one of its investments, Colossal Pictures, should be permitted to continue its hazardous financial operations. Knowing

absolutely nothing about films, Howard is assigned a short-order instructor, Miss Lester Plum (Blondell), who is the stand-in for the
company's star, Thelma Cheri (Marla Shelton).   The latter is making
a film called <u>Sex and Satan</u> which is being directed by a charlatan
named Koslofski (Alan Mowbray).

Producer Bogart is in love with Shelton who is really conspir-
ing with Mowbray and rival producer Ivor Nassau (C. Henry Gordon)
to destroy the project and cause Colossal to close.   Bogart meanwhile,
has taken to drink.

Through the tutelage of Blondell, Howard quickly learns about
film-making and uncovers the plot to destroy the studio.   In the interim, without Howard's knowledge, the bank sells the studio's stock
and fires all the employees.   Howard persuades the workers to seize
the lot for 48 hours.   He sobers up Bogart and has him re-edit the
film.   Most of Shelton's role is left on the cutting room floor, allowing the ape in the jungle epic to emerge the star.   As a result of
the shift of emphasis, the picture is a success, the studio is saved,
and Howard (as expected) finds love with Blondell.

At the time of release, there were many critics who thought
the vehicle would have benefitted from a Harold Lloyd or an Eddie
Cantor rather than a still too-prim Leslie Howard in the focal comedy
(burlesque) assignment.

THE STAR (20th Century-Fox, 1952) 90 min.

Producer, Bert E. Friedlob; director, Stuart Heisler; screen-
play, Katharine Albert and Dale Eunson; music, Victor Young; Miss
Davis' costumes, Orry-Kelly; art director, Boris Levin; camera,
Ernest Laszlo; editor, Otto Ludwig.

Bette Davis (Margaret Elliot); Sterling Hayden (Jim Johannson);
Natalie Wood (Gretchen); Warner Anderson (Harry Stone); Minor Wat-
son (Joe Morrison); June Travis (Phyllis Stone); Katherine Warren
(Mrs. Morrison); Kay Riehl (Mrs. Adams); Barbara Woodell (Peggy
Morgan); Fay Baker (Faith); Barbara Lawrence (Herself); David Al-
pert (Keith Barkley); Paul Frees (Richard Stanley).

A public auction is held to sell off the property of one-time
Oscar-winning star Margaret Elliot (Bette Davis), who has fallen on
very difficult times.   A series of bad investments, box-office duds,
and advancing age have left her a discard in the new era of picturemaking.   Her agent (Warner Anderson) cannot get her work; her
child (Natalie Wood) is kept by her ex-husband.   Adding the final blow
in her plight, she is told to pay her rent or be evicted from her
small apartment.   Her sister (Fay Baker) and her weak-willed brother-
in-law (David Alpert), both of whom she has financed for years, re-
fuse to aid her monetarily and she spends her last money getting
drunk.

She is arrested but is bailed out by a former leading man
(Sterling Hayden) who now runs a boat marina and who admits he
once loved her from a distance.   He advises her to start living as

Bette Davis in The Star (1952).

a real woman and to dismiss her past as a star. Davis consequently
takes a job as a sales clerk but is soon fired, after a fight with two
customers who have recognized her. Later she gains a screen test
for a supporting role in a film but plays the audition as a sexy young
girl, thinking it might win her the lead. Still later she witnesses her
ludicrous screen performance and breaks down in tears.

      At a party at her agent's home she talks to a young producer
who outlines a new picture concept for her; it tells of a star like
Davis who has put her career above happiness. Awakening to a new
sense of values, she leaves the party and confesses to her daughter
that she plans to start a new life for them by wedding Hayden.   At
the marina, he welcomes her and she sets out to start anew.

      Much more in the sunlight of reality than the fanciful Sunset
Boulevard (q. v.), The Star showed starkly what can happen to a celebrity once she is stripped of glamour, fame, and attention.   The
story has been told many times in reality but its finale has usually
been less pleasant in real life. "Regrettably, there is altogether too
fast and too contrived an ending to the actress's deep-seated troubles"
(Newsweek).   Time magazine appreciated that the film "offers some
authentic behind-the-scenes glimpses of movie-town activities. "

      Bette Davis' strong performance in the lead (originally, Joan
Crawford was to have starred) carries the modestly-budgeted film and

makes it believable as well as entertaining. For her efforts, she
received her ninth Academy Award nomination (but she lost the Oscar to Shirley Booth of Come Back, Little Sheba). The tenth would
come a decade later for Davis, again for portraying a has-been film
star--of a far different variety--in What Ever Happened to Baby Jane?
(q. v.).

STAR DUST (20th Century-Fox, 1940) 85 min.

        Producer, Darryl F. Zanuck; associate producer, Kenneth Mc-
gowan; director, Walter Lang; based on the story by Jesse Malo,
Kenneth Earl, and Ivan Kahn; screenplay, Robert Ellis and Helen Logan; music director, David Buttolph; songs, Mack Gordon; camera,
Peverell Marley; editor, Robert Simpson.

        Linda Darnell (Carolyn Sayres); John Payne (Bud Borden); Ro-
land Young (Thomas Brooke); Charlotte Greenwood (Lola Langdon);
William Gargan (Dane Wharton); Mary Beth Hughes (June Lawrence);
Mary Healy (Mary); Donald Meek (Sam Wellman); Jessie Ralph (Mrs.
Parker); Walter Kingsford (Napoleon); George Montgomery (Ronnie);
Billy Wayne (Cameraman); Robert Lowery (Bellboy); Paul Hurst (Lab-
oratory Man); Lynne Roberts and Elyse Knox (Girls); Tom Dugan (Bus
Driver); Fern Emmett (Secretary); Irving Bacon (Clerk); Sid Grauman
(Himself); Mantan Moreland (Waiter); Robert Shaw (Boy Leaving); Joan
Leslie (College Girl); Hal K. Dawson (Wellman's Assistant); Jody Gil-
bert (Swedish Maid); Philip Morris (Coach).

        Erstwhile movie idol Tom Brooke (Roland Young), is hired by
Dane Wharton (William Gargan), the president of Amalgamated Stu-
dios--his task is to ferret out new talent for the studio.   Young tours
the Southwest, and signs football hero Bud Borden (John Payne), and
in a small college town, he meets waitress Carolyn Sayres (Linda
Darnell).   She is a young beauty with both looks and talent.   Complications arise, though, when Young learns that Darnell is not only a
minor (16) but also the offspring of one of Young's former girlfriends
from his salad days.   He tells the movie-struck girl to forget her
Hollywood ambitions and he departs.   Nevertheless, she dispatches
her glossy picture to Gargan and forges Young's name on an accompanying note.   Gargan sends for her and she is given a screen test,
which she passes.   Soon she is caught up in the Hollywood whirl,
but regains her emotional stability when she meets and falls in love
with Payne, now a name in pictures also.
        The story for this film was supposedly based on the early ex-
periences of 20th Century-Fox contractee, Linda Darnell.   At 14 she
was sent back home to Dallas, Texas, because she was too young
for films, but a year later she returned to the film capital to obtain
a featured role in Fox's Elsa Maxwell's Hotel for Women (1939).
Apparently some of the ups-and-downs of the young actress, as depicted in the film after her arrival in tinsel town, were also suggested by Darnell's own experiences.

Billy Wayne (seated), Charlotte Greenwood and Linda Darnell in Star Dust (1940).

Whatever the source, Star Dust was a mild swipe at Hollywood and the dream factory which produced starlets and turned them into stars.   Darnell was radiant and Payne fitted well into the mold of the gridiron hero turned movie actor.   Perhaps the most captivating aspect of the film was the casting of William Gargan as studio mogul Dave Wharton.   It was a thinly disguised lampoon of Fox's own potentate, Darryl F. Zanuck, right down to the brief sequence on the polo field.

A STAR IS BORN (United Artists, 1937) Color, 111 min.

Producer, David O. Selznick; director, William A. Wellman; story, Wellman and Robert Carson; screenplay, Dorothy Parker, Alan Campbell, and Carson; color designer, Lansing C. Holden; Technicolor consultant, Natalie Kalmus; settings, Lyle Wheeler and Edward Boyle; costumes, Omar Khayyam; music, Max Steiner; assistant director, Eric Stacey; sound, Oscar Lagerstrom; special effects, Jack Cosgrove; editors, Hal C. Kern and Anson Stevenson.

Janet Gaynor (Esther Blodgett--later Vicki Lester); Fredric March (Norman Maine [Alfred Hinkel]); Adolphe Menjou (Oliver Niles); Andy Devine (Danny McGuire); May Robson (Granny); Lionel Stander (Libby); Owen Moore (Casey Burke); Elizabeth Jenns (Anita Regis); J. C. Nugent (Theodore Blodgett); Clara Blandick (Aunt Mattie); A. W. Sweatt (Alex); Peggy Wood (Central Casting Receptionist); Clarence Wilson (Justice of the Peace); Franklin Pangborn (Billy Moon); Jonathan Hale (Night Court Judge); Edgar Kennedy (Pop Randall); Pat Flaherty (Cuddles); Adrian Rosley (Harris the Makeup Man); Arthur Hoyt (Ward the Makeup Man); Edwin Maxwell (Voice Coach); Dr. Leonard Walker (Orchestra Leader at the Hollywood Bowl); Jed Prouty (Artie Carver); Guinn "Big Boy" Williams (Posture Coach); Trixie Friganza (Waitress); Paul Stanton (Academy Award Speaker); Olin Howland (Jud Baker the Rustic); Francis Ford, Kenneth Howell, and Chris-Pin Martin (Prisoners); Carole Landis and Lana Turner (Extras at Santa Anita Bar); Fred "Snowflake" Toones (Witness).

A Star Is Born had a rather time-worn and simplistic plot but producer David O. Selznick endowed the feature with such rich trappings that it developed into one of the most definitive reflections of Hollywood's look at itself. Tightly directed by William A. Wellman, with authentic Hollywood ambiance, Max Steiner's lush score, and gorgeous Technicolor, A Star Is Born is one of the very best of the Hollywood-on-Hollywood genre. Despite its 1954 re-make, which is more often seen of the two, the initial version is still the more highly regarded, by critics and audiences alike. (The third "version" with Barbra Streisand and Kris Kristofferson, may have grossed over $37 million since its 1976 release, but it bears only the slightest resemblance to the 1937 and 1954 editions in plot or quality.)

Director Wellman co-wrote the story about a young farm girl, Esther Blodgett (Janet Gaynor), who has aspirations of becoming a movie star and who comes to California. There she encounters fading movie idol Norman Maine (Fredric March). He becomes very protective of her and tutors her in acting. In the course of time, they fall in love and marry.

She begins the climb to film stardom which further matches his fall. By the time she wins an Academy Award he is no longer wanted for films and has become a disillusioned drunk, unable to cope with his wife's success or his own failure. After an arrest for drunken driving, which Gaynor is able to smooth over with the authorities, March overhears his former producer (Adolphe Menjou) tell Gaynor her husband is just a reflection of what he once was.

Not wanting to ruin his wife's career any further and perceiving no future for himself, March calmly walks into the ocean (the way actor John Bowers did a few years prior), committing suicide.

Both Gaynor and March were nominated for Oscars, but lost--respectively--to Luise Rainer (The Good Earth) and Spencer Tracy (Captains Courageous). Howard Barnes wrote in the New York Herald-Tribune of this classic entry, "Hollywood has turned brilliantly introspective in [this film].... The photoplay has its fabulous aspects, but through it runs a core of honesty that makes it the most remarkable account of picture making that has yet reached the stage or screen. The authors have achieved narrative substance and fidelity of detail...."

A STAR IS BORN (Warner Bros., 1954) Color, 181 min.

Producer, Sidney Luft; associate producer, Vern Alves; director, George Cukor; based on the screen story by William A. Wellman and Robert Carson; and the screenplay by Dorothy Parker, Alan Campbell, and Carson; new screenplay, Moss Hart; art director, Malcolm Bert; assistant directors, Earl Bellamy, Edward Graham, and Russell Llewellyn; choreography, Richard Barstow; songs, Harold Arlen and Ira Gershwin; Leonard Gershe; camera, Sam Leavitt; editor, Folmer Blangsted.

Judy Garland (Esther Blodgett - later Vicki Lester); James Mason (Norman Maine); Charles Bickford (Oliver Niles); Jack Carson (Matt Libby); Tommy Noonan (Danny McGuire); Lucy Marlow (Lola Lavery); Amanda Blake (Susan Ettinger); Irving Bacon (Graves); Hazel Shermet (Libby's Secretary); James Brown (Glenn Williams); Lotus Robb (Miss Markham); Joan Shawlee (Announcer); Dub Taylor (Driver); Louis Jean Heydt (Director); Bob Jellison (Eddie); Chick Chandler (Man in Car); Leonard Penn (Director); Blythe Daly (Miss Fusselow); Kathryn Card (Landlady); Willis Bouchey (McBride the Director); Olin Howland (Charley); Mae Marsh (Party Guest); Grady Sutton (Carver); Rex Evans (Master of Ceremonies); Tristram Coffin (Director); Henry Kulky (Cuddles); Frank Ferguson (Judge); Percy Helton (Gregory); Dale Van Sickel (Reporter); Nadene Ashdown (Esther at Age Six); Heidi Meadows (Esther at Age Three).

Four years after her dismissal from MGM, Judy Garland and her entrepreneur husband Sid Luft decided to refilm A Star Is Born as a musical. Garland had played the role of Vicki Lester in 1942 on "Lux Radio Theatre" opposite Walter Pidgeon. Eventually they interested Warner Bros. in the comeback project and hired Moss Hart to revamp the script. George Cukor, who had directed What Price Hollywood? (q. v.), the precursor to all the Star Is Born versions was signed to direct the vehicle. Before James Mason was contracted to reinterpret the Norman Maine role, Humphrey Bogart and Cary Grant had been the choices for the dramatic assignment.
    The CinemaScope color version opens at a benefit show with Esther Blodgett (Garland) as a band singer and alcoholic star Norman Maine (Mason) as a guest performer, he being under the watchful eye of publicist Matt Libby (Jack Carson). At the charity program Mason meets Garland and later tracks her down again as he is convinced she has talent. He talks studio mogul Oliver Niles (Charles Bickford) into giving her a screen test and it results in a contract.
    Soon she is transformed into a new personality, Vicki Lester, and rises from screen extra to a performer of a speciality number in a musical (a part given to her at Mason's insistence). It is not long before she becomes a celluloid sensation.
    By now Garland is enamored of Mason and they soon marry.

As time goes by, drink causes Mason to lose his studio contract, while Garland's career rises. Eventually she wins an Oscar. But at the formal ceremony her drunken husband makes a fool of himself and his wife in front of millions on TV.

Later the ex-star is arrested for drunken driving, but Garland manages to convince the law enforcers to free him without a jail sentence. Later Mason is sent to a sanatorium where he hopefully can be treated for his alcoholism and fits of depression. Back home one evening, he hears Bickford inform Garland that Mason is now nothing but a liability to everyone and that she should cut loose from him. Although she refuses to consider such a step, Mason takes his own action. He commits suicide by walking into the ocean.

Said one critic of the day, "A simply beautiful phenomenon-- a superb musicalized remake of a Hollywood classic, whose straight dramatization of the love of the two stars, she on the rise and he on the wane, was the finest of all inside-Hollywood films. "

The 1954 A Star Is Born grossed $6.1 million in distributors' domestic rentals. Many insist that the reason Judy Garland lost her Oscar bid for Best Actress of the Year (Grace Kelly won for The Country Girl) was that studio head Jack L. Warner had ordered many critical scenes of the musical to be deleted, robbing the public of many dramatic highlights.

Having achieved such a notable success in musicalizing a classic about Hollywood on Hollywood, in 1958 Garland was considered for a musical film version of All About Eve in which she would have played egocentric stage star Margo Channing. The project was to have been filmed at 20th Century-Fox by producer Jerry Wald. Regretfully it was shelved, although there would be a stage musical version of All About Eve entitled Applause! and starring Lauren Bacall.

The 1976 A Star Is Born, with Barbra Streisand and Kris Kristofferson dealt with the field of music and recording artists.

STAR-SPANGLED RHYTHM (Paramount, 1942) 99 min.

Associate producer, Joseph Sistrom; director, George Marshall; screenplay, Harry Tugend; music, Robert Emmett Dolan; songs, Johnny Mercer and Harold Arlen; art directors, Hans Dreier and Ernst Fegte; camera, Leo Tover and Theodor Sparkuhl; editor, Paul Weatherwax.

Betty Hutton (Polly Judson); Eddie Bracken (Jimmy Webster); Victor Moore (Pop Webster); Anne Revere (Sarah); Walter Abel (Frisbee); Cass Daley (Mimi); Macdonald Carey (Louie the Lug); Gil Lamb (Hi-Pockets); William Haade (Duffy); Bob Hope (Master of Ceremonies); Fred MacMurray, Franchot Tone, Ray Milland, and Lynne Overman (Men Playing Cards Skit); Dorothy Lamour, Veronica Lake, Paulette Goddard, Arthur Treacher, Walter Catlett, and Sterling Holloway (A

Opposite: James Mason, Charles Bickford (right), and Judy Garland in A Star Is Born (1954).

Paulette Goddard, Dorothy Lamour, and Veronica Lake in a publicity pose for Star-Spangled Rhythm (1942).

Sweater, A Sarong, and A Peekaboo Bang Number); Tom Dugan (Hitler); Paul Porcasi (Mussolini); Richard Loo (Hirohito); Alan Ladd (Scarface); Mary Martin, Dick Powell, and Golden Gate Quartette (Dreamland Number); William Bendix, Jerry Colonna, Maxine Ardell, Marjorie Deanne, Lorraine Miller, Marion Martin, and Chester Clute (Bob Hope Skit); Vera Zorina, Johnny Johnston, and Frank Faylen (Black Magic Number); Eddie "Rochester" Anderson, Katherine Dunham, Slim and Slam, and Woody Strode (Smart As a Tack Number); Susan Hayward (Genevieve--Priorities Number); Ernest Truex (Murgatroyd--Priorities Number); Marjorie Reynolds, Betty Rhodes, Dona Drake, Louise LaPlanche, Lorraine Miller, Donivee Lee, Don Castle, Frederic Henry, and Sherman Sanders (Swing Shift Number); Bing Crosby (Old Glory Number); Virginia Brissac (Lady from Iowa--Old Glory Number); Irving Bacon (New Hampshire Farmer--Old Glory Number); Matt McHugh (Man from Brooklyn--Old Glory Number); Peter Potter (Georgia Boy--Old Glory Number); Edward J. Marr (Heavy--Old Glory Number); Gary Crosby (Himself); Albert Dekker, Cecil Kellaway, Ellen Drew, Jimmy Lydon, Charles Smith, Francis

Gifford, Susanna Foster, Robert Preston, Christopher King, Alice
Kirby, and Marcella Phillips (Finale); Walter Dare Ware and Company
(Specialty Act); Cecil B. DeMille, Preston Sturges, and Ralph Murphy
(Themselves); Dorothy Granger, Barbara Pepper, Jean Phillips, and
Lynda Grey (Girls); Karin Booth (Kate); Eddie Dew and Rod Cameron
(Petty Officers).

Paramount resurrected the all-star musical revue concept,
popular a decade earlier in such films as Paramount on Parade and
Hollywood Revue of 1929, (qq. v.). This time around, however, the
idea was strung around the slender thread of a plotline and it endeav-
ored to promote the war effort, which was just beginning on a large
scale in World War II Hollywood. Practically every contract player
big and small on the lot was pressed into service for this feature,
which proved exceedingly popular. It spawned many imitations both
at Paramount and at other studios.

Sailor Jimmy Webster (Eddie Bracken) is coming home on
leave with his pals who think his father will give them a red-carpet
tour of Paramount Pictures. Actually, Bracken's dad, Pop Webster
(Victor Moore), is really the studio gateman, and not the executive
vice-president of the studio he has claimed to be. In a Lady for a
Day-type plot, studio telephone operator Polly Judson (Betty Hutton)
aids Moore in carrying off the deception and in doing so enlists practically every luminary at the facilities to take part in the charade,
even including the real studio head, Mr. Frisbee (Walter Abel). A
big finale had some of these stars staging a musical revue, culmina-
ting with Bing Crosby's "Old Glory" number.

Star-Spangled Rhythm afforded viewers a backstage look at the
Paramount lot plus a peak at many of the studio's top names doing
their "bit" for box-office duty and the Allied cause. It was 99 minutes of fun, and not nearly as tedious as other films that would follow the same format in the remainder of the war years.

STARLET! (Entertainment Ventures, 1969) Color, 100 min.

Producers, David F. Friedman and William Allen Castleman;
director, Richard Banter; story/screenplay, Friedman; assistant
director, Don Brodie; music supervisor, Billy Allen; sound, Sam
Kopetsky; camera, Paul Hipp; editor, Robert Freemantle.

Sheri Mann (Allison Jordan); Deirdre Nelson (Carol Yates);
Chris Mathis (Linda Ford); Stuart Lancaster (Kenyon Adler); John
Alderman (Phil Latio); Kathi Cole (Maxine Henning); Vincent Brian
(Forrest Barker); Jay Donohue (Jerry); Joe Gardner (Doug Davis);
Karen Nichols (Miss Scott); Clark Twelvetress (Cameraman); Paul
Wilmoth (Motorcycle Gang Leader); David Friedman, Billy Allen,
and Heaven's Devils (Themselves).

This is one of the few X-rated products made for the exploitation market that has delved into the area of film-making. Furthermore the movie actually deals with the tribulations of a young girl

(Shari Mann) as she tries to make her way in the field of sex-exploi-
tation motion pictures. As an incisive look at this level of picture
making, Starlet! is a satisfactory effort, despite its unabashed attempts at titillating the viewer's libido.

Most of the scenes for the picture were shot at the EVI pro-
duction company, the firm that produced such pornographic fare as
Trader Hornee, The Lustful Turk, 'Thar She Blows, and Love Thy
Neighbor and His Wife.

In 1969 Starlet! was one of six films seized by police in Ala-
bama as being of an obscene nature, the order for the seizure deriv-
ing from the state's then governer, Albert Brewer.

STARLIFT (Warner Bros. , 1951) 103 min.

Producer, Robert Arthur; director, Roy Del Ruth; story, John
Klorer; screenplay, Klorer and Karl Kamb; art director, Charles H.
Clarke; set decorator, G. W. Berntsen; technical advisers, Major
James G. Smith, USAF, MATS, Major George E. Andrews, USAF,
SAC; assistant director, Mel Dellar; songs, Ira Gershwin and George
Gershwin; Cole Porter; Joe Young and Jimmy Monaco; Edward Hey-
man and Dana Suesse; Sammy Cahn and Jule Styne; Irving Kahal and
Sammy Fain; Harry Ruskin and Henry Sullivan; Ruby Ralesin and Phil
Harris; Percy Faith; music director, Ray Heindorf; choreography,
LeRoy Prinz; costumes, Leah Rhodes; makeup, Gordon Bau; sound,
Francis J. Scheid; camera, Ted McCord; editor, William Ziegler.

Doris Day, Gordon MacRae, Virginia Mayo, Gene Nelson, and
Ruth Roman (Themselves); James Cagney, Gary Cooper, Virginia
Gibson, Phil Harris, Frank Lovejoy, Lucille Norman, Louella O.
Parsons, Randolph Scott, Jane Wyman, and Patrice Wymore (Guest
Stars); Janice Rule (Nell Wayne); Dick Wesson (Sergeant Mike Nolan);
Ron Hagerthy (Rick Williams); Richard Webb (Colonel Callan); Hayden
Rorke (Chaplain); Howard St. John (Steve Rogers); Ann Doran (Mrs.
Callan); Tommy Farrell (Turner); John Maxwell (George Norris); Don
Beddoe (Bob Wayne); Pat Henry (Theatre Manager); Gordon Polk
(Chief Usher); Jill Richards (Flight Nurse); William Hunt (Boy with
Cane); Elizabeth Flournoy (Army Nurse); Walter Brennan, Jr. (Dri-
ver); Dick Ryan (Doctor); James Brown (Non-Com).

With the onset of the Korean conflict in the early fifties, Hollywood rallied to the cause and resurrected the idea of the "Hollywood Canteen" and again attempted to entertain the troops with a
show, this time entitled "Hollywood's Operation Starlift. " Unfortunately this idea did not work out very well and the show closed after ex-
hausting the $5000 fund the various members of the film capital had
donated to the cause. When this Warner Bros. feature was issued--
after the demise of the operation--Time magazine found it to be
"guilty of the worst breach of good taste" since Hollywood had really
failed to support this charity in the first place; besides, the picture
made it seem as if Warner Bros. had been the sole guiding force
of the morale-boosting plan.

Starlift as a film was far from solid. The badly-acted tale

offered Janice Rule as film notable Nell Wayne, who, with Doris Day
and Ruth Roman, is making a personal appearance in San Francisco
when they meet two soldiers. One of the GI's, Rick Williams (Ron
Hagerthy), falls for Rule and the other (Dick Wesson) tells the girls
they are headed for Korea, although they are actually members of
a regular transport flight. Rule, Day, and Roman agree to accompany the boys to Travis Air Force Base where Rule bids farewell to
Hagerthy with a kiss. The movie star's appearance at the base
causes a sensation and other celebrities follow suit, putting on an
extravaganza show for the soldiers.

The whole process had been far better executed in Warners'
earlier Hollywood Canteen (q. v.).

STARS IN YOUR BACKYARD   see   PARADISE ALLEY

START CHEERING (Columbia, 1938) 79 min.

Director, Albert S. Rogell; story, Corey Ford; screenplay,
Eugene Solow; songs, Johnny Green and Ted Koehler; Charles Tobias,
Phil Baker, and Samuel Pokrass; Milton Drake and Ben Oakland; Jimmy Durante; choreography, Danny Dare; camera, Joseph Walker;
editor, Gene Havlick.

Jimmy Durante (Willie Gumbatz); Walter Connolly (Sam Lewis);
Joan Perry (Jean Worthington); Charles Starrett (Ted Crosley); Dr.
Craig E. Earle (Professor Quiz); Gertrude Niesen (Sarah); Raymond
Walburn (Dean Worthington); The Three Stooges (Themselves); Brod-
erick Crawford (Biff Gordon); Hal LeRoy (Tarzan Biddle); Ernest
Truex (Blodgett); Virginia Dale (Mabel); Chaz Chase (Shorty); Jimmy
Wallington (Announcer); Romo Vincent (Fatso); Gene Morgan (Coach
Burns); Louise Stanley (Flo); Arthur Loft (Librarian); Howard Hick-
man (Dr. Fosdick); Minerva Urecal (Miss Grimley); Arthur Loft
(Joe Green); Nick Lukats, Louie Prima & His Band, Johnny Green
& His Orchestra (Themselves).

Film star Ted Crosley (Charles Starrett) deserts the world of
Western movies to start a career as a college student, much to the
chagrin of the president (Walter Connolly) of his film company.
Connolly orders his agent (Jimmy Durante) to persuade Starrett to
return to Hollywood. At college Starrett finds he is the idol of all
the coeds and the enemy of all the male students. On the football
field he proves to be an athletic bust. By the finale, he willingly
agrees to return to the happier environs of the cinema.

Despite its programmer trappings, this pleasing entry turned
out to be "one of the funniest of the year's admittedly minor productions ... " (New York Times). With its fast-paced and active cast,
the picture was enjoyable from start to finish. Along the way it
poked fun at a movie star--out of his profession and into a world in
which he could not excell. Top-billed Durante offered one of his
most engaging screen performances as the harried agent, while
Western movie hero Starrett benefitted from a nice change of pace

as Ted Crosley.   Broderick Crawford was seen as a rather dimwitted
football player and the Three Stooges had some delightful slapstick
scenes during the proceedings.   Also entertaining were specialty numbers by radio's Professor Quiz (Dr. Craig E. Earle) and bandleader
Louie Prima.
          An interesting sidelight to the comedy is that Columbia hired
the cheering section at the University of Southern California to spell
out the title and credits by means of cards of contrasting shades.

THE STORY OF WILL ROGERS (Warner Bros. , 1952) Color, 109 min.

          Producer, Robert Arthur; director, Michael Curtiz; based on
the story "Uncle Clem's Boy" by Mrs. Will Rogers; screenplay, Stanley Roberts and Frank Davis; adaptor, John C. Moffitt; music, Victor
Young; assistant director, Sherry Shourds; art director, Edward Carrere; camera, Wilfrid M. Cline; editor, Folmer Blangsted.

          Will Rogers, Jr.   (Will Rogers); Jane Wyman (Betty Rogers);
Carl Benton Reid (Clem Rogers); Slim Pickens (Dusty Donovan); Eve
Miller (Cora Marshall); Noah Beery, Jr. (Wiley Post); James Glea-
son (Bert Lynn); Margaret Field (Maggie Mahoney [Sally Rogers]);
Brian Daly (Tom McSpadden); Steve Brodie (Dave Marshall); Jay Sil-
verheels (Joe Arrow); Pinky Tomlin (Orville); Mary Wickes (Mrs.
Foster); Richard Kean (Mr. Cavendish); Earl Lee (President Wilson);
William Forrest (Florenz Ziegfeld); Robert Scott Correll (Younger
Will, Jr.); Carol Ann Gainey (Younger Mary); Michael Gainey (Youn-
ger Jimmy/Young Will); Carol Nugent (Young Mary); Dub Taylor (Actor); Monte Blue (Delegate); Denver Dixon (Bit).

          One of the most accurate of Hollywood film biographies--but
alas one of the most slow-moving, was The Story of Will Rogers,
based on the book by the late comedian's wife.   Warner Bros. purchased the screen rights to it in 1941 but did not film the project
for a decade until Will Rogers, Jr. , agreed to star in the title role.
The young actor was a logical choice since he was not only the son
of the late celebrity (1879-1935), but also looked, sounded, and moved
a good deal like his father.   Michael Curtiz, a close friend of Will
Rogers, affectionately directed the color feature.   The production did
not touch on aspects of Rogers' movie career as much as it should
have, especially since Rogers had starred in both silents and sound
films.   He had been a top personality in the latter media until his
death in a plane crash in Alaska on August 13, 1935.
          The narrative opens with Rogers as a young cowpoke in Okla-
homa who decides on a fling in show business.   He begins in the
field with his lariat act, later adding comedy patter.   His rich father
(Carl Benton Reid) however, will have none of this and the boy's career decision causes a major rift between the two.   Will goes on the
road with his improving act, eventually transferring to vaudeville and
then winning lasting fame during the teens while on Broadway in the
various editions of the Ziegfeld Follies.   The chronicle covers his
rise to prominence as a commentator on national events and his de-

Eddie Cantor and Will Rogers, Jr., in The Story of Will Rogers (1952).

clining the nomination for President in 1932 when offered it by the Democrats. Sections of the story are devoted to his love for his wife Betty (Jane Wyman) and their happy life together. The picture concludes with the fatal plane crash that took Rogers' life and that of his close pal, aviator Wiley Post (Noah Beery, Jr.).

STRANDED (Sterling, 1927) 5443 ft.

Supervisor, Joe Rock; director, Phil Rosen; story, Anita Loos; continuity, Frances Guihan; titles, Wyndham Gittens; camera, Herbert Kirkpatrick; editor, Leotta Whytock.

Shirley Mason (Sally Simpson); William Collier, Jr. (Johnny Nash); John Miljan (Grant Payne); Florence Turner (Mrs. Simpson); Gale Henry (Lucille Lareaux); Shannon Day (Betty); Lucy Beaumont (Grandmother); Rosa Gore (Landlady).

Rural Miss Sally Simpson (Shirley Mason) is aided by her mother (Florence Turner) and her grandmother (Lucy Beaumont) in the quest for stardom in the movies, while her fiancé, Johnny Nash

(William Collier, Jr.) is against the plan. Traveling to Hollywood,
Mason finally wangles a job as a movie extra and becomes friends
with Lucille Lareaux (Gale Henry) a veteran film player.
     Meanwhile, Turner finds a job to send her daughter money.
Mason later winds up jobless but sends home letters describing her
professional success.   Finally a friend takes the heroine to meet
wealthy Grant Payne (John Miljan) who agrees to promote her cinema
career in return for sexual favors.   Declining his overtures, Mason
attempts to find movie work but fails and resorts to working in a
beanery.
     She then learns her mother needs money for an operation and
Mason is prepared to go to Miljan for the deal.   However, Collier
arrives on the Coast, having been summoned by Henry.   He beats
Miljan in a fight and thereafter Mason abandons his career ambitions.
She returns home with the man she loves.
     Based on an Anita Loos story, Stranded was a quickie effort
which rehashed the theme done earlier and better in films like The
Extra Girl (q. v.).   Here, though, the film was greatly aided by a
fine performance by Shirley Mason in the lead, as well as by the
winning Collier and perennial villain Miljan.

THE STUDIO MURDER MYSTERY (Paramount, 1929) 66 min.

     Director, Frank Tuttle; based on the novel by A. Channing
Edington and Carmen Ballen Edington; camera, Victor Milner; editor,
Merrill White.

     Doris Hill (Helen MacDonald); Neil Hamilton (Tony White);
Fredric March (Dick Hardell); Warner Oland (Anton Borka); Guy Oli-
ver (MacDonald); Florence Eldridge (Blanche Hardell); Chester Conk-
lin (George); Donald MacKenzie (Captain Coffin); Eugene Pallette
(Lieutenant Dirk); Jack Luden (Bob); Gardner James (Ted MacDonald);
E. H. Calvert (R. C. Grant); Lane Chandler (Bill Martin); Lawford
Davidson (Al Hemmings); Mary Foy (Miss O'Brien); Mischa Auer
(Grant's Secretary); Phillips Holmes (Film Star).

     When nasty actor Richard Hardell (Fredric March) is found
murdered, there are several suspects: his jealous wife (Florence
Eldridge); the film director (Warner Oland) whose wife died with
March's name as her last words; a starlet (Doris Hill) done wrong
by the late thespian; and the girl's studio-watchman father (Guy Oliver) and her brother (Gardner James), both of whom vowed revenge
for her undoing.   Detective Dirk (Eugene Pallette) is called in to
solve the case which becomes further complicated when a dummy is
switched for the corpse.   Also aiding the rotund detective in the
caper is studio gagman Tony White (Neil Hamilton), who cares very
much for Hill.   It is Hill, however, who is arrested for the crime
on circumstantial evidence and is later convicted by a jury.   But
Hamilton continues the investigation and eventually pins the crime on
the real culprit--Oland.
     Despite an excellent cast, the film was one of those early
talkies that did nothing but spout dialogue.   (A silent version of the

feature was also released.) Of interest, today, however, are the
many scenes of the Paramount studios of that time. This film provided the first of the several screen teamings of March and his actress wife Eldridge. New studio contractee Phillips Holmes had a
bit as a film star.

Photoplay magazine, which commissioned the original story
for the film and conducted the Studio Murder Mystery Contest, quite
naturally found the film "a corking melodrama, with plenty of dramatic kicks and numerous surprises." On the other hand, a more im-
partial source, Variety determined that it holds "enough interest and
suspense to get by as a fair programmer." Seen today, this 1929
entry seems badly dated, especially the attempts at jocularity.

STUNT PILOT (Monogram, 1939) 62 min.

Producer, Paul Malvern; director, George Waggner; based on
the cartoon character created by Hal Forrest; screenplay, Scott Darling and Joseph West; camera, Fred Jackman, Jr.; editor, Carl
Pierson.

John Trent (Tailspin Tommy); Marjorie Reynolds (Betty Lou);
Milburn Stone (Skeeter); Jason Robards, Sr. (Paul); Pat O'Malley
(Sheehan); George Meeker (Carl Martin); Wesley Barry (Glenn); Charles
Morton (Charlie).

Hal Forrest's popular comic strip character Tailspin Tommy
had been used in a film serial Tailspin Tommy (q. v.), which had a
few installments on moviemaking; the follow-up Tailspin Tommy and
the Great Air Mystery (1935) did not deal with the film business.
Both cliffhangers were produced by Universal and that studio, later
in the decade, began a series of films based on the character with
John Trent in the title role. A quartet of features developed, all of
them good, but the series did not catch on with adventure fans and
was soon dropped.
The second of the four entries was Stunt Pilot. Here Tommy
(Trent), along with pals Skeeter (Milburn Stone), Paul (Jason Robards,
Sr.), and Betty Lou (Marjorie Reynolds), are hired to make an air
war movie. During the production of a battle sequence, however,
someone switches the bullets in Trent's machinegun, substituting the
real things instead of blanks. As a result another flyer is killed
and Trent is accused of murdering him. The pals work together to
catch the actual killer who turns out to be the film's director.
The movie's star, Trent, was a former flyer and he added a
great deal of authenticity to the role of Tailspin Tommy. Also of
interest to movie and aviation enthusiasts is the inclusion of stock
footage from 1930's Hell's Angels, which served here for the air
battle which results in the homicide.

STUNTS (New Line Cinema, 1977) Color, 90 min.

Producers, Raymond Lofaro, and William Panzer; executive

Jason Robards, Sr. , John Trent, Marjorie Reynolds, and Milburn
Stone in Stunt Pilot (1939).

producers, Peter S. Davis and Robert Shaye; director, Mark L. Les-
ter; story, Lofaro, Shaye, and Michael Harpster; screenplay, Dennis
Johnson and Barney Cohen; music, Michael Kamen; assistant director,
Corky Ehlers; stunt coordinator, Paul Nuckles; assistant director,
Carol Olsen; camera, Daniel Pearl; special unit camera, Bob Bailin;
editor, Ehlers.

　　　　Robert Forster (Glen Wilson); Fiona Lewis (B. J. Parswell);
Joanna Cassidy (Patti); Darrell Fetty (Dave); Bruce Glover (Chuck
Johnson); Jim Luisi (Blake); Richard Lynch (Pete); Candice Rialson
(Judy); Malachi Throne (Earl); Ray Sharkey (Paul).

　　　　"The plot was corny when it was used 45 years ago for The
Lost Squadron [q. v.], but director Mark L. Lester manages to keep
Stunts lively and interesting despite its far-fetched and hackneyed
premise.... It will be evident to film buffs that what Lester is doing
here is updating the Howard Hawks style and thematic approach to
the world of contemporary film-making. Like Hawks' Only Angels
Have Wings, Hatari, and Red Line 7000, this is a tight-lipped action-
er about a male group involved in a dangerous trade, with sexy female camp followers admitted to the group once they accept the code
of grace under pressure" (Variety).

While on location in San Luis Obispo, California, making a police thriller, a film-making crew must cope with a maniac on the
loose. Among those present for the lensing are veteran, ace stunt
man Glen Wilson (Robert Forster); Chuck Johnson (Bruce Glover),
who proves to be a victim to the killer; Patti (Joanna Cassidy), the
victim's stunt lady wife, Paul (Ray Sharkey) an Italian who works
overtime in the bedroom after the day's filming; Dave (Darrell Fetty), a local man who earns a job with the troupe; the unfeeling director (Malachi Throne); producer Blake (Jim Luisi) and his trampish
wife Judy (Candice Rialson); and the special effects man (Richard
Lynch) who seems to be the culprit.
      Judging the final results, Variety decided, "While Hollywood
insider plots have proved to be commercially weak in the last couple
of years, this ... release has enough action to make it an okay exploitation item for double bills. "

SULLIVAN'S TRAVELS (Paramount, 1941) 90 min.

      Producer, Paul Jones; director/story/screenplay, Preston
Sturges; special effects, Farciot Edouart; camera, John Seitz; editor,
Stuart Gilmore.

      Joel McCrea (John L. Sullivan); Veronica Lake (The Girl);
Robert Warwick (Mr. Lebrand); William Demarest (Mr. Jones); Frank-
lin Pangborn (Mr. Casalsis); Porter Hall (Mr. Hadrian); Byron Foulger (Mr. Valdelle); Margaret Hayes (Secretary); Robert Greig (Sulli-
van's Butler); Eric Blore (Sullivan's Valet); Torben Meyer (The Doc-
tor); Victor Potel (Cameraman); Richard Webb (Radio Man); Charles
Moore (Chef); Almira Sessions (Ursula); Esther Howard (Miz Zeffie);
Frank Moran (Tough Chauffeur); George Renavent (Old Tramp); Jan
Buckingham (Mrs. Sullivan); Robert Winkler (Bud); Jimmy Conlin
(Trusty); Alan Bridge (The Mister); Harry Hayden (Mr. Carson); Wil-
lard Robertson (Judge); Edward Hearn (Cop at Beverly Hills Station);
Paul "Tiny" Newlan (Truck Driver); Monte Blue (Cop in Slums);
Dewey Robinson (Sheriff); Harry Seymour (Entertainer in Air Raid
Shelter); Chester Conklin (Old Bum); Emory Parnell (Man at Railroad
Shack).

      Preston Sturges turned out this comedy-drama on the eve of
World War II and it stands as one of the most stringent satires made
by Hollywood on the "relevant filmmaker, " the type who tries to use
the cinema for social change instead of entertainment. While the
character of John L. Sullivan (Joel McCrea), the director, was certainly relevant to that period, the film remains valid today as the industry seems glutted with such (well-meaning) types, the kind of
craftsman who prefers to educate than to entertain.
      After making a series of sugary box-office hits (e. g. , Ants
in Your Pants, 1939) director Sullivan (McCrea) decides to make a
"message" picture about poverty in America. He plans to trek across the land to learn firsthand about social conditions. On his initial travels he becomes trapped by two old maids (Almira Sessions

and Esther Howard), one of whom has lecherous designs on him. He escapes from them and lands back in Hollywood, where he meets a disillusioned young beauty (Veronica Lake) who is heading back home after an unsuccessful bid at breaking into films. He uses his car to escort her to the train station, but since he is dressed as a "bum," he is arrested. Finally he is cleared when his true identity is made known.

The girl then begs him to take her on his travels. Together they set out to discover the true meaning of poverty by living and traveling with hobos, sleeping in flophouses, etc. After returning to Hollywood, McCrea then decides to go on a "goodwill" mission and distribute $5 bills to hobos. But he is robbed and beaten. After a confrontation with a railroad yard guard, he loses his memory and is sent to work on a chain gang where he is abused. One night he and the other prisoners are shown a movie in a nearby church, and there watching a cartoon, he observes the delight it brings to others (especially these downtrodden prisoners). Finally he comprehends the real value of movies--to take one out of one's self. When McCrea finally is able to establish his identity, he is released and returns to the studio with a new slant on picture-making. He and the girl face a happy future together.

The New York Times rejoiced: "Sullivan's Travels is one of the screen's more 'significant' films. It is the best social comment made upon Hollywood since A Star Is Born" (q. v.). Reviewer Bosley Crowther added, "... [Sturges] makes pointed sport, in his own blithely mischievous way, of Hollywood's lavish excesses, of baldly staged publicity stunts and of motion picture producers whose notion of art is 'a little sex.' ... [T]his truly brilliant serio-comedy which makes fun of films with 'messages' carries its own paradoxical morals and its note of tragedy. Laughter, it says, is 'better than nothing in this cock-eyed caravan.'"

To be appreciated is Veronica Lake's refreshing performance as the practical-minded movie hopeful.

SUNSET BOULEVARD (Paramount, 1950) 110 min.

Producer, Charles Brackett; director, Billy Wilder; based on the story "A Can of Beans" by Brackett and Wilder; screenplay, Brackett, Wilder, and D. M. Marshman, Jr.; art directors, Hans Dreier and John Meehan; set decorators, Sam Comer and Ray Moyer; music, Franz Waxman; song, Jay Livingston and Ray Evans; assistant director, C. C. Coleman, Jr.; sound, Harry Lindgren and John Cope; process camera, Farciot Edouart; special camera effects, Gordon Jennings; camera, John F. Seitz; editorial supervisor, Doane Harrison; editor, Arthur Schmidt.

William Holden (Joe Gillis); Gloria Swanson (Norma Desmond); Erich von Stroheim (Max Von Mayerling); Nancy Olson (Betty Schaefer); Fred Clark (Sheldrake); Jack Webb (Artie Green); Lloyd Gough (Morino); Buster Keaton, Hedda Hopper, Cecil B. DeMille, Anna Q. Nilsson, H. B. Warner, Ray Evans, Jay Livingston, and Sidney

William Holden and Gloria Swanson in Sunset Boulevard (1950).

Skolsky (Themselves); Franklyn Farnum (Undertaker); Larry Blake
and Charles Dayton (Finance Men); Eddie Dew (Assistant Coroner);
Archie Twitchell (Salesman); Ruth Clifford (Sheldrake's Secretary);
Bert Moorhouse (Gordon Cole); E. Mason Hopper (Doctor/Courtier);
Stan Johnson and William Sheehan (Assistant Directors); Virginia
Randolph, Gertrude Astor, Frank O'Connor, and Eva Novak (Cour-
tiers); Gertrude Messinger (Hairdresser); John "Skins" Miller (Elec-
trician); Julia Faye (Hisham); Ken Christy (Captain of Homicide);
Howard Negley (Police Captain); Len Hendry (Police Sergeant); Jack
Perrin (Detective).

    "The film caused a great stir; I've never seen so many prom-
inent people at once in the projection room at Paramount as I saw
the first day they showed it.   Word was out that this was a stunner,
you see.   After the picture ended there were violent reactions--from
excitement to pure horror.   I remember Barbara Stanwyck kneeling
down in front of Miss Swanson and kissing the hem of her garment
in one of those ridiculous adulation things, and I still remember
Mr. Louis B. Mayer shaking his fist and saying, 'We should horse-
whip ... [Wilder].   We should throw him out of this town! He has
dirtied the nest!   He has brought disgrace on the town that is feeding
him!'   He was furious!   I don't know what the hell was so anti-Hol-
lywood in that picture ... " (Billy Wilder in The Celluloid Muse: Hollywood Directors Speak, by Charles Higham and Joel Greenberg, 1969).

It's difficult to accept Mr. Wilder's remark that he fails to recognize the pillorying of Hollywood's desperation, gaudiness, and insane ego that comprises Sunset Boulevard.   One of the cinema's true classics, this mirrored, distorted, and utterly fascinating look at Hollywood's past remains today, even after countess bastardizations and satirizations, Hollywood's most thorough lambasting.   The film is striking in its authenticity of detail (the marble floors, overly furnished rooms, innumerable narcissistic portraits of Norma Desmond emblazoning the decaying mansion at 10086 Sunset Boulevard*, almost morbid in its exhumation of long forsaken stars (Anna Q. Nilsson, H. B. Warner, Buster Keaton in the classic bridge game sequence and the great Erich von Stroheim as Norma's bondaged worshipper Max von Mayerling), and glorious in its casting of Gloria Swanson as the terrifying yet touching monster of ego, Norma Desmond.   It remains a brilliant study of the tragedy of a once-great star who refuses to accept the fact that she is as ancient and unwanted in the film capital as a Vitagraph one-reeler from the cinema's dawn.

Originally Wilder conceived of Sunset Boulevard as a burlesque, and envisioned Mae West playing Norma.   As the script became more and more serious, Mary Pickford and Pola Negri (the latter a very enthusiastic candidate), were considered, but it was Swanson who became, as Wilder phrases it, "the lucky choice."   Swanson was then 49 and insists today that she almost lost the part because "When they made the test, I looked about 30, 35, and I was very pleased."   The part of Joe Gillis, seedy script writer who becomes Norma's unhappy paramour, was originally written for Montgomery Clift, who withdrew at the last minute, upset at the prospect of being seen making love to an "elderly" woman.   William Holden replaced Clift, savoring the opportunity to play a heel and kill off his wholesome screen image which he disgustingly described as "Nice Willie."

The original print of Sunset Boulevard began in a Hollywood morgue, where the corpses are relating to each other the details of their deaths.   "By the time Holden has arrived, and they'd put the name tag on his big toe, people were helpless with mirth," recalls Wilder of the preview.   This footage was snipped and the release print storyline begins as police swamp the grounds of the mansion of legendary but forgotten silent screen great Norma Desmond (Swanson).   There is the body of an attractive, much younger man floating in her pool.   As the police haul the corpse of Joe Gillis (Holden) from the water with a hook, the cadaver's voice relates the story of his life and death via flashback.

Holden is a third-rate screenwriter, long out of work, who is trying to escape a finance company bent on repossessing his car.

---

*Though Hollywood tour buses still point out to the unknowing patrons "the house of Norma Desmond from Sunset Boulevard" Wilder himself has remarked, "The Norma Desmond house was on the corner of Wilshire and Cranshaw, and it's been torn down and replaced by Tidewater Oil.   It was the house of the richest man in the world, Mr. Paul Getty.   We had to put the rats in the pool ... ugh!"

A flat tire forces him to pull off Sunset Boulevard to hide in an old mansion's garage, as the repossessors give chase.   At first he thinks the house is deserted, but a stiff, Teutonic butler, Max von Mayerling (von Stroheim) arrives and invites Holden inside.   When the grand mistress of the manse makes an appearance, Holden learns why he has been given entrance: the woman's pet monkey has died and Holden is thought to be the undertaker.   The gaffe revealed, Holden is ordered to leave--that is until he recognizes his hostess.   "You're Norma Desmond!   You used to be in silent pictures.   You used to be big. "   "I am big!" roars Swanson.   "It's the pictures that got small. "

Learning that Holden is a film writer, she asks him to read through her script for a long-dreamed-of comeback project, Salome. Realizing that there is money to be made here, Holden agrees.   Before long, he becomes Swanson's lover and factotum, eager to cash in on her shrewdly invested fortune.   He is willing to temporarily overlook her bizarre nature and her destructive impulses--which force von Stroheim to take locks off all the doors and keep sharp objects unavailable.

The death knell for the Swanson-Holden affair begins its toll when Desmond receives a call from the office of Cecil B. DeMille, her old Paramount mentor.   She believes he wants to discuss producing the epic Salome; in actuality, his office only wants to rent her antique car as a period set piece.   In addition, Holden is attracted to Betty Schaefer (Nancy Olson), a blonde contract writer at Paramount.   When Swanson learns of this, she steals a razor and slashes her wrists.   Holden returns and the distraught ex-star is patched up and comforted.

However, Holden, sickened by the tragedy of von Stroheim (who reveals himself to be a once great director and former husband of Swanson's, having sacrificed all to become a virtual slave to her), the gloominess of the mansion, and the growing lunacy of Swanson, is now determined to reveal all to Olson, and leaves the "tomb. " Swanson follows him outside and fatally shoots him.   He plunges into the freshly-filled pool.

The next day Hollywood is agog over the killing.   Police and columnists (including the ubiquitous Hedda Hopper) arrive at the mansion, where Swanson, having slipped into total madness, believes she is about to star in a big scene for her comeback picture.   She enters the balcony area above the swarm of reporters and police, and as she notes the newsreel cameras focused on her, von Stroheim--ever sympathetic--barks, "This is the staircase of the palace!"   Following the butler/director's lead, she descends, stops the "scene, " and speaks, "I can't go on with the scene.   I'm too happy!   Mr. DeMille, do you mind if I say a few words?   Thank you.   I just want to tell you all how happy I am to be back in the studio, making a picture again! You don't know how much I've missed all of you.   And I promise you, I'll never desert you again!   Because after Salome we'll make another picture and another picture!   You see, this is my life!   It always will be!   There's nothing else ... just us ... and the cameras ... and those wonderful people out there in the dark.   All right Mr. DeMille, I'm ready for my close-up. "   And Swanson's Norma

Desmond, advancing her grotesquely made-up face and chillingly dramatic expression into the camera, fades into the screen and into the total oblivion of insanity.

For Swanson, Sunset Boulevard was the apex of her screen career.   She reaped her third Academy Award nomination (losing to Judy Holliday of Born Yesterday) and won the New York Film Critics Award for her stunning performance which many still believe to be the real Swanson.   Though she blissfully dominated the film, Holden, von Stroheim, and Olson were all pungently and respectively caddish, bizarre, and appealing, with each player also winning an Oscar nomination.   Sunset Boulevard itself was Academy-nominated for Best Picture (it lost to All About Eve) and won the number one spot on the National Board of Review's Ten Best List of 1950.

As a result of its enormous critical and popular success, Sunset Boulevard spawned a raft of Hollywood films examining filmdom's decadent past, but to date, none have been as biting, frank, or just plain entertaining as Sunset Boulevard.

SUPER-SLEUTH (RKO, 1937) 75 min.

Producer, Edward Small; director, Ben Stoloff; based on the play by Harry Segall; screenplay, Gertrude Purcell and Ernest Pagano; assistant director, Kenny Holmes; special effects, Vernon L. Walker; camera, Joseph H. August; editor, William Hamilton.

Jack Oakie (Bill Martin); Ann Sothern (Mary Strand); Eduardo Ciannelli (Professor Herman); Alan Bruce (Larry Frank); Edgar Kennedy (Lieutenant Garrison); Joan Woodbury (Doris Dunne); Bradley Page (Ralph Waring); Paul Guilfoyle (Gibbons); Willie Best (Warts); William Corson (Beckett); Alec Craig (Eddie the Doorman); Richard Lane (Barker); Paul Hurst (Motorcycle Cop); George Rosener (Policeman); Fred Kelsey (Jailer); Robert Emmett O'Connor (Casey); Phillip Morris (Sullivan); Dick Rush (Grimes).

Champion movie star Bill Martin (Jack Oakie), who specializes in detective and mystery films, takes it upon himself to solve the Poison Pen mysteries which had been plaguing the Los Angeles police. Since he has been "trained" by the movies to solve crimes, and since he believes his own press releases, Oakie sets forth on the self-appointed task.   His reward is to receive a Poison Pen note informing him he better drop the investigation, and besides, his last movie was dreadful.   Later the Poison Pen attempts to shoot Oakie but misses.   Meanwhile, Mary Strand (Ann Sothern), head of the studio's publicity department and in love with Oakie, is sent on the actor's trail to woo him back before the cameras.   In the interim, naive Oakie chooses for his ally the very man who is the Poison Pen culprit.   Eventually--and quite by accident--the dim-witted film star unmasks the villain.

Oakie had a field day in the role of Bill Martin and the resulting film was "an amusing bit of nonsense" (New York Times). With many of the picture's scenes set within the film studio, Super-Sleuth managed to capture a nice flavor of the Hollywood milieu.

SWEET BIRD OF YOUTH (MGM, 1962) Color, 120 min.

Producer, Pandro S. Berman; associate producer, Kathryn
Hereford; director, Richard Brooks; based on the play by Tennessee
Williams; screenplay, Brooks; art directors, George W. Davis and
Urie McCleary; set decorators, Henry Grace and Hugh Hunt; music
supervisor, Harold Gelman; music director, Robert Armbruster;
makeup, William Tuttle; color consultant, Charles K. Hagedon; cos-
tumes, Orry-Kelly; sound, Franklin Milton; special camera effects,
Lee Le Blanc; camera, Milton Krasner; editor, Henry Berman.

Paul Newman (Chance Wayne); Geraldine Page (Alexandra Del
Lago); Shirley Knight (Heavenly Finley); Ed Begley ("Boss" Finley);
Rip Torn (Thomas J. Finley, Jr.); Mildred Dunnock (Aunt Nonnie);
Madeleine Sherwood (Miss Lucy); Philip Abbott (Dr. George Scudder);
Corey Allen (Scotty); Barry Cahill (Bud); Dub Taylor (Dan Hatcher);
James Douglas (Leroy); Barry Atwater (Ben Jackson); Charles Arnt
(Mayor Henricks); Dorothy Konrad (Mrs. Maribelle Norris); James
Chandler (Professor Burtus H. Smith); Mike Steen (Deputy); Kelly
Thordsen (Sheriff Clark).

When this Tennessee Williams opus first appeared on Broadway in March 1959, it was a tortuous duel of the minds between the
two focal characters, an aging gigolo (Paul Newman) attempting to
break into the movies and a has-been film star (Geraldine Page) now
on dope. The drama concluded with the gigolo's being castrated for
a violation of the governor's daughter, while the ex-star was run out
of town to the promise of an unhappy future. By the time the compelling theatre piece reached the screen, the finale had been white-
washed. It made all that came before seem to be no more than one
long argument between two self-indulgent down-and-outers.

Sweet Bird of Youth is set in a small Southern town which
happens to be the home of Chance Wayne (Newman), a one-time local
high school hero who had wandered off to Hollywood looking for easy
success. He ended up as a beach boy at a swim club. Not too long
before the story opens, he has latched onto Alexandra Del Lago (Page),
a fading movie queen who finds compensation in booze, dope, sex,
and her oxygen tank. The two begin their bleak travels together.
Newman's chief desire is to ferret out enough information on Page
to blackmail her into pushing him into films.

Newman has returned home to see his loyal, bird-like Aunt
Nonnie (Mildred Dunnock) and there re-meets his high school sweetheart, Heavenly Finley (Shirley Knight) the daughter of the state's
biggest politician, Boss Finley (Ed Begley). Years before, when the
girl was 14, Newman had ended her virginity and the governor had
him thrown out of town. The stud was warned that if he ever came
back, he would indeed be sorry. Knight's brother (Rip Torn) reports
back to their father that Newman is back. After a confrontation with
Begley, in which he tells him his hopes to wed Knight, Newman is
badly beaten and his face scarred. It ends his chances for a movie
career and a life with his childhood sweetheart. For Page, the future
is not so bad. She learns that her last film was not a bust (there is

a captivating flashback to her leaving the premiere in embarrassment),
and that her career may well be on the upswing. She deserts the
no-longer attractive Newman and returns to the West Coast.
Time magazine noted, "... the picture belongs to Actress
Page. She swirls to the girls' room as if to a coronation, she cuddles her oxygen mask as a normal woman might cuddle a newborn
babe, she dimples in maidenly dither at her gigolo's advances, she
proceeds a moment later with hard-nosed efficiency to collect what
she has paid for. She is a mascaraed monument to the era of the
superstar, a veritable muse of publicity. " Ed Begley would win a
Best Supporting Actor's Oscar for his role in Sweet Bird of Youth;
Page lost the Best Actress Award to Anne Bancroft (The Miracle
Worker), and Knight was beaten in the Best Supporting Actress category by Patty Duke (The Miracle Worker).

SWINGTIME IN THE MOVIES see THE SHORT FILMS

TAILSPIN TOMMY (Universal, 1934) 12 chapters.

Director, Louis Friedlander [Lew Landers]; based on the cartoon strip by Hal Forrest; screenplay, Norman S. Hall, Vin Moore,
Basil Dickey, and Ella O'Neill.

Maurice Murphy (Tailspin Tommy Tompkins); Patricia Farr
(Betty Lou Barnes); Noah Beery, Jr. (Skeeter); Belle Daube (Mrs.
Tompkins); Lee Beggs (Deacon Grimes); Grant Withers (Milt Howe);
Walter Miller (Bruce Hoyt); Charles A. Browne (Paul Smith); Edmund Cobb (Speed Walton); John Davidson (Tiger Taggart); Monte Montague (Cliff); Jack Leonard (Al); Bud Osborne (Grease Rowley); William Desmond (Sloane).

Chapters: 1) Death Flies the Mail; 2) The Mail Goes Through;
3) Sky Bandits; 4) The Copper Room; 5) The Night Flight; 6) The
Baited Trap; 7) Tommy to the Rescue; 8) The Thrill of Death; 9)
The Earth Gods Roar; 10) Death at the Controls; 11) Rushing Waters;
12) Littleville's Big Day.

This 12 chapter serial was based on Hal Forrest's comic strip
and proved to be the only sound cliffhanger to have a movie theme
incorporated within its (sub) plot. Why the serial genre almost completely overlooked the Hollywood motif is a mystery, since using
studio facilities as backdrops would have cut the costs of such productions even further. The only silent serial to really deal with the
cinema was The Third Eye (q. v.).
Set in Littleville, the narrative tells of the many adventures
of Tailspin Tommy Tompkins (Maurice Murphy), a youthful mechanic

Opposite: Paul Newman and Geraldine Page in Sweet Bird of
Youth (1962).

who is hired by pilot Milton Howe (Grant Withers) and his partners
at the Three Points Airline to help them in a race to win a mail
contract. In doing so, Murphy becomes an enemy of Tiger Taggart
(John Davidson) who wants the government contract for his own outfit.
Soon Murphy is also a pilot with Three Points and he is in constant
battle with Davidson and his aerial pirates.

Along the way, Murphy saves a group of children by stopping
a runaway plane, prevents a train wreck, and escapes several attempts
at sabotage instigated by Davidson's chief henchman, Bruce Hoyt (Walter Miller). Finally, a famous movie producer hires Murphy to make
an aerial movie and obtains backing for the production from the owners of the Three Points Airline who mortgage their property to get
the funds. Davidson then tries to shut down the filming, hoping to
take over the mortgage. The villain arranges for Miller to bomb an expensive set. Murphy learns of the scheme, however, and follows Miller
and photographs the sabotage for use in the movie. Then he rounds up
Davidson and his gang after Miller's plane tailspins and crashes.

In the late thirties, Universal would make four features concerning Tailspin Tommy; one of them, Stunt Pilot (q. v.), dealt with
moviemaking.

TALENT SCOUT (Warner Bros. , 1937) 67 min.

Director, William Clemens; story, George Bilson; screenplay,
Bilson and William Jacobs; song, M. K. Jerome and Jack Scholl;
camera, Rex Wimpy; editor, Terry Morse.

Donald Woods (Steve Stewart); Jeanne Madden (Doris Pierce
[Mary Brannigan]); Fred Lawrence (Raymond Crane); Rosalind Mar-
quis (Bernice Fox); Joseph Crehan (A. J. Lambert); Charles Halton
(M. B. Carter); Teddy Hart (Moe Jerome); Mary Treen (Janet Mor-
ris); Al Herman (Jack School); Helen Valkis (Ruth); John Pearson
(Jed Hudkins); Frank Faylen (Master of Ceremonies); John Harron
(Charlie); Mary Doyle (Miss Grant); Harry Fox (Robert Donnolly);
Joan Blondell, Patricia Ellis, and Allen Jenkins (Nightclub Patrons);
Paul Panzer (Bit).

"Everything about this piece of make believe has the stamp
of the quick once over, and lightly" (Variety).
Talent scout Steve Stewart (Donald Woods) discovers Mary
Brannigan (Jeanne Madden) and believes she is screen star material.
He maneuvers her a movie test at Apex Pictures (from which he has
been fired) but she flops. However, a later club singing date for
the small-town girl leads to a celluloid audition and this time she
is approved by studio executives. Meanwhile publicist Woods, who
is falling in love with Madden--renamed Doris Pierce, the "sweet-
heart of the movies"--arranges for her to date screen lead Raymond
Crane (Fred Lawrence). The fabricated romance evolves into the
real thing, and Woods must stand on the sidelines while Madden and
Lawrence wed.
Of interest today is the nightclub scene which reveals Joan
Blondell, Allen Jenkins, and Patricia Ellis among the ringsiders.

Paul Panzer (moustache), Fred Lawrence, and Jeanne Madden in
Talent Scout (1937).

THE TALK OF HOLLYWOOD (Sono Art-World Wide, 1929) 6586 ft.

Presenters, Samuel Zierler and Harry H. Thomas; director,
Mark Sandrich; story, Sandrich and Nat Carr; dialogue, Darby Aaron-
son; sound, George Osthmann and John Dolan; camera, Walter
Strenge; editor, Russell Shields.

Nat Carr (J. Pierpont Ginsburg); Fay Marbé (Adore Renee);
Hope Sutherland (Ruth); Sherline Oliver (John Applegate); Edward Le
Saint (Edward Hamilton); Gilbert Marbé (Reginald Whitlock); John
Troughton (Butler); Goodman and His Orchestra and the Leonidoff
Ballet (Themselves).

This early talkie was perhaps the first sound feature to aim
its targets at Hollywood and it chose a most topical facet--the transition from silent pictures to sound ones and the inherent problems
therein.   Unfortunately the picture itself was as static as the situation
it was kidding.   It led Photoplay magazine to write, "This would be
the talk of any town--it's so bad.   Intended as a comedy, it evolves
a tragedy." The film also included a most cruel dig--it satirized
the temperamental movie star type, with a character called Adore
Renee, hardly much of a coverup for French actress Renee Adoree,
whose career was destroyed by sound films and who died in the early
thirties.

Producer J. Pierpont Ginsburg (Nat Carr) intends to make a

successful talking film in order to raise enough money to pay for his
daughter's expensive wedding to a lawyer.   He hires a noted film actress to head the cast (Fay Marbé), but she fails to appear at the
shooting.   Also, wrong actors are brought in, and the production is
continually delayed.   Finally filming gets underway; but after a day
of what seemed to be satisfactory shooting, it is learned that the
soundstage microphones were not working properly.   Eventually the
film is completed, but at a preview, the drunk projectionist mixes
up the reels, and the showing is a disaster.   The distributors are
uninterested in the property, except for one man with a sense of
humor, who regards the effort as an out-and-out takeoff on talkies.
He orders many prints of the film and through him the movie is a
huge success.

TARGETS (Paramount, 1968) Color, 90 min.

Producer, Peter Bogdanovich; associate producer, Daniel Selznick; director, Bogdanovich; story, Polly Platt and Bogdanovich;
screenplay, Bogdanovich; production designer, Platt; sound, Sam
Koeptzky; camera, Laszlo Kovacs.

Boris Karloff (Byron Orlok); Tim O'Kelly (Bobby Thompson);
Nancy Hsueh (Jenny); James Brown (Robert Thompson, Sr.); Sandy
Baron (Kip Larkin); Arthur Peterson (Ed Loughlin); Mary Jackson
(Charlotte Thompson); Tanya Morgan (Ilene Thompson); Monty Landis
(Marshall Smith); Paul Condylis (Drive-In Manager); Mark Dennis
(Salesman in Second Gun Shop); Stafford Morgan (Salesman in First
Gun Shop); Peter Bogdanovich (Sammy Michaels); Daniel Ades (Chauf-
feur); Tim Burns (Walter); Warren White (Grocery Boy); Geraldine
Baron (Larkin's Girl); Mike Farrell (Man in Phone Booth); Jay Daniel
(Snack Bar Attendant); James Morris (Man with Pistol).

In this release Hollywood examines the confusion of movie
fiction with real life.   Would you believe a killer was captured because he thought a movie monster came to life to hunt him as he
stalks his potential victims?
The storyline begins as youthful filmmaker Sammy Michaels
(Peter Bogdanovich) attempts to convince aged horror movie star
Byron Orlok (Boris Karloff) to make a low-budget terror picture for
him.   Karloff, however, will have none of the project; insisting he
is tired of selling his name to make low-grade quickies and that real
horror is far more significant in today's world than the foolish monsters he has portrayed on the screen.   Finally, though, he does
agree to make a personal appearance at a drive-in theatre exhibiting
one of his recent efforts.   At the open-air cinema is Bobby Thompson
(Tim O'Kelly), a clean-cut young man, who earlier in the day had
lost control and shot his wife, father, a grocery boy, and a number

Opposite: Fay Marbé, Hope Sutherland, and Nat Carr in The Talk
of Hollywood (1929).

Nancy Hsueh and Peter Bogdanovich in Targets (1968).

___

of motorists.   He had escaped from his perch on the top of a huge
gas tank and come to the drive-in to continue his sniper activities,
taking a stand on the screen tower.

Soon after Karloff arrives for the festivities, O'Kelly begins
his random killings again.   Karloff, however, gains entry into the
young man's sanctuary and confronts him.   The sight of the living
monster man so frightens the sniper that he lapses into a catatonic
state; the reign of terror is over.

Writer-director Bogdanovich (who also played the young director in Targets) made this feature in 25 days at a cost of $130,000,
using a five-day commitment for Boris Karloff's services which he
had purchased from Roger Corman.   This scenario was based on an
actual sniper spree incident in Texas in 1966.   The Paramount release contained footage of Karloff in Corman's The Terror (1963) and
from an earlier film, The Criminal Code (1930)--employed to give
the new project "scenes" from prior Byron Orlok footage.

The role of Orlok was perhaps Karloff's finest screen portrayal.   When Targets was first released, Paramount added an anti-gun
prologue which would be deleted upon later distribution, once the film
had gained critical praise for its stark substance and for Karloff's
performance in particular.

In New York magazine, Judith Crist lauded the two portraitures
offered in this film, "We get a good look at a segment of the moviemaking world through the star, his colleagues and his entourage; we
get a thorough look at the 'normal' aspects of middle-class family
life, the non-communication of the family that lives together with
mechanical comforts and constantly blaring radio or television sets
to fill the silences that might be used for talk or thought or even a
close look at another human being."

When Targets was issued in Great Britain, 14 minutes were
shorn from the running time.

THE TEXAS STREAK (Universal, 1926) 6259 ft.

Presenter, Carl Laemmle; director/story/screenplay, Lynn
Reynolds; camera, Edward Newman.

Hoot Gibson (Chad Pennington); Blanche Mehaffey (Amy Hollis);
Alan Roscoe (Jefferson Powell); James Marcus (Colonel Hollis); Jack
Curtis (Jiggs Cassidy); George "Slim" Summerville (Swede Sonberg);
Les Bates (Pat Casey); Jack Murphy (Jimmy Hollis); William H.
Turner (Charles Logan).

Tom Mix kidded the motion pictures in some of his early
short films for Selig, such as Sagebrush Tom (1915) and A Mix-Up
in Movies and Shooting Up the Movies (both 1916). Other than these
Mix shorts the Western film genre did not often interpolate a movie
plot within its confines. Then came Hoot Gibson's The Texas Streak,
made as part of his popular oater series for Universal.

Here hard-riding Chad Pennington (Gibson) and his pals (Slim
Summerville and Jack Curtis) are extras working for a movie outfit
shooting on location in Arizona. They lose their railroad tickets and
are stranded in the area. Gibson takes a job as a guard for a sur-
veying company, and winds up involved with local ranchers' difficul-
ties over water rights. He soon is bewitched by the comely daughter
(Blanche Mahffey) of one of the ranchers (James Marcus) and attempts
to solve the troubles. He finally accomplishes his mission; rounding
up the culprit. As a result he wins the girl's hand in marriage.
Due to the publicity surrounding his accomplishments, he is given
a contract by a movie studio to star in Westerns.

THANK YOUR LUCKY STARS (Warner Bros, 1943) 127 min.

Producer, Mark Hellinger; director, David Butler; story,
Everett Freeman and Arthur Schwartz; screenplay, Norman Panama,
Melvin Frank, and James V. Kern; songs, Arthur Schwartz and
Frank Loesser; orchestral arranger, Ray Heindorf; music adaptor,
Heinz Roemheld; orchestrator, Maurice de Packh; vocal arranger,
Dudley Chambers; choreography, LeRoy Prinz; assistant director,
Phil Quinn; art directors, Anton Grot and Leo K. Kuter; set deco-
rator, Walter F. Tilford; gowns, Milo Anderson; makeup, Perc West-

Eddie Cantor in Thank Your Lucky Stars (1943).

more; sound, Francis J. Scheid and Charles David Forrest; special
effects, H. F. Koenekamp; camera, Arthur Edeson; editor, Irene
Morra.

Eddie Cantor (Himself/Joe Simpson); Joan Leslie (Pat Dixon);
Dennis Morgan (Tommy Randolph); Humphrey Bogart, Bette Davis,
Olivia de Havilland, Errol Flynn, John Garfield, Ida Lupino, Ann
Sheridan, Dinah Shore, Alexis Smith, Spike Jones & His City Slick-
ers, Jack Carson, Alan Hale, and George Tobias (Themselves); S. Z.
Sakall (Dr. Schlenna); Hattie McDaniel (Gossip); Ruth Donnelly (Nurse
Hamilton); Edward Everett Horton (Farnsworth); Joyce Reynolds (Girl
with Book); Richard Lane (Barney Jackson); Don Wilson (Announcer);
Henry Armetta (Angelo); Willie Best (Soldier); Jack Mower and Creigh-
ton Hale (Engineers); Frank Faylen (Sailor); Mike Mazurki (Olaf);
Noble Johnson (Charlie the Indian); Marjorie Hoshelle and Anne O'Neal
(Maids); Mary Treen (Fan); James Burke (Interne Guard); Boyd Ir-
win (Man); Errol Flynn Number: Monte Blue, Fred Kelsey, Bobby
Hale, Buster Wiles, Henry Iblings, Dudley Kuzelle and Ted Billings
(Pub Characters).

This was Warner Bros'. big wartime extravaganza which
boasted every major star on the lot in cameo appearances.   Despite
the sugar-thin plot and the vaudeville nature of the proceedings, it
adds up to 127 minutes of very pleasant entertainment.
    Singer Tommy Randolph (Dennis Morgan) and his girlfriend/
songwriter Pat Dixon (Joan Leslie) are blessed with a none-too-bright
cabdriver friend (Eddie Cantor).   Their major aim is to get Morgan
into show business.   Fortunately the cabbie is a dead ringer for Eddie Cantor and he convinces two producers putting on a wartime benefit show that he is really the banjo-eyed star, and that Morgan is
his protégé.   Believing the taxi driver, the producers hire Morgan
for the program.   Meanwhile the real Cantor tries to take over the
show and causes so much havoc that the producers have him abducted
and committed to a hospital.   Naturally Cantor escapes and arrives
at the show just as Morgan is about to do his stint.   The young
vocalist is such a hit that Cantor gladly accepts the acclaim for having
"discovered" him.
    Fortunately the sticky plot was surrounded by many solid num-
bers performed excellently by the Warners' stable of personalities.
The best in the lot were: "Ice Cold Katie" featuring Hattie McDaniel
and Willie Best, Bette Davis' rendition of "They're Either Too Young
or Too Old," Jack Carson and Alan Hale's hammy routine, "Goin'
North," and Errol Flynn singing "That's What You Jolly Well Get."
    James Agee wrote in The Nation, "Thank Your Lucky Stars is
the loudest and most vulgar of the current musicals.   It is also the
most fun, if you are amused when show people kid their own idiom...."

THAT'S ENTERTAINMENT! [part I] (MGM/United Artists, 1974) Color,
    132 min.

Executive producer, Daniel Melnick; producer/director/script,

Elizabeth Taylor in <u>That's Entertainment!</u> (1974).

Jack Haley, Jr.; additional music adaptor, Henry Mancini; music
supervisor, Jesse Kaye; assistant directors, Richard Bremerkamp,
David Silver, and Claude Binyon, Jr.; film librarian, Mort Feinstein;
sound re-recording, Hal Watkins, Aaron Rochin, Lyle Burbridge,
Harry W. Tetrick, and William L. McCaughey; camera, Gene Polito,
Ernest Laszlo, Russell Metty, Ennio Guarnieri, and Allan Green;
opticals, Robert Hoag and Jim Liles; editors, Bud Friedgen and David
E. Blewitt.

Fred Astaire, Bing Crosby, Gene Kelly, Peter Lawford, Liza
Minnelli, Donald O'Connor, Debbie Reynolds, Mickey Rooney, Frank
Sinatra, James Stewart, and Elizabeth Taylor (Narrators/Hosts).

Extracts from: The Hollywood Revue ("Singin' in the Rain"--
Cliff Edwards); Speak Easily ("Singin' in the Rain"--Jimmy Durante);
Little Nellie Kelly ("Singin' in the Rain"--Judy Garland); Singin' in
the Rain ("Singin' in the Rain"--Gene Kelly, Donald O'Connor, and
Debbie Reynolds); Broadway Melody ("Broadway Melody"--Charles
King); Rosalie ("Rosalie"--Eleanor Powell); Rose-Marie ("Indian Love
Call "--Jeanette MacDonald and Nelson Eddy); The Great Ziegfeld ("A
Pretty Girl Is Like a Melody"--Dennis Morgan (dubbed by Allan Jones)
and Virginia Bruce); Broadway Melody of 1940 ("Begin the Beguine"--
Fred Astaire and Eleanor Powell); It Happened in Brooklyn ("The
Song's Gotta Come from the Heart"--Frank Sinatra and Jimmy Dur-
ante); Cynthia ("Melody of Spring"--Elizabeth Taylor); Thousands
Cheer ("Honeysuckle Rose"--Lena Horne); Take Me Out to the Ball
Game ("Take Me Out to the Ball Game"--Frank Sinatra and Gene
Kelly); Words and Music ("Thou Swell"--June Allyson); Good News
("Varsity Drag" and "French Lesson"--June Allyson and Peter Law-
ford); Two Weeks with Love ("Aba Daba Honeymoon"--Debbie Rey-
nolds and Carleton Carpenter); A Date With Judy ("It's a Most Unusual Day"--Elizabeth Taylor, Jane Powell, Wallace Beery, Selena
Royle, Robert Stack, George Cleveland, Scotty Beckett, Jerry Hunter,
and Leon Ames); The Harvey Girls ("On the Atcheson, Topeka and
Santa Fe"--Judy Garland and Ray Bolger); Free and Easy ("It Must
Be You"--Robert Montgomery and Lottice Howell); The Hollywood Revue ("I've Got a Feelin' for You"--Joan Crawford); Reckless ("Reckless"--Jean Harlow (dubbed by Virginia Verrell)); Suzy ("Did I Remember"--Jean Harlow and Cary Grant); Born to Dance ("Easy to
Love"--James Stewart and Eleanor Powell); Idiot's Delight ("Puttin'
on the Ritz"--Clark Gable); Broadway to Hollywood (montage dance
number--Mickey Rooney); Broadway Melody of 1938 ("You Made Me
Love You"--Judy Garland); Babes in Arms ("Babes in Arms"--Doug-
las McPhail and Chorus); Babes on Broadway ("Hoedown"--Judy Gar-
land and Mickey Rooney); Strike Up the Band ("Do the La Conga"--Judy
Garland and Mickey Rooney); Babes on Broadway ("Waitin' for the
Robert E. Lee" and "Babes on Broadway"--Judy Garland and Mickey
Rooney); Strike Up the Band ("Strike Up the Band"--Judy Garland
and Mickey Rooney); Ziegfeld Follies ("The Babbitt and the Bromide"--
Gene Kelly and Fred Astaire); The Barkleys of Broadway ("They
Can't Take That Away from Me"--Fred Astaire and Ginger Rogers);
Dancing Lady ("Rhythm of the Day"--Fred Astaire and Joan Crawford);

The Band Wagon ("I Guess I'll Have to Change My Plans"--Fred
Astaire and Jack Buchanan); Royal Wedding ("Sunday Jumps"--Fred
Astaire); The Barkleys of Broadway ("Shoes with Wings On"--Fred
Astaire); Royal Wedding ("You're All the World to Me"--Fred Astaire);
The Band Wagon ("Dancing in the Dark"--Fred Astaire and Cyd Cha-
risse); Pagan Love Song ("Pagan Love Song"--Esther Williams); Bath-
ing Beauty (production number--Esther Williams); Million Dollar Mer-
maid (production number--Esther Williams); Three Little Words
["I Wanna Be Loved by You"--Debbie Reynolds (dubbed by Helen
Kane) and Carleton Carpenter]; Small Town Girl ("I Gotta Hear That
Beat"--Ann Miller); The Toast of New Orleans ("Be My Love"--
Mario Lanza and Kathryn Grayson); Singin' in the Rain ("Make 'em
Laugh"--Donald O'Connor); Show Boat ("Cotton Blossom"--cast; "Make
Believe"--Kathryn Grayson and Howard Keel; "Ol' Man River"--Wil-
liam Warfield); The Band Wagon ("By Myself"--Fred Astaire); The
Pirate ("Be a Clown"--Gene Kelly and the Nicholas Brothers); Living
in a Big Way (dance number--Gene Kelly); The Pirate ("Mack the
Black"--Gene Kelly); On the Town ("New York, New York"--Frank
Sinatra, Gene Kelly, and Jules Munshin); Anchors Aweigh ("The Wor-
ry Song"--Gene Kelly and Jerry the Mouse); Singin' in the Rain ("Sing-
in' in the Rain" and "Broadway Melody"--Gene Kelly); In the Good Old
Summertime ("In the Good Old Summertime"--Judy Garland, Van
Johnson, and Liza Minnelli); La Fiesta Santa Barbara ("La Cucaracha"
--The Gumm Sisters with Judy Garland); Every Sunday ("Opera Ver-
sus Jazz"--Judy Garland and Deanna Durbin); Broadway Melody of
1938 (dance--Judy Garland and Buddy Ebsen); The Wizard of Oz ("We're
Off to See the Wizard"--Judy Garland; "If I Only Had a Brain"--
Judy Garland, Ray Bolger, Jack Haley, and Bert Lahr; "Over the
Rainbow"--Judy Garland); Meet Me in St. Louis ("The Trolley Song"--
Judy Garland; "Under the Bamboo Tree"--Judy Garland and Margaret
O'Brien; "The Boy Next Door"--Judy Garland); Summer Stock ("Get
Happy"--Judy Garland); Going Hollywood ("Going Hollywood"--Bing
Crosby); High Society ("Well, Did You Ever?"--Bing Crosby and
Frank Sinatra; "True Love"--Bing Crosby and Grace Kelly); Hit the
Deck ("Hallelujah"--Kay Armen, Debbie Reynolds, Jane Powell, Ann
Miller, Tony Martin, Russ Tamblyn, and Vic Damone); Seven Brides
for Seven Brothers ("Barn-Raising Ballet"--cast); Gigi ("Gigi"--Louis
Jourdan; "Thank Heaven for Little Girls"--Maurice Chevalier); An
American in Paris ("An American in Paris"--Gene Kelly and Leslie
Caron).

THAT'S ENTERTAINMENT: Part II (MGM/United Artists, 1976) Color,
133 min.

Producers, Saul Chaplin and Daniel Melnick; new sequences
director, Gene Kelly; commentary, Leonard Gershe; production designer, John De Cuir; music director/music arranger, Nelson Riddle; music supervisor, Harry V. Lojewski; special lyrics, Howard
Dietz and Saul Chaplin; assistant director, William R. Poole; animators, Hanna-Barbera Productions; sound, Bill Edmondson; sound re-
recording, Hal Watkins and Aaron Rochin; camera, George Folsey;
editors, Bud Friedgen and David Blewitt; contributing editors, David
Bretherton and Peter C. Johnson.

Fred Astaire, Gene Kelly, and Sammy Cahn (Hosts).

Extracts from: The Band Wagon ("That's Entertainment"--
Fred Astaire, Nanette Fabray, Oscar Levant, Jack Buchanan, and Cyd
Charisse; "Triplets"--Astaire, Fabray, and Buchanan); For Me and My
Gal ("For Me and My Gal"--Judy Garland and Gene Kelly); Lady Be
Good ("Fascinatin 'Rhythm"--Eleanor Powell; Broadway Melody of
1936 ("I've Got a Feeling You're Fooling"--Robert Taylor); Two-
Faced Woman ("La Chica Chaca"--Greta Garbo); The Belle of New
York ("I Wanna Be a Dancin' Man"--Fred Astaire); Lili ("Hi-Lili,
Hi-Lo"--Leslie Caron); The Pirate ("Be a Clown"--Judy Garland and
Gene Kelly), Kiss Me Kate ("From This Moment On--Ann Miller,
Tommy Rall, Carol Haney, Bobby Van, Bob Fosse, and Jeanne Coyne);
Silk Stockings ("All of You"--Fred Astaire and Cyd Charisse); Seven
Brides for Seven Brothers ("Lonesome Polecat"--Howard Keel); Love-
ly to Look At ("Smoke Gets in Your Eyes"--Kathryn Grayson, Marge
Champion, and Gower Champion); Easter Parade ("Easter Parade--
Fred Astaire and Judy Garland; "Steppin' Out with My Baby"--Fred
Astaire; "A Couple of Swells"--Fred Astaire and Judy Garland); Going
Hollywood ("Temptation"--Bing Crosby and Fifi D'Orsay); Listen,
Darling ("Zing Went the Strings of My Heart"--Judy Garland); Cabin
in the Sky ("Taking a Chance on Love"--Ethel Waters and Eddie
"Rochester" Anderson); Born to Dance ("Swingin' the Jinx Away"--
Eleanor Powell); New Moon ("Stouthearted Men"--Nelson Eddy; "Lover
Come Back to Me"--Nelson Eddy and Jeanette MacDonald); Hollywood
Party ("Inka Dinka Doo"--Jimmy Durante); Girl Crazy ("I Got Rhythm"--
Judy Garland and Mickey Rooney); Songwriters Revue ("Songwriters
Revue of 1929"--Jack Benny); The Broadway Melody ("Wedding of the
Painted Doll"--original troupe); Lady Be Good ("Lady Be Good"--Ann
Sothern and Robert Young); Broadway Serenade ("Broadway Serenade"--
Lew Ayres and Al Shean; "For Every Lonely Heart"--Jeanette Mac-
Donald); Words and Music ("The Lady Is a Tramp"--Lena Horne;
"Manhattan"--Mickey Rooney, Tom Drake, and Marshall Thompson);
Three Little Words ("Three Little Words"--Fred Astaire and Red
Skelton); The Great Waltz ("Tales from the Vienna Woods"--Fernand
Gravet and Miliza Korjus); Singin' in the Rain ("Good Morning"--Gene
Kelly, Debbie Reynolds, and Donald O'Connor; "Broadway Rhythm"--
Gene Kelly and Cyd Charisse); An American in Paris ("Concerto in
I"--Oscar Levant; "I Got Rhythm"--Gene Kelly; "Our Love Is Here
to Stay"--Gene Kelly and Leslie Caron; "I'll Build a Stairway to
Paradise"--Georges Guetary); Meet Me in St. Louis ("Have Yourself
a Merry Little Christmas"--Judy Garland and Margaret O'Brien); Love
Me Or Leave Me ("Ten Cents a Dance"--Doris Day and James Cag-
ney); The Tender Trap ("The Tender Trap"--Frank Sinatra); Till the
Clouds Roll By ("Old Man River"--Frank Sinatra; "The Last Time I
Saw Paris"--Dinah Shore); Anchors Aweigh ("I Fall in Love Too Eas-
ily"--Frank Sinatra; "I Begged Her"--Frank Sinatra and Gene Kelly);
It Happened in Brooklyn ("I Believe"--Frank Sinatra, Jimmy Durante,
and Billy Roy); High Society ("You're Sensational"--Frank Sinatra and
Grace Kelly; "Now You Has Jazz"--Bing Crosby and Louis Armstrong);
The Merry Widow (1934) ("Maxim's" and "Girls, Girls, Girls"--Maur-
ice Chevalier; "The Merry Widow Waltz"); The Merry Widow (1952)

("Can-Can"--Gwen Verdon and dancers); Invitation to the Dance ("Sinbad"--Gene Kelly); Small Town Girl ("Take Me to Broadway"--Bobby Van); Annie Get Your Gun ("There's No Business Like Show Business"--Betty Hutton, Howard Keel, Keenan Wynn, and Louis Calhern); It's Always Fair Weather ("I Like Myself"--Gene Kelly); Gigi ("I Remember It Well"--Maurice Chevalier and Hermione Gingold); The Barkleys of Broadway ("Bouncin' the Blues"--Fred Astaire and Ginger Rogers); Easy to Love ("Water Ski Ballet"--Esther Williams); Bud Abbott and Lou Costello in Hollywood (Bit); Adam's Rib (Spencer Tracy and Kathryn Hepburn); A Day at the Races (The Three Marx Brothers); A Night at the Opera (The Three Marx Brothers); A Tale of Two Cities (Bit); Bombshell (Jean Harlow); Boom Town (Spencer Tracy and Clark Gable); Boys Town (Spencer Tracy and Mickey Rooney); China Seas (Robert Benchley); Dancing Lady (Bit); David Copperfield (W. C. Fields); Dinner at Eight (Jean Harlow); Gone With the Wind (Vivien Leigh and Clark Gable); Goodbye Mr. Chips (Bit); Grand Hotel (Greta Garbo and John Barrymore); Billy Rose's Jumbo (Jimmy Durante); Lassie Come Home (Roddy McDowall); Laurel and Hardy's Laughing Twenties (Bits); Ninotchka (Greta Garbo); Pat and Mike (Spencer Tracy and Katharine Hepburn); The Philadelphia Story (Katharine Hepburn and Cary Grant); Private Lives (Bit); Saratoga (Jean Harlow and Clark Gable); Strange Cargo (Bit); Tarzan, the Ape Man (Johnny Weissmuller); The Thin Man (William Powell); Two Girls and a Sailor (Bit); White Cargo (Bit); Without Love (Bit); Ziegfeld Girl (Bit); and scenes from the travelogues: Hong Kong, Hub of the Orient; Stockholm, Pride of Sweden; Beautiful Banff and Lake Louise; Land of the Taj Mahal; Colorful Guatemala; Japan, In Cherry Blossom Time; Ireland, the Emerald Isle; Switzerland, the Beautiful; Picturesque Udaipur; Old New Orleans; A Day on Treasure Island; Madeira, Island of Romance; Copenhagen, City of Towers.

These two compilation features embody many of the choicest musical scenes from Metro-Goldwyn-Mayer films from the dawn of the talkies until the sixties. In addition, the first of the two entries boasted a number of star host/hostesses in specially filmed introductions providing occasional insight into their years at MGM during its golden age. Of the duo, the first one, produced by Jack Haley, Jr., is by far the better. It includes the choicest of the studio's song-and-dance numbers along with a well-paced variety of various musical sequences filled with gaudy visuals.

That's Entertainment! was a box-office giant with a gross of over $12 million in U.S. and Canadian rental alone. There were scenes from dozens of MGM films, from Hollywood Revue (q.v.) to Gigi, plus loads of MGM newsreel and promotional footage. Among the varied scenes were montage shots from various versions of the song "Singin' in the Rain" used by Metro in assorted features over the years, footage of Joan Crawford singing, compilations of Gene Kelly dancing in a myriad of films, frames upon frames of Esther Williams in her exotic swims, the mind boggling sight of Fred Astaire dancing on walls in Royal Wedding (1951), and many, many more delightful and nostalgia-oriented sequences. Watching Astaire walk among the ruins of the train station set from The Band Wagon (1952),

Peter Lawford ambling midst the faded Tate College locale from
Good News (1947), and Mickey Rooney wandering on the remains of
Carvel street from the Hardy Family series brought back wistful
memories for many viewers.

Focus on Film magazine called the movie "a gigantic trailer"
only it was a trailer in reverse; instead of introducing a movie, it
reprised dozens of the best musicals turned out by Hollywood's premiere film factory during its long-ago heyday.

That's Entertainment: Part II proved to be a more-than-ade-
quate box-office item, but it possessed none of the drawing power of
its predecessor.   Although it contained a myriad of musical numbers
(those not used in the initial film, along with new sequences directed
by Gene Kelly and starring Kelly and Fred Astaire), the new documentary was poorly edited and badly lacked the cohesion of the original.   For many, there was just too much of Kelly and Astaire.

Many viewers were puzzled by the film's ads which listed, for
example, Elizabeth Taylor as a star of That's Entertainment: Part
II, yet she is glimpsed in only one brief close-up from Ivanhoe. Tony
Martin is mentioned in the final credits as a star of the picture, yet
he does not appear in the proceedings at all.   It proved how drasti-
cally the film had been re-edited after initial showings.

For many the best moments of the follow-up film were not
the clips of Katharine Hepburn and Spencer Tracy from some of their
joint Metro hits, but the opening credits, which in motif spoofed many
of the genres so dear to Hollywood.   Sadly the originality of the opening bit of the picture was not carried throughout the rest of the program.

THAT'S RIGHT--YOU'RE WRONG (RKO, 1939) 91 min.

Producer/director, David Butler; story, Butler and William
Conselman; screenplay, Conselman and James V. Kern; art director,
Van Nest Polglase; music arranger, George Dunning; songs, Walter
Donaldson, Johnny Burke, and Frankie Masters; James Kern, Hy
Heath, Johnny Lange, and Lew Porter; Charles Newman and Sammy
Stept; Jerome Brainin and Allan Roberts; Dave Franklin; assistant
director, Fred A. Flecke; special effects, Vernon L. Walker; cam-
era, Russell Metty; editor, Irene Morra.

Lucille Ball (Sandra Sand); Dennis O'Keefe (Chuck Deems);
Kay Kyser & His Band (Themselves); Adolphe Menjou (Stacey Del-
more); May Robson (Grandma); Edward Everett Horton (Tom Village);
Roscoe Karns (Mal Stamp); Moroni Olsen (J. D. Forbes); Hobart
Cavanaugh (Dwight Cook); Ginny Simms (Ginny); Harry Babbitt (Harry);
Sully Mason (Sully); Ish Kabibble (Ish); Dorothy Lovett (Miss Cos-
grave); Fred Othman, Erskine Johnson, Sheilah Graham, Hedda Hop-
per, Jimmy Starr, and Feg Murray (Themselves); Kathryn Adams
(Elizabeth); Horace McMahon and Elliott Sullivan (Hoods).

When Kay Kyser of radio fame was signed to a RKO movie
contract, the studio found it impossible to cast him in any film genre

in which he would be believable.   Finally the studio concocted a
scenario which required him to be a non-actor and then used his in-
ability at thespian activities as the comedy crux of the 91-minute
affair.   As a result, That's Right, You're Wrong--which earned its
title from a phrase from Kyser's radio show--was a huge success
and resulted in other features starring the popular bandleader, including the Hollywood genre effort Playmates (q. v.).

Here Kyser signs a movie contract with Four Star Pictures
and brings his band to the West Coast.   When the temperamental
head of the studio (Adolphe Menjou) is confronted with Kyser's lack
of screen presence, he is irate, and refuses to cast him in a film.
Kyser finally performs a test scene from Romeo and Juliet, but the
audition is a fiasco.   Menjou is now more determined than ever to
be rid of the bandleader.   All looks bad for Kay until his manager
(Dennis O'Keefe) falls in love with a high-strung female star (played
with enormous comic zest by Lucille Ball).   To keep her happy, the
studio must keep Kyser on the payroll.   Finally he is put into a
feature and his debut proves a hit, since audiences find his realistic
non-acting quite amusing.

THE THIRD EYE (Pathé, 1920) 15 chapters.

Director, James W. Horne; story, H. H. Van Loan.

With: Eileen Percy, Warner Oland, Jack Mower, Olga Grey,
and Mark Strong.

Chapters: (1) The Poisoned Dagger, (2) The Pendulum of
Death, (3) In Destruction's Path, (4) Daggers of Death, (5) The Black
Hand Bag, (6) The Death Spark, (7) The Crook's Ranch or The Double
Trap, (8) Trails of Danger or Dangerous Trails (9) The Race for
Life, (10) The House of Terrors (11) The Long Arm of Vengeance,
(12) Man Against Man, (13) Blind Trails of Justice, (14) At Bay,
(15) Triumph of Justice.

This is the first American serial and the only silent chapter-
play to deal with the movie industry.   The 15-chapter entry is also
noted for being one of the first pictures to combine the murder-
mystery motif with a movie studio background, a formula which would
become popular after the onset of the sound era.

Eileen Percy starred as a vivacious movie actress who is
loved by Warner Oland, the head of a group of crooks.   When she
refuses to help him in his nefarious deeds and rejects his advances,
the evil Oland commits a murder in her movie studio.   The shadow
of guilt falls on Percy.   Later the police discover the actual killing
was recorded on film, although it is not known who operated the
camera during the murder.   When a reel of film is found, it "shows"

Opposite: Hedda Hopper, Feg Murray, Lucille Ball, and Adolphe
Menjou in That's Right--You're Wrong (1940).

Eileen killing the victim. However, her boyfriend (Jack Mower) par-
ticipates in the continuing battle to demonstrate her innocence. Finally a scrap of film is discovered which confirms Oland committed the
crime.
     The title of this serial refers to a camera lens, in this case
the third eye which saw who committed the crime.

THREE FOR BEDROOM C (Warner Bros. , 1952) Color, 74 min.

     Associate producer, Edward L. Alperson, Jr.; director, Mil-
ton H. Bren; based on the novel by Goddard Lieberson; screenplay,
Bren; music, Heinz Roemheld; camera, Ernest Laszlo; editor, Arthur Hilton.

     Gloria Swanson (Ann Haven); James Warren (Oli J. Thrumm);
Fred Clark (Johnny Pizer); Hans Conreid (Jack Bleck); Steve Brodie
(Conde Marlow); Janine Perreau (Barbara); Ernest Anderson (Fred
Johnson); Margaret Dumont (Mrs. Hawthorne).

     After her tremendous success in Sunset Boulevard (q. v.), vet-
eran cinema queen Gloria Swanson was offered a number of film vehicles but refused most of them because they would cast her as an
older woman or the mother of grown offspring. Finally she decided
to do this farce, in which she played the mother of a teenage daughter. Somewhere along the way, everything went wrong and the end
result was an exceedingly mundane farce which received few bookings.
     Shot in Natural Color, Swanson appeared as Ann Haven, a
movie great who becomes miffed at her latest studio assignment.
With her young daughter (Janine Perreau) she boards a train bound
for Hollywood. The star, however, did not bother to make reservations, and, after taking possession of Bedroom C in the sleeping
coach, she and her child discover the compartment is also occupied
by a rather shy biochemistry professor (James Warren) who is on his
way to Cal-Tech to deliver a lecture. After the expected misunder-
standings have been dealt with, a romance develops between the demanding luminary and the intellectual soul. By the end of the trek
they realize they are in love. Ho-hum.

365 NIGHTS IN HOLLYWOOD (Fox, 1934) 74 min.

     Producer, Sol Wurtzel; director, George Marshall; story, Jim-
my Starr; screenplay, William Conselman and Henry Johnson; songs,
Sidney Clare and Richard Whiting; choreography, Sammy Lee; music,
Whiting; camera, Harry Jackson.

     James Dunn (Jimmy Dale); Alice Faye (Alice Perkins); Frank
Mitchell (Percy); Jack Durant (Clarence); John Qualen (Professor

James Warren and Gloria Swanson in Three for Bedroom C (1952).

Ellenbogen); John Bradford (Adrian Almont); Frank Melton (Frank Young); Grant Mitchell (J. Walter Delmar); Ray Cooke (Assistant Director); Addison Richards (Assistant District Attorney); Arthur Housman (Drunk); Enid Gray (Old Lady); Ernest Wood (Agent); Gloria Roy (Waitress); Carl Stockdale (Bookkeeper); Frank Conroy (Executive); Betty Bryson (Ingenue).

An acting school in Hollywood is controlled by a crook named J. Walter Delmar (Grant Mitchell). To attract prospective students to the bogus academy, he employs former screen idol Adrian Almont (John Bradford). Alice Perkins (Alice Faye) arrives at the school with two pals, Percy (Frank Mitchell) and Clarence (Jack Durant), who work as ice men. About the same time Frank Young (Frank Melton) appears on the scene willing to invest in a movie.

Grant Mitchell decides to produce a film to star Faye with alcoholic director Jimmy Dale (James Dunn) in charge of the project. But Grant Mitchell incorporates a clause in the contract with Dunn that if the filming should halt for any reason, all of the money on the project will go to the bogus promoter.

Dunn, hoping to make a comeback, remains sober and the film moves along smoothly. To mess up the situation, Grant Mitchell has Bradford abduct Faye. She is left stranded out of town, but her

ice men pals find her.   The picture is resumed and soon she and
Dunn realize they want one another.
  In the finale the police arrest Grant Mitchell and Bradford.
The picture turns out to be a huge hit, returning Melton's investment
and re-establishing Dunn's career.
  This thin satire on Hollywood acting academies and get-rich-
quick-schemers was given the necessary zest by director George
Marshall and by songwriters Richard Whiting and Sidney Clare.   The
tunes "Yes to You" and "My Future Star" were presented in well-
staged production numbers highlighting the musical abilities of blondized
Faye, then a rapidly rising commodity on the Hollywood scene.

THREE LITTLE WORDS (MGM, 1950) Color, 103 min.

  Producer, Jack Cummings; director, Richard Thorpe; based
on the lives of Bert Kalmar and Harry Ruby; screenplay, George
Wells; art directors, Cedric Gibbons and Urie McCleary; choreogra-
phy, Hermes Pan; music director, Andre Previn; orchestrator, Leo
Arnaud; songs, Kalmar and Harry Puck; Kalmar, Harry Ruby, and
Herman Ruby; Kalmar, Ruby, and Ted Snyder; Edgar Leslie and
Ruby; Kalmar, Ruby, and Herbert Stothart; Arthur Freed and Nacio
Herb Brown; camera, Harry Jackson; editor, Ben Lewis.

  Fred Astaire (Bert Kalmar); Red Skelton (Harry Ruby); Vera-
Ellen (Jessie Brown Kalmar); Arlene Dahl (Eileen Percy Ruby); Keen-
an Wynn (Charlie Kope); Gale Robbins (Terry Lordel); Gloria DeHaven
(Mrs. Carter DeHaven); Phil Regan (Himself); Harry Shannon (Clana-
han); Debbie Reynolds (Helen Kane); Carleton Carpenter (Dan Healy);
Paul Harvey (Al Masters); George Metkovich (Al Schacht); Harry
Mendoza (The Great Mendoza); Pierre Watkins (Philip Goodman);
Harry Barris (Party Pianist); Syd Saylor (Barker); Alex Gerry (Mar-
ty); Harry Ruby (Baseball Player); Anita Ellis (Singing Voice of Jessie Brown Kalmar); Helen Kane (Singing Voice of Helen Kane).

  Three Little Words relates the "story" of songwriters Bert
Kalmar and Harry Ruby.   Like most such screen biographies it
touched fleetingly on the film work of the two gentlemen.   Unlike
most such biopics, however, this feature was far from dull or mundane.   It greatly benefitted from a sensible scenario, excellent music, and the expert dancing of Fred Astaire and Vera-Ellen.
  The main storyline emphasis was on Kalmar's (Astaire's)
career and his rise from a Tin Pan Alley lyricist to writing Broadway and finally Hollywood musicals.   In this latter section of the film
Debbie Reynolds plays the role of Helen Kane, with the latter supply-
ing the vocal for her trademark Kalmar-Ruby hit theme song, "I
Wanna Be Loved by You. "   Not to be overlooked is Red Skelton's
well-modulated performance as Harry Ruby.   Skelton, a personal
friend of the songwriter, limited his slapstick proclivity to a display
of enthusiasm for Ruby's great love--baseball.
  The New York Times heralded this Metro color showcase as
"a grand musical, well-nigh flawless.... "

Fred Astaire and Red Skelton in <u>Three Little Words</u> (1950).

THE THRILL HUNTER (Columbia, 1933) 58 min.

Director, George B. Seitz; story/dialogue, Harry O. Hoyt; assistant director, Sam Nelson; sound, Glenn Rominger; camera, Ted Tetzlaff; editor, Gene Milford.

Buck Jones (Buck Crosby); Dorothy Revier (Marjorie Lane); Edward LeSaint (Jackson); Eddie Kane (Levine); Arthur Rankin (Roy Lang); Frank La Rue (Hall); Robert Ellis (Blake); Harry Semels (Lon Norton); Al Smith (Sheriff); John Ince (Mayor Thomas); Alf James (Samuel Nebit); Harry Todd (Baggage Man); Willie Fung (Wung Lo); Jim Corey (Deputy Jim); Frank Ellis, Hank Bell, Joe Ryan, and

---

Opposite: choreographer Sammy Lee, chorus girls, and director George Marshall on the set of <u>365 Nights in Hollywood</u> (1934).

Glenn Strange (Cowboy Actors); Art Mix (Cleveland the Double); Buddy Roosevelt (Marjorie's Chauffeur); Buffalo Bill, Jr. [Jay Wilsey] (Pilot).

Buck Jones was one of the most stalwart of all cowboy stars and quite often his action Westerns took on a somber overtone. Still he could also kid his image and he did so in a most satisfying manner in The Thrill Hunter. It was a breezy action film played more for comedy and fast pacing than for gunplay.

Jones was Buck Crosby, a long-winded cowpoke who saves a girl (Dorothy Revier) on a runaway wagon only to find she is a film star doing some scouting for a movie location. She invites Buck to dinner with the company and over the meal he spins many tall yarns, which impresses the troupe's producers. Riding home, Jones comes across the bodies of two bandits who have shot one another over stolen loot. Later he is given credit for having killed the marauders and is made a town hero--even the local swimming pool is renamed after him. Due to his "heroism" Buck is signed to star in Revier's new film for Celebrated Pictures and he is whisked off to Hollywood to live happily ever after.

Once on the film set Buck is outfitted in flashy Western regalia. "I look like a lily of the valley" he complains. He also finds the film he is to star in is a mixed blessing at best. Having convinced the director that he is an ace race driver, Buck proceeds to wreck a racing vehicle. Then he boasts that he can pilot a plane and when he is required to do so in the storyline, he takes a practice outing in a model plane at a local circus (failing miserably). The next day on the set he wrecks the company plane. He is revealed as a fraud and is fired. He is also rejected by Revier with whom he has fallen in love.

Jones returns to his hometown where he is still regarded as a hero. He encounters two remaining members of the Blake gang, unknown to him, the survivors of the bandits he supposedly shot. The duo kidnap Buck and try to force him to reveal the hiding place of the money they had stolen. When the crooks learn that Jones has given a clue to the booty's whereabouts to Revier (due in town soon for location shooting), the outlaws kidnap her. But Buck escapes from his bondage and gives chase. He comandeers a private plane, overcomes the bandits, and rescues Revier. She now accepts his affections.

TILL THE CLOUDS ROLL BY (MGM, 1946) Color, 137 min.

Producer, Arthur Freed; director, Richard Whorf; Judy Garland's numbers directed by Vincente Minnelli; story, Guy Bolton; adaptor, George Wells; screenplay, Myles Connolly and Jean Holloway; assistant director, Wally Worsley; art directors, Cedric Gibbons and Daniel B. Cathcart; set decorators, Edwin B. Willis and Richard Pefferle; music director, Lennie Hayton; orchestrator, Conrad Salinger; vocal arranger, Kay Thompson; songs, Jerome Kern and Oscar Hammerstein II; Kern and P. G. Wodehouse; Kern and Edward Laska;

Joan Wells, Van Heflin, and Robert Walker in Till the Clouds Roll
By (1946).

Kern and Herbert Reynolds; Kern, Otto Harbach, and Hammerstein
II; Kern and Harbach; Kern and B. G. De Sylva; Kern and Ira Gershwin; Kern and Dorothy Fields; sound, Douglas Shearer; special effects, Warren Newcombe; camera, Harry Stradling and George J.
Folsey; editor, Albert Akst.

Robert Walker (Jerome Kern); Judy Garland (Marilyn Miller);
Lucille Bremer (Sally); Joan Wells (Sally as a Girl); Van Heflin
(James I. Hessler); Paul Langton (Oscar Hammerstein); Dorothy Patrick (Mrs. Jerome Kern); Mary Nash (Mrs. Muller); Harry Hayden
(Charles Frohman); Paul Maxey (Victor Herbert); Rex Evans (Cecil
Keller); William "Bill" Phillips (Hennessey); Dinah Shore (Julie San-
derson); Van Johnson (Band Leader); June Allyson, Angela Lansbury,
and Ray McDonald (Guest Performers); Maurice Kelly, Cyd Charisse,
and Gower Champion (Dance Specialties); Ray Teal (Orchestra Conductor); Wilde Twins (Specialty); Showboat William Halligan (Captain
Andy); Tony Martin (Ravenal); Kathryn Grayson (Magnolia); Virginia
O'Brien (Ellie); Lena Horne (Julie); Caleb Peterson (Joe); Bruce Cow-

ling (Steve); Frank Sinatra and Johnny Johnston (Finale); William Forrest (Motion Picture Director); Herschel Graham, Fred Hueston, Dick Earle, Larry Steers, Reed Howes, James Darrell, and Charles Griffin (Opening Night Critics); Byron Foulger (Frohman's Secretary); Margaret Bert (Maid); Ann Codee (Miss Laroche); James Finlayson (Candy Vendor); Arnaut Brothers (Bird Act); Russell Hichsk (Motion Picture Producer); Stanley Andrews (Doctor); Sally Forrest and Mary Hatcher (Chorus Girls).

Till the Clouds Roll By was a very long (137-minute) and colorful musical biography of songwriter Jerome Kern (1885-1945), played by Robert Walker. The film opens at a party following the successful Broadway bow of Show Boat in the late twenties. After the party, Kern asks to be driven to the old brownstone house where he began his musical writing career; from there he relives his life in flashbacks. Included is his personal happiness--marrying the girl (Dorothy Patrick) he truly loves, his Broadway successes, and his writing for the movies at MGM. The picture culminates with the "filming" of Show Boat and a series of musical presentations of various Kern tunes.

Walker was not particularly interesting as Kern--nor was he aided by the pious scenario which wanted to elevate the composer to a semi-diety. The opulent production values of the film, however, more than compensated for the draggy storyline. The film was well-photographed in Technicolor and the various big-name guest artists added much to the proceedings, as did the re-creations of various segments from Show Boat. Among the highlights of the latter were Caleb Petersen singing "Ol' Man River" (reprised in the finale by Frank Sinatra) and Kathryn Grayson and Tony Martin dueting "Make Believe." Kern's death during the making of this film resulted in a production shutdown, script rewrites, and a prevailing tone of reverential awe towards the late composer. But audiences did not mind the blend, it grossed $4.5 million in the U.S. and Canada alone.

Cue magazine's analysis stated, "The story itself, not unlike most film biographies, is a success story--told simply and unaffectedly, and not in the embarrassingly fawning fashion characteristic of certain other recent endeavors along these lines.... It's a glorious, lively and grand entertainment, not to be missed." If many critics and some filmgoers found the Sinatra finale singing "Ol' Man River" in a white satin dress suit to be tasteless, there was general accord that Judy Garland (as Marilyn Miller) shone in her production numbers, "Look for the Silver Lining" and "Who?"

TOO MUCH, TOO SOON (Warner Bros., 1958) 121 min.

Producer, Henry Blanke; director, Art Napoleon; based on the book by Diana Barrymore and Gerold Frank; screenplay, Art and Jo Napoleon; music, Ernest Gold; assistant director, George Vieira; art director, John Beckman; set decorator, George James Hopkins; costumes, Orry-Kelly; makeup, Gordon Bau; dialogue supervisor, Eu-

John Dennis, Dorothy Malone, and Errol Flynn in Too Much, Too Soon (1958).

gene Busch; sound, Francis E. Stahl; camera, Nick Musuraca and Carl Guthrie; editor, Owen Marks.

Dorothy Malone (Diana Barrymore); Errol Flynn (John Barrymore); Efrem Zimbalist, Jr. (Vincent Bryant); Ray Danton (John Howard); Neva Patterson (Michael Strange); Murray Hamilton (Charlie Snow); Martin Milner (Lincoln Forrester); John Dennis (Walter Gerhardt); Edward Kemmer (Robert Wilcox); Robert Ellenstein (Gerold Frank); Kathleen Freeman (Miss Magruder); John Doucette (Crowley); Michael Mark (Patterson); Francis DeSales and Jay Jostyn (Imperial Pictures Executives); Herb Ellis and Louis Quinn (Assistants); Robert S. Carson (Associate); James Elsegood (Diana's Tango Partner); Bess Flowers and Charles Evans (Guests); Gail Bonney (Nurse).

"Nothing could be duller. But is there, somewhere in the sky, a Happy Drinking Ground from which John Barrymore can view this impersonation of his splendid self by Errol Flynn? That would make it all worthwhile," wrote Hollis Alpert of Saturday Review in his critique of Too Much, Too Soon. It was based on Diana Barrymore's scandalously frank autobiography, a tome written in conjunction with Gerold Frank (co-writer of Lillian Roth's best selling I'll Cry Tomorrow). The sad panorama of Barrymore's lonely life and Diana's worship-turned-loathing of her celebrated father turned the

book into a successful publication.   The film was not nearly so pungent as the tome.   In fact, it was a limp, emasculated version,
giving in to whitewashing to avoid potential law suits from still-living
parties.

Originally Warner Bros. offered the part of Diana Barrymore
to Carroll Baker, who refused it.   Another potential choice for the
role was Anne Baxter.   But it was Dorothy Malone (Best Supporting
Actress winner for 1956's Written on the Wind) who played in this
boozed-up soap opera.   The narrative covers superficially the lone-
liness and insecurity suffered by Diana, despite her heritage--father:
acclaimed actor John Barrymore (Errol Flynn); mother: laureated
poetess Michael Strange (Neva Patterson).   The treatment of Diana's
three marriages was cinematically uneven: husband no. 1: Bram-
well Fletcher was still very much alive and still involved in show
business, hence a new character by the name of Vincent Bryant (Efrem Zimbalist, Jr.) replaced his chapter in Diana's love life. Spouse
no. 2, tennis player John Howard (Ray Danton) worried the studio
less, and was presented under his own name as a sadistic lout (". . .
one of the most heinous villains since Walter Lang in The Birth of a
Nation, " huffed Films in Review).   Since her last husband, actor
Robert Wilcox, was dead, he was fair game to be presented--via
actor Edward Kemmer--as a drunken, pathetic leech.   The latter
segment of the biopic centered almost exclusively on Diana's grotesque drunk binges.   But in Hollywood tradition it managed to close
on an optimistic note, with the Barrymore offspring apparently taking
hold of herself.   (Tragically, the optimistic finale was not fulfilled in
real life; Diana Barrymore died on January 25, 1960, a gaggle of
empty bottles beside her bed.)

The movie is crammed with distortions and inaccuracies.
(Diana is presented as having made only one film, actually she made
six as a Universal contract player; the mansion presented as Barrymore's home was actually on the other side of town from the star's
bizarre Tower Road domain.)   However, the picture is almost sal-
vaged by the presence of Flynn as Barrymore himself.   In actuality,
Flynn and Barrymore were close friends.   (Director Raoul Walsh
would delight in telling and retelling of the night he and some cronies
snatched Barrymore's corpse from the funeral parlor and propped
him up in Flynn's living room while the actor was out for the evening.)   Director Art Napoleon vetoed Flynn's use of the uncanny imitation he had perfected of his late chum as too hammy.   Nevertheless, the veteran swashbuckler still provided one of his most masterful acting jobs as the declining, alcohol-ridden star.   While the
New York Times noted that Ms. Malone "is a winsome, earnest
protagonist--but no Susan Hayward" (of I'll Cry Tomorrow, q. v.),
the review cheered Flynn, who "steals the picture, lock stock, and
keg.   It is only in the scenes of his savage disintegration . . . that
the picture approaches real tragedy. "

TRAIL OF ROBIN HOOD (Republic, 1950) Color, 67 min.

Producer, Edward J. White; director, William Witney; screenplay, Gerald Geraghty; songs, Jack Elliott and Foy Willing; camera, John MacBurnie; editor, Tony Martinelli.

Roy Rogers (Himself); Trigger (The Smartest Horse in the Movies); Penny Edwards (Toby); Gordon Jones (Splinters); Jack Holt (Himself); Emory Parnell (J. Corwin Aldridge); Clifton Young (Mitch); James Magill (Murtagh); Carol Nugent (Sis); George Chesebro (George); Edward Cassidy (Sheriff); Foy Willing & the Riders of the Purple Sage (Themselves); Rex Allen, Allan "Rocky" Lane, Monte Hale, William Farnum, Tom Tyler, Ray Corrigan, Kermit Maynard, and Tom Keene (Guest Cowboy Stars).

Toward the end of his tenure at Republic, Roy Rogers made a second feature which dealt with the movie industry. (The first was Bells of Rosarita, q. v.) This outing not only showcased Rogers, but featured long-time movie star Jack Holt, along with a group of Republic's top cowboy film players in guest appearances.

Here Roy comes up against a gang of Christmas tree rustlers who are making trouble for an old-time movie idol (Holt) who owns the ranch on which the trees are being grown. At the entertaining finale, Roy and Holt are joined by Rex Allen, Ray Corrigan, William Farnum, Monte Hale, Tom Keene (aka Richard Powers), Allan "Rocky" Lane, Kermit Maynard, and George Chesebro. The latter informs the group he has been a villain in Holt's features for two decades but would now like to get on the right side of the law and help his coworker. Together the star-clustered troupe of sagebrush cavaliers alight on the rustlers and set everything right for their grateful pal.

This staunch cast alone represents a huge segment of Hollywood's Western heritage. Besides Rogers, who was the forties' most popular screen cowboy, there was Farnum who dates back in movies to the 1914 classic version of The Spoilers; Chesebro, a longtime veteran villain of B oaters who himself starred in low-budget Westerns in the twenties; Maynard, the stuntman-star brother of Ken Maynard; and Keene, who had starred in a fine series of RKO Westerns in the thirties, including Scarlet River (q. v.).

TWO WEEKS IN ANOTHER TOWN (MGM, 1962) Color, 107 min.

Producer, John Houseman; associate producer, Ethel Winant; director, Vincente Minnelli; based on the novel by Irwin Shaw; screenplay, Charles Schnee; music, David Raksin; assistant director, Erich von Stroheim, Jr. ; art directors, George W. Davis and Urie McCleary; set decorators, Henry Grace and Keogh Gleason; color consultant, Charles K. Hagedon; Miss Charisse's gowns, Pierre Balmain; wardrobe, Walter Plunkett; makeup, William Tuttle; sound, Franklin Milton; special camera effects, Robert R. Hoag; camera, Milton Krasner; editors, Adrienne Fazan and Robert J. Kern.

Kirk Douglas (Jack Andrus); Edward G. Robinson (Maurice Kruger); Cyd Charisse (Carlotta); George Hamilton (David Drew);

Dahlia Lavi (Veronica); Claire Trevor (Clara Kruger); Rosanna
Schiaffino (Barzelli); James Gregory (Brad Byrd); Joanna Roos (Janet
Bark); George Macready (Lew Jordan); Mino Doro (Tucino); Stefan
Schnabel (Zeno); Vito Scotti (Assistant Director); Tom Palmer (Dr.
Cold Eyes); Erich von Stroheim, Jr. (Ravinski); Leslie Uggams
(Chanteuse).

This movie about picturemaking fails at the same subject and
with the same basic cast of talent that The Bad and the Beautiful
(q. v.) succeeded at so triumphantly.   (In fact, scenes of Kirk Douglas and Lana Turner from The Bad and the Beautiful are incorporated in a screening room sequence.)   This time the plot revolves
around has-been actor Jack Andrus (Kirk Douglas), who after having
spent three years in a sanatorium for alcoholism caused by an auto
crash, a divorce, and a fading career, is offered a smallish part in
a feature being shot in Rome.   The director (of the movie-within-a-
movie) is Maurice Kruger (Edward G. Robinson) who had supervised
some of Douglas' great successes in the past.

In Rome, Douglas finds the production a hectic one and not
totally in Robinson's control.   The latter is about to lose the project
if he goes over budget while his actors battle each other and his
lovely leading lady (Rosanna Schiaffino) struggles with her microsco-
pic English vocabulary.   Robinson asks Douglas to supervise the
soundtrack dubbing of the film and this helps him emotionally, even
after his glamourous ex-wife (Cyd Charisse) arrives on the scene
to try to regain control of his life and income.

Later at an anniversary party, Robinson's shrewish wife (Claire
Trevor) accuses Robinson of having an affair with his young leading
lady and the old man suffers a heart attack.   Douglas is then per-
suaded to finish directing the movie, which he does, although he
loses Robinson's friendship in the process.   Finally,   emotionally
free of both Robinson and Charisse, Douglas returns to the U. S. with
a bright future ahead as a director.

Douglas had enjoyed a great success in the genre in The Bad
and the Beautiful, but Two Weeks in Another Town was more on par
with his later genre entry, the mundane soap opera, Jacqueline Susann's Once Is Not Enough (q. v.).   Douglas was unable to breathe
much life into the character of Jack Andrus, although both Robinson
and Trevor were superb as the battling Krugers, and Charisse had a
good change of pace as the venomous Carlotta, the ex-wife.   What
could have been a substantial look at the American-European copro-
duction activities was totally overlooked in this specious melodrama.
It seemed here the filmmakers were more interested in a heavy,
neurotic love story than in the finer points of picturemaking.

The New York Times dismissed it: "... a drippy drama on
a theme of degradation ... "; while Variety reported, "... the film
is desperately in need of simpler, nicer people. "   Perhaps Time
magazine wrote it best: "The movie business has long suffered a
fascination with its own filth. ...   [This movie] leaves the customer
to assume that Hollywood, no matter where you find it, is hell, and
the people who run it are devils. "

UNCENSORED MOVIES see THE SHORT FILMS

VALENTINO (Columbia, 1951) Color, 91 min.

Producer, Edward Small; director, Lewis Allen; screenplay,
George Bruce; music, Heinz Roemheld; camera, Harry Stradling;
editor, Daniel Mandell.

Anthony Dexter (Rudolph Valentino); Eleanor Parker (Joan
Carlisle); Richard Carlson (William King); Patricia Medina (Lila
Reyes); Joseph Calleia (Luigi Verducci); Dona Drake (Maria Torres);
Lloyd Gough (Eddie Morgan); Otto Kruger (Mark Towers); Marietta
Canty (Tillie); Paul Bruyar (Photographer); Eric Wilton (Butler).

This Edward Small production was supposedly three years in
the making while undergoing over a dozen major script changes. The
end result should have been a definitive pictorial history of the great
silent screen lover, but it turned out to be one of the more disappointing films ever produced in the genre. Except for the use of the
star's name and the titles of a few of his films, the chronicle is
complete fiction--it has scarcely any basis in fact or even legend.
Not only was Rudolph Valentino abused by life but the industry which
he helped to make famous could not bother to present even a half-
factual portrait of the sad and tormented star.
        According to this fantasy, Valentino came to the U.S. from
Italy after World War I and on the boat met and romanced movie
figure Joan Carlisle (Eleanor Parker) who was traveling incognito.
In New York City Rudy finds a job as a dishwasher but loses it and
takes up dancing as a gigolo. Again he meets the mysterious woman
from the boat. This time he learns her identity and that her companion is famous film director Bill King (Richard Carlson). They
arrange for him to play a bit in a feature being shot at Fort Lee,
New Jersey, and there he attracts another cinema actress, Lila Reyes
(Patricia Medina).
        Despite the distractions, Valentino is only enchanted with Carl-
isle and he departs for Hollywood to try his luck in the film mecca.
There he meets Reyes again and he has the inspiration to audition
for the lead in The Four Horsemen of the Apocalypse. He does so
by performing a tango dance at a party for the film's producer.
Rudy wins the main role in the major picture and is an "overnight"
success. But even fame cannot dampen his love for Joan with whom
he later stars in The Sheik.
        Not wanting to destroy Joan's marriage to Bill, Rudy tries to
avoid her, but when she comes to him he accepts her offer of love.
But she has been followed by a newsman and their rendezvous makes
national headlines. Humiliated, Rudy returns to New York. On the
way he suffers from severe stomach pains and dies when he arrives
in Manhattan.
        The finale depicts "the lady in black" putting flowers on his
grave.
        Except for Anthony Dexter's striking resemblance to Valentino,

Patricia Medina, Dona Drake, Anthony Dexter, and Eleanor Parker
in a publicity pose for Valentino (1951).

there was no semblance of reality in this dry tale. The New York
Times succinctly labeled it "silly, corny, gaudily-colored hoopla...."

VALENTINO (United Artists, 1977) Color, 132 min.

        Producers, Irwin Winkler and Robert Chartoff; associate pro-
ducer, Harry Benn; director, Ken Russell; screenplay, Russell and
Mardik Martin; art directors, Philip Harrison, Malcolm Middleton,
and Tim Hutchinson; set dresser, Ian Whittaker; costumes, Shirley
Russell; choreography, Gillian Gregory and Michael Vernon; assistant
director, Jonathan Benson; makeup, Peter Robb-King; music, Ferde
Grofe and Stanley Black; words of parody to songs, Ken Russell;
dialogue coach, Marcella Markham; sound, John Mitchell; process
projection, Charles Staffell; camera, Peter Suschitsky; editor, Stuart
Baird.

Rudolf Nureyev and Michelle Phillips in the sheik's tent in <u>Valentino</u>
(1977).

Rudolf Nureyev (Rudolph Valentino); Leslie Caron (Nazimova);
Michelle Phillips (Natasha Rambova); Carol Kane ("Fatty's" Girl);
Felicity Kendal (June Mathis); Seymour Cassel (George Ullman); Peter
Vaughan (Rory O'Neil); Huntz Hall (Jesse Lasky); David De Keyser
(Joseph Schenck); Alfred Marks (Richard Rowland); Anton Diffring
(Baron Long); Jennie Linden (Agnes Ayres); William Hootkins ("Fat-
ty"); Bill McKinney (Jail Cop); Don Fellows (George Melford); John
Justin (Sidney Olcott); Linda Thorson (Billie Streeter); June Bolton
(Bianca De Saulles); Penny Milford (Lorna Sinclair); Dudley Sutton
(Willie); Robin Brent Clarke (Jack De Saulles); Anthony Dowell (Vas-
lav Nijinsky); James Berwick (Flight Referee); Marcella Markham
(Hooker); Leland Plamer (Marjorie Tain); John Alderson (Cop); Hal
Galili (Harry Fischbeck); Percy Herbert (Studio Guard); Nicolette
Marvin (Marsha Lee); Mark Baker (Assistant Director); Mildred Shay
(Old Lady); Lindsay Kemp (Mortician); John Ratzenberger, Norman
Chancer, and Robert O'Neil (Newshounds); Christine Carlson (Tango
Dancer).

August 23, 1976, was the fiftieth anniversary of the death of
Italian-born Rudolph Valentino, who had died at the age of 31. In
"celebration," United Artists a week earlier had begun production of
the British-filmed Valentino, ballyhooed as the film which would finally reveal the true story of the "Great Lover of the Silent Screen."
To direct this would-be incisive study of Hollywood's great legend,
the producers selected none other than Ken Russell, who had delivered
to filmgoers the very unorthodox (and for many, foolish, excessive,
and distorted) studies of Tchaikovsky (The Music Lovers, 1970),
Mahler (1974), and others. With his past track record in mind, industry observers and movie enthusiasts alike were concerned how
impassioned Russell would handle the still-mysterious and ambiguous
life of the silent pictures' greatest hero. When Russell announced
that acclaimed ballet star Rudolf Nureyev would star in the vehicle
(in his dramatic acting debut), fears mounted.
It all proved to be justified trepidation. Judith Crist lambast-
ed the movie in her New York Post review: "... [it] is an opulent
exercise in mindlessness, an extravaganza of bad taste that is as
pretentious as it is boring.... The screenplay ... starts out by defining Valentino as 'a pansy' and a 'wop' (an odd term in the face
of Nureyev's Slavic looks and Russian accent), and proceeds to prove
him a boob and a ham."
This fictionalized chronicle opens at Valentino's garish funeral
in New York, where amidst the hysteria, reporters pressure four
women mourners into revealing the "true" account of the star's amazing life. From Bianca De Saulles (June Bolton), the wife of a gang-
land figure, Valentino's early years in New York are detailed: his
days as a taxi dancer in a Manhattan ballroom, his insistence that
he will not sell his love, and how he longs to grow oranges in California. The narrative is then picked up by June Mathis (Felicity Kendal), the screen writer and editor who had faith in the man's capacity
to become a great screen personality. She reveals how Valentino--
in California as the partner of an alcoholic ballroom danseuse--steals
away Fatty Arbuckle's (William Hootkins') girl (Carol Kane) and from

her gains an insight into the qualities needed to become a filmland
player. While his hasty marriage to the actress is a well-publicized
failure and joke (adding to his growing legend as a "pink powderpuff")
he becomes a movie sensation via The Four Horsemen of the Apocalypse.
         If one could stomach (or tolerantly forgive) the needless twist-
ing of facts into ridiculous fancy up to this point in haphazard chronicle, one loses all patience with Russell's baroque production when
Leslie Caron is introduced as Alla Nazimova.   Perhaps because Pola
Negri is still alive, and Nazimova, the great Russian actress and
bizarre personality, is long deceased, it was decided to blend the
two images together, giving Nazimova many of the qualities and situations attributed over the years to Valentino's relationship with
Negri.   Thrown into the melee is Natasha Rambova (Michelle Phillips), the youngish step-daughter of an American cosmetics tycoon,
who as a dancer and designer grew to have tremendous power over
Valentino, both as his second wife and as his controller in all artistic matters.   The scenario suggests that Nazimova and Rambova
indulge in an off-again, on-again lesbian relationship.
         For most of the two hours-plus of absurdities, there are con-
tinual references to Valentino's alleged impotence, his supposed homo-
sexuality, his ambivalence to success, his domination by strong-willed
women, and most of all his confusion as to his own movie image.
At no time does Russell take a stand in defining the star's complex
character, merely titillating the viewer with offensive, self-indulgent
orgies of puerile creativity: a jailhouse sequence where the im-
prisoned Valentino is tossed into the vomit and excrement of animal-
istic prisoners who are about to rape him when the sequence ends
(Ken Russell would lambast the United Artists task force for elimi-
nating segments of the offensive jail cell scene: "I'm going to be
judged by the critics for someone else's amateurish, butchering cutting.   I don't like being judged on something that is not my work."
Later, portions of the deleted jail scenes were restored.), the nude
mating scene between Valentino and Rambova in the tent set for The
Sheik, the decadent behavior of the supremely theatrical Nazimova
who ogles Rambova openly, etc.
         There are fussily elaborate scenes of moviemaking-within-the-
movie as Valentino appears in a string of hits, including The Four
Horsemen, The Sheik, Monsieur Beaucaire, etc., and as he copes
with such studio figures as Jesse Lasky (Huntz Hall).   Much attention
is given to the near-fatal beating he suffers in the ring as he boxes,
battles, and beats pugnacious reporter Rory O'Neil (Peter Vaughan),
who has openly questioned his manliness.   It is indicated that this
grueling canvas match contributed to the screen star's demise.
         Crist in her Post attack on Russell's film, rightfully remarks
that "there is a total lack of affection for the people, the era or the
medium involved.   There is barely a suggestion that the authors are
exploring a phenomenon ('A man who wants to be a farmer--turned
into a god,' Valentino remarks ruefully at one point), none that they
are considering the brief career of a sex symbol or commenting on
the tinsel of the town.   There is only exploitation--with an eye on the
box-office."

The dialogue, like the plotline, is filled with clichés, many of them laughable. Valentino to Lasky, "I made you millions and you offer me trash." Nazimova to Rambova, "Fellow artists should only play jokes on studio bosses, not on each others." Mathis re Valentino, "Valentino is the ticket to a far away romance." Mathis' boss re the actor, "This guy doesn't want a screen test, he wants a sex test." Perhaps the most appropriate line of dialogue occurs when Michelle Phillips is visiting Valentino on The Four Horsemen set and remarks, "What an awful lot of horseshit!"

If the casting of ex-Bowery Boy Huntz Hall as Paramount executive Jesse Lasky seemed pointless*, one can only wonder what prompted Russell to indulge in the whim of assigning Nureyev to interpret the Sheik of the Screen. Granted, both individuals were graceful dancers but there the similarities ended. What Nureyev brought to the screen was a poor imitation of Ricardo Montalban on an off day.

With three such sad versions of Valentino's life already filmed (including the 1951 Valentino and 1975's TV drama, The Legend of Valentino, qq. v.) one can only hope that someday a more authentic and caring account of the enigmatic screen figure will be offered to the public, and that by that day people still care.

VALLEY OF THE DOLLS (20th Century-Fox, 1967) Color, 123 min.

Producer, David Weisbart; director, Mark Robson; based on the novel by Jacqueline Susann; screenplay, Helen Deutsch and Dorothy Kingsley; art directors, Jack Martin Smith and Richard Day; set decorators, Walter M. Scott and Raphael G. Bretton; gowns, Travilla; makeup, Ben Nye; assistant director, Eli Dunn; music adaptor/conductor, Johnny Williams; songs, Andre and Dory Previn; orchestrator, Herbert Spencer; choreography, Robert Sidney; sound, Don J. Bassman and David Dockendorf; special effects, L. B. Abbott, Art Cruickshank, and Emil Kosa, Jr.; camera, William H. Clothier; editor, Dorothy Spencer.

Barbara Parkins (Anne Welles); Patty Duke (Neely O'Hara); Paul Burke (Lyon Burke); Sharon Tate (Jennifer North); Tony Scotti (Tony Polar); Martin Milner (Mel Anderson); Charles Drake (Kevin Gillmore); Alex Davion (Ted Casablanca); Lee Grant (Miriam); Naomi Stevens (Miss Steinberg); Robert H. Harris (Henry Bellamy); Jacqueline Susann (Reporter); Robert Viharo (Director, Mike Angel (Man in Hotel Room)); Barry Cahill (Man in Bar); with: Joey Bishop (Master of Ceremonies at Telethon); George Jessel (Master of Ceremonies at

*Jesse Lasky, Jr., in trade paper interviews was dismayed at the depiction of his father in Valentino, claiming it was a "caricature" of the man who was a second generation Californian and did not have a Brooklyn accent as in the film. Lasky, Jr., stated of the film: "... as a portrayal of Hollywood it's grotesque."

Patty Duke and Susan Hayward in <u>Valley of the Dolls</u> (1967).

Grammy Awards); <u>and</u> Susan Hayward (Helen Lawson); Robert Street (Choreographer); Leona Powers (Woman at Martha Washington Hotel); Norman Burton (Neely's Director in Hollywood); Margot Stevenson (Anne's Mother); Marvin Hamlisch (Pianist); Billy Beck (Man Sleeping in Movie House); Judith Lowry (Aunt Amy); Peggy Rea (Neely's Voice Coach).

While it may be pointless to lambast a film which grossed $20 million, it is equally impossible to praise <u>Valley of the Dolls,</u> a gaudy splattering of sex and sin set against a Hollywood and Broadway background. Adapted, of course, from the best-selling novel of Jacqueline Susann (who played a brief cameo as a reporter), the Mark Robson-directed feature somehow lost the punch of Susann's sizzling novel of three girls embroiled in the seemier side of show business and their eventual tragic reliance on barbiturates ("dolls"). As played by Barbara Parkins (Anne Welles), Patty Duke (Neely O'Hara), and Sharon Tate (Jennifer North), all revealing flawless make-ups, lovely hair styles, and woeful histrionic incompetence, the trio of heroines became crude caricatures of their novel counterparts. (When the book had first come out, critics and readers played the parlor game of trying to decipher which traits of which characters were borrowed from Broadway and Hollywood originals.)
    The basic kernel of the tale traces the rise and fall of each girl in the show business world. Parkins' tragic flaw is her infatuation with writer/producer Lyon Burke (played with sticky male oomph by Paul Burke); though he weds her (after the inevitable seduction), his wandering eye soon causes him to stray and Parkins to sprawl about the California beach, drugged and deliriously heartbroken. Tate's on-screen problems are twofold: a singer husband (Tony Scotti), whose incarceration in an expensive sanatorium following a degenerative mental disease pushes her into European sex films; and a cancerous breast, which launches her into suicide. As for Duke's Neely, she performs a Judy Garland-ish plunge; after being ordered by her studio to "sparkle, Neely, sparkle, " she becomes addicted, consumptive, and obviously a hopeless lush.
    "Atrocious" best describes most of the <u>Valley</u> performances, especially Duke, who interprets her part without any subtlety. Glowing in the film, however, was Susan Hayward, who replaced Judy Garland, as Helen Lawson, an Ethel Merman-like Broadway luminary who, though doomed to a lonely life and the reputation of being the stage's most loathesome bitch, has remained an impeccable professional. In the film's most sensational sequence, Duke snatches aging Hayward's red wig off her cropped gray head, tries to flush the piece down a toilet, and leaves the ashen star stranded in the powder room with a Who's Who of the Broadway scene just outside the ladies' room door.
    Critical attacks on <u>Valley of the Dolls</u> (the <u>New York Times</u> called it "an unbelievably hackneyed and mawkish mishmash of backstage plots.... ") did nothing to drain the box-office appeal. If there were any indulgent filmgoers who took any of the celluloid proceedings seriously, it only confirmed the decades-old belief that all show business celebrities dine exclusively on dope, sex, and drink, and that the road to success is hell.

There followed in 1971 a sequel in name only, Beyond the
Valley of the Dolls, produced and directed by Russ Meyer and pri-
marily concerned with a Los Angeles hermaphrodite named "Super
Sex" and the world of rock music stars.

VARIETY GIRL (Paramount, 1947) 83 min. [color sequence]

Producer, Daniel Dare; director, George Marshall; screenplay,
Edmund Hartmann, Frank Tashlin, Robert Welch, and Monte Brice;
art directors, Hans Dreier and Robert Clatworthy; set decorators,
Sam Comer and Ross Dowd; Puppetoon sequence, George Pal; music
director, Joseph J. Lilley; music associate, Troy Sanders; orchestrator, N. Van Cleave; music for Puppetoon sequence, Edward Plumb;
songs, Frank Loesser; assistant director, George Templeton; sound,
Gene Merritt and John Cope; process camera, Farciot Edouart;
special effects, Gordon Jennings; camera, Lionel Lindon and Stuart
Thompson; editor, LeRoy Stone.

Mary Hatcher (Catherine Brown); Olga San Juan (Amber La-
Vonne); DeForest Kelley (Bob Kirby); William Demarest (Barker);
Frank Faylen (Stage Manager); Frank Ferguson (J. R. O'Connell);
Russell Hicks, Crane Whitley, Charles Coleman, Hal K. Dawson,
and Eddie Featherston (Men at Steam Bath); Catherine Craig (Secre-
tary); Bing Crosby, Bob Hope, Gary Cooper, Ray Milland, Alan Ladd,
Barbara Stanwyck, Paulette Goddard, Dorothy Lamour, Veronica
Lake, Sonny Tufts, Joan Caulfield, William Holden, Lizabeth Scott,
Burt Lancaster, Gail Russell, Diana Lynn, Sterling Hayden, Robert
Preston, John Lund, William Bendix, Barry Fitzgerald, Cass Daley,
Howard da Silva, Billy de Wolfe, Macdonald Carey, Arleen Whelan,
Patric Knowles, Mona Freeman, Cecil Kellaway, Johnny Coy, Vir-
ginia Field, Richard Webb, Stanley Clements, Cecil B. DeMille,
Mitchell Leisen, Frank Butler, George Marshall, Roger Dann, Pearl
Bailey, the Mulcays, Spike Jones & His City Slickers, Mikhail Ra-
sumny, Rae Paterson, George Reeves, Wanda Hendrix, Sally Rawlin-
son, Nanette Parks, Adra Verna, Patricia Barry, and June Harris
(Themselves); Nella Walker (Mrs. Webster); Glenn Tryon (Bill Far-
ris); Jack Norton (Brown Derby Busboy); Harry Hayden (Grauman's
Chinese Theatre Stage Manager); Eric Alden (Makeup Man); Edgar
Dearing and Ralph Dunn (Cops); Raymond Largay (Director of Variety
Club).

Variety Girl was a decidedly minor piece of fluff that was designed as a tribute to the Variety Clubs of America, an organization
founded in 1928 by movie theatre owners in Pittsburgh, Pennsylvania,
to aid underprivileged children. While the film's "heart" was in the
right place, it was not an elevating or entertaining outing; even the
huge roster of Paramount stars were unable to salvage many of the
mundane script situations.
     The wispy narrative thread concerns two screen-struck girls,
Catherine Brown (Mary Hatcher) and Amber LaVonne (Olga San Juan)
who descend on Hollywood seeking movie careers. They soon are

Alan Ladd and Dorothy Lamour in <u>Variety Girl</u> (1947).

visiting various Hollywood landmarks: the Brown Derby, Grauman's Chinese Theatre, and Paramount Studios.   At the latter site they become involved with many of the lot's stars and better-known technicians.   The picture concludes at a Variety Club function, where the girls are rewarded with their career wish; it develops that Hatcher is the original Variety Girl, the first child adopted and helped by the Club.

In the course of the 83 minutes of unremarkable screen fare there is: Gary Cooper looking bored atop his horse, Paulette Goddard enjoying a luxurious bubble bath, Dorothy Lamour and Alan Ladd in the "Tallahassee" airplane production song number, Burt Lancaster and Lizabeth Scott in a minor spoof of circus sharpshooters, Diana Lynn, Lamour, Cooper, and Barry Fitzgerald as a barbershop quartet (singing "Harmony"), and walk-on cameos by the likes of Ray Milland and Veronica Lake.

The <u>New York Herald-Tribune</u> concluded, "the foundation of the humor here is a Hollywood attempt to kid itself, but the film's incidents rarely rise above a half-hearted slapstick."

VILLA OF THE MOVIES see **THE SHORT FILMS**

A VITAGRAPH ROMANCE see THE SHORT FILMS

THE VOICE OF HOLLYWOOD see THE SHORT FILMS

W. C. FIELDS AND ME (Universal, 1976) Color, 112 min.

Producer, Jay Weston; director, Arthur Hiller; based on the book by Carlotta Monti with Cy Rice; screenplay, Bob Merrill; assistant directors, Frederic Brost and Gary D. Daigler; production designer, Robert Boyle; set decorator, Arthur Jeph Parker; consultant, Monti; music, Henry Mancini; costumes, Edith Head and Bib Jobe; makeup, Stan Winston; sound, John Kean; sound re-recording, Robert L. Hoyt; special camera effects, Albert Whitlock; camera, David M. Walsh; editor, John C. Howard.

Rod Steiger (W. C. Fields); Valerie Perrine (Carlotta Monti); John Marley (Harry Bannerman); Jack Cassidy (John Barrymore); Bernadette Peters (Melody); Dana Elcar (Dockstedter); Paul Stewart (Florenz Ziegfeld); Billy Barty (Ludwig); Allan Arbus (Gregory La Cava); Milt Kamen (Chasen); Louis Zorich (Gene Fowler); Andrew Parks (Claude Fields); Hank Rolike (Leon); Kenneth Tobey (Parker); Paul Mantee (Edward); Elizabeth Thompson (Woman Patient); Eddie Firestone (Private Detective); Linda Purl (Ingenue); Clay Tanner (Assistant Director); George Loros (Schmidt).

For 14 years, willowy brunette Carlotta Monti served W. C. Fields as mistress and secretary, foresaking her career as a starlet with apparent glee to become the lover and companion to the famed comedian. When Fields died on Christmas day of 1946, he left Carlotta $25 a week for life, his antique roadster (which Miss Monti still rides up and down Sunset Boulevard), and a bevy of memories which the lady later transformed into a book, W. C. Fields and Me, penned with Cy Rice. Miss Monti's revelations about her late amour proved a popular book and Universal hoped to cash in on the nostalgia craze by filming the property. The result was--in the words of Vincent Canby (New York Times)--a "dreary exhibition of incompetence, beside which the recent Gable and Lombard [q. v.] becomes one of the towering achievements of the world cinema. "
W. C. Fields and Me proved to be a seemingly endless distortion of the life and times of William Claude Dukinfield (1879-1946). Tracing the comedian's career from his Broadway tenure with Florenz Ziegfeld to his death in a Hollywood sanatorium, the film revels in outrageously fictional episodes (e. g. Fields' arriving impoverished in Hollywood with a benign dwarf [Billy Barty], while, in actuality, he drove to Hollywood in 1931 in a new Lincoln car carrying $350,000 in $1,000 bills).
For many it was unfortunate that Rod Steiger was cast as the bulbous-nosed, alcoholic comedian. The actor's exhaustive "method" approach to the part (he did capture the vocal inflections well) carried a melancholy smile which diluted the great man's magnificent misanthropic aura. More unforgiveable was the casting of Valerie Perrine,

Rod Steiger in <u>W. C. Fields and Me</u> (1976).

former Las Vegas chorine who had freshly scored in Lenny (1974).
The actress complained bitterly throughout production about the necessity of wearing, for example, a garter belt or a girdle to flatter her
period costumes, publically referring to the still very-much-alive
Miss Monti as "kinda weird. " For whatever reasons, Perrine interpreted Monti--in the words of the aforementioned Canby of the Times--
as "either a masochist or mental deficient. "

    Not content to malign Fields alone, the film fractured such
other Hollywood legends as John Barrymore (admittedly played smoothly by Jack Cassidy), writer Gene Fowler (Louis Zorich), director
Gregory La Cava (Allan Arbus), and restauranteur Dave Chasen (Milt
Kamen). Shining in the 111 minutes of fiction was Paul Stewart as a
classy Florenz Ziegfeld, who provided some desperately needed dignity, and Bernadette Peters as Fields' treacherous vaudeville partner
Melody.

    It is truly an absurd situation when Hollywood takes the life
of one of its most colorful and unforgettable habitués and shellacks
it with fictional muck which demotes the character from the excep-
tional to the mundane. But then, has not Hollywood been performing
that self-denigration for years? As Time magazine sadly reported of
the box-office dud, "... if its creators had backed up to the fact
that there was no honest way to make a PG movie out of life and art
which was strictly R-rated, they might have turned out a film worthy
of the peculiar old master himself. "

THE WAY WE WERE (Columbia, 1973) Color, 118 min.

    Producer, Ray Stark; associate producer, Richard Roth; dir-
ector, Sydney Pollack; based on the novel by Arthur Laurents; screenplay, Laurents; assistant director, Howard Koch, Jr. ; production designer, Stephen Grimes; set decorator, William Kiernan; music, Marvin Hamlisch; song, Hamlisch, Marilyn Bergman, and Alan Bergman;
titles, Phil Norman; sound, Jack Solomon; camera, Harry Stradling,
Jr. ; supervising editor, Margaret Booth.

    Barbra Streisand (Katie Morosky); Robert Redford (Hubbell
Gardiner); Bradford Dillman (J. J.); Lois Chiles (Carol Ann); Patrick
O'Neal (George Bissinger); Viveca Lindfors (Paula Reisner); Allyn
Ann McLerie (Rhea Edwards); Murray Hamilton (Brooks Carpenter);
Herb Edelman (Bill Verso); Diana Ewing (Vicki Bissinger); Sally Kirk-
land (Pony Dunbar); Marcia Mae Jones (Peggy Vanderbilt); Don Keefer
(Actor); George Gaynes (El Morocco Captain); Eric Boles (Army Cor-
poral); Barbara Peterson (Ash Blonde); Roy Jenson (Army Captain);
Robert Gerringer (Dr. Short); Susie Blakely (Judianne); Ed Power
(Airforce); Suzanne Zenor (Dumb Blonde); Dan Seymour (Guest); Don
Koll (Extra).

    The setting for this elaborate piece of nostalgia was the two-
decade period between the late thirties and the mid-fifties, with much
of the storyline occurring in Hollywood. The film capital of this time
spanned the period from the hedonistic days of economic recovery

when everyone went to the movies and scriptwriters lined up at identical typewriters with their identical thoughts and identical phraseology
belching out the pap for the masses, to the post-"witch hunt" era
when movies were fighting a losing battle with their archenemy television.   The Way We Were is a bittersweet tale of love and political
alienation draped against this background.

Hubbell Gardiner (Robert Redford) is a non-political college
student with a talent for prose who meets a pro-Communist activist
Katie Morosky (Barbra Streisand) and, to his amazement and hers,
is later greatly attracted to the kookie young woman.   Streisand ad-
mires Redford's writing ability but not his political detachment.
When they meet again in New York after he has written a best-selling
novel, they fall in love and the iconoclastic girl sublimates her politics in order to nurture the man's career.

They go to Hollywood where he settles into the profitable, if
creatively unrewarding, life of a scenarist.   By the early fifties,
pregnant Streisand finds herself once again involved in politics as
her indignation about the House Committee on UnAmerican Activities
investigations of "Reds" in California leads her on a crusade to Washington, D.C., to protest the situation--all of this against the wishes
of her firmly-entrenched screenwriter husband.   Returning west she
is caught by a mob of anti-Reds and is badly shaken.

It is then that the couple realize their marriage is doomed
and they agree to separate after the birth of their child.   Years later
they meet again in Manhattan, each with a new life.   Although they
have a twinge of love for one another, each realizes the future must
be led separately.

As a love story, The Way We Were was superb and the performances of its superstar leads were credible.   Streisand was Oscar-nominated, though most thought Redford, not nominated, bested
her.   The title tune proved to be a best-selling record for Streisand
and an Oscar winner; making a celebrity of its composer, Marvin
Hamlisch.   The film was stylishly made and grossed $25 million in
distributors' domestic rentals.   It was still in release in 1976, just
weeks before making its TV debut.

Films in Review critic Michael Deskey, summed it up thusly:
"The film is not profound, but somehow, at this particular time, it
strikes a nostalgic resonance that makes it thoroughly moving and enjoyable. "   The portrait painted of the talented writer stagnated in es-
tablishment-bound Hollywood evoked just enough F. Scott Fitzgerald
to cement the movie's credibility without overshadowing the story with
spectors of that tragic writer's fate.

WEEK-END AT THE WALDORF   see   IN PERSON

WE CAN'T HAVE EVERYTHING (Paramount, 1918) 6 reels

Producer/director, Cecil B. DeMille; based on the novel by

Opposite: Barbra Streisand and Robert Redford in The Way We Were
(1973).

Rupert Hughes; screenplay, William C. DeMille; camera, Alvin Wyckoff; editors, DeMille and Anne Bauchens.

Kathlyn Williams (Charity Coe Cheever); Elliott Dexter (Jim Dyckman); Wanda Hawley (Kedzie Thropp); Sylvia Breamer (Zada L'Etoile); Thurston Hall (Peter Cheever); Raymond Hatton (Marquis of Strathdene); Tully Marshall (The Director); Theodore Roberts (The Sultan); James Neill (Detective); Ernest Joy (Heavy); Billy Elmer (Props); Charles Ogle and Sylvia Ashton (Kedzie's Parents).

A society woman, Charity Cheever (Kathlyn Williams), is badly neglected by her millionaire husband (Peter Cheever) who is having an affair with a dancer.   Williams, however, is also sought after by young millionaire Jim Dyckman (Elliott Dexter), but she informs him they cannot wed.   The eligible bachelor then relates to movie star Kedzie Thropp (Wanda Hawley) who vamps him into marriage.
Williams does later divorce her husband and then discovers that Dexter has wed the film notable.   Meanwhile Hawley has become bored with her new spouse and wants out of the marriage in order to marry the Marquis of Strathdene (Raymond Hatton).   Hawley divorces Dexter, names Williams as "the other woman," and then marries Hatton.   She then discovers that she will enjoy no honeymoon as the nobleman must return to France to join his wartime regiment.   In the meantime, Dexter and Williams go abroad to marry.
Within the framework of this supposedly topical story of the vagaries of the very rich, there is quite a bit of attention devoted to moviemaking.   Wanda Hawley is shown on the movie set making a desert epic with Theodore Roberts as the sultan, Tully Marshall as a D. W. Griffith-type director, and Hawley as a harem girl.   This cloak-and-sandal epic, however, is presented as a rather tacky effort and the film-within-the-film offers some amusing aspects of shoe-string film-making.   One such facet was the lensing of an unexpected fire at the Lasky Studio and interpolating it into the movie-within-a-movie footage.

WHAT EVER HAPPENED TO BABY JANE?   (Warner Bros. , 1962) 132 min.

Executive producer, Kenneth Hyman; producer/director, Robert Aldrich; based on the novel by Henry Farrell; screenplay, Lukas Heller; art director, William Glasgow; set decorator, George Sawley; assistant director, Tom Connors; makeup, Jack Obringer and Monty Westmore; choreography, Alex Romero; music, Frank De Vol; sound, Jack Solomon; special effects, Don Steward; camera, Ernest Haller; editor, Michael Luciano.

Bette Davis (Jane Hudson); Joan Crawford (Blanche Hudson); Victor Buono (Edwin Flagg); Anna Lee (Mrs. Bates); Maidie Norman (Elvira Stitt); Marjorie Bennett (Mrs. Flagg); Dave Willock (Ray Hudson); Ann Barton (Cora Hudson); Barbara Merrill (Liza Bates); Julie Allred (Young Jane Hudson); Gina Gillespie (Young Blanche Hudson); Bert Freed (Producer); Wesley Addy (Director).

Within 11 days of issuance this black-and-white picture re-couped its million-dollar-plus budget and then went on to gross over $4 million domestically. It was the "sleeper" film of 1962. The macabre offering reactived the careers of both Bette Davis and Joan Crawford, setting the way for the grand dames to journey on further excursions into grand guignol cinema. Heaped in nostalgia and just a side-street off Sunset Boulevard (q. v.), the bizarre feature proved to be one of the most captivating looks Hollywood has taken at the price of fame and its fleeting rewards.

The narrative involves sisters Jane (Davis) and Blanche Hudson (Crawford) who exist as recluses in their Hollywood mansion. In the heyday of vaudeville Davis had been a big child star, but had failed to make a success in the talkies, while Crawford had become the biggest name in Hollywood. Then a freak car accident had left Crawford a hopeless cripple.

For three decades the hate-drenched duo had lived in their dinosaur of a house, Crawford trying to cling to reality. Davis, who had been blamed for the accident, has lost herself in drink and fantasy. When Davis learns that Crawford plans to have her committed, she retaliates by keeping her a prisoner until the neurotic young pianist (Victor Buono), hired by Davis, finds Crawford in a near-death condition.

After murdering the cleaning lady who tries to help her sister, Davis flees with Crawford to Malibu Beach. There a strange ballet-like horror tale is played out on the sand. Dying, Crawford confesses to Davis that she was responsible for the accident that made her a cripple all these years. Completely unbalanced by now, Davis leaves Crawford to expire. As she watches the other bathers gather around, she believes she is back on stage as a child and dances as the police arrive to find the prostrate body of Crawford.

Both Davis and Crawford contributed sharply-delineated characterizations as the aged, outlandish movie star sisters. Davis and Buono were nominated for Oscars. Although neither of these two won the coveted statue, the film did earn Academy Awards for set design and costumes.

It was the cold, piercing examination of a starkly mad side of Hollywood that offered audiences their greatest reward--that and the opportunity of seeing two great (and always rival) actresses playing to the hilt their substantial assignments. Scenes from Crawford's Sadie McKee (MGM, 1934) were used in the pictures as were sequences from Davis' Parachute Jumper and Ex-Lady (both Warner Bros. , 1933).

As a companion piece to Sunset Boulevard, What Ever Happened to Baby Jane? is a stark testimony to how far adrift bruised ego can wander after the years of adolation stop. Being a has-been in any profession is damaging enough; but to drop from the heights in show business where every emotion is magnified a thousandfold, is near cataclysmic.

WHAT PRICE HOLLYWOOD? (RKO-Pathé, 1932) 87 min.

Executive producer, David O. Selznick; associate producer,

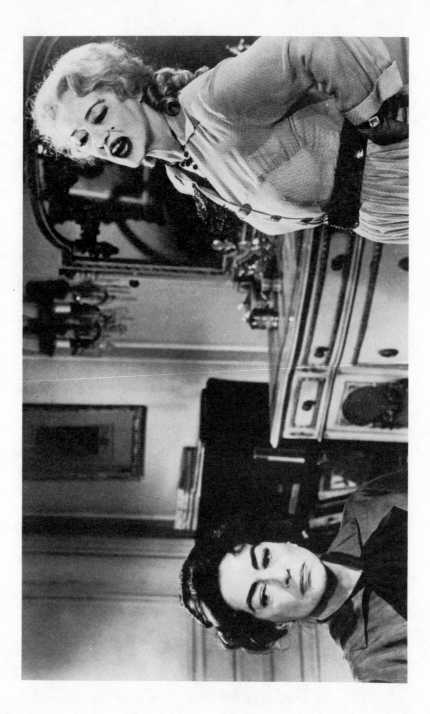

Constance Bennett and Lowell Sherman in <u>What Price Hollywood?</u>
(1932).

Pandro S. Berman; director, George Cukor; based on the story by
Adela Rogers St. John; adaptors, Gene Fowler and Rowland Brown;
screenplay, Jane Murfin and Ben Markson; art director, Carroll
Clark; music director, Max Steiner; montages, Slavko Vorkapich;
costumes, Margaret Pemberton; camera, Charles Rosher; editor,
Jack Kitchin.

Constance Bennett (Mary Evans); Lowell Sherman (Maximilian
Carey); Neil Hamilton (Lonny Borden); Gregory Ratoff (Julius Saxe);
Brooks Benedict (Muto); Louise Beavers (Bonita the Maid); Eddie Anderson (James); Bryant Washburn (Washed-Up Star); Florence Roberts
(Diner); Gordon DeMain (Yes Man); Heinie Conklin (Car Owner); Eddie Dunn (Doorman at Grauman's Chinese Theatre); Phil Teal (Jimmy
the Assistant Director).

As president of RKO Radio Pictures, David O. Selznick planned
this vehicle by Adela Rogers St. John as a comeback picture for
Clara Bow.   But the famous "It" Girl and RKO were unable to come
to terms and sleek, sophisticated Constance Bennett inherited the
meaty role.   The concept of intermingling the rise to success and

---

Opposite: Joan Crawford and Bette Davis in <u>What Ever Happened to
Baby Jane?</u> (1962).

the fall from fame apparently intrigued Selznick greatly, for he would employ it again in his later thirties' success, A Star Is Born (q. v.).

Mary Evans (Bennett) is a waitress at the Brown Derby Restaurant in Hollywood. There she meets drunken but debonair film director Maximilian Carey (Lowell Sherman). This important film figure arranges a screen test for her. Step by step she climbs the Hollywood ladder and becomes a star known as "America's Pal. "

With stardom she also acquires a husband, handsome polo player Lonny Borden (Neil Hamilton), but she places him second to her career. Hamilton will not endure this subordinate status and leaves Bennett just prior to the birth of their son.

Director Sherman, now a has-been, makes a scene at Bennett's home and there commits suicide. As a result a scandal develops which promises to ruin her film career. With her infant son she flees to rural France where she intends to live in obscurity. Hamilton follows, however, and they are reconciled. They now look forward to a happy future together with their child.

Although this feature would emerge as a major/minor landmark in the history of Hollywood-on-Hollywood films, at the time, the "witty and biting parody of the film colony" (John Baxter, Hollywood in the Thirties, 1968) earned some rebukes. The New York Times insisted, "Parts of What Price Hollywood? are very amusing, intentionally, and others are despite themselves. Sections of it are very sorrowful, in the bewildered manner of a lost scenario writer, and yet others are quite agreeable.... Lest there be confusion, What Price Hollywood? is not all bad. The early scenes, where Mr. Sherman is a director on the downward glide and Mary is a waitress going up, are very amusing. Mr. [Gregory] Ratoff's caricature of the screen magnate is also excellent throughout. "

Interestingly, George Cukor, in his first job at RKO, directed this effort as he would its distant cousin, the second version of A Star Is Born (q. v.).

WHAT'S THE MATTER WITH HELEN? (United Artists, 1971) Color, 101 min.

Executive producer, Edward S. Feldman; producers, George Edwards and James C. Pratt; director, Curtis Harrington; screenplay, Henry Farrell; assistant director, Claude Binyon, Jr. ; costumes, Morton Haack; choreography, Tony Charmoli; art director, Eugene Lourie; set decorator, Jerry Wunderlich; sound, Al Overton, Jr. ; camera, Lucien Ballard; editor, William H. Reynolds.

Debbie Reynolds (Adelle Bruckner); Shelley Winters (Helen Hill); Dennis Weaver (Lincoln Palmer); Agnes Moorehead (Sister Alma); Michael MacLiammoir (Hamilton Starr); Sammee Lee Jones (Winona Palmer); Robbi Morgan (Rosalie Greenbaum); Helene Winston (Mrs. Greenbaum); Molly Dodd (Mrs. Rigg); Peggy Rea (Mrs. Schultz); Yvette Vickers (Mrs. Barker); Paulle Clarke (Mrs. Plumb); Pamelyn Ferdin (Kiddy Master of Ceremonies); Debbie Van DenHouten (Sue Anne Scultz); Tammy Lee (Charlene Barker); Teresa de Rose

Shelley Winters and Debbie Reynolds in What's the Matter with Helen? (1971).

(Donna Plumb); Swen Swenson (Gigolo); Timothy Carey (Tramp); Minta Durfee Arbuckle (Old Lady); Douglas Deane (Fanatical Man).

Based on a screenplay by Henry Farrell (who had written the novel What Ever Happened to Baby Jane?), this psychological horror film sought to follow in the same profitable path as the earlier Bette Davis-Joan Crawford vehicle.   Unfortunately it came too late in the cycle and lacked the horrific atmosphere expected of such screen fare.   On the plus side, it did offer a glow of nostalgia and it did rather convincingly recreate the tinsel world which was the periphery of thirties' Hollywood where a child star like Shirley Temple could emerge from the type of dancing school herein depicted.

To escape the stigma of a murder committed by their respective offsprings, Adelle Bruckner (Debbie Reynolds) and Helen Hill (Shelley Winters) leave their small town and come to Hollywood. Once there, Reynolds establishes dancing classes for small girls, with Winters accompanying on the organ (her specialty is "Goody, Goody").   In the background is a mysterious figure who seems to be

stalking the two women.   As time goes by, success comes to the
school and romance comes to Reynolds in the form of Lincoln Palmer
(Dennis Weaver).   As the two women drift apart, Winters becomes
deeply involved with revivalist Sister Alma (Agnes Moorehead).   At
the finale she is found at the organ playing a rousing rendition of
"Goody, Goody" as Weaver finds the corpse of Reynolds.   The de-
mented, overweight Winters is the killer.

In the Village Voice, Michael Kerbel wrote of director Curtis
Harrington, "Quite interesting is his evocation of the '30's through
both newsreels and a careful re-creation of the Hollywood milieu--
done with a friendly mockery that seems to come from an artist
having a love-hate relationship with Hollywood."

THE WHOLE TRUTH (Columbia, 1958) 84 min.

Producer, Jack Clayton; director, John Guillermin; based on
the stage and television play by Philip Mackie; screenplay, Jonathan
Latimer; assistant director, Ronald Spencer; art director, Tony
Masters; music, Mischa Spoliansky; music director, Lambert William-
son; makeup, Roy Ashton; wardrobe, Bridget Sellers; sound, F. Ryan,
Bob Jones, and John Aldred; camera, Wilkie Cooper; editor, Gerry
Hambling.

Stewart Granger (Max Paulton); Donna Reed (Carol Paulton);
George Sanders (Inspector Carliss); Gianna Maria Canale (Gina Ber-
tini); Michael Shillo (Inspector Simon); Richard Molinas (Gilbert);
Peter Dyneley (Willy Reichel); John Van Eyssen (Archer); Philip
Vickers (Jack Leslie); Jimmy Thompson (Assistant); Hy Hazell
(American Woman); Carlo Justini (Leading Man); Agnes Lauchlan
(English Woman); Jacques Cey (Barman); Hugo De Varnier (Hotel Re-
ceptionist); Yves Chanteau (Rouget); Jean Driant (Servant).

Adventure star Stewart Granger headlined the cast of this
British-lensed Columbia product which also included two other ex-
MGM luminaries, Donna Reed and George Sanders.   The movie was
based on the stage and TV play by Philip MacKie and Picturegoer
magazine noted, "It's a neat enough thriller, but hardly worth the
while of its star cast."   The Whole Truth was good item for the
foreign markets, but for the U.S. it held little appeal and was soon
relegated to TV.

Film idol Max Poulton (Granger), is a bit down on his luck.
He goes on location to Italy for his latest epic.   There he initiates
a love affair with fiery co-star Gina Bertini (Gianna Maria Canale).
After the duo come to an unhappy parting, the girl is found murdered
with an ax in her back.   Granger is naturally a major suspect in the
homicide.   His wife (Reed) arrives on the scene only to be hurt by
the belated news of the amorous encounter, although she believes
her spouse to be innocent of the killing.   Scotland Yard Inspector
Carliss (Sanders) however, is out to entrap Granger as the wrong-
doer.   On the other hand, the movie actor believes that Sanders
himself might be the needed clue to the solution of the case.

Donna Reed and George Sanders in <u>The Whole Truth</u> (1958).

The mixture of the international cast and the random bits of "authentic" film-making sequences, gave the film a slight flavor of the industry, but it all seemed too contrived to have much verisimilitude.

One can only wonder why in decades past, the formula of mixing film-making-within-a-film had so often to be mixed with an on-the-set-murder. Did the scripters feel that a true study of the dreary grind of moviemaking would be too dull on its own to capture the audience's interest?

THE WILD PARTY (American International, 1975) Color, 100 min.

Presenter, Samuel Z. Arkoff; executive producers, Edgar Lansbury and Joseph Beruh; producer, Ismail Merchant; associate producer, George Manasse; director, James Ivory; based on the poem by Joseph Moncure March; screenplay/original songs, Walter Marks; dance music, Louis St. Louis; music sequences staged by Patricia Birch; music, Larry Rosenthal; art director, David Nichols; assistant director, Edward Folger; costumes, Ron Talsky, Ralph Lauren, and Ronald Kolodgie; camera, Walter Lassally; editor, Kent McKinney.

James Coco and Jennifer Lee in The Wild Party (1974).

James Coco (Jolly Grimm); Raquel Welch (Queenie); Perry King (Dale Sword); Tiffany Bolling (Kate); Royal Dano (Tex); David Dukes (James Morrison); Dena Dietrich (Mrs. Murchison); Regis Cordic (Mr. Murchison); Jennifer Lee (Madeline True); Marya Small (Bertha); Bobo Lewis (Wilma); Annette Ferra (Nadine); Eddie Laurence (Kreutzer); Tony Paxton (Sergeant); Waldo K. Berns (Policeman); Nino Faso (Nurse); Baruch Lumet (Tailor); Martin Kove (Editor); Ralph Manza (Fruit Dealer); Lark Geib (Rose); Frederick Franklyn (Sam); J. S. Johnson (Morris); Don De Natale (Jackie the Dancer); Phil D'Armano (Skipper).

The Wild Party was supposed to be a re-staging of the famous orgy of the early twenties in which Roscoe "Fatty" Arbuckle was accused of murdering starlet Virginia Rappe. Any similarity, however, between this film and the event was purely coincidental. In fact, about the only real similarity was that Arbuckle and Jolly Grimm (James Coco) were both fat. Arbuckle was at the zenith of his screen career when the tragedy occurred in San Francisco, while Coco's Grimm is depicted as a faded has-been still clinging to the glories of stardom through false hopes for his latest picture.

The events of this color, 100-minute offering, take place during a 24-hour period and are narrated in rhyme (!) by the character of writer James Morrison (David Dukes). The narrative has Coco and mistress Queenie (Raquel Welch) inviting a number of moguls and others of the Hollywood crowd to his mansion to witness his first new film in five years, Brother Jasper. Coco prays the picture will re-establish him as a first-ranking star and will give him the status to keep fickle Welch's interest. Many of the invited, however, do not arrive, as another gala is being held--at Pickfair--the same evening. Those who do appear at Coco's mansion are not overly impressed with Coco's new photoplay; the fact that it is a silent at a time (1929) when talkies are all the rage seals its fate.

Dismayed, Coco drinks heavily and disgusted Welch is attracted to fast-rising stud star, Dale Sword (Perry King). Coco is later almost involved in a major brawl when he is caught kissing the nymphet sister of a guest. When he discovers that Welch has gone to bed with King, he loses control of his emotions. In a wild fit of rage, Coco kills both Welch and King, and injures Dukes, who is revealed writing the tragic account from his hospital bed.

The Wild Party was such a poor offering that it received very scant theatrical release in the U.S. (it was quickly shunted to home box-office). A cut and poorly re-edited version was premiered on NBC-TV on February 12, 1977, and the picture was a disaster all over again. Among the more embarrassing moments were Welch singing "Singapore Sally" and dancing to the tune "Queenie." Only Coco as Jolly Grimm turned in a half-way decent lead performance; Royal Dano was quite competent as Coco's loyal assistant, Tex.

Without a doubt, much of the blame lies with American-born director James Ivory, who gained more of his cinema fame making motion pictures in India (e.g. The Householder, 1962; Shakespeare Wallah, 1964; Bombay Talkie, 1970; etc.). It seems to be accepted form in Hollywood to have someone not deeply steeped in the virtues and vices of the industry's past direct such a history-ladden exercise on screen (e.g. Tony Richardson's The Loved One, John Schlesinger's The Day of the Locust, and Ken Russell's Valentino, qq. v.).

WILL SUCCESS SPOIL ROCK HUNTER? (20th Century-Fox, 1957) Color, 94 min.

Producer/director, Frank Tashlin; based on the play by George Axelrod; screenplay, Tashlin; art directors, Lyle Wheeler and Leland Fuller; music, Cyril J. Mockridge; song, Bobby Troup; music director, Lionel Newman; orchestrator, Edward B. Powell; wardrobe designer, Charles Le Maire; assistant director, Joseph E. Rickards; special camera effects, L. B. Abbott; camera, Joe MacDonald; editor, Hugh S. Fowler.

Jayne Mansfield (Rita Marlowe); Tony Randall (Rock Hunter); Betsy Drake (Jenny); Joan Blondell (Violet); John Williams (Le Salle, Jr.); Henry Jones (Rufus); Lili Gentle (April); Mickey Hargitay (Bobo); Georgia Carr (Calypso Number); Groucho Marx (Surprise Guest); Dick Whittinghill (TV Interviewer); Ann McCrea (Gladys); Lida Piazza (Jr.'s Secretary); Bob Adler and Phil Chambers (Mailmen); Larry Kerr (Mr.

Ezzarus); Sherill Terry (Annie); Carmen Nisbit (Breakfast Food Demonstrator); Don Corey (Voice of Ed Sullivan); Benny Rubin (Theatre Manager); Minta Durfee and Edith Russell (Scrub Women).

As written by George Axelrod and produced on Broadway in 1955, Will Success Spoil Rock Hunter? was a satirical jab at the movie medium.   When 20th Century-Fox bowdlerized it, however, the lampoon had been switched from movies to television and the latter industry's lifeblood, commercials.

Advertising executive Rock Hunter (Tony Randall) is about to lose his company's biggest client, a lipstick company.   He saves the account by luring blonde bombshell movie star Rita Marlowe (played by Jayne Mansfield recreating her stage success) into endorsing the product.   Unfortunately for Randall, Mansfield falls in love with him, much to his chagrin.   The movie life quickly becomes too much for introspective Randall.   After fainting at the altar during his thus aborted marriage to Mansfield, he winds up retiring to a chicken farm and marrying his former girlfriend (Betsy Drake).

The Rita Marlowe character as played to the hilt and the bust by Mansfield, was a broad caricature of Marilyn Monroe.   (In the film Betsy Drake even does an imitation of MM.)   As such, it is an engaging view of the sex symbol phenomenon.   As a satire on TV, however, it was less successful.   As Gordon Gow describes in Hollywood in the Fifties (1971), "It burlesqued the brain-washing commercials, among other things, and the best laugh it raised came during the credit titles when a girl was seen with an active washing machine, extolling its powers while desperately trying to extricate a pair of trousers from its tenacious interior and being hauled into the cauldron herself.   If the manner was generally too broad, the reproaches against gullibility and the readiness of communication outlets to exploit the susceptible en masse were part of a useful trend, which had been evident in a desultory way for quite some time. "

The zestiest performance in the film was offered by Joan Blondell as Mansfield's visually-expressive confidante/masseuse. Note the surprise guest appearance by Groucho Marx.

British release title: Oh, for a Man!

WINDY RILEY GOES TO HOLLYWOOD see THE SHORT FILMS

WINGS OVER WYOMING see HOLLYWOOD COWBOY

WITH A SONG IN MY HEART (20th Century-Fox, 1952) Color, 117 min.

Producer, Lamar Trotti; director, Walter Lang; story/screenplay, Trotti; music director, Alfred Newman; choreography, Billy Daniel; songs, Lorenz Hart and Richard Rodgers; Lew Brown and Sammy Fain; Arthur Freed and Nacio Herb Brown; Irving Caesar and Vincent Youmans; June Hershey and Don Swander; James Bland;

Susan Hayward and Richard Allan in <u>With a Song in My Heart</u> (1952).

Dan Emmett; Frank Loesser and Arthur Schwartz; Peggy Lee and
Dave Barbour; Sammy Cahn and Jule Styne; George M. Cohan; Bud
Green, B. G. De Sylva, and Ray Henderson; De Sylva, Al Jolson,
and Joseph Meyer; Fred Fisher; Katherine Lee Bates and Samuel A.
Ward; Gus Kahn, Fud Livingston, and Matty Malneck; Ira and George
Gershwin; Leo Robin and Ralph Rainger; Don George and Charles
Henderson; Newman and Eliot Daniel; E. A. Fenstad and Lincoln
Colcord; Ballard MacDonald and James F. Hanley; Ted Koehler and
Harold Arlen; Max Showalter and Jack Woodford; Ken Darby; art
directors, Lyle Wheeler and Earle Hagen; costumes, Charles Le
Maire; camera, Leon Shamroy; editor, J. Watson Webb.

Susan Hayward (Jane Froman); Rory Calhoun (John Burn);
David Wayne (Don Ross); Thelma Ritter (Clancy); Robert Wagner
(G. I. Paratrooper); Helen Westcott (Jennifer March); Una Merkel
(Sister Marie); Richard Allan (Dancer); Max Showalter (Guild); Lyle
Talbot (Radio Director); Leif Erickson (General); Stanley Logan (Dip-
lomat); Jane Froman (The Singing Voice of Jane Froman); Frank Sul-
ly (Texas); George Offerman, Jr. (Muleface); Ernest Newton (Special-
ty); William Baldwin (Announcer); Carlos Molina, Nestor Paiva, and
Emmett Vogan (Doctors); Maud Wallace (Sister Margaret); Dick Ryan
(Officer); Douglas Evans (Colonel).

Singer Jane Froman had a very brief film career in the later thirties. Her main source of show business activity was the stage and radio before setting off on a very successful tour entertaining servicemen during World War II. It was on this Allied trek in 1943 that she was involved in a plane accident in which she nearly lost a leg. The crash necessitated many operations and it was years before she could return to work.

The screen biography, With a Song in My Heart, starring dynamic Susan Hayward in the title role, played up the fact that Froman had been a "movie star" but it mostly revolved around the war tour, her accident, and heroic recovery. Froman herself sang the songs on the soundtrack of the film, including "The Right Kind of Love," "Get Happy," "Tea for Two," "It's a Good Day," and the color picture proved to be one of the top ten grossers of 1952. The film provided Hayward with her third Academy Award nomination (she lost the Best Actress Oscar to Shirley Booth of Come Back, Little Sheba). The fourth would derive from I'll Cry Tomorrow (q. v.), and like that film, this entry had basically little to do with the complex Hollywood scene other than relating the life story of a personality who had been in films only for a short period.

WITHOUT RESERVATIONS (RKO, 1946) 107 min.

Producer, Jesse L. Lasky; director, Mervyn LeRoy; based on the novel by Jane Allen and Mae Livingston; screenplay, Andrew Solt; art directors, Albert S. D'Agostino and Ralph Berger; set decorators, Darrell Silvera and James Altwies; music, Roy Webb; music director, C. Bakaleinikoff; sound, Clem Portman and Francis M. Sarver; montages, Harold Palmer and Harold Stine; special effects, Vernon L. Walker and Russell A. Culley; camera, Milton Krasner; editor, Jack Ruggiero.

Claudette Colbert (Kit); John Wayne (Rusty); Don DeFore (Dink); Anne Triola (Connie); Phil Brown (Soldier); Frank Puglia (Ortega); Thurston Hall (Baldwin); Dona Drake (Dolores); Fernando Alvarado (Mexican Boy); Charles Arnt (Salesman); Cary Grant (Himself); Louella Parsons (Herself); Jack Benny (Guest Performer); Charles Evans (Jerome); Harry Hayden (Mr. Randall); Lela Bliss (Mrs. Randall); Griff Barnett (Train Conductor); Esther Howard (Sarah); Oscar O'Shea (Conductor); Ruth Roman (Girl in Negligee); Sam McDaniel (Freddy); Harry Holman (Gas Station Attendant); Eric Alden (Chauffeur); Cy Kendall (Bond's Man); Raymond Burr (Paul Gill).

Kit (Claudette Colbert), author of a best seller, is en route to Hollywood to adapt her work for the screen. In the sleeping car on the train she encounters two Marine flyers, Rusty (John Wayne) and Dink (Don DeFore), who pan her book. The boys do not know her identity, but she immediately envisions one of them, Wayne, for the lead in the picture and wires her producer. Rather than lose sight of the two pilots, she leaves her reserved drawing room accommodation in Chicago and boards their train minus her baggage.

Don DeFore, Claudette Colbert, and John Wayne in Without Reservations (1945).

That evening the trio become drunk, build an airplane out of furniture, and cause so much havoc, that they are thrown off the train. The men then purchase a second-hand auto, and the three pals travel westward. In New Mexico, Colbert cashes a check but is tossed into jail because it is thought she is impersonating a famous writer--herself. Wayne and DeFore sell the car and bail her out, but Wayne later leaves her, thinking he has been played for a fool.

In Hollywood, Colbert succumbs to the social whirl and meets Louella Parsons, Cary Grant, and Jack Benny (playing themselves). A news item in a gossip magazine linking Colbert with an actor upsets Wayne who comes to California. When Colbert meets him again, she knows that her future lies with him.

Although a deft movie comedy, Without Reservations presented several distortions and misconceptions regarding authors and the screen. The major fallacy states that it is the original author who usually adapts his or her work to the screen (they generally do not) and that authors are given the red-carpet treatment by the film industry, who listen patiently to their every interpretation of how their writings should be transferred to the screen. All of this is rarely true, especially in the decade when this feature was produced.

WON-TON-TON, THE DOG WHO SAVED HOLLYWOOD (Paramount, 1976) Color, 92 min.

Producers, David V. Picker, Arnold Schulman, and Michael Winner; associate producer, Tim Zinnemann; director, Winner; screenplay, Schulman and Cy Howard; art director, Ward Preston; set decorator, Ned Parsons; assistant directors, Charles Okun and Arne Schmidt; makeup, Philip Rhodes; dogs trained by Karl Miller; sound, Bob Post; camera, Richard H. Kline; editor, Bernard Gribble.

Dennis Morgan (Tour Guide); Shecky Greene (Tourist); Phil Leeds and Cliff Norton (Dog Catchers); Madeline Kahn (Estee Del Ruth); Teri Garr (Fluffy Peters); Romo Vincent (Short Order Cook); Bruce Dern (Grayson Potchuck); Sterling Holloway (Old Man on Bus); William Benedict (Man on Bus); Dorothy Gulliver (Old Woman on Bus); William Demarest (Studio Gatekeeper); Art Carney (J. J. Fromberg); Virginia Mayo (Miss Battley); Henny Youngman (Manny Farber); Rory Calhoun (Philip Hart); Billy Barty (Assistant Director); Henry Wilcoxon (Silent Film Director); Ricardo Montalban and Richard Arlen (Silent Film Stars); Jackie Coogan and Johnny Weissmuller (Stagehands); Aldo Ray (Stubby Stebbins); Ethel Merman (Hedda Parsons); Yvonne De Carlo (Cleaning Woman); Joan Blondell (Landlady); Andy Devine (Priest in Dog Pound); Broderick Crawford (Special Effects Man); Jack La Rue (Silent Film Villain); Dorothy Lamour (Visiting Film Star); Phil Silvers (Murray Fromberg); Nancy Walker (Mrs. Fromberg); Gloria DeHaven and Ann Miller (President's Girls); Louis Nye (Radio Interviewer); Stepin Fetchit (Dancing Butler); Ken Murray (Souvenir Salesman); Rudy Vallee (Autograph Hound); George Jessel (Awards Announcer); Rhonda Fleming (Rhoda Flaming); Dean

Stockwell (Paul Lavell); Dick Haymes (James Crawford); Tab Hunter
(David Hamilton); Robert Alda (Richard Entwhistle); Eli Mintz (Tail-
or); Ron Leibman (Rudy Montague); Fritz Feld (Rudy's Butler); Ed-
ward Ashley (Another Butler); Jane Connell (Waitress); Janet Blair
(President's Girl #3); Dennis Day (Singing Telegraph Man); Mike
Mazurki (Studio Guard); The Ritz Brothers (Cleaning Women); Jesse
White (Rudy's Agent); Carmel Myers and Jack Carter (Journalists);
Jack Bernardi (Fluffy's Escort); Victor Mature (Nick); Barbara
Nichols (Nick's Girl); Army Archerd (Premiere MC); Fernando Lamas
(Premiere Male Star); Zsa Zsa Gabor (Premiere Female Star); Cyd
Charisse (President's Girl #4); Huntz Hall (Moving Man); Doodles
Weaver (Man in Mexican Film); Pedro Gonzales-Gonzales (Mexican
Projectionist); Eddie Le Veque (Prostitute Customer); Edgar Bergen
(Professor Quicksand); Ronny Graham (Mark Bennett); Morey Amster-
dam and Eddie Foy, Jr. (Custard Pie Stars); Peter Lawford (Slap-
stick Star); Patricia Morison and Guy Madison (Stars at Screening);
Regis Toomey (Burlesque Stagehand); Alice Faye (Secretary at Gate);
Ann Rutherford (Grayson's Studio Secretary); Milton Berle (Blind
Man); John Carradine (Drunk); Keye Luke (Cook in Kitchen); Walter
Pidgeon (Grayson's Butler); Augustus Von Schumacher (Won-Ton-Ton).

Won-Ton-Ton is a dog who was done wrong. Paramount ballyhooed this most talented of animals with an extravagant publicity campaign, a mounting with all the trimmings, and the promise of future
stardom. Then it let him down by allowing the film to die a quick
death.

While far from a classic of any sort, Won-Ton-Ton has moments of entertainment, helped by cameos of dozens of Hollywood's
past greats (photographed, unfortunately, at their worst), along with
the ingratiating presence of the canine star himself. Paramount was
unable to decide on a proper marketing procedure for the picture--
should it be geared for adults or kiddies?--and let it drift into a
midway limbo.

In the Hollywood of 1923, an enterprising police dog (later
dubbed Won-Ton-Ton) escapes from the pound. He befriends an out-
of-work starlet Estee Del Ruth Madeline Kahn). Later, J. J.
Fromberg (Art Carney), the president of New Era Pictures, wants
the dog to star in a film--Carney has witnessed the dog's heroic
rescue of his starlet friend from a lecherous stagehand (Aldo Ray).
Meanwhile tour-bus guide Grayson Potchuck (Bruce Dern), erstwhile
writer-director, saves the dog from a return trip to the pound. With
the clandestine aid of Kahn, Dern makes films with the dog and the
animal becomes the sensation of the industry.

Meanwhile, Kahn, pursuing her own acting aspirations, is discovered by transvestite matinee idol Rudy Montague (Ron Leibman),
who agrees to costar with Kahn and the dog--both of whom upstage
him. Later Leibman tries unsuccessfully to have them both killed.
When the film--about General Custer--is released, it is a bust, and
everyone is out of work.

Finally Kahn becomes a star in her own right by acting in
comedies for Mark Bennett (Ronny Graham), but she has to give up
the dog. He is later rejected from a doggie act and wanders about

aimlessly.   Thereafter, Won-Ton-Ton is found at the beach by Kahn
and Dern, who have now wed.

As a burlesque on Hollywood, movie making, and canine stars
(obviously Rin-Tin-Tin), the film is occasionally pleasant, but most
moviegoers devoted their time trying to name the dozens of (aging)
stars who passed by too quickly in a myriad of cameos.   Perhaps
best were the Ritz Brothers (as cleaning ladies on the wrong set),
Victor Mature (as Nick the hit man), and Aldo Ray.

WORLD PREMIERE (Paramount, 1941) 70 min.

Producer, Sol C. Siegel; director, Ted Tetzlaff; story, Earl
Felton and Gordon Kahn; screenplay, Felton; camera, Dan Fapp; editor, Archie Marshek.

John Barrymore (Duncan DeGrasse); Frances Farmer (Kitty
Carr); Eugene Pallette (Gregory Martin); Virginia Dale (Lee Morri-
son); Ricardo Cortez (Mark Saunders); Sig Rumann (Franz von Bush-
master); Don Castle (Joe Bemis); William Wright (Luther Skinkley);
Fritz Feld (Muller); Luis Alberni (Signor Scaletti); Cliff Nazarro
(Peters); Andrew Tombes (Nixon).

This unassuming B picture was a zany satire on wartime propaganda films, but unfortunately it was suppressed and quickly forgotten because it was released on the eve of World War II.   The
picture took stabs at the use of the movie medium for "educational"
purposes, a situation which came true in World War II as it had
during the Great War of the teens.

John Barrymore was featured as madcap movie producer Duncan DeGrasse who has just completed a film entitled The Earth's on
Fire.   He wants to debut this political intrigue opus in Washington,
D. C.   To drum up publicity for this goal he has his public relations
people send him letters from fictitious fifth columnists, threatening
to sabotage the film.   In reality the Axis assigns two bungling spies
(Luis Alberni and Sig Rumann) to secure a print of the film and
splice in Nazi propaganda.   Despite causing a lot of trouble, the enemy agents are captured, and Barrymore's film is saved.

Charles Higham and Joel Greenberg in Hollywood in the Forties
(1968) term the picture "an almost forgotten comic masterpiece. "
It was the initial directorial effort of cinematographer Ted Tetzlaff
and it was a sterling debut in which he made effective use of the
camera to emphasize the comedy points.   Aging John Barrymore
carried off the role of the bizarre producer with hambone glee.   Frances Farmer, in one of her final solid film jobs, seemed a bit typecast as a snobbish and jealous movie actress who is afraid her leading man (Ricardo Cortez) will upstage her.

Opposite: Gloria DeHaven, Art Carney, Phil Silvers, and Bruce Dern
in Won-Ton-Ton, the Dog Who Saved Hollywood (1976).

John Barrymore, Cliff Nazarro, and Ricardo Cortez in World Premiere (1941).

THE WORLD'S A STAGE (Principal, 1922) 5,700 ft.

Director, Colin Campbell; story, Elinor Glyn; screenplay,
Colin Campbell and George Bertholon; camera, Dal Clawson and Byron Haskin.

Dorothy Phillips (Jo Bishop); Bruce McRae (John Brand); Kenneth Harlan (Wallace Foster); Otis Harlan (Richard Manseld Bishop);
Jack McDonald (Property Man).

Popular screen star Jo Bishop (Dorothy Phillips) falls in love
with and marries a salesman, rather than her old suitor.   Later
Phillips recognizes her error when the husband turns into an alcoholic
who will not work and who exists from her income.   The former beau
tries to straighten out the husband, with little success, and he also

tries to comfort the distraught movie personality.   Finally the spouse is drowned accidentally, and the suitor and Phillips are free to wed.

Fashionable Elinor Glyn penned this domestic melodrama which is an interesting relic as a study of marriage values in the early twenties.   Also it fostered what became the cliche of how unhappy movie people can be by marrying outside their social circle.   In its primitive ways, the film is a distant forerunner of story situations in A Star Is Born.

THE WORLD'S GREATEST LOVER (20th Century-Fox, 1977) Color, 89 min.

Producer, Gene Wilder; co-producer, Terence Marsh and Chris Greenbury; associate producer, Frank Baur; director/screenplay, Wilder; assistant director, Mel Dellar; production designer, Marsh; art director, Steve Sardanis; set decorator, John Franco, Jr.; make-up, Bill Tuttle; choreography, Alan Johnson; music, John Morris; orchestrator, Ralph Burns; song, Wilder; costumes, Ruth Myers; stunt coordinator, Mickey Gilbert; sound, Theodore Soderberg and Jack Solomon; special effects, Logan Frazee and Terry Frazee; camera, Gerald Hirschfeld; supervising editor, Greenbury; editor, Anthony A. Pellegrino.

Gene Wilder (Rudy Valentine); Carol Kane (Annie); Dom DeLuise (Adolph Zitz); Fritz Feld (Hotel Manager); Cousin Buddy (Cousin Buddy); Robert E. Ball (Bald Man); Carol Arthur (Woman in Record Store); Candice Azzara (Anne Calassandro); Carl Ballantine (Uncle Harry); Stanley Brock, James Hong, Frank O'Brien, Richard Karron, and Randolph Dobbs (Yes Men); Warren Burton (Greta Ga-Ga); Matt Collins (Rudolph Valentino); Lou Cutell (Mr. Kipper); Danny DeVito (Assistant Director); Richard Dimitri (Tony Lassiter); Josip Elic (Headwaiter); Melissa Fellen (Cousin Corrine); Ricky Fellin (Cousin Max); James Gleason (Room Clerk); Ronny Graham (Director); Michael Huddleston (Barber); Richard Karron (Bodyguard); Art Mendelli (Jail-or); Sidney Miller (Man at the Table); Jorge Moreno (Mexican Gang-ster); Jack Riley (Projectionist); Rolfe Sedan (Conductor); Florence Sundstrom (Aunt Tillie); Richard Roth (Chico); Pat Ast (Italian War-drobe Lady/Bakery Lady); Patrick Regan (Assistant Director); Pavla Ustinov (Leading Lady); Al Wyatt Sr. (Arab Wrangler); Nick Dimitri (Assistant Director--Seaside/Boyfriend).

It is 1926 and Adolph Zitz (Dom DeLuise), volatile head of Rainbow Pictures, decides to compete with Paramount's Rudolph Valentino by launching a contest to find a new screen matinee idol and star him in a plush photoplay entitled The World's Greatest Lover. Among those drawn to Hollywood by the contest are Rudy Valentine (Gene Wilder), an unemotionally unstable refugee from Milwaukee and his young wife Annie (Carol Kane).   Hardly have they settled in Hollywood than Kane departs to find her true love--Rudolph Valentino (Matt Collins), leaving Wilder to cope with life and his pending audition alone.

The manic head of Rainbow Studios (DeLuise) is so determined to find his Latin Lover rival, that he blithely tests thousands of candidates, most of whom have no talent whatsoever for screen acting. By a fluke of outrageous fate and luck, Wilder is among the three finalists in the contest. Meanwhile, Kane has gone on location with the Valentino film unit and there made love to whom she assumed was the great matinee idol. In reality, it was Wilder who had followed her and made friends with the film star, who loaned him the star tent for the rendezvous.

Wonder of wonders, Wilder is so convincing in his final audition (actually because he is bemoaning the loss of Kane who has announced she is returning to the Midwest) that he is selected as Rainbow Pictures' hope for the future. However, Wilder rides off the set and pursues the train carrying Kane. She disembarks and they ride off into the sunset together.

In the same year that saw the release of the dismal, tasteless, Valentino (q. v.) by Ken Russell, this comedy seemed far better than it was. As with most of the screen mayhem produced by Mel Brooks (e. g. Silent Movie, Blazing Saddles, qq. v.) and his factory of talent (including Wilder and Marty Feldman, both of whom have launched out on their own as star/directors) the proceedings are very uneven, the comedy barbs of seesawing levels, and the end results often anticlimactic. The World's Greatest Lover is no exception.

There are some quite funny set pieces: Wilder swimming in his hotel sunken living room, the chaos on the bakery assembly line, the actor going berserk during his screen audition, the elaborate seduction scene in the tent (where Wilder sends-up Valentino's "pink powderpuff" image), etc. (There is an end title card which thanks Federico Fellini for his encouragement--Wilder's way of acknowledging the Italian filmmaker's consent for him to lampoon his 1952 The White Sheik.)

Of major importance is that within the comedy scenario--and the terribly broad, even overbearing caricatures by DeLuise, Huddleston, Graham, et al--there are many salient points made about Hollywood in the twenties, especially the general public's fantasy about how each and everyone can become a movie star if he really so desires. The sequence in which a sartorially proud Wilder departs the train in Los Angeles to discover hundreds of other screen contest applicants in similar white suits makes its mark, as does the audition scenes in which bored screen dames must suffer through screen test after test with untutored, crude candidates.

Wilder evidently has great affection for the Flapper period and treats it royally: hotel scenes, costumes, backlot ambiance. If anything, it was Wilder's insistence on assuming too many production tasks which vitiated the potential of the lampoon. As Variety analyzed, "This time the individual sketchpieces ... emerge as varyingly humorous episodes strung out on a skimpy story line. "

As for Matt Collins' impersonation of Valentino, the fashion model had the proper exotic looks and theatrical presence, but the script (fortunately or otherwise) refrained from having him engage in much more than a bit of pantomime acting. His limited footage, however, gave seventies' viewers a far closer approximation of the sexual chemistry created by the Latin Lover than did Nureyev, Franco Nero, or Anthony Dexter in past and present Hollywood entries on the legendary screen figure.

If low-brows found this film amusing, critics such as Arthur Knight of the Hollywood Reporter did not. In his "thumbs down" on the picture he explained, "It turns out to be The Guardsman without the wink, a Wilder comedy in which the second bananas get all the best lines. And not even Marty Feldman is quite so addicted to popping the eyeballs for comic effect as Wilder.... The conveyor belt in the mechanized bakery scene that opens the film only reminded me how much better Chaplin did it in Modern Times. The sequences with the flooded sunken living room had the potential for a marvelous Keaton sight gag, but with none of Keaton's fecund comic invention. Wilder's character in this film has a lot in common with Harold Lloyd's bespectacled innocent--except that Wilder himself is so obsessed with his own sexiness and going it 'by the numbers,' that all innocence is lost. On the other hand, John Morris has provided a lilting, nostalgic--if occasionally anachronistic--score that repeatedly helps the film find its bearings." (Knight also points out the factual error in the plotline--by 1926 Rudolph Valentino was no longer at Paramount; he had joined United Artists.)

YOKEL BOY (Republic, 1942) 69 min.

   Associate producer, Robert North; director, Joseph Santley; based on the play by Russel Crouse; screenplay, Isabel Dawn; music director, Cy Feuer; songs, Lew Brown, Charles Tobias, and Sammy Stept; Caesar Petrillo, Nelson Shawn, and Edward Ross; camera, Ernest Miller; editor, Edward Mann.

   Joan Davis (Molly Malone); Albert Dekker (Bugsie Malone); Eddie Foy, Jr. (Joe Ruddy); Alan Mowbray (R. B. Harris); Roscoe Karns (Al Devers); Mikhail Rasumny (Amatoff); Lynne Carver (Vera Valaize); Tom Dugan (Professor); Marc Lawrence (Trigger); Florence Wright (Receptionist); Pierre Watkin (Johnson); Charles Lane (Cynic); Cyril Ring (Reporter); Betty Blythe (Woman Reporter); Lois Collier (Stewardess); Tim Ryan (Waiter); Harry Hayden (Bank President); Anne Jeffreys and Mady Lawrence (Witnesses at Wedding); Rod Bacon and Arthur O'Connell (Assistant Directors); Charles Quigley (Policeman); Emmett Vogan (Doctor).

   As a publicity stunt to promote a new gangster film, a movie studio brings to Hollywood a hillbilly boy (Eddie Foy, Jr.) who claims to have seen more movies than anyone in the U.S. The studio churns out loads of publicity about how this "dimwit" can accurately predict upcoming movie tastes due to his vast knowledge of the cinema. As his first prediction, Foy advises the studio to hire a real gangster to play a crimeland chieftain on the screen. The company obliges and Bugsie Malone (Albert Dekker) is put on the payroll. But trouble develops when the hood's none-too-bright sister Molly (Joan Davis) arrives on the scene and proceeds to take over the film. Foy, how-

Roscoe Karns, Joan Davis, and Eddie Foy, Jr., in Yokel Boy (1942).

ever, tumbles romantically for Davis and the two characters--who deserve one another--wind up in each other's arms.

Yokel Boy was very fragile in the comedy department and one reviewer noted that it "works hard to be funny. " Perhaps one of the reasons Yokel Boy emerged such a labored farce--with the likes of Alan Mowbray as a very broad caricature of a studio head--is that the picture was plagued with pre-production problems.   Republic had acquired the screen rights to the Russel Crouse play as a Judy Canova vehicle, she having starred in the 1939 Broadway hit version. Although under contract to Republic, Canova refused the film role, despite the fact her first starring role for the company had been in another Hollywood-oriented comedy, Scatterbrain (q. v.), which had been a big success.   After Joan Davis was hired as a replacement, the emphasis of the property was switched to the Foy role and the end result provided none of the fresh appeal which had made the play so popular.

YOUNG AND BEAUTIFUL (Mascot, 1934) 63 min.

Director, Joseph Santley; story/adaptors, Santley and Milton Krims; screenplay, Dore Schary; additional dialogue, Al Martin and Colbert Clark; sound, Karl Zint; camera, John Stumar; editor, Thomas Scott.

William Haines (Bob Preston); Judith Allen (June Dale); Joseph M. Cawthorne (Herman Cline); John Miljan (Gordon Douglas); Vince Barnett (Sammy); Hazel Hayes, Jean Carmen, Katherine Williams, Judith Arlen, Lu Anne Meredith, Lucille Lund, Jean Gale, Betty Bryson, Dorothy Drake, Ann Hovey, Neoma Judge, and Lenore Keef (Wampas Baby Stars); Ted Fio Rito and His Orchestra (Themselves); Shaw and Lee (Piano Movers); James Bush (Dick); Warren Hymer (Champion); Franklin Pangborn (Radio Announcer); James Burtis (Farrell); and: Syd Saylor, Greta Meyer, Fred Kelsey, Andre Beranger, Ray Mayer, Roy Russell, and Edward Hearn.

June Dale (Judith Allen) is a promising film starlet who falls in love with studio press agent Bob Preston (William Haines). Haines, not realizing that she adores him, plans to make her into a big star with a lot of high-powered publicity stunts.   In this respect he is successful, but Allen still longs to abandon her career and wed Haines. Eventually this set of cross-purposes causes Allen to believe that Haines does not care for her at all and she decides to elope with a wealthy playboy.   Realizing his error, and acknowledging that he loves her, Haines proposes to her and the wedding is set.   Haines, however, cannot resist one final publicity gimmick and he obtains an entire squadron of military planes to be a part of their honeymoon entourage.

In the twilight of the silent days and in the period of the early talkies, star William Haines made quite a number of Hollywood-related films at MGM: Excess Baggage, Show People, A Man's Man, Hollywood Revue of 1929, Free and Easy (qq. v.).   But by the mid-

thirties his career was on the skids and this puny effort was the
first of two comeback pictures he did for Mascot Pictures. Although
Motion Picture Herald graciously claimed, "Nat Levine's first try at
feature production is quite promising," Haines detested both of the
two quickies he did for the producer (the other film was The Marines
Are Coming) and he retired from films permanently thereafter. (He
became a very successful interior decorator in Hollywood.)
        Young and Beautiful was obviously a rush production which
gave little thought to details. It was filmed for quick theatrical playoff and profit, making good use of the residue of Haines' marquee
draw (he had been off the screen for nearly two years since the ending of his MGM contract). To be noted, Young and Beautiful features
the Wampas Baby Stars of 1934 in its cast along with one of the more
popular bands of the day, Ted Fio Rito and His Orchestra.

THE YOUNGEST PROFESSION (MGM, 1943) 82 min.

        Producer, B. F. Ziedman; director, Edward Buzzell; based
on the book by Lillian Day; screenplay, George Oppenheimer, Charles
Lederer, and Leonard Spigelgass; art directors, Cedric Gibbons and
Edward Carfagno; set decorators, Edwin B. Willis and Helen Conway;
music, David Snell; assistant director, Julian Silberstein; sound, Wilhelm W. Brockway; camera, Charles Lawton; editor, Ralph Winters.

        Virginia Weidler (Jean Lyons); Edward Arnold (Mr. Lawrence
Lyons); John Carroll (Hercules); Jean Porter (Patricia Drew); Marta
Linden (Mrs. Edith Lyons); Dick Simmons (Douglas Sutton); Ann Ayars
(Susan Thayer); Agnes Moorehead (Miss Featherstone); Marcia Mae
Jones (Vera Bailey); Raymond Roe (Schuyler); Scotty Beckett (Junior
Lyons); Jessie Grayson (Lilybud); Greer Garson, Walter Pidgeon,
William Powell, Robert Taylor, and Lana Turner (Guest Stars);
Beverly Tyler (Thyra Winters); Patricia Roe (Polly); Marjorie Gate-
son (Mrs. Drew); Thurston Hall (Mr. Drew); Aileen Pringle (Miss
Farwood); Nora Lane (Hilda); Mary Vallee (Mary); Gloria Tucker
(Gladys); Ann MacLean (Ann); Shirley Coates and Mary McCarty
(Girls); Mark Daniels (Les Peterson); William Tannen (Hotel Clerk);
Edward Buzzell (Man in Theatre); Leonard Carey (Valet); Sara Haden
(Salvation Army Lass); Ray Teal (Taxi Driver); Dorothy Morris (Sec-
retary).

        This second-class feature was designed as a starring vehicle
for growing moppet star Virginia Weidler. To bolster its box-office
chances (it debuted at Radio City Music Hall), several MGM contract
stars made token appearances. Nevertheless, it remained "at best
flyweight fare" (New York Times).
        The anemic storyline focused on Jean Lyons (Weidler), a New
York City teenager who heads an autograph club called Guiding Stars,
Ltd. With pal Patricia Drew (Jean Porter) she devotes her time to
haunting railroad terminals and hotels trying to obtain movie celebrities' autographs. Since most of Weidler's romantic illusions and
feelings toward life in general have evolved from film-watching, she

Raymond Roe, Jean Porter, Virginia Weidler, and John Carroll in The Youngest Profession (1943).

---

soon gets herself and her parents (Edward Arnold and Marta Linden) in a pack of trouble when she attempts to remedy various domestic problems.

The "treat" of this precious package was the passing appearances of the likes of Greer Garson, William Powell, Walter Pidgeon, Robert Taylor, and Lana Turner, all giving autographs to the enterprising--if hardly endearing--Miss Weidler, and a few of them offering a bit of homey advice to the precocious miss. In its vague way, The Youngest Profession tried to show that movie personalities were real people concerned with real problems, and that glamour was not their only stock-in-trade.

YOU'RE MY EVERYTHING (20th Century-Fox, 1949) Color, 94 min.

Producer, Lamar Trotti; director, Walter Lang; story, George Jessel; screenplay, Trotti and Will H. Hays, Jr.; art directors, Lyle Wheeler and Leland Fuller; set decorators, Thomas Little and Ernest

Anne Baxter and Dan Dailey in a publicity pose for You're My Everything (1949).

Lansing; music director, Alfred Newman; orchestrators, Herbert Spencer and Earle Hagen; song, Mack Gordon and Josef Myrow; assistant director, Gaston Glass; makeup, Ben Nye, Frank Prehoda, and Ernie Parks; choreography, Nick Castle; costumes, Bonnie Cashin; sound, George Leverett and Roger Heman; special effects, Fred Sersen; camera, Arthur E. Arling; editor, J. Watson Webb, Jr.

Dan Dailey (Timothy O'Connor); Anne Baxter (Hannah Adams); Anne Revere (Aunt Jane); Stanley Ridges (Mr. Mercer); Shari Robinson (Jane); Henry O'Neill (Professor Adams); Selena Royle (Mrs. Adams); Alan Mowbray (Joe Blanton); Robert Arthur (College Boy); Mack Gordon (Song Writer); Buster Keaton (Butler); Phyllis Kennedy (Elizabeth); Chester Jones (Butler); Hal K. Dawson (Ticket Seller); Charles Lane (Mr. Pflum); Robert Emmett Keane (Architect); Ruth Clifford (Nurse); J. Farrell MacDonald (Doorman); Rita La Roy

(Fashion Editor); Patricia Weil (Jane at Age Three); Sherry Jackson (Jane at Age Six); Jack Mulhall (Leading Man).

Vaudeville entertainer Timothy O'Connor (Dan Dailey) meets, falls in love with, and marries pretty Hannah Adams (Anne Baxter), who happens to be from a wealthy family.   Eventually Dailey wins a break in Hollywood--during the twenties--but he does not fare well in films.   Ironically, wife Baxter does, however, and soon becomes a star of flapper movies and popular screen fare.

With the coming of sound, the situation reverses and it is Dailey, with his stage experience, who becomes a big star in screen musicals, while Baxter's career slips away.   When the musical cycle does die out, Dailey is also washed up in pictures, but by then the duo have saved enough money to live comfortably.

Their young daughter, Jane (Shari Robinson), though, wants to be in the movies and the couple disagree about it--choice--Dailey wants her in films and Baxter doesn't.   As a result, the couple separate.   Robinson manages to get her chance in movies and she becomes a sensation.   Finally Baxter and Dailey are reconciled.

You're My Everything, taking its title from a popular Russ Columbo standard song of the early thirties, was a conglomerate look at Hollywood during the transitional stage from silent to sound film-making.   As Hannah, Baxter was a combination of all the flap-per-age movie stars, especially Clara Bow; while Dailey as Timothy was the stereotype of the numerous song-and-dance men who invaded the film capital with the coming of sound.   In a brief sequence de-voted to silent comedy, Buster Keaton appeared as a butler.   In the course of the picture, Baxter performed the Charleston (à la Joan Crawford of Our Dancing Daughters, 1928) and there was a produc-tion number of "On the Good Ship Lollipop" from Shirley Temple's Bright Eyes (1935).

The conception of the film was based on an idea by George Jessel, and Anne Baxter replaced Jeanne Crain in the title role. The picture proved a financial success grossing $2.4 million in dis-tributors' rentals in the U.S. and Canada alone.

ABOUT THE AUTHORS
AND THE STAFF

JAMES ROBERT PARISH, California-based freelancer and corporation administrator, was born in Cambridge, Massachusetts. He attended the University of Pennsylvania and graduated as a Phi Beta Kappa with an honors degree in English. A graduate of the University of Pennsylvania Law School, he is a member of the New York Bar. As president of Entertainment Copyright Research Co., Inc., he headed a major researching facility for the media industries. Later he was a reporter for film trade papers. He is the author of such books as The RKO Gals, Hollywood's Great Love Teams, The Hollywood Character Actors, The Tough Guys, and Actors' Television Credits (1950-72 & Supplement). Among his coauthorship credits are: The Cinema of Edward G. Robinson, Liza!, Leading Ladies, The MGM Stock Company, Hollywood Players: The Thirties, The Great Spy Pictures, The Great Science Fiction Pictures, and Film Directors: A Guide to Their American Films.

MICHAEL R. PITTS is a freelance writer and journalist who resides with his wife Carolyn in Anderson, Indiana, where he works for the Anderson Herald newspaper and is the film reviewer for local channel 7 television. A graduate of Ball State University in Muncie, Indiana, with a B.S. in History and a M.A. in journalism, Mr. Pitts formerly worked in public education and public relations. With Mr. Parish he has written: The Great Spy Pictures, Film Directors: A Guide to Their American Films, The Great Gangster Pictures, The Great Western Pictures, and The Great Science Fiction Pictures. He has also written Radio Soundtracks: A Reference Guide; Hollywood on Record: The Film Stars' Discography; and Famous Movie Detectives. Mr. Pitts has been published in cinema journals both here and abroad.

GREGORY W. MANK is a 1972 graduate of Mt. St. Mary's College, Emmitsburg, Maryland, with a B.A. in English. He has assisted Mr. Parish as a Research Associate on the volumes Great Movie Heroes, The Elvis Presley Scrapbook, Hollywood Players: the Forties, Great Child Stars, The Tough Guys, The Hollywood Beauties, The Hollywood Dependables, and The Funsters, and is the coauthor (with Mr. Parish) of The Best of MGM. A contributor to Films in Review and Cinefantastique magazines, Mr. Mank resides in Delta, Pennsylvania, and is also active as an actor and an instructor.

433

DeWITT BODEEN was born in Fresno, California.   After grad-
uation from UCLA, he was an actor and playwright at the Pasadena
Playhouse.   In 1941 he was placed under contract at RKO as a screenwriter.   His first project, Cat People, was a hit.   Two other films
that he wrote for producer Val Lewton--Curse of the Cat People and
Seventh Victim--are highly regarded today as cult films.   Among his
other screen writing credits are The Yellow Canary, The Enchanted
Cottage, Night Song, and I Remember Mama, the last three for producer Harriet Parsons.   He has collaborated on the scenarios for
Mrs. Mike and Billy Budd and has written more than 50 teleplays.
He is coauthor of The Films of Cecil B. DeMille and The Films of
Maurice Chevalier and authored From Hollywood and More from Hol-
lywood.   He was final associate editor for the reference volume Who
Wrote the Movie (and What Else Did He Write)? and has authored the
novel 13 Castle Walk.

JOHN ROBERT COCCHI has been viewing and collating data on
motion pictures since an early age and is now regarded as one of the
world's most energetic film researchers.   He is the New York editor
of Boxoffice Magazine.   He was research associate on The American
Movies Reference Book: The Sound Era, The Fox Girls, Good Dames,
The MGM Stock Company, The Hollywood Character Actors, and a
contributing editor to The Films of Jeanette MacDonald and Nelson
Eddy.   He has written cinema history articles for such journals as
Film Fan Monthly, Films in Review, and Screen Facts, and is the
author of The Western Pictures Quiz Book.   Mr. Cocchi is cofounder
of one of New York City's leading film societies.

New York-born FLORENCE SOLOMON attended Hunter College
and then joined Ligon Johnson's copyright research office.   Later she
was appointed director for research at Entertainment Copyright Research Co., Inc., and is presently a reference supervisor at ASCAP's
Index Division in New York City.   Ms. Solomon has collaborated on
such volumes as The American Movies Reference Book: The Sound
Era, TV Movies, The Great Movie Series, Vincent Price Unmasked,
Film Directors Guide: Western Europe, The Elvis Presley Scrapbook, and several others.   She is a niece of the noted sculptor, the
late Sir Jacob Epstein.

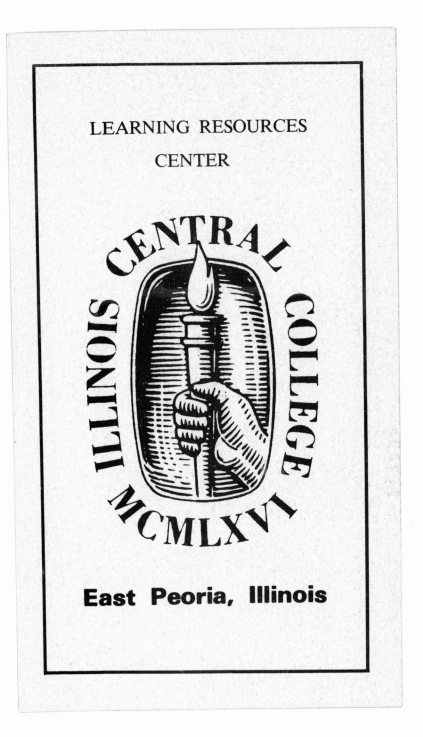

LEARNING RESOURCES CENTER

ILLINOIS CENTRAL COLLEGE MCMLXVI

East Peoria, Illinois